User's PC

The PC User's Mac

PC user—get things done on a Mac!

Elaine J. Marmel

The Mac User's PC/The PC User's Mac

Library of Congress Catalog Card Number: 93-077144

International Standard Book Number: 0-672-48545-1

95 94 93 4 3 2 1

Interpretation of the printing code: the rightmost double-digit number is the year of the book's printing; the rightmost single-digit number is the number of the book's printing. For example, a printing code of 93-1 shows that the first printing of the book occurred in 1993.

The Mac User's PC/The PC User's Mac is based on Lotus 1-2-3 for DOS, Lotus 1-2-3 for Macintosh, Lotus 1-2-3 for Windows, Microsoft Excel for Apple Macintosh, Microsoft Excel for Windows, Microsoft Word for DOS, Microsoft Word for Apple Macintosh, Microsoft Word for Windows, WordPerfect for DOS, WordPerfect for Macintosh, WordPerfect for Windows, MS-DOS, Microsoft Windows, and Apple's family of Macintosh and Performa computers.

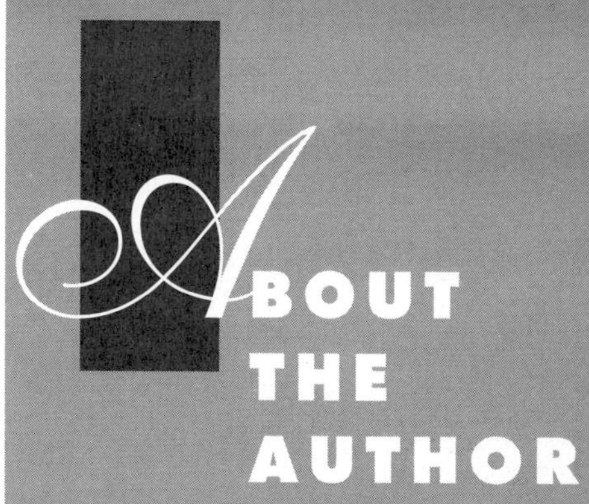

About the Author

Elaine J. Marmel

Elaine Marmel is president of Marmel Enterprises, Inc., an organization which provides PC and Macintosh software training and support and specializes in assisting small- to medium-sized businesses to computerize their accounting systems.

Elaine is the author of *Word for Windows 2 QuickStart, Quicken 1.0 for Windows Quick Reference, Quicken 6 for DOS Quick Reference,* and *Using Quicken 2.0 for Windows,* and a contributing author to *Look Your Best with 1-2-3* and *Using Ami Pro 3 for Windows,* Special Edition.

Elaine left her native Chicago for the warmer climes of Florida (by way of Cincinnati, Ohio; Jerusalem, Israel; Ithaca, New York; and Washington, D.C.) where she basks in the sun with her PC, her Mac, and her cats, Tonto and Cato. Elaine also enjoys cross-stitching, and she sings in an internationally recognized barbershop chorus, the Toast of Tampa.

Publisher

Mike Britton

Developmental Editor

Laura Wirthlin

Editors

Dave Ciskowski

Pamela Wampler

Laura Wirthlin

Technical Editors

Dave Ciskowski

Gloria Schuler

Cover Designer

Scott Cook

Interior Designer

Scott Cook

Interior Illustrator

Roger Morgan

Production Team

Jeanne Clark, Tim Cox, Mark Enochs, Joelynn Gifford, Tim Groeling, Phil Kitchel, Tom Loveman, Michael J. Nolan, Joe Ramon, Carrie Roth, Mary Beth Wakefield, Barbara Webster, Kelli Widdifield

Dedicated to Terry Higdon, for courage and bravery and, most of all, friendship.

I would like to thank the following people:

Brian Low and Mike Pearse of Lotus Corporation for background technical help on the various versions of Lotus 1-2-3.

Earl Martin and the staff at TechForce for providing evaluation copies of software.

Glenda Kilpatrick for information on Clipper.

Gloria Schuler for the excellent technical editing job she did (although she enjoyed it far too much, and I think she ought to give the money back) and for providing an ear when I needed one.

Dave Ciskowski for keeping me on the right track with outstanding technical comments.

Pamela Wampler for her gentle guidance to help me make this a better book.

Laura Wirthlin for the opportunity to write this book.

Trademark Acknowledgments

This book mentions too many companies and products to list every trademark on this page. Because we are environmentalists, and because paper is a valuable (and costly) commodity, we limit our trademark acknowledgments to the following statements:

All terms mentioned in this book that are known to be trademarks or service marks have been appropriately capitalized. Hayden cannot attest to the accuracy of this information. Use of a term in this book should not be regarded as affecting the validity of any trademark or service mark.

IBM is a registered trademark of International Business Machines. Lotus and 1-2-3 are registered trademarks of Lotus Development Corporation. Microsoft, Microsoft Excel, Microsoft Windows, Microsoft Word, and MS-DOS are registered trademarks of Microsoft Corporation. WordPerfect is a registered trademark of WordPerfect Corporation. Apple, Mac, Macintosh, and Performa are registered trademarks of Apple Computer, Inc.

THE MAC USER'S PC CONTENTS

We Want to Hear from You

What our readers think of Hayden is crucial to our sense of well-being. If you have any comments, no matter how great or small, we'd appreciate your taking the time to send us a note, fax us a fax, rhyme us a rhyme, and so on.

We can be reached at the following address:

Hayden Books
11711 North College Avenue
Carmel, Indiana 46032
(317) 573-6880 voice
(317) 573-2583 fax

If this book has changed your life, please write and describe the euphoria you've experienced. Do you have a book idea? Please contact us at the above address.

The war between the Macintosh and the PC continues, each side claiming its own computer as the best. Which computer *is* the best? This book does not answer that question. It doesn't even try. (If this text sounds familiar, then you have read the introduction to *The PC User's Mac*. This introduction is the same, so you can skip ahead to Chapter 1 if you want.)

Who Should Use This Book?

Are you a Mac user who has been forced to use a PC, if only for a small task such as copying a file from a hard disk to a floppy disk? If you're lucky, perhaps Windows started automatically. But, if not, what does `C>` (or `C:\>`) mean? What's the blinking square or underline next to it? Maybe you see a menu, but where's the mouse pointer? How do you find the file you want, let alone copy it to a floppy disk?

Or, are you a PC user confronted with the task of using a Macintosh? Are you trying to use a Macintosh, for example, to copy a file to a floppy disk that you can take to your PC and use? Oh, sure, your friend the Mac user keeps telling you how easy the Macintosh is. But where's your DOS prompt? Or where's the menu you always use to start programs? And what do all the pictures mean? Is this Windows on the Macintosh? How do you find what you're looking for? How do you use the mouse?

In either case, you may have found yourself in an environment that's entirely unfamiliar. This book is created for Mac users who are experienced on Macs but have an occasional need to work on a PC, and for PC users who are experienced on PCs but have a similar occasional need to work on a Mac. This book will not make you an expert at either the PC or the Macintosh—it does not provide an exhaustive look at either computer. This book covers software that exists for both platforms; for example, you will find chapters on WordPerfect for DOS, WordPerfect for Windows, and WordPerfect for the Mac (and, yes, I did have trouble keeping them all straight after a while!). This book will help you get by when you have to use the computer with which you are not familiar, and, I hope, this book will prepare you to read other books (or even the manuals) with greater understanding.

What Does This Book Contain?

The book consists of two parts, and you use each part independently. In fact, this book can be viewed as two books in one: *The Mac User's PC* and *The PC User's Mac*. In each part of the book, you find information that helps you identify the parts and understand the basic differences between the Macintosh and the PC. You learn to start popular programs; get help in those programs; open, edit, print, and save files in the programs; copy the files to a floppy disk; and exit the programs. You also learn to transfer and translate files between Macs and PCs.

The Mac User's PC

This part of the book, *The Mac User's PC*, contains 13 chapters that describe a typical IBM-compatible PC and how to use popular PC programs, plus a glossary of common PC terms.

You may not want to read *The Mac User's PC* from front to back (or front to middle). But because Chapters 1 and 2 contain basic background information about PC hardware, be sure to read these chapters first. Then, read the chapters that pertain to the PC software you need to use. Some of the information may be repetitive; for example, each chapter about a Windows-based program contains basic information about using Windows. This repetition is intentional. Because Chapters 3 through 9 are independent and self-contained, you can rely on one chapter alone to use a particular software package. This way, you don't have to hunt for information throughout the book.

Chapter 1, "Examining the Parts of a PC," focuses on the PC hardware. You learn to identify what you typically see when you look at the PC from the front and from the back.

Chapter 2, "Turning On the PC and Starting a Program," first explains, in a general way, the differences in philosophy behind the original construction of the Macintosh and the PC. To help you identify the PC environment in which you are working, this chapter describes the various screens you might see when you start a PC. You then learn how to start a program in each of these environments. Chapter 2 also contains tips on starting programs not specifically covered in this book.

Chapters 3 through 9 contain the same basic information for different popular software programs: how to get help in the program; how to open, edit, save, and print a file; how to copy a file to a floppy disk; and how to exit from the program. In Chapter 3, you learn about WordPerfect for DOS; in Chapter 4, about WordPerfect for Windows. Chapter 5 covers Microsoft Word for

DOS. Chapter 6 covers Microsoft Word for Windows. Chapter 7 discusses Microsoft Excel for Windows. Chapter 8 describes Lotus 1-2-3 for DOS, and Chapter 9 describes Lotus 1-2-3 for Windows.

In Chapter 10, "Avoiding Database Programs," you learn what a database program is and what it can do for you. You also learn why you shouldn't use somebody else's database unless you really know what you're doing. You learn the names of some of the more popular database programs so that you can avoid them while working on someone else's PC.

In Chapter 11, "Working with the MS-DOS Shell," you learn how to use the MS-DOS Shell, which is one of the PC environments described in Chapter 2. (In Chapter 2, you learned how to identify the MS-DOS Shell screen.) In this chapter, you learn to understand the MS-DOS Shell screen and to use the MS-DOS Shell to view, copy, and print files, and to start programs. The MS-DOS Shell is available to any user working under MS-DOS Version 4.0 or later. (In Chapter 2, you also learned how to identify the version of DOS you are using.) Even if the MS-DOS Shell doesn't appear when you start the computer, you may want to try using it if it is available.

Chapter 12, "Working with Basic DOS Commands (When All Else Fails)," teaches you the basics of the dreaded DOS. You review how to identify the version of DOS with which you are working, and learn how to copy and erase files. You also learn about directories and how to list their contents, switch to another directory, make a new directory, and delete a directory. PC users also may want to review this chapter. (But then again, maybe not.)

In Chapter 13, "Transferring and Translating Files between a Mac and a PC," you learn some of the ways you can move a file from a Macintosh to a PC or from a PC to a Macintosh.

The PC Glossary provides definitions of popular PC terms, and this part of the book concludes with a comprehensive index of *The Mac User's PC.*

The PC User's Mac

The other part of the book, *The PC User's Mac*, contains nine chapters that describe a typical Macintosh and how to use popular Macintosh programs, plus a glossary of common Macintosh terms.

You may not want to read *The PC User's Mac* from front to back (or front to middle) either. But because Chapters 1 and 2 contain basic background information about Mac hardware, be sure to read these chapters first. Then, read the chapters that pertain to the Mac software you need to use.

Chapter 1, "Examining the Parts of a Mac," focuses on the Macintosh hardware. You learn to identify what you typically see when you look at the Macintosh from the front and from the back.

Chapter 2, "Turning On the Mac and Starting a Program," first explains, in a general way, the differences in philosophy behind the original construction of the PC and the Macintosh. In this chapter, you learn to experiment with the Macintosh without fear of "breaking" things. This chapter also describes what you typically see when you turn on a Macintosh, and you learn the basics of using a mouse. You also learn how to start a program on a Mac.

Chapters 3 through 6 contain the same basic information for different popular software programs: how to get help in the program; how to open, edit, save, and print a file; how to copy a file to a floppy disk; and how to exit from the program. In Chapter 3, you learn about WordPerfect for the Mac. Chapter 4 covers Microsoft Word for the Mac. Chapter 5 discusses Microsoft Excel for the Mac. Chapter 6 describes Lotus 1-2-3 for the Mac.

In Chapter 7, "Avoiding Database Programs," you learn what a database program is and what it can do for you. You also learn why you shouldn't use somebody else's database unless you really know what you're doing. You learn the names of some popular database programs so that you can avoid them while working on someone else's Macintosh.

In Chapter 8, "Working with Disks, Folders, and Files," you learn how to use the Finder on the Desktop to manage disks, folders, and files. You first review how to identify, select, and open disks, folders, and files. Then, you learn how to create disks, folders, and files; rename, move, and copy folders and files; use the Trash; and get help.

In Chapter 9, "Transferring and Translating Files between a PC and a Mac," you learn some of the ways you can move a file from a PC to a Macintosh and from a Macintosh to a PC.

The Mac Glossary provides definitions of popular Macintosh terms, and the other part of the book concludes with a comprehensive index of *The PC User's Mac.*

Conventions Used in This Book

The conventions used in this book were established to help you use the book more easily.

Information that appears onscreen and information that you type appears in a `special typeface`.

Shortcut keys for choosing menus, commands, and dialog box options appear in **boldface type**. (Remember that to choose a menu in a Windows-based application, you hold down the Alt key as you press the shortcut key.)

When you see two or more keys separated by a plus sign (+), you hold down the first key(s) as you press the last key. When you see two or more keys separated by a comma (,), you press the keys in sequence.

Terms that appear in the glossary appear in **boldface type**.

ONE

TWO

THREE

FOUR

FIVE

SIX

SEVEN

EIGHT

NINE

TEN

ELEVEN

TWELVE

THIRTEEN

GLOSSARY

Examining the Parts of a PC

You have received the dreaded assignment: on Mary's PC, find a file and print it. All you know about a PC is that there's one sitting on Mary's desk. And until now, that's all you ever wanted to know. But now you must use Mary's PC. The first step is to identify what you see when you look at the PC. In this chapter, you learn about the hardware you can view from the outside of the computer.

Looking at the Computer from the Front

A typical IBM-compatible PC closely resembles your Macintosh (at least physically) from the front—unless you use a Mac Classic or a Performa 200. In most cases, you should see these three pieces of equipment: a monitor, a keyboard, and a box containing other hardware components. For lack of a better term, the box containing these other hardware components is called "the box" throughout this book (just think of this as another technical term). Occasionally, you may see a mouse. In Figure 1.1, you see a typical IBM-compatible PC. Not all IBM-compatible computers look the same, but you will see the same types of buttons, lights, and so on, on most IBM-compatible PCs.

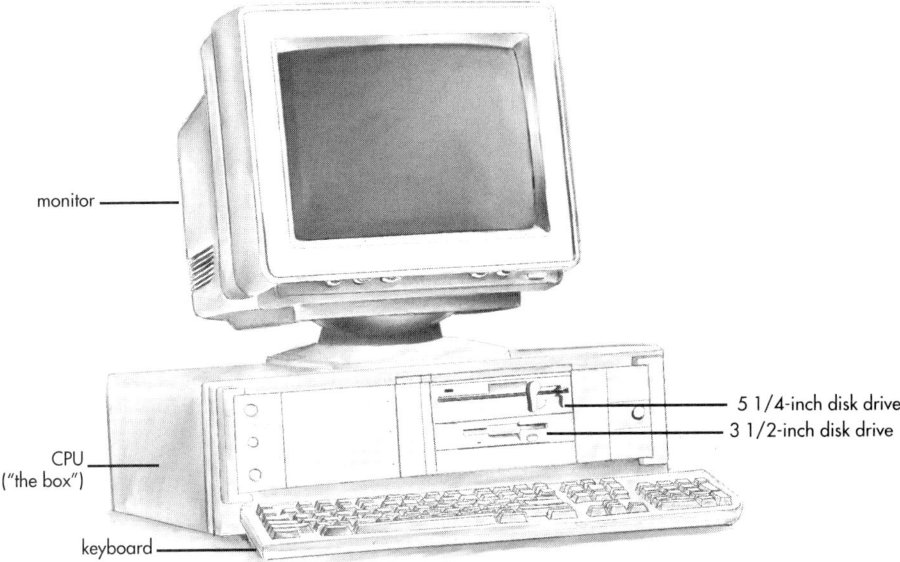

Figure 1.1. A typical IBM-compatible PC.

The Front of the Monitor

Many PC users place the monitor on top of the box. In some cases, the box is designed to stand horizontally beside the monitor or on the floor, so the PC user can place the monitor directly on the desk.

As on a Mac, the monitor usually has a switch you can use to turn the monitor on or off. The switch may be somewhere on the rim around the front of the monitor, or the switch may be on the back of the monitor. Usually, the monitor has a light somewhere on the front that lets you know whether it is on or off (see Figure 1.2). The light is usually green when the monitor is on.

Also, the monitor usually has controls you can use to adjust the brightness of the image and the contrast (see Figure 1.2). These controls may be on the front or the back of the monitor and work like the brightness and contrast knobs on your television set and the controls on your Mac.

Figure 1.2.

A typical monitor and its parts.

The Front of the Box

Many PC users place the box underneath the monitor on top of the desk. In some cases, the box is designed to stand horizontally beside the monitor or on the floor.

Inside the box, you might find, among other hardware items, the **Central Processing Unit** (**CPU**), memory chips, disk drives, and connection ports. Because you probably will not need to open the box (at least I *hope* you won't need to open the box), this section focuses on what you might see from the outside of the box. As you see from Figure 1.3, you will find an on/off switch, several lights, and one or more floppy disk drives somewhere on the outside of the box. Most of these items also appear on your Mac, but not all the items look the same.

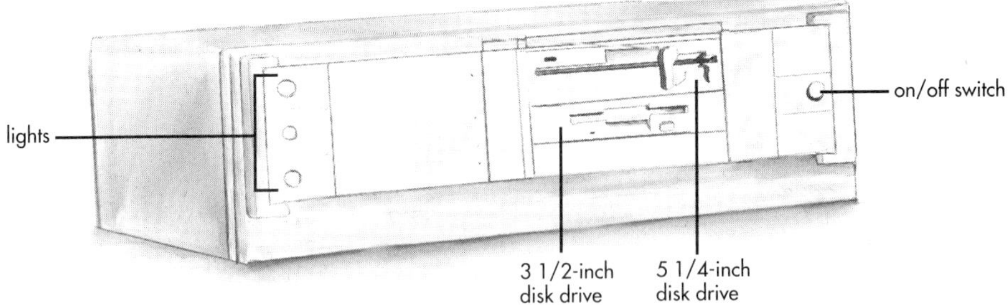

Figure 1.3.
A typical IBM-compatible CPU box.

The on/off switch can take a variety of shapes and appear in any number of places. You may find the on/off switch on the front of the computer, or the switch may appear on either side or on the back of the computer. If the on/off switch appears on the back, it usually is located close to the right or left side of the back. On some computers (like mine), the on/off switch is the only button that doesn't have a label on the front of the computer. (Do you suppose the manufacturer assumed that if I couldn't find the on/off switch, I ought to stick to yellow pads and not try to use a computer?) The on/off switch may work like a light switch that you push up or down or from side to side, or the switch may work like a push button that has two positions—in for on and out for off.

Generally, you also see some lights on the box. Usually one light is green when the computer is turned on; this light indicates that electrical power is running to the computer. A second light may appear green or red; this light flickers when an action is taking place on the hard disk drive. You may not see this light if the PC doesn't have a hard disk drive or if the manufacturer chose not to include this light. A third light, usually marked "Turbo," may appear yellow, green, or red if the computer is operating in turbo mode, which is a faster speed. Most PCs operate, by default, in turbo mode because most programs perform very well in this mode. Occasionally, you will see a button that controls whether the PC is operating in turbo mode. If your software doesn't seem to be working properly, check to see whether the computer is operating in turbo mode, and, if not, press the Turbo button.

You also may see a button marked "Reset," which functions similarly to the Reset button on a Mac. You use this button when you want to restart the computer without using the on/off switch. Using the Reset button is often referred to as performing a "warm boot" on the computer; using the on/off switch is referred to as performing a "cold boot" on the computer. Usually, you use the Reset button if your keyboard seems to freeze and you cannot close a program as the manufacturer intended. If you use the Reset button while working in a program, you will lose all the changes you have made since the last time you saved your data. Use the Reset button only in emergencies.

You also may see one or more floppy disk drives. Most IBM-compatible PCs can use two different sizes of floppy disks: 5 1/4-inch or 3 1/2-inch. Figure 1.4 shows a 5 1/4-inch disk; Figure 1.5 shows a 3 1/2-inch disk.

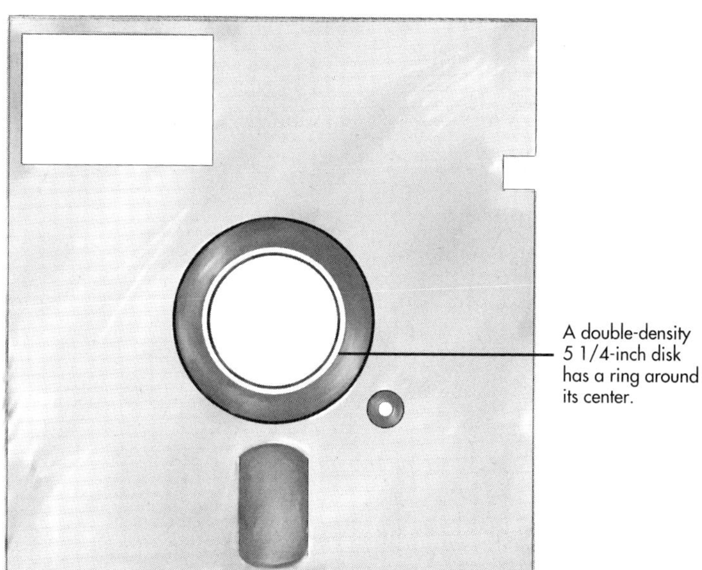
A double-density
5 1/4-inch disk
has a ring around
its center.

Figure 1.4.

A double-density 5 1/4-inch disk.

A double-density 3 1/2-inch
disk has one hole along its
side.

Figure 1.5.

A double-density 3 1/2-inch disk.

In most cases, if a computer contains both sizes of disk drives, the 5 1/4-inch disk drive is referred to as "drive A," and the 3 1/2-inch disk drive is referred to as "drive B." Again, in most cases, drive A is above drive B. Unlike a Mac SuperDrive, a PC's 5 1/4-inch disk drive always includes some kind of "door" you must close after you insert the disk into the drive. The door may be a handle you turn or a button you push. A PC's 3 1/2-inch disk drive operates more like a SuperDrive; when you insert a disk into the drive, the drive "grabs" the disk. To remove a disk from either drive, you don't use a software command like you do on a Mac. Instead, you open the 5 1/4-inch disk drive's door and slide out the disk or push the 3 1/2-inch disk drive's button to eject the disk. Again, the 3 1/2-inch disk drive performs more like a SuperDrive because when you press the button that ejects the disk, the disk pops out.

In addition to using two different sizes of disks, PCs, like Macs, can two different capacities of disks. The capacities are referred to as

"high density" and "double density." You see very few differences visually between high-density and double-density disks for a given size. The disks in Figures 1.4 and 1.5 are both double-density disks.

You can tell the difference between a high-density 5 1/4-inch disk and a double-density 5 1/4-inch disk by looking at the center of the disk. If the center has a ring (as shown in Figure 1.4), the disk is a double-density disk. If you don't see a ring in the center of the disk, the disk is a high-density disk.

As with a Mac disk, you can tell the difference between a high-density 3 1/2-inch disk and a double-density 3 1/2-inch disk by the number of square holes you see on the sides of the disk. If you see a square hole on only one side of the disk (as shown in Figure 1.5), you are looking at a double-density disk. If you see a square hole on each side of the disk, you are looking at a high-density disk.

High-density disks hold more information than double-density disks—you can store 1.2M of information on a high-density 5 1/4-inch disk, and 1.44M of information on a high-density 3 1/2-inch disk. (The difference is negligible.)

On double-density disks, however, the difference in capacity becomes quite noticeable. A double-density 5 1/4-inch disk can hold only 360K of information, while a double-density 3 1/2-inch disk can hold twice that amount—720K (unlike a Mac disk, which holds 800K).

In some cases, near the floppy disk drives, you may see a third drive (which doesn't appear in either Figure 1.1 or Figure 1.3). This drive may be an internal tape drive used to back up the hard disk. The tape onto which the backups are stored resides in a cartridge and resembles a cassette tape. If you are using a PC as an occasional user, you probably won't have any need to use the tape drive to make a backup. If you need to use the tape drive, see the user's guide that came with the tape drive.

The Keyboard

Most keyboards have 102 keys and are similar to the keyboard in Figure 1.6.

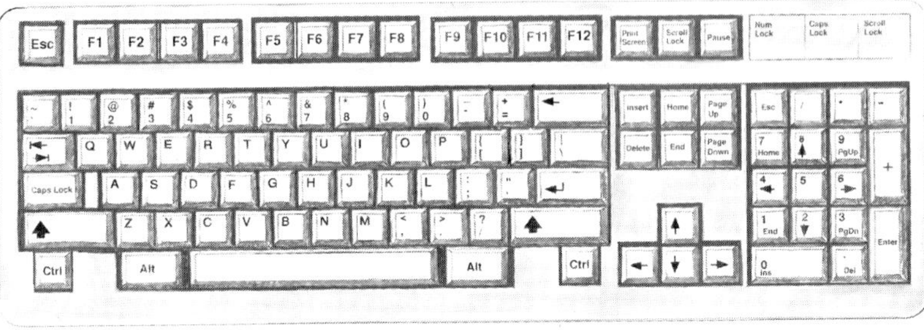

Figure 1.6.

A typical IBM-compatible PC keyboard.

For the sake of discussion, you can think of the keys on the keyboard in six different groups:

- The alphanumeric keys
- The editing keys
- The cursor-movement keys
- The numeric keypad
- The function keys
- The special-purpose keys

In the following sections, you learn about the functions of each of these groups of keys as if you were using them to perform actions in application software. Be aware, however, that the actions of most keys can be redefined by application software. Some keys, such as the alphanumeric keys, typically retain their actions as you

move from one software package to another. Other keys, such as the function keys, usually change their actions as you move from one piece of software to another.

The Alphanumeric Keys

The **alphanumeric keys** on a PC keyboard are arranged similarly to the way they appear on a typewriter (see Figure 1.7).

Figure 1.7.
The alphanumeric keys.

The alphanumeric keys produce letters and symbols. These keys operate, for the most part, like the keys on a typewriter. When enabled, the Caps Lock key lets you produce uppercase letters for the 26 alphabetic characters without pressing the Shift key. If you want to produce one of the symbols that appears in the top row of the alphanumeric keys (above the numbers), however, you still must press the Shift key.

The Editing Keys

The **editing keys**—Backspace, Del, and Ins—enable you to modify text you already have typed (see Figure 1.8). On some keyboards, you may see "Delete" and "Insert." In this book, you will see the keys referred to as "Del" and "Ins," particularly because the Del key is *not* the same key as the Delete key on a Mac keyboard. The Delete key on a Mac keyboard is the same as the Backspace key on a PC keyboard.

Figure 1.8.
The editing keys.

The **cursor** is the DOS equivalent of the insertion point in a Windows or Macintosh program, and designates the location where your next action will take place. In most DOS-based programs, the cursor appears as a blinking underline, a blinking square, or as a video bar (a highlight).

Both the Backspace key and the Del key enable you to remove characters you have typed. The Backspace key operates like the Delete key on a Mac keyboard and deletes the character immediately to the left of the cursor. The Del key deletes the character on which the cursor is resting.

When you type on a PC, you type in one of two modes: overtype (also called "typeover") mode or insert mode. In **overtype mode**, each character you type replaces any character that currently exists at the cursor location. In **insert mode**, each character you type is inserted at the current cursor location and any existing characters move to the right. The Ins key is a toggle switch that enables you to switch between overtype mode and insert mode. Each application program defines the mode (overtype or insert) in which you start by default, but you can simply press the Ins key to switch to the other mode.

The Cursor-Movement Keys

If the keyboard is an extended keyboard, it contains two sets of editing and **cursor-movement keys**: one set on the numeric keypad on the right side of the keyboard, and another set of gray

editing and cursor-movement keys between the numeric keypad and the alphanumeric keys (see Figure 1.9).

Figure 1.9.
The cursor-movement keys.

Cursor-movement keys are also called **directional keys**. You can use the gray directional keys (the ones between the numeric keypad and the alphanumeric keypad) simply by pressing the keys. The directional keys on the numeric keypad, however, are active only when the Num Lock feature is not turned on. To turn on or off Num Lock, press the Num Lock key, which is a toggle switch. If the Num Lock light is on, for example, press the Num Lock key to turn off the feature (and the light).

Pressing the arrow keys moves the cursor in the direction that the arrow key points. Most often, pressing the Home key moves the cursor to the upper left corner of the screen or to the left end of the current line. Pressing the End key typically moves the cursor to the end0 of the current line. Pressing the PgUp key usually causes the previous screen's information to reappear. Pressing the PgDn key usually causes the following screen's information to appear. The Tab key works like the Tab key on a typewriter, and typically moves the cursor to the next preset tab stop.

On an extended keyboard, you will see two Enter keys—one where you usually see the Return key on a typewriter or on an Apple extended keyboard, and one on the numeric keypad. On a PC keyboard, both Enter keys operate the same way. The Enter key serves many different functions. At a DOS prompt, you use the Enter key to send a command to the computer—that is, you press Enter to indicate that you're done typing the command and that

DOS should perform the command. In a word-processing program, pressing Enter usually causes the cursor to move to the beginning of the next line. In a spreadsheet program, pressing Enter places information you typed into a cell.

The Numeric Keypad

The **numeric keypad** (see Figure 1.10) actually serves two purposes: to enter numbers or to move the cursor. When the Num Lock light is turned on and you press a key on the numeric keypad, a number appears onscreen. When the Num Lock light is turned off and you press a key on the numeric keypad, the cursor changes positions.

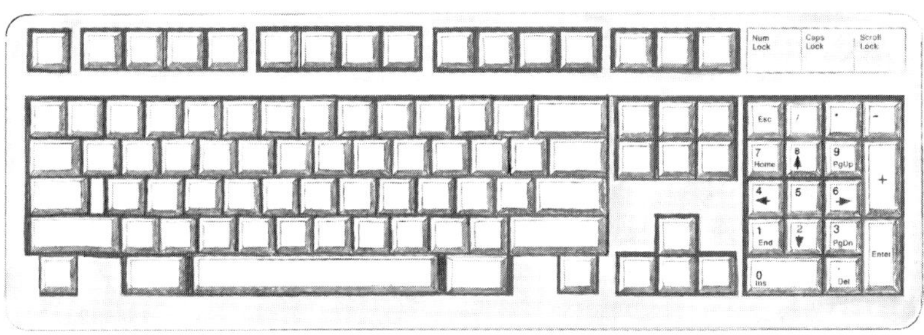

Figure 1.10. The numeric keypad.

You can use the gray keys on the numeric keypad for mathematical operations:

+	Add
-	Subtract
*	Multiply
/	Divide

Note that, on some PC keyboards, you must make sure that the Num Lock light is on or these keys won't work.

The Function Keys

Usually, you see **function keys** across the top of the keyboard (see Figure 1.11), although on some keyboards, these function keys appear on the left side of the keyboard.

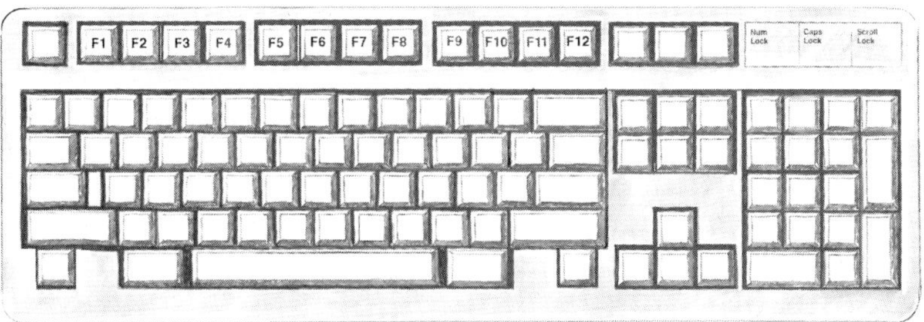

Figure 1.11.

The function keys.

The purpose of the function keys changes from one software package to another; most programs use these keys to simplify work by assigning commonly used tasks to the function keys. In many software packages, for example, pressing F1 displays help information.

Special-Purpose Keys

You usually see the Esc key somewhere near the upper left corner of the keyboard ("Esc" is an abbreviation for "escape") . The Esc key is often (but not always) defined by software programs to cancel the current action.

The keyboard contains several other special-purpose keys, only a few of which you may have an occasion to use (see Figure 1.12).

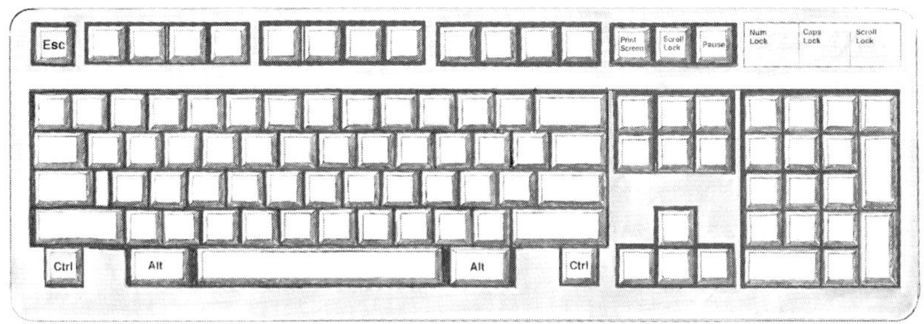

Figure 1.12.

The special-purpose keys.

The **Alt key** has no function by itself ("Alt" is an abbreviation for "alternate"). When pressed in combination with another key, the Alt key may generate a special action in the current software package. The **Ctrl key** operates like the Alt key ("Ctrl" is an abbreviation for "control"). By itself, the Ctrl key has no function, but when used in combination with another key, the Ctrl key also may generate a special action in the current software package.

Looking at the Computer from the Back

You may never need (or want) to look at a PC from the back. (In fact, you may decide to let somebody else do it for you if you think it's necessary.) In WordPerfect for DOS, for example, you may see a message that the PC isn't communicating with the printer and that you should check to make sure the cable is connected. Usually, this message appears when you didn't turn on the printer, or, in the case of a laser printer, when you turned on the printer after you started the computer. This misleading message may make you *think* you need to look at the back of the PC when, in fact, you don't. (You can solve this problem by saving your document, shutting down WordPerfect and the computer, and restarting everything, making sure that you turn on the printer a few seconds before you turn on the computer.)

On the other hand, you may want to fix a problem that requires you to look at the back of a PC. So, I have included information to identify the parts you may find on the back of a PC. Not all PCs look alike from the back, but most have the standard basic parts described in this section. Also, the parts may not appear in the same place you see in the figures.

The back of a typical IBM-compatible PC resembles the drawing in Figure 1.13.

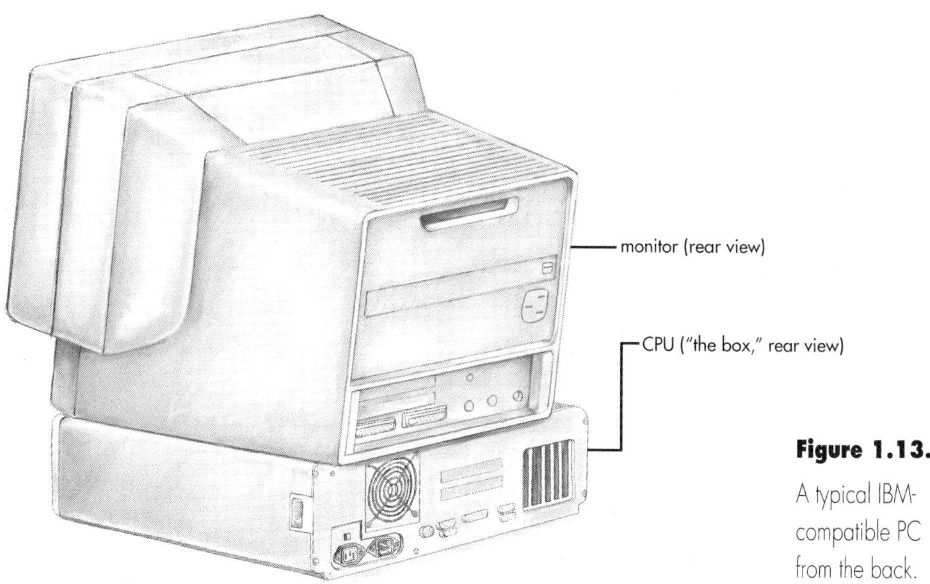

Figure 1.13.

A typical IBM-compatible PC from the back.

Unless you use a Mac Classic or a Performa 200, a typical IBM-compatible PC closely resembles your Macintosh (physically) from the back. In most cases, you should see two pieces of equipment—the monitor and the box that contains other hardware components. When you look at the back of the PC, you see cables running out of connectors, ports, and slots. In the figures that appear in this section, however, you don't see the cables; you see the actual connectors, ports, and slots that appear on the back of the equipment.

The Back of the Monitor

The back of a PC monitor is very similar to the back of a Mac monitor (except the back of the Mac Classic and the Performa 200). On the back of the monitor (see Figure 1.14), you see a cable that enables you to connect the monitor to the video port on the CPU box. You also see the connector for the cable that connects the monitor to a source of electricity.

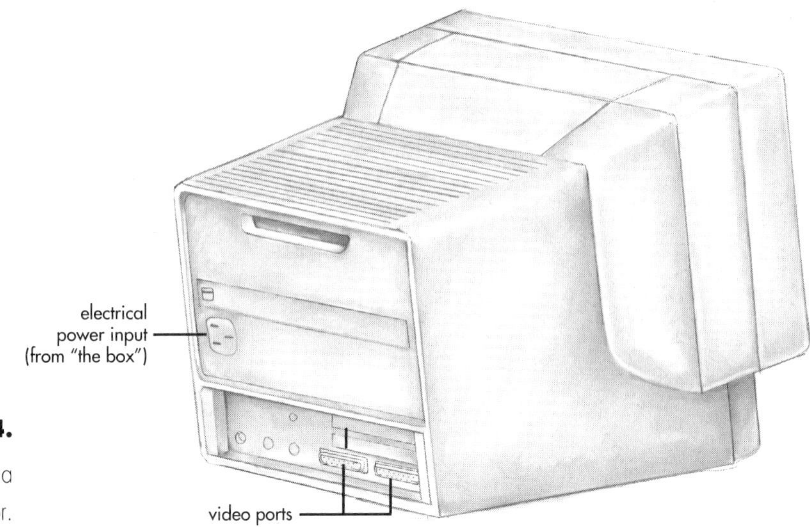

Figure 1.14.
The back of a typical monitor.

The Back of the Box

On the back of the box, you see a variety of connectors, ports, and slots (see Figure 1.15). The position of these various connectors, ports, and slots may change from PC to PC, but, in general, the appearance of each is similar.

Typically, you see two power connectors, one input and one output. You use the bottom connector, the input, to connect the PC to a source of electricity. You can use the top connector, the output, to connect a monitor to the power supply of the computer.

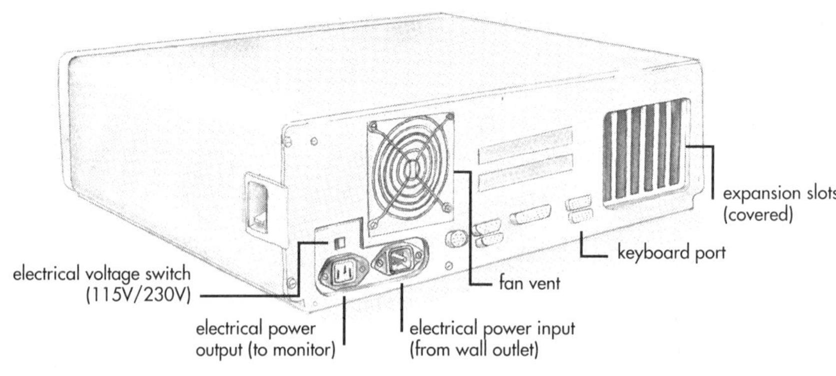

Figure 1.15.
The back of a typical PC CPU box.

You then can leave the monitor switched on all the time, and let the on/off switch on the box determine whether electricity flows to the monitor. In this way, when you turn on the PC, you also turn on the monitor; similarly, when you turn off the PC, you also turn off the monitor.

The fan vent appears next to the power connectors. The fan vent cools the computer's power supply, which generates significant heat.

You use the five-pin keyboard port, shown next to the fan vent in Figure 1.15, to connect the keyboard cable to the box.

RS232 ports are serial ports you can use to connect to the PC devices that run in serial mode, such as a serial mouse. Most serial ports are nine-pin ports. The first serial port is named COM1, while the second serial port is named COM2. On some PCs, you also may see 25-pin serial ports.

You usually use a 25-pin parallel port to connect a printer to the PC. You may see more than one parallel port on some PCs; the first parallel port is called LPT1, the second parallel port is called LPT2, and so on. You can identify the difference between a 25-pin serial port and a 25-pin parallel port based on the gender of the port's connector. If the connector is male, the port is serial. If the connector is female, the port is parallel.

The display connectors enable you to connect the monitor to the box. Use the 15-pin connector to attach a monitor that sends analog signals. Use the 9-pin connector to attach a monitor that sends digital signals.

Finally, the series of metal strips are slot covers that cover the expansion slots inside the PC to keep them free from dust and debris. You use expansion slots like NuBus slots on a Mac—to add additional pieces of equipment, such as a modem, a fax board, or a network board, to a PC. Various IBM-compatible PCs have varying numbers of expansion slots. Note that when you use an expansion slot, you no longer use its slot cover, so you won't see slot covers over the expansion slots that contain additional hardware items. Also, some of the items you add may contain additional ports, and you may, therefore, see ports on the back of the PC that are not described here.

Chapter Summary

In this chapter, you learned to identify the parts of a PC, both from the front and the back. You learned that although IBM-compatible PCs do not all look the same, they each contain some basic elements in common.

In general, a PC closely resembles a Mac physically, except for the Mac Classic or the Performa 200. And, even the Mac Classic and the Performa 200 have basically the same parts: a monitor, a keyboard, and a box. The greatest differences between the two types of computers are:

- You turn on a PC by using a button or switch somewhere on the box, but you often can turn on a Mac by pressing a key on the keyboard (although all Macs also have a switch on the box).

- On a PC, floppy disk drives (and hard disk drives) have letter names.

- When you insert a 5 1/4-inch floppy disk into a PC's disk drive, you must close the drive door.

- On a PC, you remove a floppy disk from the disk drive by using the hardware. On a Mac, you remove a floppy disk from the disk drive by using a software command.

- On a PC extended keyboard, you can use the numeric keypad as directional keys if you turn off the Num Lock feature.

The next chapter explains the differences in philosophy behind the original construction of the PC and the Macintosh. Also, because you may find yourself in one of many PC environments, the chapter helps you identify the various PC environments; the chapter describes the screens you might see when you start a PC. Chapter 2 also shows you how to start a program in each of these environments.

Turning On the PC and Starting a Program

When you turn on a Mac, the computer performs an automatic startup process. After the startup process, you see the Desktop. Different things may appear on the Desktop, but the Desktop always remains onscreen.

When you turn on a PC, the computer also performs an automatic startup process. What you see at the end of the startup process, however, may be a menu, or the MS-DOS Shell, or Microsoft Windows, or a DOS prompt. From any of these screens, you then can start a program. To help you understand *why* you may see any of a variety of screens, the first section in this chapter briefly examines the difference in design philosophies that makes PCs different from Macs. After that, you learn to turn on a PC, and then how to start a program from any of the screens that may appear at the end of the computer's automatic startup process.

Understanding Design Philosophies: PC vs. Macintosh

As you already know, the Macintosh and the PC work very differently. Of course, technology is responsible for the major differences in the way these computers process information, but their design philosophies account for the differences in technology.

When IBM builds a computer, it attempts to build the most flexible computer available. An IBM-compatible personal computer will do almost anything you want it to—you just have to learn how to tell it what you want it to do. And that means *everyone*, end users and programmers alike, must learn how to tell the computer what they want it to do. Typically, people tend to view flexibility as a "good" thing; however, flexibility has its price.

First, no specific standards exist that require software developers to make their programs look alike or operate in the same basic way. For this reason, developers have few restrictions and can work freely to design programs as they want. As users move from one program to another, they must learn how to operate each program from the ground up. Further, although PCs offer a great deal of flexibility to the users, this flexibility comes at the price of added complexity—the users must be well versed in making the computer do what they want them to. This requirement usually means that users must learn, at a minimum, some basics about operating systems. And any PC user will tell you that working with the operating system on a PC is not a user-friendly experience.

On the other hand, the driving design philosophy behind the Macintosh was to make the computer user-friendly. And, as any Mac user will tell you, the Mac is easy to use. In the user-friendly environment, many of the details of how the software works have been predetermined. The users find that, regardless of the programs they are using, they can accomplish certain basic tasks by using the same basic commands. But, as with the PC's design philosophy, user-friendliness has its price—lack of flexibility. Mac programmers must operate under certain constraints.

Rather than focusing on which approach is better (which is a debate that's been going on for years), this chapter focuses on how a Mac user can adjust to an unfamiliar, flexible PC environment.

Although the screens you see in DOS-based programs don't typically look alike and the commands that perform similar functions often have different names, most of the tasks you perform are similar from one program to another. Therefore, when working in the PC environment, look for similar commands (for example, "open" and "retrieve") and try them. Remember that you probably won't hurt anything as long as you don't delete files. Don't be afraid to experiment.

Turning On the PC

Starting a PC is a two-step process: you turn on the power and then watch while the computer runs through its automatic startup routine. In this section, you review how to turn on a PC and learn what happens during the automatic startup process.

Turning On the Power

As you learned in Chapter 1, you can find an on/off switch on a PC somewhere on the outside of the box. The on/off switch can take a variety of shapes and appear in any number of places. You may find the on/off switch on the front of the computer, on either side of the computer, or on the back of the computer. If the on/off switch appears on the back, it usually is located close to the right or left side of the back. The on/off switch may work like a light switch that you push up or down or from side to side, or the switch may work like a push button that has two positions—in for on and out for off.

In addition to turning on the power for the box, you may need to turn on the power for the monitor. The on/off switch on the monitor may be located somewhere on the rim around the front of the monitor or on the back of the monitor. Usually, the monitor has a light somewhere on the front that indicates whether the monitor is on or off. The light is usually green when the monitor is on.

Watching the Startup Process

Starting a PC is also called **booting** the PC. I once read in a college computer textbook that this term supposedly comes from the expression "pulling yourself up by your bootstraps." (No, it didn't make any sense to me, either.) As on a Mac, when you boot a PC, the computer executes a set of boot instructions and certain events *always* happen. On a PC, however, when the computer reaches a specified point, the user can define what happens next. To keep things simple during this discussion, I assume that you are working on a stand-alone PC, rather than on a networked PC.

When you turn on a PC, you see the computer follow these steps:

1. The computer takes an inventory of its hardware parts.

2. The computer searches for the operating system.

3. The computer searches for a configuration file and, if found, executes its instructions.

4. The computer searches for an automatic execution file and, if found, executes the instructions.

The first two steps always happen. The last two steps happen only if the PC owner has defined a configuration file and an automatic execution file, both of which are optional to the computer's operation.

During the first step, instructions stored in the hardware chips (the ROM) tell the computer to take an inventory and test the parts of the computer to make sure that they are working properly. The computer tests the memory chips and the keyboard. You can see the memory test onscreen (numbers flash by). On newer PCs, you can't see the keyboard test, but on older PCs, you may notice the Num Lock, Caps Lock, and Scroll Lock lights flash on. Then, you see the lights on the floppy disk drives light up, one at a time. If you have two floppy disk drives, you see the light on drive A flash on first, and then the light on drive B. After testing the floppy disk drives, the computer tests the hard disk drive to make sure that it's working, and you see the hard disk drive light go on.

After testing the hardware components, the computer performs the second step: searching for the DOS (disk operating system) file, COMMAND.COM. The computer reads drive A, searching for a disk containing COMMAND.COM. If no disk is found in drive A, the computer searches drive C. (In the network environment, most users use a boot disk in drive A; therefore, the search for an operating system on drive C doesn't occur.) Again, if you watch while the computer boots, you will see the light for drive A, then the light for drive C.

PC NOTE

If you place a disk that doesn't contain COMMAND.COM into drive A, the computer displays a message that drive A contains a nonsystem disk. You should remove the disk and press any key to continue the startup process.

Until now, the sequence of events has been standard; all the preceding events happen on any PC whenever you boot it. The next boot instruction tells the computer to perform the third step: to look for a configuration file, CONFIG.SYS, and, if it finds the file, to execute the instructions in the file. The CONFIG.SYS file typically contains instructions for loading a mouse driver or for handling memory. The instructions in the CONFIG.SYS file are similar to loading extensions (INITs) on a Mac and affect the way in which the computer operates and enables programs to operate. Because the CONFIG.SYS file can be created and modified by the owner of the PC, different things may happen, depending on whose PC you are using.

After executing any instructions found in the CONFIG.SYS file, the computer performs the fourth step: looking for the AUTOEXEC.BAT file, which also can be created and modified by the owner of the PC. If the computer finds an AUTOEXEC.BAT file, it executes the instructions in that file. The AUTOEXEC.BAT file typically contains instructions that the owner wants the computer to perform when booting. These instructions may include starting memory-resident programs (programs that are available, even inside other programs, by touching a few keys) and loading menus or programs. If, for example, the PC owner works almost exclusively in WordPerfect for DOS, he might include in the AUTOEXEC.BAT file an instruction that starts WordPerfect for DOS; then, whenever he boots the computer, WordPerfect for DOS starts.

Starting a Program

Typically, based on instructions included in the PC's AUTOEXEC.BAT file, you might see any of the following items onscreen when the computer finishes the boot process:

- A menu
- The MS-DOS Shell
- Microsoft Windows
- A DOS prompt

The way you start a program on a PC depends on which of the above items appears onscreen after the boot process. In the following sections, you learn to identify which of the environments appears on your screen after the boot process ends. You learn how to start a program from any of these screens, except the MS-DOS Shell. If you find you are working in the MS-DOS Shell, refer to Chapter 11, which is devoted to using the MS-DOS Shell to start programs and perform other DOS commands.

Using a Menu To Start a Program

Many PC users depend on menus to help them start programs. Typically, those PC users include a statement in the AUTOEXEC.BAT file to start the menu program. The menu then

appears immediately after the computer executes the AUTOEXEC.BAT file.

Because many menu programs are available on the market and users can create their own menus, you may not see the same menu on the different PCs you use. Direct Access is a popular menu program you may encounter; Figure 2.1 shows the Direct Access menu as an example of a menu program.

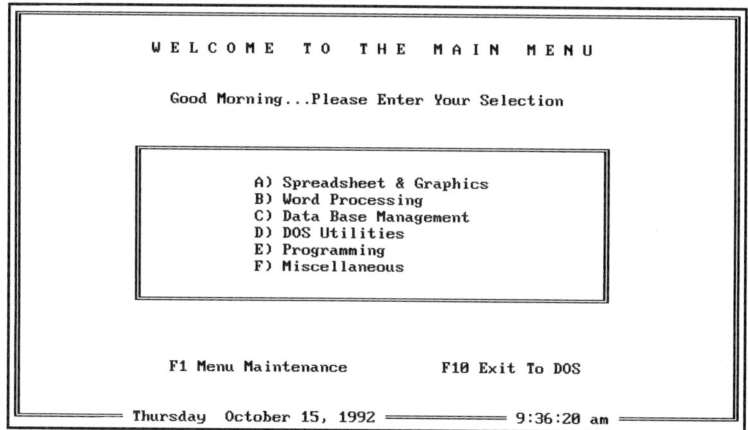

Figure 2.1.

The Direct Access menu.

Most menu programs work in basically the same way. To choose a menu command, you press a number or a letter or a function key associated with the program you want to start, or you press an arrow key to highlight the name of the program you want to start and then press the Enter key. Unfortunately (for a Mac user), most DOS-based menu programs don't support the use of a mouse to choose a program from the menu.

If you don't see the name of the program you want to start on the menu, you must start the program from a DOS prompt. In most cases, the menu you see also has a command that exits from the menu to DOS. If you need to start the program from the DOS prompt, choose the command that exits to DOS and then see "Using the DOS Prompt To Start a Program" later in this chapter. (If the menu does not contain a command that exits to DOS, see "Using the DOS Prompt To Start a Program" for information on bypassing the menu to get to DOS.)

Identifying the MS-DOS Shell

As part of DOS Version 4.0 and 5.0, Microsoft supplied the MS-DOS Shell to simplify using DOS. In this section, you learn to identify the various versions of the MS-DOS Shell screen that may appear after the AUTOEXEC.BAT file is executed. After you determine that you are looking at the MS-DOS Shell, refer to Chapter 11 for detailed information on using the MS-DOS Shell to start DOS-based programs and to perform DOS commands.

The default view of the MS-DOS Shell for Version 5.0, the Program/File Lists view, looks like the view in Figure 2.2.

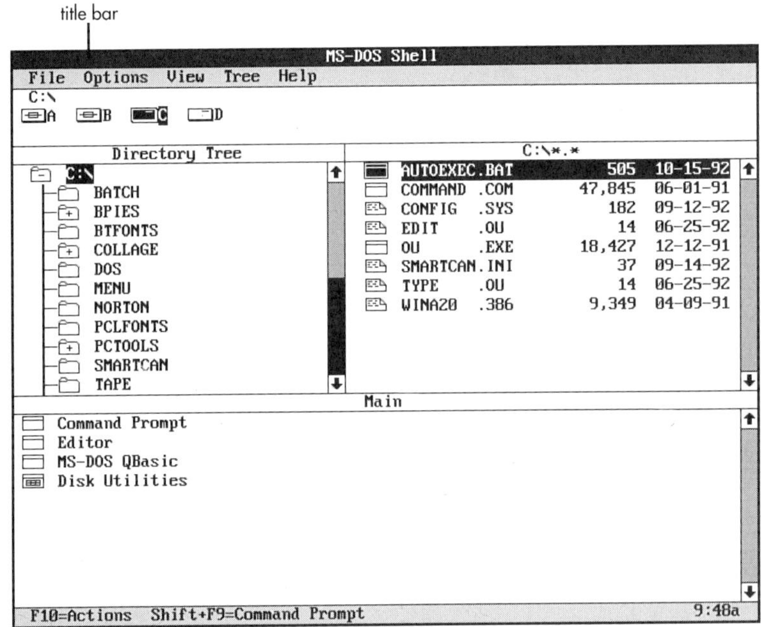

Figure 2.2.

The default view of the MS-DOS Shell, Version 5.0.

Or, because users can control the appearance of the MS-DOS Shell, you may see a screen like one of the screens in Figures 2.3, 2.4, 2.5, or 2.6. On all these screens, the title bar appears at the top of the screen. The title bar always contains the name of the program that is running. In this case, `MS-DOS Shell` appears in the title bar of Figures 2.2, 2.3, 2.4, 2.5, and 2.6.

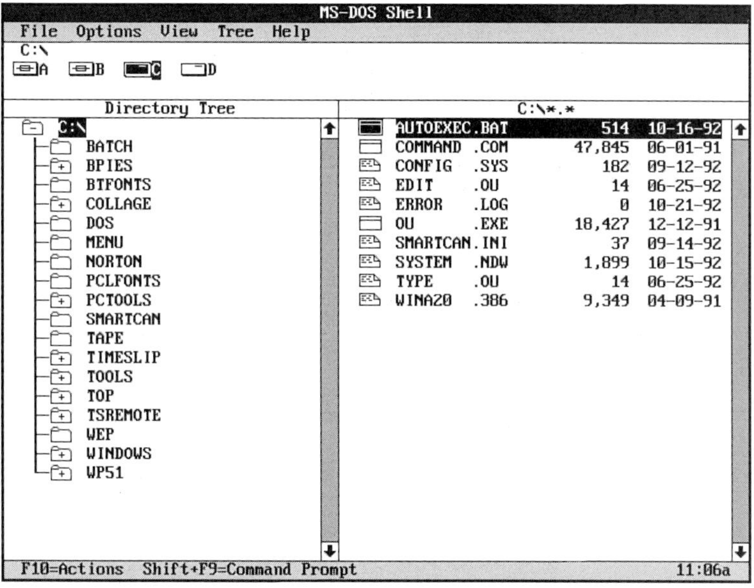

Figure 2.3. The Single File List view of the MS-DOS Shell.

```
                              MS-DOS Shell
 File  Options  View  Tree  Help
 C:\
 A  B  C  D
          Directory Tree                        C:\*.*
   C:\                                AUTOEXEC.BAT       514  10-16-92
    BATCH                             COMMAND .COM    47,845  06-01-91
    BPIES                             CONFIG  .SYS       182  09-12-92
    BTFONTS                           EDIT    .OU         14  06-25-92
    COLLAGE                           ERROR   .LOG         0  10-21-92
    DOS                               OU      .EXE    18,427  12-12-91
    MENU                              SMARTCAN.INI        37  09-14-92
    NORTON                            SYSTEM  .NDW     1,899  10-15-92
    PCLFONTS                          TYPE    .OU         14  06-25-92
    PCTOOLS                           WINA20  .386     9,349  04-09-91
 A  B  C  D
          Directory Tree                        C:\*.*
   C:\                                AUTOEXEC.BAT       514  10-16-92
    BATCH                             COMMAND .COM    47,845  06-01-91
    BPIES                             CONFIG  .SYS       182  09-12-92
    BTFONTS                           EDIT    .OU         14  06-25-92
    COLLAGE                           ERROR   .LOG         0  10-21-92
    DOS                               OU      .EXE    18,427  12-12-91
    MENU                              SMARTCAN.INI        37  09-14-92
    NORTON                            SYSTEM  .NDW     1,899  10-15-92
    PCLFONTS                          TYPE    .OU         14  06-25-92
 F10=Actions  Shift+F9=Command Prompt                          11:06a
```

Figure 2.4. The Dual File List view of the MS-DOS Shell.

```
                              MS-DOS Shell
 File  Options  View  Tree  Help
 C:\WP51\BOOKORG
 A  B  C  D
                                                     *.*
                            000UT                 20,318  07-05-91   2:08p
 File                       000UT    .ORG         22,857  10-14-91  10:14a
   Name   : 000UT           01START               44,797  07-05-91   1:19p
   Attr   : ....            01START  .WP5         61,694  09-27-91   3:14p
 Selected            C      02ENTRY               39,713  06-27-91   2:15p
   Number:           1      02ENTRY  .WP5         65,452  09-27-91   2:53p
   Size  :         514      02PC-01  .PCX         24,656  10-15-92   9:37a
 Directory                  02PC-01B .PCX          8,143  10-15-92   9:36a
   Name  : BOOKORG          02PC-02  .PCX         48,865  10-15-92   9:48a
   Size  :     573,066      02PC-07  .PCX         45,125  10-15-92  11:39a
   Files :          30      03CLINFO .WP5         86,960  09-27-91   3:10p
 Disk                       03EDIT                25,638  06-27-91   2:17p
   Name  : DRIVE_C          03PC-01  .PCX         48,865  10-15-92   9:48a
   Size  : 105,097,216      03PC-06  .PCX         41,140  10-15-92   9:56a
   Avail :  29,593,600      04CLINFO              69,928  07-05-91   1:22p
   Files :       3,015      04CLTRAN .WP5         37,594  09-27-91   3:10p
   Dirs  :          81      04PC-01  .PCX          6,568  10-15-92  11:53a
                            04PC-02  .PCX         23,140  10-15-92  11:55a
                            04PC-07  .PCX         62,289  10-15-92  11:55a
                            05CLTRAN              38,196  07-05-91   1:27p
                            05CRIT   .WP5         31,295  10-01-91  12:41p
                            05PC-01  .PCX         45,125  10-15-92  11:39a
                            05PC-06  .PCX         29,351  10-15-92  10:39a
 F10=Actions  Shift+F9=Command Prompt                              11:07a
```

Figure 2.5.

The All Files view of the MS-DOS Shell.

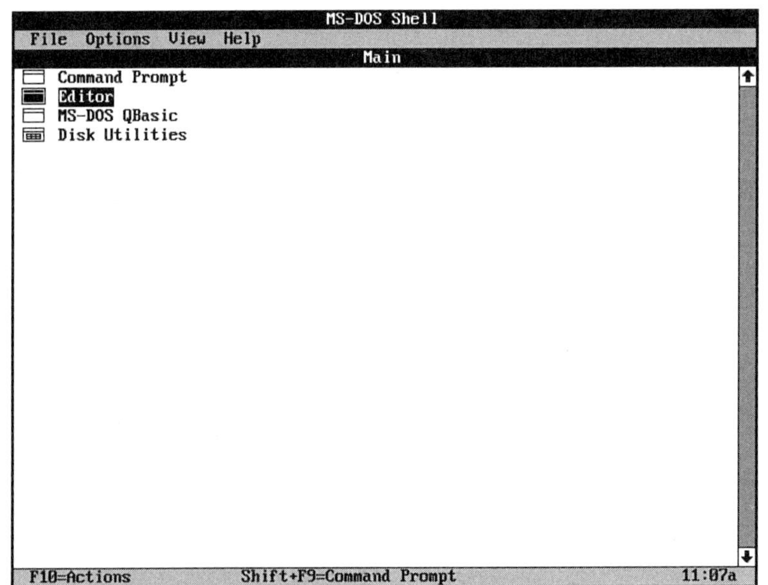

Figure 2.6.

The Program List view of the MS-DOS Shell.

You can use the MS-DOS Shell to do more than just start programs; you also can use it to copy or print files and perform other basic DOS functions. Even if you don't see the MS-DOS Shell when you start the computer, you still can start the MS-DOS Shell from a DOS prompt if you are using DOS Version 4.0 or later. (Later in this chapter, in the section "Using the DOS Prompt To Start a Program," you learn to identify the version of DOS you are using.) Chapter 11 contains detailed information on starting and using the MS-DOS Shell.

PC NOTE

If the MS-DOS Shell configuration includes enabling the Task Swapper, you may see an additional area called the Active Task List on either the default view or the Program List view.

Using Microsoft Windows To Start a Program

You also may see Microsoft Windows appear after the computer executes the AUTOEXEC.BAT file. Microsoft Windows is an operating environment that, in the world of DOS, provides a graphical user interface (also called GUI, pronounced "gooey") with which you can use either a mouse or a keyboard. Windows most closely resembles the Desktop on a Mac. Figure 2.7 shows a sample opening screen in Windows 3.1.

Because the IBM world is flexible and users can define what actually appears, not all Windows screens look the same. Most, however, show the Program Manager (which you can identify by checking the title bar at the top of the screen), although some third-party vendors have created their own versions of the Program Manager. If, for example, the Norton Desktop for Windows is running, you see `Norton Desktop` in the title bar, with a screen that appears similar to the one in Figure 2.8.

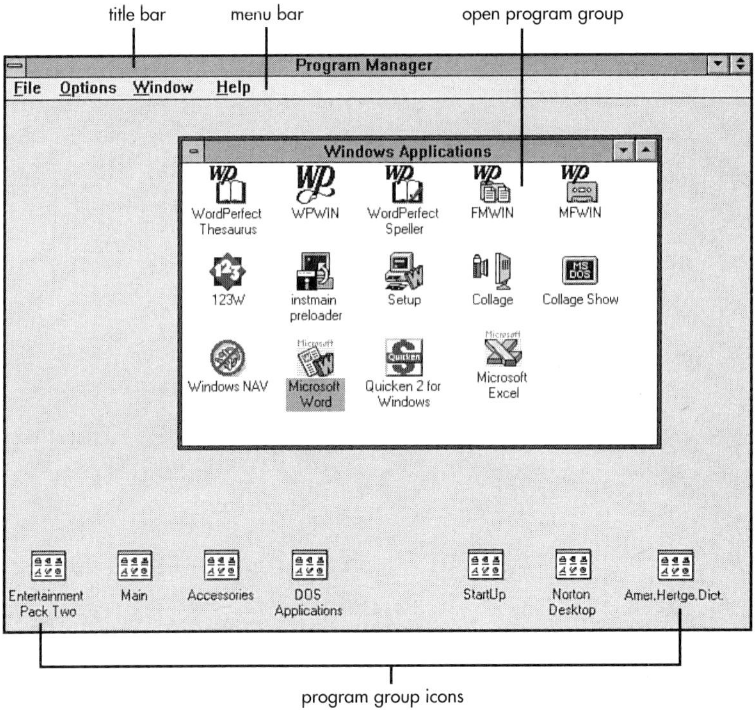

title bar
menu bar
open program group

program group icons

Figure 2.7.

A typical Windows opening screen.

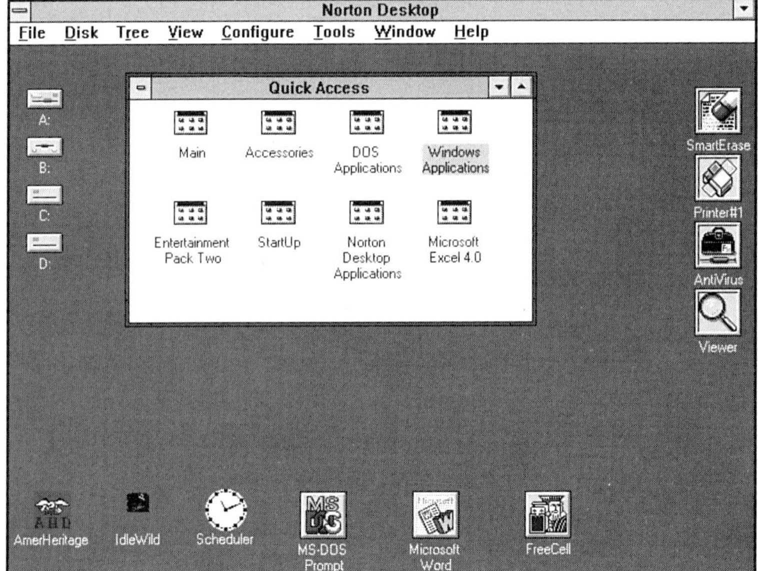

Figure 2.8.

A sample Norton Desktop for Windows screen.

Because most Windows users use the default Program Manager, though, the rest of this discussion refers to the default Windows Program Manager.

In addition to providing a graphical user interface, Windows also permits the user to perform multitasking. **Multitasking** enables the user to perform two or more functions simultaneously. In a multitasking environment, for example, the user can send data over a modem and work in a word processor while the data transmission takes place. To provide multitasking, the operating environment must manage the memory of the computer. Each program must obtain enough memory to perform its functions; otherwise, the user is warned that sufficient memory is unavailable to perform all the requested tasks. DOS alone does not provide the capability to multitask.

Windows and its Program Manager manage the allocation of the computer's memory among various programs. To take advantage of the capabilities of Windows, programs must be written to operate in the Windows environment. Programs that were written to run under DOS alone can run under Windows, but cannot take advantage of all the Windows' capabilities.

If you find yourself in Microsoft Windows, you can use Windows to start the program you want to run. Chapters 4, 6, 7, and 9 include a more detailed review of Windows basics. The rest of this section provides enough information to help you start a program in Windows.

Operating a Mouse in Windows

In the Windows environment, you can use a mouse or the keyboard to start programs, choose commands from menus, and choose options in dialog boxes. In Windows, a mouse looks and operates somewhat differently from a mouse on a Macintosh. A PC mouse has at least two mouse buttons. Unless otherwise instructed, you use the left mouse button. To use a mouse to choose an item in Windows, follow these steps:

1. Slide the mouse until the mouse pointer points to the item you want to choose.

2. Press and release a mouse button—usually the left mouse button—one time.

The action you perform in step 1 is known as **pointing**, and the action you perform in step 2 is known as **clicking**. You can click either the left or the right mouse button, as defined by the software program you are using. Most of the time, to choose an item, you click the left mouse button. You also may want to double-click. To **double-click**, you press and release the left mouse button twice in rapid succession. Occasionally, you may want to drag an item to move it from one location to another. To **drag**, point to the item you want to drag. Then, press and hold the left mouse button while sliding the mouse to move the mouse pointer to the new location.

Working with Menus and Commands in Windows

Just below the title bar in Figure 2.7, you see the menu bar. The menu bar contains menus, and each menu contains the commands you use in Windows. To see and use the commands, you can open a menu by using the mouse or the keyboard.

To open a menu by using the mouse, point to the menu you want to open and click the left mouse button. Windows opens the menu. To choose a command by using the mouse, point to the command and click the left mouse button. Windows executes the command.

Note the difference in the way clicking works in Windows compared to on a Mac. In Windows, for the most part, you don't need to hold down the mouse button while trying to open a menu and choose a command; the menus usually remain open after you release the mouse button. On a Mac, if you release the mouse button, the menu from which you were trying to choose a command closes.

You also can use the keyboard to open a menu and choose a command. First, you activate the menu bar by pressing the Alt key. A **reverse video bar** (or **highlight**) appears on the name of the first menu, **F**ile. Then, you can open a menu and choose a command in two ways:

- You can use the hot key shortcuts. Each menu and command contains an underlined letter, also called a **hot key**. You can press that key to open the menu or execute the command. When you press the W key, for example, the Program Manager opens the **W**indow menu and displays the commands available on that menu. In this book, all references to hot keys appear in boldface type.

- You can press one of the arrow keys on the keyboard to point to a menu or command, and then press the Enter key to choose it. When you press an arrow key, the reverse video bar moves. Continue pressing the arrow key until the reverse video bar appears on top of the menu or command to which you want to point. For example, you can press the Alt key to activate the menu bar and then press the left-arrow key twice to point to the **W**indow menu. Remember, when you use the arrow keys to point to a menu or command, you must press Enter to open that menu or choose that command.

Starting a Program from the Program Manager

The Program Manager contains program groups, which can appear as open windows or as icons. In Figure 2.7, the Windows Applications program group appears as an open window and all the other program groups appear as icons at the bottom of the screen.

Each program group contains icons that represent programs. You use these icons to start their programs. (To start a program, the program group must be open so that you can see the icon that represents the program you want to start.)

To use the mouse to open a program group that appears as an icon, double-click on the icon. To start a program in that group, double-click on the icon representing the program in the program group window. The Program Manager starts the program.

To use the keyboard to open a program group that appears as an icon, follow these steps:

1. Press the **Alt** key to activate the menu bar.

2. Press **W** to open the **W**indow menu.

   The Program Manager displays the commands on the Window menu (see Figure 2.9).

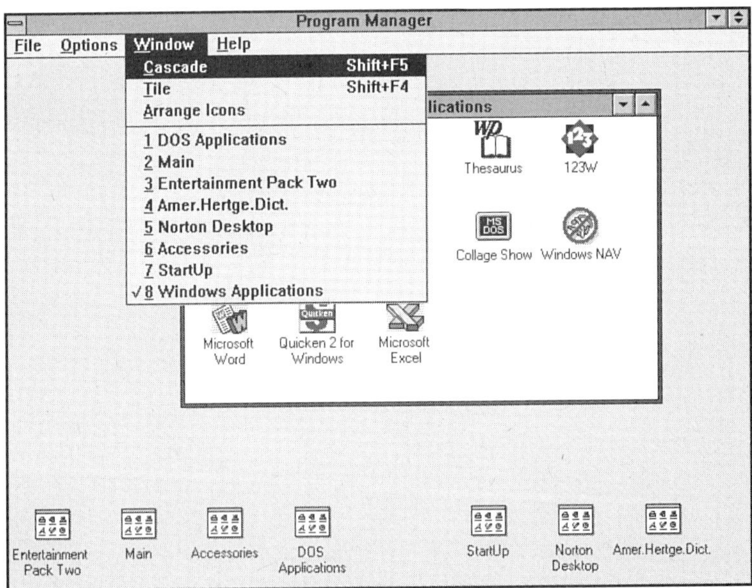

Figure 2.9. The **W**indow menu.

3. From the numbered list that appears below the line in the **W**indow menu, press a number to choose the program group you want to open (or use the arrow keys to highlight it and then press Enter).

   Windows opens the specified program group.

To start a program by using the keyboard, use the arrow keys to point to the program you want to start. Then, press Enter. The Program Manager starts the program.

Using the DOS Prompt To Start a Program

After the boot process ends, you might see `C>` or `C:\>`, followed by a small blinking square or underline (see Figure. 2.10).

Figure 2.10.

The DOS prompt.

You are looking at a DOS prompt. The **DOS prompt** identifies the default disk drive on which DOS will operate if you enter a command. The DOS prompt also includes the **cursor**, the blinking square or underline, which designates the place where your commands will appear when you type. If the DOS prompt appears as `C>` or `C:\>`, DOS will operate on drive C when you enter a command. The DOS prompt `C>` or `C:\>` is often referred to as "the C prompt." If you place a disk in drive A and switch to drive A (by typing A: and then pressing Enter), the DOS prompt changes to A> or A:\> (an A prompt), and DOS will perform any commands you enter on the disk in drive A. (To switch back to drive C, type C: and press Enter.)

You use DOS commands to instruct the computer to perform actions. When you type a DOS command, the character case doesn't matter—you can use uppercase, lowercase, or a combination of the two. In this book, however, all DOS commands appear in uppercase. This convention helps you easily identify the text you need to type to use that command.

If a menu program does not enable you to exit to DOS, you can reboot the computer and force the PC to bypass the menu and display a DOS prompt instead. After you see the drive lights flash on during the boot process, press and hold down the Ctrl key and press the Pause key. When you press Pause as you hold down Ctrl, Pause acts as the break key. You should see this message onscreen:

```
Terminate Batch Job (Y/N)?
```

Press the Y key to stop the computer from executing the AUTOEXEC.BAT file and loading the menu. You then will see a DOS prompt.

If you are using MS-DOS Version 4.0 or 5.0, you may want to try to use the MS-DOS Shell (described in Chapter 11). To find out what version of MS-DOS you are using, type VER at the C prompt and press Enter. (VER stands for version.) DOS returns a message similar to the one displayed in Figure 2.11.

To start a program from the C> prompt, you must know the directory in which the program is stored and the name of the file that starts the program. A **directory** is similar to a folder on a Mac. Users define directories in which to store related programs and data. For more information on directories, see "Storing Information on Disks" in Chapter 12. In the installation instructions for a program, the manufacturer usually suggests a directory name in which to store the program files; most users accept these suggestions. You use a portion of the program file name to start the

program. Table 2.1 lists the directory names and program file names of several popular DOS-based software programs.

```
C:\>ver

MS-DOS Version 5.00

C:\>
```

Figure 2.11. The DOS message after you issue the VER command.

Table 2.1. Default directories and startup files of several DOS-based programs.

Software Package	Directory	Startup File Name
WordPerfect for DOS Version 4.2 and earlier	\WP	WP.EXE
WordPerfect for DOS Version 5.0	\WP50	WP.EXE
WordPerfect for DOS Version 5.1	\WP51	WP.EXE
Lotus 1-2-3 Release 2.01 and earlier	\123	123.COM
Lotus 1-2-3 Release 2.2	\123R22	123.EXE
Lotus 1-2-3 Release 2.3	\123R23	123.EXE
Lotus 1-2-3 Release 2.4	\123R24	123.EXE
Lotus 1-2-3 Release 3.0	\123R3	123.EXE
Lotus 1-2-3 Release 3.1 and 3.1+	\123R31	123.EXE
dBASE (all versions)	DBASE	DBASE.EXE
Q&A	\QA	QA.EXE

Note that all file names are divided into two parts, separated by a period (.). The second part of the name is called the **extension**. You can use the extension to distinguish files that start programs from files that contain data. Files that start programs have extensions of EXE, COM, or BAT. When you use a program name to start a program, you type just the first part of the name; you don't type the extension. If you don't know the name of the program file or directory containing your program file, and it doesn't appear in Table 2.1, check the installation instructions in the user's guide for that program.

After you identify the name of the directory and the program file, use the following commands to start the program. Start from a C> prompt and substitute the correct directory name for *DIRNAME* and the first part of the program name for *PROGNAME* (the italics indicate variable information):

```
CD\DIRNAME
PROGNAME
```

Be sure to type only the requested information on one line, and then press Enter at the end of the line. For example, after you type `CD\` and the name of the directory containing the program file, press Enter.

To start WordPerfect 5.1 from the C> prompt, for example, type the following DOS commands:

```
CD\WP51
WP
```

Be sure to press Enter after typing `CD\WP51` and again after typing `WP`. DOS starts WordPerfect 5.1.

Chapter Summary

In this chapter you learned how to turn on a PC and how to identify the operating environment in which you find yourself after the computer completes its startup process. You learned that the on/off switch for a PC is not on the keyboard, as it may be on our Mac, but on the box. You learned that the beginning of the startup process for the PC is similar to the startup process for a Mac. On a PC, however, a user can define two files—a configuration file and an automatic execution file—that determine how the computer functions and what screens appear at the end of the startup process.

Chapters 3 through 9 in *The Mac User's PC* focus on specific software packages. You should read the chapters that pertain to the software you want to use. Chapter 10 tells you about database programs you may want to avoid if you are working on someone else's PC. If, after starting the computer, you find yourself in the MS-DOS Shell, read Chapter 11. If you find yourself at a DOS prompt, you may want to read Chapter 12. If you need to transfer and translate files between a Mac and a PC, read Chapter 13.

ONE

TWO

THREE

FOUR

FIVE

SIX

SEVEN

EIGHT

NINE

TEN

ELEVEN

TWELVE

THIRTEEN

GLOSSARY

Working with WordPerfect for DOS Files

In the first two chapters of *The Mac User's PC*, you learned about the physical appearance of a PC, how to turn on a PC, how to recognize what you may see onscreen, and how to start programs. In this chapter, you will learn very basic information about using WordPerfect for DOS. This chapter is not intended to make you an expert at using WordPerfect for DOS; this chapter simply teaches you how to perform some basic tasks. You will learn how to open, edit, save, and print a WordPerfect for DOS document; how to copy a WordPerfect for DOS file to a floppy disk; and how to exit the program properly. And you will learn one other important thing—how to get help in WordPerfect for DOS so that you can teach yourself to do the things that aren't covered in this book! In fact, this chapter starts by showing you how to get help.

Using an appropriate technique you learned in Chapter 2, start the WordPerfect for DOS program (or see Chapter 11 for information on starting a program from the MS-DOS Shell). The rest of the discussion in this chapter refers to WordPerfect 5.1, but if you are using an earlier version, you will still be able to follow along. The screen didn't change dramatically between versions even though the features available in the program (and therefore the commands available on some menus) changed.

When you start WordPerfect for DOS, you see the main screen, which looks like the screen in Figure 3.1.

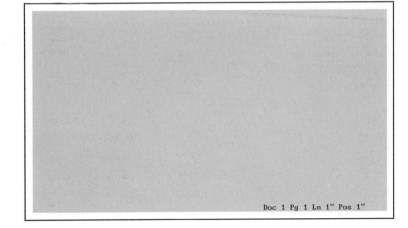

Figure 3.1.
The opening WordPerfect for DOS screen.

Getting Help in WordPerfect for DOS

As the old saying goes, there's good news and there's bad news. Some of the good news is that WordPerfect for DOS relies heavily on the function keys to execute commands. So, because you also can execute WordPerfect for the Mac commands by using the function keys, this technique probably is already familiar. The bad news is that the commands in WordPerfect for DOS are almost entirely unfamiliar unless you have been using the WordPerfect 5.x keyboard in WordPerfect for the Mac (which you probably aren't doing if you're using WordPerfect for the Mac). But, the rest of the good news is that WordPerfect for DOS contains an excellent online Help facility.

You can start the Help program in WordPerfect for DOS by pressing the Help key (F3). In WordPerfect 5.1, the help you receive is context-sensitive. If you are looking at a menu when you press F3, for example, the help you get is about that menu. In WordPerfect for DOS Version 5.0 or earlier, you see the opening Help screen when you press F3 (this screen also appears in WordPerfect 5.1 when you press F3 from the main screen). If you press F3 and don't see a screen similar to the screen in Figure 3.2, try pressing F1. If

you are using WordPerfect for DOS Version 5.0 or later, the PC's owner may have changed the Help key to F1.

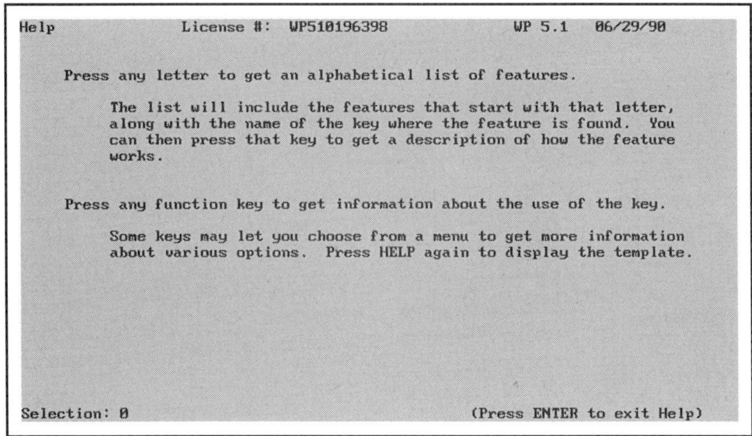

Help License #: WP510196398 WP 5.1 06/29/90

Press any letter to get an alphabetical list of features.

The list will include the features that start with that letter, along with the name of the key where the feature is found. You can then press that key to get a description of how the feature works.

Press any function key to get information about the use of the key.

Some keys may let you choose from a menu to get more information about various options. Press HELP again to display the template.

Selection: 0 (Press ENTER to exit Help)

Figure 3.2.

The opening Help screen.

As you see from the information on the opening Help screen, you can access an alphabetical listing of features in WordPerfect for DOS. This listing displays the features, their WordPerfect for DOS keys, and their keystrokes. To look up a feature, press the letter of the alphabet associated with the function you want to perform. If you want to copy something, for example, press C for "Copy." The screen in Figure 3.3 appears.

Features [C]	WordPerfect Key	Keystrokes
Cancel	Cancel	F1
Cancel Hyphenation Code	Home	Home,/
Cancel Print Job(s)	Print	Shft-F7,4,1
Capitalize Block (Block On)	Switch	Shft-F3,1
Cartridges and Fonts	Print	Shft-F7,s,3,4
Case Conversion (Block On)	Switch	Shft-F3
Center Block (Block On)	Center	Shft-F6
Center Justification	Format	Shft-F8,1,3,2
Center Page (Top to Bottom)	Format	Shft-F8,2,1
Center Tab Setting	Format	Shft-F8,1,8,c
Center Text	Center	Shft-F6
Centered Text With Dot Leaders	Center	Shft-F6,Shft-F6
Centimeters, Units of Measure	Setup	Shft-F1,3,8
Change Comment to Text	Text In/Out	Ctrl-F5,4,3
Change Default Directory	List	F5,=,Dir name,Enter
Change Font	Font	Ctrl-F8
Change Supplementary Dictionary	Spell	Ctrl-F2,4
Change Text to Comment (Block On)	Text In/Out	Shft-F5
Character Sets	Compose	Ctrl-v or Ctrl-2
Character Spacing	Format	Shft-F8,4,6,3

More... Press c to continue.

Selection: 0 (Press ENTER to exit Help)

Figure 3.3.

The first Help Topics screen for the letter C.

The screen is divided into three columns. The left column lists the Help topic (or the action you want to perform). The middle column lists the name of the WordPerfect for DOS function key that performs the action in the first column (more on this in just a moment). The right column lists the keystrokes for performing the action in the left column.

Notice that "Copy" doesn't appear—yet. At the bottom of the screen, WordPerfect for DOS tells you to press C again to see more topics for that letter. When you finally see "Copy," you will notice these options for the topic (see Figure 3.4): `Copy Block` (two methods); `Copy File(s)`; `Copy, Keyboard`; and `Copy Text`.

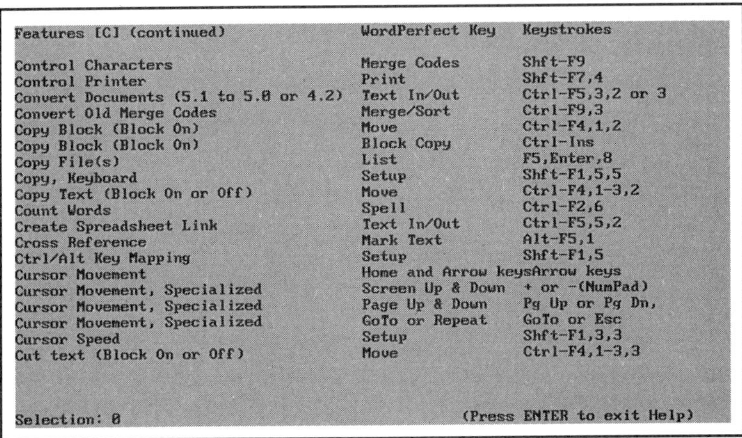

Features [C] (continued)	WordPerfect Key	Keystrokes
Control Characters	Merge Codes	Shft-F9
Control Printer	Print	Shft-F7,4
Convert Documents (5.1 to 5.0 or 4.2)	Text In/Out	Ctrl-F5,3,2 or 3
Convert Old Merge Codes	Merge/Sort	Ctrl-F9,3
Copy Block (Block On)	Move	Ctrl-F4,1,2
Copy Block (Block On)	Block Copy	Ctrl-Ins
Copy File(s)	List	F5,Enter,8
Copy, Keyboard	Setup	Shft-F1,5,5
Copy Text (Block On or Off)	Move	Ctrl-F4,1-3,2
Count Words	Spell	Ctrl-F2,6
Create Spreadsheet Link	Text In/Out	Ctrl-F5,5,2
Cross Reference	Mark Text	Alt-F5,1
Ctrl/Alt Key Mapping	Setup	Shft-F1,5
Cursor Movement	Home and Arrow keys	Arrow keys
Cursor Movement, Specialized	Screen Up & Down	+ or -(NumPad)
Cursor Movement, Specialized	Page Up & Down	Pg Up or Pg Dn,
Cursor Movement, Specialized	GoTo or Repeat	GoTo or Esc
Cursor Speed	Setup	Shft-F1,3,3
Cut text (Block On or Off)	Move	Ctrl-F4,1-3,3

Selection: 0 (Press ENTER to exit Help)

Figure 3.4.

The Help Topics screen that includes options for "Copy."

The opening Help screen (refer to Figure 3.2) also tells you how to get help for a function key: press the function key after starting the Help program. You also can consult the middle column of the Help Topics screen, which contains the name of the WordPerfect for DOS function key that performs the action in the first column. Remember that the function keys on the keyboard can be (and usually are) redefined by the software to help you perform common actions in the software.

Because WordPerfect for DOS depends heavily on the function keys, the software comes with a template you can place on the

keyboard next to the function keys for easy reference. This template is similar to the template in Figure 3.5. Each function key description is limited to four words, and each word is printed in red, blue, green, or black.

WordPerfect®
for IBM® Personal Computers

Column Left/Right	Home, ←/→	
Compose	2	
Delete to End of Ln/Pg	End/PgDn	
Delete Word	Backspace	
Hard Page	Enter	
◆Margin Release	Tab	
Pull-Down Menus		
Screen Up/Down	–/+ (num)	
Word Left/Right	←/→	

ISBN 1-55692-464-X
© WordPerfect Corp. 1989 TMUS/WP5110Q—11/89

Shell	Spell	Screen	Move	*Ctrl*	Text In/Out	Tab Align	Footnote	Font	*Ctrl*	Merge/Sort	Macro Define		
Thesaurus	Replace	Reveal Codes	Block	*Alt*	Mark Text	Flush Right	Columns/Table	Style	*Alt*	Graphics	Macro		
Setup	◆Search	Switch	◆Indent◆	*Shift*	Date/Outline	Center	Print	Format	*Shift*	Merge Codes	Retrieve		
Cancel	◆Search	Help	◆Indent		List	Bold	Exit	Underline		End Field	Save	Reveal Codes	Block
F1	*F2*	*F3*	*F4*		*F5*	*F6*	*F7*	*F8*		*F9*	*F10*	*F11*	*F12*

Figure 3.5.

A sample of the WordPerfect for DOS template.

The words on the template represent the commands in WordPerfect for DOS. These commands perform the various actions listed as Help topics on the Help screens. At various places on the template, you will see columns with the color-coded words "Ctrl," "Shift," and "Alt." You use these color-coded words in combination with function keys to execute commands in WordPerfect for DOS. For example, press Ctrl+F3 to start the Speller. Table 3.1 summarizes the way you use the function keys in WordPerfect for DOS.

Table 3.1.

Function keys and WordPerfect for DOS commands.

Color	Keystroke
Red	Hold down the Ctrl key and press the appropriate function key.
Blue	Hold down the Alt key and press the appropriate function key.
Green	Hold down the Shift key and press the appropriate function key.
Black	Press the appropriate function key.

OK, so what do you do if your template isn't color-coded? Just remember that all the commands are listed in the same order for each function key—the top action is red, the second is blue, the third is green, and the fourth is black.

And what do you do if you don't have a template? WordPerfect for DOS has incorporated an onscreen representation of the template within its online Help facility. From the main screen, press F3 twice to see the Help screen that appears in Figure 3.6.

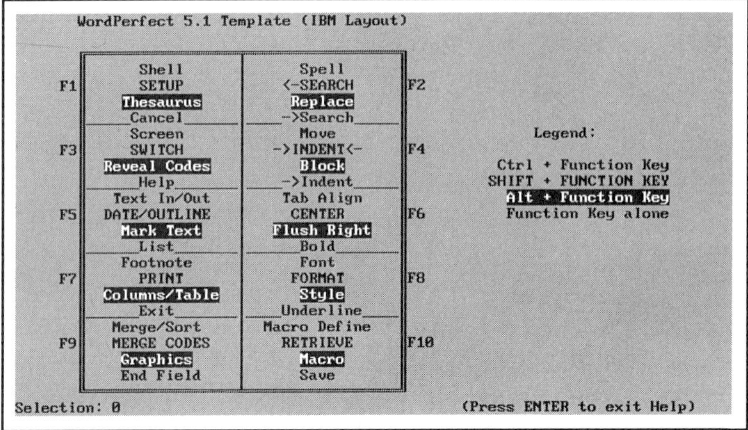

Figure 3.6.

The Help screen that shows the commands assigned to each function key.

Identifying WordPerfect for DOS Screen Parts

As a matter of expediency, let's review the parts of the WordPerfect for DOS screen. As you can see from Figure 3.7, the screen is primarily blank except for the status bar, which appears in the lower right corner.

From the status bar, you can identify the **document** in which you are working (WordPerfect refers to a file as a document) and the current location of the cursor. (The **cursor** is a small blinking underline that appears in the upper left corner of the screen, and indicates where text will appear when you type.) When you first

start WordPerfect for DOS, you always see an empty document screen on which you can start creating a new document. The status bar indicates that you are working in Document 1, and that the cursor is located on Page 1, Line 1 inch, at Position 1 inch. This position indicates that one-inch margins already exist on all sides of the page. (POS may be blinking if the Num Lock feature is on.)

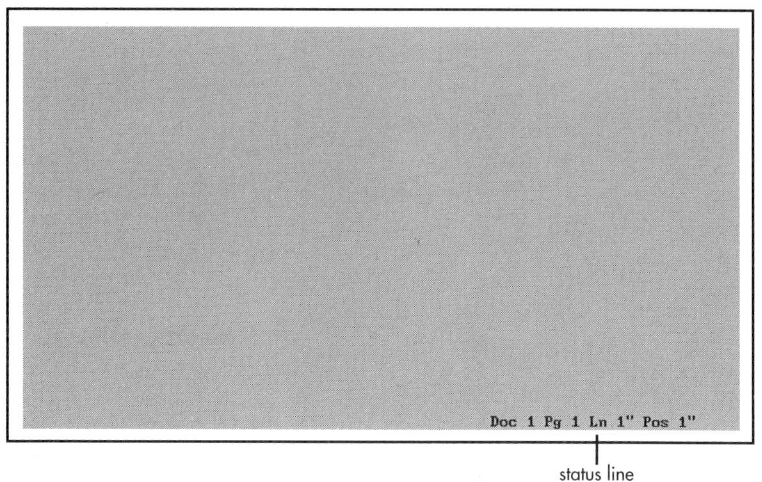

Figure 3.7. The main WordPerfect for DOS screen.

PC NOTE

For versions earlier than 5.0, WordPerfect for DOS expresses the cursor location in units that work well with nonproportional fonts such as Courier and Prestige Elite. In Versions 5.0 and later, you can customize the program to use these special units, and therefore the status bar may not display measurements in inches.

Until you type, you cannot move the cursor, not even by using the arrow keys.

Opening a WordPerfect for DOS File

Suppose that someone brings you a letter, asks you to make some minor changes to it, and then wants you to print the revised letter. In this section, you learn how to open (retrieve) a WordPerfect for DOS document. In the next three sections, you learn how to edit, save, and print a WordPerfect for DOS document.

In WordPerfect for DOS, opening a document is called **retrieving**. You can retrieve a document in WordPerfect for DOS in two ways. One method works when you know the exact file name for the document. The other method works when you *don't* know the exact file name. To retrieve a document for which you know the exact file name, follow these steps:

1. Press **Shift**+**F10**.

   A prompt appears at the bottom of the screen, asking you to type the name of the document you want to retrieve.

2. Type the file name for the document you want to retrieve, and then press **Enter**.

   WordPerfect for DOS retrieves and displays the document. Most users set up WordPerfect for DOS so that the name of the document appears at the bottom of the screen.

If you don't know the file name for the document, you can use WordPerfect for DOS's List Files screen and menu. To find and retrieve the document this way, follow these steps:

1. Press **F5**, and then press **Enter**.

   WordPerfect for DOS displays the List Files screen in Figure 3.8. Notice the menu commands at the bottom of the screen. The default menu command is **6 L**ook.

```
11-05-92  04:22p                 Directory C:\WP51\WPDATA\*.*
Document size:    13,078   Free: 31,565,824 Used:     637,531     Files:       68

 .    Current     <Dir>                        |  ..    Parent      <Dir>
 ADDENDUM.CPX    13,921  04-13-90 11:52a       |  ADDENDUM.IBE    14,258  04-13-90 10:15a
 BARDI   .        7,415  07-23-92 02:38p       |  BARDI   .SAM     7,474  07-23-92 02:49p
 BEZEMEK .        3,357  12-12-91 05:23p       |  BOX     .        8,942  09-08-90 09:48a
 BPI     .        6,438  10-16-91 09:47a       |  BUSPLAN .OUT     8,594  04-04-90 08:07a
 CABLEVAL.        6,870  07-30-90 05:43p       |  CERTIFIC.       34,758  11-12-90 04:18p
 CITMAINT.RFP    24,170  04-12-90 03:30p       |  CITPLAN .AMD     4,193  06-17-89 11:38p
 CITRUS  .DB      7,688  03-07-90 06:41p       |  CLEMSON .       16,597  07-27-90 10:52a
 CLEMSON .LTR     4,896  07-27-90 12:38p       |  CLIENT  .LST     7,326  09-26-91 12:45p
 CONDOTUR.        3,599  07-23-90 02:57p       |  CPAS    .        1,837  10-16-91 10:18a
 DEPTREV .        2,905  04-06-90 08:22a       |  DOCTORS .        4,450  11-13-90 08:39a
 DOLRFP  .       89,712  04-09-90 07:09p       |  EXPOTIME.ADD     2,209  10-30-91 12:39p
 FICPA   .        3,912  09-11-90 10:35a       |  FLCCAB  .NET     6,228  11-27-89 10:18a
 FLCITRUS.LTR     2,758  03-29-89 09:19a       |  FLCITRUS.OUT     5,676  05-26-89 03:22p
 FLCITRUS.PLN    20,711  05-29-89 12:18a       |  FLCITRUS.PRP    11,123  03-29-89 10:00a
 FLCOSTS .STA     2,674  05-29-89 12:18a       |  FLFOLLOW.LTR     5,152  07-23-90 02:59p
 FLFOLLOW.PRP    24,616  10-06-89 10:18a       |  FLHARD  .SPC     1,124  05-27-89 12:34p
 FORM    .       12,484  09-08-90 08:40a       |  GUNS    .        6,230  09-17-91 09:58a
 HISBPI  .        5,994  10-11-90 09:05p       ▼  HORIZON .YE      5,984  08-21-91 11:47a

1 Retrieve; 2 Delete; 3 Move/Rename; 4 Print; 5 Short/Long Display;
6 Look; 7 Other Directory; 8 Copy; 9 Find; N Name Search: 6
```

menu line

Figure 3.8. The List Files screen.

PC NOTE

Each menu choice in WordPerfect for DOS contains both a number and a bold letter. You can choose from a menu by typing either the number or the bold letter.

2. Press the arrow keys to highlight the file name of a document.

3. Press **6** or **L** to choose the **L**ook command, and then press **Enter**.

   WordPerfect for DOS selects the default menu command **L**ook, and displays the contents of the file (see Figure 3.9). Notice that, at the bottom of the screen, you see the Look menu instead of a document name.

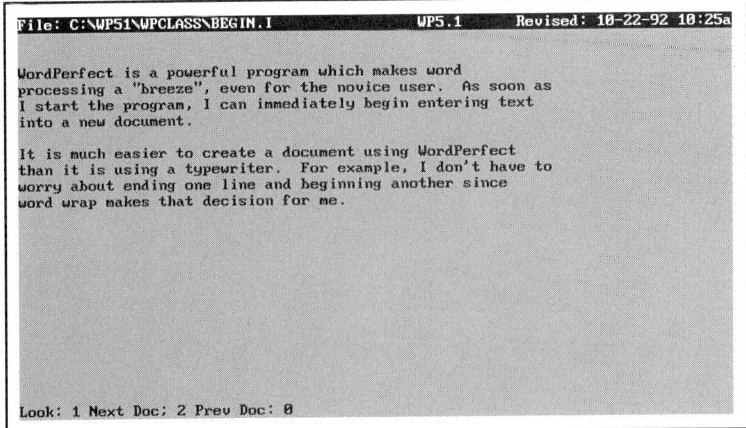

File: C:\WP51\WPCLASS\BEGIN.I WP5.1 Revised: 10-22-92 10:25a
WordPerfect is a powerful program which makes word
processing a "breeze", even for the novice user. As soon as
I start the program, I can immediately begin entering text
into a new document.
It is much easier to create a document using WordPerfect
than it is using a typewriter. For example, I don't have to
worry about ending one line and beginning another since
word wrap makes that decision for me.
Look: 1 Next Doc; 2 Prev Doc: 0

Figure 3.9. A document viewed from the List Files screen.

4. To return to the List Files screen, press **Enter**.

5. Continue this process until you find the document you need to edit.

6. With the file name of the correct document highlighted, press **1** or **R** to choose the **R**etrieve command and open the document.

> **PC NOTE**
>
> Remember, each menu choice in WordPerfect for DOS contains both a number and a bold letter. You can choose from a menu by typing either the number or the bold letter.

WordPerfect for DOS displays the document on the main screen, ready for you to edit. As you can see in Figure 3.10, the name of the document appears at the bottom of the screen.

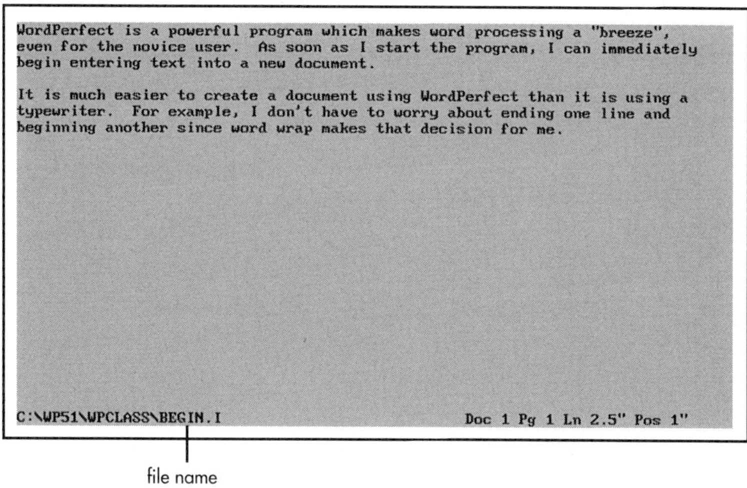
WordPerfect is a powerful program which makes word processing a "breeze",
even for the novice user. As soon as I start the program, I can immediately
begin entering text into a new document.
It is much easier to create a document using WordPerfect than it is using a
typewriter. For example, I don't have to worry about ending one line and
beginning another since word wrap makes that decision for me.
C:\WP51\WPCLASS\BEGIN.I
Doc 1 Pg 1 Ln 2.5" Pos 1"
file name

Figure 3.10. The WordPerfect for DOS main screen after retrieving a document.

A word of caution: As you can see from Figure 3.9, it is easy to confuse the screen in which you can just "look" at a document (the viewing screen) with the main screen in which you can edit a document. When you look at a document from the List Files screen, you might think you can edit the document. In fact, you can move the cursor by pressing the up- and down-arrow keys, but you cannot edit the document until you *retrieve* it. To distinguish between the editing screen and the viewing screen, note the following features of the *viewing* screen only:

- You can move the cursor up or down, but not left or right.
- A reverse video bar appears at the top of the viewing screen, identifying the name of the file and some statistics about when the file was last updated.
- The file name does not appear at the bottom of the screen. (Instead, the Look menu appears at the bottom of the screen. Using this menu, you can look at the next or previous document on the List Files screen.)

Performing Basic Editing in WordPerfect for DOS

After you type something in a new document or you retrieve a document you want to edit (one that already contains text), you can use the arrow keys in combination with other keys to move around. Table 3.2 summarizes the most commonly used ways in which you can move around a WordPerfect for DOS document.

Table 3.2.

Cursor-movement keys (in an existing document).

Key(s)	Effect
→, ←, ↓, or ↑	Moves right, left, down, or up one character.
Ctrl+→	Moves right one word.
Ctrl+←	Moves left one word.
Ctrl+↓	Moves down one paragraph.*
Ctrl+↑	Moves up one paragraph.*
Alt+↓	Moves down one sentence.*
Alt+↑	Moves up one sentence.*
End	Moves to the end of the current line.
Home, →	Moves to the end of the current line.
Home, ←	Moves to the beginning of the current line.
Home, ↓	Moves to the bottom of the current screen.
Home, ↑	Moves to the top of the current screen.
Home, Home, ↓	Moves to the end of the document.
Home, Home, ↑	Moves to the beginning of the document.
PgDn	Moves to the top of the next page.
PgUp	Moves to the top of the previous page.

*If the PC User has indicated to WordPerfect for DOS that an enhanced keyboard is installed.

By default, when you type in WordPerfect for DOS, you are working in insert mode. In **insert mode**, WordPerfect for DOS places characters at the current location of the cursor and moves all existing characters to the right. Alternatively, you can press the Ins key to switch to typeover mode. In **typeover mode**, WordPerfect for DOS places characters at the current location of the cursor and types over characters that exist at that location, removing them. The Ins key works like a **toggle switch**: press it once to change from insert mode to typeover mode; press it a second time to change back from typeover mode to insert mode.

You can use the Backspace key to delete the character immediately to the left of the cursor. You can use the Del key to delete the current character (the character under the cursor). WordPerfect for DOS also provides shortcuts for deleting words, lines, pages, and text you select. For more information, see WordPerfect for DOS Help.

Just as in WordPerfect for the Mac, when you want to "operate" on text (for example, to apply bold or underline character formatting), you select the text. Selecting text in WordPerfect for DOS is called **blocking**. To select text, follow these steps:

1. Position the cursor at the beginning of the text you want to select.

2. Press the Block key (either **F12** or **Alt**+**F4**).

3. Move the cursor (by using the arrow keys or the key combinations listed in Table 3.2) until the text you want to select is highlighted.

Saving a WordPerfect for DOS File

After you have made changes, you will want to save your work. You may want to save it to a different file, leaving the original intact. In this section, you learn about the two ways you can save a document, and you learn how to save the document under a name different from its original name.

You can save your work in two ways: by pressing F10 or by pressing F7. If you simply want to save the document and then continue working on it, press F10. If you want to save the document and either exit WordPerfect for DOS or clear the screen to begin working on another document, press F7.

Regardless of which method you choose, WordPerfect for DOS may prompt you with a series of questions about saving the document. The next two sections take you through the decision-making process involved when you save a document.

Using F10 To Save a Document

After you press the F10 key to save a file, WordPerfect for DOS displays the `Document to be saved:` prompt at the bottom of the screen. The steps you take depend on the result you're trying to achieve.

If you decide not to save the document, press F1 to cancel. (Note that you can press F1 at any point in the process to abort the saving process.)

If you are saving a new document, the prompt will appear blank. Follow these steps:

1. At the prompt, type a name for the document.

   You can use up to 11 characters in the name. The first part of the name can contain no more than 8 characters; the second part of the name, the **extension**, can contain no more than 3 characters. For more information on the rules for naming files in DOS, see Chapter 12.

2. Press **Enter**.

   WordPerfect for DOS saves the document with the name you typed and returns to the screen containing the document you just saved.

If you are saving an existing document, the prompt will contain the current name for the document. To save the document under a *different* name, follow these steps:

1. Type a new name at the prompt (right over the name that appears).

2. Press **Enter**.

   WordPerfect for DOS saves the current version of the document under the new name. The version that existed before you made changes still exists under its original name.

You might want to leave the original document available in cases where your changes may not be final. If you are unsure of the changes you have made, for example, and somebody else is going to come back and check your work, you might want to keep the original document. You then can show the person your version, and let him or her decide which version to continue using.

To save an existing document under a *same* name, follow these steps:

1. Press **Enter** to save the existing document under the same name.

WordPerfect for DOS displays the question `Replace existing file?`

2. Press **Y** to replace the existing version of the document with the new version you have created during editing.

   WordPerfect for DOS saves the current version of the document, using the name of the original document. The original version no longer exists.

   If you do not want to replace the original version of the document, press **N** or **F1** (to cancel saving).

   If you press **N**, WordPerfect for DOS then redisplays the `Document to be saved:` prompt, and you can supply a different name (see the preceding set of steps).

Note that changing the location of a document (for example, saving the document to a floppy disk when it was originally stored on the hard disk) falls into the category of saving an existing document under a different name.

Using F7 To Save a Document

Use F7 to save a document if you want to exit from WordPerfect for DOS or if you are finished working on the current document and you want to clear the screen so that you can start or retrieve a new document. When you press F7 to save a document, the process is similar to the process when you press F10; however, you see an additional question.

If you decide not to save the document, press F1 to cancel. (Note that you can press F1 at any point in the process to abort the saving process.)

If you are saving a new document, the prompt will appear blank. Follow these steps:

1. At the prompt, type a name for the document.

   You can use up to 11 characters in the name. The first part of the name can contain no more than 8 characters; the second part of the name, the **extension**, can contain no more than 3 characters. For more information on the rules for naming files in DOS, see Chapter 12.

2. Press **Enter**.

   WordPerfect for DOS saves the document with the name you typed, and then displays the prompt `Exit WP?`

3. Press **Y** to exit from WordPerfect for DOS. Press **N** to remove the saved document from the screen but remain in WordPerfect for DOS on a new blank document screen.

If you are saving an existing document, the prompt will contain the current name for the document. To save the document under a *different* name, follow these steps:

1. Type a new name at the prompt (right over the name that appears).

2. Press **Enter**.

   WordPerfect for DOS saves the current version of the document under the new name. The version that existed before you made changes still exists under its original name. WordPerfect then displays the prompt `Exit WP?`

3. Press **Y** to exit from WordPerfect for DOS. Press **N** to remove the saved document from the screen but remain in WordPerfect for DOS on a new blank document screen.

You might want to leave the original document available in cases where your changes may not be final. If you are unsure of the changes you have made, for example, and somebody else is going to come back and check your work, you might want to keep the original document. You then can show the person your version, and let him or her decide which version to continue using.

To save an existing document under a *same* name, follow these steps:

1. Press **Enter** to save the existing document under the same name.

   WordPerfect for DOS displays the question `Replace existing file?`

2. Press **Y** to replace the existing version of the document with the new version you have created during editing.

   WordPerfect for DOS saves the current version of the document, using the name of the original document. The original version no longer exists.

   If you do not want to replace the original version of the document, press **N** or **F1** (to cancel saving).

   If you press **N**, WordPerfect for DOS then redisplays the `Document to be saved:` prompt, and you can supply a different name (see the preceding set of steps). WordPerfect for DOS then displays the prompt `Exit WP?`

3. Press **Y** to exit from WordPerfect for DOS. Press **N** to remove the saved document from the screen but remain in WordPerfect for DOS on a new blank document screen.

Note that changing the location of a document (for example, saving the document to a floppy disk when it was originally stored on the hard disk) falls into the category of saving an existing document under a different name.

Printing a WordPerfect for DOS File

You can print a WordPerfect for DOS document in two ways. You can print from the List Files screen, or you can print from the main screen by using the Print menu.

Printing from the List Files Screen

To print all or part of a document from the List Files screen, follow these steps:

1. Press **F5**, and then press **Enter**.

   WordPerfect for DOS displays the List Files screen.

2. Press the arrow keys to highlight the document you want to print.

3. Press **4** or **P** to choose the **P**rint command.

   WordPerfect for DOS replaces the menu at the bottom of the screen with a prompt, as shown in Figure 3.11. This prompt suggests that you print the entire document.

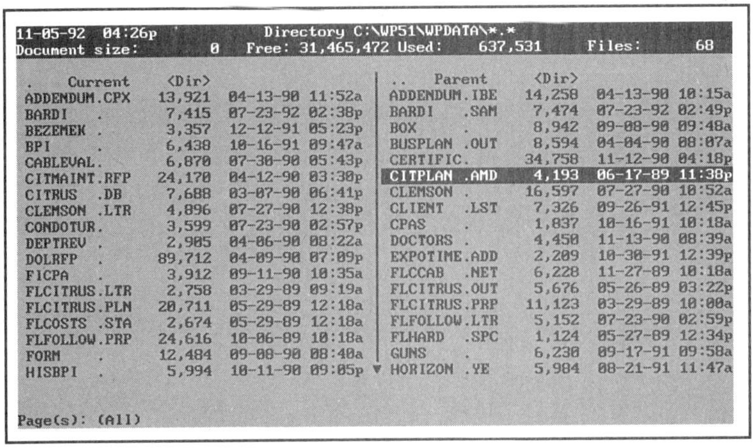

```
11-05-92  04:26p              Directory C:\WP51\WPDATA\*.*
Document size:          0  Free: 31,465,472 Used:    637,531      Files:      68

 .    Current     <Dir>                          ..    Parent     <Dir>
ADDENDUM.CPX    13,921  04-13-90 11:52a  | ADDENDUM.IBE   14,258  04-13-90 10:15a
BARDI    .       7,415  07-23-92 02:38p  | BARDI    .SAM   7,474  07-23-92 02:49p
BEZEMEK  .       3,357  12-12-91 05:23p  | BOX      .      8,942  09-08-90 09:48a
BPI      .       6,438  10-16-91 09:47a  | BUSPLAN  .OUT   8,594  04-04-90 08:07a
CABLEVAL.        6,870  07-30-90 05:43p  | CERTIFIC.      34,758  11-12-90 04:18p
CITMAINT.RFP    24,170  04-12-90 03:30p  | CITPLAN  .AMD   4,193  06-17-89 11:38p
CITRUS   .DB     7,688  03-07-90 06:41p  | CLEMSON  .     16,597  07-27-90 10:52a
CLEMSON  .LTR    4,896  07-27-90 12:38p  | CLIENT   .LST   7,326  09-26-91 12:45p
CONDOTUR.        3,599  07-23-90 02:57p  | CPAS     .      1,837  10-16-91 10:18a
DEPTREV  .       2,905  04-06-90 08:22a  | DOCTORS  .      4,450  11-13-90 08:39a
DOLRFP   .      89,712  04-09-90 07:09p  | EXPOTIME.ADD    2,209  10-30-91 12:39p
FICPA    .       3,912  09-11-90 10:35a  | FLCCAB   .NET   6,228  11-27-89 10:18a
FLCITRUS.LTR     2,758  03-29-89 09:19a  | FLCITRUS.OUT    5,676  05-26-89 03:22p
FLCITRUS.PLN    20,711  05-29-89 12:18a  | FLCITRUS.PRP   11,123  03-29-89 10:00a
FLCOSTS  .STA    2,674  05-29-89 12:18a  | FLFOLLOW.LTR    5,152  07-23-90 02:59p
FLFOLLOW.PRP    24,616  10-06-89 10:18a  | FLHARD   .SPC   1,124  05-27-89 12:34p
FORM     .      12,484  09-08-90 08:40a  | GUNS     .      6,230  09-17-91 09:58a
HISBPI   .       5,994  10-11-90 09:05p  ▼ HORIZON  .YE    5,984  08-21-91 11:47a

Page(s): (All)
```

Figure 3.11. The List Files screen after choosing the **P**rint command from the menu.

4. If you want to print the entire document, press **Enter**. If you want to print a group of pages, an individual page, or both, type the number(s) of the page(s) you want to print and then press **Enter**. To print, for example, pages 4 through 11, type 4-11. To print page 13, type 13. To print pages 3 through 8 and page 14, type 3-8,14.

   WordPerfect for DOS prints the document.

Printing the Active Document

You also can print a document that appears onscreen. Perhaps you created a new document or retrieved and edited an existing document that you now want to print. To print the document currently onscreen, press Shift+F7. WordPerfect for DOS displays the Print menu shown in Figure 3.12. As you can see, this menu is a full-screen menu; although you no longer see the document, it is still there.

To return to the document without printing, press Enter, Esc, F1 (Cancel), or F7 (Exit).

```
Print

     1 - Full Document
     2 - Page
     3 - Document on Disk
     4 - Control Printer
     5 - Multiple Pages
     6 - View Document
     7 - Initialize Printer

Options

     S - Select Printer                    HP LaserJet Series II
     B - Binding Offset                    0"
     N - Number of Copies                  1
     U - Multiple Copies Generated by      WordPerfect
     G - Graphics Quality                  Medium
     T - Text Quality                      High

Selection: 0
```

Figure 3.12.

The Print menu.

Because you probably won't need most of the commands on the Print menu, only the commands you are likely to use are described in this section.

If you have a monitor that is capable of displaying graphics, you can preview your document before you print it. When you preview a document, you can check its layout and alignment. Press 6 or V to choose the **V**iew Document command. WordPerfect for DOS displays a version of your document onscreen. The version of the document you see is similar to the one in Figure 3.13.

Although you cannot edit on this screen, you can see the document as it will print. If the text and graphics are not aligned properly on this screen, they won't be aligned properly when you print. You can press 1 to enlarge the view 100%, 2 to enlarge the view 200%, 3 to see the full page (as shown in Figure 3.13), or 4 to see facing pages (as in a book) of a long document. To return to the Print menu, press the spacebar. To return to the document, press the Exit key (F7).

To print more than one copy of the current document, press **N** to choose Number of Copies. Then, type the number of copies you want to print and press Enter.

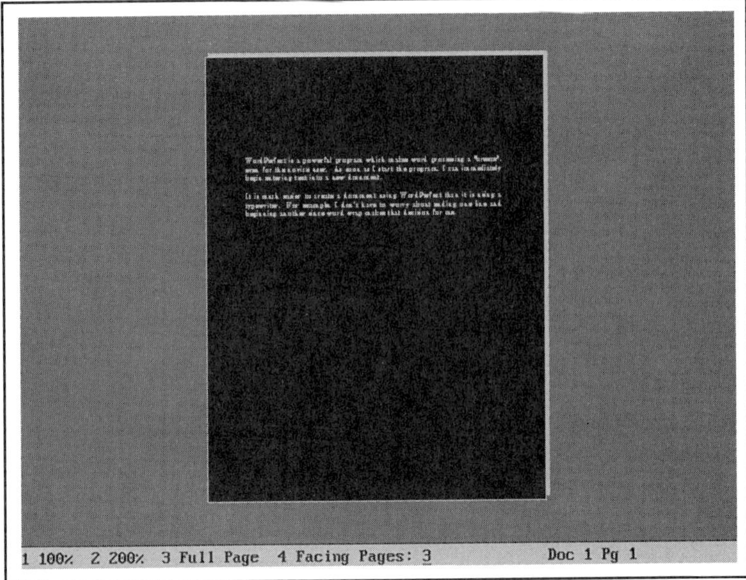

Figure 3.13. The View Document screen.

To print, choose one of the following options:

- If you want to print the entire document, press 1 or choose **F**ull Document.
- If you want to print only the page on which the cursor is resting, press 2 or choose **P**age.
- If you want to print a selection of pages, press 5 or choose **M**ultiple Pages. Then, type the numbers of the pages you want to print. You can type a group of pages, an individual page, or both. To print, for example, pages 4 through 11, type 4-11. To print page 13, type 13. To print pages 3 through 8 and page 14, type 3-8,14.

WordPerfect for DOS prints your selection.

Copying a WordPerfect for DOS File to a Floppy Disk

You may find that you need to copy a WordPerfect for DOS file to a floppy disk. You may need to print a file on another PC, for example. Using the **C**opy command on the List Files menu is the easiest way to copy a WordPerfect for DOS file to a floppy disk. Follow these steps:

1. Insert a formatted disk into the floppy disk drive.

2. Press **F5**, and then press **Enter**.

   WordPerfect for DOS displays the List Files screen (see Figure 3.14).

```
11-05-92  04:22p                Directory C:\WP51\WPDATA\*.*
Document size:    13,078   Free: 31,565,824 Used:     637,531       Files:       68

 .     Current    <Dir>                        |  ..     Parent    <Dir>
 ADDENDUM.CPX   13,921  04-13-90 11:52a        |  ADDENDUM.IBE   14,258  04-13-90 10:15a
 BARDI   .       7,415  07-23-92 02:38p        |  BARDI   .SAM    7,474  07-23-92 02:49p
 BEZEMEK .       3,357  12-12-91 05:23p        |  BOX     .       8,942  09-08-90 09:48a
 BPI     .       6,438  10-16-91 09:47a        |  BUSPLAN .OUT    8,594  04-04-90 08:07a
 CABLEVAL.       6,870  07-30-90 05:43p        |  CERTIFIC.      34,758  11-12-90 04:18p
 CITMAINT.RFP   24,170  04-12-90 03:30p        |  CITPLAN .AMD    4,193  06-17-89 11:38p
 CITRUS  .DB     7,688  03-07-90 06:41p        |  CLEMSON .      16,597  07-27-90 10:52a
 CLEMSON .LTR    4,896  07-27-90 12:38p        |  CLIENT  .LST    7,326  09-26-91 12:45p
 CONDOTUR.       3,599  07-23-90 02:57p        |  CPAS    .       1,837  10-16-91 10:18a
 DEPTREV .       2,905  04-06-90 08:22a        |  DOCTORS .       4,450  11-13-90 08:39a
 DOLRFP  .      89,712  04-09-90 07:09p        |  EXPOTIME.ADD    2,209  10-30-91 12:39p
 FICPA   .       3,912  09-11-90 10:35a        |  FLCCAB  .NET    6,228  11-27-89 10:18a
 FLCITRUS.LTR    2,758  03-29-89 09:19a        |  FLCITRUS.OUT    5,676  05-26-89 03:22p
 FLCITRUS.PLN   20,711  05-29-89 12:18a        |  FLCITRUS.PRP   11,123  03-29-89 10:00a
 FLCOSTS .STA    2,674  05-29-89 12:18a        |  FLFOLLOW.LTR    5,152  07-23-90 02:59p
 FLFOLLOW.PRP   24,616  10-06-89 10:18a        |  FLHARD  .SPC    1,124  05-27-89 12:34p
 FORM    .      12,484  09-08-90 08:40a        |  GUNS    .       6,230  09-17-91 09:58a
 HISBPI  .       5,994  10-11-90 09:05p        ▼  HORIZON .YE     5,984  08-21-91 11:47a

1 Retrieve; 2 Delete; 3 Move/Rename; 4 Print; 5 Short/Long Display;
6 Look; 7 Other Directory; 8 Copy; 9 Find; N Name Search: 6
```

Figure 3.14.

The List Files screen.

3. Press the arrow keys to highlight the file you want to copy to a floppy disk.

4. Press **8** or press **C** to choose the **C**opy command from the List Files menu at the bottom of the List Files screen.

   WordPerfect for DOS prompts you to identify the location to which you want to copy the file (see Figure 3.15).

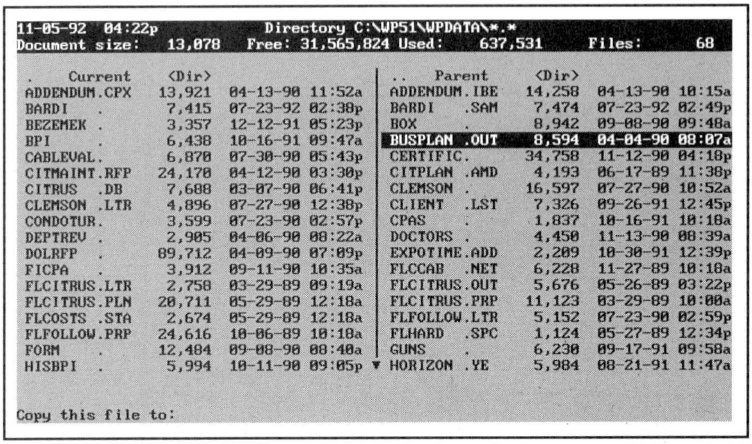

```
11-05-92  04:22p              Directory C:\WP51\WPDATA\*.*
Document size:    13,078   Free: 31,565,824 Used:     637,531      Files:       68

 .    Current     <Dir>                           |  ..    Parent      <Dir>
 ADDENDUM.CPX    13,921  04-13-90 11:52a  |  ADDENDUM.IBE    14,258  04-13-90 10:15a
 BARDI   .        7,415  07-23-92 02:38p  |  BARDI   .SAM     7,474  07-23-92 02:49p
 BEZEMEK .        3,357  12-12-91 05:23p  |  BOX     .        8,942  09-08-90 09:48a
 BPI     .        6,438  10-16-91 09:47a  |  BUSPLAN .OUT     8,594  04-04-90 08:07a
 CABLEVAL.        6,870  07-30-90 05:43p  |  CERTIFIC.       34,758  11-12-90 04:18p
 CITMAINT.RFP    24,170  04-12-90 03:30p  |  CITPLAN .AMD     4,193  06-17-89 11:38p
 CITRUS  .DB      7,688  03-07-90 06:41p  |  CLEMSON .       16,597  07-27-90 10:52a
 CLEMSON .LTR     4,896  07-27-90 12:38p  |  CLIENT  .LST     7,326  09-26-91 12:45p
 CONDOTUR.        3,599  07-23-90 02:57p  |  CPAS    .        1,837  10-16-91 10:18a
 DEPTREV .        2,905  04-06-90 08:22a  |  DOCTORS .        4,450  11-13-90 08:39a
 DOLRFP  .       89,712  04-09-90 07:09p  |  EXPOTIME.ADD     2,209  10-30-91 12:39p
 FICPA   .        3,912  09-11-90 10:35a  |  FLCCAB  .NET     6,228  11-27-89 10:18a
 FLCITRUS.LTR     2,758  03-29-89 09:19a  |  FLCITRUS.OUT     5,676  05-26-89 03:22p
 FLCITRUS.PLN    20,711  05-29-89 12:18a  |  FLCITRUS.PRP    11,123  03-29-89 10:00a
 FLCOSTS .STA     2,674  05-29-89 12:18a  |  FLFOLLOW.LTR     5,152  07-23-90 02:59p
 FLFOLLOW.PRP    24,616  10-06-89 10:18a  |  FLHARD  .SPC     1,124  05-27-89 12:34p
 FORM    .       12,484  09-08-90 08:40a  |  GUNS    .        6,230  09-17-91 09:58a
 HISBPI  .        5,994  10-11-90 09:05p  ▼  HORIZON .YE      5,984  08-21-91 11:47a


Copy this file to:
```

Figure 3.15. The Copy File prompt.

5. Type A: (or the name of the floppy disk drive into which you inserted a disk), and then press **Enter**.

   WordPerfect for DOS copies the file to the floppy disk.

Exiting WordPerfect for DOS

You use the Exit key (F7) to close the WordPerfect for DOS program. Follow these steps:

1. Press **F7**.

   WordPerfect for DOS asks whether you want to save the document that is currently onscreen (see Figure 3.16). Or, if appropriate, WordPerfect for DOS displays a message in the

lower right corner of the screen, telling you that you haven't made any changes to the document since the last time you saved it.

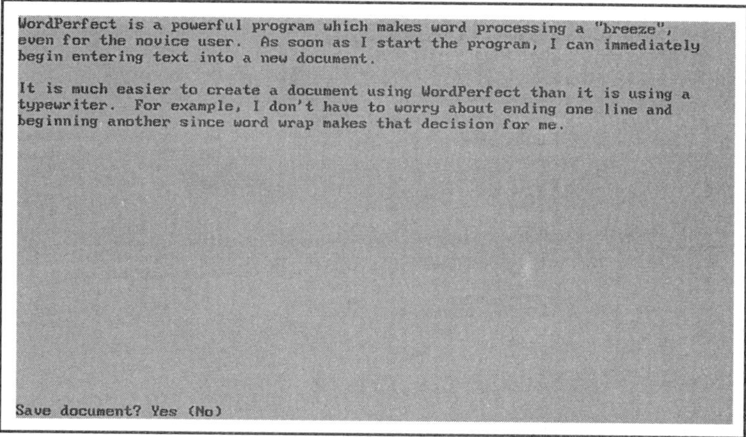

Figure 3.16. The `Save document?` prompt.

2. If you want to save the document, press **Y** and follow the steps described earlier in this chapter for saving documents. If you don't want to save the document, press **N**.

   WordPerfect for DOS then displays a screen similar to the one in Figure 3.17. The prompt asks whether you want to exit from the program.

```
WordPerfect is a powerful program which makes word processing a "breeze",
even for the novice user.  As soon as I start the program, I can immediately
begin entering text into a new document.

It is much easier to create a document using WordPerfect than it is using a
typewriter.  For example, I don't have to worry about ending one line and
beginning another since word wrap makes that decision for me.

Exit WP? No (Yes)                                (Cancel to return to document)
```

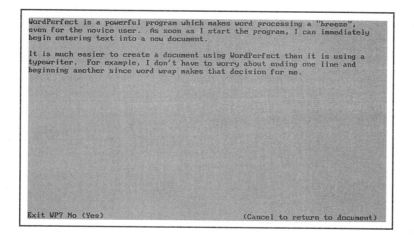

Figure 3.17. The `Exit WP?` prompt.

3. Press **Y** to exit from WordPerfect for DOS.

   A menu, the DOS prompt, or the DOS Shell appears.

Usually, you can turn off the PC safely when you see the screen you saw before you started WordPerfect for DOS.

Chapter Summary

In this chapter, you learned how to use the excellent online Help facility in WordPerfect for DOS. You learned how to retrieve, edit, save, and print a WordPerfect for DOS document. You also learned how to copy a WordPerfect for DOS file to a floppy disk, and how to exit from WordPerfect for DOS.

As you noticed in this chapter, there is, unfortunately, very little resemblance between WordPerfect for DOS and WordPerfect for the Mac unless you have been using the WordPerfect 5.x keyboard in WordPerfect for the Mac. Some terms changed, but others are the same:

- In WordPerfect for DOS, you *retrieve* a document; in WordPerfect for the Mac, you *open* a document.
- In WordPerfect for DOS, you *block* text on which you want to operate; in WordPerfect for the Mac, you *select* the text.
- In both packages, you *save, print,* and *copy* documents.
- You *exit* from WordPerfect for DOS, but you *quit* from WordPerfect for the Mac.

In the next chapter, you learn how to work with WordPerfect for Windows files. As you know, Chapters 3 through 9 in *The Mac User's PC* focus on specific software packages. You should read the chapters that pertain to the software you want to use. Chapter 10 tells you about database programs you may want to avoid. Chapter

11 discusses the MS-DOS Shell. Refer to Chapter 12 for information on file-naming conventions imposed on WordPerfect for DOS by the operating system, and to learn about basic DOS commands. If you need to transfer and translate files between a Mac and a PC, read Chapter 13.

Working with WordPerfect for Windows Files

In the first two chapters of *The Mac User's PC*, you learned about the physical appearance of a PC, how to turn on a PC, how to recognize what you may see onscreen, and how to start programs. In this chapter, you will learn very basic information about using WordPerfect for Windows. This chapter is not intended to make you an expert at WordPerfect for Windows; this chapter simply teaches you how to perform some basic tasks. You will learn how to open, edit, save, and print a WordPerfect for Windows document; how to copy a WordPerfect for Windows file to a floppy disk; and how to exit the program properly. And you will learn one other important thing—how to get help in WordPerfect for Windows so that you can teach yourself to do the things that aren't covered in this book!

When your read this chapter, be aware that there are unfortunately few similarities between WordPerfect for Windows and WordPerfect for the Mac.

Before you can start WordPerfect for Windows, you must start Microsoft Windows. Let's review some basic information about Windows.

Reviewing Windows Basics

Microsoft Windows is an operating environment that, in the world of DOS, provides a graphical user interface (also called GUI, pronounced "gooey") with which you can use either a mouse or a keyboard. Windows most closely resembles the Desktop on a Macintosh. Figure 4.1 shows a sample opening screen in Windows 3.1.

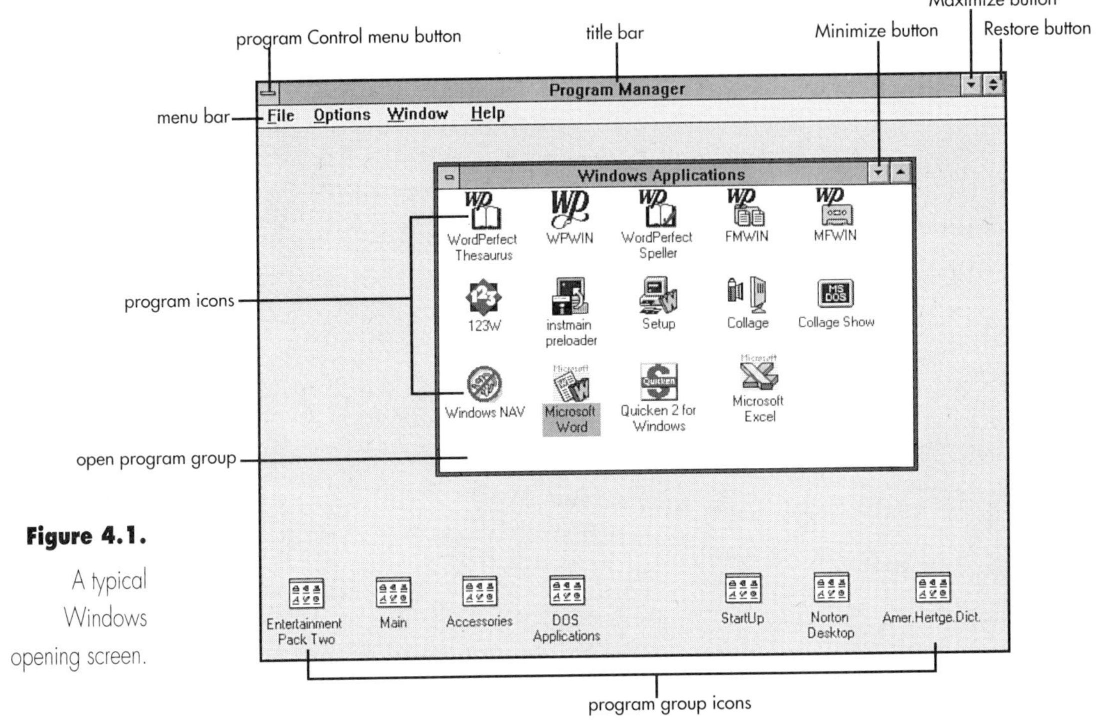

Figure 4.1.

A typical Windows opening screen.

If Microsoft Windows doesn't appear onscreen when you start the PC, type `WIN` at the DOS prompt.

As you learned in Chapter 2, Windows permits the user to perform multitasking. **Multitasking** enables the user to perform two or more functions simultaneously. To support multitasking, Windows and its Program Manager provide a way to manage the memory of the computer. Each program obtains enough memory to perform its functions; otherwise, Windows warns the user that sufficient memory is not available to perform all the requested tasks.

You can use a mouse or the keyboard to navigate in Windows, and you start programs from the Program Manager in Windows.

Understanding the Program Manager Screen

When you start Windows, the **Program Manager** appears. (At the very top of every Windows screen, you see in the **title bar** the name of the program that is currently running. In Figure 4.1, `Program Manager` appears in the title bar.)

At the left end of the title bar, you see the program **Control menu button**, a small box that contains a hyphen. You can use the Control menu to change the size of the screen that displays the Program Manager, to close the Program Manager, and to switch to another program.

At the right end of the title bar, you see two buttons. Rather than using the Control menu, you can click on these buttons to change the size of the screen that displays the Program Manager:

- Choose the **Minimize button** to reduce the entire Program Manager screen to an icon. If you minimize a program, you choose its icon to return the program to the size it was before you minimized it.

- If the Program Manager fills the entire screen (as it does in Figure 4.1), you see the Restore button (rather than the Maximize button). Choose the **Restore button** to reduce the Program Manager screen to a size somewhere between minimum and maximum (see Figure 4.2).

- If the Program Manager does not fill the entire screen but appears similar to Figure 4.2, you see the Maximize button (rather than the Restore button). Choose the **Maximize button** to enlarge the Program Manager to fill the entire screen.

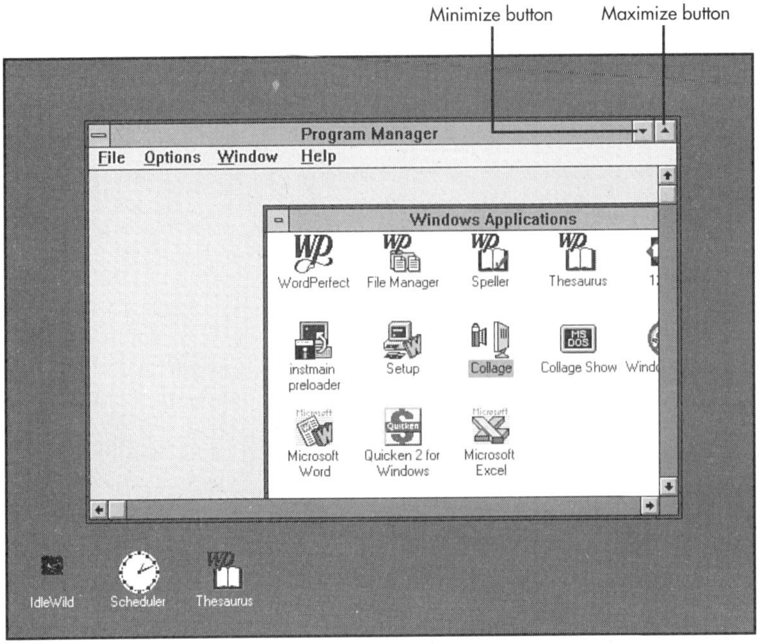

Minimize button Maximize button

Figure 4.2.

The Program Manager when it doesn't fill the entire screen.

Just below the title bar, you see the **menu bar**. The menu bar contains **menus**, and each menu contains the **commands** (also referred to as "menu commands") you use in Windows—but more about these in a moment.

The Program Manager contains **program groups**, which can appear either as open windows or as icons. In Figures 4.1 and 4.2, the Windows Applications program group appears as an open window while all the other program groups appear as **icons** at the bottom of the screen. Notice that the Windows Applications program group (and any open program group) also has a title bar, a Control menu, and Minimize and Maximize (or Restore) buttons. Open program groups do not, however, have menu bars.

Each program group contains icons that represent programs. You use these icons to start the programs. To start a program, the program group must be open so that you can see and access the icon that represents the program you want to start.

Navigating in Windows

When working in Windows, you can use the mouse or the keyboard to perform certain tasks. In the following sections, you will find instructions on how to use the mouse and the keyboard to open menus, **choose** commands from menus, choose options in dialog boxes, and start programs.

In Windows, a mouse operates differently from a mouse on a Macintosh. Before you learn the specifics of performing each of the previously mentioned actions, let's review the way in which a mouse operates in Windows.

Operating a Mouse in Windows

Using a mouse in Windows is a two-step process. To use a mouse to choose an item in Windows, follow these steps:

1. Slide the mouse until the mouse pointer points to the item you want to choose.

2. Press and release a mouse button—usually the left mouse button—one time.

The action you perform in step 1 is known as **pointing**, and the action you perform in step 2 is known as **clicking**. You can click either the left or the right mouse button, as defined by the software program you are using. Most of the time, to choose an item, you click the left mouse button. You also may have occasion to double-click. To **double-click**, you press and release the left mouse button twice in rapid succession. Occasionally, you may need to drag an item to move it from one location to another. To **drag**, point to the item you want to drag. Then, press and hold down the left mouse button as you slide the mouse to move the item to the new location.

Note the difference in the way clicking works in Windows compared to on a Mac. In Windows, for the most part, you don't need to hold down the mouse button while opening a menu and choosing a command; the menu remains open after you release the mouse button. On a Mac, when you release the mouse button, the menu from which you were trying to choose a command closes.

Working with Menus and Commands in Windows

The menu bar appears just below the title bar. Each menu contains the commands you use in Windows. To see the commands, you can open a menu by using the mouse or the keyboard.

To open a menu by using the mouse, point to the menu you want to open and click the left mouse button. Windows opens the menu. Unlike a menu on a Mac, the menu remains open when you release the mouse button, and the first command on the menu appears highlighted. To choose a command by using the mouse, point to the command and click the left mouse button. Windows executes the command.

You also can use the keyboard to open a menu and choose a command. First, you activate the menu bar by pressing the Alt key. A **reverse video bar** (or **highlight**) appears on the name of the first menu, **F**ile. Then, you can open a menu and choose a command in two ways:

- You can use the hot key shortcuts. Each menu and command name contains an underlined letter, also called a **hot key**. You can press that key to open the menu or execute the command. When you press the W key, for example, the Program Manager opens the **W**indow menu and displays the commands available on that menu. In this book, all references to hot keys appear in boldface type.

- You can press one of the arrow keys on the keyboard to point to a menu or command, and then use the Enter key to choose it. When you press an arrow key, the reverse video bar moves. Continue pressing the arrow key until the reverse video bar highlights the menu or command to which you want to point. For example, you can press the Alt key to activate the menu bar and then press the left-arrow key two times to point to the **W**indow menu command. Remember, when you use the arrow keys to point to a menu or command, you must press Enter to open that menu or choose that command.

PC NOTE

If you activate the menu bar and then press the right-arrow key four times, you highlight the Control menu. The Control menu contains the commands that control the size of the Program Manager screen. To open the Control menu after you have highlighted it, press Enter. If you have any open program group windows and you activate the menu bar and then press the right-arrow key five times, you highlight the Control menu of the group window. Again, press Enter to open that Control menu.

Working with Dialog Boxes in Windows

Ellipses (...) appear after some commands on the menus. The program requires additional information about these commands before it can execute them. When you choose a command that includes an ellipsis, a **dialog box** (in which you supply the additional required information) appears.

The dialog boxes that appear when you choose a command from the Program Manager's **F**ile menu are not typical of the dialog boxes you see and use in application programs. So, there's not

much point in describing one of those dialog boxes. Instead, Figure 4.3 displays a more typical dialog box that contains a representative sample of types of dialog box options. Each dialog box is different, and most dialog boxes provide only some of these options.

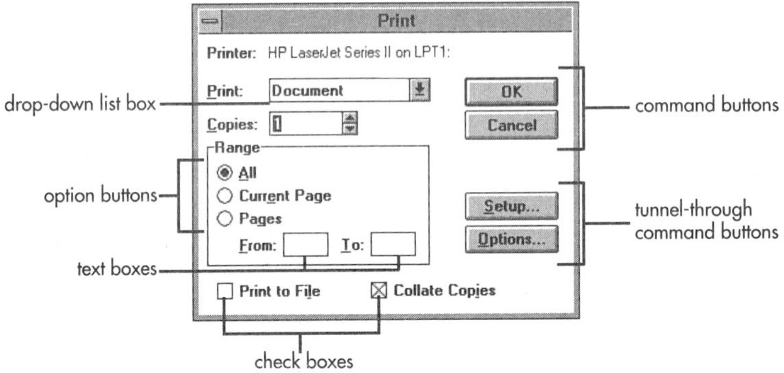

Figure 4.3.

A typical Print dialog box.

PC NOTE

You may notice a dotted line surrounding an option. This line indicates the current mouse pointer position. If you are using the keyboard rather than a mouse, you can use the Tab key to move around in a dialog box.

A **list box** contains a list of options. You may see one of two kinds of list boxes in a dialog box. The **P**rint list box in Figure 4.3 is an example of a drop-down list box, and is closed when the dialog box appears. To open a **drop-down list box**, click on the down arrow at the right end of the box; or, hold down the Alt key and type the underlined letter in the list box name. The other type of list box is already open when the dialog box appears. To choose an item from either type of list box, click on the item; or, press the down arrow key to point to the item, and then press Enter. If the list box is not long enough to display all the available items in the list, click the down arrow or press and hold the down-arrow key to move beyond the items that appear in the box.

An **option button** is a small round button you use to choose one option from a group of related options. A black dot appears in the button of the current option. To choose an option button, click on the option button; or, hold down the Alt key and type the underlined letter in the option name. In the Range area, the **A**ll, Curr**e**nt Page, and Pa**g**es buttons are option buttons.

A **check box** is a small square box you use to choose an option. You can choose more than one check box from a group of related options. An X appears in the check boxes of the activated options. To choose a check box, click on the check box; or, hold down the Alt key and type the underlined letter in the option name. To deactivate the option and remove the X from the box, choose the check box again. In Figure 4.3, the Print to Fi**l**e and Collate Cop**i**es check boxes appear at the bottom of the dialog box.

A **text box** is a rectangular box in which you enter text. When a dialog box that contains a text box opens, the current text is usually selected. To replace the selected text, simply type the new information. In Figure 4.3, the Range area contains two text boxes (**F**rom and **T**o). The **C**opies box is also a text box.

A **command button** is an oblong button that performs an action. To choose a command button, click on the button; or, use the Tab key to move the mouse pointer to the button and press Enter. In Figure 4.3, the OK button accepts the settings in the dialog box. The Cancel button cancels your changes to the settings in the dialog box. The default command button, which changes from dialog box to dialog box, has a darker outline than the other command buttons. As on a Mac, if you press Enter, you choose the highlighted command button.

A **tunnel-through command button** is a button that contains an ellipsis(...) and opens another dialog box. To choose a tunnel-through command button, click on the button; highlight the button and press Enter; or, hold down the Alt key and then type the underlined letter. In Figure 4.3, the **S**etup and **O**ptions buttons are tunnel-through command buttons.

Starting a Program in Windows

As mentioned earlier, all programs reside in program groups in Windows. To start a program, its program group cannot appear minimized as an icon; the program group must be open.

To use the mouse to open a program group that appears as an icon, double-click on the program group icon.

To use the keyboard to open a program group that appears as an icon, follow these steps:

1. Press the **Alt** key to activate the menu bar.

2. Press **W** to open the **W**indow menu.

   The Program Manager displays the choices on the **W**indow menu (see Figure 4.4). You see a check mark next to the currently selected program group.

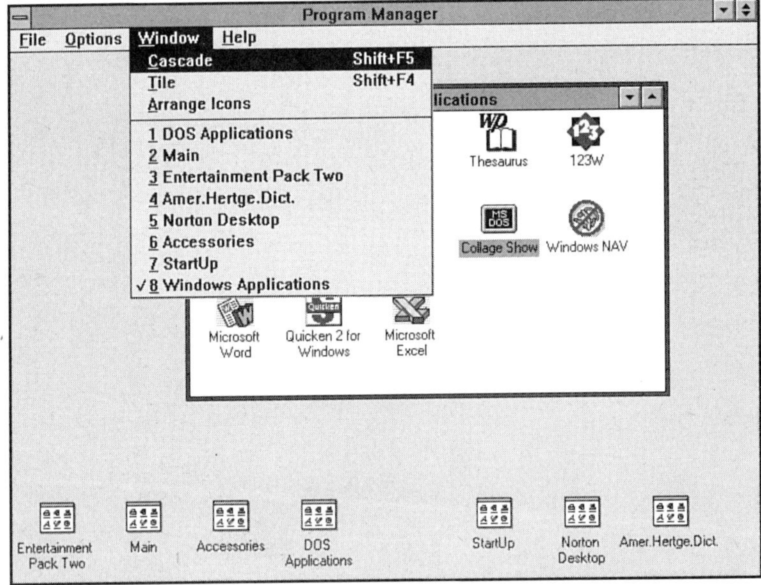

Figure 4.4.
The Window menu.

3. From the numbered options in the **W**indow menu, press a number to choose the program group you want to open.

   Windows opens the specified program group.

After you open the program group, you can start a program. To start a program by using the mouse, double-click on the icon for the program in the program group window. The Program Manager starts the program.

To start a program by using the keyboard, use the arrow keys to point to the program you want to start. Then, press Enter. The Program Manager starts the program.

Using one of the techniques just described, open the program group containing the WordPerfect for Windows program icon and start WordPerfect for Windows. You may find the program icon in the Windows Applications group or in a WordPerfect for Windows group. Or, you may find WordPerfect for Windows somewhere altogether different—the owner of the PC may have a different technique for organizing programs.

Identifying WordPerfect for Windows Screen Parts

When you first start WordPerfect for Windows, you see the default screen, which looks like the screen in Figure 4.5.

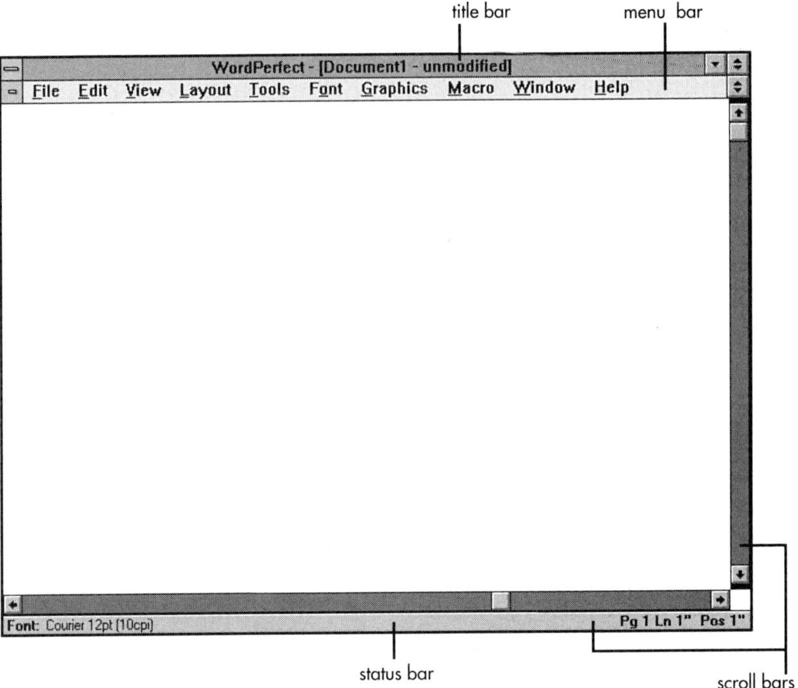

Figure 4.5.
The opening screen of WordPerfect for Windows.

PC NOTE

If, on the opening screen, you see only the program name in the title bar at the top of the screen and you see a separate document title bar, then the document window is not maximized. To maximize the document window, open the *document* Control menu (the one on the left end of the document title bar, not the one above the menu bar) and choose the Ma**x**imize command. Or, click the document Maximize button, which appears at the right end of the document title bar.

As in the opening Windows screen, you see in the **title bar** the name of the program that is currently running, `WordPerfect`, and the name of the current file (also called a **document**), `[Document1 - unmodified]`. The WordPerfect for Windows program Control menu appears to the left of the title bar, and the program Minimize and Restore buttons appear to the right of the title bar.

Just below the title bar, you see the **menu bar** for WordPerfect for Windows. At the left end of the menu bar, you see the document Control menu; you can use this Control menu to change the size of only the document portion of the screen. At the right end of the menu bar, you see the document Restore button. Initially, when you start the program, the document portion of the window is maximized.

Along the right edge and toward the bottom of the screen, you see the horizontal and vertical scroll bars, which have arrows at both ends and a scroll box somewhere along the scroll bar. Using a mouse, you can click the arrows or drag the scroll box on the horizontal scroll bar to move the view of a document right or left. Or, you can click the arrows or drag the scroll box on the vertical scroll bar to move the view of a document down or up.

At the bottom of the screen, you see the status bar. The status bar tells you, at the left, what font you are currently using and, at the right, the current location of the insertion point, the flashing black vertical bar. The **insertion point** represents the current location of the mouse pointer and shows you where text will appear when you type. When you start WordPerfect for Windows, you always see an empty document screen, on which you can start creating a new document. On the empty document screen, the status bar always indicates, as you can see in Figure 4.5, that the insertion point is located on Page 1, Line 1 inch, at Position 1 inch. This position indicates that one-inch margins already exist on all sides of the page.

WordPerfect for Windows comes with some additional features that users can define to appear onscreen; you may see some of these features on your screen. Figure 4.6 shows some of these features.

Just below the menu bar, you see the default Button Bar. WordPerfect for Windows uses the Button Bar to assign commonly performed tasks to buttons. You must use a mouse to select a button on the Button Bar. In addition, the Button Bar can be customized, so the buttons in Figure 4.6 may not appear on your screen.

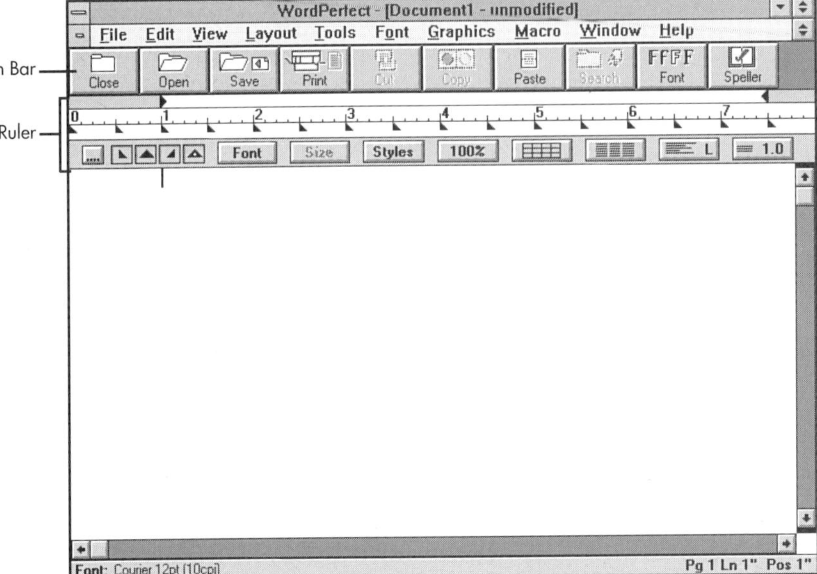

Figure 4.6. The WordPerfect for Windows screen with additional features.

Below the Button Bar, you see the Ruler. You must use a mouse to perform an action on the Ruler. Remember, however, that you can use the menus and the keyboard to perform any action you can perform by using the mouse on the Ruler.

The Ruler actually consists of three parts. You use the top part of the ruler to set the left and right margins. You use the middle part of the Ruler to move and remove tab stops. You use the Ruler buttons on the bottom of the Ruler to perform a variety of functions:

- The first button from the left edge of the Ruler enables you to set dot leader tabs (tabs preceded by a dotted line).
- The next four buttons enable you to add tabs to the middle part of the Ruler.
- The Font button enables you to choose a different font.
- The Size button enables you to change the size of proportional fonts.

- The Styles button enables you to apply a predefined style to text.

- The 100% button enables you to change the amount of text that appears onscreen while you edit. You can choose from 50%, 75%, 100%, 150%, 200%, or Page Width.

- The Table button (the fourth button from the right edge of the Ruler) enables you to insert a table into your text.

- The Columns button enables you to change the text from one column into as many as five columns.

- The Justification button enables you to determine how your text will align: left-, center-, or right-aligned, or justified between the left and right margins.

- The Spacing button enables you to set the line spacing at single, 1 1/2, or double spacing.

Getting Help in WordPerfect for Windows

WordPerfect for Windows contains an excellent online Help facility. In this section, you learn the basics of using Help in WordPerfect for Windows.

The **H**elp menu contains several commands, two of which should be of particular interest to you: **H**ow Do I and **I**ndex. If you choose the **H**ow Do I command, you see a list of the most common WordPerfect tasks. You can choose the topics to get help about those tasks.

If you don't see what you want in the How Do I list, you can try using the Help Index. You can display the Help Index in WordPerfect for Windows by pressing F1 or by opening the **H**elp menu and choosing the **I**ndex command (see Figure 4.7). In WordPerfect for Windows, the help you receive is context-sensitive—if you are looking at a command on a menu and you press F1, the help you get is about that command.

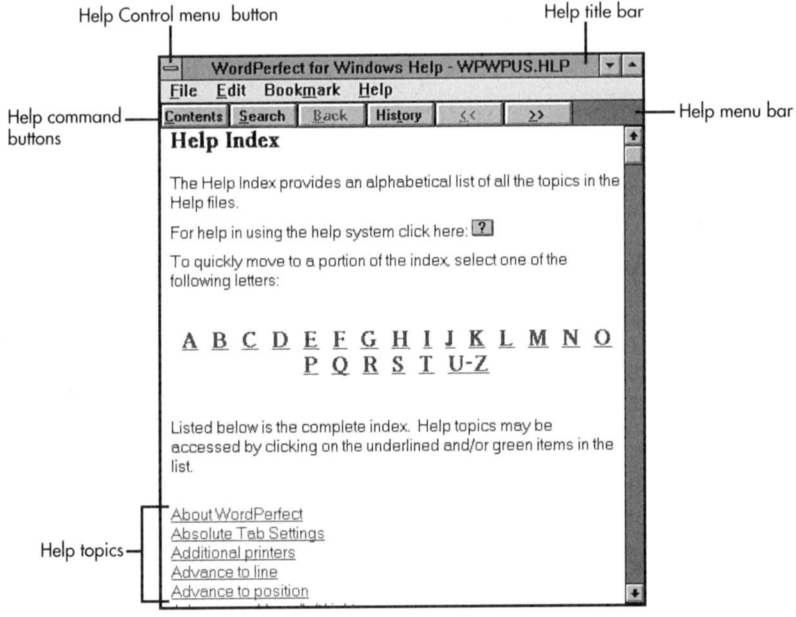

Figure 4.7.

The Help Index window.

As you can see from the information that appears in the Help Index window, you can use an alphabetical listing of topics in WordPerfect for Windows Help. You can choose a letter of the alphabet to move directly to that list of topics. If you want to copy something, for example, use the mouse to click on `C`; or press the Tab key until you highlight `C`, and then press Enter. The screen in Figure 4.8 appears.

In the lower portion of the Help Index window, you see the topics listed. You can choose a topic directly from the list. Using the mouse, you can click on the scroll arrows to move the topics in the window until you see the topic about which you want help. To

choose the topic, click on it. Using the keyboard, you can press the down-arrow key to move the topics in the window. To choose the topic, press the Tab key to highlight the topic and then press Enter.

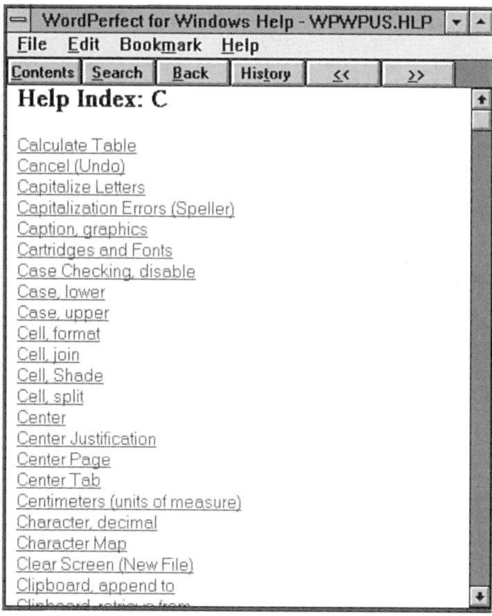

Figure 4.8.

The Help topics for the letter **C**.

You can use the **S**earch button in the Help Index window to open the Search dialog box in Figure 4.9. and search for topics you specify.

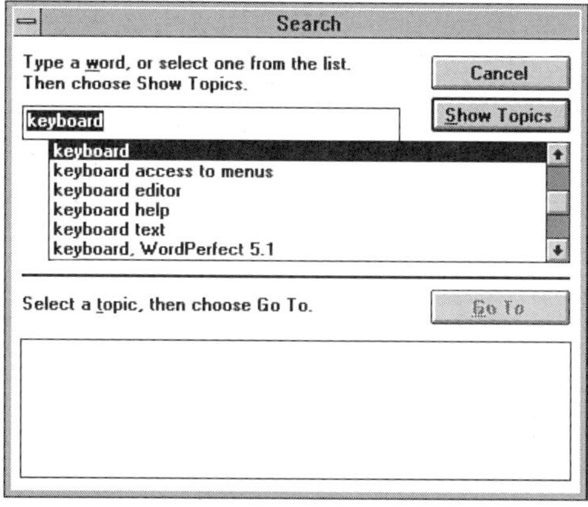

Figure 4.9.

The Help Search dialog box.

To use the Search dialog box, follow these steps:

1. Type a **w**ord that represents the topic for which you want to search.

   As you type, WordPerfect for Windows Help highlights the topic that most closely matches the characters you type.

2. Choose the **S**how Topics button.

   WordPerfect for Windows Help displays the topics that most closely match the characters you typed. The topics appear in the bottom portion of the dialog box.

3. Choose a topic from the list, and then choose the **G**o To button.

   WordPerfect for Windows Help displays the topic you chose.

You can print the information that appears in Help windows by choosing the **P**rint Topic command on the **F**ile menu in the Help window.

If you find a Help topic to which you might want to return later (without having to remember how you got there in the first place), you can create a bookmark for the topic. Follow these steps:

1. When viewing the topic you want to mark, open the Book**m**ark menu on the Help window's menu bar.

2. Choose the **D**efine command.

   WordPerfect for Windows Help displays the Bookmark Define dialog box in Figure 4.10. The name of the topic you are viewing appears in the **B**ookmark Name text box.

3. If you want to change the bookmark name, type a new name; otherwise, WordPerfect for Windows Help will use the topic name as the bookmark name.

Figure 4.10.
The Bookmark Define dialog box.

4. Choose OK.

   WordPerfect for Windows stores the topic name on the Book**m**ark menu.

When you open the Book**m**ark menu again, you see below the **D**efine command the topic for which you stored a bookmark. If you choose the topic from the Book**m**ark menu, WordPerfect for Windows Help displays the topic.

After viewing several topics, you can use the **C**ontents button to redisplay the Help Index window. Or, you can use the **B**ack button to redisplay in reverse order the topics you viewed. You also can return directly to any topic you display by choosing the His**t**ory button. When you choose the His**t**ory button, WordPerfect for Windows Help displays the Help History window, in which you can see every topic you viewed since you started Help. If you looked at a topic more than once, it appears more than once in the Help History window. To go to a topic listed in the Help History Window, double-click on the topic; or, use the arrow keys to point to the topic and then press Enter.

PC NOTE

If you close Help, WordPerfect for Windows also closes the history of your Help session and no longer maintains the history of the Help screens you viewed. When you open Help again, WordPerfect for Windows starts the history over again.

You can learn more about how to use the WordPerfect for Windows Help facility by opening the **H**elp menu on the Help window's menu bar and choosing **H**ow To Use Help.

Opening a WordPerfect for Windows File

Suppose that someone brings you a letter, asks you to make some minor changes to it, and then wants you to print the revised letter. In this section, you learn how to open an existing WordPerfect for Windows document. In the next three sections, you learn how to edit, save, and print a WordPerfect for Windows document.

You can open a document in WordPerfect for Windows in two ways. You can open the document into its own new document window, or you can retrieve the document into the current document window at the insertion point.

Opening a Document

To open an existing document into its own document window, follow these steps:

1. Open the **F**ile menu and choose the **O**pen command. You also can choose the Open button on the Button Bar. Or, if you are using the WordPerfect for DOS keyboard, you can press **Shift+F10**. If you are using the CUA keyboard (more on that later), you can press **F4**.

   WordPerfect for Windows displays the Open File dialog box in Figure 4.11.

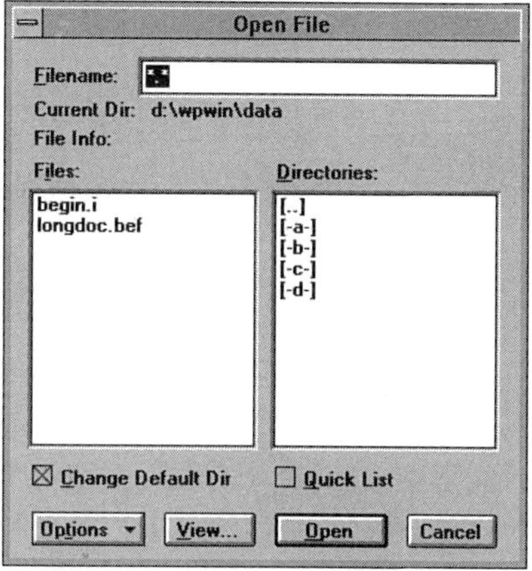

Figure 4.11.

The Open File dialog box.

2. Choose the name of the document you want to open from the F**i**les list, or type the file name of the document you want to open in the **F**ilename text box.

3. If you want, you can make sure that you have chosen the right document by choosing the **V**iew button to preview the document.

   WordPerfect for Windows displays the currently highlighted document in the View window. You don't have to close the View window—after you open a document, WordPerfect for Windows closes both the Open File dialog box and the View window.

4. Choose the **O**pen button.

   The document appears onscreen, and you can edit it.

You can open up to nine documents at one time. The document that contains the insertion point is called the **active document**, and you are looking at it in the **active window**.

Retrieving a Document

You can combine two documents by retrieving a document rather than opening it. When you retrieve, WordPerfect for Windows doesn't open a new window before opening the document you choose. Therefore, you effectively "merge" two documents together when you retrieve. They both appear together in the same window onscreen. During each WordPerfect for Windows session, the first document window you see after starting the program is blank; therefore, you accomplish the same task whether you retrieve or open. *After* you create or edit a document during the current WordPerfect for Windows session, retrieving serves a different purpose than opening.

To retrieve a document, follow the same steps you used to open a document, but in step 1 open the **F**ile menu and choose the **R**etrieve command (there are no shortcuts on the keyboard or the Button Bar). WordPerfect for Windows displays the Retrieve File dialog box, which looks and operates exactly like the Open File dialog box in Figure 4.11. Continue with steps 2 through 4, but choose the **R**etrieve button in step 4.

If, for some reason, you must type a new document and you don't want to close the one you're working on, start in a clean window by choosing the **N**ew command from the **F**ile menu.

Performing Basic Editing in WordPerfect for Windows

By default, when you type in WordPerfect for Windows, you are working in insert mode. In **insert mode**, WordPerfect for Windows places characters at the current location of the insertion

point and moves all existing characters to the right. You can press the Ins key to switch to typeover mode. In **typeover mode**, WordPerfect for Windows places characters at the current location of the insertion point and types over characters that exist at that location, removing them. The Ins key works like a toggle switch: press it once to change from insert mode to typeover mode; press it a second time to change back from typeover mode to insert mode.

You can use the Backspace key to delete the character immediately to the left of the insertion point. You can use the Del key to delete the character immediately to the right of the insertion point.

Moving around a Document

You move around a WordPerfect for Windows document by clicking the mouse or by pressing the directional keys (the arrow keys, and Home, End, PgUp, and PgDn). The action you perform when you press these keys, however, depends on whether the CUA (Common User Access) keyboard or the WordPerfect for DOS keyboard is active. Also, you may notice some slight differences between the way you move around a WordPerfect for Windows document and the way you move around a WordPerfect for the Mac document.

When installing WordPerfect for Windows, the user can choose to use the CUA keyboard or the WordPerfect for DOS keyboard. Most Windows programs use the CUA keyboard, which has standardized functions across programs for certain keys. The CUA keyboard ensures some standardization within Windows; pressing certain function keys and the directional keys in any Windows program produces the same results.

By installing the WordPerfect for DOS keyboard, however, users who are switching from WordPerfect for DOS can use the same function keys to execute commands in WordPerfect for Windows. This valuable learning aid can help WordPerfect for DOS users be productive almost immediately in WordPerfect for Windows.

Unless you have been using the WordPerfect 5.x keyboard in WordPerfect for the Mac, you probably will be most comfortable using the CUA keyboard. The CUA keyboard's actions most closely resemble the commands you use in WordPerfect for the Mac.

To find out which keyboard is active, press F4. If you see the Open File dialog box, the CUA keyboard is active. If, instead, the insertion point moves to the first tab stop, the WordPerfect for DOS keyboard is active.

Table 4.1 summarizes the most common ways in which you can use the CUA version of the keyboard to move around a WordPerfect for Windows document.

Table 4.1. CUA insertion point-movement keys (in an existing document).

Key(s)	Effect
→, ←, ↓, or ↑	Moves right, left, down, or up one character.
Ctrl+→	Moves right one word.
Ctrl+←	Moves left one word.
Ctrl+↓	Moves down one paragraph.
Ctrl+↑	Moves up one paragraph.
Home	Moves to the beginning of the current line.
End	Moves to the end of the current line.
PgDn	Moves down to the top of the next window.
PgUp	Moves up to the top of the preceding window.

Table 4.2 summarizes the most common ways in which you can use the WordPerfect for DOS version of the keyboard to move around a WordPerfect for Windows document.

Table 4.2.
WordPerfect for DOS insertion point-movement keys (in an existing document).

Key(s)	Effect
→, ←, ↓, or ↑	Moves right, left, down, or up one character.
Ctrl+→	Moves right one word.
Ctrl+←	Moves left one word.
Ctrl+↓	Moves down one paragraph.
Ctrl+↑	Moves up one paragraph.
End	Moves to the end of the current line.
Home,→	Moves to the end of the current line.
Home,←	Moves to the beginning of the current line.
Home,↓	Moves down to the top of the next window.
Home,↑	Moves up to the top of the preceding window.
Home,Home,↓	Moves to the end of the document.
Home,Home,↑	Moves to the top of the document.
PgDn	Moves to the top of the next page.
PgUp	Moves to the top of the preceding page.

Selecting Text

You may want to make changes to the appearance of text. For example, you may want certain text to appear underlined, in italics, or in boldface type; you may want to change the alignment of certain text; or you may want to delete certain text.

In WordPerfect for Windows, you select text when you want to "operate" on it—that is, when you want to format, align, edit, or even print text. **Selecting** is the process of highlighting the text so that WordPerfect for Windows can identify the text on which you want to work. You select text in WordPerfect for Windows similarly to the way you select text in WordPerfect for the Mac.

To use the mouse to select text, you drag across the text. Follow these steps:

1. Place the insertion point at the beginning of the text you want to select. Click and hold down the left mouse button.

2. Slide the mouse to the right.

   As you slide the mouse, a reverse video bar appears over the text you are selecting.

3. Continue sliding the mouse until you reach the end of the text you want to select.

4. Release the left mouse button.

   The text you selected is highlighted—a reverse video bar appears over it.

You can select a word by double-clicking on it; you can select a sentence by triple-clicking on it; and you can select a paragraph by quadruple-clicking on it. You can cancel a selection by clicking the mouse anywhere else onscreen.

To use the keyboard to select text, follow these steps:

1. Place the insertion point at the beginning of the text you want to select.

2. Enter Select mode. If you are using the WordPerfect for DOS keyboard, press **F12**. If you are using the CUA keyboard, press **F8**.

   `Select Mode` appears in the status bar at the bottom of the screen.

3. Use the **Shift** key combined with directional keys to select text. Use Table 4.1 or Table 4.2 (as appropriate) to identify the text you want to select. For example, to select one word to the right, press **Shift**+**Ctrl**+→.

4. Perform the action on the selected text. For example, underline the text.

5. Exit Select mode by pressing **F12** or **F8** again.

You can cancel a selection by exiting Select mode or by choosing the **U**ndo command from the **E**dit menu.

Using the Function Keys To Execute Commands

As the old saying goes, there's good news and bad news. Some of the good news is that you can use either menus or function keys in WordPerfect for Windows to execute commands. So, because you also can execute commands in WordPerfect for the Mac by using either menus or function keys, this method is familiar. The bad news is that the commands in WordPerfect for Windows are basically unfamiliar to you unless you have been using the WordPerfect 5.x keyboard in WordPerfect for the Mac. For a Mac user, that's not likely. But, the rest of the good news is that WordPerfect for Windows contains an excellent online Help facility to help you learn the purpose of the commands you can execute by using the menus and by using the function keys.

You may see a template similar to the one in Figure 4.12 on the keyboard next to the function keys. If your template came with the software or was purchased, you see words printed in red, green, blue, or black ink next to each function key.

Figure 4.12.

Sample templates for WordPerfect for Windows.

WordPerfect® for Windows™
CUA™ Compatible

Cancel	Esc	Top of Doc	Home
Undo	Z	Bottom of Doc	End
Cut	X	Column ←/→	←/→
Copy	C	Page Up	PgUp
Paste	V	Page Down	PgDn
Bold	B	Del EOL	Del
Italics	I	Hard Page	Enter
Underline	U	WP Characters	W
Normal	N	Print Doc	P

74 - 4 0-74
© WordPerfect Corp. 1991 TMUSWWP51XID—10/91

	F1	F2	F3	F4		F5	F6	F7	F8		F9	F10	F11	F12
Ctrl+Sh	Preferences •		Draft Mode •	Clear •	Ctrl+Sh	Date Code •	Prev Doc •	Double Indent •		Ctrl+Sh	Document •	Macro Stop •	Vertical Line •	Sort •
Ctrl	Speller	Replace	Redisplay	Close	Ctrl	Date Text	Next Doc	Hanging Indent	Margins	Ctrl	Tables	Macro Record	Horizontal Line	Merge
Alt+Sh			Ruler •		Alt+Sh	Paragraph Def •	Prev Window •	Decimal Tab •	Special Codes •	Alt+Sh	Columns •		Text Box Edit •	
Alt	Thesaurus	Search Prev	Reveal Codes	Exit	Alt	Paragraph Num	Next Window	Flush Right	Styles	Alt	Page	Macro Play	Text Box Create	Generate
Shift	Help: What Is?	Search Next	Save	New	Shift	Print Preview	Prev Pane	Center	Select Cell	Shift	Line		Figure Edit	Define
	Help	Search	Save As	Open		Print	Next Pane	Indent	Select		Font	Menu Bar	Figure Retrieve	Mark Text

WordPerfect® for Windows™
WP 5.1 for DOS Compatible

Cancel	Esc	Top of Doc	Home,Home↑
Undo	Z	Bottom of Doc	Home,Home↓
Cut	X	Column ←/→	←/→
Copy	C	Page Up	PgUp
Paste	V	Page Down	PgDn
Bold	B	Del EOL	End
Italics	I	Hard Page	Enter
Underline	U	WP Characters	W
Normal	N	Print Doc	P

74 - 4 0-74
© WordPerfect Corp. 1991 TMUSWWP51XID—10/91

	F1	F2	F3	F4		F5	F6	F7	F8		F9	F10	F11	F12
Ctrl+Sh	Prev Pane •		Draft Mode •	Select Paragraph •	Ctrl+Sh			Clear •		Ctrl+Sh		Macro Stop •		
Ctrl	Next Pane	Speller	Redisplay	Select Sentence	Ctrl		Decimal Tab	Footnote	Font	Ctrl	Merge/Sort	Macro Record		
Alt+Sh		Search Prev •	Prev Doc •	Select Cell •	Alt+Sh	Generate •	Next Window •	Print Preview •	Special Codes •	Alt+Sh				
Alt	Thesaurus	Replace	Reveal Codes	Select	Alt	Mark Text	Flush Right	Tables/Columns	Styles	Alt	Graphics	Macro Play	Draft Mode	
Shift	Preferences	Search Next	Next Doc	Double Indent	Shift	Date/Outline	Center	Print	Layout	Shift	Merge	Open	Ruler	Select Cell
	Help	Search	Undelete	Indent		File Manager	Bold	Close	Underline		End Field	Save As	Reveal Codes	Select

The words on the template represent commands you use in WordPerfect for Windows to perform the various actions listed on the menus. At various places on the template, you see columns with the color-coded words "Ctrl," "Shift," and "Alt" (and combinations of Ctrl+Shift and Alt+Shift). You can use the key combinations indicated on the template to execute the command without opening a menu. For example, on the CUA keyboard, press Ctrl+F1 to start the Speller. Table 4.3 summarizes the way you use the function keys in WordPerfect.

Table 4.3. Function keys and WordPerfect commands.

Color	Key(s)
Red with green dot	Hold down the Ctrl key and the Shift key as you press the appropriate function key.
Red	Hold down the Ctrl key as you press the appropriate function key.
Blue with green dot	Hold down the Alt key and the Shift key as you press the appropriate function key.
Blue	Hold down the Alt key as you press the appropriate function key.
Green	Hold down the Shift key as you press the appropriate function key.
Black	Press the appropriate function key.

OK, so what do you do if your template isn't color-coded or you don't have a template? WordPerfect has incorporated an onscreen representation of the template for either keyboard within its online Help facility. Open the **H**elp menu and choose the **K**eyboard command. To see the Help window that displays the CUA template (see Figure 4.13), choose `CUA Keyboard Template`. To see the Help window that displays the WordPerfect for DOS template (see Figure 4.14), choose `DOS Keyboard Template`. When you view these images onscreen, you see a four-color image; the colors correspond to the information provided in Table 4.3.

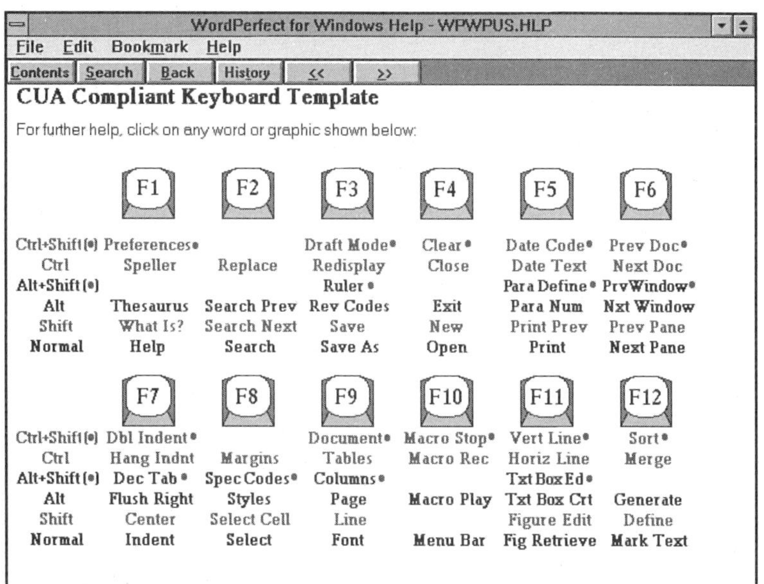

Figure 4.13. The Help window showing the CUA template.

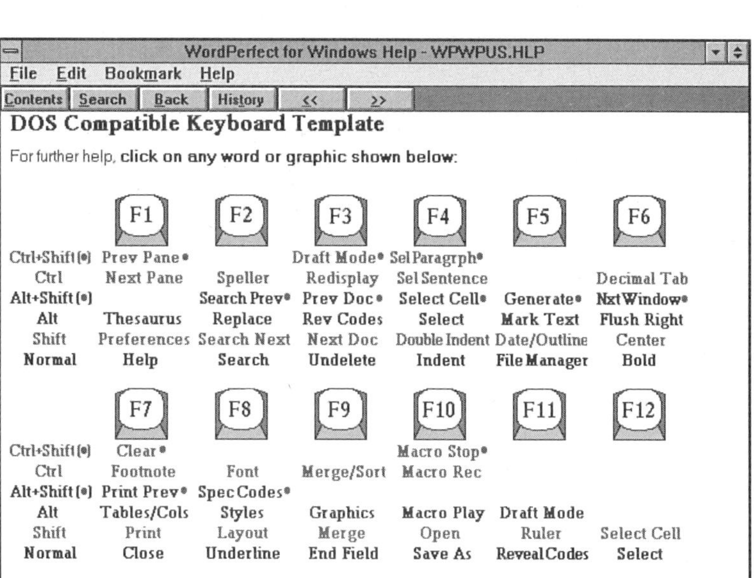

Figure 4.14. The Help window showing the WordPerfect for DOS template.

Saving a WordPerfect for Windows File

After you have made the changes you need to make, you will want to save the document. WordPerfect for Windows provides three ways to save a document, and each of these ways is described in this chapter. One of these methods enables you to save a document using a different name. Because you may not want to overwrite the work that existed before you edited, you may want to read the sections on these three methods before you use any of them.

- You can use the **C**lose command to save the document under its current name and then "put away" the document (remove it from the screen).
- You can use the **S**ave command to save the document under its current name and then continue working on the document.
- You can use the Save **A**s command to save the document under a different name. You may want to save the document under a different name to avoid changing the original.

When you exit from WordPerfect for Windows, the program also prompts you to save any documents that contain changes before you exit—but more about that later in this chapter.

Using the Close Command

You can use the **C**lose command when you finish working with a document and you want WordPerfect for Windows to save the document and put it away.

To close a document, open the **F**ile menu and choose the **C**lose command. Or, you can click the Close button on the Button Bar. If

you are using the WordPerfect for DOS keyboard, you also can press F7. If you are using the CUA keyboard, you also can press Ctrl+F4.

If you have not made any changes to the document since the last time you saved it, WordPerfect for Windows simply removes the document from the screen. If, however, you have made changes, WordPerfect for Windows displays the dialog box in Figure 4.15.

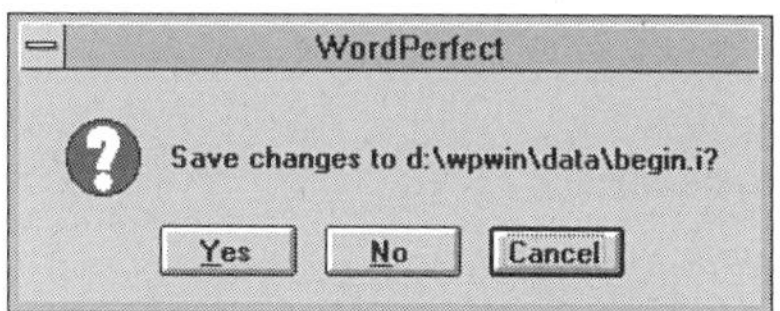

Figure 4.15.
The `Save changes to?` dialog box.

If you choose **Y**es, WordPerfect for Windows saves the changes you have made and removes the document from the screen. If you choose **N**o, WordPerfect for Windows *does not* save the changes you made since the last time you saved, but WordPerfect for Windows *does* remove the document from the screen. If you choose Cancel, WordPerfect for Windows *does not* save the changes you made since the last time you saved and *does not* remove the document from the screen.

Using the Save Command

You can use the **S**ave command to save the active document under its current name and then continue working on the document. When you use the **S**ave command, WordPerfect for Windows saves the changes you have made to a disk (either hard or floppy) and leaves the document onscreen.

To save a document by using the **S**ave command, open the **F**ile menu and choose the **S**ave command. Or, you can choose the Save button from the Button Bar. If you are using the CUA keyboard, you also can press Shift+F3. WordPerfect for Windows saves the document. (If you pay close attention to the status bar at the bottom of the screen, you will see a message that indicates WordPerfect for Windows is saving the document.)

Using the Save As Command

You might want to leave the original document available in cases where your changes may not be final. If you are unsure of the changes you have made, for example, and somebody else is going to come back and check your work, you might want to keep the original document. You then can show the person your version, and let him or her decide which version to continue using.

To save your version of an existing document and leave the original version intact, follow these steps:

1. Open the **F**ile menu and choose the Save **A**s command. If you are using the WordPerfect for DOS keyboard, you can press **F10**. If you are using the CUA keyboard, you can press **F3**.

   WordPerfect for Windows displays the Save As dialog box in Figure 4.16.

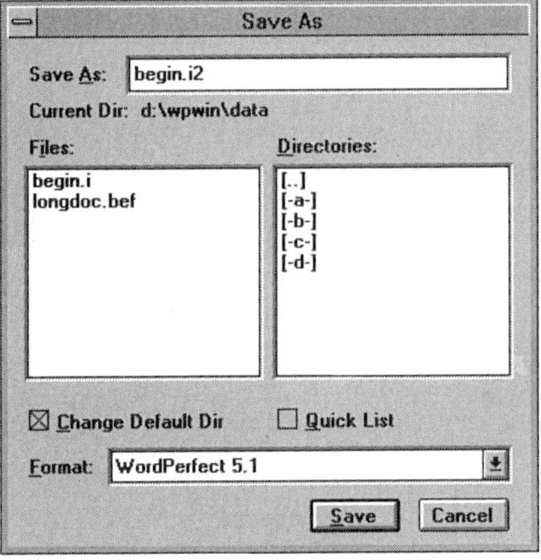

Figure 4.16. The Save As dialog box.

2. Type the new name for the document in the Save **A**s text box. You can use up to 11 characters for the name you want to assign to the document. The first part of the name can contain no more than 8 characters; the **extension** can contain no more than 3 characters.

For more information on the rules DOS imposes when you name a file on a PC, see Chapter 12. (Yes, it is DOS that imposes file name rules. It's even DOS that does the saving.)

If you choose a name that appears in the F**i**les list box, WordPerfect for Windows asks whether you want to replace that document. Because you probably don't want to replace the original version, choose **N**o and then type another name—preferably one that doesn't appear in the F**i**les list box.

3. If you want, you can use the **F**ormat list box to choose a format other than WordPerfect in which to save the document. For example, you could choose to save the document as a Word for Windows document.

4. Choose the **S**ave button.

   WordPerfect for Windows saves your document under the name you specify, leaving the original version (under the original name) intact.

Printing a WordPerfect for Windows File

After you have edited and saved the document, you may need to print it. But before you print the document, you may want to see onscreen the way it will look when you print it. To preview a document in WordPerfect for Windows and then print it, open the document and then open the **F**ile menu and choose Print Pre**v**iew. If you are using the WordPerfect for DOS keyboard, you can press Alt+Shift+F7 to choose Print Pre**v**iew. If you are using the CUA keyboard, you can press Shift+F5 to choose Print Pre**v**iew.

WordPerfect for Windows displays the layout of your document as it will appear when you print it (see Figure 4.17).

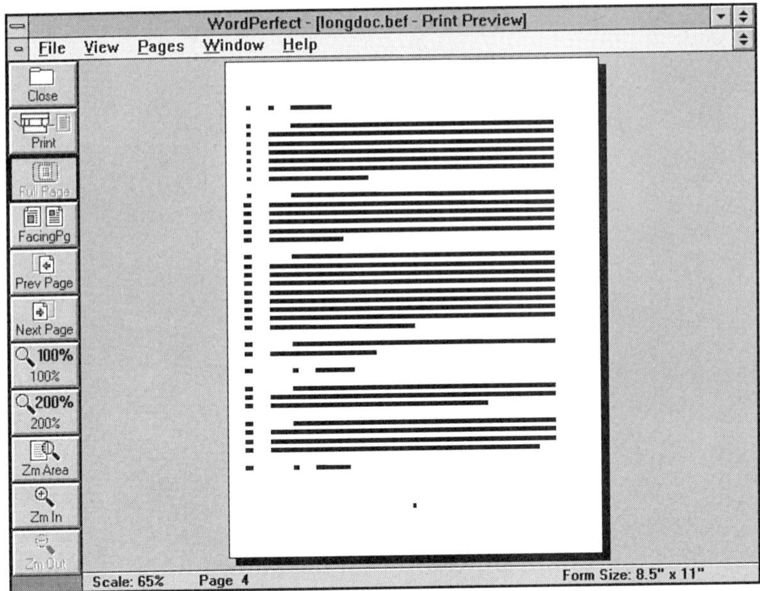

Figure 4.17.

A sample Print Preview screen.

Although you cannot edit on this screen, you can see the layout of the document as it will print. If the text and graphics are not aligned properly on this screen, they won't be aligned properly when you print. You can use the Print Preview Button Bar along the side of the window or the menus at the top of the window to perform the following tasks:

- You can use buttons on the Button Bar or commands on the **V**iew menu to enlarge the view by 100% or 200%, or to zoom in and out on areas of the page.

- You can use the buttons on the Button Bar or commands on the **P**ages menu to see the full page (as shown in Figure 4.17), to see the next or preceding page, or to see facing pages (as in a book) of a long document.

- You can choose the Close button from the Button Bar or the **C**lose command from the **F**ile menu to return to the editing window. If you are using the WordPerfect for DOS keyboard,

you also can press F7. If you are using the CUA keyboard, you also can press Ctrl+F4.

- You can choose the Print button on the Button Bar or the **P**rint command from the **F**ile menu to print the document. If you are using the WordPerfect for DOS keyboard, you also can press Shift+F7 to print. If you are using the CUA keyboard, you also can press F5 to print. WordPerfect for Windows displays the Print dialog box in Figure 4.18.

PC NOTE

If you want to print the document without previewing it, you can display the Print dialog box in any of the following ways: open the **F**ile menu and choose the **P**rint command, choose the Print button from the Button Bar, press Shift+F7 if you are using the WordPerfect for DOS keyboard, or press F5 if you are using the CUA keyboard.

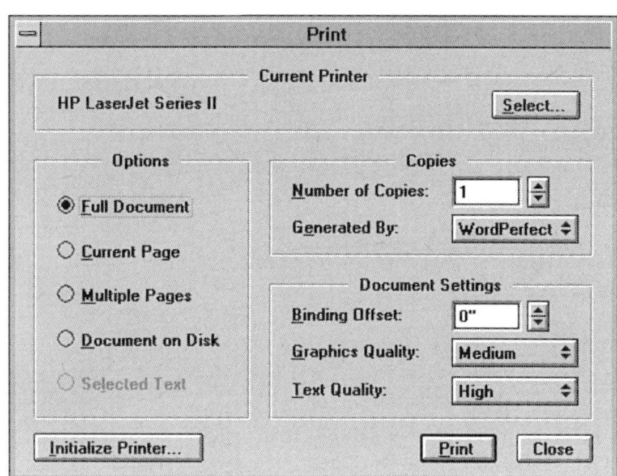

Figure 4.18. The Print dialog box.

Although there are many choices in the Print dialog box, the ones you are most likely to use are the choices in the Options box and the **N**umber of Copies option in the Copies box.

From the choices in the Options box, you can print the **F**ull Document, the **C**urrent Page, **M**ultiple Pages, a **D**ocument on Disk, or Se**l**ected Text:

- If you choose **F**ull Document, WordPerfect for Windows prints all of the active document.

- If you choose **C**urrent Page, WordPerfect for Windows prints the current page of the active document.

- If you choose **M**ultiple Pages, WordPerfect for Windows enables you to identify specific pages to print. When you choose the **P**rint command button, WordPerfect for Windows displays the Multiple Pages dialog box, in which you type in the **R**ange text box the numbers of the pages you want to print. You can type a group of pages, an individual page, or both. To print, for example, pages 4 through 11, type 4-11. To print page 13, type 13. To print pages 3 through 8 and page 14, type 3-8,14.

- If you choose **D**ocument on Disk, you can print a document you haven't opened. If you choose this option, you must complete the Document on Disk dialog box after choosing the **P**rint command button. In the **F**ilename text box, identify the document you want to print and, in the **R**ange text box, identify the range of pages you want to print. It is easier to open the document and print all or part of the document.

- The Se**l**ected text option is available only if you highlighted text before you opened the Print dialog box. If you highlighted text, you can print just the highlighted text in the active document by using this option.

You can print more than one copy of the choice you indicated in the Options box of the Print dialog box. Simply enter the number of copies in the **N**umber of Copies text box.

Copying a WordPerfect for Windows File to a Floppy Disk

You may find that you need to copy a WordPerfect for Windows file to a floppy disk. You may need to print a file from another PC, for example. Using the WordPerfect File Manager is the easiest way to copy a WordPerfect for Windows document to a floppy disk. Alternatively, you can use DOS commands, which you can find in Chapter 12.

The WordPerfect File Manager is actually a separate application program that enables you to perform a variety of functions. You may want to explore some of these functions on your own. To use the WordPerfect File Manager to copy a file to a floppy disk, follow these steps:

1. Insert a formatted disk into the floppy disk drive.

2. Open the **F**ile menu and choose the **F**ile Manager command.

   WordPerfect for Windows displays the WordPerfect File Manager (see Figure 4.19), the directory structure on the current drive. For more information on directory structure, see Chapter 12. At this point, all you need to know is where the files in the current WordPerfect for Windows directory are listed. The files appear in the rightmost portion of the window that contains information; they are *not* enclosed in brackets ([ ]).

   If the document you want to copy doesn't appear in the rightmost portion of the window, you may need to change to a different drive or directory. You probably *won't* need to change to a different drive or directory, but you can use either the mouse or the keyboard to change to a different drive or directory. You can use the mouse to change to a different drive by double-clicking in the Drives pane. You can use the mouse to change to a different directory, an item enclosed in brackets ([ ]), by double-clicking on the directory. You can use the keyboard to change to a different directory by opening the **F**ile menu and choosing the Chan**g**e Directory command. (From the Change Directory dialog box, you also can change drives.)

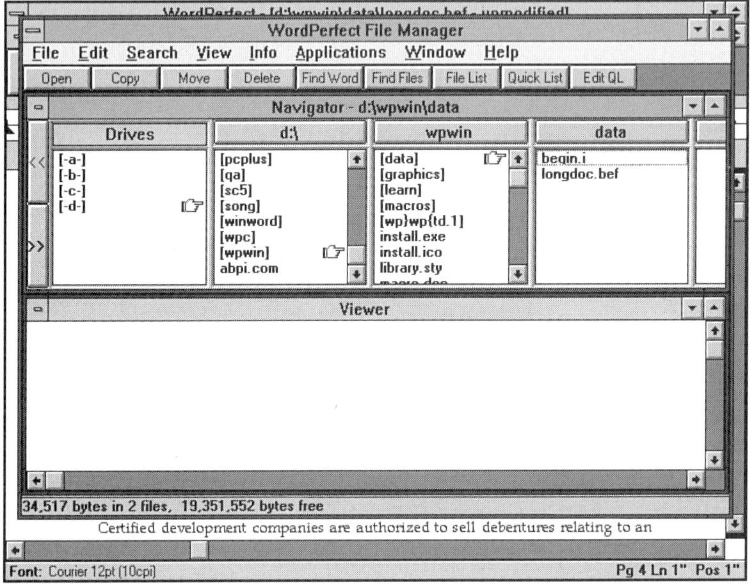

Figure 4.19. The WordPerfect File Manager.

3. Highlight the file you want to copy to a floppy disk. Using the mouse, click on the file. Using the keyboard, press the **Tab** key until you see the dotted outline in the correct pane. Then, press the arrow keys to highlight the correct file.

   When a file is highlighted, its contents appear in the Viewer portion of the File Manager window, which is the lower pane.

4. Choose the Copy button from the Button Bar, or open the **F**ile menu and choose the **C**opy command.

   WordPerfect for Windows displays the Copy File(s) dialog box in Figure 4.20.

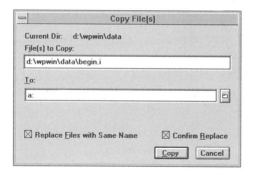

Figure 4.20.
The Copy File(s) dialog box.

5. In the **T**o text box, type `A:` (or the name of the floppy drive into which you inserted the disk).

6. Choose the **C**opy button.

   WordPerfect for Windows copies the file to the floppy disk. Because the Replace **F**iles with Same Name check box and the Confirm **R**eplace check box both contain `X`'s, any files on the floppy disk that already have the same name as the file you selected will be overwritten when you copy. But, before any files are overwritten, WordPerfect for Windows asks whether to overwrite the existing file on the floppy disk.

7. Open the **F**ile menu and choose the E**x**it command to close the File Manager.

Exiting WordPerfect for Windows

When you are finished using WordPerfect for Windows, you can exit by choosing the E**x**it command from the **F**ile menu. If you are using the CUA keyboard, you also can press Alt+F4 to exit from WordPerfect for Windows. If any of the open documents contain changes you didn't save, WordPerfect for Windows displays a dialog box that asks whether you want to save the changes to the document in question before you exit. Choose **Y**es to save the changes and exit. Choose **N**o to ignore the changes and exit. Choose Cancel to return to editing in WordPerfect for Windows.

When you exit from WordPerfect for Windows, you return to Windows. You can exit from Windows by choosing the E**x**it Windows command from the **F**ile menu or by pressing Alt+F4.

You safely can shut off the PC after exiting from Windows.

Chapter Summary

In this chapter, you learned how to use the excellent online Help facility in WordPerfect for Windows. You learned to open, retrieve, edit, save, and print a WordPerfect for Windows document. You also learned how to copy a document to a floppy disk and how to exit from WordPerfect for Windows.

As you noticed in this chapter, there is, unfortunately, very little resemblance between WordPerfect for Windows and WordPerfect for the Mac unless you have been using the WordPerfect 5.x keyboard in WordPerfect for the Mac (not likely for a Mac user). Primarily, the terminology is the same. In both packages, you open, save, print, and copy documents and select text. In both packages, you can use function keys or menus to execute commands.

In the next chapter, you learn how to work with Word for DOS files. As you know, Chapters 3 through 9 in *The Mac User's PC* focus on specific software packages. You should read the chapters that pertain to the software you want to use. Chapter 10 tells you about database programs you may want to avoid. Chapter 11 discusses the MS-DOS Shell. Refer to Chapter 12 for information on file-naming conventions imposed on WordPerfect for Windows by the operating system, and to learn about basic DOS commands. If you need to transfer and translate files between a Mac and a PC, read Chapter 13.

Working with Word for DOS Files

In the first two chapters of *The Mac User's PC*, you learned about the physical appearance of a PC, how to turn on a PC, how to recognize what you may see onscreen, and how to start programs. In this chapter, you will learn very basic information about using Microsoft Word for DOS. This chapter is not intended to make you an expert at Word for DOS; this chapter simply teaches you how to perform some basic tasks. You will learn how to open, edit, save, and print a Word for DOS document; how to copy a Word for DOS file to a floppy disk; and how to exit the program properly. And you will learn one other important thing—how to get help in Word for DOS so that you can teach yourself to do the things that aren't covered in this book!

You should feel at home with Word for DOS, relatively speaking. Although the screens don't resemble one another physically, the functioning of Word for DOS and Word for the Mac is quite similar.

Using an appropriate technique you learned in Chapter 2, start the Word program (or see Chapter 11 for information on starting programs from the MS-DOS Shell). This discussion covers Word 5.5, but if you are working with an earlier version, you should still be able to follow along.

Identifying Word for DOS Screen Parts

When you first start Word for DOS, you see the default screen, which looks like the screen in Figure 5.1. Note that many of the items on the default screen are customizable and therefore may not appear on your screen.

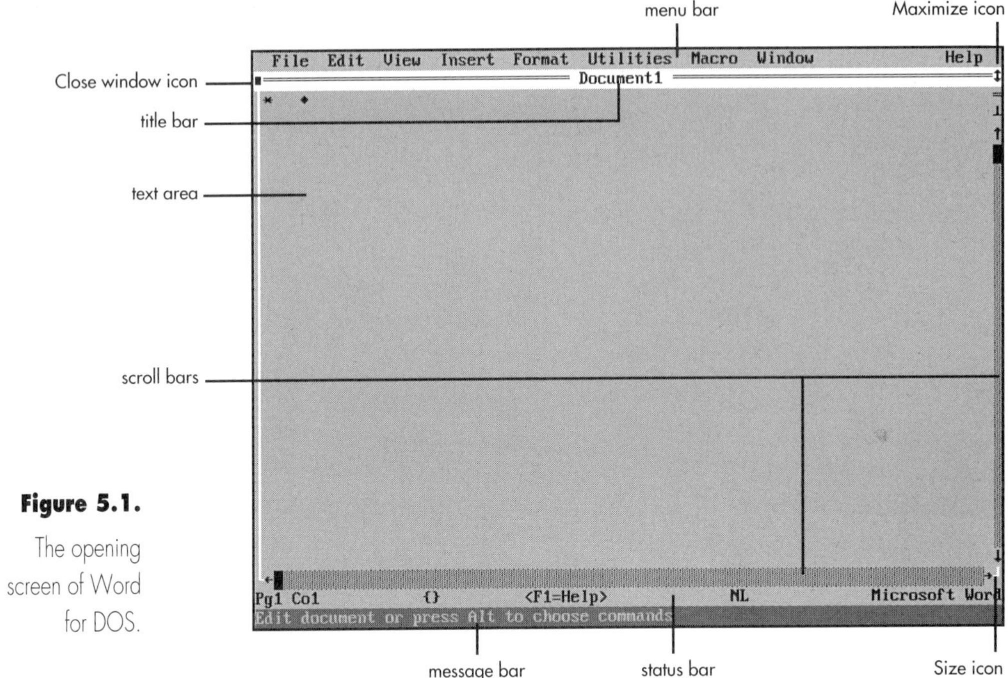

Figure 5.1.
The opening screen of Word for DOS.

As in Word for the Mac, you see the **menu bar** at the top of the screen. On the Help menu, about which you learn more later in this chapter, you will find commands that help you learn to use Word for DOS.

Below the menu bar, you see the **title bar** for the current document. When you start Word for DOS, you always see an empty document screen on which you can create a new document. The name of the first empty document, `Document1`, appears in the title bar. Each new empty window you open is named incrementally—Document2, Document3, Document4, and so on. You can open up to nine documents at one time.

At the left end of the title bar, you see the Close window icon, which works just like the Close box in Word for the Mac. If you click on the Close window icon, the current window closes. At the right end of the menu bar, you see the Maximize icon. More about this icon in just a moment.

You may see the style area at the left side of the text area (the appearance of this feature is optional). The style area identifies the styles applied to each paragraph. In addition, the left edge of the text area contains an invisible selection bar, which you can use to select text just as you do in Word for the Mac, but more on this later in the chapter.

Just below the text area and along its right side, you see the horizontal and vertical scroll bars, which have arrows at both ends and a scroll box somewhere along the scroll bar. You can use the scroll arrows or the scroll box with a mouse to move through a document. Using a mouse, you can click on the scroll arrows or drag the scroll box on the horizontal scroll bar to move the view of a document right or left. Or, you can click on the arrows or drag the scroll box on the vertical scroll bar to move the view of a document down or up.

At the intersection of the horizontal and vertical scroll bars, you see the Size icon. You can use the Size icon the same way you use the Size box in Word for the Mac. If you drag the Size icon, you can change the size of the document window.

The Size icon brings us back to the Maximize icon. If you use the Size icon to reduce the size of the document window, you can click on the Maximize icon to maximize the size of the document window. Initially, when you start the program, the document portion of the window is maximized. If you click on the Maximize icon, the letters `MX` appear in the status bar. If you click on the Maximize icon again, the letters `MX` disappear from the status bar.

The status bar, which appears just below the horizontal scroll bar, is divided into four parts (see Figure 5.2).

At the left end of the status bar, you see the current position of the **cursor**, which is a blinking underline. (The diamond shape represents an end marker—the end of the text you have typed). The cursor works just like the insertion point in Word for the Mac—the cursor indicates where text will appear when you type.

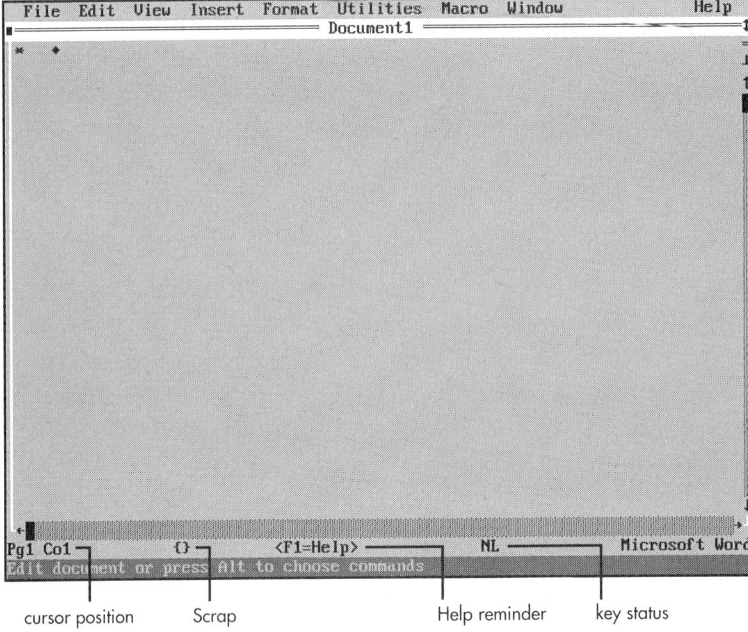

Figure 5.2.

The parts of the status bar.

Next to the cursor position information, you see the Scrap. You can compare the Scrap to the Clipboard in Word for the Mac. In the Scrap, you see the first and last characters of the most recently cut or copied text. If you choose the **P**aste command from the **E**dit menu, you can insert the contents of the Scrap into your document.

Next to the Scrap on the status bar, you see the Help reminder, which supplies context-sensitive Help.

And, next to the Help reminder, you see the key status information. In this location, you see codes that provide information about the keyboard; for example, if the NumLock key is pressed down, you see `NL` in the key status information area. You also see codes that provide information about the window; for example, after you click on the Maximize icon, `MX` appears in the key status information area. Later in this chapter, when you learn to get help, you learn how to identify the codes that may appear in the key status part of the status bar.

Just below the status bar, you see the message bar. The message bar provides brief help on actions you can perform.

Word for DOS comes with some additional features that users can define to appear onscreen; you may see some of these features on your screen. Figure 5.3 shows some of these features.

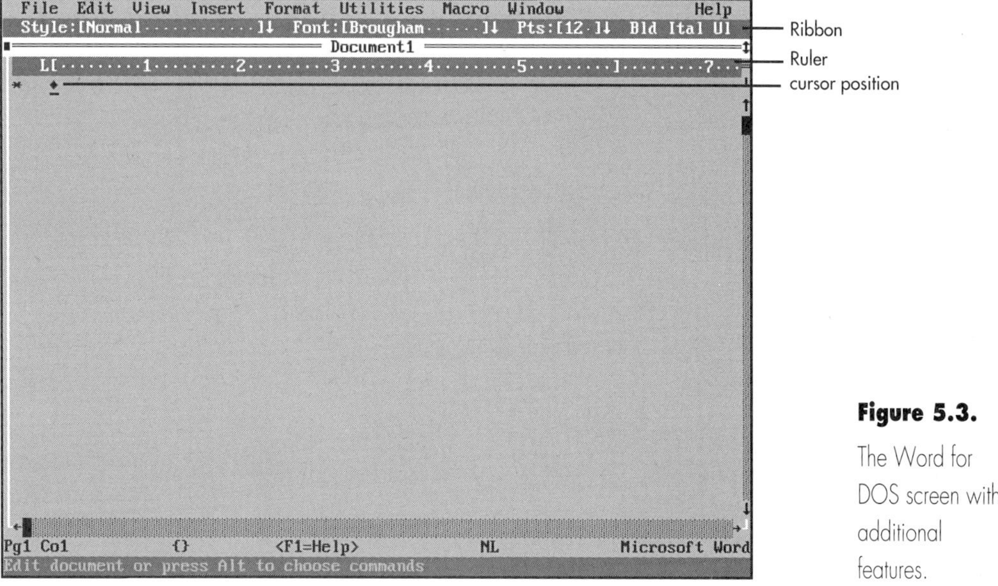

Figure 5.3.

The Word for DOS screen with additional features.

Just below the menu bar, you see the Ribbon. You can use the Ribbon to perform common tasks without opening the menus. Working from the left end of the Ribbon, you can perform the following tasks:

- Use the Style drop-down list to change the predefined style of the current paragraph or of selected text.
- Use the Font drop-down list to change the font.
- Choose the point size of a font.
- Add boldface, italic, or underline formatting to the selected text.

Below the Ribbon, you see the Ruler. You can use the Ruler to set, move, and remove tab stops and indents, as well as add or delete leader characters.

Using a Mouse in Word for DOS

While working in Word for DOS, you can use the mouse or the keyboard to perform certain tasks. In the following sections, you will find instructions on how to use the mouse and the keyboard to **choose** commands from menus, choose options in dialog boxes, and start programs.

In Word for DOS, a mouse operates differently from a mouse on a Macintosh. Before you learn the specifics of performing each of the previously mentioned actions, let's review the way in which a mouse operates in Word for DOS.

Using a mouse in Word for DOS is a two-step process. To use a mouse to **choose** an item in Word for DOS, follow these steps:

1. Slide the mouse until the mouse pointer points to the item you want to choose.

2. Press and release a mouse button—usually the left mouse button—one time.

The action you perform in step 1 is known as **pointing**, and the action you perform in step 2 is known as **clicking**. You can click either the left or the right mouse button, as defined by Word for DOS. Most of the time, to choose an item, you click the left mouse button. You also may have occasion to double-click. To **double-click**, you press and release the left mouse button twice in rapid succession.

Note the difference in the way clicking works in Word for DOS compared to on a Mac. In Word for DOS, for the most part, you don't need to hold down the mouse button while trying to open a menu and choose a command; the menu remains open after you release the mouse button. On a Mac, when you release the mouse button, the menu from which you were trying to choose a command closes.

Working with Menus in Word for DOS

You use the menus on the menu bar to execute commands. The menu bar appears at the top of the screen, and each menu contains the commands you use in Word for DOS. To execute a command, you open a menu and choose the command. You can use either the mouse or the keyboard to open a menu.

To open a menu by using the mouse, point to the menu you want to open and click the left mouse button. Word for DOS opens the menu. Unlike on a Mac, the menu remains open when you release the mouse button, and the first command on the menu appears highlighted. To choose a command from a menu by using the mouse, point to the command and click the left mouse button. Word for DOS executes the command.

You also can use the keyboard to open a menu and choose a command. First, you activate the menu bar by pressing the Alt key. A **reverse video bar** (or **highlight**) appears on the name of the first menu, **F**ile. Then, you can open menus and choose menu commands in one of two ways:

- You can use the hot key shortcuts. Each menu and command contains a bold letter, also called a **hot key**. You can press that key to open the menu or execute the command. When you press the **W** key, for example, Word for DOS opens the

Window menu and displays the commands available on that menu. In this book, all references to hot keys appear in boldface type.

- You can press one of the arrow keys on the keyboard to point to a menu or command, and then press the Enter key to choose it. When you press an arrow key, the reverse video bar moves. Continue pressing the arrow key until the reverse video bar appears on top of the menu or command to which you want to point. For example, you can press Alt to activate the menu bar, and then press the left-arrow key twice to point to the Window menu. Remember, when you use the arrow keys to point to a menu or command, you must press Enter to open that menu or choose that command.

You can bypass menus by pressing the key combinations that appear on the menu next to the commands. For example, on the **F**ile menu, the key combination Alt+Ctrl+F2 appears next to the **O**pen command. These key combinations work just like they do on the Mac: hold down the first key(s) as you press the last key. Pressing Alt+Ctrl+F2 is the equivalent of opening the **F**ile menu and choosing the **O**pen command. As an occasional user of Word for DOS, you may not have much use for these key combinations because you must memorize them to use them.

Working with Dialog Boxes in Word for DOS

Ellipses (...) appear after some commands on the menus. The program requires additional information about these commands before it can execute them. When you choose a command that includes an ellipsis, a **dialog box** (in which you supply the additional required information) appears.

Figure 5.4 displays a typical dialog box that contains the types of options you might see. Each dialog box is different, and most dialog boxes provide only some of these types of options.

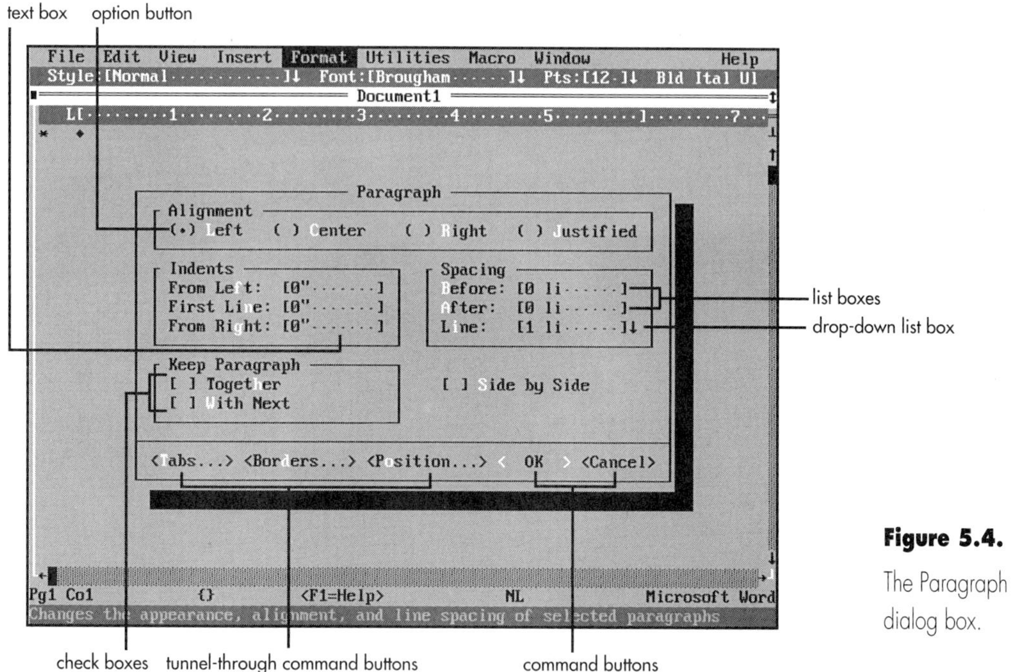

Figure 5.4.

The Paragraph dialog box.

To move around in a dialog box by using the mouse, click on the area in which you want to work. If you are using a keyboard instead of a mouse, you can use the Tab key to move around in a dialog box.

A **list box** contains a list of options. You may see two kinds of list boxes in a dialog box. The L**i**ne list box (in the Spacing area) in Figure 5.4 is an example of a drop-down list box, and is closed when the dialog box appears. To open a drop-down list box, click on the down arrow at the right end of the box; or type the bold letter in the list box name. The other type of list box is already open when the dialog box appears. To choose an item from either type of list box, click on the item or press the down-arrow key to point to the item and then press Enter. If the list box is not long enough to display all the available items in the list, press and hold the down-arrow key to move beyond the items that appear in the box.

An **option button** is a small round button you use to choose one option from a group of related options. A black dot appears in the button of the current option. To choose an option button, click on the option button; or, type the bold letter in the option name. In Figure 5.4, **L**eft, **C**enter, **R**ight, and **J**ustified are options in the Alignment area, and **L**eft is the current option.

A **check box** is a pair of brackets ([ ]) you use to choose an option. You can choose more than one check box from a group of related options. An X appears in the check boxes of the activated options. To choose a check box, click on the check box; or type the bold letter in the option name. To deactivate the option and remove the X from the box, choose the check box again. In Figure 5.4, the options that appear in the Keep Paragraph area are check boxes.

A **text box** is a rectangular box in which you enter text. When a dialog box that contains a text box opens, the current text usually is selected. To replace the selected text, simply type the new information. In Figure 5.4, all the options in the Indents area are text boxes.

A **command button** appears enclosed within angle brackets (< >) and performs an action. To choose a command button, click on the button; or, use the Tab key to move the mouse pointer to the button and press Enter. In Figure 5.4, the OK button accepts the settings in the dialog box. The Cancel button cancels your changes to the settings in the dialog box.

A **tunnel-through command button** is a command button that contains an ellipsis (...) and opens another dialog box. To choose a tunnel-through command button, click on the button; highlight the button and press Enter; or type the bold letter. In Figure 5.4, the **T**abs, Bor**d**ers, and P**o**sition buttons are tunnel-through command buttons.

Getting Help in Word for DOS

If the person who installed Word for DOS also installed the online tutorials, you may find a command on the **H**elp menu for teaching yourself to use Word for DOS. If you choose **L**earning Word from the **H**elp menu, you start a tutorial on using Word for DOS. Each lesson in the tutorial provides estimated completion times, and you can choose the lessons you want to complete. You will need about three hours to complete the entire tutorial.

PC NOTE

If you don't see the tutorial on the **H**elp menu and you can find the original program disks, you can install just the tutorial. Make sure that you are looking at a DOS prompt (exit from any programs you are running). Place the first disk into the floppy disk drive (I'll assume it's drive A), change to that drive by typing A: (substitute the letter of your floppy drive if necessary and include the colon), and press Enter. Then, type **SETUP** and press Enter. You will see instructions onscreen, and you can choose to install *only* the tutorial.

In addition to this online tutorial, Word for DOS contains an excellent online Help facility. You can display the Help Index in Word for DOS by pressing F1 or by opening the **H**elp menu and choosing the **I**ndex command (see Figure 5.5). In Word for DOS, the help you receive is context-sensitive—if you are looking at a command on a menu and you press F1, the help you get is about that menu command.

When you view the Help Index window, you see command buttons for Help topics. If the information in the Help window is too long to fit in one Help window, you see a scroll bar on the right side of the window. Using the mouse, you can click on the scroll arrows to move the information in the window so that you can read it all. To view information on a Help topic, click on it. Using the keyboard, you can press the down-arrow key to move the topics in the window. Then, use the Tab key to highlight the topic about which you want help and press Enter. Or, you can press the first letter of a topic; Word for DOS Help takes you to the first topic in the list that begins with that letter. You then can use the arrow keys to scroll down the list; when you highlight the topic about which you want to read, press Enter.

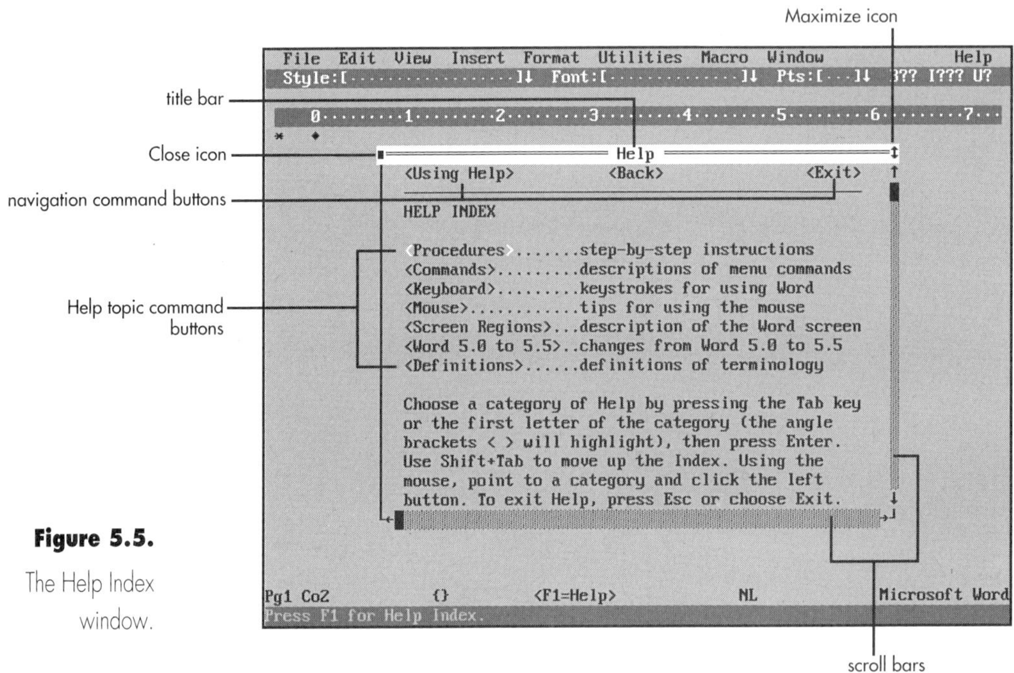

Figure 5.5. The Help Index window.

As you can see from the information in Table 5.1 and in the Help Index window, you can choose command buttons in the Help Index window to view lists of topics organized in assorted ways.

Table 5.1. Help Index window command buttons.

Command Button	Effect
Procedures button	Displays an alphabetical index of topics. Each of the topics in the Procedures Index provides step-by-step instructions for the topic.
Commands button	Displays a list of the commands that appear on each menu.
Keyboard button	Displays a list of topics related to the keyboard.
Mouse button	Displays a list of topics related to the mouse.
Screen Regions button	Displays an onscreen graphic of the Word for DOS screen. You can click on various parts of the graphic to view information on the function of the screen part. For example, you can click on the letters in the status bar to view definitions of the letters that might appear in the key status portion.
Word 5.0 to Word 5.5 button	Displays a list of topics related to the differences between the two versions of Word for DOS. (As an occasional user of Word for DOS, it's not likely that you will need this information, unless, of course, you're working in Word 5.0 and reading this chapter, which is based on Word 5.5.)
Definitions button	Displays an alphabetical list of terms. If you choose a term from the list, you will see its definition.

After you choose a topic, you will see other topics listed in the Help information. You can choose those other topics for additional information. If you choose any word that appears in angle brackets within the Help text, you will see a definition of that word. If you choose any of the additional topics listed at the end of the Help information, Word for DOS Help switches to the Help information for that topic. At the top of each Help window, you see the following command buttons that you use to navigate through Help:

- The Index button, which appears on every Help screen except the first, redisplays the opening Help Index window.
- The Back button redisplays the last Help window you viewed.
- The Exit button closes the Help window.

Opening a Word for DOS File

Suppose that someone brings you a letter, asks you to make some minor changes to it, and then wants you to print the revised letter and mail it. In this section, you learn how to open an existing Word for DOS document. In the next three sections, you learn how to edit, save, and print a Word for DOS document.

You can open up to nine documents at one time. The document that contains the cursor is called the **active document**, and you are viewing it in the **active window**. When you start Word for DOS, Document1 always appears. You can start typing a new document in Document1. If you open an existing document without typing in Document1, the existing document replaces Document1.

To open an existing document, follow these steps:

1. Open the **F**ile menu and choose the **O**pen command. You also can press **Alt**+**Ctrl**+**F2**.

   Word for DOS displays the Open dialog box in Figure 5.6. By default, Word for DOS displays documents created in Word for DOS format in the current directory.

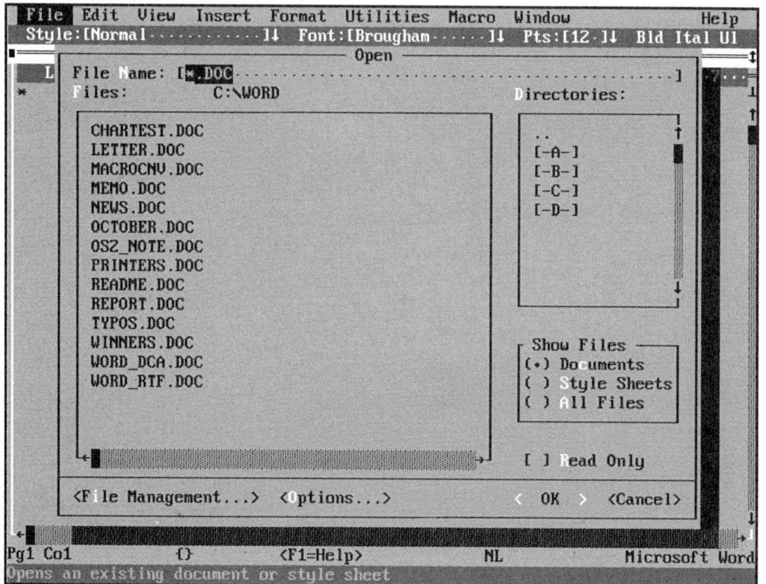

Figure 5.6. The Open dialog box.

2. Choose the name of the document you want to open from the list on the left side of the dialog box.

   If the document you want to open doesn't appear in the list, the document may be saved in another directory. You can type the file name of the document you want to open, including the entire path name, in the File **N**ame text box. Or, you can switch to a different directory by clicking on the drive identifier and then modifying the directory path name that appears in the File **N**ame text box. See Chapter 12 for more information on path names.

3. Choose the OK button.

   The document appears onscreen, and you can edit it.

If you must type a new document, start in an empty window by choosing the **N**ew command from the **F**ile menu.

Performing Basic Editing in Word for DOS

By default, when you type in Word for DOS, you are working in insert mode. In **insert mode**, Word for DOS places characters at the current location of the cursor and moves all existing characters to the right. You can press the Ins key to switch to **overtype mode**. In **overtype mode**, Word for DOS places characters at the current location of the cursor and types over characters that exist at that location, removing them. The Ins key works like a toggle switch: press the key once to change from insert mode to overtype mode; press the key a second time to change back from overtype mode to insert mode. If you switch to overtype mode, the letters OT appear in the key status portion of the status bar.

You can use the Backspace key to delete the character immediately to the left of the cursor. You can use the Del key to delete the character immediately above the cursor.

Moving around a Document

You move around in a Word for DOS document by pressing the directional keys (the arrows keys, Home, End, PgUp, and PgDn). Table 5.2 summarizes the most common ways in which you can use the keyboard to move around in a Word for DOS document.

Table 5.2. Directional keys in an existing document.

Key(s)	Effect
→ and ←	Moves right or left one character.
↑ and ↓	Moves up or down one line.
Ctrl+→	Moves right one word.
Ctrl+←	Moves left one word.
Ctrl+↓	Moves down one paragraph.
Ctrl+↑	Moves up one paragraph.
Home	Moves to the beginning of the current line.
End	Moves to the end of the current line.
PgDn	Moves to the same cursor position in the next window.
PgUp	Moves to the same cursor position in the preceding window.

Selecting Text

You may want to make changes to the appearance of text. For example, you may want certain text to appear underlined, in italics or in boldface type; you may want to change the alignment of certain text; or you may want to delete certain text.

As in Word for the Mac, in Word for DOS, you select text when you want to "operate" on it—that is, when you want to format, align, delete, or even print text. **Selecting** is the process of highlighting the text so that Word for DOS can identify the text on which you want to work. Selection techniques in Word for DOS closely resemble selection techniques in Word for the Mac.

To use the mouse to select text, you drag the mouse pointer. Follow these steps:

1. Place the cursor in front of the text you want to select. Click and hold down the left mouse button.

2. Slide the mouse to the right.

   As you slide the mouse, a reverse video bar (a highlight) appears over the text you are selecting.

3. Continue sliding the mouse until you reach the end of the text you want to select.

4. Release the left mouse button.

   The text you selected is highlighted—a reverse video bar appears over it.

You can use the following shortcuts with the mouse to select a word, a sentence, or a paragraph:

- To select a word, double-click on it.

- To select a sentence, hold down the Ctrl key as you click the left mouse button anywhere in the sentence you want to select.

- To select a line or groups of lines, you can use the selection bar. The selection bar isn't visible; however, when you move the mouse pointer into the selection bar, the mouse pointer changes to an arrow pointing up and to the right. Place the mouse pointer next to the line you want to select, and then click the left mouse button. Word for DOS highlights the line. If you want to select more than one line, don't just click the left mouse button; drag the mouse until all the lines you want to select are highlighted.

- To select a paragraph or groups of paragraphs, you can use the selection bar. Place the mouse pointer in the selection bar next to the paragraph you want to select and double-click the left mouse button. If you want to select more than one paragraph, don't just click the left mouse button; drag the mouse until all the paragraphs you want to select are highlighted.

You can cancel a selection by clicking the mouse anywhere else onscreen.

To select text by using the keyboard, follow these steps:

1. Use the arrow keys to place the cursor (the blinking underline) at the beginning of the text you want to select.

2. Use the **Shift** key combined with directional keys to select text. You can use Table 5.2 to review how to select the appropriate block of text. For example, to select one word to the right, press **Shift**+**Ctrl**+→.

You can cancel a selection by pressing any arrow key.

Saving a Word for DOS File

After you have made the changes you need to make, you will want to save the document. Word for DOS provides three ways to save a document, just like Word for the Mac. One of these methods lets you save a document using a different name. Because you may not want to overwrite the work that existed before you edited, you may want to read the detail sections on these three methods before you use any of them.

- You can use the Close command to save the document under its current name and then "put away" the document (remove it from the screen).

- You can use the Save command to save the document under its current name and then continue working on the document.
- You can use the Save **A**s command to save the document under a different name. You may want to save the document under a different name to avoid changing the original.

When you exit from Word for DOS, the program also prompts you to save any documents that contain changes before you exit—but more about that later in this chapter.

Using the Close Command

As in Word for the Mac, you can use the **C**lose command when you finish working with a document and you want Word for DOS to put away the document. When you choose the **C**lose command, Word for DOS also gives you the option of saving any changes you might have made before Word for DOS puts away the document. To use the **C**lose command, open the **F**ile menu and choose the **C**lose command; or, click on the Close icon on the document window.

If you haven't made any changes to the document since the last time you saved it, Word for DOS simply removes the document from the screen. If, however, you have made changes, Word for DOS displays the dialog box in Figure 5.7.

If you choose **Y**es, Word for DOS saves the changes you have made and removes the document from the window. If you choose **N**o, Word for DOS *does not* save the changes you made since the last time you saved, but Word for DOS *does* remove the document from the window. If you choose Cancel, Word for DOS *does not* save the changes you made since the last time you saved and *does not* remove the document from the window.

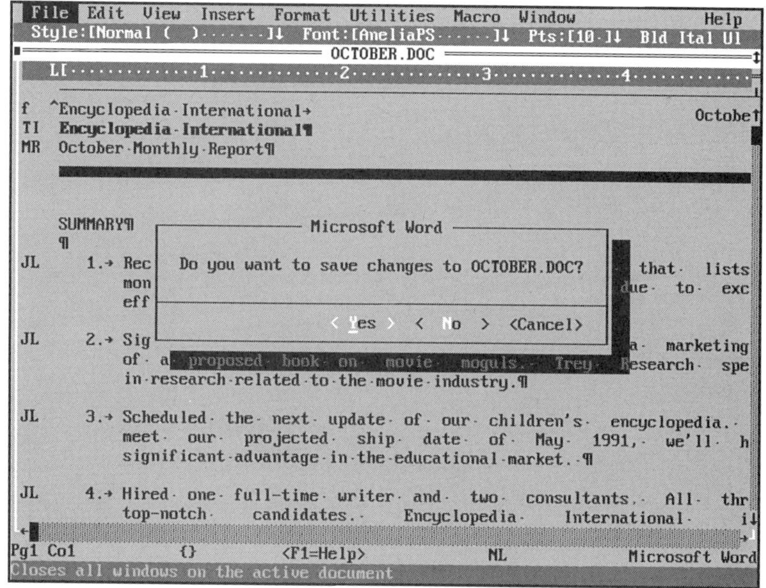

Figure 5.7.

The `Do you want to save changes to?` dialog box.

If you have multiple documents open and you want to remove all of them from view, you can use the Close All command on the **F**ile menu. The C**l**ose All command works just like the **C**lose command, but asks you whether you want to save changes to any open documents that contain modifications since you last saved.

Using the Save Command

Also as in Word for the Mac, you can use the **S**ave command to save the document in the active window. When you use the **S**ave command, Word for DOS saves the changes you have made to a disk (either hard or floppy) and leaves the document onscreen so that you can continue to work on it.

To save a document by using the **S**ave command, open the **F**ile menu and choose the **S**ave command. Or, you can press Alt+Shift+F2. If you are saving an existing document that already has a name, Word for DOS saves the document. (If you pay close attention to the status bar at the bottom of the screen, you will see a message that indicates Word for DOS is saving the document.)

If you are saving a new document that doesn't yet have a name, Word for DOS displays the Save As dialog box discussed in the next section.

Using the Save As Command

You might want to leave the original document available in cases where your changes may not be final. If you are unsure of the changes you have made, for example, and somebody else is going to come back and check your work, you might want to keep the original document. You then can show the person your version, and let him or her decide which version to continue using.

To save your version of an existing document and leave the original version intact, follow these steps:

1. Open the **F**ile menu and choose the Save **A**s command, or press **Alt+F2**.

   Word for DOS displays the Save As dialog box in Figure 5.8.

2. Type the new name for the document in the File **N**ame text box. You can use up to 11 characters for the name you want to assign to the document. The first part of the name can contain no more than 8 characters; the **extension** can contain no more than 3 characters.

   For more information on the rules DOS imposes when you name a file on a PC, see Chapter 12. (Yes, it is DOS that imposes file name rules. It's even DOS that does the saving.)

   If you choose a name that appears in the list box, Word for DOS asks whether you want to replace that document.

3. Choose OK.

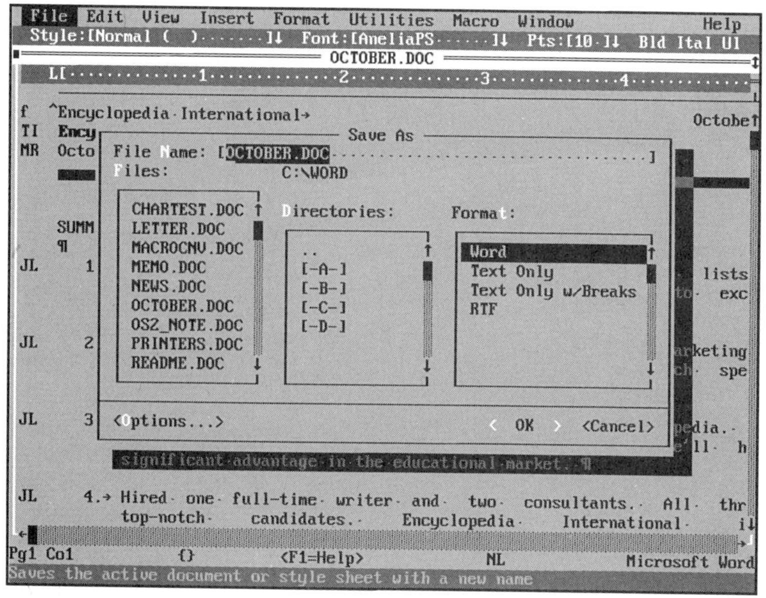

Figure 5.8.

The Save As dialog box.

Word for DOS saves the document under the name you specified in the File **N**ame text box, leaving the original version (under the original name) intact.

The Summary Information dialog box appears as it does in Word for the Mac. The Summary Information dialog box enables you to attach additional information to the document. You can use this information later if you need to search for text but are not sure about the document in which the text appears. Completing the Summary Information dialog box is optional, just as in Word for the Mac. Choose OK to close the dialog box.

Printing a Word for DOS File

After you have edited and saved the document, you may need to print it. Before you print the document, you may want to see onscreen the way the document will look when you print it. You

can preview a document in Word for DOS the same way you preview a document in Word for the Mac. To preview a document in Word for DOS and then print it, open the **F**ile menu and choose Print Pre**v**iew. Word for DOS displays the layout of your document as it will appear when you print it (see Figure 5.9).

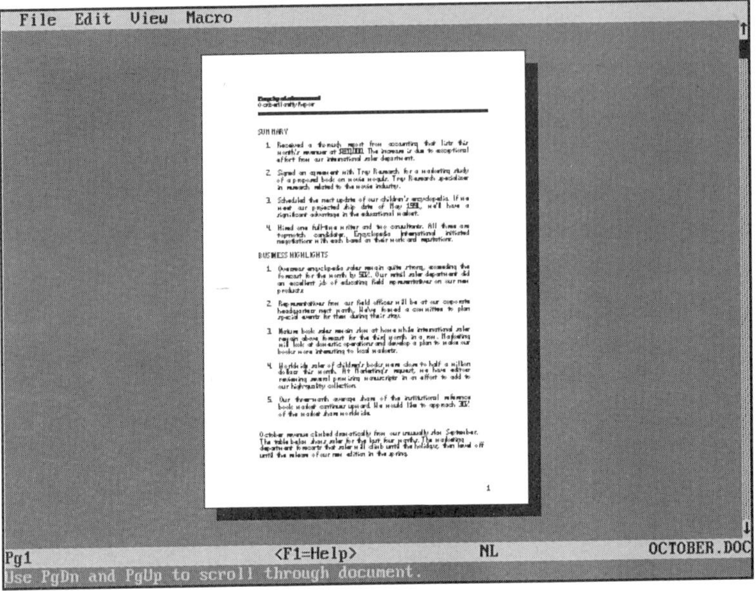

Figure 5.9.

A sample Print Preview screen.

You cannot edit on this screen, but you can see the layout of the document as it will print. If the text and layout are not aligned properly on this screen, they won't be aligned properly when you print. You can use the menus along the top of the Print Preview window to adjust the view, return to the editing window, or print the document:

- You can use the **V**iew menu to see one page at a time (as shown in Figure 5.9), two pages at a time, or two facing pages (as in a book) of a long document.

- You can return to the editing window by pressing the Esc key or by choosing the Exit Preview command from the **F**ile menu.

- You can print the document by choosing the **P**rint command from the **F**ile menu. Word for DOS displays the Print dialog box in Figure 5.10.

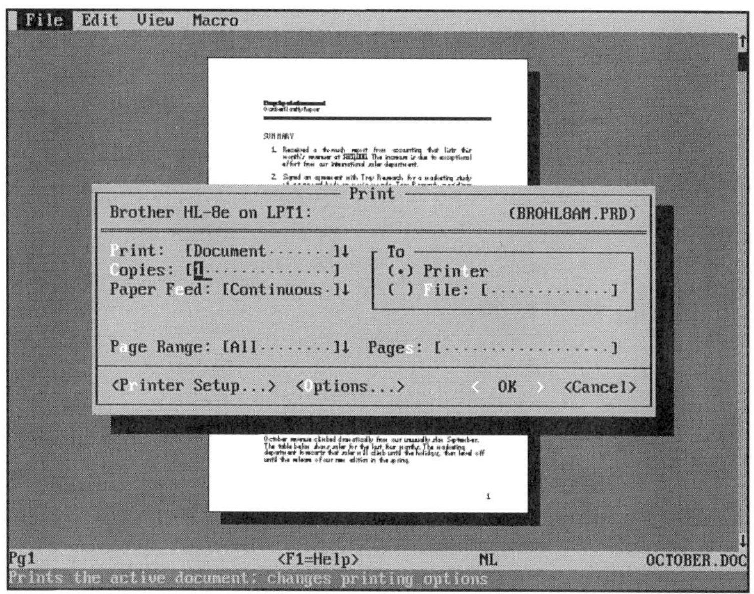

Figure 5.10.

The Print dialog box.

Although there are several choices in this dialog box, the ones you are most likely to use are the choices in the P**a**ge Range list box and the **C**opies text box.

From the choices in the Page Range options box, you can choose the pages you want to print:

- To print the entire document, choose **A**ll.
- To print selected pages, choose the Pa**g**es text box and then specify the page numbers.
- To print only selected text, select the text and then choose **S**election from the Page Range list box.

To print more than one copy of the choice you indicated in the Page Range list box of the Print dialog box, change the number of copies in the **C**opies text box.

You can open the Print dialog box (see Figure 5.9) without previewing by choosing the **P**rint command from the **F**ile menu or by pressing Shift+F9.

Copying a Word for DOS File to a Floppy Disk

You may find that you need to copy a Word for DOS file to a floppy disk. You may need to print a file from another PC, for example. Using the Save As dialog box is the easiest way to copy a Word for DOS document onto a floppy disk. Alternatively, you can use DOS commands, which you can find in Chapter 12.

Earlier in this chapter, you learned to use the Save As dialog box to save a new document or to save an existing document under a different name. When you use the Save As command to copy a file, in effect you save the file to a different disk. Remember that the following set of steps saves the current document to a *different* disk. If you also want to save the current document to the hard disk, first use either the **S**ave or Save **A**s command (as you learned earlier) to save to the hard disk. Then, use the following set of steps to save the current document to a different disk.

To use the Save As dialog box to copy a file to a floppy disk, follow these steps:

1. Insert a formatted disk into the floppy disk drive.

2. Open the **F**ile menu and choose the Save **A**s command, or press **Alt**+**F2**.

Word for DOS displays the Save As dialog box (see Figure 5.11), showing the files in the current directory at the left. The name of the current document appears highlighted in the File **N**ame text box at the top of the dialog box; the current directory name appears just below the File **N**ame text box.

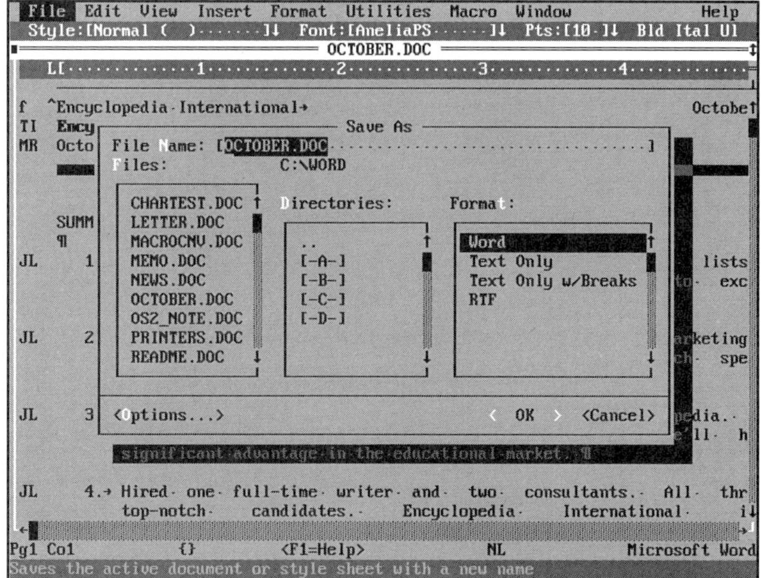

Figure 5.11.

The Save As dialog box.

3. In the **D**irectories list, double-click on the letter of the floppy drive that contains the formatted floppy disk.

   The path specified under the File **N**ame text box changes to the name of the floppy disk drive you selected, while the document name that appears in the File **N**ame text box remains unchanged.

4. If you want, type a new name for the document in the File **N**ame text box. The new name will be assigned to the document on the floppy disk. The original file on the hard disk will retain its original name.

5. Choose OK.

Word for DOS saves the file to the floppy disk. If a file of that name already exists on the floppy disk, Word for DOS prompts you to replace the file on the floppy disk or cancel the operation. If you replace the version on the floppy disk, you write over it and it is gone forever; if you have ANY doubts, cancel the operation.

You may see the Summary Information dialog box. Make any changes you want to this dialog box, or choose OK to accept the information you see in the dialog box.

When you complete these steps, Word for DOS places a copy of the current document on the floppy disk. Remember, if you want a copy of the current document on the hard disk, save it first to the hard disk by using the **S**ave or the Save **A**s command discussed earlier in this chapter.

Exiting Word for DOS

When you are finished using Word for DOS, you can exit by choosing the E**x**it command from the **F**ile menu or by pressing Alt+F4. If any of your open documents contain changes you didn't save, Word for DOS displays a dialog box asking whether you want to save the changes to the document before you exit. Choose **Y**es to save the changes and exit. Choose **N**o to ignore the changes and exit Word for DOS. Choose Cancel to return to editing in Word for DOS.

When you exit from Word for DOS, you return to DOS (or a menu or the MS-DOS Shell). From this point, you safely can shut off the PC.

Chapter Summary

In this chapter, you learned how to use the excellent online Help facility in Word for DOS. You also learned how to open, edit, save, and print a Word for DOS document; how to copy a Word for DOS file to a floppy disk; and how to exit from Word for DOS.

As you have seen, apart from the appearance of the screens, Word for DOS and Word for the Mac are quite similar. You find familiar commands on the menus, and you use all the same basic commands to perform the functions of opening, saving, and printing a document. You can use the keyboard to move around a Word for DOS document in many of the same ways you move around a Word for the Mac document; the basic dissimilarity appears on the keyboard itself—the keyboard of a PC doesn't have a Command key.

In the next chapter, you learn how to work with Word for Windows files. As you know, Chapters 3 through 9 in *The Mac User'sPC* focus on specific software packages. You should read the chapters that pertain to the software you want to use. Chapter 10 tells you about database programs you may want to avoid. Chapter 11 discusses the MS-DOS Shell. Refer to Chapter 12 for information on file-naming conventions imposed on Word for DOS by the operating system and to learn about basic DOS commands. If you need to transfer and translate files between a Mac and a PC, read Chapter 13.

Working with Word for Windows Files

In the first two chapters of *The Mac User's PC*, you learned about the physical appearance of a PC, how to turn on a PC, how to recognize what you may see onscreen, and how to start programs. In this chapter, you will learn very basic information about using Microsoft Word for Windows. This chapter is not intended to make you an expert at Word for Windows; this chapter simply teaches you how to perform some basic tasks. You will learn how to open, edit, save, and print a Word for Windows document; how to copy a Word for Windows file to a floppy disk; and how to exit the program properly. And you will learn one other important thing—how to get help in Word for Windows so that you can teach yourself to do the things that aren't covered in this book!

You should feel at home with Word for Windows, relatively speaking. Although the screens are not identical, the functioning of Word for Windows and Word for the Mac is quite similar.

Before you can start Word for Windows, you must start Microsoft Windows. Let's review some basic information about Windows.

Reviewing Windows Basics

Microsoft Windows is an operating environment that, in the world of DOS, provides a graphical user interface (also called GUI, pronounced "gooey") with which you can use either a mouse or a keyboard . The Microsoft Windows screen most closely resembles the Desktop on a Macintosh. Figure 6.1 shows a sample opening screen in Windows 3.1.

If Microsoft Windows doesn't appear onscreen when you start the PC, type `WIN` at the DOS prompt.

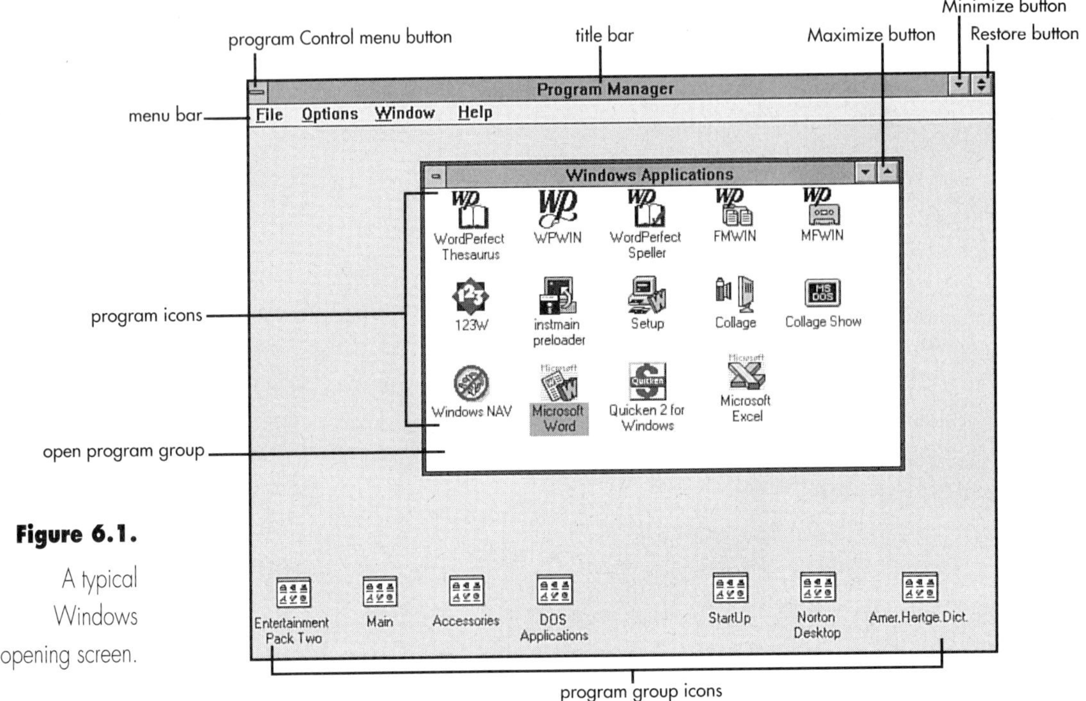

Figure 6.1.

A typical Windows opening screen.

As you learned in Chapter 2, Windows permits the user to perform multitasking. **Multitasking** enables the user to perform two or more functions simultaneously. To support multitasking, Windows and its Program Manager provide a way to manage the memory of the computer. Each program obtains enough memory to perform its functions; otherwise, Windows warns the user that sufficient memory is unavailable to perform all the requested tasks.

You can use a mouse or the keyboard to navigate in Windows, and you start programs from the Program Manager in Windows.

Understanding the Program Manager Screen

When you start Windows, the **Program Manager** appears. At the very top of every Windows screen, you see in the **title bar** the name of the program that is currently running. In Figure 6.1, `Program Manager` appears in the title bar.

At the left end of the title bar, you see the program **Control menu button**, a small box that contains a hyphen. You can use the program Control menu to change the size of the screen that displays the Program Manager, to close the Program Manager, and to switch to another program.

At the right end of the title bar, you see two buttons. Rather than using the Control menu, you can click on these buttons to change the size of the screen that displays the Program Manager:

- Choose the **Minimize button** to reduce the entire Program Manager screen to an icon. If you minimize a program, you choose its icon to return the program to the size it was before you minimized it.

- If the Program Manager fills the entire screen (as it does in Figure 6.1), then you see the Restore button (rather than the Maximize button). Choose the **Restore button** to reduce the Program Manager screen to a size somewhere between minimum and maximum (see Figure 6.1).

- If the Program Manager does not fill the entire screen but appears similar to Figure 6.2, then you see the Maximize button (rather than the Restore button). Choose the **Maximize button** to enlarge the Program Manager to fill the entire screen.

Just below the title bar, you see the **menu bar**. The menu bar contains **menus**, and each menu contains the **commands** (also called "menu commands") you use in Windows—but more about these in a moment.

The Program Manager contains **program groups**, which can appear either as open windows or as icons. In Figures 6.1 and 6.2, the Windows Applications program group appears as an open window while all the other program groups appear as **icons** at the bottom of the screen. Notice that the Windows Applications program group (and any open program group) also has a title bar, a Control menu, and Minimize and Maximize (or Restore) buttons. Open program groups do not, however, have menu bars.

Each program group contains icons that represent programs. You use these icons to start the programs. To start a program, the program group must be open so that you can see and access the icon that represents the program you want to start.

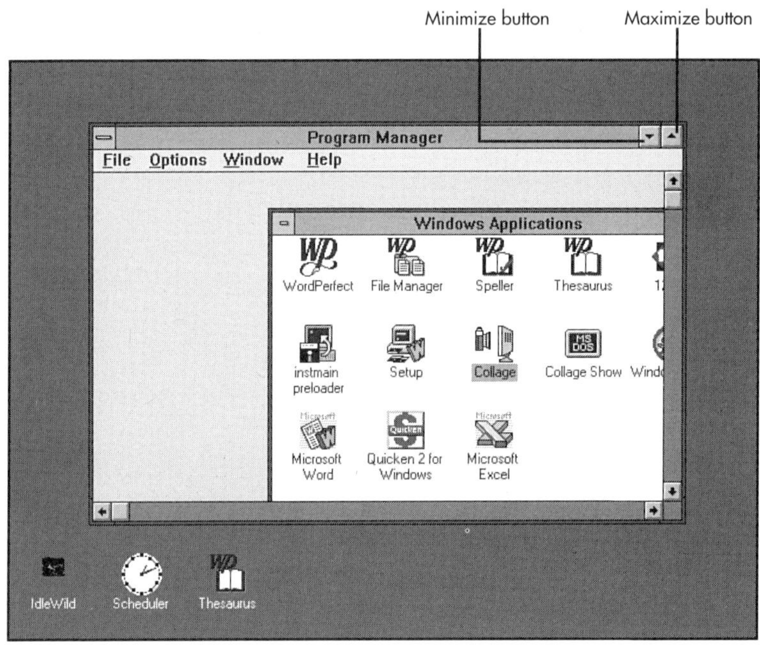

Figure 6.2. The Program Manager when it doesn't fill the entire screen.

Navigating in Windows

While working in Windows, you can use the mouse or the keyboard to perform certain tasks. In the following sections, you will find instructions on how to use the mouse and the keyboard to open menus, **choose** commands from menus, choose options in dialog boxes, and start programs.

In Windows, a mouse operates differently from a mouse on a Macintosh. Before you learn the specifics of performing each of the previously mentioned actions, let's review the way in which a mouse operates in Windows.

Operating a Mouse in Windows

Using a mouse in Windows is a two-step process. To use a mouse to choose an item in Windows, follow these steps:

1. Slide the mouse until the mouse pointer points to the item you want to choose.

2. Press and release a mouse button—usually the left mouse button—one time.

The action you perform in step 1 is known as **pointing**, and the action you perform in step 2 is known as **clicking**. You can click either the left or the right mouse button, as defined by the software program you are using. Most of the time, to choose an item, you click the left mouse button. You also may have occasion to double-click. To **double-click**, you press and release the left mouse button twice in rapid succession. Occasionally, you may need to drag an item to move it from one location to another. To **drag**, point to the item you want to drag. Then, press and hold the left mouse button while sliding the mouse to move the mouse pointer to the new location.

Note the difference in the way clicking works in Windows compared to on a Mac. In Windows, for the most part, you don't need to hold down the mouse button while opening a menu and choosing a command; the menu remains open after you release the mouse button. On a Mac, when you release the mouse button, the menu from which you were trying to choose a command closes.

Working with Menus and Commands in Windows

The menu bar appears just below the title bar. The menus contain the commands you use in Windows. To see the commands, you can open a menu by using the mouse or the keyboard.

To open a menu by using the mouse, point to the menu you want to open and click the left mouse button. Windows opens the menu. Unlike a menu on a Mac, the menu remains open when you release the mouse button, and the first command on the menu appears highlighted. To choose a command by using the mouse, point to the command and click the left mouse button. Windows executes the command.

You also can use the keyboard to open a menu and choose a command. First, you activate the menu bar by pressing the Alt key. A **reverse video bar** (or **highlight**) appears on the name of the first menu, **F**ile. Then, you can open a menu and choose a command in two ways:

- You can use the hot key shortcuts. Each menu and command contains an underlined letter, also called a **hot key**. You can press that key to open the menu or execute the command. When you press the W key, for example, the Program Manager opens the **W**indow menu and displays the commands available on that menu. In this book, all references to hot keys appear in boldface type.

- You can press one of the arrow keys on the keyboard to point to a menu or command, and then press the Enter key to choose it. When you press an arrow key, the reverse video bar moves. Continue pressing the arrow key until the reverse video bar appears on top of the menu or command to which you want to point. For example, you can press Alt to activate the menu bar, and then press the left-arrow key twice to point to the **W**indow menu. Remember, when you use the arrow keys to point to a menu or command, you must press Enter to open that menu or choose that command.

PC NOTE

If you activate the menu bar and then press the right-arrow key four times, you highlight the Control menu. The Control menu contains the commands that control the size of the Program Manager screen. To open the Control menu after you have highlighted it, press Enter. If you have any open program group windows and you activate the menu bar and then press the right-arrow key five times, you activate the Control menu of the group window. Again, press Enter to open that Control menu.

Working with Dialog Boxes in Windows

Ellipses (...) appear after some commands on the menus. The program requires additional information about these commands before it can execute them. When you choose a command that includes an ellipsis, a **dialog box** (in which you supply the additional required information) appears.

The dialog boxes that appear when you choose a command from the Program Manager's **F**ile menu are not typical of the dialog boxes you see and use in application programs. So, there's not much point in describing one of those dialog boxes. Instead, Figure 6.3 displays a more typical dialog box that contains a representative sample of types of dialog box options. Each dialog box is different, and most dialog boxes provide only some of these options.

PC NOTE

You may notice a dotted line surrounding an option. This line indicates the current mouse pointer position. If you are using the keyboard rather than a mouse, you can use the Tab key to move around a dialog box.

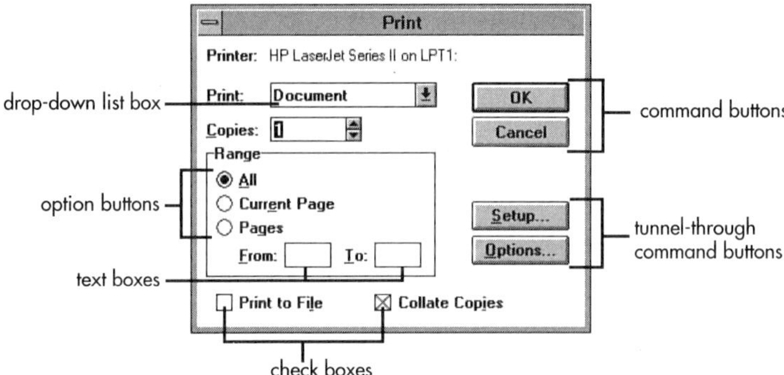

Figure 6.3. A typical dialog box.

A **list box** contains a list of options. You may see two kinds of list boxes in a dialog box. The **P**rint list box in Figure 6.3 is an example of a **drop-down list box**, and is closed when the dialog box appears. To open a drop-down list box, click on the down arrow at the right end of the box; or, hold down the Alt key and type the underlined letter in the list box name. The other type of list box is already open when the dialog box appears. To choose an item from either type of list box, click on the item; or, press the down-arrow key to point to the item and then press Enter. If the list box is not long enough to display all the available items in the list, click the down arrow or press and hold the down-arrow key to move beyond the items that appear in the box.

An **option button** is a small round button you use to choose one option from a group of related options. A black dot appears in the button of the current option. To choose an option button, click on the option button; or, hold down the Alt key and type the underlined letter in the option name. In the Range area, the **A**ll, Curr**e**nt Page, and Pa**g**es buttons are option buttons.

A **check box** is a small square box you use to choose an option. You can choose more than one check box from a group of related options. An X appears in the check boxes of the activated options. To choose a check box, click on the check box; or, hold down the Alt key and type the underlined letter in the option name. To deactivate the option and remove the X from the box, choose the check box again. In Figure 6.3, the Print to Fi**l**e and Collate Cop**i**es check boxes appear at the bottom of the dialog box.

A **text box** is a rectangular box in which you enter text. When a dialog box that contains a text box opens, the current text is usually selected. To replace the selected text, simply type the new information. In Figure 6.3, the Range area contains two text boxes (**F**rom and **T**o). The **C**opies box also is a text box.

A **command button** is an oblong button that performs an action. To choose a command button, click on the button; or, use the Tab key to highlight the button and press Enter. In Figure 6.3, the OK button accepts the settings in the dialog box. The Cancel button cancels your changes to the settings in the dialog box. The default command button, which changes from dialog box to dialog box, appears highlighted (an outline appears darker than the other buttons). As on a Mac, if you press Enter, you choose the highlighted command button.

A **tunnel-through command button** is a command button that contains an ellipsis (...) and opens another dialog box. To choose a tunnel-through command button, click on the button; highlight the button and press Enter; or, hold down the Alt key and then type the underlined letter. In Figure 6.3, the **S**etup and **O**ptions buttons are tunnel-through command buttons.

Starting a Program in Windows

As mentioned earlier, all programs reside in program groups in Windows. To start a program, its program group cannot appear minimized as an icon; the program group must be open.

To use the mouse to open a program group that appears as an icon, double-click on the icon.

To use the keyboard to open a program group that appears as an icon, follow these steps:

1. Press the **Alt** key to activate the menu bar.

2. Press **W** to open the **W**indow menu.

The Program Manager displays the choices on the **W**indow menu (see Figure 6.4). You see a check mark next to the currently selected program group.

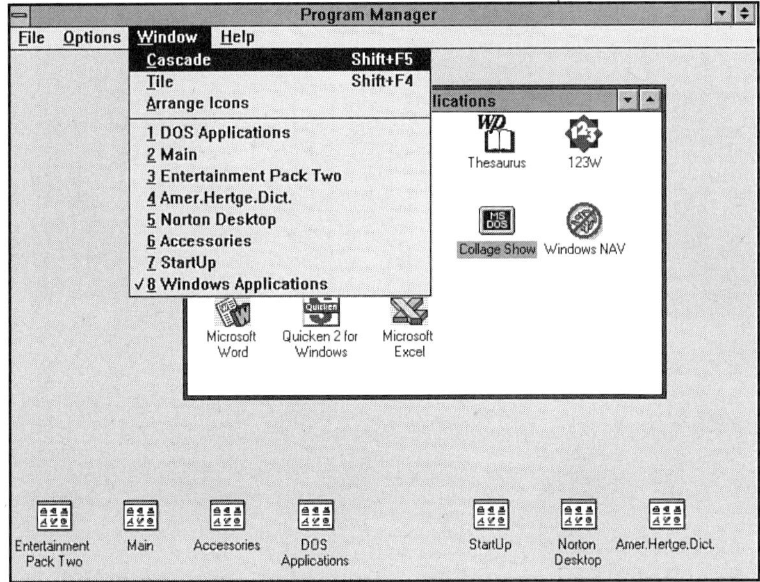

Figure 6.4.

The **W**indow menu.

3. From the numbered options in the **W**indow menu, press a number to choose the program group you want to open.

   Windows opens the specified program group.

After you open the program group, you can start a program. To start a program by using the mouse, double-click on the icon representing the program in the program group window. The Program Manager starts the program.

To start a program by using the keyboard, use the arrow keys to point to the program you want to start. Then, press Enter. The Program Manager starts the program.

Using one of the techniques just described, open the program group containing the Word for Windows program icon and then start Word for Windows. You may find the program icon in the Windows Applications group or in a Word for Windows group. Or, you may find Word for Windows somewhere altogether different because the owner of the PC has a different technique for organizing programs.

Identifying Word for Windows Screen Parts

When you first start Word for Windows, you see the default screen, which looks like the screen in Figure 6.5.

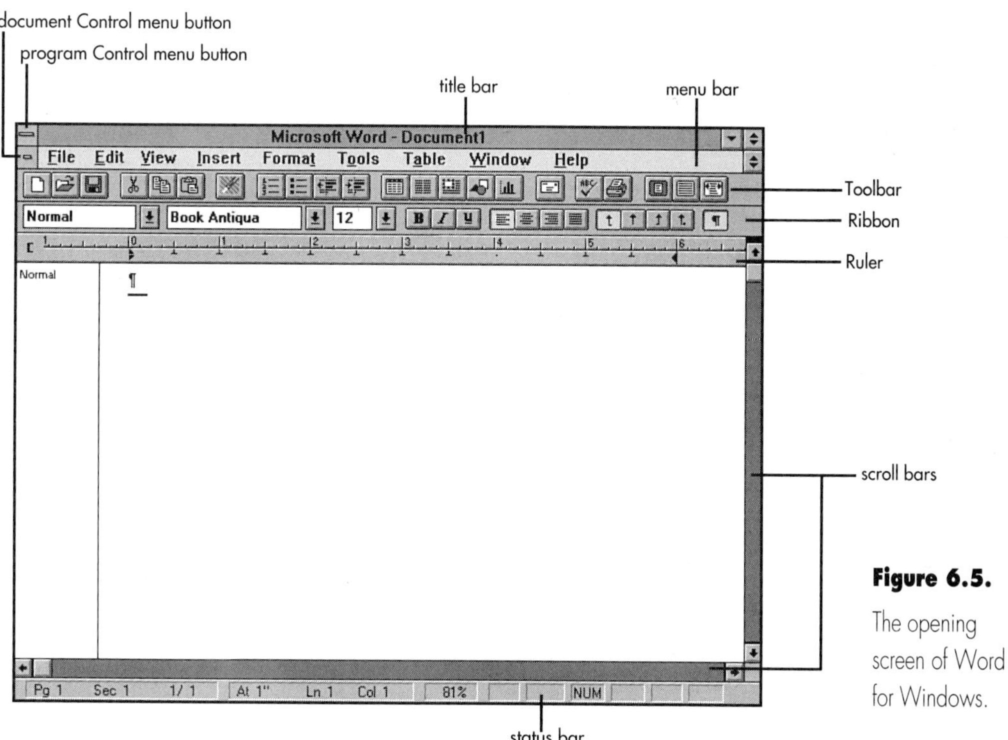

Figure 6.5.

The opening screen of Word for Windows.

PC NOTE

If, on the opening screen, you see only the program name in the title bar at the top of the screen and you see a separate document title bar, then the document window is not maximized. To maximize the document window, open the *document* Control menu (the one at the left end of the document title bar, not the one above the menu bar) and choose the Ma**x**imize command. Or, click the document Maximize button, which appears at the right end of the document title bar.

As in the opening Windows screen, you see in the **title bar** the name of the program that is currently running, `Microsoft Word` (along with the name of the current document, `Document1`). The Word for Windows program Control menu appears to the left of the title bar, and the program Minimize and Restore buttons appear to the right of the title bar.

Just below the title bar, you see the **menu bar** for Word for Windows. At the left end of the menu bar, you see the document Control menu; you can use this Control menu to change the size of only the document portion of the screen. At the right end of the menu bar, you see the document Restore button. Initially, when you start the program, the document portion of the window is maximized.

Just below the menu bar, you see the default Toolbar. Word for Windows uses the Toolbar to assign commonly performed tasks to buttons. You must use a mouse to select a button on the Toolbar. Remember, however, that you also can use the keyboard and menus to perform all the tasks assigned to buttons on the Toolbar. In addition, the Toolbar can be customized, so the buttons on the default Toolbar in Figure 6.5 may not appear on your screen.

Below the Toolbar, you see the Ribbon and the Ruler. You must use a mouse to perform an action on the Ribbon or the Ruler. Remember, however, that you can use the menus and the keyboard to

perform any action you can perform by using the mouse and the Ribbon or the Ruler.

You can use the Ribbon to perform a variety of functions, as shown in Figure 6.6.

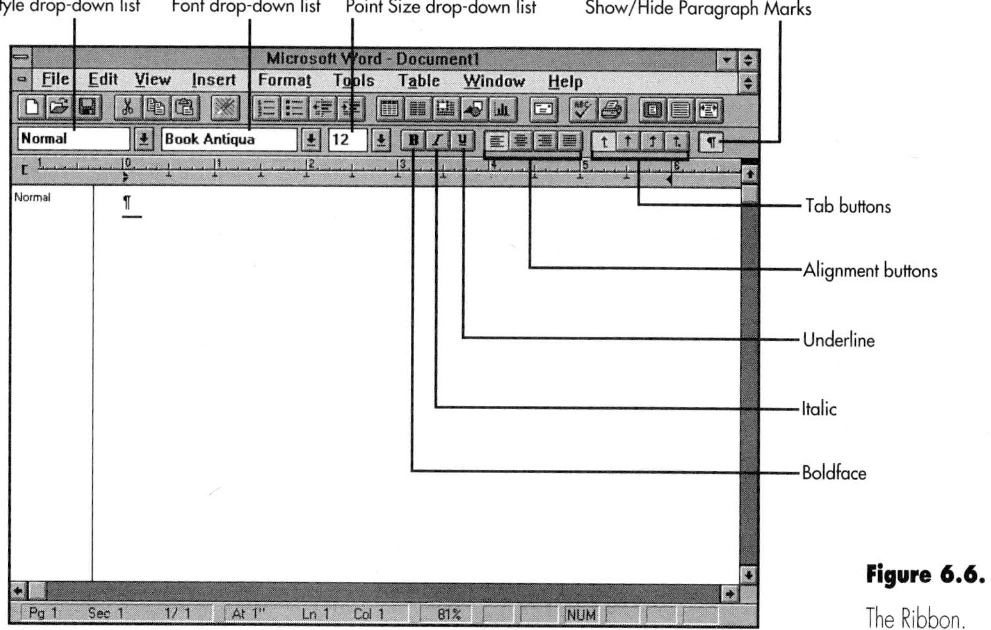

Figure 6.6.
The Ribbon.

Working from the left end of the Ribbon, you can perform the following tasks:

- Use the Style drop-down list to change the style of the current paragraph or of selected text.
- Use the Font drop-down list to change the font.
- Choose the point size of a font.
- Add boldface, italic, or underline formatting to selected text.

- Align the current or selected paragraphs left, center, right, or justified between the left and right margins.
- Choose left, center, right, or decimal tabs before you set a tab stop on the Ruler.
- Display onscreen marks that identify the ends of paragraphs.

You can use the Ruler to move the left and right margins. You also can use the Ruler to set, move, and remove tab stops.

When you start Word for Windows, you see an empty document, in which you can start creating a new document. On the left side of Figures 6.5 and 6.6, you see the style area. The style area does *not* appear on the default Word for Windows opening screen. Because the style area is quite useful for editing, however, I have included it in the figures. You will learn more about using the style area when you learn about selecting text later in this chapter.

At the bottom of the screen, you see the status bar. The status bar tells you the current location of the insertion point, the flashing black vertical bar. The **insertion point** represents the current location of the mouse pointer and shows you where text will appear when you type. In the left portion of the status bar, you see the current page number, the current section number, and what page you are viewing out of the total number of pages. The next part of the status bar tells you how far vertically, in both inches and lines, the insertion point appears from the top of the page. You also see the number of the column in which the insertion point appears, which tells you how far along the line horizontally the insertion point appears.

Just above the status bar and along the right side of the screen, you see the horizontal and vertical scroll bars, which have arrows at both ends and a scroll box somewhere along the scroll bar. Using a mouse, you can click the arrows or drag the scroll box on the

horizontal scroll bar to move the view of a document right or left. Or, you can click the arrows or drag the scroll box on the vertical scroll bar to move the view of a document down or up.

Getting Help in Word for Windows

Word for Windows contains both online tutorials and an online Help facility. In this section, you learn the basics of using Help in Word for Windows.

First, notice that you can use commands on the **H**elp menu to teach yourself to use Word for Windows. If you choose **G**etting Started from the **H**elp menu, you start a short tutorial on the basics of using Word for Windows. If you choose **L**earning Word from the **H**elp menu, you start a more extensive tutorial with more advanced options.

In addition to these online tutorials, Word for Windows includes an excellent online Help facility. You can display the Help Index in Word for Windows by pressing F1 or by opening the **H**elp menu and choosing the **I**ndex command (see Figure 6.7). In Word for Windows, the help you receive is context-sensitive—if you are looking at a command on a menu and you press F1, the help you get is about that command.

When you view the Help Index window, you see the Help topics. On a color monitor, these topics appear in green and are underlined. To choose a topic, click on it. Using the keyboard, press the Tab key to highlight the topic about which you want help, and then press Enter. When you view a topic, the information may be too long to fit in one Help window. In that case, you will see a scroll bar on the right side of the window; you can use the scroll bar to view the rest of the information. (On the Help Index window, no scroll bar appears because all the topics fit in the Help window; but on other Help windows, you may see a scroll bar.) Using the mouse, you can click on the scroll arrows to move the topics in the window until you see the topic about which you want help. Using the keyboard, you can press the down-arrow key to move the topics in the window.

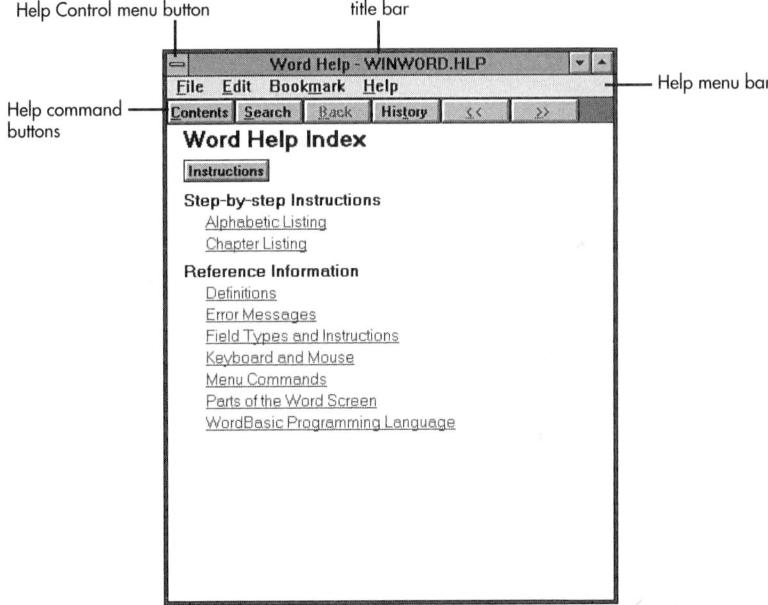

Figure 6.7.

The Help Index window.

As you can see from the Help Index window, the Help Index offers two methods for getting help: Step-by-step Instructions and Reference Information. You can access the step-by-step instructions by using an alphabetical listing of topics in Word for Windows Help; or, you can use a listing of topics organized in the same way that the chapters appear in the Word for Windows User's Guide.

You also can use the Reference section of the Help Index window to find definitions of terms and meanings of error messages you may encounter while working in Word for Windows. When viewing a particular Help topic, you also may see a word underlined with a dotted line. If you choose the word, Word for Windows displays its definition. Press Enter or click on the word again to remove the definition.

The Reference section also can help you find information about parts of the Word for Windows screen and about the mouse and the keyboard. You can use the Menu Commands topic in the Reference section to get help about a specific command that appears on one of the Word for Windows menus. Or, rather than using the Help Index, you can get help about the command by pointing to it and pressing F1. More advanced users may want to use the Reference section to find out about field types and programming in WordBasic, the Word for Windows macro language.

You can use the **S**earch button in the Help Index window to open the Search dialog box shown in Figure 6.8. and search for topics you specify.

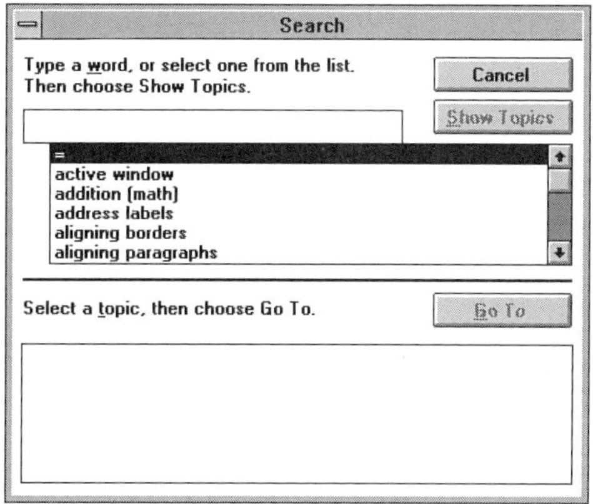

Figure 6.8.

The Help Search dialog box.

To use the Search dialog box, follow these steps:

1. Type a **w**ord that represents the topic for which you want to search.

   As you type, Word for Windows Help highlights the topic in the list that most closely matches the characters you type.

2. Choose the **S**how Topics button.

   In the bottom portion of the dialog box, Word for Windows Help displays the topics that most closely match the characters you typed.

3. Choose a topic from the list, and then choose the **G**o To button.

   Word for Windows Help displays the topic you chose.

You can print the information that appears in Help windows by choosing the **P**rint Topic command on the Help window's **F**ile menu.

If you find a Help topic to which you might want to return later (without having to remember how you got there in the first place), you can create a bookmark for the topic. Follow these steps:

1. While viewing the topic you want to mark, open the Book**m**ark menu on the Help window's menu bar.

2. Choose the **D**efine command.

   Word for Windows Help displays the Bookmark Define dialog box shown in Figure 6.9. The name of the topic you are viewing appears in the **B**ookmark Name text box.

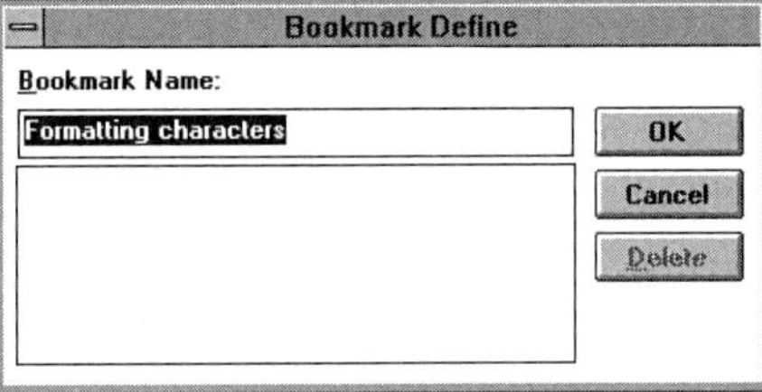

Figure 6.9. The Bookmark Define dialog box.

3. If you want to change the bookmark name, type a new name; otherwise, Word for Windows Help will use the topic name as the bookmark name.

4. Choose OK.

   Word for Windows stores the topic name on the Book**m**ark menu.

When you open the Book**m**ark menu again, you see below the **D**efine command the topic for which you stored a bookmark. If you choose the topic from the Book**m**ark menu, Word for Windows Help displays the topic.

After viewing several topics, you can use the **C**ontents button to redisplay the Help Index window. Or, you can use the **B**ack button to redisplay in reverse order the topics you viewed. You also can return directly to any topic you display by choosing the His**t**ory button. When you choose the His**t**ory button, Word for Windows Help displays the Help History window, in which you can see every topic you viewed since you started Help. If you looked at a topic more than once, it appears more than once in the Help History window. To go to a topic listed in the Help History Window, double-click on the topic; or, use the arrow keys to point to the topic and then press Enter.

PC NOTE

If you close Help, Word for Windows also closes the history of your Help session and no longer maintains the history of the Help screens you viewed. When you open Help again, Word for Windows starts the history over again.

You can learn more about how to use the Word for Windows Help facility by opening the **H**elp menu on the Help window's menu bar and choosing **H**ow To Use Help.

Opening a Word for Windows File

Suppose that someone brings you a letter, asks you to make some minor changes to it, and then wants you to print the revised letter. In this section, you learn how to open an existing Word for

Windows document. In the next three sections, you learn how to edit, save, and print a Word for Windows document.

You can open up to nine documents at one time. The document that contains the insertion point is called the **active document**, and you are looking at it in the **active window**. When you start Word for Windows, Document1 always appears. You can start typing a new document in Document1. If you open an existing document without typing in Document1, the existing document replaces Document1.

You open a document in Word for Windows in much the same way you open a document in Word for the Mac. To open an existing Word for Windows document, follow these steps:

1. Open the **F**ile menu and choose the **O**pen command. You also can choose the Open Button on the Toolbar (the second button from the left), or you can press **Ctrl+F12**.

   Word for Windows displays the Open dialog box shown in Figure 6.10.

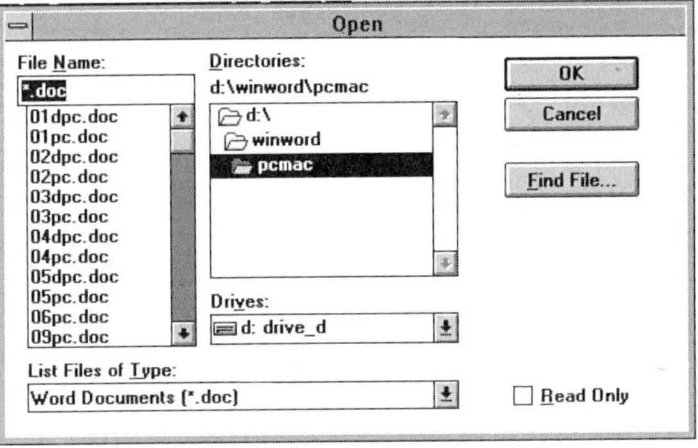

Figure 6.10. The Open dialog box.

2. Choose the name of the document you want to open from the list, or type the file name of the document you want to open in the File **N**ame text box. If necessary, change the drive or the directory so that the file you want to open appears in the File **N**ame list box. To change to a floppy disk drive, open the

Drives drop-down list box, and choose the drive from the list. To change to another directory, double-click on a directory listed in the **D**irectories list box. The files in the list change to display the contents of the newly selected directory.

3. Choose OK.

   The document appears onscreen, and you can edit it.

If you're not sure of the document's name, you can preview the contents of a document before you open it. To preview the contents of a document, you can use the **F**ind File button in the Open dialog box or the **F**ind File command on the **F**ile menu. Follow these steps:

1. Choose the **F**ind File button from the Open dialog box, or choose the **F**ind File command from the **F**ile menu.

   Word for Windows displays the Find File dialog box in Figure 6.11

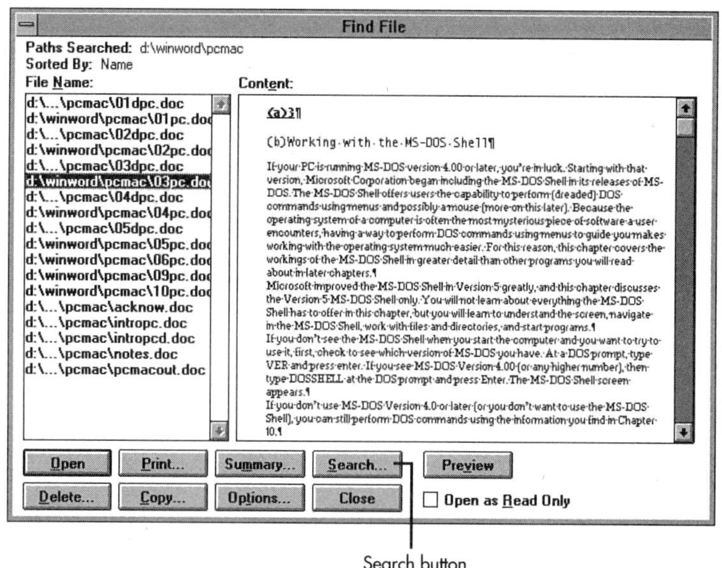

Figure 6.11. The Find File dialog box.

2. In the File **N**ame list, highlight the name of the document you want to preview. If the name of the file you want to preview does not appear in the File **N**ame list, change the search path by choosing the **S**earch button.

   Word for Windows displays the Search dialog box (see Figure 6.12).

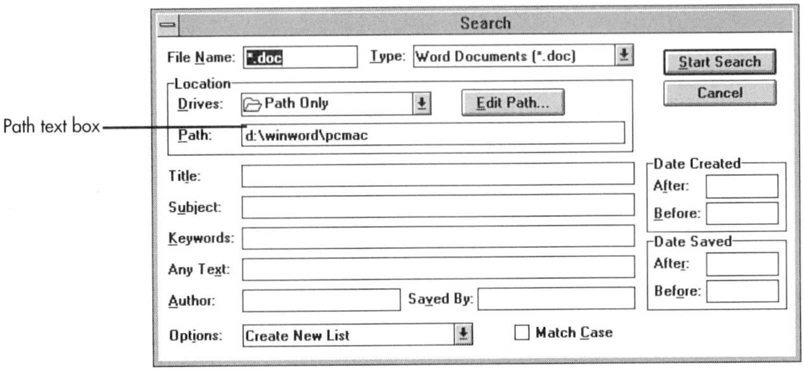

Figure 6.12. The Search dialog box.

   In the Search dialog box, you must type the correct name in the **P**ath text box (for more information on paths, see Chapter 12). After the path is set correctly, choose the **S**tart Search button.

   Word for Windows redisplays the Find File dialog box, showing the path you designated in the Search dialog box.

3. View the contents of the document you highlighted in the Contents portion of the Find File dialog box. If the currently highlighted document is not the one you want to open, highlight a different document in the list until you find the one you want to open.

4. After you find the document you want to open, you can open it from the Find File dialog box by choosing the **O**pen button.

   Word for Windows closes the Find File dialog box and opens the document you chose.

If you must type a new document, start in an empty window by choosing the **N**ew command from the **F**ile menu. You also can choose the New icon from the Toolbar (the first icon on the left).

Performing Basic Editing in Word for Windows

By default, when you type in Word for Windows, you are working in insert mode. In **insert mode**, Word for Windows places characters at the current location of the insertion point and moves all existing characters to the right. You can press the Ins key to switch to overtype mode. In **overtype mode**, Word for Windows places characters at the current location of the insertion point and types over characters that exist at that location, removing them. The Ins key works like a toggle switch: press it once to change from insert mode to overtype mode; press it a second time to change back from overtype mode to insert mode.

You can use the Backspace key to delete the character immediately to the left of the insertion point. You can use the Del key to delete the character immediately to the right of the insertion point.

Moving around a Document

You move around a Word for Windows document by clicking the mouse or by pressing the directional keys (the arrow keys, and Home, End, PgUp, and PgDn).Table 6.1 summarizes the most common ways in which you can use the keyboard to move around in a Word for Windows document.

Table 6.1. Directional keys in an existing document.

Key(s)	Effect
→ and ←	Moves right or left one character.
↑ and ↓	Moves up or down one line.
Ctrl+→	Moves right one word.
Ctrl+←	Moves left one word.
Ctrl+↓	Moves down one paragraph.
Ctrl+↑	Moves up one paragraph.
Home	Moves to the beginning of the current line.
End	Moves to the end of the current line.
PgDn	Moves down to the top of the next window.
PgUp	Moves up to the top of the preceding window.

Selecting Text

You may want to make changes to the appearance of text. For example, you may want certain text to appear underlined, in italics, or in boldface type; you may want to change the alignment of certain text; or you may want to delete certain text.

In Word for Windows, you select text when you want to "operate" on it—that is, when you want to boldface, underline, center, or even print text. **Selecting** is the process of highlighting the text so that Word for Windows can identify the text on which you want to work.

To use the mouse to select text, you drag the mouse pointer. Follow these steps:

1. Place the insertion point in front of the text you want to select. Click and hold down the left mouse button.

2. Slide the mouse to the right.

   As you slide the mouse, a reverse video bar (a highlight) appears over the text you are selecting.

3. Continue sliding the mouse until you reach the end of the text you want to select.

4. Release the left mouse button.

   The text you selected is highlighted—a reverse video bar appears over it.

You can use some shortcuts with the mouse to select a word, a sentence, or a paragraph:

- To select a word, double-click on it.

- To select a sentence, hold down the Ctrl key as you click the left mouse button anywhere in the sentence.

- To select a paragraph or groups of paragraphs, you can use the selection bar. The selection bar is an unmarked area to the left of the style area. You place the mouse pointer in the selection bar when you want to select paragraphs or groups of paragraphs. When you move the mouse pointer into the selection bar, the mouse pointer changes into an arrow pointing up and to the right. Place the mouse pointer next to the paragraph you want to select and click the left mouse button. Word for Windows highlights the paragraph. If you want to select more than one paragraph, don't just click the left mouse button—drag the mouse until all the paragraphs you want to select are highlighted.

You can cancel a selection by clicking the mouse anywhere else onscreen.

To select text by using the keyboard, follow these steps:

1. Place the insertion point at the beginning of the text you want to select.

2. Use the **Shift** key combined with directional keys to select text starting at the current location of the insertion point. You can use Table 6.1 to review how to select the appropriate block of text. For example, to select one word to the right, press **Shift**+**Ctrl**+→.

You can cancel a selection by pressing any arrow key.

Executing Commands

Typically, to execute a command, you open a menu and choose the command. You can use the mouse and keyboard techniques described earlier in this chapter to open menus and choose commands. If the command you want to execute appears on the Toolbar, you also can use the Toolbar to choose the command.

On the menus, you may notice that key combinations appear next to certain commands. These key combinations are hot keys—you use them as shortcuts to bypass the menu when choosing a command. For example, if you want to move the insertion point to a specific place in the document (for example, page 5), you can open the **E**dit menu and choose the **G**o To command, or, you simply can press F5.

Saving a Word for Windows File

After you have made the changes you need to make, you will want to save the document. Like Word for the Mac, Word for Windows provides three ways to save a document, and each of these ways is described in this chapter. One of these methods lets you save a document using a different name. Because you may not want to overwrite the work that existed before you edited, you may want to read the sections on these three methods before you use any of them.

- You can use the **C**lose command to save the document under its current name and then "put away" the document (remove it from the screen).

- You can use the **S**ave command to save the document under its current name and then continue working on the document.

- You can use the Save **A**s command to save the document under a different name. You may want to save the document under a different name to avoid changing the original.

When you exit from Word for Windows, the program also prompts you to save any documents that contain changes before you exit—but more about that later in this chapter.

Using the Close Command

As in Word for the Mac, you can use the **C**lose command when you finish working with a document and you want Word for Windows put it away. When you choose the **C**lose command, Word for Windows also gives you the option of saving any changes you might have made before Word for Windows puts away the document. To close a document, open the **F**ile menu and choose the **C**lose command.

If you have not made any changes to the document since the last time you saved it, Word for Windows simply removes the document from the screen. If, however, you have made changes, Word for Windows displays the dialog box in Figure 6.13.

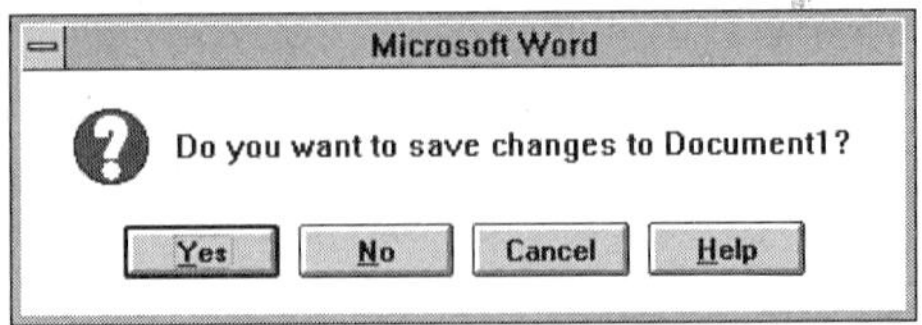

Figure 6.13.
The Do you want to save changes to? dialog box.

If you choose **Y**es, Word for Windows saves the changes you have made and removes the document from the screen. If you choose **N**o, Word for Windows *does not* save the changes you made since the last time you saved, but Word for Windows *does* remove the document from the screen. If you choose Cancel, Word for Windows *does not* save the changes you made since the last time you save and *does not* remove the document from the screen.

Using the Save Command

Also as in Word for the Mac, you can use the **S**ave command to save the document in the active window. When you use the **S**ave command, Word for Windows saves the changes you have made to a disk (either hard or floppy) and leaves the document onscreen so that you can continue to work on it.

To save a document by using the **S**ave command, open the **F**ile menu and choose the **S**ave command. Alternatively, you can choose the Save button from the Toolbar (the third button from the left), or you can press Shift+F12. If you are saving an existing document that already has a name, Word for Windows saves the document. (If you pay close attention to the status bar at the bottom of the screen, you will see a message that indicates Word for Windows is saving the document.) If you are saving a new document that doesn't yet have a name, Word for Windows displays the Save As dialog box discussed in the next section.

Using the Save As Command

You might want to leave the original document available in cases where your changes may not be final. If you are unsure of the changes you have made, for example, and somebody else is going to come back and check your work, you might want to keep the original document. You then can show the person your version, and let him or her decide which version to continue using.

You can save a Word for Windows document under another name similarly to the way you save a Word for the Mac document under a different name. To save your version of an existing document and leave the original version intact, follow these steps:

1. Open the **F**ile menu and choose the Save **A**s command, or press **F12**.

   Word for Windows displays the Save As dialog box in Figure 6.14.

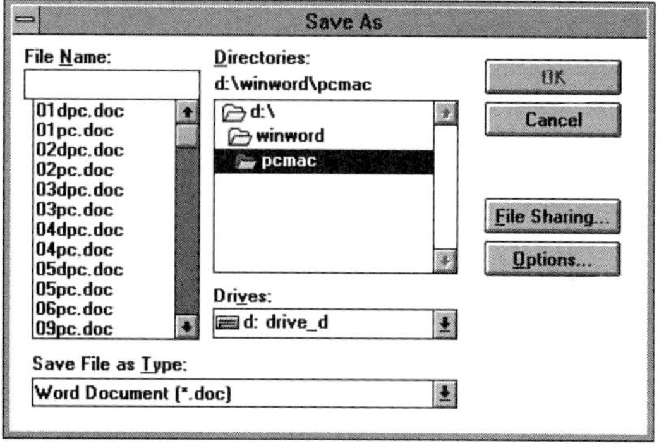

Figure 6.14.

The Save As dialog box.

2. Type the new name for the document in the File **N**ame text box. You can use up to 11 characters for the name you want to assign to the document. The first part of the name can contain no more than 8 characters; the **extension** can contain no more than 3 characters.

For more information on the rules DOS imposes when you name a file on a PC, see Chapter 12. (Yes, it is DOS that imposes file name rules. It's even DOS that does the saving.)

If you choose a name that appears in the list box, Word for Windows asks whether you want to replace that document. If you replace the document, you *overwrite* the original version, which, of course, is the exact thing you were trying to avoid doing. So, choose **N**o to return to the dialog box and try a different name; or choose Cancel to close the dialog box without saving at all. Then, you can try again.

3. If you want, you can use the Save File As **T**ype list box to choose a format other than Word for Windows in which to save the document. For example, you could choose to save the document as a Word for Macintosh document.

4. Also, if you want, you can save the file to a floppy disk by changing the drive that appears in the Dri**v**es list box.

5. Choose OK.

   Word for Windows saves the document under the name you specified in the File **N**ame text box, leaving the original version (under its original name) intact.

Printing a Word for Windows File

After you have edited and saved the document, you may need to print it. But before you print the document, you may want to see onscreen the way it will look when you print it. You can preview a Word for Windows document the same way you preview a Word for the Mac document. To preview a document in Word for Windows and then print it, open the **F**ile menu and choose Print Pre**v**iew. Word for Windows displays the layout of your document as it will appear when you print it (see Figure 6.15).

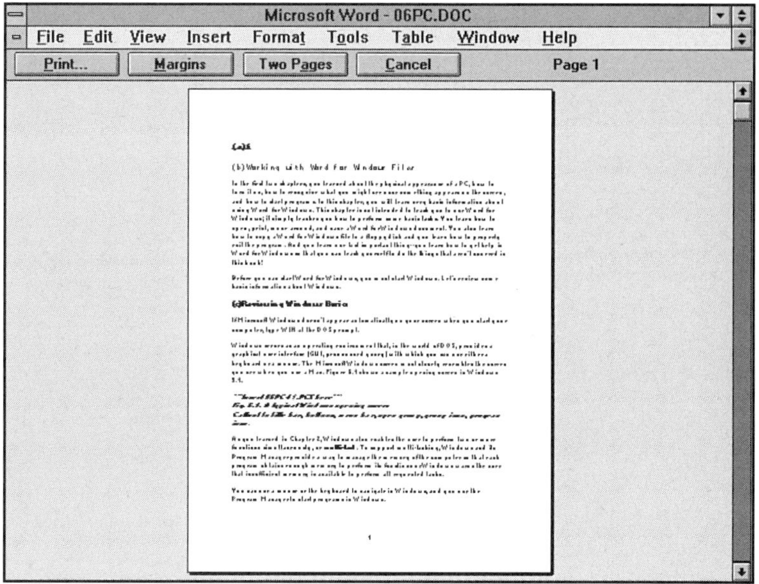

Figure 6.15.

A sample Print Preview screen.

Although you cannot edit on this screen, you can change the margins and see how the layout will appear when printed. If the text and graphics are not aligned properly on this screen, they won't be aligned properly when you print. You can use the command buttons along the top of the Print Preview window to perform the following tasks:

- You can use the **M**argins button to hide or display the margins of your document. When you display margins, you can change them by dragging with the mouse.

- You can use the P**a**ge button to see the full page (as shown in Figure 6.15), or to see two facing pages (as in a book) of a long document.

- You can use the **C**ancel button to return to the editing window.

- You can use the **P**rint button to print the document. Word for Windows displays the Print dialog box in Figure 6.16.

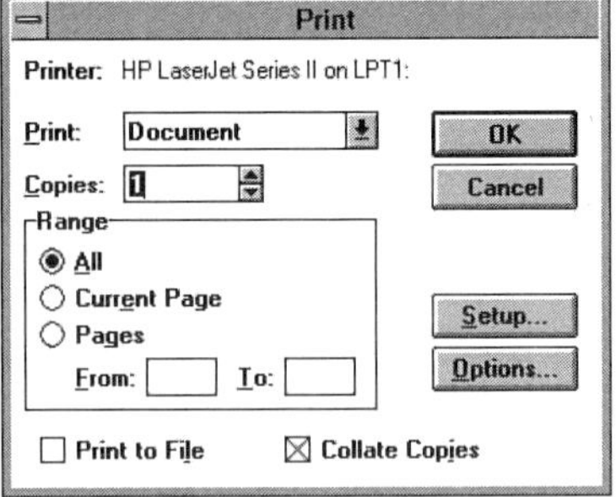

Figure 6.16.
The Print dialog box.

Although there are several choices in the Print dialog box, the ones you are most likely to use are the choices in the Range options box and the **C**opies text box.

From the choices in the Range options box, you can choose the pages you want to print:

- To print the entire document, choose **A**ll.
- To print only the page on which the insertion point appears, choose Curr**e**nt Page.

> **PC NOTE**
>
> If you selected text before opening the Print dialog box, you won't see Curr**e**nt Page as a choice in the Range box. Instead, you will see S**e**lection. If you choose S**e**lection, Word for Windows prints only the text you selected.

- To print selected pages, choose Pa**g**es and then specify the page numbers in the **F**rom and **T**o text boxes.

You can print more than one copy of the choice you indicated in the Range options box of the Print dialog box. Simply change the number of copies in the **C**opies text box.

To open the Print dialog box (see Figure 6.16) without previewing the document, choose the **P**rint command from the **F**ile menu, or press Ctrl+Shift+F12. If you know that you want to use the default settings that appear in the Print dialog box (if you want to print one copy of the entire document in the active window), you can print the document without opening the Print dialog box; simply choose the Print button from the Toolbar (the fourth button from the right).

Copying a Word for Windows File to a Floppy Disk

You may find that you need to copy a Word for Windows file to a floppy disk. You may need to print a file from another PC, for example. Using the Find File dialog box is the easiest way to copy a Word for Windows file to a floppy disk. Alternatively, you can use DOS commands, which you can find in Chapter 12.

Earlier in this chapter, when you were learning to open a document, you used the Find File dialog box to preview a document before you opened it. To use the Find File dialog box to copy a file to a floppy disk, follow these steps:

1. Insert a formatted disk into the floppy disk drive.

2. Open the **F**ile menu and choose the **F**ind File command.

   Word for Windows displays the Find File dialog box (see Figure 6.17), showing the files listed in the directory on the search path. The **search path** is the drive and directory Word for Windows uses when looking for files.

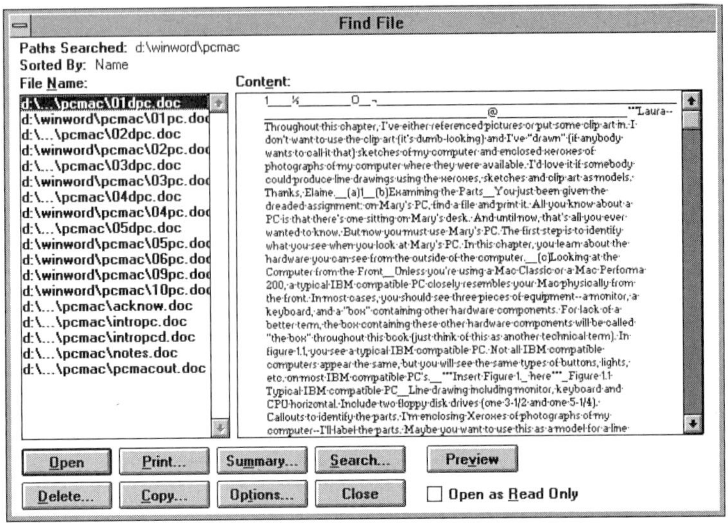

Figure 6.17.

The Find File dialog box.

You probably won't need to change to a different drive or directory, but you can change the search path from the Search dialog box. Use the **S**earch button to open the Search dialog box in Figure 6.18.

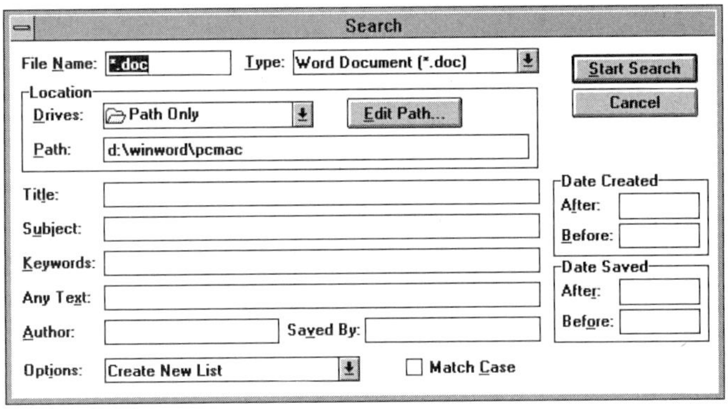

Figure 6.18.

The Search dialog box.

Type the correct path name in the **P**ath text box. (See Chapter 12 for more information on paths.) If you change the path, choose the **S**tart Search button to close the Search dialog box and redisplay the Find File dialog box. If you don't change the path, choose Cancel.

Word for Windows redisplays the Find File dialog box.

3. In the File **N**ame list, highlight the file you want to copy to a floppy disk. To highlight the file by using the mouse, click on the file. To highlight the file by using the keyboard, press the down-arrow key.

   When a file is highlighted, its contents appear in the Contents portion of the Find File dialog box.

4. Choose the **C**opy button.

   Word for Windows displays the Copy dialog box in Figure 6.19.

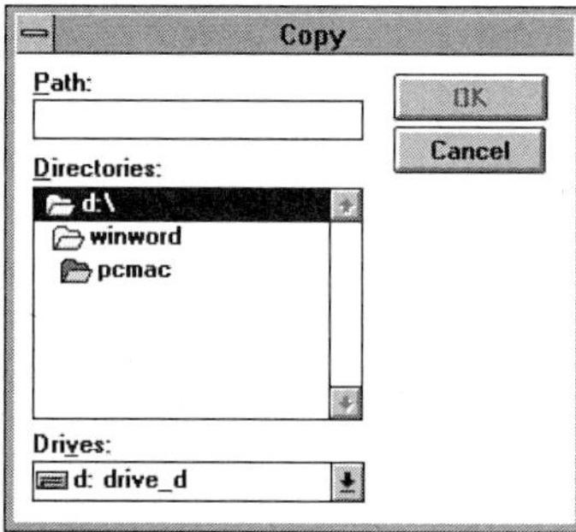

Figure 6.19.
The Copy dialog box.

5. To copy the file to the floppy disk under the same name it has on the hard disk, type `A:` (or the name of the floppy drive into which you inserted a disk) in the **P**ath text box. Then, click on OK.

   Word for Windows copies the file to the floppy disk. If a file with the same name already exists on the floppy disk, you will see a dialog box that asks whether you want to replace files on the floppy disk with files of the same name on the hard disk. If you *don't* want to write over a file on the floppy disk, choose **N**o. Word for Windows redisplays Find File dialog box. You choose the **C**opy button again and either can insert a new floppy disk or type a file name after you type `A:` in the **P**ath text box.

6. Choose the Close button to close the Find File dialog box.

Exiting Word for Windows

When you are finished using Word for Windows, you can exit by choosing the E**x**it command from the **F**ile menu or by pressing Alt+F4. If any of the open documents contain changes you didn't save, Word for Windows displays a dialog box asking whether you want to save the changes to the document in question before you exit. Choose **Y**es to save the changes and exit. Choose **N**o to ignore the changes and exit Word for Windows. Choose Cancel to return to editing in Word for Windows.

When you exit from Word for Windows, you return to Windows. You can exit from Windows by choosing the E**x**it Windows command from the **F**ile menu or by pressing Alt+F4.

You safely can shut off the PC after exiting from Windows.

Chapter Summary

In this chapter, you learned how to use the excellent online Help facility in Word for Windows. You learned to open, edit, save, and print a document. You also learned how to copy a document to a floppy disk and how to exit from Word for Windows.

As you noticed in this chapter, many of the commands you use in Word for the Mac are also available in Word for Windows. The keyboard commands are different because of differing keyboards, but you can use the mouse to find and execute commands you are accustomed to using, such as the **O**pen command, the **C**lose command, the **S**ave command, and the Save **A**s command. In Chapter 13, you will learn that Word for Windows can be particularly useful if you are transferring files between a PC and a Mac because of the many different conversion filters included with Word for Windows.

In the next chapter, you learn how to work with Microsoft Excel for Windows files. As you know, Chapters 3 through 9 in *The Mac User's PC* focus on specific software packages. You should read the chapters that pertain to the software you want to use. Chapter 10 tells you about database programs you may want to avoid. Chapter 11 discusses the MS-DOS Shell. Refer to Chapter 12 for information on file-naming conventions imposed on Word for Windows by the operating system, and for information on basic DOS commands. If you need to transfer and translate files between a Mac and a PC, read Chapter 13.

Working with Excel for Windows Files

In the first two chapters of *The Mac User's PC*, you learned about the physical appearance of a PC, how to turn on a PC, how to recognize what you may see onscreen, and how to start programs. In this chapter, you will learn very basic information about using Microsoft Excel for Windows. This chapter is not intended to make you an expert at Excel for Windows; this chapter simply teaches you how to perform some basic tasks. You will learn how to open, edit, print, and save an Excel for Windows worksheet; how to copy an Excel for Windows file to a floppy disk; and how to exit the program properly. And you will learn one other important thing—how to get help in Excel for Windows so that you can teach yourself to do the things that aren't covered in this book!

And, there's some wonderful news for Mac users. Excel for Windows is almost identical to Excel for the Mac. The major difference you will notice is that the PC keyboard doesn't have a Command key like your Mac keyboard does. Even the Help facility is almost identical.

Before you can start Excel for Windows, you must start Microsoft Windows. Let's review some basic information about Windows.

Reviewing Windows Basics

Microsoft Windows is as an operating environment that, in the world of DOS, provides a graphical user interface (also called GUI, pronounced "gooey") with which you can use either a mouse or a keyboard. The Microsoft Windows screen most closely resembles the Desktop on a Macintosh. Figure 7.1 shows a typical opening screen in Windows 3.1.

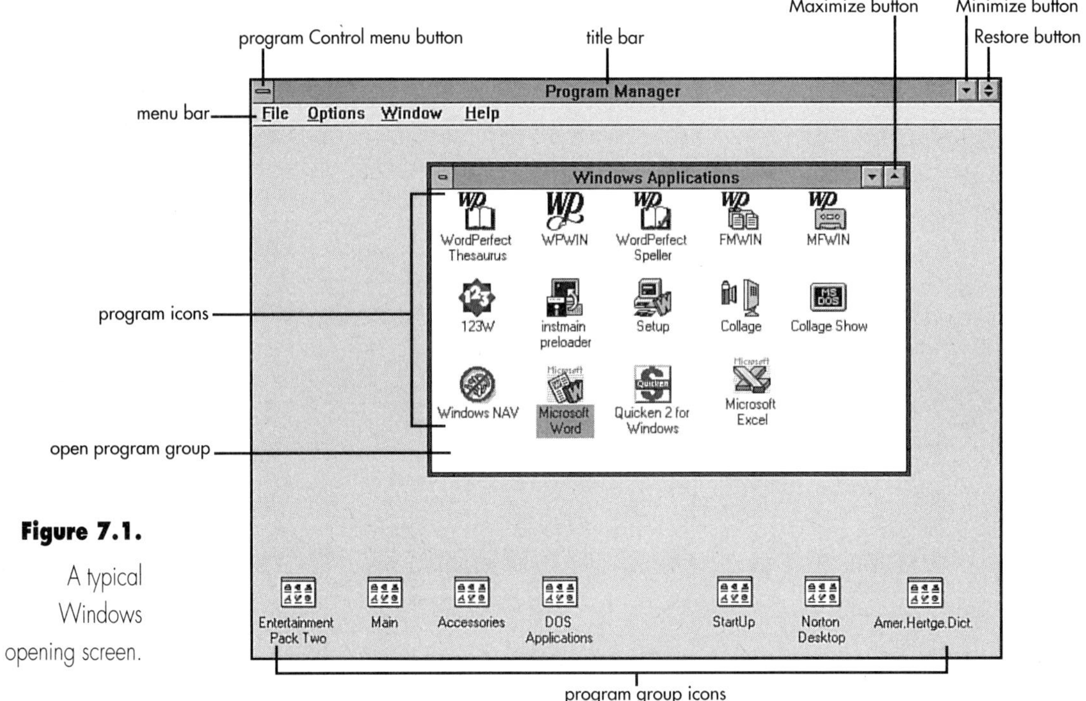

Figure 7.1.

A typical Windows opening screen.

If Microsoft Windows doesn't appear onscreen when you start the PC, type **WIN** at the DOS prompt.

As you learned in Chapter 2, Windows permits the user to perform multitasking. **Multitasking** enables the user to perform two or more functions simultaneously. To support multitasking, Windows and its Program Manager provide a way to manage the memory of the computer. Each program obtains enough memory to perform its functions; otherwise, Windows warns the user that sufficient memory is unavailable to perform all the requested tasks.

You can use a mouse or the keyboard to navigate in Windows, and you start programs from the Program Manager in Windows.

Understanding the Program Manager Screen

When you start Windows, the **Program Manager** appears. At the very top of every Windows screen, you see in the **title bar** the name of the program that is currently running. In Figure 7.1, `Program Manager` appears in the title bar.

At the left end of the title bar, you see the program **Control menu button**, a small box that contains a hyphen. You can use the program Control menu to change the size of the screen that displays the Program Manager, to close the Program Manager, and to switch to another program.

At the right end of the title bar, you see two buttons. Rather than using the Control menu, you can click on these buttons to change the size of the screen that displays the Program Manager:

- Choose the **Minimize button** to reduce the entire Program Manager screen to an icon. If you minimize a program, you choose its icon to return the program to the size it was before you minimized it.

- If the Program Manager fills the entire screen (as it does in Figure 7.1), then you see the Restore button (rather than the Maximize button). Choose the **Restore button** to reduce the Program Manager screen to a size somewhere between minimum and maximum (see Figure 7.2).

- If the Program Manager does not fill the entire screen but appears similar to Figure 7.2, then you see the Maximize button (rather than the Restore button. Choose the **Maximize button** to enlarge the Program Manager to fill the entire screen.

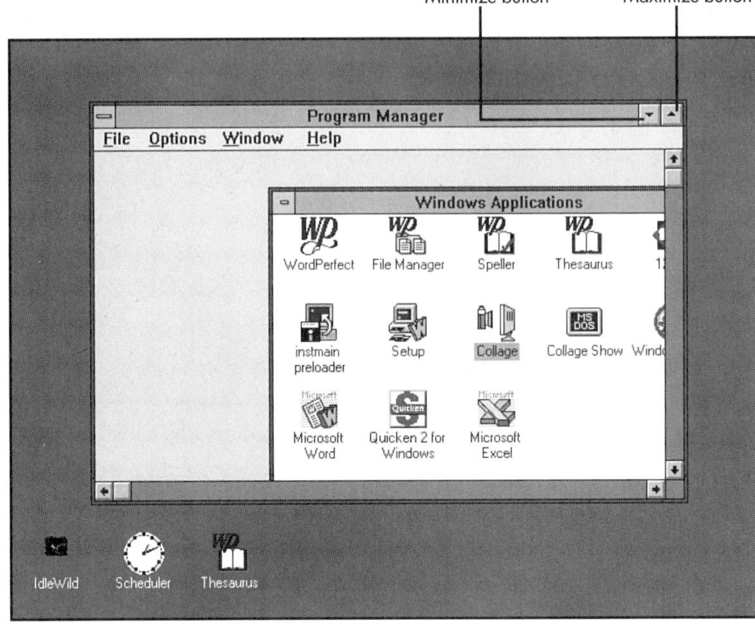

Figure 7.2.

The Program Manager when it doesn't fill the entire screen.

Just below the title bar, you see the **menu bar**. The menu bar contains **menus**, and each menu contains the **commands** (also called "menu commands") you use in Windows—but more about these in a moment.

The Program Manager contains **program groups**, which can appear either as open windows or as icons. In Figures 7.1 and 7.2, the Windows Applications program group appears as an open window while all the other program groups appear as **icons** at the bottom of the screen. Notice that the Windows Applications program group (and any open program group) also has a title bar, a Control menu, and Minimize and Maximize (or Restore) buttons. Open program groups do not, however, have menu bars.

Each program group contains icons that represent programs. You use these icons to start the programs. To start a program, the program group must be open so that you can see and access the icon that represents the program you want to start.

Navigating in Windows

While working in Windows, you can use the mouse or the keyboard to perform certain tasks. In the following sections, you will find instructions on how to use the mouse and the keyboard to open menus, **choose** commands from menus, choose options in dialog boxes, and start programs.

In Windows, a mouse operates differently from a mouse on a Macintosh. Before you learn the specifics of performing each of the previously mentioned actions, let's review the way in which a mouse operates in Windows.

Operating a Mouse in Windows

Using a mouse in Windows is a two-step process. To use a mouse to choose an item in Windows, follow these steps:

1. Slide the mouse until the mouse pointer points to the item you want to choose.

2. Press and release a mouse button—usually the left mouse button—one time.

The action you perform in step 1 is known as **pointing**, and the action you perform in step 2 is known as **clicking**. You can click either the left or the right mouse button, as defined by the software program you are using. Most of the time, to choose an item, you click the left mouse button. You also may have occasion to double-click. To **double-click**, you press and release the left mouse button twice in rapid succession. Occasionally, you may need to drag an item to move it from one location to another. To **drag**, point to the item you want to drag. Then, press and hold the left mouse button while sliding the mouse to move the mouse pointer to the new location.

Note the difference in the way clicking works in Windows compared to on a Mac. In Windows, for the most part, you don't need to hold down the mouse button while opening a menu and choosing a command; the menu remains open after you release the mouse button. On a Mac, when you release the mouse button, the menu from which you were trying to choose a command closes.

Working with Menus and Commands in Windows

The menu bar appears just below the title bar. Each menu contains the commands you use in Windows. To see the commands, you can open a menu by using the mouse or the keyboard.

To open a menu by using the mouse, point to the menu you want to open and click the left mouse button. Windows opens the menu. Unlike a menu on a Mac, the menu remains open when you release the mouse button, and the first command on the menu appears highlighted. To choose a command by using the mouse, point to the command and click the left mouse button. Windows executes the command.

You also can use the keyboard to open a menu and choose a command. First, you activate the menu bar by pressing the Alt key. A **reverse video bar** (or **highlight**) appears on the name of the first menu, **F**ile. Then, you can open a menu and choose a command in two ways:

- You can use the hot key shortcuts. Each menu and command contains an underlined letter, also called a **hot key**. You can press that key to open the menu or execute the command. When you press the W key, for example, the Program Manager opens the **W**indow menu and displays the commands available on that menu. In this book, all references to hot keys appear in boldface type.

- You can press one of the arrow keys on the keyboard to point to a menu or command, and then press the Enter key to choose it. When you press an arrow key, the reverse video bar moves. Continue pressing the arrow key until the reverse video bar appears on top of the menu or command to which you want to point. For example, you can press the Alt key to activate the menu bar, and then press the left-arrow key twice to point to the Window menu. Remember, when you use the arrow keys to point to a menu or command, you must press Enter to open that menu or choose that command.

PC NOTE

If you activate the menu bar and then press the right-arrow key four times, you highlight the Control menu. The Control menu contains the commands that control the size of the Program Manager screen. To open the Control menu after you have highlighted it, press Enter. If you have any open program group windows and you activate the menu bar and then press the right-arrow key five times, you activate the Control menu of the group window. Again, press Enter to open that Control menu.

Working with Dialog Boxes in Windows

Ellipses (...) appear after some commands on the menus. The program requires additional information about these commands before it can execute them. When you choose a command that includes an ellipsis, a **dialog box** (in which you supply the additional required information) appears.

The dialog boxes that appear when you choose a command from the Program Manager's **F**ile menu are not typical of the dialog boxes you see and use in application programs. So, there's not

much point in describing one of those dialog boxes. Instead, Figure 7.3 displays a more typical dialog box that contains a representative sample of types of dialog box options. Each dialog box is different, and most dialog boxes provide only some of these options.

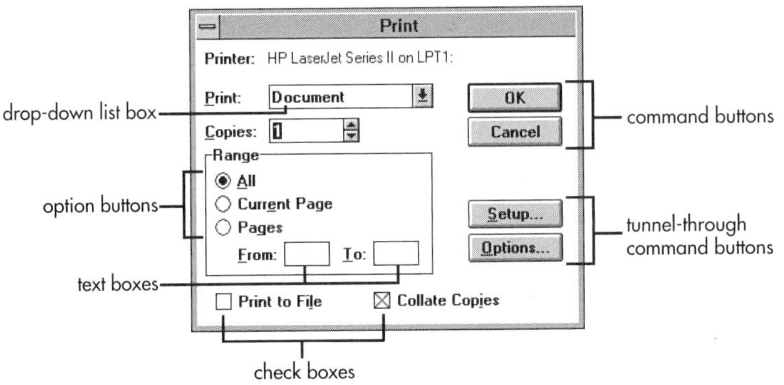

Figure 7.3.

A typical dialog box.

PC NOTE

You may notice a dotted line surrounding an option. This line indicates the current mouse pointer position. If you are using the keyboard rather than a mouse, you can use the Tab key to move around a dialog box.

A **list box** contains a list of options. You may see two kinds of list boxes in a dialog box. The Print list box in Figure 7.3 is an example of a **drop-down list box**, and is closed when the dialog box appears. To open a drop-down list box, click on the down arrow at the right end of the box; or, hold down the Alt key and type the underlined letter in the list box name. The other type of list box is already open when the dialog box appears. To choose an item from either type of list box, click on the item; or, press the down-arrow key to point to the item and then press Enter. If the list box is not long enough to display all the available items in the list, click the scroll arrow or press and hold the down-arrow key to move beyond the items that appear in the box.

An **option button** is a small round button you use to choose one option from a group of related options. A black dot appears in the button of the current option. To choose an option button, click on the option button; or, hold down the Alt key and type the underlined letter in the option name. In the Range area, the **A**ll, Curr**e**nt Page, and Pa**g**es buttons are option buttons.

A **check box** is a small square box you use to choose an option. You can choose more than one check box from a group of related options. An X appears in the check boxes of the activated options. To choose a check box, click on the check box; or, hold down the Alt key and type the underlined letter in the option name. To deactivate the option and remove the X from the box, choose the check box again. In Figure 7.3, the Print to Fi**l**e and Collate Cop**i**es check boxes appear at the bottom of the dialog box.

A **text box** is a rectangular box in which you enter text. When a dialog box that contains a text box opens, the current text is usually selected. To replace the selected text, simply type the new information. In Figure 7.3, the Range area contains two text boxes (**F**rom and **T**o). The **C**opies box also is a text box.

A **command button** is an oblong button that performs an action. To choose a command button, click on the button; or, use the Tab key to highlight the button and press Enter. In Figure 7.3, the OK button accepts the settings in the dialog box. The Cancel button cancels your changes to the settings in the dialog box. The default command button, which changes from dialog box to dialog box, appears highlighted (its outline appears darker than the other buttons). As on a Mac, if you press Enter, you choose the highlighted command button.

A **tunnel-through command button** is a button that contains ellipses (...) and opens another dialog box. To choose a tunnel-through command button, click on the button; highlight the button and press Enter; or, hold down the Alt key and type the underlined letter. In Figure 7.3, the **S**etup and **O**ptions buttons are tunnel-through command buttons.

Starting a Program in Windows

As mentioned earlier, all programs reside in program groups in Windows. To start a program, its program group cannot appear minimized as an icon; it must be open.

To use the mouse to open a program group that appears as an icon, double-click on the icon.

To use the keyboard to open a program group that appears as an icon, follow these steps:

1. Press the **Alt** key to activate the menu bar.

2. Press **W** to open the **W**indow menu.

   The Program Manager displays the choices on the **W**indow menu (see Figure 7.4). You see a check mark next to the currently selected program group.

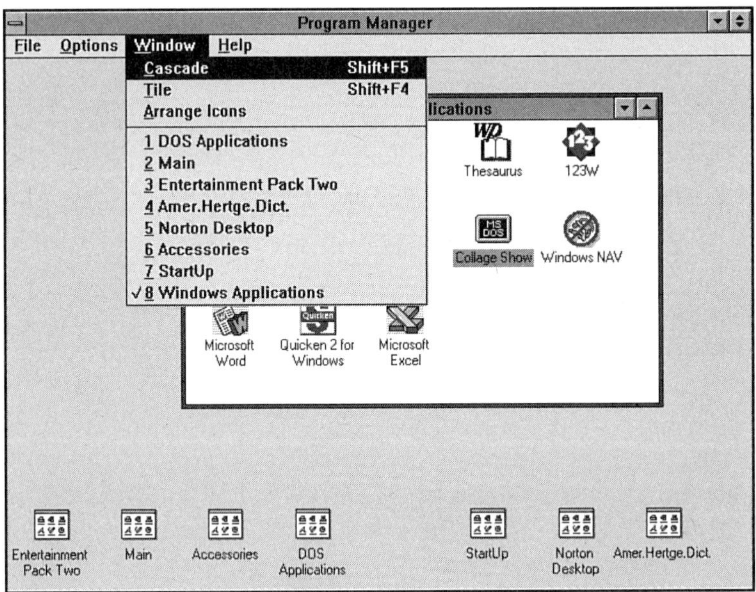

Figure 7.4.
The **W**indow menu.

3. From the numbered options in the **W**indow menu, press a number to choose the program group you want to open.

   Windows opens the specified program group.

After you open the program group, you can start a program. To start a program by using the mouse, double-click on the icon representing the program in the program group window. The Program Manager starts the program.

To start a program by using the keyboard, use the arrow keys to point to the program you want to start. Then, press Enter. The Program Manager starts the program.

Using one of the techniques just described, open the program group containing the Excel for Windows program icon and then start Excel for Windows. You may find the program icon in the Windows Applications group or in an Excel for Windows group. Or, you may find Excel for Windows somewhere altogether different because the owner of the PC has a different technique for organizing programs.

Identifying Excel for Windows Screen Parts

When you first start Excel for Windows, you see the default screen, which looks like the screen in Figure 7.5 or Figure 7.6.

In Figure 7.5, you see the program name `Microsoft Excel` along with the name of the current worksheet, `Sheet1`, in the **title bar** because the worksheet window is maximized. The Excel for Windows program Control menu appears to the left of the title bar, and the program Minimize and Restore buttons appear to the right of the title bar. Just below the title bar, you see the **menu bar** for Excel for Windows. At the left end of the menu bar, you see the worksheet Control menu; you can use this Control menu to change the size of just the worksheet portion of the screen. At the right end of the menu bar, you see the worksheet Restore button.

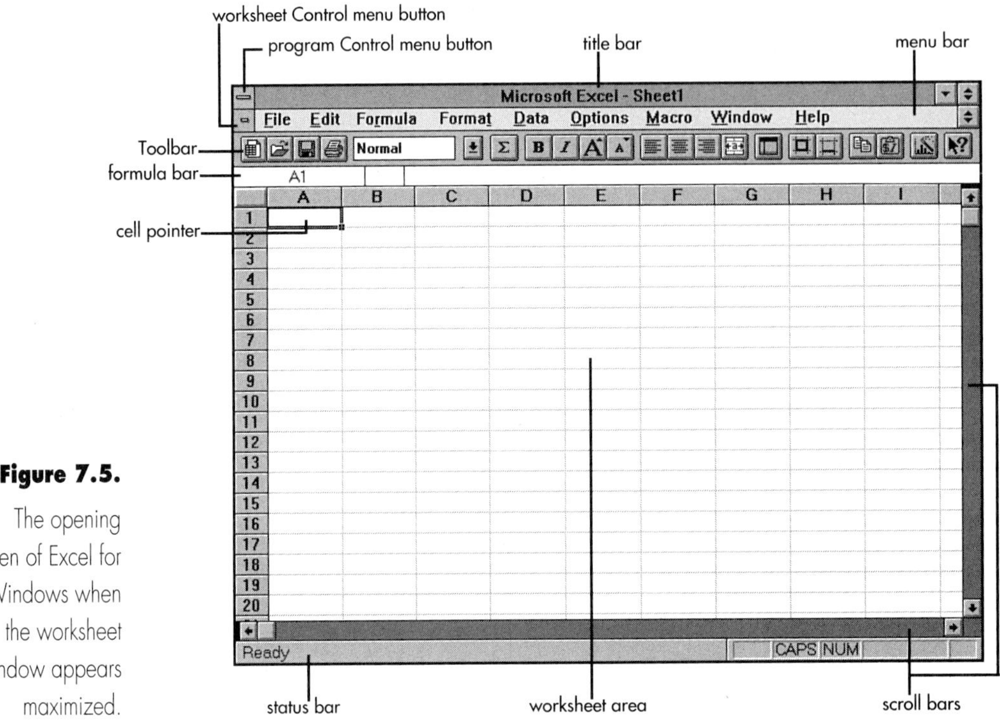

Figure 7.5. The opening screen of Excel for Windows when the worksheet window appears maximized.

In Figure 7.6, you see only the program name in the title bar at the top of the screen and you see a separate worksheet title bar because the worksheet window is not maximized. The Excel for Windows program Control menu appears to the left of the program title bar, and the program Minimize and Restore buttons appear to the right of the program title bar. Just below the program title bar, you see the menu bar for Excel for Windows.

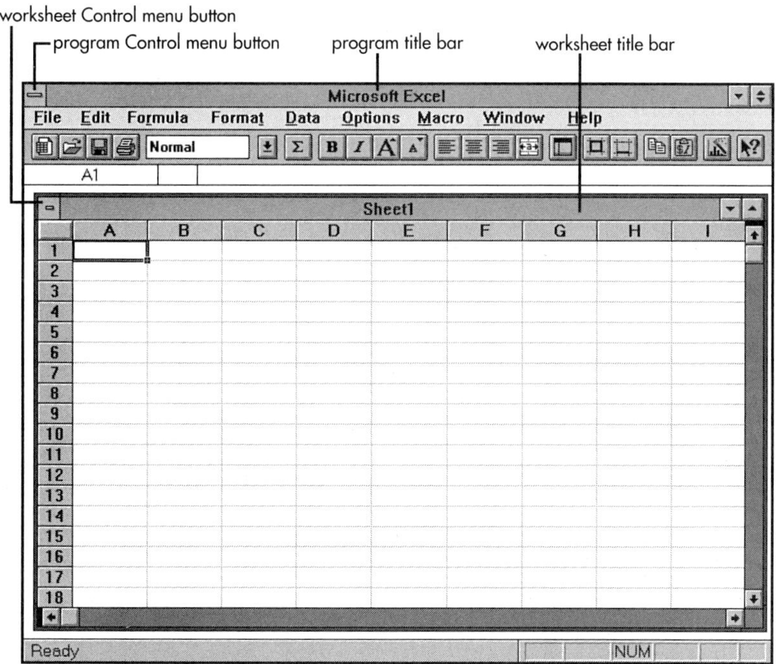

Figure 7.6. The opening screen of Excel for Windows when the worksheet window does not appear maximized.

PC NOTE

To maximize the worksheet window, open the worksheet Control menu and choose the Ma**x**imize command. Or, click the worksheet Maximize button, which appears at the right end of the worksheet title bar.

Just below the menu bar, you see the default Toolbar. Excel for Windows uses the Toolbar to assign commonly performed tasks to buttons. You must use a mouse to select a button on the Toolbar. Remember, however, that you also can use the keyboard and menus to perform all the tasks assigned to buttons on the Toolbar. In addition, the Toolbar can be customized, so the buttons on the default Toolbar in Figure 7.7 may not appear on your screen.

Figure 7.7. The default Toolbar.

Working from the left end of the Toolbar, you can perform the following tasks:

- Start a new worksheet.
- Open an existing worksheet.
- Save a worksheet.
- Print a worksheet.
- Use the Style drop-down list to change the appearance of the active cell or selected cells.
- Add a column or row of cells, all of which contain numbers.
- Apply boldface or italic character formatting to the active cell or selected cells.
- Increase or decrease the size of the font in the active cell or selected cells.
- Set left-, center-, or right-alignment for the active cell or selected cells, or center across selected cells.
- Automatically format cells based on the last automatic formatting you applied.
- Add a border around the outermost ends of the active cell or selected cells.
- Add a border to the bottom of the active cell or selected cells.
- Copy the active cell or selected cells to the Clipboard.

- Paste the formats of the cells you copied to the Clipboard into the active cell or selected cells.

- Start the ChartWizard so that you can create or edit a chart.

- Get context-sensitive Help about the area where you point and click.

Below the Toolbar, you see the formula bar. From the formula bar, you can identify the current location of the cell pointer, and, if the active cell contains any information, you see that information in the formula bar. When you type in a cell, whatever you type appears in the formula bar. You use the formula bar to edit the contents of a cell.

When you start Excel for Windows, you see an empty worksheet, in which you can start creating a new worksheet. The worksheet area consists of lettered columns and numbered rows. The intersection of a column and a row is called a **cell**; you enter information into cells. The cell pointer, the darker rectangular outline, identifies the **active cell**—the location where text or numbers will appear when you type. You refer to a cell by its cell address, the name of its column and row. In Figure 7.5, the cell pointer is resting in cell A1.

At the bottom of the screen, you see the status bar. The status bar is divided into two parts. The left end of the status bar informs you about the current operation or command you are executing. The right end of the status bar shows you whether the Caps Lock and Num Lock features are on.

Just above the status bar and along the right side of the screen, you see the horizontal and vertical scroll bars, which have arrows at either end and a scroll box somewhere along the scroll bar. Using a mouse, you can click the arrows or drag the scroll box on the horizontal scroll bar to move the view of a worksheet right or left. Or, you can click the arrows or drag the scroll box on the vertical scroll bar to move the view of a worksheet down or up.

Getting Help in Excel for Windows

Excel for Windows contains both online tutorials and an online Help facility. In this section, you learn the basics of using Help in Excel for Windows.

First, notice that you can use commands on the **H**elp menu to teach yourself to use Excel for Windows. If you choose **I**ntroducing Microsoft Excel from the **H**elp menu, you start a short tutorial on the basics of using Excel for Windows. If you choose L**e**arning Microsoft Excel from the **H**elp menu, you start a more extensive tutorial with more advanced options.

In addition to these online tutorials, Word for Windows includes an excellent online Help facility. You can display the Help Contents window in Excel for Windows by pressing F1 or by opening the **H**elp menu and choosing the **C**ontents command (see Figure 7.8). In Excel for Windows, the help you receive is context-sensitive—if you are looking at a command on a menu and you press F1, the help you get is about that command.

When you view the Help Contents window, you see the Help topics. On a color monitor, these topics appear in green and are underlined. If the list of topics is too long to fit in one Help window, you can use the scroll bar on the right side of the window to view the rest of the topics. Using the mouse, you can click on the scroll arrows to move the topics in the window until you see the topic about which you want help. To choose the topic, click on it. Using the keyboard, you can press the down-arrow key to move the topics in the window. To choose the topic, press the Tab key to highlight the topic and then press Enter.

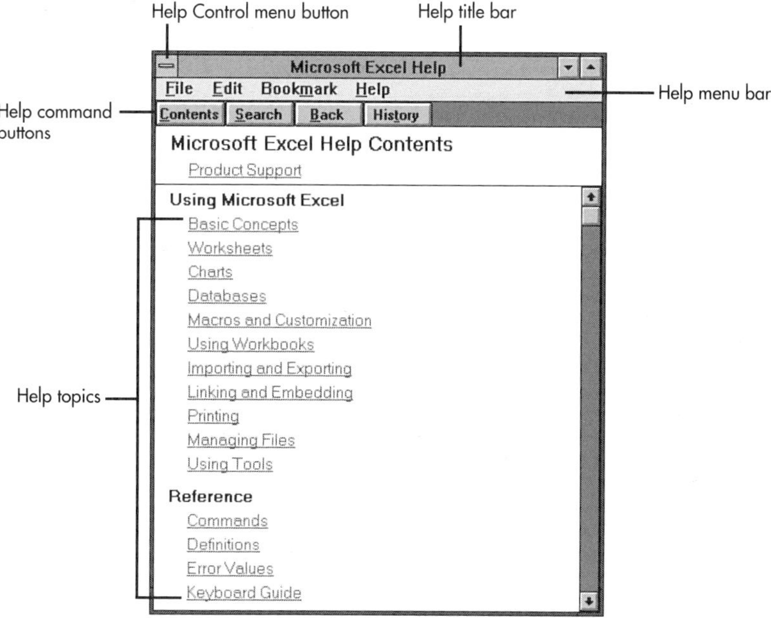

Figure 7.8. The Help Contents window.

As you can see in the Help Contents window, you can get step-by-step instructions by using an organizational approach (the topics listed under `Using Microsoft Excel`) or by using a reference approach (the topics listed under `Reference`).

You also can use the Reference section of the Help Contents window to find definitions of terms and meanings of error messages you may encounter while working in Excel for Windows. When viewing a particular Help topic, you also may see a word underlined with a dotted line. If you choose that word, Excel for Windows displays its definition. Press Enter or click on the word again to remove the definition.

The Reference section also can help you find information about parts of the Excel for Windows screen and about the mouse and the keyboard. You can use the Commands topic in the Reference section to get help about a specific command that appears on one of the Excel for Windows menus. Or, rather than using the Help Contents window, you can get help about the command by pointing to it and pressing F1.

You can use the **S**earch command on the **H**elp menu or the **S**earch button in the Help Contents window to open the Search dialog box shown in Figure 7.9 and search for topics you specify.

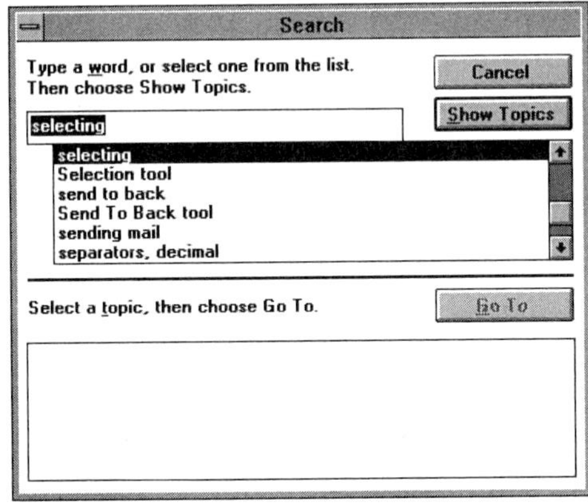

Figure 7.9. The Search dialog box.

To use the Search dialog box, follow these steps:

1. Type a **w**ord that represents the topic for which you want to search.

   As you type, Excel for Windows Help highlights the topic that most closely matches the characters you type.

2. Choose the **S**how Topics button.

   In the bottom portion of the dialog box, Excel for Windows Help displays the topics that most closely match the characters you typed.

3. Choose a topic from the list, and then choose the **G**o To button.

   Excel for Windows Help displays the topic you chose.

You can print the information that appears in Help windows by choosing the **P**rint Topic command on the Help window's **F**ile menu.

If you find a topic in Help to which you might want to return later (without having to remember how you got there in the first place), create a bookmark for the topic. Follow these steps:

1. While viewing the topic you want to mark, open the Book**m**ark menu on the Help window's menu bar.

2. Choose the **D**efine command.

   Excel for Windows Help displays the Bookmark Define dialog box shown in Figure 7.10. The name of the topic you are viewing appears in the **B**ookmark Name text box.

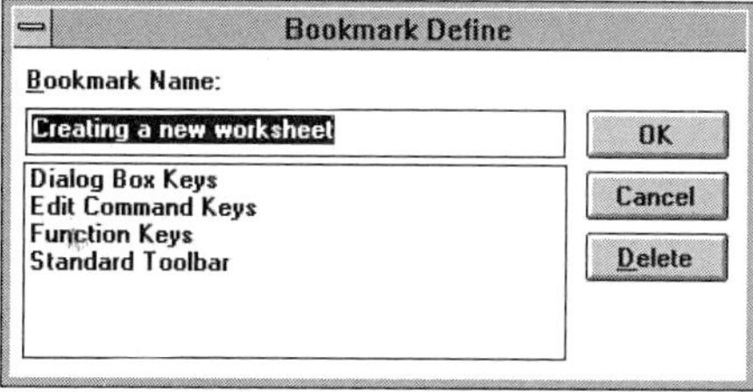

Figure 7.10. The Bookmark Define dialog box.

3. If you want to change the bookmark name, type a new name; otherwise, Excel for Windows Help will use the topic name as the bookmark name.

4. Choose OK.

   Excel for Windows stores the topic name on the Book**m**ark menu.

When you open the Book**m**ark menu again, you see below the **D**efine command the topic for which you stored a bookmark. If you choose the topic from the Book**m**ark menu, Excel for Windows Help displays the topic.

After viewing several topics, you can use the **C**ontents button to redisplay the Help Contents window. Or, you can use the **B**ack button to redisplay in reverse order the topics you viewed. You also can return directly to any topic you displayed by choosing the His**t**ory button. When you choose the His**t**ory button, Excel for Windows Help displays the Help History window, in which you can see every topic you viewed since you started Help. If you looked at a topic more than once, it appears more than once in the Help History window. To go to a topic listed in the Help History window, double-click on the topic; or, use the arrow keys to point to the topic and then press Enter.

PC NOTE

If you close Help, Excel for Windows also closes the history of your Help session and no longer maintains the history of the Help screens you viewed. When you open Help again, Excel for Windows starts the history over again.

You can learn more about how to use the Excel for Windows Help facility by opening the **H**elp menu on the Help window's menu bar and choosing **H**ow to Use Help.

Opening an Excel for Windows File

Suppose that someone brings you a worksheet, asks you to make some minor changes to it, and then wants you to print the revised worksheet. In this section, you learn how to open an existing Excel for Windows worksheet. In the next three sections, you learn how to edit, save, and print an Excel for Windows worksheet.

You can open more than one worksheet at a time. The worksheet that contains the insertion point is called the **active worksheet**,

and you are looking at it in the **active window**. When you start Excel for Windows, Sheet1 always appears. You can start typing a new worksheet in Sheet1. If you open an existing worksheet without typing in Sheet1, the existing worksheet becomes the active worksheet, but you can switch back to Sheet1 by using commands on the **W**indow menu.

You open a document in Excel for Windows in much the same way you open a document in Excel for the Mac. To open an existing Excel for Windows worksheet, follow these steps:

1. Open the **F**ile menu and choose the **O**pen command. You also can choose the Open button on the Toolbar (the second button from the left), or you can press **Ctrl**+**F12**.

   Excel for Windows displays the Open dialog box (see Figure 7.11).

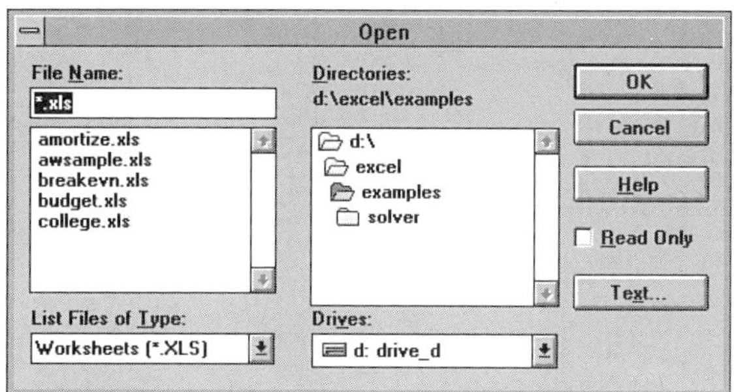

Figure 7.11.
The Open dialog box.

2. Choose the name of the worksheet you want to open from the list, or type the file name of the worksheet you want to open in the File **N**ame text box. If necessary, change the drive or the directory so that the worksheet file you want to open appears in the File **N**ame list box. To change to a floppy disk drive, insert the floppy disk into the drive, open the Dri**v**es drop-down list box, and choose the drive from the list. To change to another directory, double-click on a directory listed in the **D**irectories list box. The files in the list change to display the worksheets in the newly selected directory.

PC NOTE

Worksheet file names end with the extension XLS. If you want to look only at worksheets, open the List Files of **T**ype list box and choose Worksheets (*.XLS). Be aware, however, that the user also can create a **workbook**, which is a collection of worksheets that are conceptually related to one another. Workbook file names end in XLW. When you retrieve a workbook, you retrieve all the worksheets in the workbook.

3. Choose OK.

   The worksheet appears onscreen, and you can edit it.

Performing Basic Editing in Excel for Windows

In this section, you learn about basic editing in Excel for Windows. You learn how to move around a worksheet, how to enter information into a cell, how to change the contents of a cell, how to select a group of cells, and how to execute commands.

Moving around a Worksheet

You move around an Excel for Windows worksheet by clicking the mouse or by pressing the directional keys (the arrow keys, and Home, End, PgUp, and PgDn). Table 7.1 summarizes the most common ways in which you can use the keyboard to move around an Excel for Windows worksheet.

PC NOTE

Excel for Windows enables you to use many different keys on the keyboard to perform functions. The keystrokes you see in Table 7.1 are basic editing keystrokes. For more information on other keystrokes available, see Excel for Windows Help, discussed earlier in this chapter.

Table 7.1.

Directional keys in a worksheet.

Key(s)	Effect
→ and ←	Moves right or left one cell—right or left one column.
↑ and ↓	Moves up or down one cell—up or down one row.
PgDn	Moves down one window.
PgUp	Moves up one window.
Ctrl+PgDn	Moves right one window.
Ctrl+PgUp	Moves left one window.
Home	Moves to the first cell in the current row.
Ctrl+Home	Moves to the beginning of the worksheet.
Ctrl+End or End+Home	Moves to the last non-empty cell in the worksheet.
End	Turns on or off End Mode.
End+arrow key	Moves right, left, up, or down to the last non-empty cell.

Entering Information into a Cell

Entering text or numbers into a worksheet is a three-step process. To enter text or numbers into a worksheet, follow these steps:

1. Position the cell pointer on the cell into which you want to type text or numbers.

2. Type the text or numbers.

   When you type, Excel for Windows activates the formula bar, and the text or numbers you type appear in the formula bar. When Excel for Windows activates the formula bar, you also see the Accept and Cancel buttons (see Figure 7.12).

Cancel button

Accept button

Microsoft Excel

File Edit Formula Format Data Options Macro Window Help

Normal

A17 Returns and

AWSAMPLE.XLS

	A	B	C	D	E	F
5						
6	Revenues					
7	Product Sales	325,421	331,929	338,568	345,339	
8	Rentals	81,335	82,982	84,642	86,335	
9	Maintenance Fees	48,813	49,789	58,785	51,881	
10		455,569	464,700	481,995	483,555	
11						
12	Cost of Sales					
13	Material Costs	177,688	181,234	184,858	188,555	
14	Packaging Costs	7,107	7,249	7,394	7,542	
15	Shipping Costs	11,194	11,418	11,644	11,879	
16	Sales Commissions	16,271	16,596	233,361	23,828	
17	Returns and					
18		212,260	216,497	437,257	231,804	
19						
20						
21						
22						
23						

Edit NUM

Figure 7.12.

The formula bar when activated.

3. To accept what you typed, press an arrow key (to accept and move to another cell), press the **Enter** key, or click the Accept button in the formula bar.

To cancel what you typed, press the **Esc** key or choose the Cancel button in the formula bar.

By default, when you enter text into a cell, Excel for Windows left-aligns the text in the cell. Also by default, when you enter numbers into a cell, Excel for Windows right-aligns the numbers in the cell.

Changing the Contents of a Cell

You can use the Backspace key to delete the character immediately to the left of the insertion point. You can use the Del key to delete the character immediately to the right of the insertion point. (The **insertion point**, the flashing black vertical bar, tells you where text will appear when you type.)

You can replace the contents of a cell simply by typing over what currently appears in the cell, or you can edit the contents of the cell. To edit the contents of the cell, position the cell pointer on the cell you want to edit. Then press F2 or click on the cell's contents in the formula bar. If you press F2, the insertion point appears at the end of the cell's contents. If you click on the cell's contents in the formula bar, the insertion point appears at the location you clicked.

While you are editing a cell, you are working in insert mode. In **insert mode**, Excel for Windows places characters at the current location of the insertion point and moves all existing characters to the right. You can press the Ins key to switch to overtype mode. In **overtype mode**, Excel for Windows places characters at the current location of the insertion point and types over characters that exist at that location, removing them. The Ins key works like a toggle switch: press it one time to change from insert mode to overtype mode; press it a second time to change back from overtype mode to insert mode.

Selecting Cells

You may want to add the contents of a group of cells or make changes to the appearance of the worksheet. For example, you may want the contents of certain cells to appear in italics or in boldface type. You may want to change the alignment of the contents of certain cells or delete the contents of certain cells.

In Excel for Windows, you select a cell or contiguous group of cells when you want to "operate" on the cell(s)—for example, when you want to add a column or row or center the information in the cell(s). **Selecting** is the process of highlighting the cell(s) so that Excel for Windows can identify the cell(s) on which you want to work. You can select more than one cell as long as the selection is contiguous.

PC NOTE

In some operations, you must select cells more than one time to complete the command. To copy cells, for example, you first must select the range of cells you want to copy; then, you must select the target location of cells where you want the copy to appear.

To select cells by using the mouse, you drag the mouse pointer. Follow these steps:

1. Position the mouse pointer on the first cell you want to select. Click and hold down the left mouse button.

2. Slide the mouse in the direction of the other cells you want to select.

   As you slide the mouse, a reverse video bar (a highlight) appears over all the cells you are selecting except the first cell. You can slide the mouse diagonally to select a rectangle that contains more than one row and more than one column of cells.

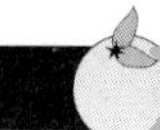

3. Continue sliding the mouse until you reach the end of the cells you want to select.

4. Release the left mouse button.

   The cells you want to select appear highlighted—a reverse video bar appears over them.

In Figure 7.13, cells B7 through B9 are selected. When referring to a block of cells (such as B7 through B9), Excel for Windows uses the notation `B7:B9`.

	A	B	C	D	E	F
1						
2	PROFIT AND LOSS PROJECTION - 1989					
3						
4		Q1	Q2	Q3	Q4	
5						
6	Revenues					
7	Product Sales	325,421	331,929	338,568	345,339	
8	Rentals	81,335	82,982	84,642	86,335	
9	Maintenance Fees	48,813	49,789	58,785	51,881	
10		455,569	464,700	481,995	483,555	
11						
12	Cost of Sales					
13	Material Costs	177,688	181,234	184,858	188,555	
14	Packaging Costs	7,107	7,249	7,394	7,542	
15	Shipping Costs	11,194	11,418	11,644	11,879	
16	Sales Commissions	16,271	16,596	233,361	23,828	
17	Returns & Allowances	32,500	33,100	33,800	34,500	
18		244,760	249,597	471,057	266,304	

Figure 7.13.

The selected cells.

Now suppose that the selection should have included cells B7:E9. If you didn't select all the cells you meant to select, you can use a shortcut to extend a selection. Press F8. In the status bar, `EXT` appears (see Figure 7.14).

Place the mouse pointer on the last selected cell and drag in the direction you want to extend the selection. Excel for Windows adds the new cells to the original selection. Press F8 again to deactivate the selection extender.

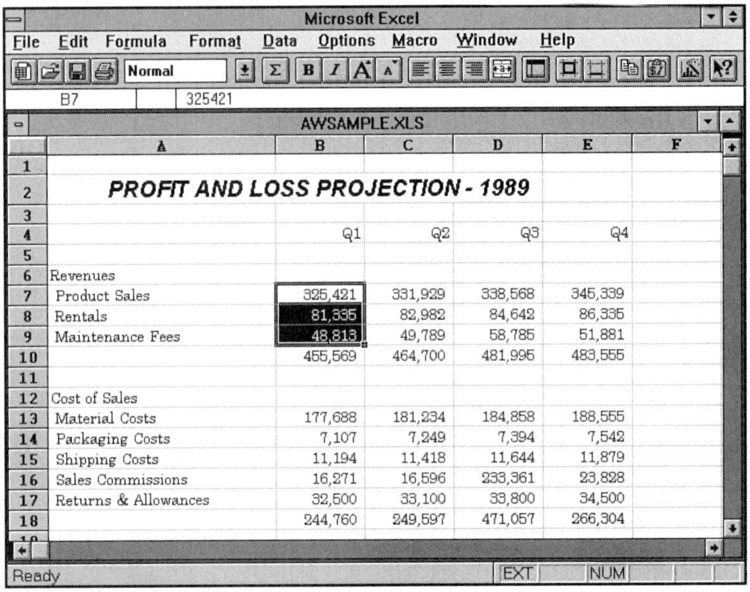

Figure 7.14.

The status bar after pressing F8 to activate the selection extender.

You can cancel a selection by clicking the mouse anywhere else onscreen.

To select cells by using the keyboard, move the cell pointer to the first cell you want to select (refer to Table 7.1 for more information). Then, use the keystrokes in Table 7.2 to select additional cell(s).

Table 7.2.

Selecting cells by using the keyboard.

Key(s)	Effect
Any arrow key	Selects the current cell.
Shift+arrow key	Extends the selection by one cell in the direction of the arrow.
Ctrl+Shift+arrow key	Extends the selection to the last non-empty cell in the direction of the arrow.
Shift+Home	Extends the selection to the beginning of the row.
Ctrl+Shift+Home	Extends the selection to the beginning of the worksheet.

Key(s)	Effect
Ctrl+Shift+End	Extends the selection to the last non-empty cell of the worksheet.
Ctrl+Shift+PgUp	Extends the selection left one window.
Ctrl+Shift+PgDn	Extends the selection right one window.
Shift+PgUp	Extends the selection up one window.
Shift+PgDn	Extends the selection down one window.
Ctrl+spacebar	Selects the entire current column.
Shift+spacebar	Selects the entire current row.
Ctrl+Shift+spacebar	Selects the entire worksheet.
Shift+Backspace	Collapses the selection to the active cell.

You can cancel a selection by pressing any arrow key.

Executing Commands

Typically, to execute a command, you open a menu and choose the command. You can use the mouse and keyboard techniques described earlier in this chapter to open menus and choose commands. If the command you want to execute appears on the Toolbar, you also can use the Toolbar to choose the command.

On the menus, you may notice that key combinations appear next to certain commands. These key combinations are hot keys—you use them as shortcuts to bypass menus when choosing a command. For example, if you want to move the cell pointer to a specific place in the worksheet (a cell you named previously, for example), you can open the **F**ormula menu and choose the **G**o To command, or, you simply can press F5.

Excel for Windows also provides a shortcut menu for the most common operations performed on selected cells. To activate the shortcut menu, follow these steps:

1. Select the cells.

2. Place the mouse pointer over the group of selected cells and press the *right* mouse button.

   Excel for Windows displays the shortcut menu.

To cancel the shortcut menu, press the Esc key or click the *right* mouse button. (If you click the *left* mouse button, you also cancel the selection.)

Saving an Excel for Windows File

After you have made the changes you need to make, you will want to save the worksheet. Like Excel for the Mac, Excel for Windows provides three ways to save a worksheet, and each of these ways is described in this chapter. One of these methods lets you save a worksheet using a different name. Because you may not want to overwrite the work that existed before you edited, you may want to read the sections on these three methods before you use any of them.

- You can use the Close command to save the worksheet under its current name, and then "put away" the document (remove it from the screen).

PC NOTE

When you work with a workbook, the **C**lose command becomes the **C**lose Workbook command. The **C**lose Workbook command works just like the **C**lose command.

- You can use the Save command to save the worksheet under its current name, and then continue working on it.

- You can use the Save As command to save the worksheet under a different name. You may want to save the worksheet under a different name to avoid changing the original.

When you exit from Excel for Windows, the program prompts you to save any worksheets that contain changes before you exit—but more about that later in this chapter.

Using the Close Command

As in Excel for the Mac, you can use the **C**lose command when you finish working with a worksheet and you want Excel for Windows to put away the worksheet. When you choose the **C**lose command, Excel for Windows also gives you the option of saving any changes you might have made before putting away the worksheet. To close a worksheet, open the **F**ile menu and choose the **C**lose command.

If you haven't made any changes to the worksheet since the last time you saved it, Excel for Windows simply removes the worksheet from the screen. If, however, you have made changes, Excel for Windows displays the dialog box in Figure 7.15.

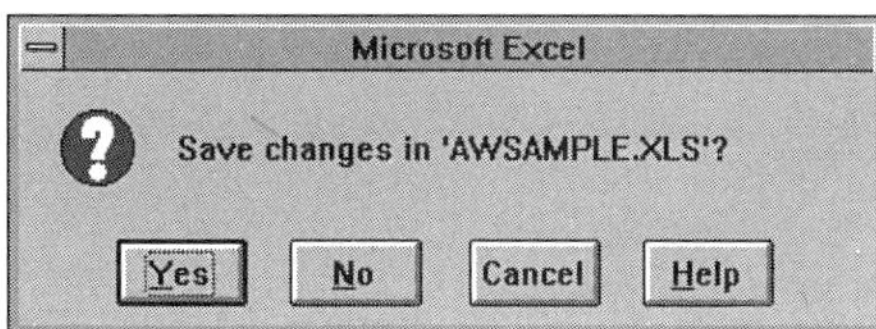

Figure 7.15.
The `Save changes in?` dialog box.

If you choose **Y**es, Excel for Windows saves the changes you have made and removes the worksheet from the screen. If you choose **N**o, Excel for Windows *does not* save the changes you have made since the last time you saved, but Excel for Windows *does* remove the worksheet from the screen. If you choose Cancel, Excel for

Windows *does not* save the changes you have made since the last time you save and *does not* remove the worksheet from the screen.

Using the Save Command

Also as in Excel for the Mac, you can use the **S**ave command to save the worksheet in the active window. When you use the **S**ave command, Excel for Windows saves the changes you have made to a disk (either hard or floppy) and leaves the worksheet onscreen so that you can continue to work on it.

To save a worksheet by using the **S**ave command, open the **F**ile menu and choose the **S**ave command. Alternatively, you can choose the Save button from the Toolbar (the third button from the left), or you can press Shift+F12. If you are saving an existing worksheet that already has a name, Excel for Windows saves the worksheet. (If you pay close attention to the status bar at the bottom of the screen, you will see a message that indicates Excel for Windows is saving the worksheet.) If you are saving a new worksheet that doesn't yet have a name, Excel for Windows displays the Save As dialog box discussed in the next section.

Using the Save As Command

You might want to leave the original worksheet available in cases where your changes may not be final. If you are unsure of the changes you have made, for example, and somebody else is going to come back and check your work, you might want to keep the original worksheet. You then can show the person your version, and let him or her decide which version to continue using.

You can save an Excel for Windows worksheet under another name similarly to the way you save an Excel for the Mac worksheet under a different name. To save your version of an existing worksheet and leave the original version intact, follow these steps:

1. Open the **F**ile menu and choose the Save **A**s command, or press **F12**.

   Excel for Windows displays the Save As dialog box in Figure 7.16.

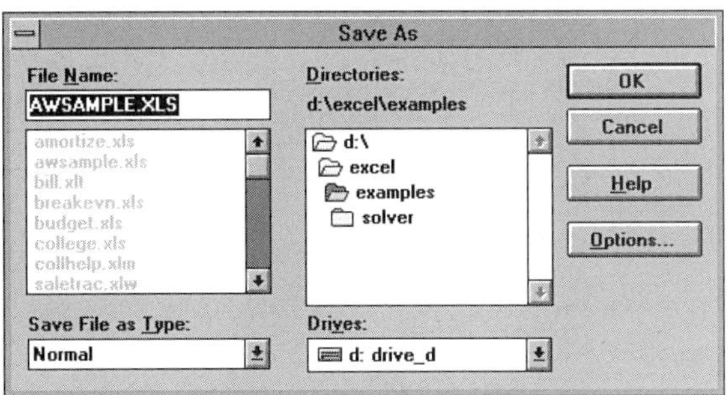

Figure 7.16.
The Save As dialog box.

2. Type the new name for the worksheet in the File **N**ame text box. You can use up to 11 characters for the name you want to assign to the worksheet. The first part of the name can contain no more than 8 characters; the **extension** can contain no more than 3 characters.

   For more information on the rules DOS imposes when you name a file on a PC, see Chapter 12. (Yes, it is DOS that imposes file name rules. It's even DOS that does the saving.)

   If you choose a name that appears in the list box, Excel for Windows asks whether you want to replace that worksheet. If you replace the document, you *overwrite* the original version, which, of course, is the exact thing you were trying to avoid doing. So, choose **N**o to return to the dialog box and try a different name; or choose Cancel to close the dialog box without saving at all. Then, you can try again.

3. If you want, you can use the Save File As **T**ype list box to choose a format other than Excel for Windows in which to save the worksheet. For example, you could choose to save it as a Macintosh Text or CSV file.

4. Also if you want, you can save the file to a floppy disk by changing the drive that appears in the Dri**v**es list box.

5. Choose OK.

   Excel for Windows saves the worksheet under the name you specified in the File **N**ame text box, leaving the original version (under its original name) intact.

Printing an Excel for Windows File

After you have edited and saved the worksheet, you may need to print it. But before you print the document, you may want to see onscreen the way it will look when you print it. You can preview an Excel for Windows worksheet the same way you preview an Excel for the Mac worksheet. To preview a worksheet in Excel for Windows and then print it, open the **F**ile menu and choose Print Pre**v**iew. Excel for Windows displays the layout of your worksheet as it will appear when you print it (see Figure 7.17).

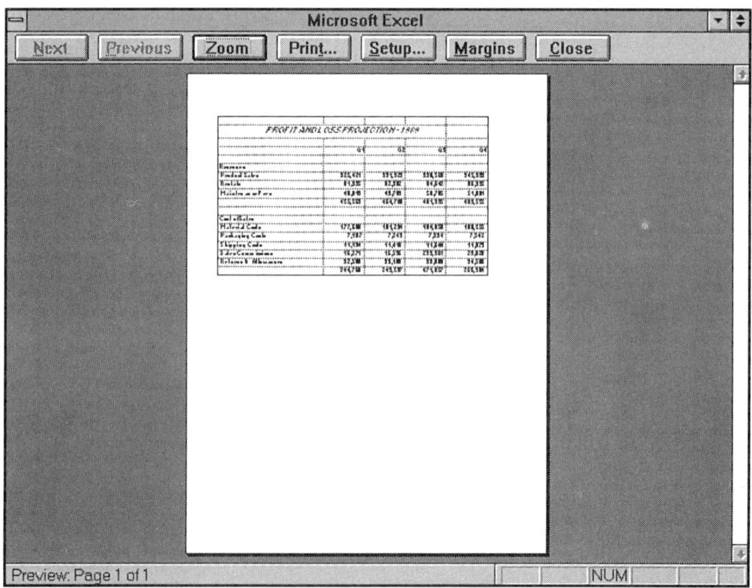

Figure 7.17. A sample Print Preview screen.

Note that the Print Preview screen in Excel for Windows is almost identical to the Print Preview screen in Excel for the Mac. Although you cannot edit on this screen, you can change the margins and see how the layout will appear when printed. If, for example, you see gridlines appearing around the cells, the gridlines will print. You can use the command buttons along the top of the Print Preview window to perform the following tasks:

- You can use the **Z**oom button to switch to the full-page view (as shown in Figure 7.17), or to see the detailed information that appears in the cells.
- You can use the **S**etup button to open the Page Setup dialog box (see Figure 7.18) to adjust page setup information, such as whether gridlines print.

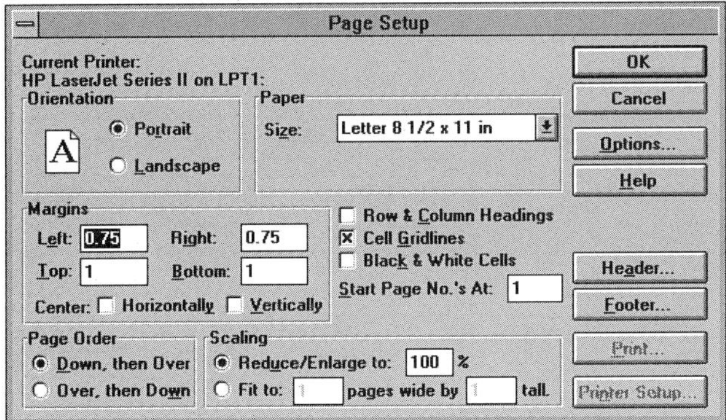

Figure 7.18.

The Page Setup dialog box.

- You can use the **M**argins button to hide or display the margins of your worksheet. When you display margins, you can change them by dragging with the mouse.
- You can use the **C**lose button to return to the editing window without printing.
- You can use the Prin**t** button to print the worksheet. Excel for Windows closes the Print Preview screen and displays the Print dialog box in Figure 7.19.

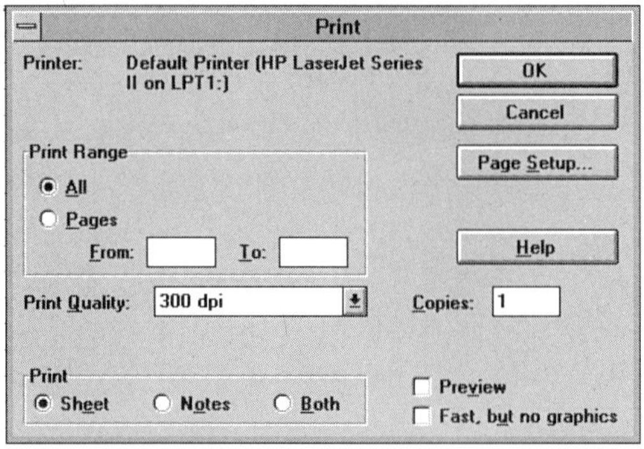

Figure 7.19. The Print dialog box.

Note that you can open the Page Setup dialog box from the Print dialog box by choosing the Page **S**etup button. Also, you can preview the worksheet before you print by checking the Pre**v**iew check box.

Although there are several choices in the Print dialog box, the ones you are most likely to use are the choices in the Print Range area and the **C**opies text box.

From the choices in the Print Range area, you can choose the pages you want to print:

- To print the entire worksheet, choose **A**ll.
- To print selected pages, choose **P**ages and then specify the page numbers in the **F**rom and **T**o text boxes.

You can print more than one copy of the choice you indicated in the Range options box of the Print dialog box. Simply change the number of copies in the **C**opies text box.

To open the Print dialog box (see Figure 7.19) without previewing the worksheet, choose the **P**rint command from the **F**ile menu, or press Ctrl+Shift+F12.

PC NOTE

When you preview a worksheet and then choose the **P**rint button from the Preview window, Excel for Windows displays the Print dialog box. When you open the Print dialog box and choose the Pre**v**iew check box, Excel for Windows displays the Preview window; however, when you choose the **P**rint button from the Preview window, Excel for Windows *does not* redisplay the Print dialog box before printing the worksheet.

If you know that you want to use the default settings that appear in the Print dialog box (if you want to print one copy of the entire worksheet in the active window), you can print the worksheet without opening the Print dialog box; simply choose the Print button from the Toolbar (the fourth button from the right).

Copying an Excel for Windows File to a Floppy Disk

You may find that you need to copy an Excel for Windows file to a floppy disk. You may need to print a file on another PC, for example. Using the Save As dialog box is the easiest way to copy an Excel for Windows file to a floppy disk. Alternatively, you can use DOS commands, which you can find in Chapter 12.

Earlier in this chapter, when you were learning to save a worksheet, you used the Save **A**s command on the **F**ile menu to open the Save As dialog box. To use the Save **A**s command to copy a file to a floppy disk, follow these steps:

1. Insert a formatted disk into the floppy disk drive.

2. Open the worksheet you want to copy to the floppy disk so that it appears in the active window.

3. Open the **F**ile menu and choose the Save **A**s command.

   Excel for Windows displays the Save As dialog box (shown in Figure 7.20).

4. Open the Dri**v**es list box and choose the letter of the floppy disk drive into which you inserted the disk.

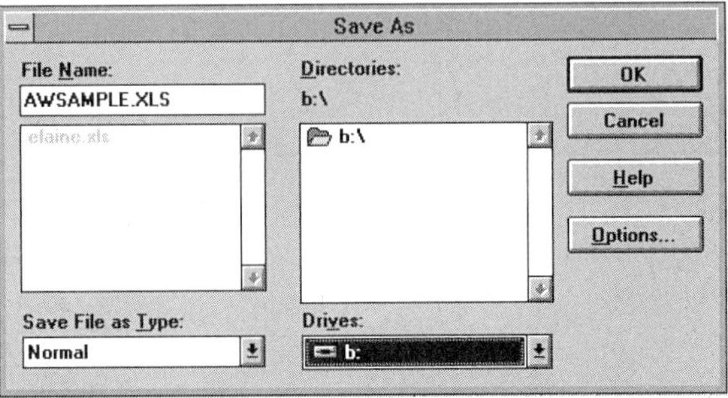

Figure 7.20. The Save As dialog box with drive B selected.

5. In the File **N**ame text box, type the name you want to give the file on the floppy disk. To give the file the same name on the floppy disk as it has on the hard disk, don't type anything. Choose OK.

   Excel for Windows copies the file to the floppy disk. If a file with the same name already exists on the floppy disk, you will see a dialog box that asks whether you want to replace the file on the floppy disk. If you *don't* want to write over a file on the floppy disk, choose **N**o. Excel for Windows redisplays the Save As dialog box. You then can insert a new floppy disk or type a different file name.

Exiting Excel for Windows

When you are finished using Excel for Windows, you can exit by choosing the E**x**it command from the **F**ile menu or by pressing Alt+F4. If any of the open worksheets contain changes you didn't save, Excel for Windows displays a dialog box asking whether you want to save the changes to the worksheet before you exit. Choose **Y**es to save the changes and exit. Choose **N**o to ignore the changes and exit. Choose Cancel to return to editing in Excel for Windows.

When you exit from Excel for Windows, you return to Windows. You can exit from Windows by choosing the E**x**it Windows command from the **F**ile menu or by pressing Alt+F4.

You safely can shut off the PC after exiting from Windows.

Chapter Summary

In this chapter, you learned how to use the excellent online Help facility in Excel for Windows. You learned how to open, edit, save, and print an Excel for Windows worksheet. You learned how to copy an Excel for Windows file to a floppy disk, and you learned how to exit from Excel for Windows.

Excel for Windows is almost completely identical to Excel for the Mac (that, in your author's humble opinion, is the *definition* of cross-platform software—no learning curve!). I found the biggest difference between the two packages to be the shortcut keys that appear on the menus. In Excel for Windows, many of the shortcut keys include a function key. But the basic tasks (using Help; opening, editing, saving, and printing a worksheet; and exiting) are almost identical in the two programs.

In the next chapter, you learn how to work with Lotus 1-2-3 for DOS files. As you know, Chapters 3 through 9 in *The Mac User's PC* focus on specific software packages. You should read the chapters that pertain to the software you want to use. Chapter 10 tells you about database programs you may want to avoid. Chapter 11 discusses the MS-DOS Shell. Refer to Chapter 12 for information on file-naming conventions imposed on Excel for Windows by the operating system, and for information on working with basic DOS commands. If you need to transfer and translate files between a PC and a Mac, read Chapter 13.

Working with 1-2-3 for DOS Files

In the first two chapters of *The Mac User's PC*, you learned about the physical appearance of a PC, how to turn on a PC, how to recognize what you might see onscreen, and how to start programs. In this chapter, you will learn very basic information about using Lotus 1-2-3 for DOS. This chapter is not intended to make you an expert at 1-2-3 for DOS; it simply teaches you how to perform some basic tasks. You will learn how to open, edit, print, and save a 1-2-3 for DOS worksheet; copy a 1-2-3 for DOS file to a floppy disk, and exit the program properly. And you will learn one other important thing—how to get help in 1-2-3 for DOS so that you can teach yourself to do the things that aren't covered in this book.

While you read this chapter, be aware that there are unfortunately few similarities between 1-2-3 for DOS and 1-2-3 for the Mac.

Using an appropriate technique you learned in Chapter 2, start the 1-2-3 for DOS program (or see Chapter 11 for information on starting programs from the MS-DOS Shell). The rest of the discussion in this chapter refers to Lotus 1-2-3 Version 2.4, but if you are using a different version, you still can follow along.

Identifying 1-2-3 for DOS Screen Parts

When you start 1-2-3 for DOS, you see the main screen, which looks like the screen in Figure 8.1.

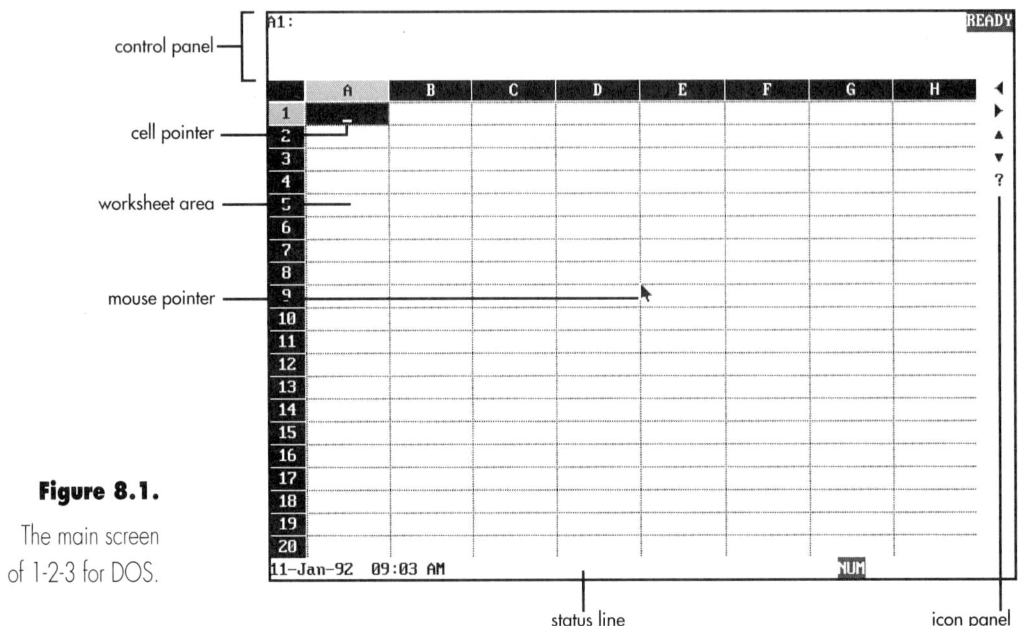

Figure 8.1.

The main screen of 1-2-3 for DOS.

If a mouse driver was loaded when you turned on the PC, you can use the mouse or the keyboard to move around 1-2-3 for DOS, choose commands from menus, and choose options from dialog boxes. If you see a small rectangle or an arrow pointing up and slightly to the left in the center of the screen, as shown in Figure 8.1, a mouse is available. If you don't see a rectangle or an arrow, a mouse is not available.

For purposes of discussion, you can think of the screen as divided into four sections:

- The worksheet area
- The status line
- The control panel
- The icon panel

The Worksheet Area

The center area of the screen (where the mouse pointer appears if a mouse driver is loaded) is the worksheet area. As in 1-2-3 for the Mac, the worksheet area consists of lettered columns and numbered rows. The intersection of a column and a row is called a **cell**; you enter information into cells. The **cell pointer**, a rectangular video bar (shown in Figure 8.1), identifies the **active cell**—the location where text or numbers will appear when you type. You refer to a cell by its cell address, the name of its column and row. In Figure 8.1, the cell pointer is in cell A1.

The Status Line

Below the worksheet area, you see the status line, which is similar to the status window in 1-2-3 for the Mac. At the left end of the status line, you see the date and time of the computer's internal clock. At the right end of the status line, you see status indicators, which tell you when you have pressed certain keys, or when certain worksheet conditions exist. In Figure 8.1, for example, you see the `NUM` status indicator, telling you that you have pressed the Num Lock key. You also might see, for example, `CALC`, which tells you that 1-2-3 for DOS must recalculate the formulas in the worksheet. You can display a complete list of the status indicators by using the Help facility in 1-2-3 for DOS, which you learn about in the next section.

The Control Panel

Above the worksheet area, you see the control panel, which is similar to the console in 1-2-3 for the Mac and displays information about your work and about what 1-2-3 for DOS is doing. The control panel consists of three lines. At the left end of the first line of the control panel, you see information about the active cell and its contents. In Figure 8.1, you see only A1, indicating that the cell pointer is in cell A1, which contains nothing. At the right end of the first line of the control panel, you see the mode indicator, which identifies the current mode in which 1-2-3 for DOS is operating. In Figure 8.1, 1-2-3 for DOS is in READY mode.

Information does not appear on all three lines of the control panel at all times. To complicate the issue further, what you see on the second and third line of the control panel depends on what you are doing. For example, when you start to type something in cell A1, the text you type appears on the second line of the control panel, as shown in Figure 8.2. The mode indicator changes to LABEL.

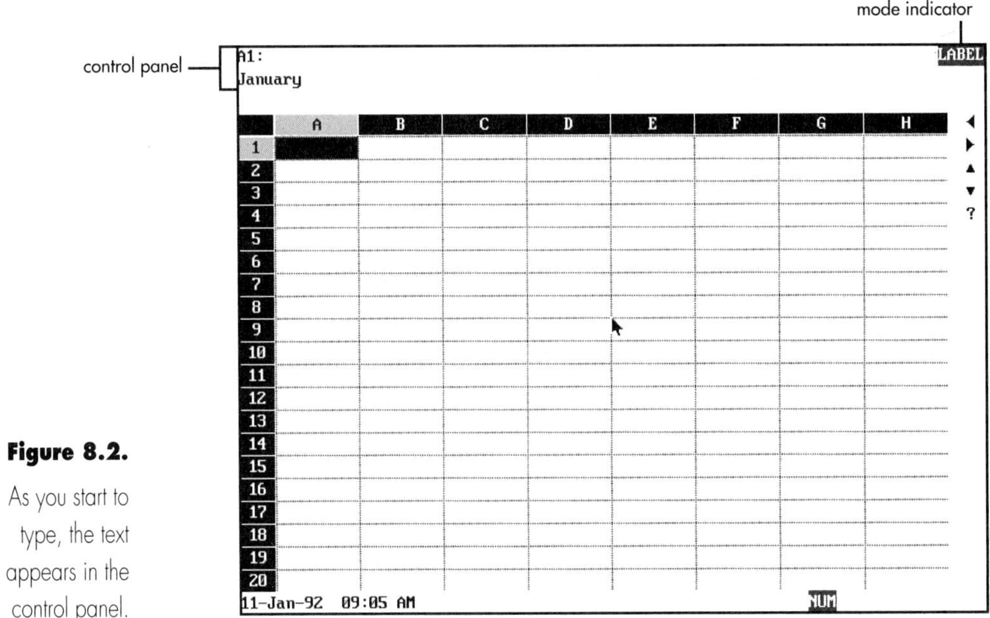

Figure 8.2.

As you start to type, the text appears in the control panel.

PC NOTE

If you start to type a number, the mode indicator changes to VALUE.

If you activate the **menu bar**, however, 1-2-3 for DOS's commands and related information appear in the second and third

lines of the control panel. You use the commands to perform various operations in 1-2-3 for DOS. When you activate the menu bar, the mode indicator changes to MENU (see Figure 8.3).

Main menu

mode indicator

```
A1:                                                                          MENU
Worksheet  Range  Copy  Move  File  Print  Graph  Data  System  Add-In  Quit
Global  Insert  Delete  Column  Erase  Titles  Window  Status  Page  Learn
11-Jan-92   09:06 AM                                              NUM
```

Figure 8.3.

The Main menu for 1-2-3 for DOS.

PC NOTE

You can activate menus with the mouse by sliding the mouse pointer into the control panel area. The 1-2-3 for DOS Main menu appears if you last selected a command from the 1-2-3 for DOS Main menu; if you last selected from the Wysiwyg Main menu, you must use the keyboard to activate the 1-2-3 for DOS Main menu. Using the keyboard, you can activate the 1-2-3 for DOS Main menu by pressing the forward slash key (/) or by pressing the less than sign (<). To use the < key, however, you must press Shift, so all lazy people (including me) use the forward slash key. (You can return to READY mode by pressing the Esc key until the menus disappear.)

You can choose commands from the menus by using the keyboard or a mouse. You learn how to choose commands from menus later in this chapter.

The second line of the control panel contains the actual menu choices. Again, what you see on the third line of the control panel depends on what menu choice you highlight on the second line of the control panel. In some cases, on the third line of the control panel, you see the submenus that will appear if you choose the highlighted menu choice. In the situation shown in Figure 8.3, for example, if you choose the Worksheet command from the Main menu, 1-2-3 for DOS displays another menu, containing the commands **G**lobal, **I**nsert, **D**elete, **C**olumn, **E**rase, **T**itles, **W**indow, **S**tatus, **P**age, and **L**earn; the mode indicator remains `MENU`.

Alternatively, as shown in Figure 8.4, you may see some descriptive text on the third line of the control panel.

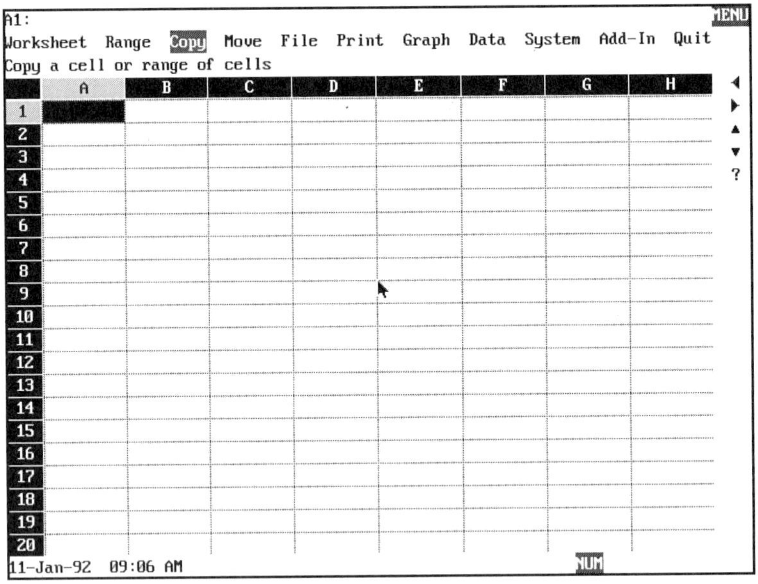

Figure 8.4.

The control panel when the **C**opy command is highlighted.

When descriptive text appears in the third line of the control panel, 1-2-3 for DOS does not display a submenu if you choose the highlighted command; instead, 1-2-3 for DOS executes the highlighted command. If you choose the **C**opy command, for example, 1-2-3 for DOS starts the process of copying information from one cell to another, and the mode indicator changes to `POINT`.

Version 2.2 of 1-2-3 for DOS came with a companion spreadsheet publishing product called Allways, which enabled the user to format, print, and add graphics to worksheets. In Releases 2.3 and 2.4, Wysiwyg replaced Allways. Wysiwyg is an acronym for What You See Is What You Get. Wysiwyg is a separate software program that users attach to 1-2-3 for DOS. Wysiwyg affects the appearance of the worksheet and lets users make worksheets more attractive by including, for example, boldface or underlining. Wysiwyg has its own set of menus and commands; compare the menus you see in Figure 8.5 to the menus that appear in Figure 8.3.

```
A1:                                                              WYSIWYG
Worksheet  Format  Graph  Print  Display  Special  Text  Named-Style  Quit
Column  Row  Page
     A     B     C     D     E     F     G     H
1
2
3
4
5
6
7
8
9
10
11
12
13
14
15
16
17
18
19
20
11-Jan-92  09:07 AM                                        NUM
```

menus

Figure 8.5.

The Wysiwyg Main menu.

PC NOTE

To activate the Wysiwyg Main menu by using the keyboard, press the colon (:) key. To activate the Wysiwyg Main menu by using the mouse, slide the mouse pointer into the control panel area. The Wysiwyg menu appears if you last selected a command from the Wysiwyg menu; if you last selected from the 1-2-3 for DOS Main menu, you must use the keyboard to activate the Wysiwyg menu. You can return to READY mode by pressing Esc until the menus disappear.

To perform various formatting and spreadsheet publishing activities, you use the Wysiwyg menus.

The Icon Panel

On the right side of the screen, you may see icons in the icon panel, as shown in Figure 8.1. Or, you may see SmartIcons, as shown in Figure 8.6.

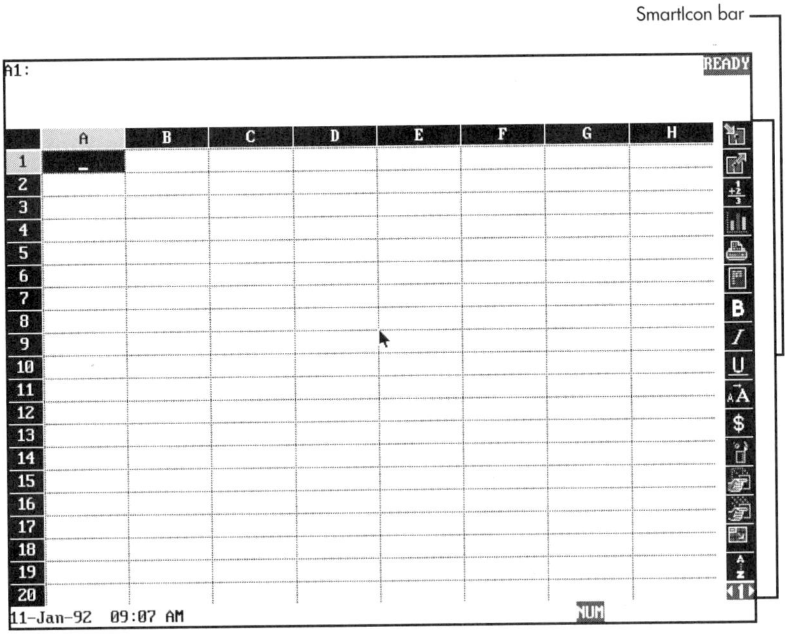

SmartIcon bar

Figure 8.6.

The 1-2-3 for DOS screen with SmartIcons.

You can use the icons in the icon panel only if you are using a mouse. You can use the SmartIcons, however, if you are using the keyboard *or* a mouse. You use the icons in the icon panel to navigate around the worksheet area. You also can use the SmartIcons to navigate around the worksheet area, but, more often, you use the SmartIcons as shortcuts to execute commands and bypass menus. You learn more about using the icon panel and the SmartIcons in the next section.

Working with 1-2-3 for DOS Menus

You can use the keyboard or a mouse to activate menus and choose commands. To activate the 1-2-3 for DOS Main menu by using the keyboard, press the forward slash key (/) or the less than sign (<). To activate the Wysiwyg Main menu, press the colon (:) key.

To activate a menu and choose a command by using the keyboard, follow these steps:

1. Select the cell or cells on which you want to operate.

2. Press **/** to activate the 1-2-3 for DOS Main menu, or press **:** to activate the Wysiwyg Main menu.

   The appropriate Main menu appears.

3. Press the right- and left-arrow keys to highlight the command.

   On the second line of the control panel, you see the Main menu choices. The third line of the control panel identifies submenus that will appear if you choose the currently highlighted menu choice. For example, if you chose the **W**orksheet command from the 1-2-3 for DOS Main menu, you would see another menu containing the commands **G**lobal, **I**nsert, **D**elete, **C**olumn, **E**rase, **T**itles, **W**indow, **S**tatus, **P**age, and **L**earn. If no submenus exist (as they don't for the **C**opy command), you see a brief explanation of the command.

4. Press **Enter** to choose the command.

Alternatively, you can press the first letter of the name of the command. The first letter of the command acts as a **hot key**, and automatically chooses the command. You won't be able to read the help information that appears when you highlight the command, but you won't need to press Enter to choose the command. For example, if you want to choose the **C**opy command from the 1-2-3 for DOS Main menu, you can press C. In this book, the hot key letters appear in boldface type.

To activate a menu by using a mouse, you move the mouse pointer into the control panel area. The menu that appears depends on the menu from which you most recently made a selection. By default, the 1-2-3 for DOS Main menu appears when you start the program and first move the mouse pointer into the control panel area. To activate the Wysiwyg Main menu, first use the keyboard (press the : key). The next time you move the mouse pointer into the control panel area, the Wysiwyg Main menu appears. To switch back to the 1-2-3 for DOS Main menu, again use the keyboard (press / or <); the next time you move the mouse pointer into the control panel area, the 1-2-3 for DOS Main menu appears.

To choose a command from a menu by using the mouse, click on the command.

The menu structure in 1-2-3 for DOS is basically hierarchical; if you choose a command from a menu, you may be presented with another menu, and if you choose a command from the second menu, a third menu might appear.

PC NOTE

You cannot move the cell pointer around the worksheet area while a menu appears in the control panel. To remove the menu from the control panel by using the keyboard, press Ctrl+Break (on the front of the Pause key, you should see the word "Break"), or press the Esc key until the menus disappear. To remove the menu from the control panel by using the mouse, move the mouse pointer out of the control panel.

Using SmartIcons To Bypass Menus

You may see the SmartIcons on the right side of the 1-2-3 for DOS screen, as shown in Figure 8.7.

A1: {Page} [W24] READY

	A	B	C	D	E	F
1						
2		PROFIT AND LOSS PROJECTION – 1989				
3						
4		Q1	Q2	Q3	Q4	
5						
6	Revenues					
7	Product Sales	325,421	331,929	338,568	345,339	
8	Rentals	81,335	82,982	84,642	86,335	
9	Maintenance Fees	48,813	49,789	58,785	51,881	
10		455,569	464,700	481,995	483,555	
11						
12	Cost of Sales					
13	Material Costs	177,688	181,234	184,858	188,555	
14	Packaging Costs	7,107	7,249	7,394	7,542	
15	Shipping Costs	11,194	11,418	11,644	11,879	
16	Sales Commissions	16,271	16,596	233,361	23,828	
17		212,260	216,497	437,257	231,804	
18						
19						
20						

11-Jan-92 09:12 AM NUM

SmartIcon bar

Figure 8.7.

The SmartIcons.

Working from the top of the SmartIcon bar, you can perform the following tasks:

- Save the current worksheet.
- Open an existing worksheet.
- Add the cells in the nearest adjacent range.
- Open the graph window.
- Print the specified range.
- Preview the specified print range.

- Apply boldface formatting to the selected cells.
- Apply italic formatting to the selected cells.
- Apply single-underline formatting to the selected cells.
- Change the font of the information in the selected cells.
- Apply currency ($) formatting to the selected cells.
- Erase the selected cells.
- Select the target range to copy.
- Select the target range to move.
- Copy the selected range.
- Sort the database.
- Identify the SmartIcon bar as the first (of 7).

You can use the SmartIcons to move around the worksheet area; but, most often, you use the SmartIcons to shorten the process of performing a command with the menus. You can use a mouse or the keyboard to choose a SmartIcon.

Because the SmartIcon bar can be customized, you may not see onscreen the same icons as you see in Figure 8.7. Although you see only one SmartIcon bar onscreen at one time, 1-2-3 for DOS actually has seven SmartIcon bars, each containing additional shortcuts for tasks you perform. At the bottom of the SmartIcon bar, you see a number. That number represents the number of the SmartIcon bar you are viewing. Because you are an occasional user of 1-2-3 for DOS, you probably won't need to use too many icons on any SmartIcon bar other than the first one.

The easiest way to work with the SmartIcons is by using a mouse. To find out the function of a SmartIcon, point to the SmartIcon and press the *right* mouse button. A description of the SmartIcon's purpose appears on the third line of the control panel. To choose a SmartIcon, click on it. To cycle through the other SmartIcon bars, click the arrow on either side of the number at the bottom of the SmartIcon bar.

Using the keyboard to work with the SmartIcons is a little trickier than using a mouse. If the SmartIcons appear automatically when you start 1-2-3 for DOS, then you can activate them by pressing *one* of the following four key combinations:

- Alt+F7
- Alt+F8
- Alt+F9
- Alt+F10

The only way to know which key combination you need is to try each one until you see a screen like the screen in Figure 8.8.

```
A1: {Page} [W24]                                                    ICONS
Use ↑ ↓ → ← to select an icon.  Press ENTER to use the icon.
Saves the current worksheet file to a disk
```

	A	B	C	D	E	F
1						
2		PROFIT AND LOSS PROJECTION – 1989				
3						
4		Q1	Q2	Q3	Q4	
5						
6	Revenues					
7	Product Sales	325,421	331,929	338,568	345,339	
8	Rentals	81,335	82,982	84,642	86,335	
9	Maintenance Fees	48,813	49,789	58,785	51,881	
10		455,569	464,700	481,995	483,555	
11						
12	Cost of Sales					
13	Material Costs	177,688	181,234	184,858	188,555	
14	Packaging Costs	7,107	7,249	7,394	7,542	
15	Shipping Costs	11,194	11,418	11,644	11,879	
16	Sales Commissions	16,271	16,596	233,361	23,828	
17		212,260	216,497	437,257	231,804	
18						
19						
20						

```
11-Jan-92  09:12 AM                                       NUM
```

Figure 8.8.

The screen when you activate the SmartIcons by using the keyboard.

To select a SmartIcon on the current SmartIcon bar by using the keyboard, press the up- or down-arrow key to highlight the appropriate icon. As you highlight each icon, a description of its purpose appears on the third line of the control panel. Press Enter to choose the highlighted icon. To change to one of the other six SmartIcon bars, press the left- or right-arrow key.

So, let's see what advantages you gain by using the SmartIcons. Suppose that you want the totals in cells B10..E10 to appear in boldface type with a single underline. To use the menus to apply this formatting, follow these steps:

1. Using the keyboard or a mouse, select cells B10..E10.

2. Press the colon (**:**) key to activate the Wysiwyg Main menu.

3. Choose **F**ormat from the Main menu.

4. Choose **B**old from the **F**ormat menu.

5. Choose **S**et from the **B**old menu.

   1-2-3 for DOS applies boldface formatting to the range and returns to READY mode.

6. Press the colon (**:**) key to reactivate the Wysiwyg Main menu (or slide the mouse pointer into the control panel).

7. Choose **F**ormat from the Main menu.

8. Choose **U**nderline from the **F**ormat menu.

9. Choose **S**ingle from the **U**nderline menu.

   1-2-3 for DOS underlines the range and returns to READY mode.

Nine steps. Now, to accomplish the same two tasks by using the SmartIcons and a mouse, follow these steps:

1. Using a mouse (or the keyboard), select cells B10..E10.

2. Click on the Bold SmartIcon (the seventh icon from the top).

   1-2-3 for DOS applies boldface formatting the range and returns to READY mode.

3. Click on the Underline SmartIcon (the ninth icon from the top).

   1-2-3 for DOS underlines the range and returns to READY mode.

Three steps. But, suppose that you don't have a mouse available (or maybe you don't have to suppose). To use the SmartIcons and the keyboard, follow these steps:

1. Using the keyboard, select cells B10..E10.

2. Activate the SmartIcon bar (by pressing **Alt**+**F7**, **Alt**+**F8**, **Alt**+**F9**, or **Alt**+**F10**).

3. Press the down-arrow key to highlight the Bold SmartIcon (the seventh icon from the top).

4. Press **Enter** to select the Bold SmartIcon.

   1-2-3 for DOS applies boldface formatting to the range and returns to READY mode.

5. Activate the SmartIcon bar (by pressing **Alt**+**F7**, **Alt**+**F8**, **Alt**+**F9**, or **Alt**+**F10** again).

6. Press the down-arrow key to highlight the Underline SmartIcon (the ninth icon from the top).

7. Press **Enter** to select the Underline SmartIcon.

1-2-3 for DOS underlines the range and returns to READY mode.

Seven steps—not a lot of savings over the menus, but some.

Getting Help in 1-2-3 for DOS

1-2-3 for DOS contains an online Help facility you can use by pressing F1 (see Figure 8.9). In 1-2-3 for DOS, the help you receive is context-sensitive—if you are looking at a menu when you press F1, for example, the help you get is about that menu.

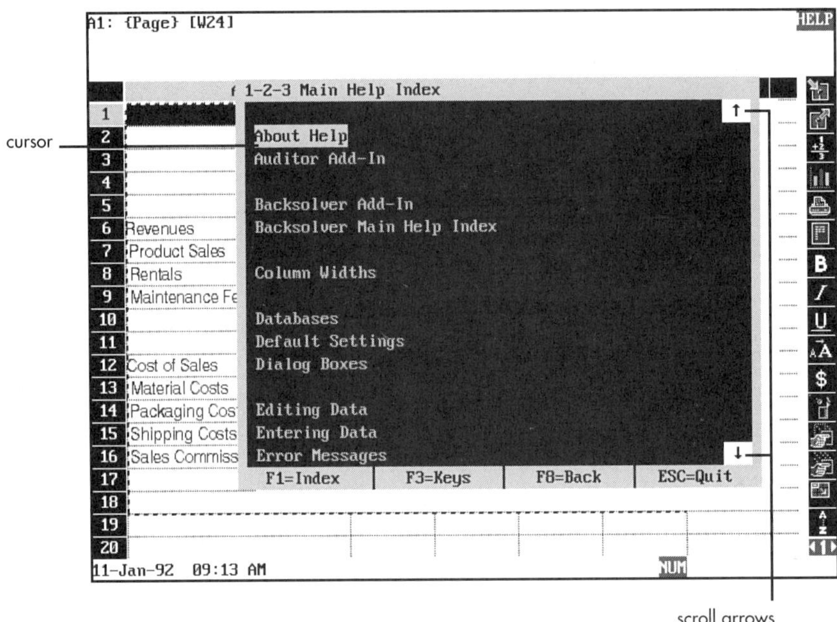

Figure 8.9.

The opening Help screen.

The opening Help screen in 1-2-3 for DOS displays an index of topics for which Help is available. To use the keyboard to select a topic, press the up- and down-arrow keys to move the **cursor**, a reverse video bar, to the topic you want to view and then press

Enter. To use the mouse to select a topic, slide the mouse until the mouse pointer points to the topic you want to view and then click the left mouse button. Moving the cursor (whether by using the keyboard or a mouse) is called **pointing**.

If the topic you want to view doesn't appear in the window, press the up- or down-arrow key. Or, click on the up or down scroll arrow on the right side of the Help window until the topic appears.

If you are using a color monitor, you may notice words that appear in red (both in the index and when you view a topic). The words in red are cross-reference topics—topics related to the topic you are currently viewing. You can press the down-arrow key, the right-arrow key, or the Tab key to move the cursor to highlight the next cross-reference topic. You can press the up-arrow key, the left-arrow key, or Shift+Tab to highlight the preceding cross reference-topic.

You can press the End key to move to the end of the current topic in the Help window; you can press the Home key to move to the beginning of the current topic in the Help window. You can press PgUp and PgDn to scroll through the Help window one window length at a time. You can press F8 or the Backspace key to cycle backward through the topics you have viewed since you started the Help program. You can press F1 to redisplay the Help index, and you can press the Esc key to exit Help.

1-2-3 for DOS also remembers the last topic you viewed the last time you used the Help facility. To view that topic, press Ctrl+F1 (rather than F1) to start Help.

Opening a 1-2-3 for DOS File

Suppose that someone brings you a 1-2-3 for DOS worksheet, asks you to make some minor changes to it, and then wants you to print the revised worksheet. In this section, you learn how to open an existing 1-2-3 for DOS worksheet. In the next three sections, you learn how to edit, save, and print a 1-2-3 for DOS worksheet.

To open an existing worksheet, follow these steps:

1. Press **/** or **<** to activate the 1-2-3 for DOS Main menu, and choose the **F**ile command.

2. Choose the **R**etrieve command from the **F**ile menu. You also can choose the Retrieve SmartIcon (the second icon from the top).

   In the third line of the control panel, 1-2-3 for DOS displays the names of the first five available worksheets (see Figure 8.10).

available worksheets

```
List  ◄  ►  ▲  ▼  ?  ..  A:  B:  C:  D:                                   FILES
Name of file to retrieve: D:\123R24\123DATA\*.wk?
AWSAMPLE.WK1   BAL.WK1        BALB.WK1       BRKB.WK1       BUDB.WK1
```

	A	B	C	D	E	F
1						
2		PROFIT AND LOSS PROJECTION – 1989				
3						
4		Q1	Q2	Q3	Q4	
5						
6	Revenues					
7	Product Sales	325,421	331,929	338,568	345,339	
8	Rentals	81,335	82,982	84,642	86,335	
9	Maintenance Fees	48,813	49,789	58,785	51,881	
10		455,569	464,700	481,995	483,555	
11						
12	Cost of Sales					
13	Material Costs	177,688	181,234	184,858	188,555	
14	Packaging Costs	7,107	7,249	7,394	7,542	
15	Shipping Costs	11,194	11,418	11,644	11,879	
16	Sales Commissions	16,271	16,596	233,361	23,828	
17		212,260	216,497	437,257	231,804	
18						
19						
20						

```
11-Jan-92  09:14 AM                                             NUM
```

Figure 8.10. The names of the worksheets you can retrieve.

To see additional available worksheets, press the right-arrow key.

1-2-3 for DOS scrolls the names along the third line of the control panel.

Or, you can press F3 to see the names of worksheet files in a columnar list format (see Figure 8.11).

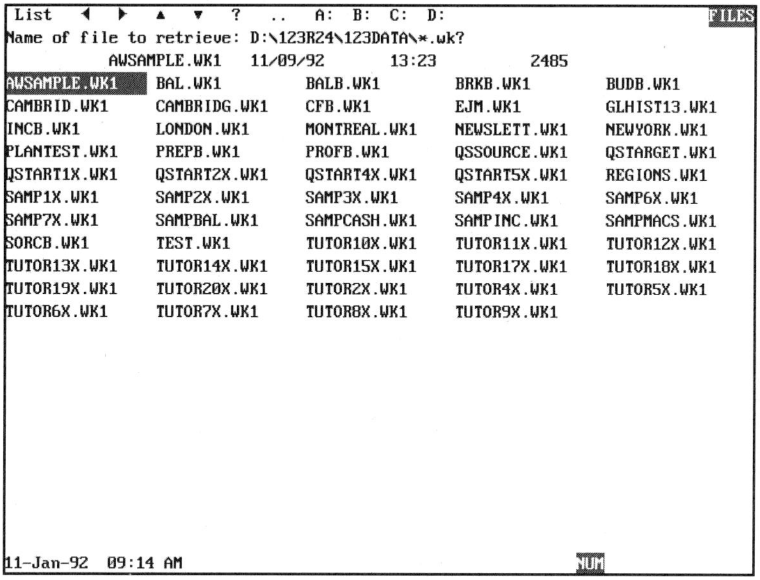

```
List  ◄  ►  ▲  ▼  ?  ..  A:  B:  C:  D:                                  FILES
Name of file to retrieve: D:\123R24\123DATA\*.wk?
           AWSAMPLE.WK1   11/09/92        13:23          2485
AWSAMPLE.WK1  BAL.WK1       BALB.WK1      BRKB.WK1      BUDB.WK1
CAMBRID.WK1   CAMBRIDG.WK1  CFB.WK1       EJM.WK1       GLHIST13.WK1
INCB.WK1      LONDON.WK1    MONTREAL.WK1  NEWSLETT.WK1  NEWYORK.WK1
PLANTEST.WK1  PREPB.WK1     PROFB.WK1     QSSOURCE.WK1  QSTARGET.WK1
QSTART1X.WK1  QSTART2X.WK1  QSTART4X.WK1  QSTART5X.WK1  REGIONS.WK1
SAMP1X.WK1    SAMP2X.WK1    SAMP3X.WK1    SAMP4X.WK1    SAMP6X.WK1
SAMP7X.WK1    SAMPBAL.WK1   SAMPCASH.WK1  SAMPINC.WK1   SAMPMACS.WK1
SORCB.WK1     TEST.WK1      TUTOR10X.WK1  TUTOR11X.WK1  TUTOR12X.WK1
TUTOR13X.WK1  TUTOR14X.WK1  TUTOR15X.WK1  TUTOR17X.WK1  TUTOR18X.WK1
TUTOR19X.WK1  TUTOR20X.WK1  TUTOR2X.WK1   TUTOR4X.WK1   TUTOR5X.WK1
TUTOR6X.WK1   TUTOR7X.WK1   TUTOR8X.WK1   TUTOR9X.WK1

11-Jan-92  09:14 AM                                             NUM
```

Figure 8.11.

The columnar list format from which you can retrieve a worksheet.

You can retrieve a file from the list on the third line of the control panel or from the columnar list that appears when you press F3.

PC NOTE

Worksheet file names end with the extension WK?, where the ? is either an S or the number 1, 2, or 3, depending on the version of 1-2-3 for DOS with which the worksheet was created.

3. Using the keyboard or a mouse, choose the name of the worksheet you want to open from the list.

The worksheet appears onscreen, and you can edit it.

Performing Basic Editing in 1-2-3 for DOS

In this section, you learn about basic editing in 1-2-3 for DOS. You learn how to move around a worksheet, how to enter information into a cell, how to change the contents of a cell, and how to select a group of cells.

Moving around a Worksheet

You move around a 1-2-3 for DOS worksheet by pressing the **directional keys** on the keyboard (the arrow keys, Home, End, PgUp, and PgDn) or, if a mouse driver is installed, by clicking the mouse.

Table 8.1 summarizes the most common ways in which you can use the keyboard to move around a 1-2-3 for DOS worksheet.

Table 8.1. Directional keys in a worksheet.

Key(s)	Effect
← or →	Moves right or left one cell—right or left one column.
↑ or ↓	Moves up or down one cell—up or down one row.
PgDn	Moves down one screen.
PgUp	Moves up one screen.
Tab or Ctrl+→	Moves right one screen.
Shift+Tab or Ctrl+←	Moves left one screen.

Key(s)	Effect
Home	Moves to cell A1.
End+Home	Moves to the last active cell in the worksheet.
End	Turns on or off End mode.
End+arrow key	Moves to the last non-empty cell in the direction of the arrow key.

If a mouse driver was installed when you started the PC, you can use it to navigate in 1-2-3 for DOS. As mentioned earlier in the chapter, if you see a small rectangle or an arrow pointing up and slightly to the left in the center of the screen, a mouse is available. If you don't see a rectangle or an arrow, a mouse is not available.

To use a mouse to move around a 1-2-3 for DOS worksheet, follow these steps:

1. Slide the mouse until the mouse pointer points to the item you want to choose.

2. Press and release a mouse button—usually the left mouse button—one time.

The action you perform in step 1 is known as **pointing**; the action you perform in step 2 is known as **clicking**. You can click the left or the right mouse button, as defined by 1-2-3 for DOS. Most of the time to choose an item, you click the left mouse button. You also may have occasion to double-click. To **double-click**, you press and release the left mouse button twice in rapid succession. Occasionally, you may need to drag an item from one location to another. Or, you may need to highlight a group of cells. To **drag**, point to the item you want to drag or the first cell you want to highlight. Then, press and hold the left mouse button while sliding the mouse to move the mouse pointer to the new location or the last cell you want to highlight.

To move to a particular cell by using a mouse, you click on that cell. To move to cell A1, for example, click on the area where column A and row 1 intersect. If you see the icon panel on the right side of the screen, you can click on any of the arrow icons to move one cell at a time in the direction of the arrow. If you click on the question mark icon, you start 1-2-3 for DOS Help, which you learned about earlier in this chapter. If you don't see the icon panel, you see the SmartIcons.

Entering Information into a Cell

Entering text or numbers into a worksheet is a three-step process that is very similar to the one you use in 1-2-3 for the Mac. To enter text or numbers into the worksheet, follow these steps:

1. Position the cell pointer on the cell into which you want to type text or numbers.

2. Type the text or numbers.

   When you type in 1-2-3 for DOS, the text or numbers appear in the control panel.

3. Press **Enter**.

   1-2-3 for DOS transfers the information you typed from the control panel to the cell.

By default, when you type text into a cell, 1-2-3 for DOS left-aligns the text in the cell. Also by default, when you type numbers into a cell, 1-2-3 for DOS right-aligns the numbers in the cell.

Changing the Contents of a Cell

You can use the Backspace key to delete the character or number immediately to the left of the cursor. You can use the Del key to delete the character or number immediately to the right of the cursor.

You can replace the contents of a cell simply by typing over what currently appears in the cell, or you can edit the contents of the cell. To type over the current contents of the cell, move the cell pointer to the cell, type, and then press Enter. 1-2-3 for DOS replaces the original contents of the cell with the new information you typed. To edit the contents of the cell, position the cell pointer on the cell you want to edit. Then, press F2. The cursor appears at the end of the cell's contents.

When you are editing a cell, you are working in insert mode. In **insert mode**, 1-2-3 for DOS places characters to the left of the cursor and moves all existing characters to the right. You can press the Ins key to switch to overtype mode. In **overtype mode**, 1-2-3 for DOS places characters at the current location of the cursor and types over characters that exist at that location, removing them. The Ins key works like a toggle switch: press the key one time to change from insert mode to overtype mode; press the key a second time to change back from overtype mode to insert mode.

Selecting Cells

You may want to add the contents of a group of cells or make changes to the appearance of the worksheet. For example, you may want the contents of certain cells to appear in italics or in boldface type. You may want to change the alignment of the contents of certain cells or delete the contents of certain cells.

In 1-2-3 for DOS, you select a cell or contiguous group of cells when you want to "operate" on the cell(s)—for example, when you want to add the column or row, or center the information in the cell(s). **Selecting** is the process of highlighting the cell(s) so that 1-2-3 for DOS can identify the cell(s) on which you want to work. You can select more than one cell as long as the selection is contiguous.

PC NOTE

In some operations, you must select cells more than one time to complete the command. To copy cells, for example, you first must select the range of cells you want to copy; then, you must select the target range of cells where the copy should appear.

To select cells by using the keyboard, follow these steps:

1. Use the directional keys to place the cell pointer in the upper left corner of the range of cells you want to select.

2. Press **F4**.

   1-2-3 for DOS activates POINT mode; the screen appears similar to the screen in Figure 8.12.

currently selected range

mode indicator

B7: (,0) 325421
Range: B7..B7

POINT

	A	B	C	D	E	F
1						
2		PROFIT AND LOSS PROJECTION – 1989				
3						
4		Q1	Q2	Q3	Q4	
5						
6	Revenues					
7	Product Sales	325,421	331,929	338,568	345,339	
8	Rentals	81,335	82,982	84,642	86,335	
9	Maintenance Fees	48,813	49,789	58,785	51,881	
10		455,569	464,700	481,995	483,555	
11						
12	Cost of Sales					
13	Material Costs	177,688	181,234	184,858	188,555	
14	Packaging Costs	7,107	7,249	7,394	7,542	
15	Shipping Costs	11,194	11,418	11,644	11,879	
16	Sales Commissions	16,271	16,596	233,361	23,828	
17		212,260	216,497	437,257	231,804	
18						
19						
20						

11-Jan-92 09:10 AM NUM

Figure 8.12. 1-2-3 for DOS in POINT mode.

3. Use the directional keys to highlight the range.

   As you press an arrow key, 1-2-3 for DOS extends the highlighted range in the worksheet area and includes the cells in the range specification that appears in the control panel.

4. When the entire range is highlighted, press **Enter**.

   1-2-3 for DOS returns to READY mode, and you can activate the menus to choose commands. Or, you can choose a SmartIcon.

You can cancel a selection by pressing the Esc key.

To select cells by using the mouse, you drag the mouse pointer. Follow these steps:

1. Place the mouse pointer on the first cell you want to select. Click and hold down the left mouse button.

2. Slide the mouse in the direction of the other cells you want to select.

   As you slide the mouse, a **reverse video bar** (or **highlight**) appears over the cells you are selecting. You can slide the mouse diagonally to select a rectangle that contains more than one row and more than one column of cells.

3. Continue sliding the mouse until you reach the end of the cells you want to select.

4. Release the left mouse button.

   The cells you want to select are highlighted—a reverse video bar appears over them.

In Figure 8.13, cells B7 through B9 are selected. When referring to a block of cells (such as B7 through B9), 1-2-3 for DOS, like 1-2-3 for the Mac, uses the notation `B7..B9`.

B7: (,0) 325421 READY

	A	B	C	D	E	F
1						
2		PROFIT AND LOSS PROJECTION – 1989				
3						
4		Q1	Q2	Q3	Q4	
5						
6	Revenues					
7	Product Sales	325,421	331,929	338,568	345,339	
8	Rentals	81,335	82,982	84,642	86,335	
9	Maintenance Fees	48,813	49,789	58,785	51,881	
10		455,569	464,700	481,995	483,555	
11						
12	Cost of Sales					
13	Material Costs	177,688	181,234	184,858	188,555	
14	Packaging Costs	7,107	7,249	7,394	7,542	
15	Shipping Costs	11,194	11,418	11,644	11,879	
16	Sales Commissions	16,271	16,596	233,361	23,828	
17		212,260	216,497	437,257	231,804	
18						
19						
20						

11-Jan-92 09:36 AM NUM

Figure 8.13.
Cells B7 through B9 are selected.

You can cancel a selection by clicking the mouse anywhere else onscreen.

Saving a 1-2-3 for DOS File

After you have made the changes you need to make, you will want to save the worksheet. Unlike 1-2-3 for the Mac, you use only one Save command to save a worksheet. And although it is easiest to save an existing worksheet under its original name, you may not want to write over the original worksheet file with your changes. Therefore, you first learn how to save a worksheet to a different name.

To save an existing worksheet under a different name, follow these steps:

1. Activate the 1-2-3 for DOS Main menu by pressing **/**.

2. Choose the **F**ile command.

   1-2-3 for DOS displays the **F**ile menu.

3. Choose the **S**ave command.

   1-2-3 for DOS displays the current name of the file on the second line of the control panel.

4. To save the worksheet using a different name, type a new name (8 characters or less, no extension) and press **Enter**.

   1-2-3 for DOS saves the file using the name you specified.

To save an existing worksheet under its original name, follow these steps:

1. Activate the 1-2-3 for DOS Main menu by pressing **/**.

2. Choose the **F**ile command.

   1-2-3 for DOS displays the **F**ile menu.

3. Choose the **S**ave command.

1-2-3 for DOS displays the current name of the file on the second line of the control panel.

4. To save the worksheet using the same name, press **Enter**.

1-2-3 for DOS displays the menu you see in Figure 8.14.

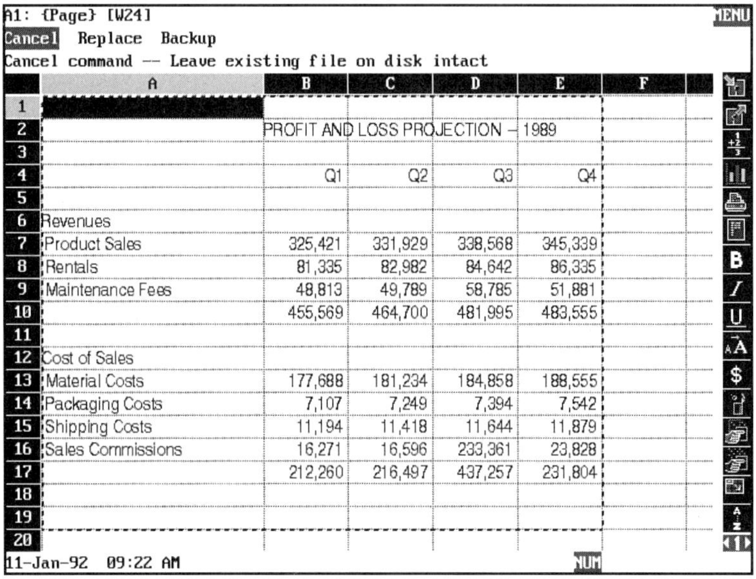

```
A1: {Page} [W24]                                                    MENU
Cancel  Replace  Backup
Cancel command -- Leave existing file on disk intact
```

	A	B	C	D	E	F
1						
2		PROFIT AND LOSS PROJECTION -- 1989				
3						
4		Q1	Q2	Q3	Q4	
5						
6	Revenues					
7	Product Sales	325,421	331,929	338,568	345,339	
8	Rentals	81,335	82,982	84,642	86,335	
9	Maintenance Fees	48,813	49,789	58,785	51,881	
10		455,569	464,700	481,995	483,555	
11						
12	Cost of Sales					
13	Material Costs	177,688	181,234	184,858	188,555	
14	Packaging Costs	7,107	7,249	7,394	7,542	
15	Shipping Costs	11,194	11,418	11,644	11,879	
16	Sales Commissions	16,271	16,596	233,361	23,828	
17		212,260	216,497	437,257	231,804	
18						
19						
20						

```
11-Jan-92  09:22 AM                                          NUM
```

Figure 8.14. The choices you see when saving a file under its original name.

5. To replace the original worksheet with the one you have modified, choose **R**eplace. To save both the original worksheet and the one you have modified, choose **B**ackup. (The original file will not automatically appear in the list that appears when you retrieve files, but an experienced 1-2-3 for DOS user will know how to retrieve it.) To abort saving, choose **C**ancel.

Printing a 1-2-3 for DOS File

After you have edited and saved the worksheet, you may want to print it. Before you print the worksheet, you may want to see onscreen the way it will look when printed. To preview and print a worksheet that includes publishing characteristics (such as boldface type or underlining), you use the **P**rint command on the Wysiwyg menu.

PC NOTE

If you use the **P**rint command on the 1-2-3 for DOS Main menu, the worksheet will print without any print enhancements (without boldface type or underlining, for example). This method is faster, but incomplete if such formatting exists in the worksheet.

To preview a worksheet onscreen and then print it, you must open the Print dialog box and make any appropriate changes. When you activate the Wysiwyg menu bar by pressing the colon (:) key and then choose the **P**rint command, 1-2-3 for DOS displays the Wysiwyg **P**rint menu in the control panel, and the Print dialog box covers up the worksheet area (see Figure 8.15).

You use the commands on the **P**rint menu to change the settings that appear in the Print dialog box. For the most part, each of the commands that appear in the control panel represent an area that appears in the Print dialog box. For example, the **R**ange command controls the Print Range information that appears in the middle of the left side of the Print dialog box; the **S**ettings command controls the information in the Settings box. To contradict myself, however, the **L**ayout command controls the information in both the Margins box and the Layout box.

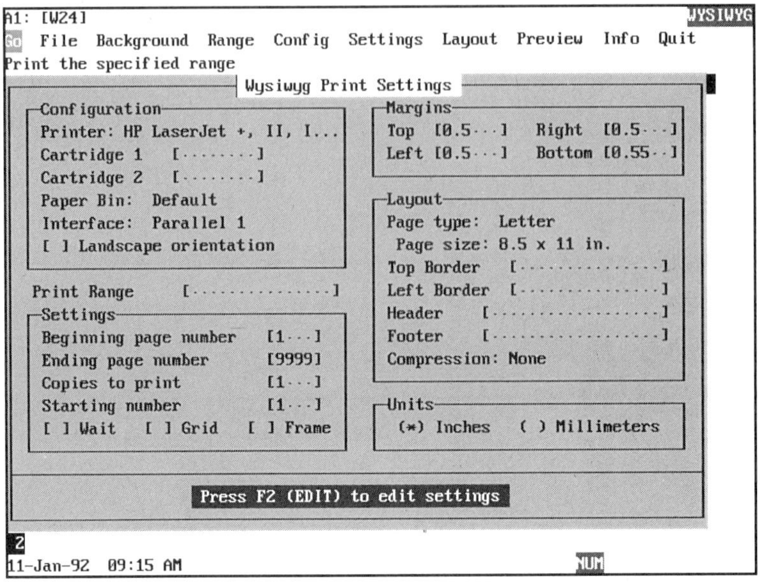

```
A1: [W24]                                                             WYSIWYG
Go  File  Background  Range  Config  Settings  Layout  Preview  Info  Quit
Print the specified range
                         Wysiwyg Print Settings
 Configuration                          Margins
 Printer: HP LaserJet +, II, I...       Top  [0.5···]   Right  [0.5···]
 Cartridge 1   [·········]              Left [0.5···]   Bottom [0.55··]
 Cartridge 2   [·········]
 Paper Bin:  Default                    Layout
 Interface:  Parallel 1                 Page type:  Letter
 [ ] Landscape orientation               Page size: 8.5 x 11 in.
                                        Top Border   [···············]
 Print Range     [················]     Left Border  [···············]
 Settings                               Header    [··················]
 Beginning page number     [1···]       Footer    [··················]
 Ending page number        [9999]       Compression: None
 Copies to print           [1···]
 Starting number           [1···]       Units
 [ ] Wait    [ ] Grid    [ ] Frame       (*) Inches    ( ) Millimeters

                   Press F2 (EDIT) to edit settings
2
11-Jan-92  09:15 AM                                            NUM
```

Figure 8.15.

The Wysiwyg **P**rint menu and the Print dialog box.

1-2-3 for DOS remembers print settings when you save a worksheet. For this reason, if you are editing an existing worksheet, you may not need to make many changes to the settings that appear in the Print dialog box because someone may already have set it up for you.

If you are unfamiliar with the meanings of the options in the dialog box, make changes using the commands on the menus; when you highlight a command, you will see Help information about the command and the options. If you are familiar with the meanings of the options in the dialog box (or if you simply hate menus), you can make changes by directly editing the dialog box.

You can use the keyboard or the mouse to work in the dialog box and select options. To use the keyboard, you must activate the dialog box by pressing F2. Then, 1-2-3 for DOS removes the menu bar from the control panel and highlights certain letters in the dialog box. To move from option to option, press the Tab key. To use the mouse, you don't activate the dialog box; you activate the option directly by clicking on it.

In the Print dialog box, you can work with the following items:

- You use a **text box** to enter text. The Beginning Page Number box is a text box. To change the information in a text box, type over the existing information or use the techniques described earlier.

- You use a **check box** to choose one or more options from a group of related alternatives. An X appears in the check boxes of the activated options. The Wait, Grid, and Frame options in the Settings box are check boxes. To choose a check box by using a mouse, click on the check box. To choose a check box by using the keyboard, press the Tab key to highlight the check box and then press the spacebar to add or remove the X.

- You use an **option box** to choose one option from a group of related options. An asterisk appears in the box of the current option; no letters appear highlighted in the option box until you press the Tab key. The Units box contains two options: **I**nches and **M**illimeters. To choose an option by using a mouse, click on the option box. To choose an option box by using the keyboard, press the Tab key to highlight the box containing the options and then press the arrow keys or type the underlined letter in the option name.

After you finish changing options by editing the dialog box directly, choose the OK button to save the changes you made.

To preview a worksheet onscreen and then print it, follow these steps:

1. Activate the Wysiwyg menu by pressing the colon (**:**) key.

2. Choose the **P**rint command.

3. From the **P**rint menu, choose the **R**ange command.

   Wysiwyg displays the **R**ange submenu.

4. Choose **S**et from the **R**ange submenu.

Wysiwyg redisplays the worksheet, enabling you to set a print range (see Figure 8.16).

A1: [W24] POINT

Specify the range to print: A1

	A	B	C	D	E	F
1						
2		PROFIT AND LOSS PROJECTION – 1989				
3						
4		Q1	Q2	Q3	Q4	
5						
6	Revenues					
7	Product Sales	325,421	331,929	338,568	345,339	
8	Rentals	81,335	82,982	84,642	86,335	
9	Maintenance Fees	48,813	49,789	58,785	51,881	
10		455,569	464,700	481,995	483,555	
11						
12	Cost of Sales					
13	Material Costs	177,688	181,234	184,858	188,555	
14	Packaging Costs	7,107	7,249	7,394	7,542	
15	Shipping Costs	11,194	11,418	11,644	11,879	
16	Sales Commissions	16,271	16,596	233,361	23,828	
17		212,260	216,497	437,257	231,804	
18						
19						
20						

11-Jan-92 09:15 AM NUM

Figure 8.16.

The worksheet when setting a print range.

5. Select the cells you want to print.

Wysiwyg redisplays the **P**rint menu and the Print dialog box.

6. Choose **P**review from the **P**rint menu.

1-2-3 for DOS displays the layout of your worksheet as it will appear when you print it (see Figure 8.17).

You cannot edit on this screen, but you can see the way the worksheet will look when it prints. If, for example, you see gridlines appearing around the cells, gridlines will print. To return to the **P**rint menu and the Print dialog box, press any key on the keyboard or click the mouse anywhere onscreen.

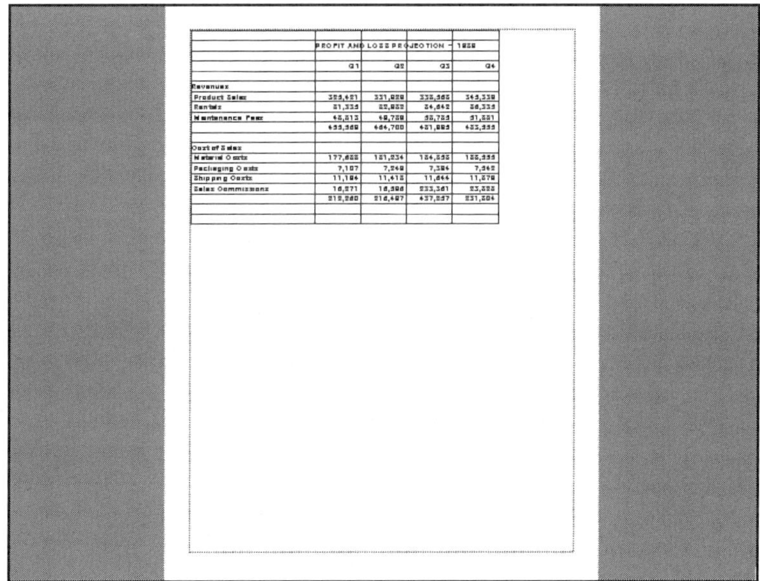

Figure 8.17.

A sample Print Preview screen.

7. Choose the **G**o command from the **P**rint menu to print the worksheet.

   1-2-3 for DOS prints the worksheet as it appeared when you previewed it.

Copying a 1-2-3 for DOS File to a Floppy Disk

You may find that you need to copy a 1-2-3 for DOS file to a floppy disk. You may need to print the file from another PC, for example. Using the **S**ave command to save the current worksheet to a floppy is the easiest way to copy a 1-2-3 for DOS worksheet to a floppy disk. Alternatively, you can use DOS commands, which you can find in Chapter 12.

Before you begin, make sure that the worksheet you want to place on a floppy disk is onscreen. If it is not onscreen, follow these basic steps (or the more detailed steps earlier in the chapter) to open it:

1. Press **/** to activate the 1-2-3 for DOS Main menu and choose the **F**ile command.

2. Choose the **R**etrieve command from the **F**ile menu.

3. Choose the file that you want to copy, and then press **Enter**.

To copy the current worksheet to a floppy disk, follow these steps:

1. Insert a formatted disk into the floppy disk drive.

2. Press **/** to activate the 1-2-3 for DOS Main menu, and then choose the **F**ile command.

3. From the **F**ile menu, choose the **S**ave command.

   1-2-3 for DOS displays the screen in Figure 8.18.

```
A1: {Page} [W24]                                              EDIT
Enter name of file to save: D:\123R24\123DATA\AWSAMPLE.WK1
```

	A	B	C	D	E	F
1						
2		PROFIT AND LOSS PROJECTION – 1989				
3						
4		Q1	Q2	Q3	Q4	
5						
6	Revenues					
7	Product Sales	325,421	331,929	338,568	345,339	
8	Rentals	81,335	82,982	84,642	86,335	
9	Maintenance Fees	48,813	49,789	58,785	51,881	
10		455,569	464,700	481,995	483,555	
11						
12	Cost of Sales					
13	Material Costs	177,688	181,234	184,858	188,555	
14	Packaging Costs	7,107	7,249	7,394	7,542	
15	Shipping Costs	11,194	11,418	11,644	11,879	
16	Sales Commissions	16,271	16,596	233,361	23,828	
17		212,260	216,497	437,257	231,804	
18						
19						
20						

```
11-Jan-92  09:22 AM                                  NUM
```

Figure 8.18. The screen you see when you choose the **S**ave command.

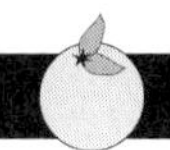

4. Press the **Esc** key three times to clear the file name from the control panel.

5. Type the name of the floppy disk drive in which you placed the disk. If you placed the floppy disk in drive A, for example, type `A:` (be sure to type the colon).

6. Type the name you want to give the file on the floppy disk, using no more than 8 characters and no extension. Then, press **Enter**.

   1-2-3 for DOS copies the file to the floppy disk. If a file with the same name already exists on the floppy disk, 1-2-3 for DOS asks whether you want to replace the file on the floppy disk. If you *don't* want to write over a file on the floppy disk, choose **C**ancel and start the process over again, either inserting a new floppy disk or typing a different file name.

Exiting 1-2-3 for DOS

When you are finished using 1-2-3 for DOS, you can exit by choosing the **Q**uit command from the 1-2-3 for DOS Main menu. 1-2-3 for DOS displays a Yes-or-No submenu asking whether you want to quit or return to editing. After you choose the **Y**es command (to say that you really want to quit), 1-2-3 for DOS checks whether the worksheet contains changes you didn't save. If the worksheet does contain changes you didn't save, 1-2-3 for DOS displays another Yes-or-No submenu asking whether you want to quit without saving the changes. Choose **Y**es to quit without saving changes, or choose **N**o to return to the worksheet. If you choose **N**o, you then can save the worksheet by using the information in the preceding section.

When you exit from 1-2-3 for DOS, you return to DOS (or a menu or the MS-DOS Shell). At this point, you safely can turn off the PC.

Chapter Summary

In this chapter, you learned how to use the online Help facility in 1-2-3 for DOS. You also learned how to open, edit, print, and save a 1-2-3 for DOS worksheet; how to copy a 1-2-3 for DOS file to a floppy disk; and how to exit from 1-2-3 for DOS.

Unless you have been using 1-2-3 Classic menus in 1-2-3 for the Mac, there are very few similarities between 1-2-3 for DOS and 1-2-3 for the Mac. If you have been using the 1-2-3 Classic menus in 1-2-3 for the Mac, then almost everything is familiar to you. But, as a Mac user, it isn't likely that you would use the 1-2-3 Classic menus in 1-2-3 for the Mac.

Both 1-2-3 for DOS and 1-2-3 for the Mac use menus. Both programs use the Save command, the Print command, and the Help command. Some of the keystroke navigation is similar, and you can use the mouse to select cells the same way in both packages. These are the only similarities I can identify. Reaching, aren't I?

In the next chapter, you learn how to work with Lotus 1-2-3 for Windows. As you know, Chapters 3 through 9 in *The Mac User's PC* focus on specific software packages. You should read the chapters that pertain to the software you want to use. Chapter 10 tells you about database programs you may want to avoid. Chapter 11 discusses the MS-DOS Shell. Refer to Chapter 12 for information on file-naming conventions imposed on 1-2-3 for DOS by the operating system, and for information on working with basic DOS commands. If you need to transfer and translate files between a PC and a Mac, read Chapter 13.

ONE
TWO
THREE
FOUR
FIVE
SIX
SEVEN
EIGHT
NINE
TEN
ELEVEN
TWELVE
THIRTEEN
GLOSSARY

Working with 1-2-3 for Windows Files

In the first two chapters of *The Mac User's PC*, you learned about the physical appearance of a PC, how to turn on a PC, how to recognize what you may see onscreen, and how to start programs. In this chapter, you will learn very basic information about using Lotus 1-2-3 for Windows. This chapter is not intended to make you an expert at 1-2-3 for Windows; this chapter simply teaches you how to perform some basic tasks. You will learn how to open, edit, print, and save a 1-2-3 for Windows worksheet; how to copy a 1-2-3 for Windows file to a floppy disk; and how to exit the program properly. And you will learn one other important thing—how to get help in 1-2-3 for Windows so that you can teach yourself to do the things that aren't covered in this book.

And, there's some good news for Mac users. 1-2-3 for Windows operates very similarly to 1-2-3 for the Mac. If you use 1-2-3 for the Mac, using 1-2-3 for Windows should be fairly easy.

Before you can start 1-2-3 for Windows, you must start Microsoft Windows. Let's review some basic information about Windows.

Reviewing Windows Basics

Microsoft Windows is an operating environment that, in the world of DOS, provides a graphical user interface (also called GUI, pronounced "gooey") with which you can use either a mouse or a keyboard. The Microsoft Windows screen most closely resembles the Desktop on a Macintosh. Figure 9.1 shows a sample opening screen in Windows 3.1.

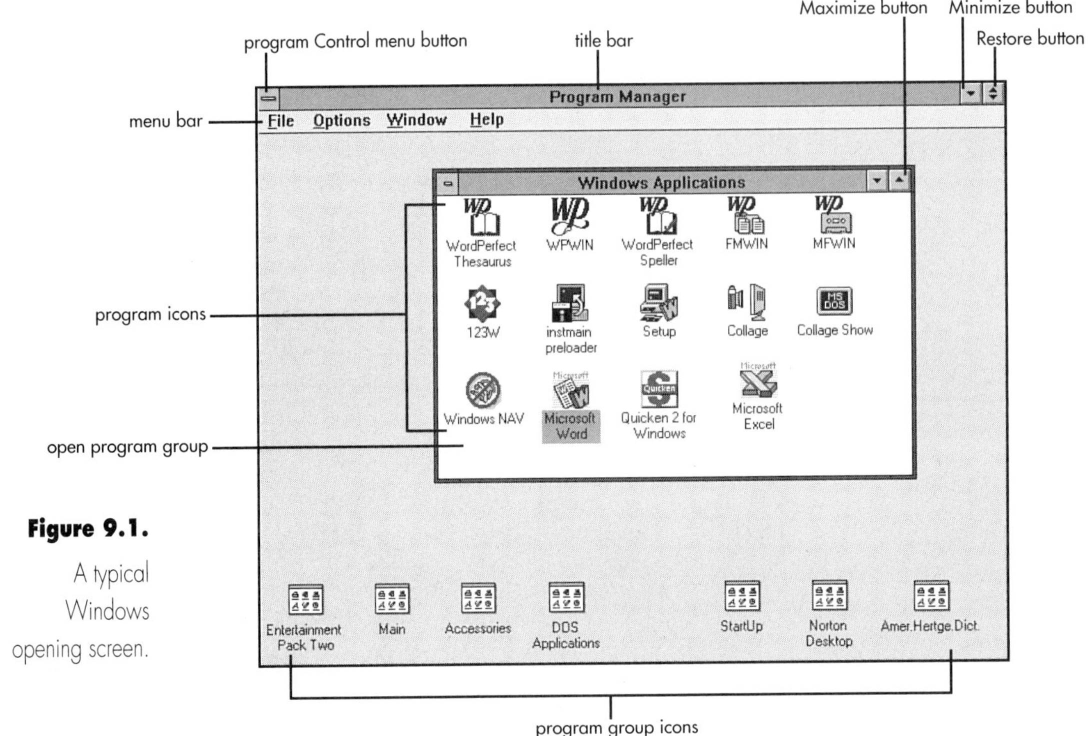

Figure 9.1.

A typical Windows opening screen.

If Microsoft Windows doesn't appear onscreen when you start the PC, type `WIN` at the DOS prompt.

As you learned in Chapter 2, Windows permits the user to perform multitasking. **Multitasking** enables the user to perform two or more functions simultaneously. To support multitasking, Windows and its Program Manager provide a way to manage the memory of the computer. Each program obtains enough memory to perform its functions; otherwise, Windows warns the user that sufficient memory is unavailable to perform all the requested tasks.

You can use a mouse or the keyboard to navigate in Windows, and you start programs from the Program Manager in Windows.

Understanding the Program Manager Screen

When you start Windows, the **Program Manager** appears. At the very top of every Windows screen, you see in the **title bar** the name of the program that is currently running . In Figure 9.1, `Program Manager` appears in the title bar.

At the left end of the title bar, you see the program **Control menu button**, a small box that contains a hyphen. You can use the program Control menu to change the size of the screen that displays the Program Manager, to close the Program Manager, and to switch to another program.

At the right end of the title bar, you see two buttons. Rather than using the Control menu, you can click on these buttons to change the size of the screen that displays the Program Manager:

- Choose the **Minimize button** to reduce the entire Program Manager screen to an icon. If you minimize a program, you choose its icon to return the program to the size it was before you minimized it.

- If the Program Manager fills the entire screen (as it does in Figure 9.1), then you see the Restore button (rather than the Maximize button). Choose the **Restore button** to reduce the Program Manager screen to a size somewhere between minimum and maximum (see Figure 9.2).

- If the Program Manager does not fill the entire screen, but appears similar to Figure 9.2, then you see the Maximize button (rather than the Restore button). Choose the **Maximize button** to enlarge the Program Manager to fill the entire screen.

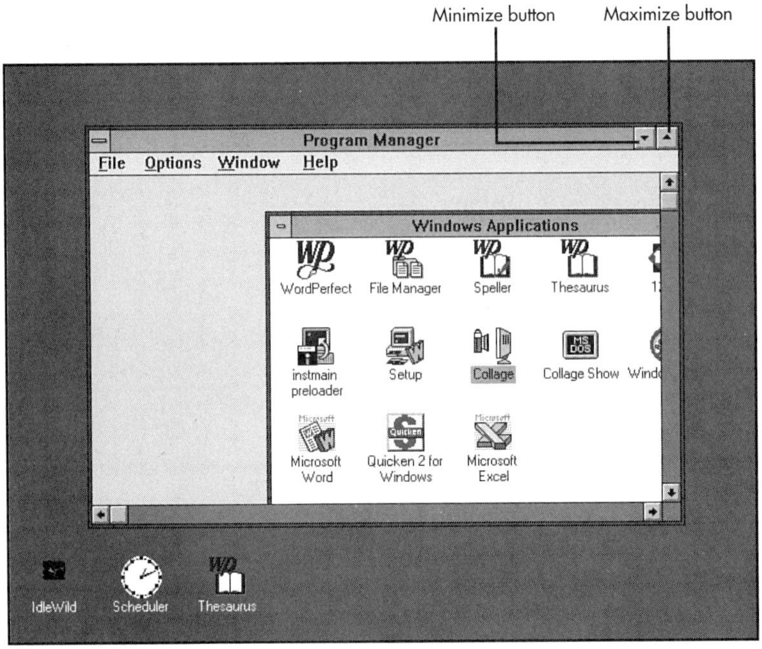

Figure 9.2.

The Program Manager when it doesn't fill the entire screen.

Just below the title bar, you see the **menu bar**. The menu bar contains **menus**, and each menu contains the **commands** (also called "menu commands") you use in Windows—but more about these in a moment.

The Program Manager contains **program groups**, which can appear either as open windows or as icons. In Figures 9.1 and 9.2, the Windows Applications program group appears as an open window while all the other program groups appear as **icons** at the bottom of the screen. Notice that the Windows Applications program group (and any open program group) also has a title bar, a Control menu, and Minimize and Maximize (or Restore) buttons. Open program groups do not, however, have menu bars.

Each program group contains icons that represent programs. You use these icons to start the programs. To start a program, the program group must be open so that you can see and access the icon that represents the program you want to start.

Navigating in Windows

While working in Windows, you can use the mouse or the keyboard to perform certain tasks. In the following sections, you will find instructions on how to use the mouse and the keyboard to open menus, **choose** commands from menus, choose options in dialog boxes, and start programs.

In Windows, a mouse operates differently from a mouse on a Macintosh. Before you learn the specifics of performing each of the previously mentioned actions, let's review the way in which a mouse operates in Windows.

Operating a Mouse in Windows

Using a mouse in Windows is a two-step process. To use a mouse to choose an item in Windows, follow these steps:

1. Slide the mouse until the mouse pointer points to the item you want to choose.
2. Press and release a mouse button—usually the left mouse button—one time.

The action you perform in step 1 is known as **pointing**, and the action you perform in step 2 is known as **clicking**. You can click either the left or the right mouse button, as defined by the software program you are using. Most of the time, to choose an item, you click the left mouse button. You also may have occasion to double-click. To **double-click**, you press and release the left mouse button twice in rapid succession. Occasionally, you may need to drag an item to move it from one location to another. To **drag**, point to the item you want to drag. Then, press and hold the left mouse button while sliding the mouse to move the mouse pointer to the new location.

Note the difference in the way clicking works in Windows compared to on a Mac. In Windows, for the most part, you don't need to hold down the mouse button while opening a menu and choosing a command; the menu remains open after you release the mouse button. On a Mac, when you release the mouse button, the menu from which you were trying to choose a command closes.

Working with Menus and Commands in Windows

The menu bar appears just below the title bar. Each menu contains the commands you use in Windows. To see the commands, you can open a menu by using the mouse or the keyboard.

To open a menu by using the mouse, point to the menu you want to open and click the left mouse button. Windows opens the menu. Unlike a menu on a Mac, the menu remains open when you release the mouse button, and the first command on the menu appears highlighted. To choose a command by using the mouse, point to the command and click the left mouse button. Windows executes the command.

You also can use the keyboard to open a menu and choose a command. First, you activate the menu bar by pressing the Alt key. A **reverse video bar** (or **highlight**) appears on the name of the first menu, **F**ile. Then, you can open a menu and choose a command in two ways:

- You can use the hot key shortcuts. Each menu and command contains an underlined letter, also called a **hot key**. You can press that key to open the menu or execute the command. When you press the W key, for example, the Program Manager opens the **W**indow menu and displays the commands available on that menu. In this book, all references to hot keys appear in boldface type.

- You can press one of the arrow keys on the keyboard to point to a menu or command, and then press the Enter key to choose it. When you press an arrow key, the reverse video bar moves. Continue pressing the arrow key until the reverse video bar appears on top of the menu or command to which you want to point. For example, you can press the Alt key to activate the menu bar, and then press the left-arrow key twice to point to the **W**indow menu. Remember, when you use the arrow keys to point to a menu or command, you must press Enter to open that menu or choose that command.

PC NOTE

If you activate the menu bar and then press the right-arrow key four times, you highlight the Control menu. The Control menu contains the commands that control the size of the Program Manager screen. To open the Control menu after you have highlighted it, press Enter. If you have any open program group windows and you activate the menu bar and then press the right-arrow key five times, you activate the Control menu of the group window. Again, press Enter to open that Control menu.

Working with Dialog Boxes in Windows

Ellipses (...) appear after some commands on the menus. The program requires additional information about these commands before it can execute them. When you choose a command that includes an ellipsis, a **dialog box** (in which you supply the additional required information) appears.

The dialog boxes that appear when you choose a command from the Program Manager's **F**ile menu are not typical of the dialog boxes you see and use in application programs. So, there's not

much point in describing one of those dialog boxes. Instead, Figure 9.3 displays a more typical dialog box that contains a representative sample of types of dialog box options. Each dialog box is different, and most dialog boxes provide only some of these options.

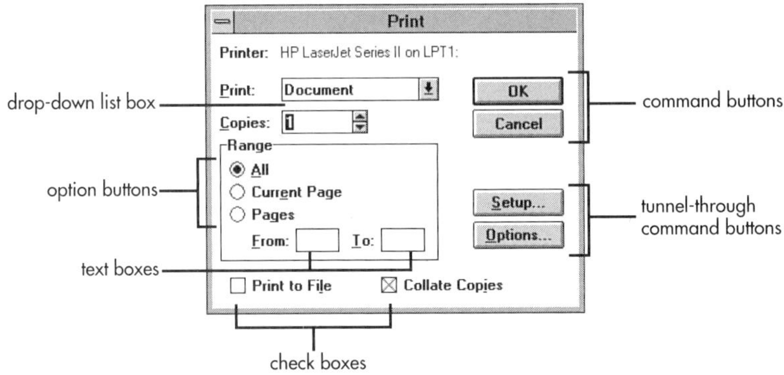

Figure 9.3.

A typical dialog box.

PC NOTE

You may notice a dotted line surrounding an option. This line indicates the current mouse pointer position. If you are using the keyboard rather than a mouse, you can use the Tab key to move around a dialog box.

A **list box** contains a list of options. You may see two kinds of list boxes in a dialog box. The **P**rint list box in Figure 9.3 is an example of a **drop-down list box** and is closed when the dialog box appears. To open a drop-down list box, click on the down arrow at the right end of the box; or, hold down the Alt key and type the underlined letter in the list box name. The other type of list box is already open when the dialog box appears. To choose an item from either type of list box, click on the item or press the down-arrow key to point to the item and then press Enter. If the list box is not long enough to display all the available items in the list, click the scroll arrow or press and hold the down-arrow key to move beyond the items that appear in the box.

An **option button** is a small round button you use to choose one option from a group of related options. A black dot appears in the button of the current option. To choose an option button, click on the option button; or, hold down the Alt key and type the underlined letter in the option name. In the Range box, the **A**ll, Curr**e**nt Page, and Pa**g**es buttons are option buttons.

A **check box** is a small square box you use to choose an option. You can choose more than one check box from a group of related options. An X appears in the check boxes of the activated options. To choose a check box, click on the check box; or, hold down the Alt key and type the underlined letter in the option name. To deactivate the option and remove the X from the box, choose the check box again. In Figure 9.3, the Print to Fi**l**e and Collate Cop**i**es check boxes appear at the bottom of the dialog box.

A **text box** is a rectangular box in which you enter text. When a dialog box that contains a text box opens, the current text is usually selected. To replace the selected text, simply type the new information. In Figure 9.3, the Range area contains two text boxes (**F**rom and **T**o), and the **C**opies box also is a text box.

A **command button** is an oblong button that performs an action. To choose a command button, click on the button; or, use the Tab key to highlight the button and press Enter. In Figure 9.3, the OK button accepts the settings in the dialog box. The Cancel button cancels your changes to the settings in the dialog box. The default command button, which changes from dialog box to dialog box, appears highlighted (its outline appears darker than the other buttons). As on a Mac, if you press Enter, you choose the highlighted command button.

A **tunnel-through command button** is a button that contains ellipses (...) and opens another dialog box. To choose a tunnel-through command button, click on the button, highlight the button and press Enter, or hold down the Alt key and type the underlined letter. In Figure 9.3, the **S**etup and **O**ptions buttons are tunnel-through command buttons.

Starting a Program in Windows

As mentioned earlier, all programs reside in program groups in Windows. To start a program, its program group cannot appear minimized as an icon; the program group must be open.

To use the mouse to open a program group that appears as an icon, double-click on the icon.

To use the keyboard to open a program group that appears as an icon, follow these steps:

1. Press the **Alt** key to activate the menu bar.

2. Press **W** to open the **W**indow menu.

   The Program Manager displays the choices on the **W**indow menu (see Figure 9.4). You see a check mark next to the currently selected program group.

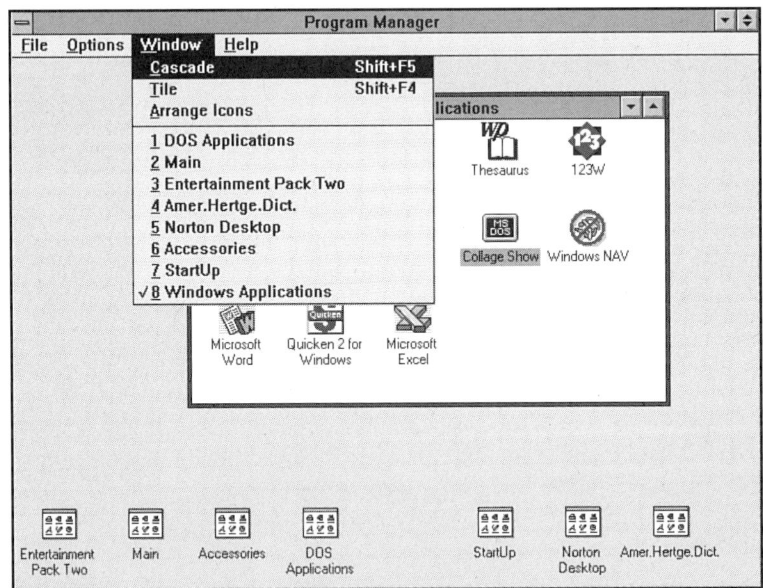

Figure 9.4. The **W**indow menu.

3. From the numbered options in the **W**indow menu, press a number to choose the program group you want to open.

   Windows opens the specified program group.

After you open the program group, you can start a program. To start a program by using the mouse, double-click on the icon representing the program in the program group window. The Program Manager starts the program.

To start a program by using the keyboard, use the arrow keys to point to the program you want to choose. Then, press Enter. The Program Manager starts the program.

Using one of the techniques just described, open the program group containing the 1-2-3 for Windows program icon and then start 1-2-3 for Windows. You may find the program icon in the Windows Applications group or in a 1-2-3 for Windows group. Or, you may find 1-2-3 for Windows somewhere altogether different because the owner of the PC has a different technique for organizing programs.

Identifying 1-2-3 for Windows Screen Parts

When you first start 1-2-3 for Windows, you see the default screen, which looks like the screen in Figure 9.5.

The top four lines of the screen are called the control panel. The control panel consists of the title bar, the menu bar, the format line, and the edit line. Like the opening Windows screen, you see the name of the program that is currently running, `1-2-3 for Windows`, in the title bar. The 1-2-3 for Windows program Control menu appears to the left of the title bar, and the program Minimize and Restore buttons appear to the right of the title bar. By default, 1-2-3 for Windows fills the screen when you start the program.

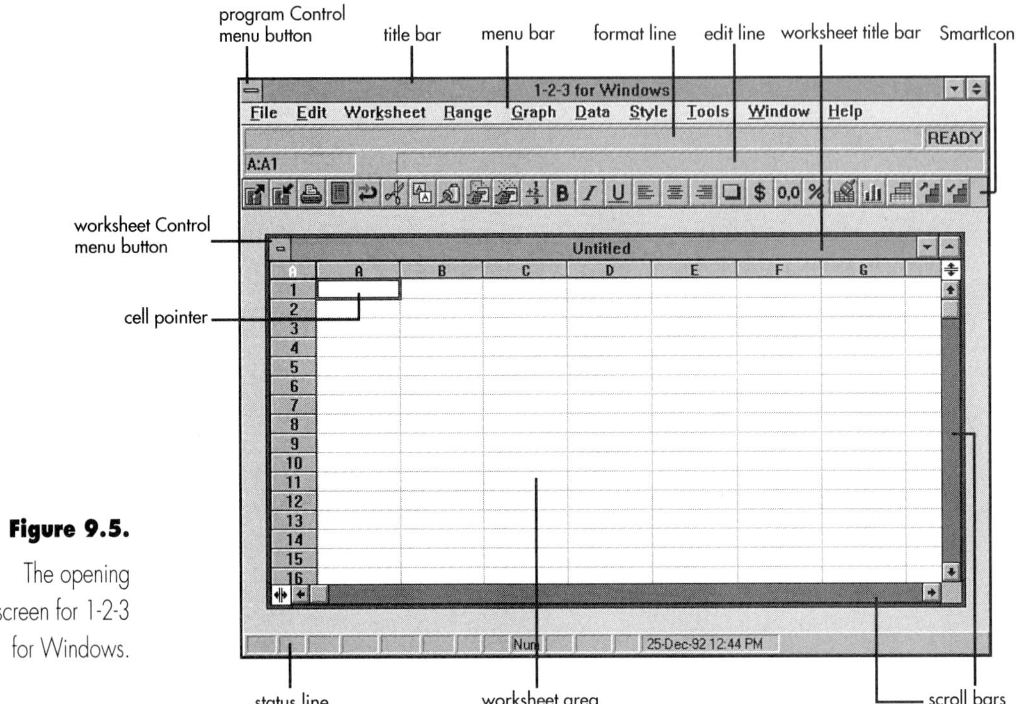

Figure 9.5.
The opening screen for 1-2-3 for Windows.

Just below the title bar, you see the **menu bar** for 1-2-3 for Windows menus. Just below the menu bar, you see the format line, where you can identify the mode in which 1-2-3 for Windows is currently operating. And just below the format line, you see the edit line, where you enter and edit data.

Just below the edit line, you see the SmartIcons, which are tools you can use as shortcuts to execute commands and bypass menus. You learn more about the SmartIcons in the next section.

Just below the SmartIcons, you see the worksheet title bar. At the left end of the worksheet title bar, you see the worksheet Control menu button; you can use this Control menu to change the amount of space assigned to the worksheet. At the right end of the worksheet title bar, you see the worksheet Maximize button. When you start the program, the worksheet portion of the window is not at its full size.

Below the worksheet title bar, you see the worksheet window. And below the worksheet window, you see the status line. For purposes of discussion, you can think of the screen as four different sections:

- The worksheet window
- The control panel
- The SmartIcons
- The status line

The Worksheet Window

The center area of the screen is the worksheet window. The worksheet window consists of lettered columns and numbered rows. The intersection of a column and a row is called a **cell**; you enter information into cells. The cell pointer, the darker rectangular outline, identifies the **active cell**—the location where text or numbers will appear when you type and press Enter. You refer to a cell by its cell address, the name of its column and row. In Figure 9.5, the cell pointer is in cell A1.

Within the worksheet window, you see panes, which are the portions of the window you can see onscreen at one time. In the **active pane** in Figure 9.5, you can see cells A1 through G16. Other cells, such as those in column H or in row 17, appear in a different pane.

The Control Panel

The control panel appears at the very top of the screen and consists of the program title bar, the menu bar, the format line, and the edit line. You open the menus to choose commands—you will learn more about working with menus later in this chapter. The format line contains some of the information you see in the status window of 1-2-3 for the Mac; in the format line, you can see the mode in which 1-2-3 is operating. The edit line contains some of the information you see in the console in 1-2-3 for the Mac and consists of two parts. At the left end of the edit line, you see the location of the cell pointer. In Figure 9.5, the cell pointer is located in cell A:A1, which is cell A1 of Sheet A. (In 1-2-3 for Windows, you can create worksheet files that consist of more than one sheet, but more about that in a moment.) In Figure 9.5, cell A:A1 contains nothing, as you can see by looking at the right side of the edit line. When you start typing or enter something into a cell, the cell's contents appear in the right side of the edit line.

In Figure 9.6, you see 456 on the right side of the edit line, because the active cell will contain the number 456 (after you press Enter).

Also in Figure 9.6, you see two new buttons to the left of the number on the edit line. These buttons appear when you type new information into a cell or when you edit the contents of the active cell. If you make a mistake while typing or editing, click on the left button (the one that looks like an X) or press the Esc key. 1-2-3 for Windows ignores your typing or editing and returns the cell's contents to what it originally contained. If you choose the right button (the one that looks like a check mark) or press Enter, 1-2-3 for Windows accepts your typing or editing and places the change in the active cell.

PC NOTE

If you start to type a number, the mode indicator on the format line changes from READY to VALUE.

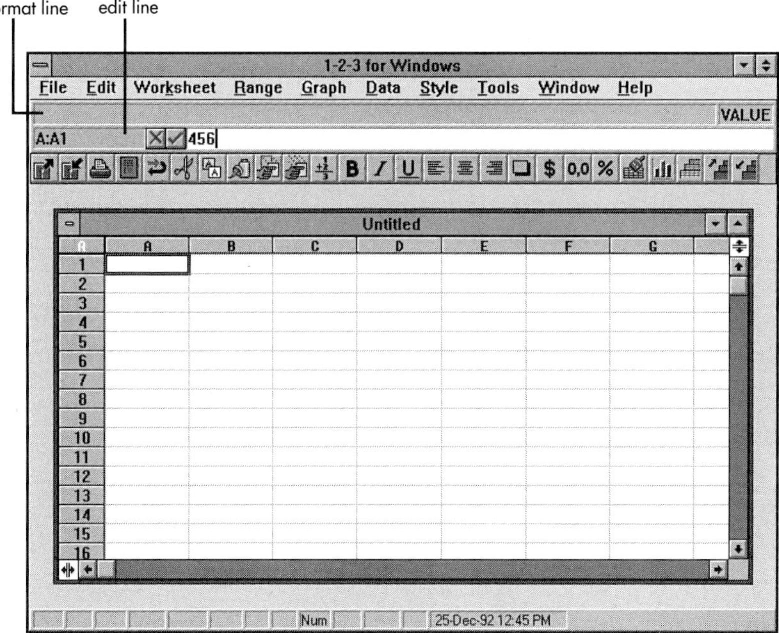

Figure 9.6.

As you start to type, the text appears in the edit line.

The SmartIcons

Just below the control panel, you see the SmartIcons. In 1-2-3 for the Mac, you can display the draw and style palettes, which don't exist in 1-2-3 for Windows. Some of the SmartIcons perform some of the functions you find on the style palette in 1-2-3 for the Mac. You can use the SmartIcons to shorten the process of performing a command. If you choose a SmartIcon, you don't have to use the menus. You choose a SmartIcon by using a mouse.

Working from the left end of the SmartIcons, you can perform the following tasks:

- Open an existing worksheet.
- Save the current worksheet.
- Print the specified range.

- Preview the print range.
- Undo the last command or action.
- Cut, copy, or paste to or from the Clipboard.
- Select the target range to copy or move.
- Add the nearest adjacent range.
- Apply boldface, italic, or underline character formatting to the active cell or selected cells.
- Set left-, center-, or right-alignment for the active cell or selected cells.
- Apply a drop shadow to the active cell or selected cells.
- Format the active cell or selected cells as currency ($), with commas ($1,000), or as percentages.
- Copy formats from the active cell to the cells you select.
- Open the graph window.
- View worksheets in perspective, three at a time. (This feature is most useful when working with three-dimensional worksheet files.)
- Move to the next or preceding worksheet in a three-dimensional worksheet file.

Because the SmartIcon bar can be customized, you may not see on your screen the same SmartIcons as you see in Figures 9.5 and 9.6. To find out the function of a SmartIcon, point to the SmartIcon and hold down the *right* mouse button. The purpose of the SmartIcon appears in the program title bar. To choose a SmartIcon, point to the SmartIcon and click the left mouse button.

The Status Line

Below the worksheet window, at the bottom of the program window, you see the status line. The status line displays information about the status of the PC. On the status line in Figures 9.5 and 9.6, for example, you see that the Num Lock feature is turned on. You also see the date and time of the computer system's internal clock.

Getting Help in 1-2-3 for Windows

1-2-3 for Windows contains an excellent online Help facility. In this section, you learn the basics of using Help in 1-2-3 for Windows.

Notice that you can choose the **U**sing Help command on the **H**elp menu to teach yourself to use Help in 1-2-3 for Windows (see Figure 9.7).

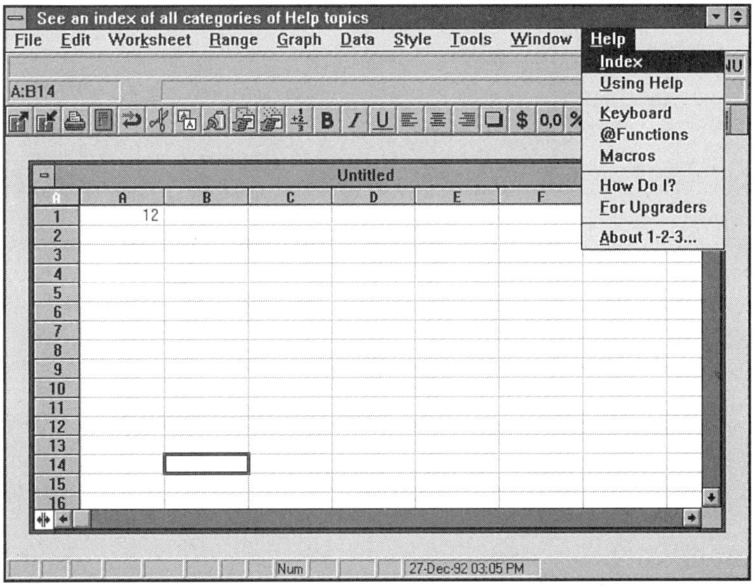

Figure 9.7.

The **H**elp menu.

You can display the Help Index window in 1-2-3 for Windows by pressing F1, or by opening the **H**elp menu and choosing the **I**ndex command (see Figure 9.8). In 1-2-3 for Windows, the help you receive is context-sensitive—if you are looking at a command on a menu and you press F1, the help you get is about that menu command.

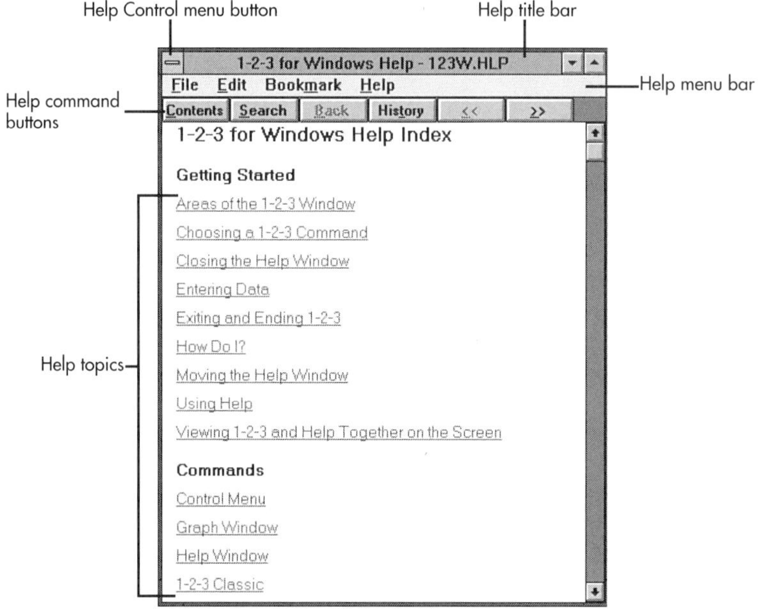

Figure 9.8.

The Help Index window.

When you view the Help Index window, you see Help topics. On a color monitor, these topics appear in green and are underlined. If the list of topics is too long to fit in one Help window, you can use the scroll bar on the right side of the window to view the rest of the topics. Using the mouse, you can click on the scroll arrows to move the topics in the window until you see the topic about which you want help. To choose the topic, click on it. Using the keyboard, you can press the down-arrow key to move the topics in the window. To choose the topic, press the Tab key to highlight the topic and then press Enter.

As you can see in the Help Index window, you can get basic information by choosing from the topics listed under `Getting Started`.

You can get help about 1-2-3 for Windows commands by choosing from the topics listed under `Commands`, or you can use Help as a reference guide by choosing from the alphabetically organized topics listed under `Reference`.

Back on the **H**elp menu (shown in Figure 9.9), you can choose the **K**eyboard command to get specific information about using the keyboard. Or, you can choose the **@**Functions command to get specific information about 1-2-3 for Windows functions. Or, you can choose the **M**acros command to get information about creating macros in 1-2-3 for Windows.

If you choose the **H**ow Do I? command, you see a window similar to the window in Figure 9.9.

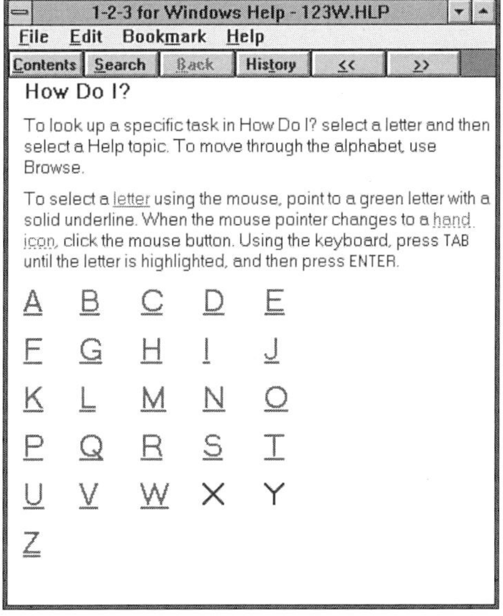

Figure 9.9.

The `How Do I?` window.

From this window, you can choose a letter to see an alphabetical listing of topics available in Help that begin with that letter.

You can use the **S**earch button in the Help window to open the Search dialog box in Figure 9.10 and search for topics you specify.

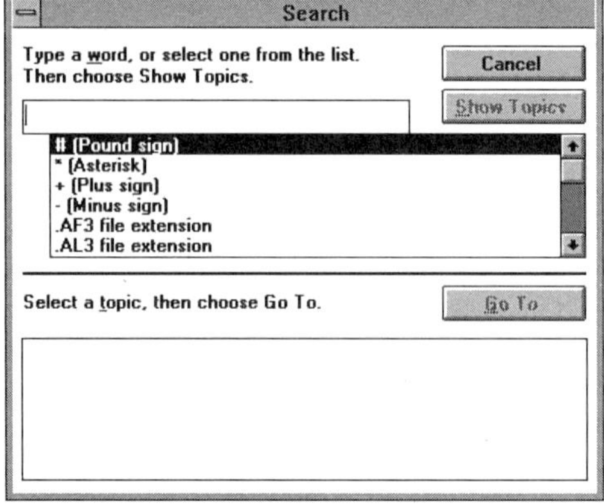

Figure 9.10. The Search dialog box.

To use the Search dialog box, follow these steps:

1. Type a **w**ord that represents the topic for which you want to search.

   As you type, 1-2-3 for Windows Help highlights the topic that most closely matches the characters you type.

2. Choose the **S**how Topics button.

   In the bottom portion of the dialog box, 1-2-3 for Windows Help displays the topics that most closely match the characters you typed.

3. Choose a topic from the list, and then choose the **G**o To button.

   1-2-3 for Windows Help displays the topic you chose.

You can print the information that appears in Help windows by choosing the **P**rint Topic command on the Help window's **F**ile menu.

If you find a topic in Help to which you might want to return later (without having to remember how you got there in the first place), create a bookmark for the topic. Follow these steps:

1. While viewing the topic you want to mark, open the Book**m**ark menu on the Help window's menu bar.

2. Choose the **D**efine command.

   1-2-3 for Windows Help displays the Bookmark Define dialog box shown in Figure 9.11. The name of the topic you are viewing appears in the **B**ookmark Name text box.

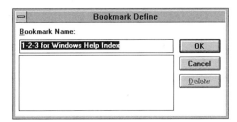

   Bookmark Define
   Bookmark Name:
   1-2-3 for Windows Help Index
   OK
   Cancel
   Delete

   Figure 9.11. The Bookmark Define dialog box.

3. If you want to change the bookmark name, type a new name; otherwise, 1-2-3 for Windows will use the topic name as the bookmark name.

4. Choose OK.

   1-2-3 for Windows stores the topic name on the Book**m**ark menu.

When you open the Book**m**ark menu again, you see below the **D**efine command the topic for which you stored a bookmark. If you choose the topic from the Book**m**ark menu, 1-2-3 for Windows Help displays the topic.

After viewing several topics, you can use the **C**ontents button to redisplay the Help Index window. Or, you can use the **B**ack button to redisplay in reverse order the topics you viewed. You also can return directly to any topic you displayed by choosing the His**t**ory button. When you choose the His**t**ory button, 1-2-3 for Windows Help displays the Help History window, in which you can see every topic you viewed since you started Help. If you looked at a topic more than once, it appears more than once in the Help History window. To go to a topic listed in the Help History window, double-click on the topic; or, use the arrow keys to point to the topic and then press Enter.

PC NOTE

If you close Help, 1-2-3 for Windows also closes the history of your Help session and no longer maintains the history of the Help screens you viewed. When you open Help again, 1-2-3 for Windows starts the history over again.

You can learn more about the 1-2-3 for Windows Help facility by opening the **H**elp menu on the Help window's menu bar and choosing **H**ow To Use Help. Or, as mentioned previously, you can choose **U**sing Help from the 1-2-3 for Windows **H**elp menu.

Opening a 1-2-3 for Windows File

Suppose that someone brings you a worksheet, asks you to make some minor changes to it, and then wants you to print the revised worksheet. In this section, you learn how to open an existing 1-2-3 for Windows worksheet. In the next three sections, you learn how to edit, save, and print a 1-2-3 for Windows worksheet.

Opening a 1-2-3 for Windows file is similar to opening a 1-2-3 for the Mac file. To open an existing 1-2-3 for Windows worksheet, follow these steps:

1. Open the **F**ile menu and choose the **O**pen command.

   1-2-3 for Windows displays the File Open dialog box (see Figure 9.12). The **F**iles list box displays the worksheets in the current directory.

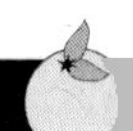

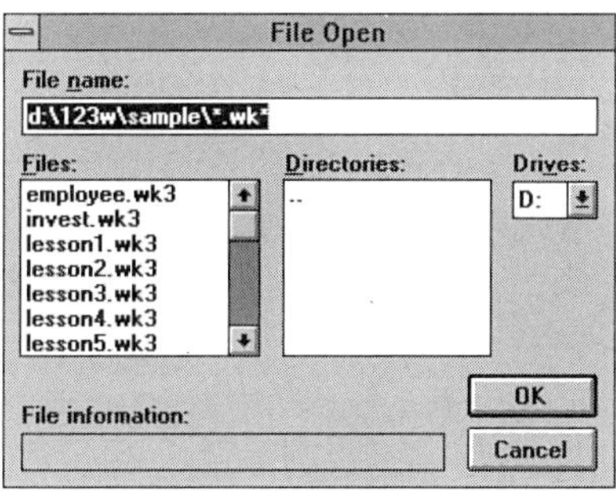

Figure 9.12.

The File Open dialog box.

2. Choose the name of the worksheet you want to open from the list or type the file name of the worksheet you want to open in the File **n**ame text box. If necessary, change the drive or the directory so that the worksheet file you want to open appears in the **F**iles list box. To change to a floppy disk drive, insert the floppy disk into the drive, open the Dri**v**es drop-down list box, and choose the drive from the list. To change to another directory, double-click on a directory listed in the **D**irectories list box. The files in the list change to display the worksheets in the newly selected directory.

3. Choose OK.

   The worksheet appears onscreen, and you can edit it.

Performing Basic Editing in 1-2-3 for Windows

In this section, you learn about basic editing in 1-2-3 for Windows. You learn how to move around a worksheet, how to enter information into a cell, how to change the contents of a cell, how to select a group of cells, and how to execute commands.

Moving around a Worksheet

You move around a 1-2-3 for Windows worksheet by clicking the mouse or by pressing the directional keys on the keyboard (the arrow keys, Home, End, PgUp, and PgDn).

For the most part, you use the same keys to move around in a worksheet in 1-2-3 for Windows as you do in 1-2-3 for the Mac. On a PC, however, you can use the numeric keypad as numbers or as directional keys. When you first start 1-2-3 for Windows, the numeric keypad produces numbers. To make the numeric keypad function as directional keys, press the Num Lock key.

Table 9.1 summarizes the most common ways in which you can use the keyboard to move around a 1-2-3 for Windows worksheet.

Table 9.1.
Directional keys in a worksheet.

Key(s)	Effect
→ or ←	Moves right or left one cell—right or left one column.
↑ or ↓	Moves up or down one cell—up or down one row.
PgDn	Moves down one window.
PgUp	Moves up one window.
Tab or Ctrl+→	Moves right one window.
Shift+Tab or Ctrl+←	Moves left one window.
Home	Moves to cell A1.
End+Home	Moves to the last active cell in the worksheet.
End	Turns on or off End mode.
End+arrow key	Moves right, left, up, or down to the last non-empty cell.

Entering Information into a Cell

To enter text or numbers into a worksheet in 1-2-3 for Windows, you use the same three-step process you use in 1-2-3 for the Mac. To enter text or numbers into a worksheet, follow these steps:

1. Position the cell pointer on the cell into which you want to type text or numbers.

2. Type the text or numbers.

   When you type, the text or numbers you type appear both in the cell and in the edit line of the control panel.

3. To accept what you typed, press **Enter** or choose the check mark button at the left end of the edit line.

By default, when you enter text into a cell, 1-2-3 for Windows left-aligns the text in the cell. Also by default, when you enter numbers into a cell, 1-2-3 for Windows right-aligns the numbers in the cell.

Changing the Contents of a Cell

You can use the Backspace key to delete the character or number immediately to the left of the insertion point. (The **insertion point**, the flashing vertical bar, indicates the place where text will appear when you type.)

You can replace the contents of a cell simply by typing over what currently appears in the cell, or you can edit the contents of the cell. To type over the current contents of the cell, move the cell pointer to the cell, type, and press Enter. 1-2-3 for Windows replaces the original contents of the cell with the new information you type. To edit the contents of the cell, position the cell pointer on the cell you want to edit. Then, click in the edit line or press F2; the insertion point appears at the end of the cell's contents.

While you are editing a cell, you are working in insert mode. In **insert mode**, 1-2-3 for Windows places characters to the left of the insertion point and moves all existing characters to the right. Press the Backspace key to delete the character immediately to the left of the insertion point; press the Del key to delete the character immediately to the right of the insertion point. When you finish making changes to the contents on the edit line, press Enter. 1-2-3 for Windows places the new information in the active cell.

Selecting Cells

You may want to add the contents of a group of cells or make changes to the appearance of the worksheet. For example, you may want the contents of certain cells to appear in italics or in boldface type. You may want to change the alignment of the contents of certain cells or delete the contents of certain cells.

In 1-2-3 for Windows, you select a cell or contiguous group of cells when you want to "operate" on the cell(s)—for example, when you want to add the column or row or center the information in the cell(s). **Selecting** is the process of highlighting the cell(s) so that 1-2-3 for Windows can identify the cell(s) on which you want to work. You can select more than one cell as long as the selection is contiguous.

PC NOTE

In some operations, you must select cells more than one time to complete the command. To copy cells, for example, you first must select the range of cells you want to copy; then, you must select the target range of cells where you want the copy to appear.

To select a single cell by using the mouse, click on the cell you want to select. To select a group of cells by using the mouse, you drag the mouse pointer. Follow these steps:

1. Position the mouse pointer on the first cell you want to select. Click and hold down the left mouse button.

2. Slide the mouse in the direction of the other cells you want to select.

   As you slide the mouse, a reverse video bar (a highlight) appears over all the cells you are selecting. You can slide the mouse diagonally to select a rectangle that contains more than one row and more than one column of cells.

3. Continue sliding the mouse until you reach the end of the cells you want to select.

4. Release the left mouse button.

   The cells you want to select appear highlighted—a reverse video bar appears over them.

In Figure 9.13, cells A:B7 through A:B9 are selected. When referring to a block of cells (such as A:B7 through A:B9), 1-2-3 for Windows, like 1-2-3 for the Mac, uses the notation `A:B7..A:B9`.

You can cancel a selection by clicking anywhere else in the worksheet.

To select cells by using the keyboard, move the cell pointer to the first cell you want to select (refer to Table 9.1 for more information). Then, use the keystrokes in Table 9.2 to select additional cell(s). You can find additional keystroke combinations for selecting cells in multisheet worksheets by using Help in 1-2-3 for Windows, which you learned about earlier in this chapter. Notice that the keystrokes in Table 9.2 bear a strong resemblance to the keystrokes you use to select cells in 1-2-3 for the Mac.

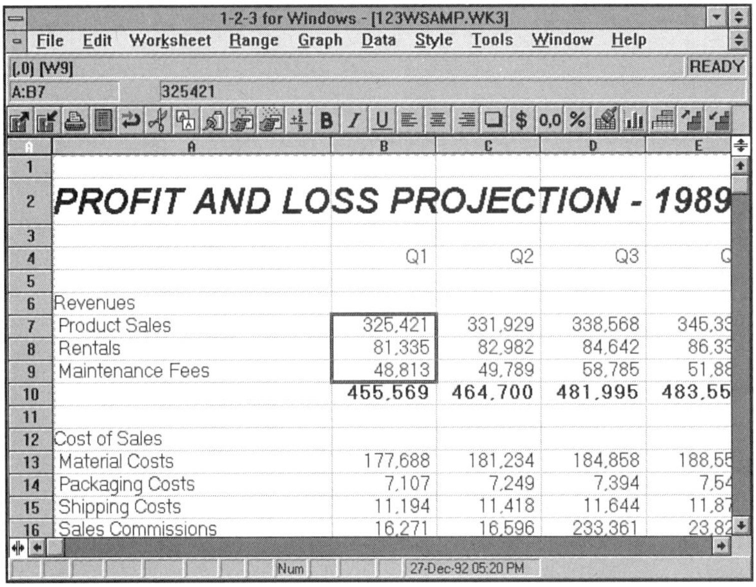

Figure 9.13. The selected cells.

Table 9.2. Selecting cells by using the keyboard.

Keys	Effect
Shift+→	Selects the active cell and the cell in the column to the right.
Shift+←	Selects the active cell and the cell in the column to the left.
Shift+↑	Selects the active cell and the cell in the row above.
Shift+↓	Selects the active cell and the cell in the row below.
Shift+Home	Selects the active cell and all cells between the active cell and cell A1.
Shift+PgUp	Selects the active cell and the pane of cells in the column above the active cell.
Shift+PgDn	Selects the active cell and the pane of cells in the column below the active cell.

You can cancel a selection by pressing any arrow key.

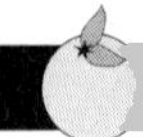

Executing Commands

1-2-3 for Windows contains both its own menus and the menus used in 1-2-3 for DOS. In 1-2-3 for Windows, the menus and commands from 1-2-3 for DOS are called the 1-2-3 Classic menus. As a user of 1-2-3 for the Mac, you probably don't make much use of 1-2-3 Classic menus, but just in case you do, you also can use them in 1-2-3 for Windows.

Assuming, however, that you use 1-2-3 for the Mac menus, here's some great news. You should find that the commands on the menus in 1-2-3 for Windows strongly resemble the commands on the menus in 1-2-3 for the Mac.

To choose a command from a 1-2-3 for Windows menu by using the mouse, click the menu to open it and then click the command you want to choose.

To choose a command from a 1-2-3 for Windows menu by using the keyboard, follow these steps:

1. Press **F10** or the **Alt** key to activate the 1-2-3 for Windows menu bar.

   The first menu on the menu bar appears highlighted, and the 1-2-3 for Windows program name is replaced in the title bar with a brief explanation of the purpose of the highlighted menu (see Figure 9.14).

2. Press the right- or left-arrow key to highlight the menu from which you want to choose a command.

3. Press the up- or down-arrow key to open the menu.

   The commands on that menu appear.

4. Press the up- or down-arrow key to highlight the command you want to choose.

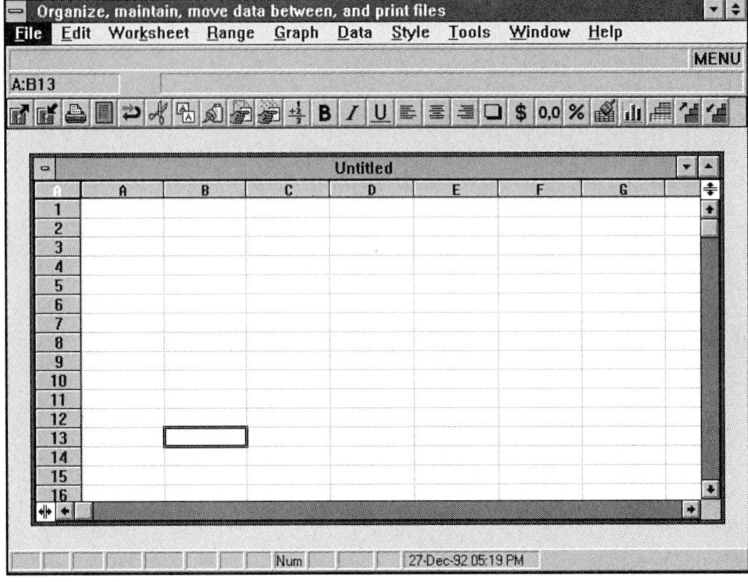

Figure 9.14. The 1-2-3 for Windows menu bar after you use the keyboard to activate it.

5. Press **Enter** to choose the command.

Alternatively, after activating the menu bar, you can press the underlined letter in the name of the menu you want to open. The first letter of the command acts as a hot key, and automatically opens the menu. You also can press the first letter of the command you want to choose. If more than one command on the menu begins with the same letter (on the **F**ile menu, for example, you see four commands that begin with P), press the letter repeatedly until the command you want to choose is highlighted. Then, press Enter to choose the command.

PC NOTE

You cannot move the cell pointer around the worksheet area while a menu is activated onscreen. To remove the menu from the screen, press Ctrl+Break or press the Esc key until the menus disappear.

Saving a 1-2-3 for Windows File

After you have made the changes you need to make, you will want to save the worksheet. Like 1-2-3 for the Mac, 1-2-3 for Windows provides three ways to save a worksheet, and each of these ways is described in this chapter. One of these methods lets you save a worksheet using a different name. Because you may not want to overwrite the work that existed before you edited, you may want to read the sections on these three methods before you use any of them.

- You can use the Close command to save the worksheet under its current name, and then "put away" the document (remove it from the screen).
- You can use the Save command to save the worksheet under its current name, and then continue working on it.
- You can use the Save As command to save the worksheet under a different name. You may want to save the worksheet under a different name to avoid changing the original.

When you exit from 1-2-3 for Windows, the program prompts you to save any worksheets that contain changes before you exit—but more about that later in this chapter.

Using the Close Command

As in 1-2-3 for the Mac, you can use the **C**lose command when you finish working with a worksheet and you want 1-2-3 for Windows to put away the worksheet. When you choose the **C**lose command, 1-2-3 for Windows also gives you the option of saving any changes you might have made before putting away the worksheet. To close a document, open the **F**ile menu and choose the **C**lose command.

If you haven't made any changes to the worksheet since the last time you saved it, 1-2-3 for Windows simply removes the worksheet from the screen. If, however, you have made changes, 1-2-3 for Windows displays the dialog box in Figure 9.15.

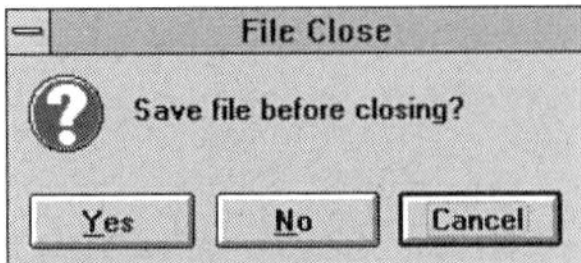

Figure 9.15. The Save file before closing? dialog box.

If you choose **Y**es, 1-2-3 for Windows saves the changes you have made and removes the worksheet from the screen. If you choose **N**o, 1-2-3 for Windows *does not* save the changes you have made since the last time you saved, but 1-2-3 for Windows *does* remove the worksheet from the screen. If you choose Cancel, 1-2-3 for Windows *does not* save the changes you have made since the last time you saved and *does not* remove the worksheet from the screen.

Using the Save Command

Also as in 1-2-3 for the Mac, use the **S**ave command to save the worksheet in the active window. When you use the **S**ave command, 1-2-3 for Windows saves the changes you have made to a disk (either hard or floppy) and leaves the worksheet onscreen so that you can continue to work on it.

To save a worksheet by using the **S**ave command, open the **F**ile menu and choose the **S**ave command. Alternatively, you can choose the Save SmartIcon (the second icon from the left). If you are saving an existing worksheet that already has a name, 1-2-3 for Windows saves the worksheet. (If you pay close attention to the status line at the bottom of the screen, you will see a message that indicates 1-2-3 for Windows is saving the worksheet.) If you are saving a new worksheet that doesn't yet have a name, 1-2-3 for Windows displays the Save As dialog box discussed in the next section.

Using the Save As Command

You might want to leave the original document available in cases where your changes may not be final. If you are unsure of the changes you have made, for example, and somebody else is going to come back and check your work, you might want to keep the original worksheet. You then can show the person your version, and let him or her decide which version to continue using.

You can save a 1-2-3 for Windows worksheet under another name similarly to the way you save a 1-2-3 for the Mac worksheet under a different name. To save your version of an existing worksheet and leave the original version intact, follow these steps:

1. Open the **F**ile menu and choose the Save **A**s command.

   1-2-3 for Windows displays the File Save As dialog box in Figure 9.16.

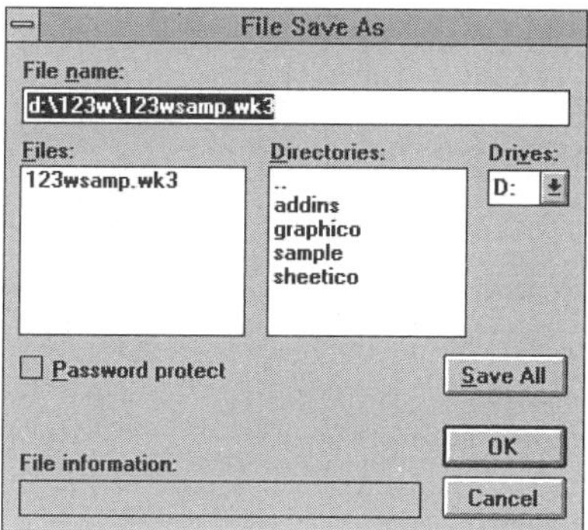

Figure 9.16.
The File Save As dialog box.

2. If you want, you can save the file to a different directory by choosing a directory from the **D**irectories list box or to a different drive by changing the drive that appears in the Dri**v**es list box. (If you want to save the file to a floppy disk drive, insert the disk before you change to the drive.)

3. Type a new name for the worksheet in the File **n**ame text box. You can use up to 11 characters for the name you want to assign to the document. The first part of the name can contain no more than 8 characters; the **extension** can contain no more than 3 characters.

   For more information on the rules DOS imposes when you name a file on a PC, see Chapter 12. (Yes, it is DOS that imposes file name rules.)

4. Choose OK.

   1-2-3 for Windows saves the worksheet under the name you specified in the File **n**ame text box, leaving the original version (under its original name) intact.

PC NOTE

If you don't type a new name in the File **n**ame text box or you type the name of a worksheet that already exists in the **F**iles list, 1-2-3 for Windows displays a dialog box telling you that the file already exists. If you choose the **R**eplace button, you write over the existing worksheet. If you choose the **B**ackup button, 1-2-3 for Windows backs up the closed version of the file and then replaces it with the version in the active window. If you choose the Cancel button, 1-2-3 for Windows redisplays the File Save As dialog box so that you can type a worksheet name in the File **n**ame text box that doesn't exist in the current directory (or so that you can switch to a different directory).

Printing a 1-2-3 for Windows File

After you have edited and saved the worksheet, you may need to print it. Printing in 1-2-3 for Windows is very similar to printing in 1-2-3 for the Mac.

Before you print the worksheet, you may want to see onscreen the way it will look when you print it. Follow these steps to preview a worksheet and then print it:

1. Open the **F**ile menu and choose the Pre**v**iew command.

   1-2-3 for Windows displays the File Preview dialog box (see Figure 9.17).

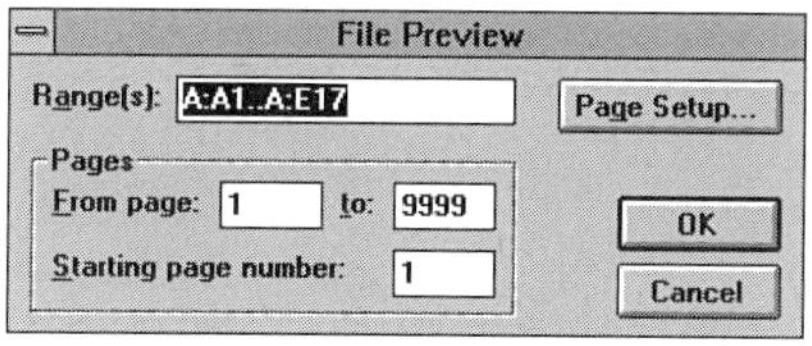

   Figure 9.17. The File Preview dialog box.

   From this dialog box, you can change the print range by typing the new print range. Or, you can choose the Pa**g**e Setup button to open the File Page Setup dialog box so that you can change page settings such as orientation, headers and footers, and margins—but more about that dialog box in a moment.

   If you choose OK, 1-2-3 for Windows displays a Print Preview screen similar to Figure 9.18.

2. Review what you see in the Print Preview screen. 1-2-3 for Windows remembers print settings when you save a worksheet. For this reason, if you are editing an existing worksheet, you may not need to change many settings—someone may have already set it up for you.

3. Click anywhere in the Print Preview screen to return to the worksheet.

If the Print Preview screen did not display what you want to print, you can make changes in the File Page Setup dialog box. If the Print Preview screen did display what you want to print, you can print by using the File Print dialog box.

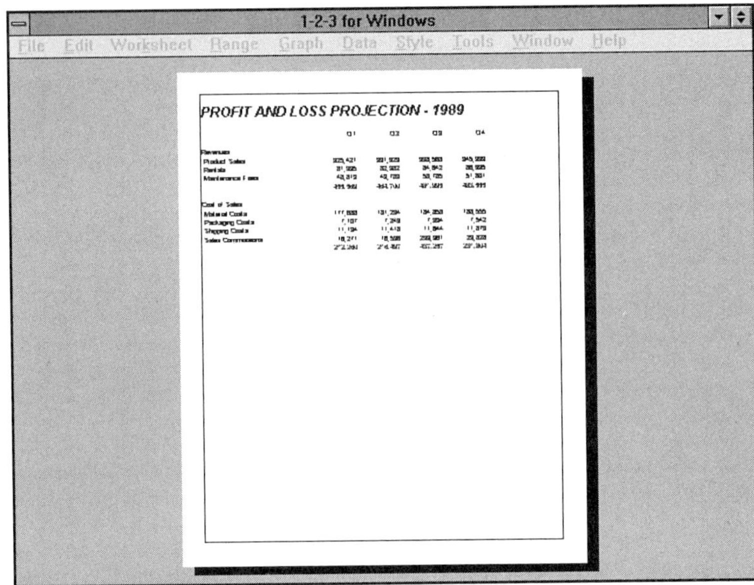

Figure 9.18.

A sample Print Preview screen.

To make changes, open the File Page Setup dialog box. You can open the File Page Setup dialog box directly (rather than opening the File Preview dialog box) by choosing Pa**g**e Setup from the **F**ile menu (see Figure 9.19).

File Page Setup

Header:

Footer:

Margins

Top: 0.5in Bottom: 0.55in

Left: 0.5in Right: 0.5in

Borders

Columns:

Rows:

Compression

Automatically fit to page

Manually size: 100

None

Options

Show worksheet frame

Show grid lines

Orientation

Landscape

Portrait

Default settings

Restore Update

Named settings

Save... Retrieve...

OK

Cancel

Figure 9.19.

The File Page Setup dialog box.

If you know that your settings are correct and you simply want to print, open the **F**ile menu and choose the **P**rint command. If you choose the **P**rint command from the **F**ile menu, 1-2-3 for Windows

displays the File Print dialog box (see Figure 9.20). Make any necessary changes, and then choose OK.

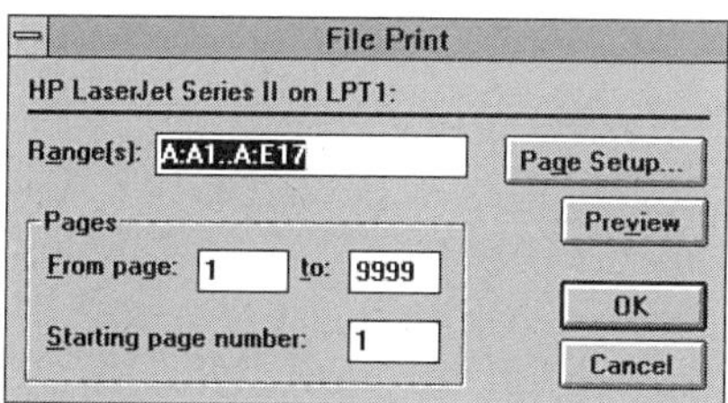

Figure 9.20. The File Print dialog box.

Copying a 1-2-3 for Windows File to a Floppy Disk

You may find that you need to copy a 1-2-3 for Windows file to a floppy disk. You may need to print a file on another PC, for example. Using the Save As dialog box is the easiest way to copy a 1-2-3 for Windows worksheet to a floppy disk. Alternatively, you can use DOS commands, which you can find in Chapter 12.

Earlier in this chapter, when you were learning to save a worksheet, you used the Save **A**s command on the **F**ile menu to open the Save As dialog box. To use the Save **A**s command to copy a file to a floppy disk, follow these steps:

1. Insert a formatted disk into the floppy disk drive.
2. Open the worksheet you want to copy to the floppy disk.
3. Open the **F**ile menu and choose the Save **A**s command.

   1-2-3 for Windows displays the File Save As dialog box (see Figure 9.21).

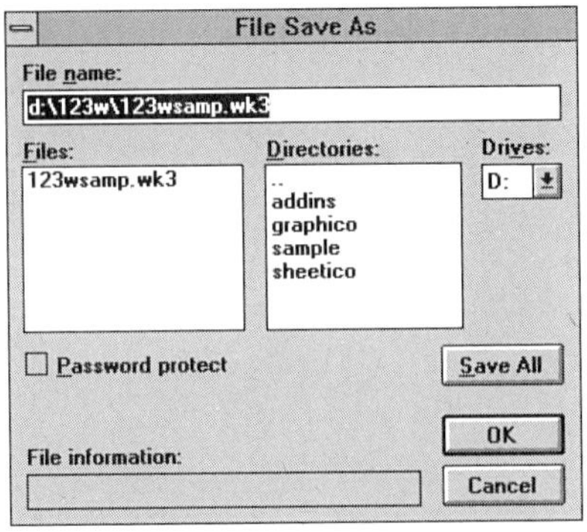

Figure 9.21.

The File Save As dialog box.

4. Open the Dri**v**es list box and choose the letter of the floppy disk drive into which you inserted the disk.

The **F**iles list box changes to display the names of files on the floppy disk in the floppy disk drive.

5. If you want, type a new name for the document in the File **N**ame text box.

The new name will be assigned to the file on the floppy disk when you save the file. The original file on the hard disk will retain its original name.

6. Choose OK.

1-2-3 for Windows copies the file to the floppy disk.

PC NOTE

If you type the name of a worksheet that already exists on the floppy disk, 1-2-3 for Windows displays a dialog box telling you that the file already exists. If you choose the **R**eplace button, you write over the existing worksheet file on the floppy disk. If you choose the **B**ackup button, 1-2-3 for Windows backs up the closed version of the file on the floppy disk and then replaces it with the version in the active window. If you choose the Cancel button, 1-2-3 for Windows redisplays the Save As dialog box so that you can type a worksheet name in the File **N**ame text box that doesn't exist on the floppy disk (or so that you can switch to a different floppy disk).

Exiting 1-2-3 for Windows

When you are finished using 1-2-3 for Windows, you can exit by choosing the Exit command from the **F**ile menu. If you saved your changes before choosing Exit from the **F**ile menu, 1-2-3 for Windows returns to the Program Manager of Windows. If, however, you made changes to the worksheet and didn't save them, 1-2-3 for Windows displays a dialog box that asks whether you want to save all files before closing. Choose the **Y**es button to save changes to any open worksheets and exit from 1-2-3 for Windows. Choose the **N**o button to exit from 1-2-3 for Windows without saving the changes to any open worksheets. Choose the Cancel button to return to the active worksheet.

When you exit from 1-2-3 for Windows, you return to Windows. You can exit from Windows by choosing the Exit Windows command from the **F**ile menu or by pressing Alt+F4.

You safely can turn off the PC after exiting from Windows.

Chapter Summary

In this chapter, you learned how to use the online Help facility in 1-2-3 for Windows. You also learned how to open, edit, save, and print a 1-2-3 for Windows worksheet; how to copy a 1-2-3 for Windows file to a floppy disk; and how to exit from 1-2-3 for Windows.

The menus and commands in 1-2-3 for Windows are very similar to the menus and commands in 1-2-3 for the Mac. 1-2-3 for Windows has the control panel, which appears where the console appears in 1-2-3 for the Mac. The format line in the control panel displays some of the information you usually see in the status window of 1-2-3 for the Mac. The edit line in the control panel displays information you usually see in the console in 1-2-3 for the Mac. In 1-2-3 for Windows, you have the SmartIcons instead of the draw and style palettes you use for drawing and text enhancement in 1-2-3 for the Mac. In 1-2-3 for Windows, you have the status line, and in 1-2-3 for the Mac, you have the status window; both display similar information. The commands you use to open, edit, save, and print a file are basically the same.

In the next chapter, you learn about database programs you may want to avoid. As you know, Chapters 3 through 9 in *The Mac User's PC* focus on specific software packages. You should read the chapters that pertain to the software you want to use. Chapter 11 discusses the MS-DOS Shell. Refer to Chapter 12 for information on file-naming conventions imposed on 1-2-3 for Windows by the operating system, and for information on working with basic DOS commands. If you need to transfer and translate files between a PC and a Mac, read Chapter 13.

Avoiding Database Programs

A strange title for a chapter, I know, but appropriate. In this brief chapter, you will learn to identify some of the more popular PC-based database design and development programs—for the express purpose of avoiding them.

Databases are repositories of related information. Typically, each entry in a database is called a **record**, and each piece of information in the record is stored in a **field**. A telephone book is a database of names, addresses, and phone numbers within a specified geographic area. A dictionary is a database of words and their meanings. A thesaurus is a database of words of related meanings.

People initially use databases (automated or otherwise) to store related information. Later, users retrieve information from the databases and, usually, sort the retrieved information in some desired order to suit a specified purpose. For example, name and address information could be sorted alphabetically to prepare an address book. Alternatively, name and address information could be sorted in ZIP code order to prepare mailing labels for a bulk mailing.

You use a database design and development program, which is generic in nature, to build a database geared toward some aspect of your job and specific to your needs. For example, you might build a database to store information about customers—their names, addresses, phone numbers, and the last time they purchased anything from you. Or, you might build a database to store information about employees—when they were hired, where they live, how much they earn, how many payroll deductions they claim, when their last performance review was, and so on.

Databases are highly personalized, both in their content and their function. When you build a database, you are "programming." In some cases, you don't perform a lot of programming, but, nevertheless, you are programming. To *use* a database, you really don't need to know how to use the database design and development program in which the database was created. Instead, you need to know how to use the database itself because each database is designed to fit the unique needs of its users.

Because database design and development programs are generic in nature, the database designer can customize the screens and functions of the database to suit his or her own needs. And, because the database designer can customize the database, it is impossible to predict the appearance of database screens. Two different people might use the same database design and development program to build databases of the same information, but the appearance and functioning of those databases are likely to be very different.

You can draw two conclusions from this discussion:

- It is impossible for me to show you the database screens you might see if you accidentally (or on purpose) start a database program.

- You are not likely to have much need to use someone else's database. In fact, unless you know how to use that database, you just might mess it up.

So, in this brief chapter, I'm going to try to familiarize you with the names (and file names) of some popular database programs, so that if you happen to start one of these programs accidentally, you can start looking for the exit command immediately.

With several of these programs, the programmer who builds the databases can create a file that starts the database program. The programmer can assign *any* name to that file, so you may accidentally start the database program without actually using any of the file names listed in the next sections. In most cases, however, regardless of the file name you use to start a database program, you will see a licensing screen, which identifies the database design and development program that the programmer used to build the database. This clue should be enough to encourage you to find the exit command.

dBASE

dBASE is a popular database design and development program that has been around for a long time (at least since 1984 that I can remember). Because it was one of the first database design and development programs available, a lot of people own and use dBASE, which increases the likelihood that you might run into it.

The latest version of dBASE is dBASE IV, but many people still use dBASE III +. If the database program was installed with the typical defaults, you might find a directory named DBASE, and in that directory, a file named DBASE.EXE, which starts the program. You also might find a file named DBASE.BAT in the **root directory** of the hard disk. Therefore, typing `DBASE` at a DOS prompt or choosing dBASE from a menu will start dBASE.

FoxPro

FoxPro has been around for a few years and was recently purchased by the Microsoft Corporation. You should be seeing a lot of advertising for FoxPro, which probably will increase its sales. Therefore, the probability that you will run into FoxPro increases. FoxPro is related to FoxBASE/Mac and is designed so that you can produce databases that work on a Mac or on a PC in either the DOS or Windows environment.

The last version of FoxPro is Version 2.0. Because the installation program doesn't suggest a directory in which to install FoxPro, this program could be installed in any directory. The name of the file that starts FoxPro is FOXPRO.EXE.

Paradox

Paradox began to gain a lot of popularity two or three years ago, and has a fairly large installed base, so you may run into Paradox. At the time of this writing, the latest releases of Paradox are Paradox 4.0 and Paradox for Windows.

If the program was installed with typical defaults, you might find a directory named PARADOX2 for Release 2, PARADOX3 for Release 3, or PDOX40 for Release 4. The name of the file that starts Paradox 4.0 is PARADOX.EXE. You start Paradox for Windows the same way you start any other Windows program.

Clipper

The process of translating program code written in a language such as BASIC or COBOL to machine language (a language only the computer can read) is called compiling. To compile code, you use, naturally, a compiler. Clipper is a compiler.

A few years ago, some of the entrenched users of dBASE found that they couldn't do everything they wanted to do in dBASE. Initially, the users migrated to Clipper to compile their dBASE code. Later, many of these users found that they didn't actually need dBASE anymore—they could write programs in any text editor and then use Clipper to compile the work.

Because Clipper is primarily a compiler, the good news for you is that you will find it difficult to do any damage with Clipper. To do anything in Clipper, you must know the correct syntax of the command that starts Clipper. If you don't, nothing happens.

The latest version of Clipper is Clipper 5.01, and, if the installer used the typical defaults, you might see a directory named CLIPPER5. All the files that start aspects of Clipper are stored in a subdirectory called \CLIPPER5\BIN. If you see these files, you should ignore them.

Q&A

Q&A is a database design and development program intended for people who don't want to program. Q&A is very easy to use, particularly for simple databases, so it has a fairly large installed base. You may run into Q&A.

The latest version of Q&A is Version 4, but many people are still using Q&A Version 3. You may find Q&A in a directory named QA4 or QA3 or QA. In the Q&A directory, you will see a file named QA.COM, which starts Q&A.

You can start Q&A by typing `QA` in the Q&A directory, by choosing QA.COM while in the MS-DOS Shell, or by selecting Q&A from a menu.

Chapter Summary

To maintain friendships, avoid database design and development programs as well as other people's databases unless you have been trained to use them. If you choose to use a database or a database design and development program, consult the user's manual that comes with that database or program—or someone who knows how that database works.

In the next chapter, you learn to understand the MS-DOS Shell screen and to use the MS-DOS Shell to view, copy, and print files, and to start programs. In Chapter 12, you learn what DOS is, how to format (initialize) disks, how to organize information on disks, and how to work with files by using basic DOS commands. In Chapter 13, you learn to transfer and translate files between a Mac and a PC.

Working with the MS-DOS Shell

If the PC is running MS-DOS Version 4.0 or later, you're in luck. Starting with that version, Microsoft Corporation began including the MS-DOS Shell in its releases of MS-DOS. The MS-DOS Shell offers you the capability to perform DOS commands by using menus and possibly a mouse (more on this later). Performing DOS commands by using menus makes working with the operating system, which is often the most mysterious piece of software a user encounters, much easier. For this reason, this chapter covers the workings of the MS-DOS Shell in somewhat greater detail than earlier chapters cover application programs.

Microsoft greatly improved the MS-DOS Shell in Version 5.0. This chapter discusses the Version 5.0 MS-DOS Shell only. You will not learn about everything the MS-DOS Shell has to offer in this chapter, but you will learn to understand the screen, to navigate in the MS-DOS Shell, to work with files and directories, and to start programs.

If you don't see the MS-DOS Shell when you start the computer and you want to try to use it, check to see which version of MS-DOS is installed. At a DOS prompt, type `VER` and press Enter. If you see `MS-DOS Version 4.0` (or any higher number), then type `DOSSHELL` at the DOS prompt and press Enter. The MS-DOS Shell appears.

If you don't use MS-DOS Version 4.0 or later (or you don't want to use the MS-DOS Shell), you still can perform DOS commands by using the information you find in Chapter 12.

Understanding the MS-DOS Shell Screen

By default, the MS-DOS Shell screen appears in text mode unless the user changes to graphics mode. In this book, the screens appear in graphics mode. The MS-DOS Shell works the same way regardless of the mode you select. If the monitor supports graphics mode, you can change to graphics mode by opening the **O**ptions menu, choosing the **D**isplay command, and selecting a graphics mode (Graphics, 25 rows, 80 columns, Low Resolution is the most effective). If you don't know whether the monitor supports graphics mode, try changing to graphics mode and see whether the screen looks "normal" to you. If it does, the monitor supports graphics mode.

Figure 11.1 shows the default view of the MS-DOS Shell screen, the Program/File Lists view, and the working sections into which it is divided.

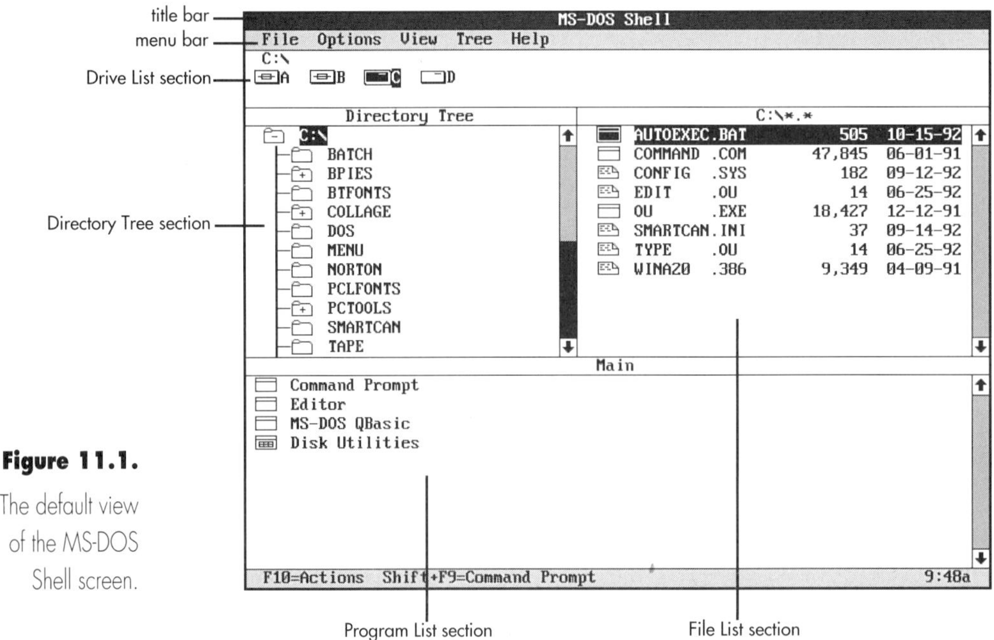

Figure 11.1.

The default view of the MS-DOS Shell screen.

As you learned in Chapter 2, the view you see of the MS-DOS Shell screen may vary if the PC owner has changed from the default view to another view. You may see any of the views in Figures 11.2 through 11.5. For the sake of clarity, this chapter assumes you are looking at the default view of the MS-DOS Shell. If you do not see the default view, change to this view by opening the **V**iew menu and choosing the Program/**F**ile Lists command.

If the Task Swapper, which is discussed later in this chapter, is enabled, you also will see the Active Task List section on the default view or the Program List view of the MS-DOS Shell.

At the top of the screen, you see the name of the program that is running, `MS-DOS Shell`, in the title bar. Directly below the title bar, you see the menu bar. The menus at the top of the MS-DOS Shell screen provide commands to perform tasks such as starting a program, copying or printing a file, or making a new directory. In this chapter, you learn about the menu commands as you learn about the tasks that use them.

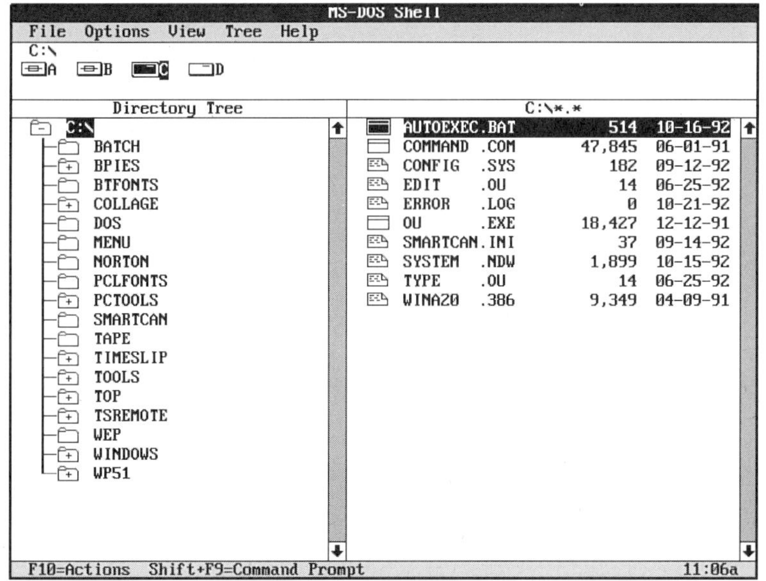

Figure 11.2.

The Single File List view of the MS-DOS Shell screen.

```
                              MS-DOS Shell
 File  Options  View  Tree  Help
 C:\
 A  B  C  D

           Directory Tree                            C:\*.*
 C:\                                 AUTOEXEC.BAT       514  10-16-92
   BATCH                             COMMAND  .COM   47,845  06-01-91
   BPIES                             CONFIG   .SYS      182  09-12-92
   BTFONTS                           EDIT     .OU        14  06-25-92
   COLLAGE                           ERROR    .LOG        0  10-21-92
   DOS                               OU       .EXE   18,427  12-12-91
   MENU                              SMARTCAN.INI        37  09-14-92
   NORTON                            SYSTEM   .NDW    1,899  10-15-92
   PCLFONTS                          TYPE     .OU        14  06-25-92
   PCTOOLS                           WINA20   .386    9,349  04-09-91

 A  B  C  D

           Directory Tree                            C:\*.*
 C:\                                 AUTOEXEC.BAT       514  10-16-92
   BATCH                             COMMAND  .COM   47,845  06-01-91
   BPIES                             CONFIG   .SYS      182  09-12-92
   BTFONTS                           EDIT     .OU        14  06-25-92
   COLLAGE                           ERROR    .LOG        0  10-21-92
   DOS                               OU       .EXE   18,427  12-12-91
   MENU                              SMARTCAN.INI        37  09-14-92
   NORTON                            SYSTEM   .NDW    1,899  10-15-92
   PCLFONTS                          TYPE     .OU        14  06-25-92
 F10=Actions  Shift+F9=Command Prompt                           11:06a
```

Figure 11.3.

The Dual File List view of the MS-DOS Shell screen.

```
                              MS-DOS Shell
 File  Options  View  Tree  Help
 C:\WP51\BOOKORG
 A  B  C  D

                                           *.*
                               00OUT             20,318  07-05-91   2:08p
 File                          00OUT    .ORG     22,857  10-14-91  10:14a
   Name  : 00OUT               01START           44,797  07-05-91   1:19p
   Attr  : ....                01START  .WP5     61,694  09-27-91   3:14p
 Selected              C       02ENTRY           39,713  06-27-91   2:15p
   Number:             1       02ENTRY  .WP5     65,452  09-27-91   2:53p
   Size  :           514       02PC-01  .PCX     24,656  10-15-92   9:37a
 Directory                     02PC-01B.PCX       8,143  10-15-92   9:36a
   Name  : BOOKORG             02PC-02  .PCX     48,865  10-15-92   9:48a
   Size  :       573,066       02PC-07  .PCX     45,125  10-15-92  11:39a
   Files :            30       03CLINFO.WP5      86,960  09-27-91   3:10p
 Disk                          03EDIT            25,638  06-27-91   2:17p
   Name  : DRIVE_C             03PC-01  .PCX     48,865  10-15-92   9:48a
   Size  :   105,097,216       03PC-06  .PCX     41,140  10-15-92   9:56a
   Avail :    29,593,600       04CLINFO          69,928  07-05-91   1:22p
   Files :         3,015       04CLTRAN.WP5      37,594  09-27-91   3:18p
   Dirs  :            81       04PC-01  .PCX      6,568  10-15-92  11:53a
                               04PC-02  .PCX     23,140  10-15-92  11:55a
                               04PC-07  .PCX     62,289  10-15-92  11:55a
                               05CLTRAN          38,196  07-05-91   1:27p
                               05CRIT   .WP5     31,295  10-01-91  12:41p
                               05PC-01  .PCX     45,125  10-15-92  11:39a
                               05PC-06  .PCX     29,351  10-15-92  10:39a
 F10=Actions  Shift+F9=Command Prompt                           11:07a
```

Figure 11.4.

The All Files view of the MS-DOS Shell screen.

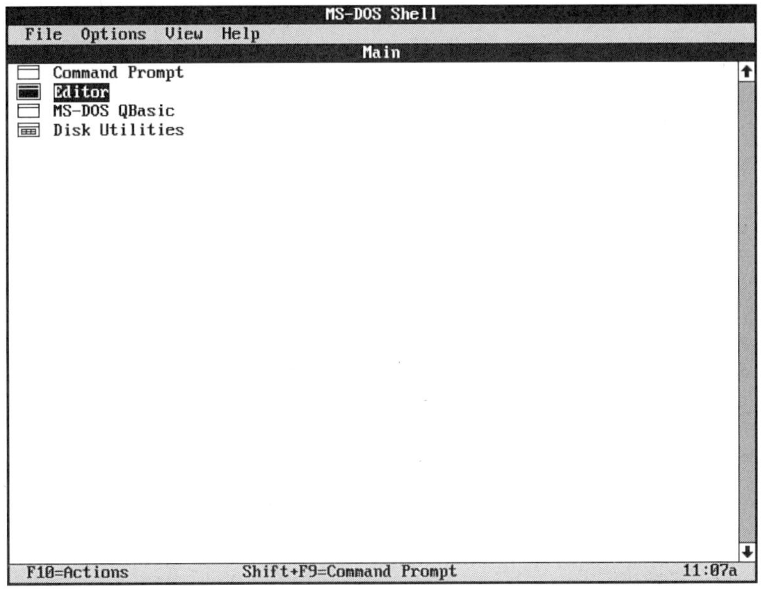

Figure 11.5.
The Program List view of the MS-DOS Shell screen.

The Drive List Section

In the Drive List section below the menu bar, the MS-DOS Shell represents as icons the disk drives available on the PC. This concept is similar to the disk icons on the Macintosh Desktop, but not quite the same. In the MS-DOS Shell Drive List section, you see *all available drives,* whether they contain disks or not. On the Macintosh Desktop, you see icons for *all available disks;* you see a floppy disk icon only when you insert a floppy disk into the floppy disk drive.

When you select a drive icon, you make that drive the current drive, and the rest of the MS-DOS Shell screen describes the information on the drive. As you can see from Figure 11.1, the floppy disk drive icons (drives A and B) are different from the hard disk drive icons (drive C).

The Directory Tree Section

The Directory Tree section's title bar contains `Directory Tree`. In this section, you see the names of the directories that exist on the current drive. (A **directory** is similar to a folder on a Mac. Users define directories in which to store related programs and data. For more information on directories, see Chapter 12.) If you change to another drive, the contents of the Directory Tree section also changes, reflecting the information on the disk in the drive to which you change.

Next to each directory name, you see an icon that looks like a file folder. If the icon contains a plus sign, then that directory contains additional **subdirectories**, or directories within directories (similar to the hierarchical folder structure you use on a Mac). Later in this chapter, you learn to expand the display so that you can see the subdirectories. By default, the MS-DOS Shell highlights `C:\`, also called the **root directory**, in the Directory Tree section.

The File List Section

In the File List section of the MS-DOS Shell screen, you see the names of the files contained in the current directory. The title bar of the File List section shows the name of the current directory, followed by the file specification. In Figure 11.1, the file specification is `*.*`; this file specification means "show all files" in the current directory. If you select another directory, the title bar of the File List section will change to display the name of the new directory; the names displayed in the File List section will change to show the files in the new directory.

Next to each file, you see one of two icons. As you will learn in Chapter 12, files contain either program instructions or data. Next to any file with an extension of EXE, COM, or BAT, you see the icon that represents a program file. Next to all other files, you see an icon that looks like a piece of paper with its upper right corner folded over. This icon represents a data file.

The Program List Section

Some people use the Program List section of the MS-DOS Shell screen to set up a menu from which to start DOS programs. This menu is similar to the one you read about in Chapter 2, and provides easy access to frequently used programs. The MS-DOS Shell enables you to group similar programs together into a program group such as Word Processing. Then, when you choose the Word Processing group, a submenu appears, listing the programs (such as WordPerfect for DOS and Microsoft Word for DOS) on the Word Processing group menu. The MS-DOS Shell also enables you to place additional program groups onto a program group menu.

The Program List section appears below the Directory Tree section and the File List section. Its title bar contains the word `Main`, which is the title of the current program group. Microsoft created the Main program group; this program group contains three program items (Command Prompt, Editor, and MS-DOS QBasic) and one program group (Disk Utilities). As you can see from Figure 11.1, programs have different icons than program groups. In the Disk Utilities program group, you find some basic DOS utilities that enable you to format disks, recover accidentally deleted files, and copy entire disks.

Navigating in the MS-DOS Shell

You can use a mouse with the MS-DOS Shell if the mouse driver was loaded before you started the MS-DOS Shell. If you see a mouse pointer onscreen as the MS-DOS Shell is loading, the mouse is available.

You can move around the sections of the MS-DOS Shell and choose items within the sections by using the mouse or the keyboard. As on a Mac, when you use the keyboard, some actions require you to hold down one key as you press another key. In this chapter, whenever you must hold down one key as you press another key to perform an action, the key names are separated by a plus sign (+). For example, if you see Shift+F9, hold down the Shift key as you press F9.

In this section, you learn to navigate in the MS-DOS Shell by using the mouse or the keyboard.

Opening and Canceling Menus

You can open and cancel menus by using the mouse or the keyboard. To open a menu by using the mouse, move the mouse pointer to the menu name (on the menu bar) and click the left mouse button. To cancel (close) the menu, click anywhere outside the menu. Remember, on the PC you don't have to hold down the mouse button like you do on the Mac.

To open a menu by using the keyboard, you first must activate the menu bar by pressing either the Alt key or F10. A reverse video bar appears on the **F**ile menu's name. Each menu name contains an underlined letter. In this book, the underlined letter appears in boldface type. You can open the menu by typing the underlined letter; or you can use the left- or right-arrow keys to **choose** (highlight) the menu and then press Enter. To open the **H**elp menu, for example, press Alt and then press H. To cancel an open menu by using the keyboard, press the Esc key.

Choosing Commands from Menus

A command appears on a menu only if the command's function is related to the current (active) MS-DOS Shell section. When you make the Directory Tree section current, for example, the open **F**ile menu appears like the menu in Figure 11.6.

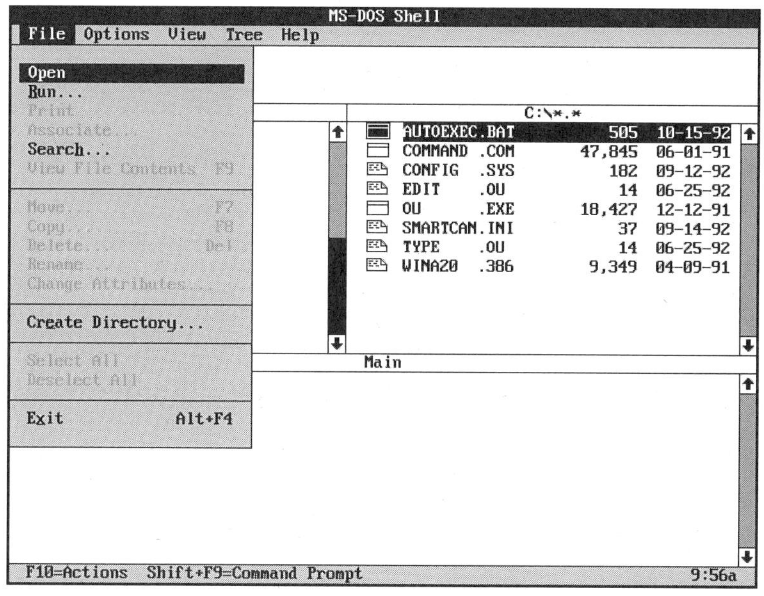

Figure 11.6. The **F**ile menu when the Directory Tree section is current.

When you make the File List section current, however, the open **F**ile menu looks like the menu in Figure 11.7.

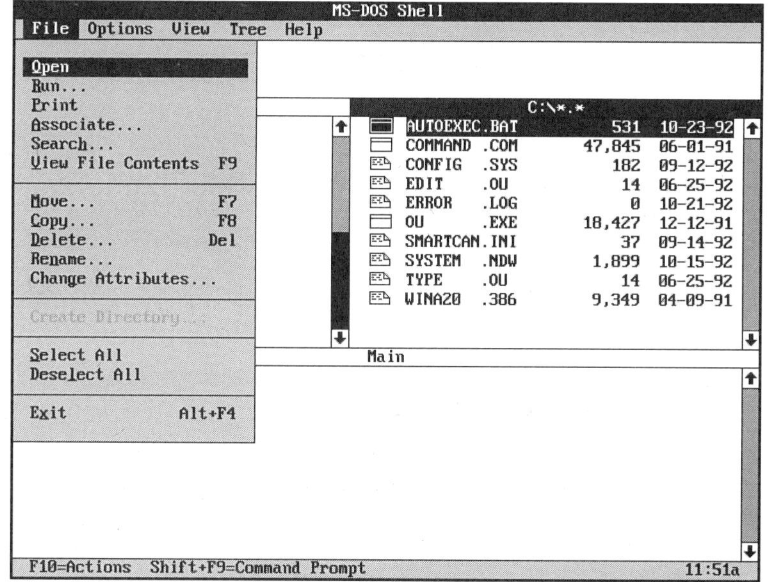

Figure 11.7. The **F**ile menu when the File List section is current.

When you make the Program List section current, the open **File** menu looks like the menu in Figure 11.8.

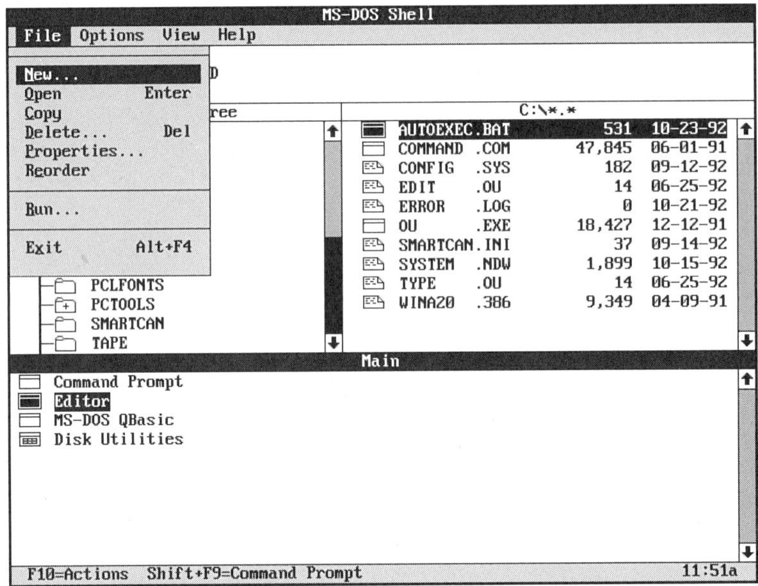

Figure 11.8. The **F**ile menu when the Program List section is current.

PC NOTE

Menus work like commands in this respect—a menu appears only if its function is related to the current MS-DOS Shell section. For example, the **T**ree menu does not appear on the menu bar when you make the Program List section current (see Figure 11.8); the **T**ree menu helps you organize the appearance of files and directories, and files and directories don't appear in the Program List section.

The commands that appear on menus have underlined letters just like the menu names that appear on the menu bar. Unavailable commands appear dimmed. You can choose an available command from a menu by using the mouse or the keyboard. Use the same techniques as described for opening a menu.

Using Dialog Boxes

As on a Mac, whenever you choose a menu command that is followed by a ellipsis (...), the MS-DOS Shell displays a **dialog box**. Also as on a Mac, you use dialog boxes to supply additional information. If you are using a mouse, you can move around a dialog box by clicking. If you are using the keyboard, you can move around by pressing Tab.

Each dialog box is different and may contain different types of options you can use to make selections and supply additional information. Typically, you will see only *some* of the items in a dialog box. Figure 11.9 shows the File Display Options dialog box with the various items labeled.

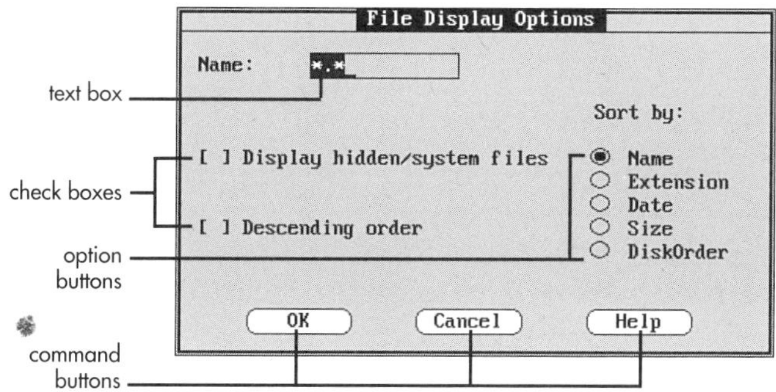

Figure 11.9. The File Display Options dialog box.

A **list box** contains a list of options. To choose from a list box by using a mouse, click on the option. To choose from a list box by using the keyboard, press the down-arrow key to point to the desired option and then press Enter.

An **option button** is a small round button you use to choose one option from a group of related options. A black dot appears in the button of the currently selected option. To choose an option button by using a mouse, click on the option button. To choose an option button by using the keyboard, tab to the group of options and press the down-arrow key to move the black dot until it appears in front of the desired option.

A **check box** is a pair of square brackets ([ ]) you use to choose an option. You can choose more than one check box from a group of related options. An X appears in the check boxes of the activated options. To choose a check box by using a mouse, click on the check box. To choose a check box by using the keyboard, use the Tab key to place the cursor in the check box and then press the spacebar. To deactivate the option and remove the X from the box, choose the check box again.

A **text box** is a rectangular box in which you enter text. When a dialog box that contains a text box opens, the current text usually is selected. To replace the text, simply type the new information.

A **command button** is an oblong button that performs an action. The OK button accepts the settings in the dialog box. The Cancel button cancels your changes to the settings in the dialog box. To choose a command button by using a mouse, click on the button. To choose a command button by using the keyboard, press Tab until the cursor appears in the button and then press Enter.

A **tunnel-through command button** is a command button that opens another dialog box. A tunnel-through command button looks like a regular command button, but has an ellipsis after the button name. To choose a command button by using a mouse, click on the button. To choose a command button by using the keyboard, press Tab until the cursor appears in the button and then press Enter.

Getting Help in the MS-DOS Shell

You can use the MS-DOS Shell's Help facility to get context-sensitive help about the currently highlighted menu item. The

Help facility also provides information about many other topics. Table 11.1 describes the seven commands on the **H**elp menu.

Table 11.1. **H**elp menu commands in the MS-DOS Shell.

Command	Effect
Index	Accesses an index of Help topics.
Keyboard	Lists the keyboard commands available in the MS-DOS Shell.
Shell Basics	Provides information about how to use the basic MS-DOS Shell functions.
Commands	Provides information about various menu commands.
Procedures	Provides information about various tasks performed by the MS-DOS Shell.
Using Help	Provides information about how to use the MS-DOS Shell's Help facility.
About Shell	Displays current version information about the MS-DOS Shell.

Working with the Sections of the MS-DOS Shell Screen

In this section, you learn how to move from section to section of the MS-DOS Shell by using a mouse or the keyboard. You also learn how to change the appearance of the MS-DOS Shell screen.

Moving around Sections of the MS-DOS Shell Screen

When you place the mouse pointer on a directory in the Directory Tree section and click the left mouse button, you make that directory the current directory; the directory appears highlighted onscreen. The files contained in that directory appear in the File List section.

To highlight a file in the File List section (or a program or program group in the Program List section), place the mouse pointer on the desired selection and click the left mouse button.

To scroll additional information into a section, use the scroll bars at the right side of the section. Each scroll bar has two main components:

- Scroll arrows located at each end of the scroll bar. If you click on the up or down arrow, the information displayed in the section moves up or down one row at a time.

- A scroll box located in the scroll bar between the scroll arrows. By dragging the scroll box, you can move through the information quickly. To drag the scroll box, place the mouse pointer on the scroll box, press and hold down the left mouse button, and then slide the mouse to move the scroll box up or down.

You also can use the Tab key to move from one section of the MS-DOS Shell screen to another. As you move, the title bar of the current (active) section appears highlighted (except the Drive List section, which has no title bar). Use the arrow keys to scroll through the items in a section and to highlight items in that section.

To make an item current (active), tab to the desired section and then use the arrow keys to highlight the item. Table 11.2 lists the keystrokes you can use to move around the MS-DOS Shell screen.

Table 11.2. Keystrokes for moving around the MS-DOS Shell screen.

Key(s)	Effect
Tab	Moves to the next section of the MS-DOS Shell screen. (In a dialog box, moves to the next item.)
Shift+Tab	Moves to the preceding section of the MS-DOS Shell screen. (In a dialog box, moves to the preceding item.)
Home	Moves to the beginning of a list or line.
End	Moves to the end of a list or line.
↓	Moves down a list one item at a time.
↑	Moves up a list one item at a time.
PgDn	Moves down a list one screen at a time.
PgUp	Moves up a list one screen at a time.
A letter (when in a list)	Moves to the next item in the list that begins with the letter you press.

Changing the Sections Displayed on the MS-DOS Shell Screen

The MS-DOS Shell enables you to specify the sections you want to see onscreen. Table 11.3 lists the five commands on the **V**iew menu that you can use to change the sections.

Table 11.3. View menu commands in the MS-DOS Shell.

Command	Effect
Single File List	The Program List section does not appear onscreen; instead you see only the Directory Tree section and the File List section.
Dual File Lists	Both the Directory Tree and the File List sections appear twice onscreen. The first set appears in its usual position; the second set replaces the Program List section. With this setup, you can view the files of two different directories simultaneously.
All Files	Neither the Directory Tree section nor the Program List section appear onscreen. Instead, you see a list of all files in all directories for the current drive.
Program/**F**ile Lists	This command is the default setting the first time you start the MS-DOS Shell. One Directory Tree section, one File List section, and one Program List section appear onscreen.
Program List	Neither the Directory Tree section nor the File List section appear onscreen. You see only the Program List section. This setup is well-suited to using the MS-DOS Shell as a menu to start programs.

Changing the Appearance of the Directory Tree Section

As noted earlier in this chapter, the directory structure on a PC is hierarchical like the folder structure on a Mac, and directories in the Directory Tree section also may contain subdirectories. You can identify a directory that contains subdirectories by the plus sign (+) contained in the icon next to the directory name.

Using the mouse, the keyboard, or the commands on the **Tree** menu, you can expand and collapse the Directory Tree section to view and hide the subdirectories. In Figure 11.10, the WINDOWS directory has been expanded to display its subdirectories.

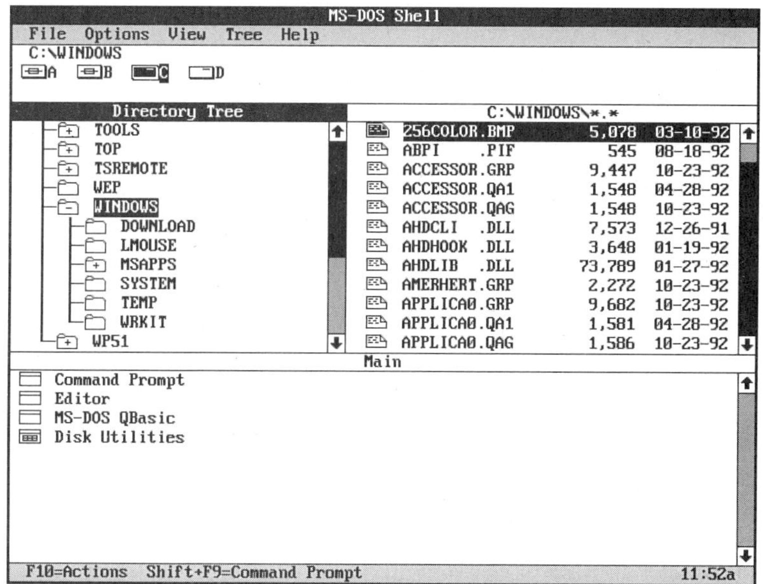

Figure 11.10. The WINDOWS directory expanded to display subdirectories.

As you can see from the icon for the MSAPPS directory in Figure 11.10, the MSAPPS subdirectory also contains subdirectories. And, when you expand a directory to display its subdirectories, the plus sign (+) in the directory's icon changes to a minus sign (-).

To expand a directory by using the mouse, click on the directory icon. (Clicking on any directory icon that contains a minus sign collapses that directory.)

You also can use commands on the **T**ree menu or their keyboard shortcuts to expand and collapse directories. Table 11.4 shows the result of choosing each command from the **T**ree menu or using its corresponding keyboard shortcut.

Table 11.4. **T**ree menu commands and keyboard shortcuts in the MS-DOS Shell.

Command	Shortcut	Effect
E**x**pand One Level	plus sign (+)	When the current directory contains a plus sign, expands the current directory to show the next level of subdirectories.
Expand **B**ranch	asterisk (*)	When the current directory contains a plus sign, expands the current directory to show all levels of subdirectories.
Expand **A**ll	Ctrl+*	Expands all directories to show all levels of all subdirectories.
Collapse Branch	minus sign (–)	When the current directory contains a minus sign, collapses the current directory to hide the next level of subdirectories.

The items on the **T**ree menu change, depending on the icon of the current directory. When the current directory's icon contains a plus sign (+), you see the first three items listed in Table 11.4 on the **T**ree menu. When the current directory's icon contains a minus sign (-), you don't see the E**x**pand One Level command, but you do see the **C**ollapse Branch command. When the current directory's

icon is empty, the Expand **A**ll command is the only available command on the **T**ree menu.

Working with Files in the MS-DOS Shell

To work with files in the MS-DOS Shell, you use commands that appear on the **F**ile menu. Remember, however, that commands appear on the **F**ile menu only if their functions are related to the current MS-DOS Shell section (review Figures 11.6 through 11.8). Therefore, different commands appear on the **F**ile menu, depending on the section you have made current. When you make the File List section current, you find commands on the **F**ile menu that enable you to print, search for, move, copy, delete, and rename files. You also find commands that enable you to run program files, change a file's attributes, and associate files with other files.

Before you can perform most of the operations listed above, you must learn how to select files. In this section, you learn how to use the MS-DOS Shell to search for, select, view, print, move, copy, and delete files. You also learn the difference between renaming and copying a file. Changing a file's attributes, associating files with other files, and renaming files are beyond the scope of this book (and beyond what you need to "get around" on a PC). In "Starting Programs" later in this chapter, you learn to use the **R**un command to start a program.

PC CAUTION

If you perform the steps in any of the following sections, *do not* perform them on the COMMAND.COM file; you could accidentally modify things so that the PC won't boot from the hard disk. Because the PC's owner would be exceptionally irate to find that the computer no longer boots from the hard disk, never use COMMAND.COM to test anything.

Searching for Files

You can search for files by using the Searc**h** command on the **F**ile menu. When you choose this command, the MS-DOS Shell displays the Search File dialog box in which you can specify a search pattern. By default, the MS-DOS Shell automatically searches the entire disk.

To find all the files with the extension BAT, for example, follow these steps:

1. Make current the Drive List section, the Directory Tree section, or the File List section.

2. Open the **F**ile menu and choose the Searc**h** command. The MS-DOS Shell opens the Search File dialog box in Figure 11.11.

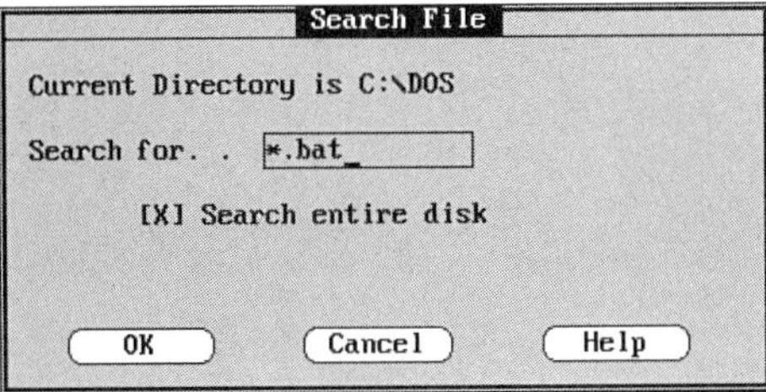

Figure 11.11. The Search File dialog box.

3. Enter the name of the file for which you want to search in the Search for text box. You can use wild cards. If you type `*.BAT`, for example, DOS searches for and displays all files that have the extension BAT.

4. Choose OK to begin the search of the entire disk.

   The results of the search appear in the Search Results list (see Figure 11.12). You then can select the file from the list as needed.

5. Press the **Esc** key to return to the main MS-DOS Shell screen.

```
MS-DOS Shell
File  Options  View  Tree  Help
Search Results for: *.BAT
C:\AUTOEXEC.BAT
C:\MENU\MAIN.BAT
C:\MENU\MENU.BAT
C:\TSREMOTE\RECEIVE.BAT
C:\TSREMOTE\SEND.BAT
C:\TSREMOTE\TSR.BAT
C:\TOP\README.BAT
C:\TAPE\DEMO.BAT
C:\NORTON\FILE1.BAT
C:\NORTON\NUDEMO.BAT
C:\COLLAGE\CLEANUP.BAT
C:\BPIES\MISC\APFIX001.BAT
C:\BPIES\MISC\DELBPI.BAT
C:\BPIES\NEWSHELL.BAT
C:\BATCH\QUIT.BAT
C:\BATCH\R.BAT
F10=Actions  Esc=Cancel                                11:56a
```

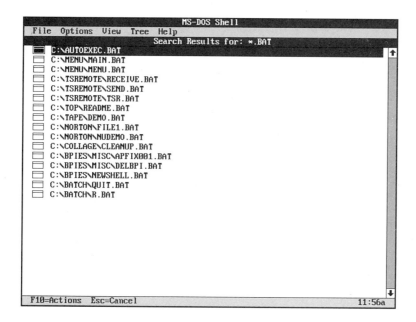

Figure 11.12. The Search Results list.

Selecting Files

Using the **S**elect All and Dese**l**ect All commands on the **F**ile menu, you can select or deselect all files in the current directory. You can select only one file or multiple files in the current directory by using the mouse or the keyboard. To select only one file, click on that file or press the arrow keys to highlight the file.

To use the mouse to select a group of files listed in sequence, click on the first file you want to select, and then hold down the Shift key as you click on the name of the last file you want to select.

To use the mouse to select a group of files that are *not* listed in sequence, click on the first file you want to select, and then hold down the Ctrl key as you click on the names of each of the other files you want to select.

You also can use the mouse to select two groups of files when the files in each group are listed sequentially in the File List section. Select the first group by following the instructions for selecting a group of files listed sequentially. Select the second group by holding down Ctrl as you click on the first file you want to include in the second group and then holding down both Ctrl and Shift as you click on the last file you want to include in the second group.

To use the keyboard to select a group of files listed in sequence, highlight the first file you want to select. Then, hold down the Shift key as you use the arrow keys to highlight the names of the other files you want to select.

To use the keyboard to select a group of files that are *not* listed in sequence, highlight the first file you want to select, and then press Shift+F8 to enter Add mode. ADD appears in the lower right corner of the MS-DOS Shell screen, indicating that you can add files to the selection. Press the arrow keys to move to the next file you want to select, and then press the spacebar to include the file in the selection. Continue this process for each file you want to include in the selection. Press Shift+F8 again to exit Add mode. ADD disappears from the bottom of the screen.

You also can use the keyboard to select two groups of files when the files in each group are listed sequentially in the File List section. To select the first group of files, follow the directions to select a group of files listed in sequence. Then, press Shift+F8 to enter Add mode. Press the arrow keys to move to the first file you want to include in the second group, and press the spacebar to start the selection of the second group. Then, hold down the Shift key as you press the arrow keys to highlight the rest of the files you want to include in the second group.

Table 11.5 describes the keys you can use to select files.

Table 11.5. File selection keys.

Key(s)	Effect
Shift+F8	Enters and exits Add mode. When Add Mode is on, ADD appears in the lower right corner of the MS-DOS Shell screen, and you can select multiple files.

Key(s)	Effect
Shift+↑	Adds the preceding file in the File List section to the selection.
Shift+↓	Adds the next file in the File List section to the selection.
Spacebar	In Add mode, starts the selection of a group of files.
Shift+spacebar	In Add mode, adds to the selection all files between the currently highlighted file and the previously selected file.
Shift+PgUp	Adds to the selection all files listed above the currently highlighted file.
Shift+PgDn	Adds to the selection all files listed below the currently highlighted file.
Ctrl+/	Selects all files in the current directory. This key combination is the equivalent of the **S**elect All command on the **F**ile menu.
Ctrl+\	Deselects all selected files, regardless of the directory. This key combination is the equivalent of the Deselect All command on the File menu.

Viewing Files

You can use the **V**iew File Contents command on the **F**ile menu to look at a file's contents.

PC NOTE

If you don't see the **V**iew File Contents command on the **F**ile menu, open the **O**ptions menu and deselect the Select **A**cross Directories command.

Usually, only text files are comprehensible. For practice, try viewing your AUTOEXEC.BAT or CONFIG.SYS file, because they are text files. Follow these steps:

1. Make current the root directory in the Directory Tree section.

2. In the File List section, highlight the AUTOEXEC.BAT file or the CONFIG.SYS file.

3. Open the **F**ile menu and choose the **V**iew File Contents command, or press the **F9** shortcut key to view the file.

   The contents of the file are shown full-screen in ASCII mode (see Figure 11.13). If the file is too big for the screen, you can press the **PgUp** and **PgDn** keys to move through the file.

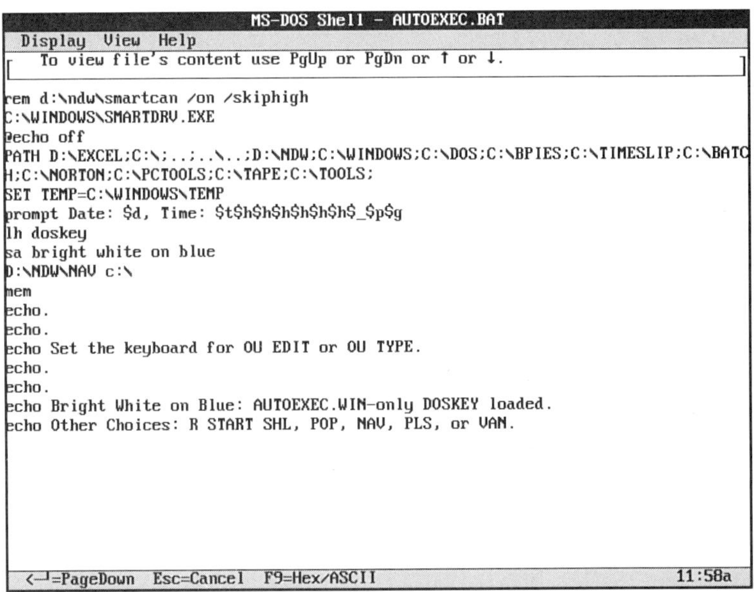

Figure 11.13.
The View screen in ASCII display mode.

4. To close the View screen, press the **Esc** key, or open the **V**iew menu and choose the **R**estore View command.

Printing Files

You can use the **P**rint command on the **F**ile menu to print files from the MS-DOS Shell.

PC NOTE

For the **P**rint command to work, you must run the DOS PRINT program *before* you start the MS-DOS Shell. If the PRINT program is not installed and you choose the **P**rint command from the **F**ile menu, the MS-DOS Shell displays a dialog box reminding you to exit the Shell and start the PRINT program.

To see how the **P**rint command works, try printing the AUTOEXEC.BAT file. The AUTOEXEC.BAT file contains the information the PC uses when you start the computer. The AUTOEXEC.BAT file is stored in the root directory. Follow these steps to try the **P**rint command:

1. Highlight the AUTOEXEC.BAT file in the root directory. If the PC doesn't have an AUTOEXEC.BAT file, highlight the CONFIG.SYS file.

2. Open the **F**ile menu and choose the **P**rint command.

   The MS-DOS Shell prints the file.

If you see a dialog box reminding you to run PRINT.COM, follow these steps:

1. Close the dialog box.

2. Press **Shift**+**F9** to exit temporarily from the MS-DOS Shell.

   The DOS prompt appears.

3. Type `PRINT` at the DOS prompt.

PC NOTE

If DOS displays the message `Bad command or file name`, you may need to change to the directory that contains your DOS commands. This directory is usually named DOS or BIN. At the DOS prompt, type **`CD\DOS`**. If `Bad command or file name` appears again, try typing **`CD\BIN`**.

4. When you see the `Name of list device [PRN]:` prompt, press **Enter**.

5. Type `EXIT` and then press **Enter** to return to the MS-DOS Shell screen.

Moving Files

When you *move* a file, you remove it from its original location and place it at a new location. When you *copy* a file, you leave the file in its original location and place an additional copy at the new location.

When working, you may create files you need to move to another directory or perhaps to another computer. To move a file or files to another computer, you first place the file(s) on a floppy disk.

If you want to move a file or files by using standard DOS commands at the DOS prompt, you must copy the file(s) to the new drive or directory and then delete the file(s) from its original location. By using the MS-DOS Shell, you can move the file(s) to a different drive or directory in one step. You can use the **M**ove command on the **F**ile menu to move files, or you can use a keyboard or mouse shortcut.

To move a file or files by using the MS-DOS Shell menus, follow these steps:

1. Select the directory that contains the file(s) you want to move from the Directory Tree section.

2. In the File List section, select the file(s) you want to move.

PC CAUTION

Do not move the COMMAND.COM file. If COMMAND.COM doesn't reside in the root directory, the PC won't boot from the hard disk. In general, never use COMMAND.COM to test anything.

3. Press **F7**, or open the **F**ile menu and choose the **M**ove command.

   The Move File dialog box appears. You see the name(s) of the file(s) you want to move in the From text box (see Figure 11.14).

Move File

From: CLEANUP.BAT

To: C:\COLLAGE

OK Cancel Help

Figure 11.14. The Move File dialog box.

4. In the To text box, type the name of the drive and directory which you want to move the file(s).

5. Choose OK to remove the file(s) from the original location and place the file(s) at the new location. Or, choose Cancel to abort the operation.

To move a file or files to a new directory or drive by using the mouse, follow these steps:

1. Place the mouse pointer on the file you want to move. If you want to move multiple files, hold down the **Ctrl** key as you click on each file.

2. Holding down the left mouse button, drag the file(s) to the appropriate directory or drive.

   As you move the mouse pointer, it changes to match the icon of the file you are moving. If you are moving multiple files, the mouse pointer changes to an icon that looks like a series of files.

3. Release the mouse button.

   The Confirm Mouse Operation dialog box asks whether you are sure you want to move the selected file(s).

4. Choose the Yes button to remove the file(s) from the original location and place the file(s) at the new location. Choose the No button to abort the operation.

If the place to which you want to move a file already contains a file with the same name as a file you want to move there, the MS-DOS Shell displays the Replace File dialog box. To complete the move operation and *write over the existing file*, choose the Yes button; otherwise, choose the No button or press the Esc key.

Copying Files

Conceptually, copying a file on a PC is similar to copying a file on a Mac. When you *copy* a file, you duplicate it. You can copy a file to the same directory (and change its name), or you can copy the file to a different directory or drive, optionally changing the file's name. When you complete a copy operation, the file exists at both the original location and the new location.

Copying a file is different from moving a file or renaming a file. When you *move* a file, you remove it from its original location. When you *rename* a file, you simply change its name—you do not create a second copy of a file, and you do not change the directory or drive on which the file is located.

To copy a file, you must supply a new location (drive, directory, or both) for the duplicate file, a new name for the duplicate file, or both. If you use a name that already exists, the MS-DOS Shell warns you that you are about to replace an existing file. Because replacing a file actually writes over the existing version, be careful when you choose a name while copying a file so that you don't inadvertently copy over a needed file.

You may want to change the contents of a file, but also leave the original intact. For this purpose, you can use the **C**opy command to make a copy of the file, and then modify the copy. You also may want to take a copy of a file to another computer (and leave a copy on the original computer). For this purpose, you can use the **C**opy command to place a copy of the file on a floppy disk. To copy the file, you can choose the **C**opy command from the MS-DOS Shell menus, or you can use a keyboard or mouse shortcut.

To use the MS-DOS Shell menus to copy a file or files, follow these steps:

1. Select the directory that contains the file(s) you want to copy from the Directory Tree section.

2. In the File List section, select the file(s) you want to copy (AUTOEXEC.BAT, for example).

3. Press **F8**, or open the **F**ile menu and choose the **C**opy command.

   The MS-DOS Shell displays the Copy File dialog box in Figure 11.15. You see the name of the file(s) you want to copy in the From text box.

4. In the To text box, type a name for the duplicate file. When you type the name, include the drive and directory. You can copy the file to the same directory under a new file name, or to a different drive or directory under either the same name or a new name.

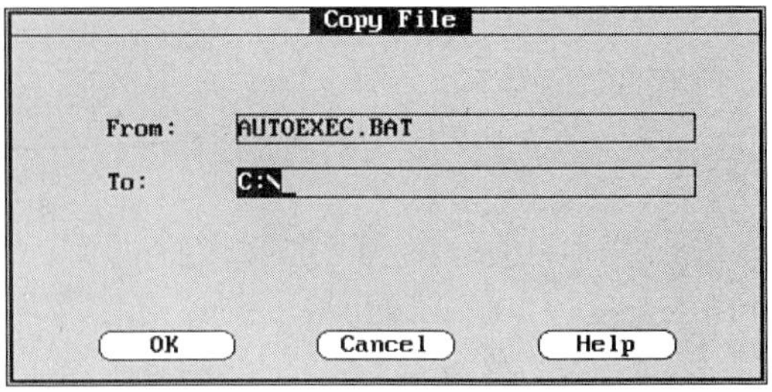

Copy File

From: AUTOEXEC.BAT

To: C:\

OK Cancel Help

Figure 11.15. The Copy File dialog box.

5. Choose OK.

   DOS copies the file(s).

You also can copy a file to another directory or drive by using a mouse shortcut. Follow these steps to drag the file to its new location:

1. Place the mouse pointer on the file you want to copy. If you want to copy multiple files, press the **Ctrl** key as you click on each file.

2. Hold down the **Ctrl** key and the left mouse button.

3. Move the mouse pointer to the appropriate directory or drive.

   As you move the mouse pointer, it changes to match the icon of the file you are copying. If you are copying multiple files, the mouse pointer changes to an icon that looks like a series of files.

4. Release the mouse button.

   The Confirm Mouse Operation dialog box appears, asking whether you are sure you want to copy the selected file(s).

5. Choose the Yes button to continue the operation. Or, choose the No button or press the Esc key to abort the operation.

If the place to which you want to copy a file already contains a file with the same name as the file you want to copy there, the MS-DOS Shell displays the Replace File dialog box. To complete the copy operation and write over the existing file, choose the Yes button; otherwise, choose the No button or press the Esc key.

Renaming Files

Both MS-DOS and the MS-DOS Shell provide a command to rename a file. When you rename a file, you simply change its name; you don't move or copy the file to a different location. You also don't make a second copy of the file. Most occasional PC users probably don't need to rename a file; instead, they need to copy a file to a new name—that is, to copy the file and change its name while copying it.

You may find, when working at someone else's PC, that you want to modify a file. You may decide, being the considerate person that you are, that you shouldn't change the original. Someone may even tell you to rename the file before you modify it.

Actually, you don't really want to rename the file; rather, you want to copy the file "to a new name." When you copy a file, you create a duplicate. To create the duplicate, you must supply a new location (drive, directory, or both) for the file, a new name for the file, or both.

Say, for example, that you want to modify ADVER.TXT, but you would rather *not* make the changes to the original file. You could copy the file ADVER.TXT to another name, such as ADVERB.TXT or ADVER.BAK. Then, you can modify the copy and leave the original untouched.

See the preceding section to learn how to make a copy of a file on which you want to work.

Because most occasional PC users don't need to rename a file, this book does not cover renaming files. If you really think you need to rename a file, see the MS-DOS User's Guide for instructions. And, as my editor says, that should stop you right in your tracks!

Deleting Files

When working on a PC, you may create a file you eventually don't need. The MS-DOS Shell enables you to delete a file by using the **D**elete command on the **F**ile menu, or by using the Del key on the keyboard.

PC CAUTION

Exercise care when deleting files. You could inadvertently delete a file you still need. If you see the Delete File dialog box and are unsure about deleting the files, cancel the operation. You always can come back at a later time (with someone who *is* sure) and delete the files. Also, be sure to back up the hard drive before you delete large numbers of files.

If you accidentally delete a file, you may be able to recover it by using the DOS 5 UNDELETE utility or a commercial disk utility program's undelete command. If you do delete a file accidentally, *you must undelete the file before you perform any other functions.* If you think you accidentally deleted a file you shouldn't have deleted, *STOP NOW.* Turn off the computer and wait until you can work with someone who knows how to recover a deleted file.

If you are *sure* you know what you're doing and want to delete a file or files by using the MS-DOS Shell menus, follow these steps:

1. Select the directory that contains the file(s) you want to delete from the Directory Tree section.

2. In the File List section, select the file(s) you want to delete.

3. Press the **Del** key, or open the **F**ile menu and choose the **D**elete command.

   The Delete File dialog box appears, with the name(s) of the file(s) listed.

4. Choose OK to delete the file(s). Or, choose Cancel to abort the operation.

Working with Directories in the MS-DOS Shell

In addition to using the MS-DOS Shell to work with files, you can use it to rename, create, and delete directories. For more information on directories, see Chapter 12. You can use DOS commands to create and delete directories, but you cannot use DOS commands to rename a directory.

Renaming Directories

The concept of renaming a directory is the same as the concept of renaming a file: you simply change the directory's name. Because occasional PC users rarely need to rename a directory, this book will not cover renaming a directory. If you really think that you need to use the MS-DOS Shell to rename a directory, see the MS-DOS User's Guide.

Creating Directories

When working at someone else's PC, you may find that you need to create several files. You may want to separate the files you create from other files on the PC. You can create a directory to hold your files. Think of a **directory** as a computer-based folder in which users place related files. People use directories to organize the files on their PCs.

Like the structure of folders on a Mac, the structure of directories created on a PC is hierarchical—you create directories *under* other directories. If you create directory B under directory A, directory B is a **subdirectory** of directory A. Directory A is the **parent directory** of directory B. When you simply want to refer to the storage unit, call it a "directory." When you want to describe relative location, use "subdirectory" and "parent directory." You learn more about directories in Chapter 12.

You can easily create directories with the MS-DOS Shell by following these steps:

1. In the Directory Tree section, select the parent directory (the directory under which you want to place your subdirectory). To create a directory under the WP51 directory, for example, select the WP51 directory in the Directory Tree section. This directory is the parent directory.

2. Open the **F**ile menu and choose the Cr**e**ate Directory command.

   The Create Directory dialog box in Figure 11.16 appears, displaying the name of the parent directory.

3. In the New directory name text box, type the name of the new directory. Do *not* include a backslash (\) as the first character of the new directory name. (When you include a backslash as the first character of the new directory name, the MS-DOS Shell displays a message in the Create Directory dialog box, instructing you to select the parent directory before you start to create a new subdirectory.)

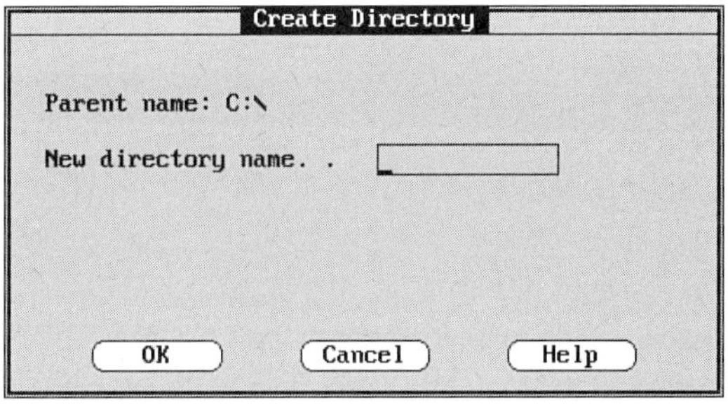

Create Directory

Parent name: C:\

New directory name. .

OK Cancel Help

Figure 11.16.
The Create Directory dialog box.

4. Choose OK to complete the operation. Or, choose Cancel to abort the operation.

For practice, create a subdirectory named MYSTUFF under the DOS directory. Follow these steps:

1. Select the DOS directory.

2. Open the **F**ile menu and choose the Cr**e**ate Directory command.

   The Create Directory dialog box appears.

3. In the New directory name text box, type `MYSTUFF`.

4. Choose OK.

   Onscreen, you see the MYSTUFF subdirectory of the DOS directory.

In the Directory Tree section, the directory icon for DOS contains a plus sign (+) to indicate that subdirectories exist for the DOS directory. Select the DOS directory and press the + key to display the MYSTUFF subdirectory. In the next section, you can use this new directory to practice deleting directories.

Deleting Directories

If you create a directory when working on someone else's PC, you may want to remove the directory when you finish using the computer.

Before you can remove a directory, you must remove all the files from that directory. You can move the files to a floppy disk, or you can delete the files from the directory. See the previous sections of this chapter for instructions.

You can delete a directory by using the Del key or the **D**elete command on the **F**ile menu—the same command you use to delete files. Follow these steps to delete an empty directory:

1. Make sure that you move or delete any files contained in the directory you want to delete. When you make current the directory that you want to delete in the Directory Tree section, the File List section should contain the message: `No files in selected directory.`

2. Select the directory you want to delete from the Directory Tree section.

3. Open the **F**ile menu and choose the **D**elete command.

   The Delete Directory dialog box asks whether you want to delete the current directory.

4. Choose the Yes button to complete the operation. Or, choose the No button or press the Esc key to abort it.

Follow these steps to delete the MYSTUFF directory you created in the previous section:

1. Select the MYSTUFF directory in the Directory Tree section. If necessary, expand the DOS directory by pressing the plus (+) key or by choosing the E**x**pand One Level command on the **T**ree menu.

2. Press the **Del** key, or open the **F**ile menu and choose the **D**elete command.

3. Delete the MYSTUFF directory by choosing the Yes button in the Delete Directory dialog box.

Starting Programs

Many PC users use the MS-DOS Shell to start programs. In the MS-DOS Shell, you can start programs from the Program List section or the File List section.

In many cases, users set up the MS-DOS Shell so that nothing appears onscreen except the Program List section. Those users probably use the MS-DOS Shell exclusively as a menu to start programs.

Starting a Program from the Program List Section

Many PC users use the Program List section of the MS-DOS Shell to set up a menu of programs. The menu commands can access individual programs or groups of programs.

When the Program List section is selected, only four menu names appear in the menu bar; the Tree menu disappears because it serves no purpose in the Program List section. Of the remaining menus, the **F**ile menu is the only one that changes its appearance (see Figure 11.17).

The Program List section may appear below the Directory Tree section and the File List section, or a user may have changed the appearance of the MS-DOS Shell screen so that the Program List section fills the entire screen (see Figure 11.18). The name of the current program group appears in the Program List section's title bar; the initial program group is `Main`.

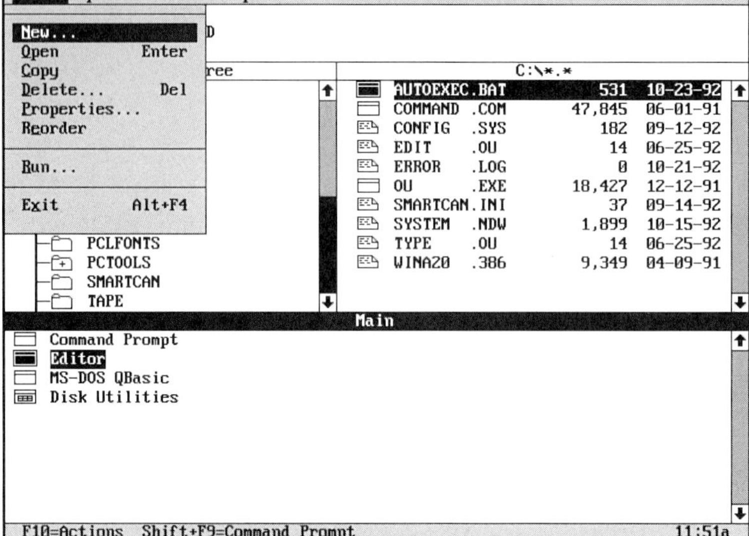

Figure 11.17.

The **F**ile menu when the Program List section is selected.

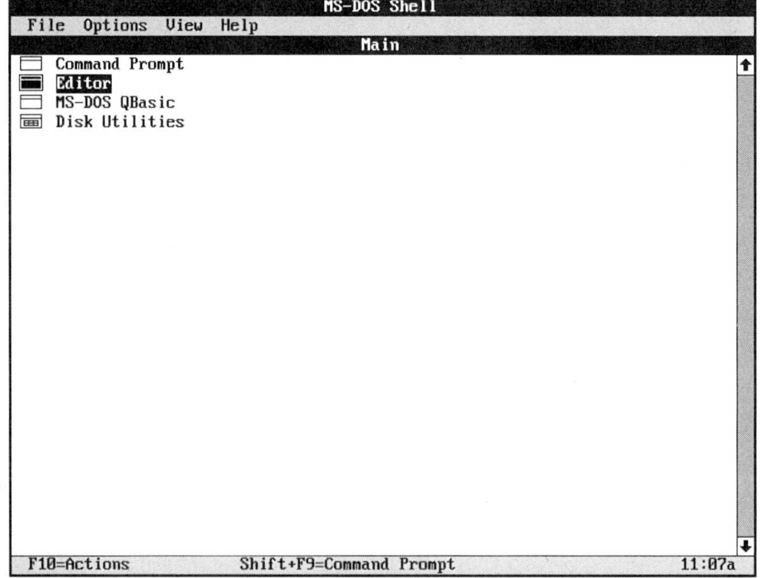

Figure 11.18.

The MS-DOS Shell screen when only the Program List section appears.

Program groups can contain both programs and other program groups. You can think of a program group as a menu choice that leads to other menu choices. The Main program group contains, for example, three program items (Command Prompt, Editor, and MS-DOS QBasic) and one program group (Disk Utilities). Notice the difference in the icons for program groups and programs.

You can start a program or open a program group from the Program List section by using the **O**pen command on the **F**ile menu. Or, you can use a mouse or keyboard shortcut. Using the mouse, double-click on the item you want to start; using the keyboard, highlight the item and press Enter. If you start a program, you can return to the MS-DOS Shell by exiting from the program. If you open a program group, you will see `Main` as an option on the Program List section menu. You can return to the Main program group by choosing `Main` from the Program List section or by pressing the Esc key.

If you don't see the name of the program you want to start listed on the menu in the Program List section, don't despair. Using the information in the next section, you still can use the MS-DOS Shell to start a DOS-based program.

PC NOTE

You *cannot* start Windows programs from within the MS-DOS Shell.

Starting a Program from the File List Section

To start a program in the MS-DOS Shell, you must know the name of the program file and the directory in which the program is located. If you do not know this information, you can use some simple strategies to figure it out.

First, note that program file names must have an extension of EXE, COM, or BAT. This criterion narrows the field. You can use the Searc**h** command on the **F**ile menu to search for all files that end in EXE, COM, or BAT to see the file names and directories of all program files.

Alternatively, you can try scanning the first few pages of the program's manual. The manufacturer usually tells you what to type at the DOS prompt to start the program. Note that you only type the *first* part of a program name to start a program at a DOS prompt. For example, if the program is named FRF.EXE, you would type only `FRF` to start the program. You could use this information and the Searc**h** command on the **F**ile menu to see the file names and directories of all files beginning with FRF.

In a program's manual, the manufacturer often suggests a directory name in which to install the program files, and most users accept these suggestions. With this information and the first part of the name of the file, you might find the file simply by scanning the directory.

If you don't have the manual for the program, you may find the information you need in Table 11.6, which lists the directory names and program file names of several popular DOS-based software programs.

Table 11.6. Default directories and startup files of several DOS-based programs.

Program	**Directory**	**Startup File Name**
WordPerfect for DOS Version 4.2 and earlier	\WP	WP.EXE
WordPerfect for DOS Version 5.0	\WP50	WP.EXE
WordPerfect for DOS Version 5.1	\WP51	WP.EXE
Lotus 1-2-3 Release 2.01 and earlier	\123	123.COM
Lotus 1-2-3 Release 2.2	\123R22	123.EXE

Program	Directory	Startup File Name
Lotus 1-2-3 Release 2.3	\123R23	123.EXE
Lotus 1-2-3 Release 2.4	\123R24	123.EXE
Lotus 1-2-3 Release 3.0	\123R3	123.EXE
Lotus 1-2-3 Release 3.1 and 3.1 Plus	\123R31	123.EXE
dBASE, all versions	DBASE	DBASE.EXE
Q&A	\QA	QA.EXE

To start a program from the File List section, follow these steps:

1. In the Directory Tree section, highlight the directory that contains the program file.

2. In the File List section, highlight the program file name.

3. Perform any of the following actions to start the highlighted program:

   Open the **F**ile menu and choose the **O**pen command.

   Double-click on the program.

   Press **Enter**.

To start Lotus 1-2-3 Release 2.4 on a computer that uses the manufacturer's suggested names, for example, highlight the 123R24 directory in the Directory Tree section. Then, in the File List section, highlight the 123.EXE file. Double-click on 123.EXE, press Enter, or open the **F**ile menu and choose the **O**pen command.

You can also use the **R**un command on the **F**ile menu to start a program. When you choose this command, the Run dialog box in Figure 11.19 appears.

Figure 11.19. The Run dialog box.

Because you have to type the entire path name for the program, use this method to start programs for which you want to specify a startup switch. In the Command Line text box, type the complete program name, including the directory in which the program is stored. For example, to start the WordPerfect program file stored on drive C in the WP51 directory, type `C:\WP51\WP`

Chapter Summary

In this chapter, you probably learned as much about the MS-DOS Shell as you ever wanted to know—maybe even *more* than you wanted to know. (If you really want to learn more, consult your MS-DOS User's Guide, or see any of the numerous books about MS-DOS—there's probably one near the computer you are using.)

You learned to understand the MS-DOS Shell screen and to navigate in the MS-DOS Shell. You learned how to search for, select, view, print, move, copy, and delete files. You did not learn how to rename a file, although you did learn that you can change a file's name when you copy it. You also learned what directories are and how to create and delete them. Last, you learned how to start a program from the MS-DOS Shell.

You learned that files on a PC are basically the same as files on a Mac, and directories on a PC are comparable to folders on a Mac. You learned that PCs, like Macs, use a hierarchical structure to organize files and directories. You learned that the MS-DOS Shell uses dialog boxes like Mac programs do, and that the contents of dialog boxes are basically similar on the two platforms.

In the next chapter, you will learn what DOS is, how to format (initialize) disks, how to organize information on disks, and how to work with files by using basic DOS commands. If you need to transfer and translate files between a Mac and a PC, read Chapter 13.

Working with Basic DOS Commands (When All Else Fails)

Working at the DOS level and using DOS commands on a PC is similar to (but more confusing than) working at the System level on a Mac.

In this chapter, you will learn what DOS is (and how to deal with the dreaded DOS prompt), how to organize information on disks, how to format (initialize) a floppy disk, and how to work with files on a PC.

What is DOS?

You can think of DOS as the software brain of the computer. DOS acts as a traffic cop, directing the activities of programs while they work. For example, DOS manages memory allocation when programs request memory.

Most of the time, the program you are using queries DOS, and the process is invisible to you. Occasionally, however, you may need to query DOS directly. You may need to query DOS to accomplish simple tasks such as checking the date and time of the computer or changing to a floppy disk drive to work with the disk in that drive.

To query DOS directly, you work at the DOS prompt and use DOS commands. The **DOS prompt** serves as a place holder that designates where you type commands. Because the DOS prompt always includes the letter of the current disk drive, you may see the DOS prompt referred to as the C prompt or the A prompt. On a PC, each drive is named with a letter of the alphabet. Drive C (or the C drive) is the name of the first hard disk drive; drive A (or the A drive) is the name of the first floppy disk drive. In most cases, the disk drives (both hard and floppy) are internal, although occasionally you may see an external disk drive. In addition, a PC may contain more than one floppy disk drive, in which case the second floppy disk drive is drive B (or, you guessed it, the B drive). You also may see an F prompt; usually (but not always), drive F represents a network drive. Whenever you see a reference to, for example, the C prompt or the A prompt, the reference means the DOS prompt on drive C or the DOS prompt on drive A.

The default DOS prompt includes the letter of the current drive and a greater than sign; for example, the default prompt that represents drive C is `C>`. Because users can customize the appearance of the DOS prompt, you may see other versions of the DOS prompt. For example, a standing favorite among many DOS users is `C:\>`, which you will see in the figures in this chapter. Next to the DOS prompt, you see a small flashing underline called the **cursor**. The cursor at the DOS prompt serves the same purpose as the insertion point on a Mac—the cursor indicates the place where characters will appear when you type.

PC NOTE

You use DOS commands to perform simple tasks such as verifying the computer's date or time or accessing information on the floppy disk in drive A. You also use DOS commands to copy files from the hard disk to a floppy disk. So, of course, you want to know where you can get a complete list of available DOS commands—an excellent question. You can get a complete list of available DOS commands from the MS-DOS User's Guide or from a number of books written about MS-DOS. (And that information alone ought to keep you from pursuing the idea!)

Trying a Few Simple DOS Commands

In this section, you get the opportunity (?) to try a few DOS commands. You learn how to get to a DOS prompt if you are looking at a menu, change to a different drive, and set the date or time on the PC.

Getting to the DOS Prompt

To try DOS commands, you must be viewing a DOS prompt. If you are working in any software package, save your work and exit. If you are in Windows, exit from Windows by pressing Alt+F4 and then choosing OK from the dialog box that asks whether you want to exit from Windows. If you're looking at a menu, exit from the menu. If you can't find a key that enables you to exit from the menu, use the following steps to try to force the PC to bypass starting the menu. Read the steps carefully before you start—you need to perform some of the steps *while* the computer is booting (restarting).

PC NOTE

Performing the following steps is equivalent to starting a Mac while holding down the Shift key so that the INITs don't load. INITs on a Mac are similar to TSRs (the acronym for Terminate/Stay Resident programs) on a PC.

1. Reboot the computer by turning it off and on with the on/off switch, or by holding down the **Ctrl** and **Alt** keys and then pressing the **Del** key (that is, by pressing **Ctrl+Alt+Del**).

2. After you see the drive lights flash on during the boot process, hold down the **Ctrl** key and press the **Pause** key (that is, press **Ctrl**+**Pause**).

   When you hold down the Ctrl key and press the Pause key, Pause acts as the Break key. You should see the following message onscreen:

   ```
   Terminate Batch Job (Y/N)?
   ```

3. Press **Y** to stop the AUTOEXEC.BAT file from executing and loading the menu.

   You then will see a DOS prompt.

All DOS commands you see in this chapter appear in uppercase letters to help you identify them quickly. When you are expected to type a command, the command appears in a special typeface as well as in uppercase letters. When you type the command, you can use either upper- or lowercase letters.

Changing to a Different Drive

PCs often have two floppy disk drives; usually (but not always), the top drive is called drive A and the bottom drive is called drive B. If a PC has two floppy disk drives, usually (but not always) one of the drives is a 5 1/4-inch disk drive and the other is a 3 1/2-inch disk drive. In the following example, you learn to change the default disk drive to drive A. If you need to change the default disk drive to drive B, substitute B for A in the following steps:

1. Insert the floppy disk into the floppy disk drive. If you are using a 5 1/4-inch disk drive, be sure to close the drive door.

2. At the C prompt, type `A:`. Don't forget to include the colon (:).

3. Press **Enter**.

   The DOS prompt changes from a C prompt to an A prompt.

To change back to drive C, follow the above steps, substituting C for A in Step 2.

Setting the Date or Time

You can use simple DOS commands to check or change the system date and time of the PC. To check or change the date the computer is using, follow these steps:

1. Make sure that you are looking at a C prompt.

2. Type `DATE`. If you make a mistake while typing, press the **Esc** key.

3. Press **Enter**.

   DOS displays a screen similar to the screen in Figure 12.1.

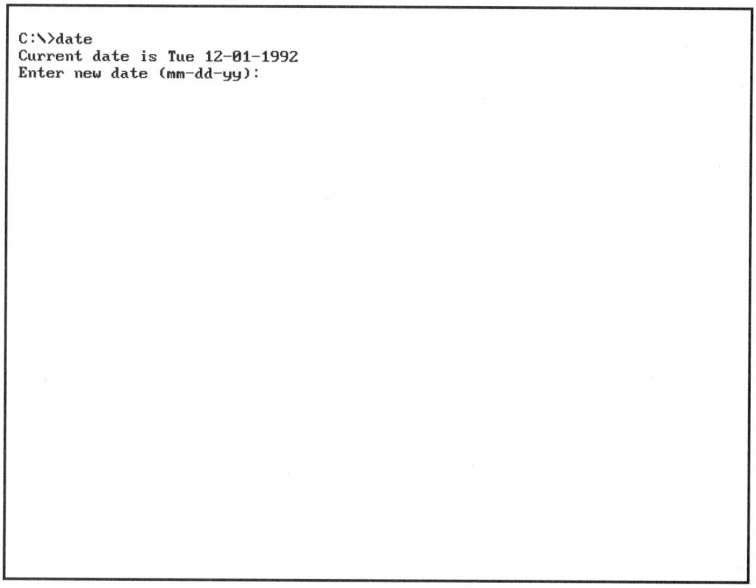

```
C:\>date
Current date is Tue 12-01-1992
Enter new date (mm-dd-yy):
```

Figure 12.1.

The screen after executing the DATE command.

4. If the date is incorrect, type the date you want the computer to use. Use the MM-DD-YY format. For example, type `06-01-93` to represent June 1, 1993. If the date is correct, skip this step and go to step 5.

5. Press **Enter**.

   DOS records the date you supplied. You can check this simply by using the DATE command again.

You can check the clock on the computer by using the TIME command. Repeat the preceding set of steps, but substitute `TIME` for `DATE` in step 2, and, in step 4, use the format HH:MM for the time. If you want, you can include the seconds (just separate the minutes and seconds with another colon). Indicate a.m. or p.m. by typing `a` or `p` at the end of the time. For example, to set the time to 4:10 p.m., type `4:10 p` at the prompt and press Enter.

Storing Information on Disks

DOS saves documents according to the specifications of the application program from which you choose the Save command. When saving, DOS places the information in a **file** on a disk. A file on a PC is comparable to a file on a Mac. Both are storage units that contain information.

You can store files on either hard disks or floppy disks, just as you can on a Mac. Floppy disks come in two physical sizes: 5 1/4 inches and 3 1/2 inches in diameter. Further, each physical size of floppy disk is available in two densities, which you use to measure the amount of information you can place on the disk. Table 12.1 shows the various sizes and densities of floppy disks and the approximate amount of information each can hold.

Size	Density	Approximate Storage Capacity
5 1/4-inch	Double	360K
5 1/4-inch	High	1.2M
3 1/2-inch	Double	720K
3 1/2-inch	High	1.4M

Table 12.1. Floppy disk storage capacities.

As you can see from the table, double-density disks hold less information than high-density disks. Many PCs use only 5 1/4-inch floppy disks; some PCs use both 5 1/4-inch and 3 1/2-inch floppy disks.

On a Macintosh, you must prepare a disk before you use it by initializing it. On a PC, you **format** a disk to prepare it for use. Just as on the Mac, you typically don't format the hard disk (and you should never format the hard disk if you are an occasional user of someone else's PC!). You limit formatting to floppy disks.

To format a floppy disk, you must use the FORMAT command. To use the FORMAT command, you must be able to find it. So, before you learn to format a floppy disk, you need to learn about how information is organized on a hard disk or a floppy disk so that you can find the FORMAT command.

Organizing Information on Disks

DOS saves documents according to the specifications of the application program from which you choose the Save command. When saving, DOS places the information in a file on a disk, either hard or floppy. You don't worry about *where* (physically, anyway) on the disk DOS places the file, because DOS keeps track of each file's location in the File Allocation Table (**FAT**). Every disk contains a FAT, which is invisible to you; the FAT acts just like the card catalog in a library—it contains name and location information for files.

On any disk, hard or floppy, you can create one or more directories to hold the files you create. A **directory** is a user-defined storage unit that people use to organize the files on their PCs. On the Mac, you store related files in folders; on a PC, you store related files in directories.

Just as folders on a Mac have a hierarchical structure, directories on a PC have a hierarchical structure. You can compare the hierarchical structure to the organizational chart of a business. The highest level directory on a disk (the president or chairman of the board of a company) is called the **root directory** (see Figure 12.2).

PC NOTE

Initially, a disk's hierarchical structure was compared to a tree's structure, with the starting point called the root. Unfortunately, the analogy is upside-down because we tend to visualize the root directory at the top of the directory structure, but a tree's roots are at the bottom of the tree. Nevertheless, in the world of PCs, the term root still represents the starting point from which you create all other directories.

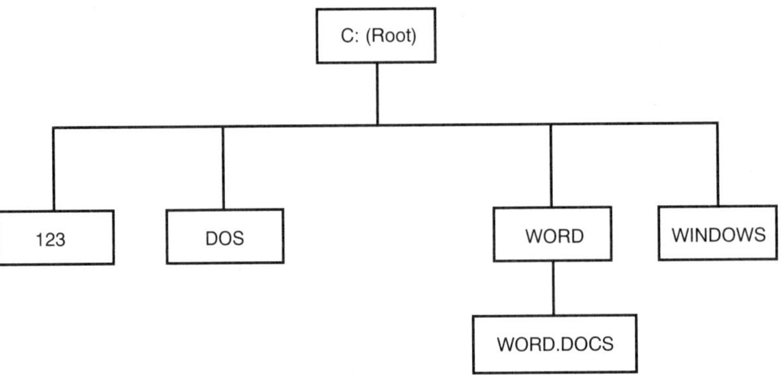

Figure 12.2. A directory organizational chart.

You create directories *under* other directories, just like you can place folders inside other folders on a Mac. If you create Directory B under Directory A, Directory B is referred to as a **subdirectory** of Directory A, and Directory A is the **parent directory** of

Directory B. When you simply want to refer to the storage unit, call it a "directory." When you want to describe relative location, use the terms "subdirectory" and "parent directory." In Figure 12.2, WORD is the parent directory of WORDDOCS, and both WORD and WORDDOCS are subdirectories of the root directory, which is represented by the drive name C:.

Understanding Paths

(Those of you who are into company politics are going to like this next part.)

Keeping in mind a company's organizational chart, you can think of a subdirectory as reporting to its parent directory (the supervisor). And, as in a chain of command, to address a subdirectory, you first must address its parent directory. DOS uses the backslash character (\) to separate one directory name from another. In Figure 12.2, the full name of the WORDDOCS directory is C:\WORD\WORDDOCS. Note that the name of the drive (C:) represents the root directory and is separated from the first subdirectory, WORD, by a backslash. The WORD directory is the parent of the subdirectory WORDDOCS, and the two directory names are separated by another backslash.

This concept of addressing a subdirectory (and the directories you have to go through along the way in the chain of command) is called specifying the **search path** or search path name. Often, users shorten search path to **path**. When you are told to specify a path, you must list the name of the directory you want to address as well as all its parent directories, separated by backslashes.

PC users often set up a default search path that DOS uses whenever the user issues a DOS command. The default search path identifies for DOS all the directories to search before DOS gives up and tells you it can't perform the command.

In Chapter 2, you learned that you can start a program by typing its program file name (without the EXE, COM, or BAT extension) at

the DOS prompt. If the directory containing the program file appears in the current search path that DOS is using to find files, you can type the program name from *any* directory and DOS will find the program file and start the program. If, however, the directory containing the program file doesn't appear in the current search path, DOS will display one of its famous cryptic error messages: `Bad command or file name`. The message simply means that DOS can't find the program file in the current subdirectory or any of the subdirectories specified in the search path.

You can use the DOS PATH command to identify the current search path DOS is using when it tries to find files. Figure 12.3 shows a sample search path.

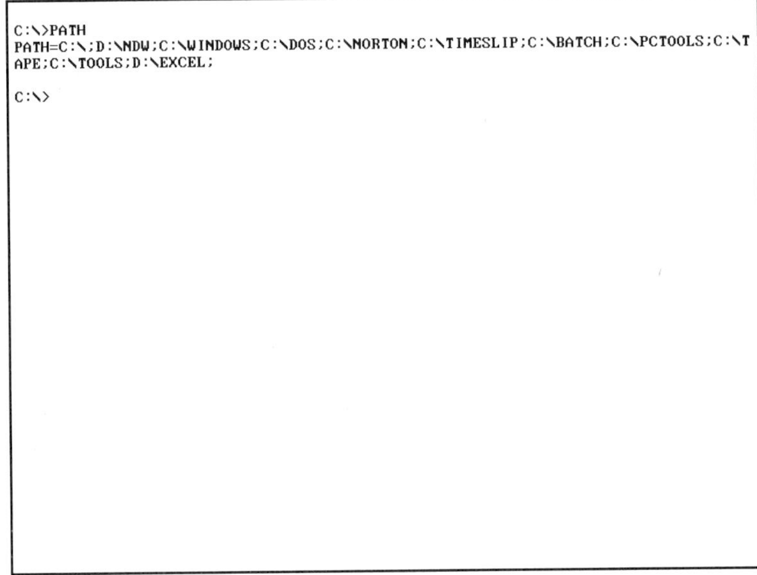

Figure 12.3.

A sample search path when you use the PATH command.

To identify the path (the list of directories) DOS searches when you issue a DOS command, type PATH at the DOS prompt. DOS displays the current search path, which includes the directories DOS searches, each separated by a semicolon (;).

You can change the current path by typing in the sequence of directories you want DOS to search, specifying the full path name for each directory, and separating the directories with a semicolon. If you try this procedure and find that things seem confused now, restart the computer by using either a cold boot (use the on/off switch to turn the computer off and then on again) or a warm boot (hold down the Ctrl and Alt keys and press the Del key). Restarting the computer restores the default path that the PC owner set up.

Listing the Contents of a Directory

You can see the contents of a directory (both the files and the directory's subdirectories) by using the DIR command. At the DOS prompt, type `DIR` and press Enter. DOS displays a listing of the files and subdirectories contained in the current directory. If you start at a C prompt, you see the files and subdirectories in the root directory. The listing may appear something like the listing in Figure 12.4.

If the directory scrolls by too quickly to read, you can make DOS pause at the end of one screen of information by typing `DIR /P`. The /P parameter tells DOS to pause; DOS stops listing files when the screen fills. You can press any key to continue the listing.

You can use the DIR command (with or without the /P parameter) whether you want to list the files on the hard disk or on a floppy disk. To list the files and directories contained on a floppy disk, place the floppy disk into the floppy disk drive, type `DIR A:` (or substitute `B:` if you want to list the files and directories on the disk in drive B), and press Enter. DOS displays a listing of the files and directories contained on the disk in the floppy disk drive. To include the /P parameter, type `DIR A: /P`.

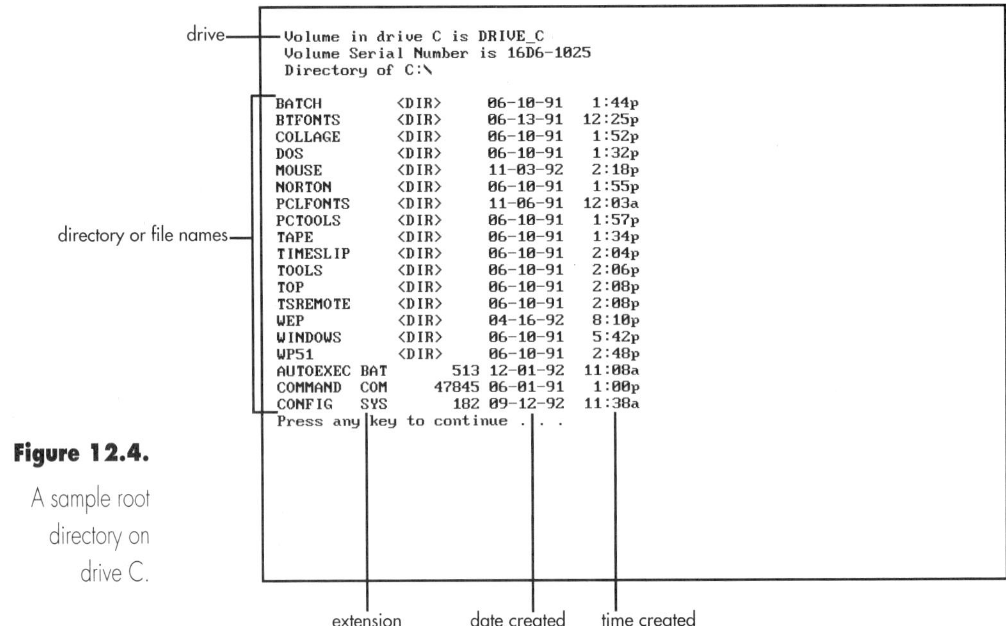

Figure 12.4.

A sample root directory on drive C.

File and directory names appear in the first column of the directory listing, and extensions appear in the second column of the directory listing. Onscreen, you don't see a period separating file or directory names from extensions, but a period is implied in the name. You can distinguish between files and directories by looking at the third and fourth columns: if the item is a file, you will see a number representing the file's size in the fourth column; if the item is a directory, you will see <DIR> in the third column. The fifth and sixth columns contain the date and time that the file or directory was created.

At the end of a directory listing, you see the number of bytes free on the disk. In Figure 12.5, the number of bytes free is 41,764,864.

```
NORTON       <DIR>      06-10-91   1:55p
PCLFONTS     <DIR>      11-06-91  12:03a
PCTOOLS      <DIR>      06-10-91   1:57p
TAPE         <DIR>      06-10-91   1:34p
TIMESLIP     <DIR>      06-10-91   2:04p
TOOLS        <DIR>      06-10-91   2:06p
TOP          <DIR>      06-10-91   2:08p
TSREMOTE     <DIR>      06-10-91   2:08p
WEP          <DIR>      04-16-92   8:10p
WINDOWS      <DIR>      06-10-91   5:42p
WP51         <DIR>      06-10-91   2:48p
AUTOEXEC BAT        513 12-01-92  11:08a
COMMAND  COM      47845 06-01-91   1:00p
CONFIG   SYS        182 09-12-92  11:38a
EDIT     OU          14 06-25-92  11:58a
OU       EXE      18427 12-12-91   1:05p
SMARTCAN INI         37 09-14-92   5:38p
TREEINFO NCD       1115 11-17-92  10:04a
TREEINFO DT        2802 11-17-92  10:04a
TYPE     OU          14 06-25-92  11:58a
WINA20   386       9349 04-09-91   5:00a
       26 file(s)       80298 bytes
                     41764864 bytes free

C:\>
```

Figure 12.5.

The end of a directory listing, showing the number of bytes available on the disk.

Changing to a Different Directory

You can change to a different directory by using the CHDIR command (CD for short). You can change to a subdirectory below the current directory or to a subdirectory that shares the same parent as the current directory. In Figure 12.6, REPORTS and MEMOS are subdirectories that share the same parent directory, WORD.

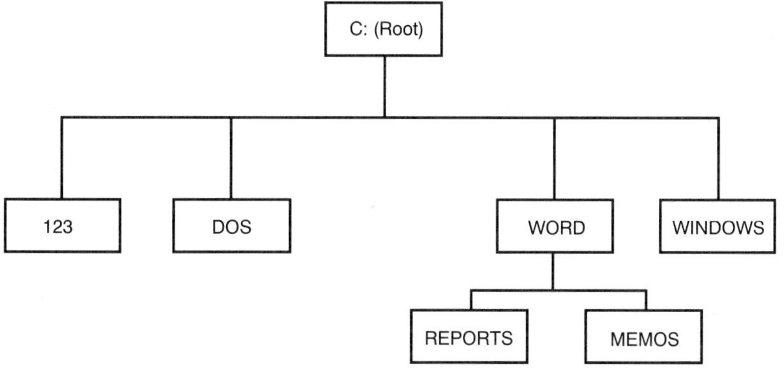

Figure 12.6.

A sample directory structure.

If you start at the root directory, you can change to the WORD directory. From the WORD directory, you can change back to the root directory, or you can change to the REPORTS directory or the MEMOS directory. If you change to the MEMOS directory, you can change back to the WORD directory, back to the root directory, or to the REPORTS directory.

At the DOS prompt, type the command, CD, the name of the directory to which you want to change, and then press Enter. Separate the command and the directory name either by a space or by a backslash (\), depending on the relationship between the current directory and the directory to which you want to change (the target directory). Use the following guidelines to help decide which separator to use:

- Use a space if the target directory is a subdirectory of the current directory. To change from the root directory to the WORD directory, type `CD WORD`, for example. To change from the WORD directory to the MEMOS directory, type `CD MEMOS`.

- Use a backslash (\) to change to a subdirectory that shares the same parent as the current directory. To change from the MEMOS directory to the REPORTS directory, for example, type `CD\REPORTS`.

Type `CD..` to change from a subdirectory to its parent directory. To change back to the root directory from *any* directory or subdirectory, type `CD\`.

Making a New Directory

When working at someone else's PC, you may decide that you would like to keep the documents you create in their own subdirectory. You can make a new subdirectory from the DOS prompt by using the MKDIR command (MD for short).

To make a subdirectory, follow these steps:

1. Change to the directory you want to be the parent of the new directory you are about to create.

2. At the DOS prompt, type `MD` followed by a space and the name of the new directory you want to create. The directory name can be no longer than 8 characters, but you can, if you want, include an extension of up to three characters. (Most PC users do not use extensions on directories.) For more information about file-naming conventions, see “Naming Files” later in this chapter.

3. Press **Enter**.

   DOS creates the new directory. You can see the directory by typing `DIR` at the DOS prompt and pressing **Enter**.

For example, to create a subdirectory named BRIEFS in the WORD directory shown in Figure 12.6, you would type the following commands from the DOS prompt at the root directory and press Enter after each command:

```
CD WORD
MD BRIEFS
```

When you then executed the DIR command, you would see three sub-directories under the WORD directory: MEMOS, REPORTS, and BRIEFS.

Formatting a Floppy Disk

Now that you understand path names, you can format a floppy disk. What’s the connection? Well, the FORMAT command, one of several commands installed with DOS, is usually contained in a directory called DOS. (Some people like to name it BIN; other users may name it something like DOS33 to represent the version of DOS they use.) Before you can format (initialize) a floppy disk, you must check to see that the directory containing the DOS commands is on the current search path, or you must change to the directory that contains the DOS commands.

To view the current search path, type `PATH` at the DOS prompt. DOS displays the current search path. Look for a directory that you think might contain DOS commands. If you don't see one, then list the directories that exist under the root directory to try to find a directory that might contain the DOS commands. To list the directories, follow these steps:

1. Change to drive C by typing `C:` and pressing **Enter**.

2. Change to the root directory of drive C by typing `CD\` and pressing **Enter**.

3. Type `DIR/P` and press **Enter** to list, one screen at a time, all the files (and subdirectories) contained in the root directory.

4. Review the information you see onscreen. Remember, you can distinguish directories from files because directories have `<DIR>` in the third column of the listing. Look for and write down the names of any directories that might contain DOS commands. If you see `Press any key to continue . . .` at the bottom of the screen, read the first screen of information that appears and then press any key on the keyboard to continue the listing. When you see the DOS prompt reappear, DOS has displayed the entire listing of the current directory.

To format a floppy disk, follow these steps:

1. Change to the drive (usually drive C) that contains the directory that contains the DOS commands. If the directory containing the DOS commands is not on the search path, type `CD` and the name of the directory containing the DOS commands. Remember to separate the CD command from the directory name with a space.

2. Insert a floppy disk in the floppy disk drive. (This example uses drive A as the floppy disk drive, but you can substitute drive B in all the steps.)

3. At the DOS prompt, type `FORMAT A:` and press **Enter**.

   DOS tells you to insert a floppy disk into the floppy disk drive (which you already have done) and press Enter.

4. Press **Enter**.

   If you are working with DOS 5, the operating system checks the disk to see whether it contains information already and, if the disk does contain information, DOS 5 tries to save the existing information on the disk so that you can unformat it, if necessary. (If you accidentally format a disk, you can try to use the DOS 5 UNFORMAT command to restore the original information on the disk.) Because the UNFORMAT command didn't exist in earlier versions of DOS, earlier versions skip this step. All versions of DOS present a warning that all data on the target disk (the floppy disk in drive A) will be destroyed. Press any key to continue.

   DOS begins formatting the disk in drive A. Onscreen, while DOS formats the disk, you may see a cylinder and head count, or you may see the percentage complete. When DOS finishes formatting the disk, DOS tells you that the format is complete and asks you to provide a volume label for the disk, which is the same thing as the name a Mac user can supply when initializing a disk.

5. Like disk names on the Mac, volume labels are optional, so you can press **Enter** without typing anything. Otherwise, type a label of no more than 11 characters.

   DOS identifies the number of bytes available on the disk and asks whether you want to format another disk.

6. To end formatting, type `N` and press **Enter**.

If you see any messages about bad sectors or invalid media, you may have tried to format a double-density disk in a high-density disk drive. Figure 12.7 shows a high-density 5 1/4-inch disk. Figure 12.8 shows a double-density 5 1/4-inch disk (note the ring in the center of the disk). Figure 12.9 shows a high-density 3 1/2-inch disk (note the holes in the two sides of the disk). Figure 12.10 shows a double-density 3 1/2-inch disk (note the hole in only one side of the disk).

Figure 12.7.
A high-density 5 1/4-inch disk.

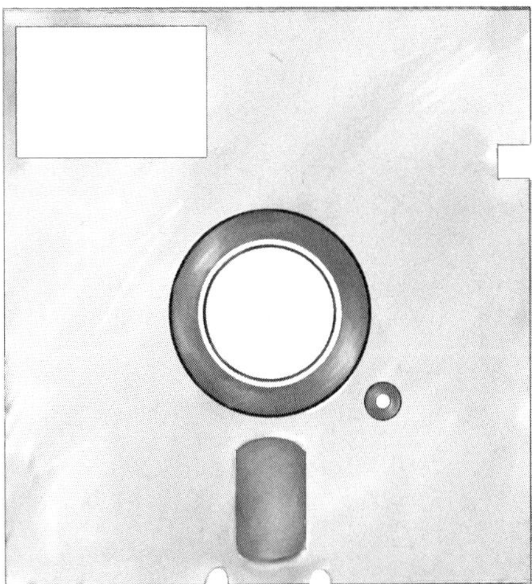

Figure 12.8.
A double-density 5 1/4-inch disk.

Figure 12.9.
A high-density 3 1/2-inch disk.

Figure 12.10.
A double-density 3 1/2-inch disk.

The command listed in step 3 in the preceding instructions should work as long as you try to format a high-density disk in a high-density drive. You cannot format high-density disks in double-density drives, but you can format double-density disks in high-density drives *if* you specify the FORMAT command correctly. If you specify the command incorrectly (and you're using DOS 5), you will see the message `This disk cannot be formatted.` (If you're using an earlier version of DOS, you will probably see a cryptic message that includes the words `Bad or invalid media.`)

If you see an error message while trying to format a double-density 5 1/4-inch disk in a high-density drive, try again, using the steps above, but substitute the following command in step 3:

```
FORMAT A: /4
```

To format a double-density 3 1/2-inch disk in a high-density drive, follow the preceding steps, but substitute the following command in step 3:

```
FORMAT A: /T:80/N:9
```

If you are using DOS 4 or later, you can use the following command in step 3 to format a double-density 3 1/2-inch disk in a high-density drive (rather than the command just listed):

```
FORMAT A: /F:720
```

Working with Files

Now for some good news—in the PC world, files are the same thing as they are in the Mac world. A file is a storage unit in which you store data, and in which software manufacturers store program code.

Unlike on a Mac, however, you must follow a number of rules when you name files (and directories) that you create on a PC.

Naming Files

The rules for naming files also apply to naming directories. Each file name and directory name can consist of two parts: the second part of the name is called the **extension**, and the first part of the name is called, for lack of anything better, the file name. On a Mac, file and folder names can contain up to 32 characters; on a PC, however, the "file name" of a file can contain no more than 8 characters, and the extension can contain no more than 3 characters. If you choose to use an extension, you must use a period (.) to separate the first name from the extension. For both first names and extensions, you can use the following characters:

A through Z

0 though 9

!@#$%^&()-{}'_~\

You must not, however, try to include either spaces or periods as part of the first name or the extension.

Certain names are reserved on the PC. You shouldn't use any of the following names for the first name of a file:

CON
AUX
COM1
COM2
COM3
COM4
LPT1
LPT2
LPT3
PRN
NUL

Also, don't use any of the following names for the extension:

COM
EXE
SYS
BAT

Renaming a File

After you name a file, you can change the name of the file by using the RENAME command. The RENAME command (REN for short) consists of three parts: the command, the current name, and the new name you want to assign. Each part is separated from the others by a space.

If, for example, you wanted to rename the file SMITH.LTR to JONES.MEM, you would type the following command from the DOS prompt of the directory that contains SMITH.LTR:

```
REN SMITH.LTR JONES.MEM
```

Remember to press **Enter** after typing the command and separate the command (REN) from the first file name (SMITH.LTR) with a space. Then, separate the first file name (SMITH.LTR) from the second file name (JONES.MEM) with a space.

Copying a File

You use the DOS COPY command to copy files from a hard disk to a floppy disk or to another directory on the hard disk. You also can copy files from one floppy disk to another floppy disk, but as an occasional PC user, you probably won't need to do this.

The syntax of the COPY command closely resembles the syntax of the REN command. The command contains three parts: the command, the current location and name of the file, and the new location. If you want, you also can include in the new location a new name you want to assign to the file. Each part is separated from the others by a space. For example, to copy the file SMITH.LTR from the MEMOS subdirectory of the WORD directory to the floppy disk in drive A without changing its name, you could type the following command at the C prompt:

```
COPY C:\WORD\MEMOS\SMITH.LTR A:
```

If you want to change the name of the file on the floppy disk in drive A, simply add a name after you type `A:`. Remember to press **Enter** after typing the command and separate the command (COPY) from the current location (C:\WORD\MEMOS\SMITH.LTR) with a space. Also include a space between the current location and the new location (A:).

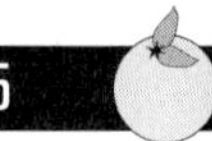

If you are already in the MEMOS subdirectory of the WORD directory, you don't need to include this location information in the COPY command. Instead, you can type the following command:

```
COPY SMITH.LTR A:
```

Suppose that you need to make some changes to SMITH.LTR, which already exists in the WORD\MEMOS directory, but you want to make a copy of the file and work on the copy. From the WORD\MEMOS directory, you could copy SMITH.LTR to a new name, such as SMITH.CPY, by using the following command:

```
COPY SMITH.LTR SMITH.CPY
```

Or, you could make your own directory under the WORD directory and then copy the file to your new directory. To change to the WORD directory from the root directory and then create a new directory (let's name it TEMP), you would use the following commands:

```
CD WORD
MD TEMP
```

To save yourself some typing, you could change to the MEMOS subdirectory. Then, you could copy SMITH.LTR from the MEMOS directory to the TEMP directory:

```
CD MEMOS
COPY SMITH.LTR C:\WORD\TEMP\SMITH.LTR
```

Note that if you don't change to the MEMOS directory or the TEMP directory, then you must spell out the location as well as the file name when you specify each part of the COPY command. You would have to type the following command:

```
COPY C:\WORD\MEMOS\SMITH.LTR C:\WORD\TEMP\SMITH.LTR
```

Also, you can change the file name when you copy the file to the new directory—just change the name that appears after C:\WORD\TEMP.

Chapter Summary

In this chapter, you probably learned more about DOS than you ever wanted to know. In fact, you may have learned why you always use a Mac—just so that you don't have to use DOS! (My editor responds with an emphatic "Right!")

You did learn that a Mac and a PC have certain similarities, though. Both store information in files, and both use a hierarchical storage structure (called directories on a PC and folders on a Mac).

You learned how to list the information on a disk or in a directory, and you learned how to change to a different directory and make your own directories. You learned about the rules that DOS imposes when you name a file or directory, and you learned how to rename a file and copy a file to a floppy disk or to a different directory on the hard disk.

Chapter 13 (the last chapter of *The MacUser's PC*) provides information on transferring and translating files from a PC to a Mac.

Transferring and Translating Files between a Mac and a PC

If you live or work in an environment where there are both Macs and PCs, someone invariably will need to move a file between the two platforms. The good news is that you can do this. And, as time has gone on, this task has become easier to accomplish. In this chapter, you will learn the basics of the simplest approach to transferring and translating files between a Mac and a PC—you will learn how to use a floppy disk and a disk (or file) translation utility to move a file between the computers and how to use application software to open the file on the "other" computer.

Remember, no matter what you do while working in this chapter, you can't "break" anything unless you start deleting files. Don't be afraid to experiment if you see something unfamiliar. (My technical editor said you would need a reminder here.)

The techniques described in this chapter work for the Mac user who needs to move a file to a PC or for the PC user who needs to move a file to a Mac. Therefore, you will find that this chapter is the same in both parts of this book. If you have read this chapter while reading *The PC User's Mac*, you don't need to read it again while reading *The Mac User's PC* (unless you really liked it).

Using Floppy Disks To Transfer Files

You may think that the most logical way to move a file from one computer to the other is to copy the file onto a floppy disk. But because both hard and floppy disks for a Mac are prepared (or "initialized" or "formatted") differently than disks for a PC, neither computer can directly read disks prepared by the other computer.

Because people sometimes need to use files on both Macs and PCs, software manufacturers have developed disk (or file) translation products that enable one computer to read disks prepared by the other computer. For both the Mac and the PC, a variety of such products exist. Apple ships PC Exchange with System 7 on Performas and Apple File Exchange with System 6.0.x and System 7 on non-Performa Macs. (PC Exchange is also available separately.) In the next two sections, you learn about using these products. Then, you will find some information on products available from other vendors.

It's important to understand that, whether you want to take a Mac file to a PC or a PC file to a Mac, you need to place the file on a DOS-formatted floppy disk. You can use PC Exchange, Apple File Exchange, or a PC to create a DOS-formatted disk.

Using PC Exchange

For users of System 7 who have PC Exchange available and enabled, transferring files is disgustingly easy. As long as PC Exchange is running, you can simply insert a DOS-formatted disk into the floppy disk drive on the Mac, and the Mac will recognize the disk as a DOS-formatted disk. You then can open the disk just like you would open any other disk and copy files to or from that disk. The Mac may not be able to read the files on the disk directly, though; you may need a file translation utility for that process. Reading the file is discussed at the end of this section. First, you learn to determine whether you have System 7 and PC Exchange. Then, you learn how to use PC Exchange to format (initialize) a DOS disk or a Mac disk. After you have a DOS-formatted disk (which the Mac will recognize), you can copy a Mac file onto the disk and then move the disk to a PC. Or, you can copy a PC file onto the disk and then move the disk back to the Mac.

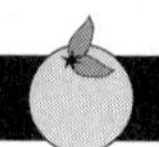

Checking for System 7

To check whether you're using System 7, switch to the Finder, open the Apple menu, and choose About This Macintosh. The window you see identifies the version of the System software with which you are working. (You can close the About This Macintosh window after you identify the version of the System software.)

Checking for PC Exchange

To check for PC Exchange the easy way, insert any DOS-formatted disk into the floppy disk drive of the Mac. If you see a disk icon that resembles the icon shown in Figure 13.1 on the Macintosh desktop, PC Exchange is installed and active. Notice that the icon is different from the typical icon you see for a floppy disk on a Mac, because it contains the letters PC in the center of the icon. If you see the dialog box shown in Figure 13.2, PC Exchange is not installed and active. (This dialog box appears when you insert an unformatted disk or a disk that the Mac cannot recognize.)

Figure 13.1. The icon for a DOS-formatted floppy disk when PC Exchange is active.

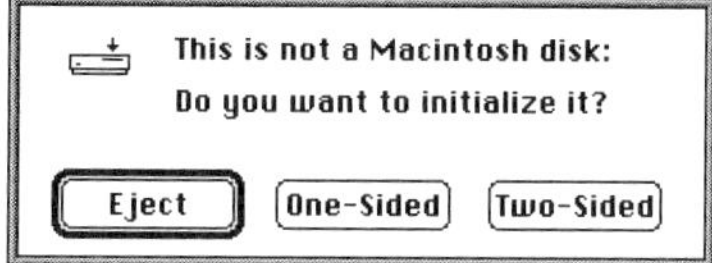

Figure 13.2. The dialog box you see when PC Exchange is not active.

If PC Exchange is not available, you can use Apple File Exchange or a third-party product to transfer files.

Formatting a Disk

If you determine that PC Exchange is installed and active, you can use PC Exchange to create a DOS-formatted disk or a Mac-formatted disk. Follow these steps:

1. Insert a disk you want to format (initialize) into the floppy disk drive on the Mac.

   If you insert a disk that has never been formatted, the Finder displays a dialog box similar to the dialog box in Figure 13.3.

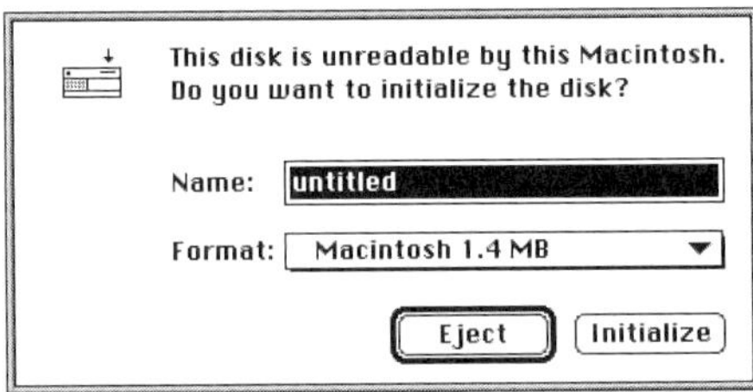

Figure 13.3. The dialog box you see when you insert a blank disk.

   If you inserted a previously formatted disk, open the **Special** menu and choose the **Erase Disk** command. The Finder displays a dialog box similar to the one in Figure 13.4.

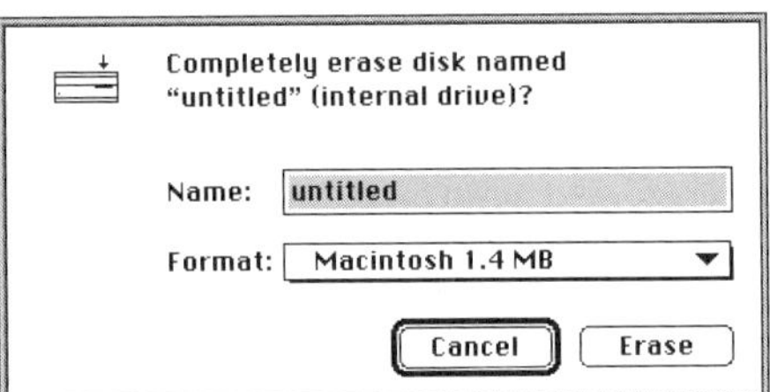

Figure 13.4. The dialog box you see when you choose the Erase Disk command from the Special menu.

2. In the Name text box, type a name you want to assign to the disk. If you plan to use this disk on a PC, use no more than 11 contiguous characters (no spaces).

3. Open the Format pop-up menu to select the format you want to assign to the disk. You can choose from Macintosh, ProDOS, or DOS. If you inserted a high-density disk, each of

the choices also shows a related density of 1.4 MB. If you inserted a double-density disk, you see related density choices of 720K for DOS and of 800K for Macintosh and ProDOS.

4. To format the disk to work on a PC, choose the DOS format.

5. If you inserted a disk that has never been formatted, choose the Initialize button. If you inserted a previously formatted disk, choose the Erase button.

   The Finder formats (or initializes) the disk.

After you have used PC Exchange to format the disk so that it can be read by either the Mac or a PC, you can copy onto the floppy disk the file(s) you want to move.

But simply creating a disk that either computer can read still doesn't mean that you will be able to open a file and use it on either computer. You still need to translate the file. The solution to this problem appears in two forms:

- Software manufacturers have developed file translation utilities as well as disk translation utilities.

- Software manufacturers of products for both the Mac and the PC often build into their products the capability to read files created on the "other" computer.

For the most part today, if you have a disk translation utility (such as PC Exchange) and the same software on both the Mac and the PC, you can easily use a floppy disk to move a file between the computers. If you don't have the same software on both computers, you may be able to use a similar software program to translate the file you transferred. For example, Microsoft Word for Windows can open not only Word for Windows documents, but also Word for DOS, Word for the Mac, WordPerfect for DOS, and WordPerfect for Windows documents (among others). So, even if you need to create a word processing document on one computer in a certain word processing program, you may be able to open the document in a different word processing program on the other computer.

In the last part of this chapter, you find sections that describe the translation process for each software program discussed in the earlier chapters of this book. If you have used PC Exchange to transfer the file to the other computer, you should refer to the section in this chapter that describes the translation process for the software in which you created the file.

Using Apple File Exchange

If you use System 6.0.x, or don't have PC Exchange, you can use Apple File Exchange to transfer files between a Mac and a PC. In addition, if you need to create a file on one computer and then transfer it to the other computer where no comparable software exists, Apple File Exchange can act as a file translator.

In this section, you learn how to start Apple File Exchange, how to use Apple File Exchange to format a DOS disk, and how to use Apple File Exchange to transfer and translate a file.

Starting Apple File Exchange

Unlike PC Exchange, Apple File Exchange is not typically running when you start the computer. In addition, unlike other programs on the Mac, you must start Apple File Exchange *before* you try to copy or translate a file; otherwise, the Mac assumes it is reading an unformatted disk and displays the dialog box that asks whether you want to initialize the disk.

Apple File Exchange is stored in the System Folder. To start Apple File Exchange, follow these steps:

1. On the Mac, make sure that the hard disk is open.

2. Open the System Folder.

3. Open the Apple File Exchange folder. If you don't see the Apple File Exchange folder, use the Find command to search for Apple File Exchange (System 6 users can use the Find File command).

4. Double-click on the Apple File Exchange application icon.

   The Apple File Exchange dialog box appears (see Figure 13.5).

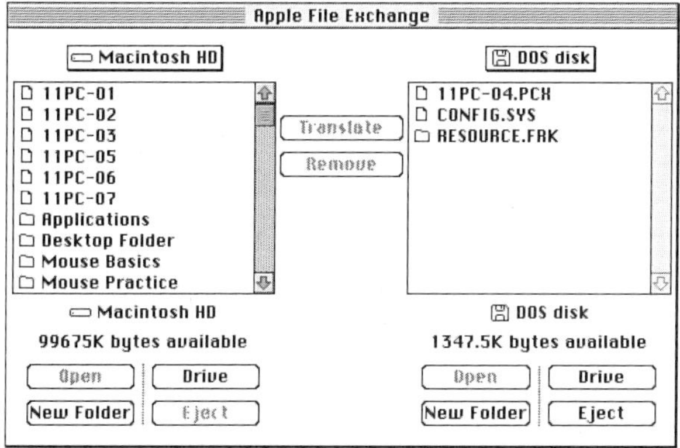

Figure 13.5. The Apple File Exchange dialog box.

Formatting a Disk

On occasion, you may need to format a DOS disk on a Mac so that you can transfer information created on the Mac to the PC. For example, if you are a Mac user and you need to supply a PC user with a file, you need to place your file on a DOS-formatted disk. Or, if you have a Mac at home and a PC at work, and you do some work at home that you want to bring to the office, you must place the file on a DOS-formatted disk. You can use Apple File Exchange to format a DOS disk (so that you can transfer a file from the Mac to a PC). Follow these steps:

1. Start Apple File Exchange as described in the preceding section.

2. Insert the disk you want to format into the floppy disk drive.

3. Choose the **Erase Disk** command from the **File** menu.

   A dialog box appears, asking whether you want to erase the information on the floppy disk (see Figure 13.6).

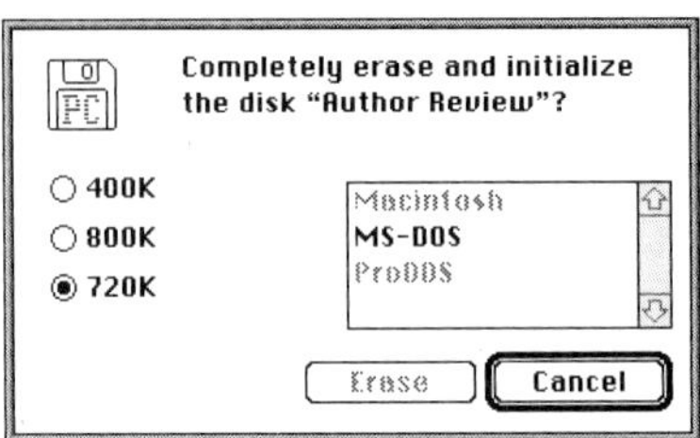

Figure 13.6.
The Apple File Exchange Erase Disk dialog box.

4. Choose a radio button on the left side of the dialog box to identify the density of the floppy disk. Use the scrolling list on the right side of the dialog box to choose the format you want Apple File Exchange to use on the floppy disk. If you inserted a high-density disk, you see only 1440K on the left side of the dialog box, but you can choose Macintosh or MS-DOS from the scrolling list on the right. If you inserted a double-density disk, the choices are 400K, 800K, or 720K. If you choose either 400K or 800K, you can choose Macintosh or ProDOS from the scrolling list on the right. If you choose 720K, you can choose only DOS from the scrolling list.

5. Click the Erase button.

   Apple File Exchange formats (initializes) the disk in the format you specified. When the process is complete, Apple File Exchange asks you to supply a name for the disk. If you plan to use the disk on a PC, limit the disk name to 11 contiguous characters (no spaces). Then, click OK.

PC NOTE

When you first place a DOS-formatted disk in the floppy disk drive, Apple File Exchange assumes you want to format the disk as an MS-DOS disk. If you, for some reason, want to format the disk as a Mac disk, choose the 800K option on the left side of the dialog box. On the right side of the dialog box, MS-DOS no longer is available, but Macintosh is.

Transferring and Translating a File

To use Apple File Exchange to transfer and translate a file between a Mac and a PC, follow these steps:

1. If you want to transfer a file from a PC to the Mac, save the PC file to a 3 1/2-inch DOS-formatted floppy disk. For more information on saving a file, see the section on saving in the chapter about the software program you are using.

2. On the Mac, start Apple File Exchange as described earlier in the chapter.

3. If you want to transfer a file from a PC to the Mac, insert the DOS-formatted floppy disk containing the file you want to transfer into the Mac's floppy disk drive. If you want to transfer a file from the Mac to a PC, format a DOS disk as described earlier in the chapter.

   On the right side of the dialog box, Apple File Exchange displays the names of the files (if any) on the floppy disk (see Figure 13.7).

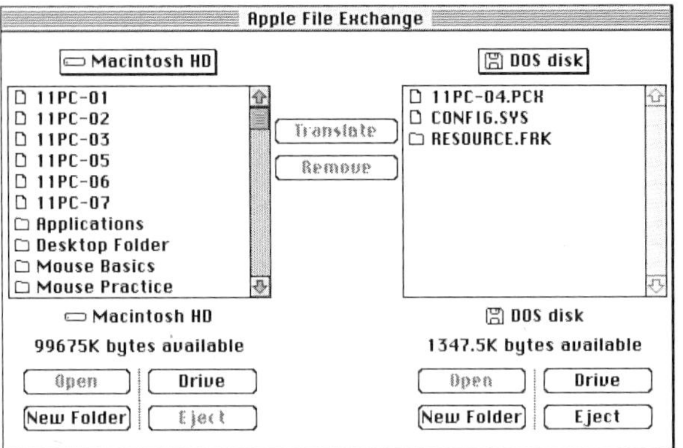

Figure 13.7. The Apple File Exchange dialog box.

4. On the left side of the window, if necessary, click on the Drive button until you display the drive on which you want to store the transferred file or from which you want to transfer a file.

PC NOTE

If you happen to switch floppy disks during this process, you may see the sides of the window switch. You can still transfer files; just make sure that you are aware of the drive *from* which you are translating and the drive *to* which you are translating.

5. On the left side of the window, open the folder into which you want to place the translated file or from which you want to transfer a file.

6. On the appropriate side of the window, highlight the name(s) of the file(s) you want to translate. You can Shift-click or Command-click to select more than one file.

7. Use the menus to make choices about the type of translation (if any) you want to perform. If you want to transfer a file from a PC to the Mac, open the **MS-DOS to Mac** menu and make sure that you see a diamond in front of the **Default format** command. If you see a check mark in front of any

other command, remove the check mark by choosing the command again.

8. When you finish setting up the translation, choose the Translate button.

   Apple File Exchange shows the progress of the translation. When the translation is complete, the dialog box reappears.

9. On the right side of the window, choose the Eject button to remove the DOS-formatted floppy disk from the floppy disk drive.

10. Open the **File** menu and choose the **Quit** command to close Apple File Exchange.

Simply transferring a file doesn't mean that you will be able to open the file and use it on the other computer. You may still need to translate the file. The solution to this problem appears in two forms:

- Software manufacturers have developed file translation utilities as well as disk translation utilities.

- Software manufacturers of products for both the Mac and the PC often build into their products the capability to read files created on the "other" computer.

For the most part today, if you use Apple File Exchange to transfer a file between the Mac and the PC, you can use the same or similar software to translate the file you transferred. For example, Microsoft Word for Windows can open not only Word for Windows documents, but also Word for DOS, Word for the Mac, WordPerfect for DOS, and WordPerfect for Windows documents (among others). So, even if you need to create a word processing document on one computer in a certain word processing program, you may be able to open the document in a different word processing program on the other computer.

In the last part of this chapter, you find sections that describe the translation process for each software program discussed in the earlier chapters of this book. If you have used Apple File Exchange to transfer the file to the other computer, you should refer to the section in this chapter that describes the translation process for the software in which you created the file.

Exploring Third-Party Translation Utilities

In addition to the two products shipped by Apple, some third-party vendors have developed disk translation utilities. You may find Access PC 2.0 on the Mac. Access PC 2.0 supports both 5 1/4- and 3 1/2-inch disks, in case you don't have a 3 1/2-inch disk drive on both computers (not the likely case, because Apple has been shipping the 3 1/2-inch SuperDrive as an internal drive on most Macs since 1989). Or, you may find DOS Mounter 3.0 on the Mac.

On the PC, you may find that hardware has been installed to let the PC "talk" to the Mac. Matchmaker, which consists of software and an internal card, enables you to connect an external Mac floppy disk drive to a PC. The PC recognizes the Mac floppy disk drive as the M drive; you basically add an "M" to the beginning of the various DOS commands you want to perform on the disk in the external Mac floppy disk drive. Or, on the PC, you may find the Deluxe Option Board and its Macintosh Control Program, which temporarily enables a PC drive to read a Mac disk.

Or, on the PC, you may find Mac-in-DOS or Mac-to-DOS, which read high-density 3 1/2-inch floppy disks. Because Mac-to-DOS also supports Mac SyQuest, Bernoulli, and erasable optical cartridges, Mac-to-DOS is most useful for transferring large files that won't fit on floppy disks.

To use most of these products, you must follow the manufacturer's instructions.

MacLinkPlus/PC is a third-party vendor product that translates files created in one format on one platform to a different format on the other platform. For example, you can use MacLinkPlus/PC to translate a PCX file created on a PC to a PICT file readable on a Mac. MacLinkPlus/PC also includes DOS Mounter, the disk translation utility mentioned previously.

Using Applications To Translate Files

In most cases, when you are transferring files between platforms, you are transferring the files between the same application on both platforms. For example, most of the time, if you need to transfer a WordPerfect for DOS file to the Mac, you want to use it in WordPerfect for the Mac.

There's good news. Most of the software vendors who manufacture products for both platforms have built into the products the capability to read files from the other platform. For this reason, you often don't need a file translation utility; you simply need a disk translation utility that lets the Mac work with a DOS-formatted disk. Because I have already discussed those utilities in the previous sections, in this section I will focus on what you do inside each software program to translate a file to the format of the corresponding program on the other platform.

There's more good news. It's usually very easy to move between platforms. Follow these two basic rules when transferring files:

- Regardless of the platform you are transferring from, start with a DOS-formatted disk. You can format the disk on the PC or on the Mac (by using a disk translation utility such as PC Exchange or Apple File Exchange to create a DOS-formatted disk).

- If you are using Apple File Exchange as your disk translation utility, you must translate the PC-based files and store them on your hard disk (in the folder of your choice) before you try to open the files in Mac programs.

Translating a WordPerfect for DOS File

Translating a WordPerfect for DOS file to WordPerfect for the Mac is very easy and works well. Follow these steps:

1. On the PC, save the open file by pressing **F7** or **F10**, making sure that you place the file on a DOS-formatted floppy disk. For more information on saving in WordPerfect for DOS, see Chapter 3 of *The Mac User's PC.*

2. On the Mac, make sure that the disk translation utility is active, and insert the DOS disk into the floppy disk drive. If you're using Apple File Exchange, make sure that you "translate" the file you want to open in WordPerfect for the Mac, and place the file in a folder of your choice on the Mac hard disk. Then, quit Apple File Exchange.

3. Start WordPerfect for the Mac by using one of the techniques described in Chapter 2 of *The PC User's Mac.*

4. Choose the **Open** command from the **File** menu. For more information on opening in WordPerfect for the Mac, see Chapter 3 of *The PC User's Mac.*

   WordPerfect for the Mac displays the Open dialog box in Figure 13.8.

5. In the Show pop-up menu, choose All to see all files. (WordPerfect for the Mac defaults to showing only WordPerfect for the Mac files.)

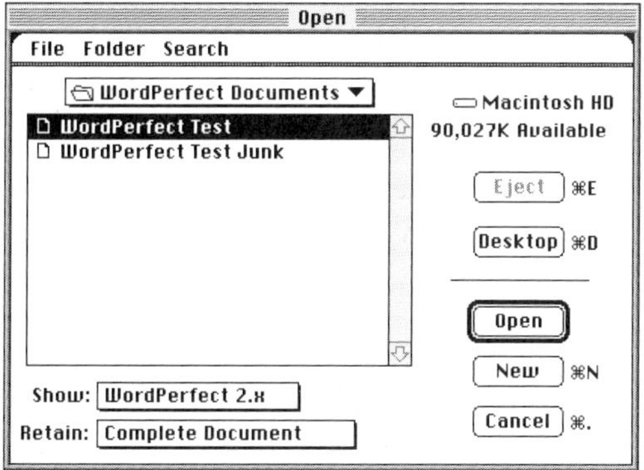

Figure 13.8.
The Open dialog box.

6. Choose the Desktop button on the right side of the dialog box.

7. Navigate to the WordPerfect for DOS file. If you are using Apple File Exchange, you already copied the WordPerfect for DOS file to someplace on the hard disk. If you are using PC Exchange, the WordPerfect for DOS file may be on the floppy disk.

8. In the scrolling list, highlight the WordPerfect for DOS file you want to open. Then choose the Open button on the right side of the dialog box.

   WordPerfect for the Mac translates and opens the WordPerfect for DOS document.

PC TIP

WordPerfect for the Mac translates the file using the default font in WordPerfect for the Mac, *not* the font you were using in WordPerfect for DOS. You may want to consider changing the font in WordPerfect for DOS to your WordPerfect for the Mac default font before you create the file, or you may want to change fonts in WordPerfect for the Mac after you translate the file.

Translating a WordPerfect for Windows File

Translating a WordPerfect for Windows file to WordPerfect for the Mac is very easy and works well. Follow these steps:

1. On the PC, save the file by using the Save **A**s command on the **F**ile menu, making sure that you place the file on a DOS-formatted floppy disk. For more information on saving in WordPerfect for Windows, see Chapter 4 of *The Mac User's PC.*

2. On the Mac, make sure that the disk translation utility is active, and insert the DOS disk into the floppy disk drive. If you're using Apple File Exchange, make sure that you "translate" the file you want to open in WordPerfect for the Mac, and place the file in a folder of your choice on the Mac hard disk. Then, quit Apple File Exchange.

3. Start WordPerfect for the Mac by using one of the techniques described in Chapter 2 of *The PC User's Mac.*

4. Choose the **Open** command from the **File** menu. For more information on saving in WordPerfect for the Mac, see Chapter 3 of *The PC User's Mac.*

   WordPerfect for the Mac displays the Open dialog box in Figure 13.9.

5. In the Show pop-up menu, choose All to see all files. (WordPerfect for the Mac defaults to showing only WordPerfect for the Mac files.)

6. Choose the Desktop button on the right side of the dialog box.

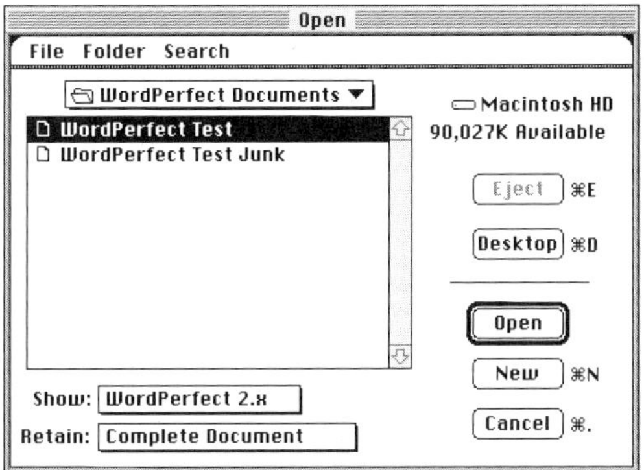

Figure 13.9.

The Open dialog box.

7. Navigate to the DOS file. If you are using Apple File Exchange, the DOS file is somewhere on the hard disk. If you are using PC Exchange, the DOS file may be on the floppy disk.

8. In the scrolling list, highlight the WordPerfect for Windows file you want to open. Then, choose the Open button on the right side of the dialog box.

   WordPerfect for the Mac translates and opens the WordPerfect for Windows document.

PC TIP

WordPerfect for the Mac translates the file using the default font in WordPerfect for the Mac, *not* the font you were using in WordPerfect for Windows. You may want to consider changing the font in WordPerfect for Windows to your WordPerfect for the Mac default font before you create the file, or you may want to change fonts in WordPerfect for the Mac after you translate the file.

Translating a WordPerfect for the Mac File

Translating a WordPerfect for the Mac file to WordPerfect for DOS or WordPerfect for Windows is only a little more complicated than saving a file in WordPerfect for the Mac. Follow these steps:

1. In WordPerfect for the Mac, use the **Open** command on the **File** menu to open the file you want to move to WordPerfect for DOS or WordPerfect for Windows. For more information on opening in WordPerfect for the Mac, see Chapter 3 of *The PC User's Mac.*

2. Open the **File** menu and choose the **Save As** command. For more information on saving in WordPerfect for the Mac, see Chapter 3 of *The PC User's Mac.*

   The Save As dialog box in Figure 13.10 appears.

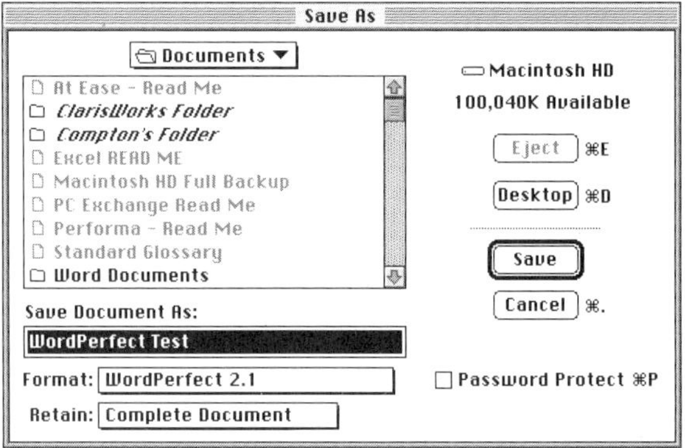

Figure 13.10. The Save As dialog box.

3. From the Format pop-up menu, choose the appropriate version of WordPerfect for DOS (Version 4.2, Version 5.0, or Version 5.1) or WordPerfect for Windows (Version 5.1).

4. Click in the Save Document As text box and type a name for the file. Be sure to follow DOS naming conventions—eight characters for the first name, a period, then three characters for the extension. (For more information on DOS file-naming conventions, see Chapter 12 of *The Mac User's PC*.)

5. Choose the Save button.

   WordPerfect for the Mac saves the file on the hard disk in the format you specified.

6. Make sure that the disk translation utility is active, and insert (and, if necessary, format) a DOS disk into the floppy disk drive. See the first part of this chapter for more information on disk translation utilities and formatting DOS disks.

7. If PC Exchange is active, copy (by dragging) the file from the hard disk to the floppy disk. If Apple File Exchange is active, navigate to the file you want to move to the PC and "translate" it to the DOS-formatted floppy disk.

8. Eject the floppy disk from the floppy disk drive on the Mac and place the disk into the floppy disk drive on the PC.

9. Using one of the methods described in Chapter 2 of *The Mac User's PC*, start WordPerfect for DOS or WordPerfect for Windows.

10. Retrieve or open the file as you usually would in WordPerfect for DOS (press **F10**) or WordPerfect for Windows (use the **Open** command on the **File** menu). For more information on retrieving or opening in WordPerfect for DOS or Word Perfect for Windows, see Chapter 3 or 4 of *The Mac User's PC*.

Translating a Word for DOS File

Translating a Word for DOS file to Word for the Mac is fairly easy. Follow these steps:

1. On the PC, save the file by using the Save **A**s command on the **F**ile menu, making sure that you place the file on a DOS-formatted 3 1/2-inch floppy disk. For more information on saving in Word for DOS, see Chapter 5 of *The Mac User's PC.*

2. On the Mac, make sure that the disk translation utility is active, and insert the DOS disk into the floppy disk drive. If you're using Apple File Exchange, make sure that you "translate" the file you want to open in Word for the Mac, and place the file in a folder of your choice on the Mac hard disk. Then, quit Apple File Exchange.

3. Start Word for the Mac by using one of the techniques described in Chapter 2 of *The PC User's Mac.*

4. Choose the **Open** command from the **File** menu. For more information on opening in Word for the Mac, see Chapter 4 of *The PC User's Mac.*

   Word displays the Open dialog box in Figure 13.11.

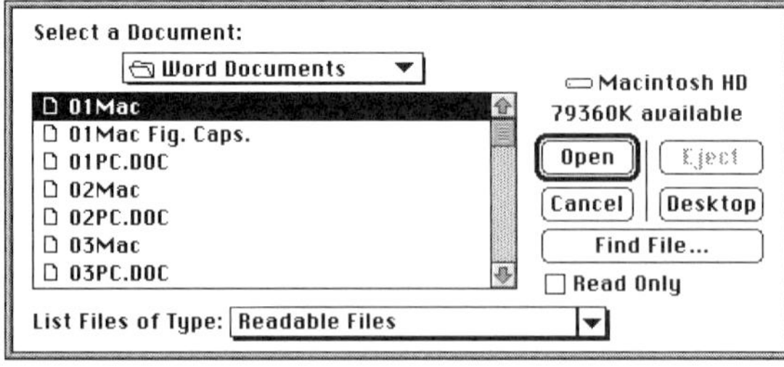

Figure 13.11.
The Open dialog box.

5. Choose the Desktop button on the right side of the dialog box.

6. Navigate to the DOS file. If you are using Apple File Exchange, you already copied the DOS file to someplace on the hard disk. If you are using PC Exchange, the DOS file may still be on the floppy disk.

7. In the scrolling list, highlight the Word for DOS file you want to open. Then choose the Open button on the right side of the dialog box.

   Unless you copied NORMAL.STY along with the document onto the floppy disk (and, unless NORMAL.STY has been modified, you *won't* be able to find it on the PC to copy it to the floppy disk), a message appears at the bottom of the dialog box that asks you to find and attach the style sheet NORMAL.STY. If you didn't copy NORMAL.STY, choose the Ignore button.

   Word for the Mac translates and opens the Word for DOS document.

Translating a Word for Windows File

Translating a Word for Windows file to Word for the Mac is only a little more complicated than saving a file in Word for Windows. Follow these steps:

PC NOTE

You may have some trouble (for example, Type 1 errors) transferring a Word for Windows file to Word for the Mac without first converting the file to Word for the Mac format. In these steps, therefore, you save the Word for Windows file as a Word for the Mac file before you try to open the file in Word for the Mac.

1. On the PC, in Word for Windows, open the file you want to move to the Mac. For more information on opening in Word for Windows, see Chapter 6 of *The Mac User's PC.*

2. Open the **F**ile menu and choose the Save **A**s command. For more information on saving in Word for Windows, see Chapter 6 of *The Mac User's PC.*

   The Save As dialog box in Figure 13.12 appears.

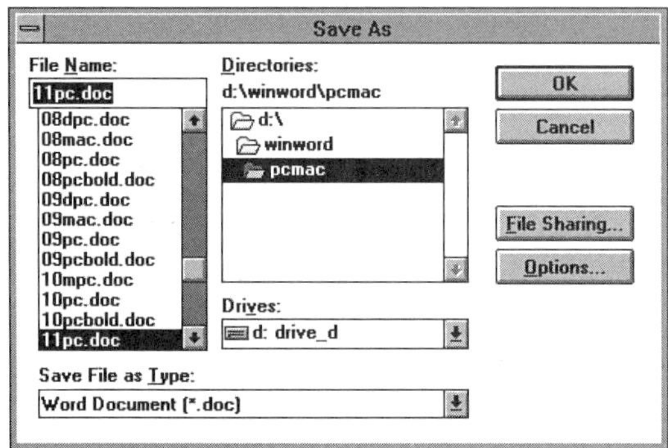

Figure 13.12. The Save As dialog box.

3. Insert the 3 1/2-inch DOS-formatted disk on which you want to store the translated file into the floppy disk drive.

4. Open the Dri**v**es drop-down list box and choose the floppy disk drive.

5. Open the Save File as **T**ype drop-down list box and choose Word for the Macintosh (4.0 or 5.0, depending on the version you use on the Mac).

6. Choose OK.

   Word for Windows saves the file in Word for the Mac format.

7. On the Mac, make sure that the disk translation utility is active, and insert the DOS disk into the floppy disk drive. If you're using Apple File Exchange, make sure that you "translate" the file you want to open in Word for the Mac,

and place the file in a folder of your choice on the Mac hard disk. Then, quit Apple File Exchange.

8. Start Word for the Mac by using one of the techniques described in Chapter 2 of *The PC User's Mac.*

9. Choose the **Open** command from the **File** menu. For more information on opening in Word for the Mac, see Chapter 4 of *The PC User's Mac.*

   Word displays the Open dialog box in Figure 13.13.

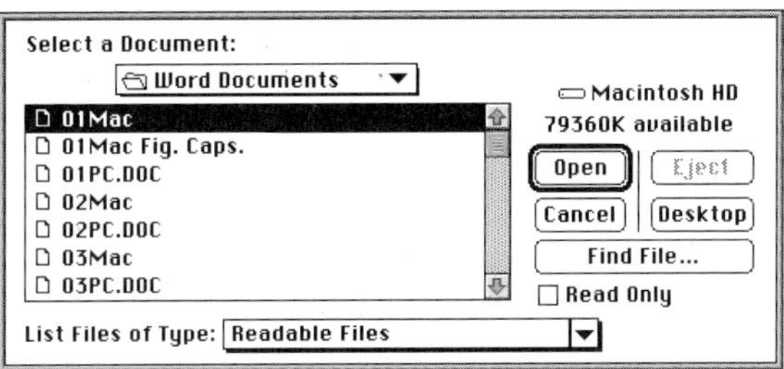

Figure 13.13.
The Open dialog box.

10. Choose the Desktop button on the right side of the dialog box.

11. Navigate to the DOS file. If you are using Apple File Exchange, you already copied the DOS file to someplace on the hard disk. If you are using PC Exchange, the DOS file may still be on the floppy disk.

12. In the scrolling list, highlight the DOS file you want to open on the left side of the dialog box. Then, choose the Open button on the right side of the dialog box.

    Word for the Mac translates and opens the Word for Windows document.

Translating a Word for the Mac File

Translating a Word for the Mac file to Word for DOS or Word for Windows is only a little more complicated than saving a file in Word for the Mac. Follow these steps:

1. In Word for the Mac, use the **Open** command on the **File** menu to open the file you want to move to Word for DOS or Word for Windows. For more information on opening in Word for the Mac, see Chapter 4 of *The PC User's Mac.*

2. Open the **File** menu and choose the **Save As** command. For more information on saving in Word for the Mac, see Chapter 4 of *The PC User's Mac.*

   The Save As dialog box in Figure 13.14 appears.

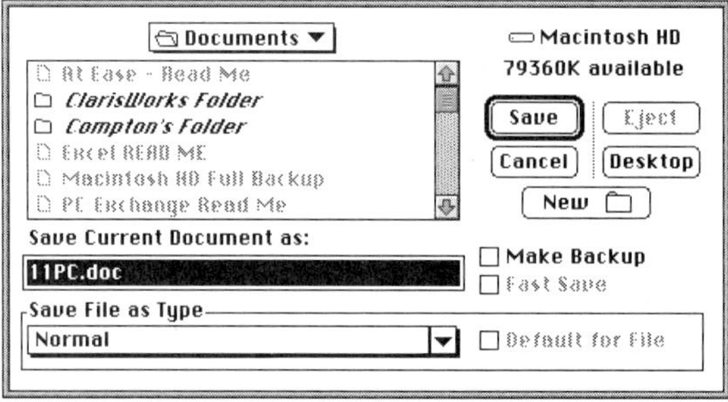

Figure 13.14.
The Save As dialog box.

3. Open the Save File as Type pop-up menu and choose the appropriate version of Word for Windows (Version 1.0 or Version 2.0) or Word for DOS.

4. Click in the Save Current Document As text box and type a name for your file. Be sure to follow the DOS naming conventions—eight characters for the first name, a period, then three characters for the extension. (For more information on DOS file-naming conventions, see Chapter 12 of *The Mac User's PC.*)

PC NOTE

When you translate a file to Word for DOS format, you see a dialog box asking you to attach a style sheet to the document. Because you probably don't have a separate style sheet on the Mac, you can't attach one, so choose No. When you open the document in Word for DOS, you may need to do some reformatting.

5. Choose the Save button.

   Word for the Mac saves the file to the hard disk in the format you specified.

6. Make sure that the disk translation utility is active, and insert (and, if necessary, format) a DOS disk into the floppy disk drive. See the first part of this chapter for more information on disk translation utilities and formatting DOS disks.

7. If PC Exchange is active, copy (by dragging) the file from the hard disk to the floppy disk. If Apple File Exchange is active, navigate to the file you want to move to the PC and "translate" it to the DOS-formatted floppy disk.

8. Eject the floppy disk from the floppy disk drive on the Mac and place the disk into the floppy disk drive on the PC.

9. Using one of the techniques described in Chapter 2 of *The Mac User's PC*, start Word for DOS or Word for Windows.

10. Use the **O**pen command on the **F**ile menu to open the document in Word for DOS or Word for Windows. For more information on opening in Word for DOS or Word Perfect for Windows, see Chapter 5 or 6 of *The Mac User's PC.*

PC TIP

In step 5, if you are translating to Word for Windows, you can save the document as a Normal type of document, in which case Word for the Mac saves the document in Word for the Mac format. When you open the document in Word for Windows, Word for Windows recognizes the Mac format and suggests that you convert the file from Word for the Mac. Simply choose OK. The conversion to Word for Windows format works equally well whether you convert in Word for the Mac or in Word for Windows.

Translating an Excel for Windows File

Translating an Excel for Windows file to Excel for the Mac is very easy and works well because both versions of Excel use the same file format. Follow these steps:

1. On the PC, use the Save **A**s command on the **F**ile menu to save the file, making sure that you place the file on a floppy disk. For more information on saving in Excel for Windows, see Chapter 7 of *The Mac User's PC.*

2. On the Mac, make sure that the disk translation utility is active, and insert the DOS disk into the floppy disk drive. If you're using Apple File Exchange, make sure that you "translate" the file you want to open in Excel for the Mac, and place the file in a folder of your choice on the Mac hard disk. Then, quit Apple File Exchange.

3. Start Excel for the Mac by using one of the techniques described in Chapter 2 of *The PC User's Mac.*

4. Choose the **Open** command from the **File** menu. For more information on opening in Excel for the Mac, see Chapter 5 of *The PC User's Mac.*

   Excel displays the Open dialog box shown in Figure 13.15.

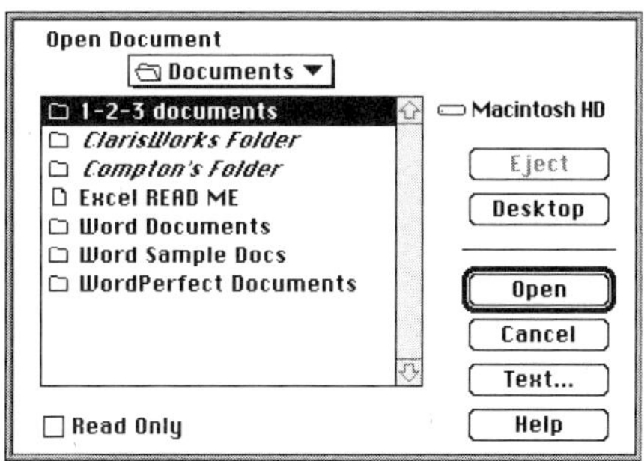

Figure 13.15.
The Open dialog box.

5. Choose the Desktop button on the right side of the dialog box.

6. Navigate to the Excel for Windows file. If you are using Apple File Exchange, you already copied the Excel for Windows file to someplace on the hard disk. If you are using PC Exchange, the Excel for Windows file may still be on the floppy disk.

7. In the scrolling list, highlight the Excel for Windows file you want to open. Then, choose the Open button from the right side of the dialog box.

   Excel for the Mac opens the worksheet.

Translating an Excel for the Mac File

Translating an Excel for the Mac file to Excel for Windows is only a little more complicated than saving a file in Excel for the Mac. Follow these steps:

1. In Excel for the Mac, use the **Open** command on the **File** menu to open the file you want to move to Excel for Windows. For more information on opening in Excel for the Mac, see Chapter 5 of *The PC User's Mac.*

2. Open the **File** menu and choose the **Save As** command. For more information on saving in Excel for the Mac, see Chapter 5 of *The PC User's Mac.*

   The Save As dialog box in Figure 13.16 appears.

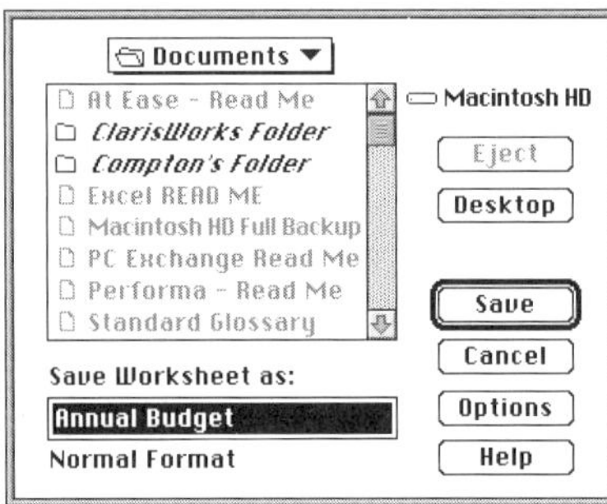

Figure 13.16.
The Save As dialog box.

3. Click in the Save Worksheet As text box and type a name for your file. Be sure to follow the DOS naming conventions—eight characters for the first name, a period, then XLS as the three-character extension. (For more information on DOS file-naming conventions, see Chapter 12 of *The Mac User's PC.*)

4. Choose the Save button.

   Excel for the Mac saves the file to the hard disk.

5. Make sure that the disk translation utility is active, and insert (and, if necessary, format) a DOS disk into the floppy disk drive. See the first part of this chapter for more information on disk translation utilities and formatting DOS disks.

6. If PC Exchange is active, copy (by dragging) the file from the hard disk to the floppy disk. If Apple File Exchange is active, navigate to the file you want to move to the PC and "translate" it to the DOS-formatted floppy disk.

7. Eject the floppy disk from the floppy disk drive on the Mac and place the disk into the floppy disk drive of the PC.

8. Using one of the methods described in Chapter 2 of *The Mac User's PC*, start Excel for Windows.

9. Use the **O**pen command on the **F**ile menu to open the document in Excel for Windows. For more information on opening in Excel for Windows, see Chapter 7 of *The Mac User's PC*.

   Excel for Windows opens the worksheet.

Translating 1-2-3 for DOS Files

To translate PC versions of Lotus 1-2-3 files, you use Lotus 1-2-3 for the Mac. Translating 1-2-3 files created on a PC is not difficult. At this time, however, 1-2-3 for the Mac cannot translate all files created with all PC versions of 1-2-3. You can translate all files created by 1-2-3 Release 3.x and 1-2-3 for Windows (see the next section), but you are limited to translating only worksheet files created by Release 2.x. You cannot translate formatting files for 1-2-3 Release 2.x, which have an extension of FMT or ALL. Worksheet files have an extension of WK1.

When you use Release 2.x of 1-2-3 to create publishing and presentation information, you create that information using one of three add-in products: Allways, Impress, or Wysiwyg. The publishing and presentation information is not stored in the worksheet file with your data; it is stored in a file with an extension of ALL or FMT. The data in your worksheet is stored in a file with an extension of WK1.

You can translate Release 2.x worksheet files, but you cannot translate Release 2.x publishing and presentation files.

To translate Lotus 1-2-3 Release 2.x files, follow these steps:

1. On the PC, use the **S**ave command on the **F**ile menu to save the file, making sure that you place the file on a floppy disk. For more information on saving in 1-2-3 for DOS, see Chapter 8 of *The Mac User's PC.*

2. On the Mac, make sure that the disk translation utility is active, and insert the DOS disk into the floppy disk drive. If you're using Apple File Exchange, make sure that you "translate" the file you want to open in 1-2-3 for the Mac, and place the file in a folder of your choice on the Mac hard disk. Then, quit Apple File Exchange.

3. Start 1-2-3 for the Mac by using one of the techniques described in Chapter 2 of *The PC User's Mac.*

4. Choose the **Open** command from the **File** menu. For more information on opening in 1-2-3 for the Mac, see Chapter 6 of *The PC User's Mac.*

   1-2-3 for the Mac displays the Open dialog box.

5. From the Show pop-up menu, choose All Types.

   1-2-3 displays all files in the scrolling list.

6. Choose the Desktop button on the right side of the dialog box.

7. Navigate to the 1-2-3 for DOS file. If you are using Apple File Exchange, you already copied the 1-2-3 for DOS file to someplace on the hard disk. If you are using PC Exchange, the 1-2-3 for DOS file may still be on the floppy disk.

The Open dialog box you see should now appear similar to the one in Figure 13.17.

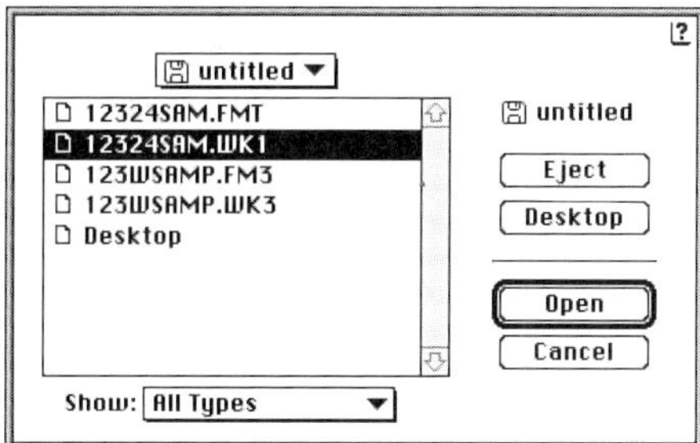

Figure 13.17. The Open dialog box after choosing the file type to show and navigating to the 1-2-3 for DOS file.

8. In the scrolling list, highlight the name of the WK1 file you want to open. Then choose the Open button on the right side of the dialog box.

1-2-3 for the Mac opens the 1-2-3 Release 2.x file. None of the formatting you applied using 1-2-3 Release 2.x appears.

PC CAUTION

Any PIC files (graphs) and CGM files (clip art pictures) used in the worksheet *will not* translate from the PC. Instead, you will see gray squares representing these files. If you save the files and then move them back to the PC, you still will see gray squares wherever you had included graphs or clip art.

Translating a 1-2-3 for Windows File

You can translate all files created by Lotus 1-2-3 Release 3.x and Lotus 1-2-3 for Windows; the process for translating either kind of file is the same. When you add publishing and presentation information to any worksheet you create in any release of Lotus 1-2-3, the publishing and presentation information is stored in a separate formatting file, while the data is stored in a worksheet file. Typically, formatting files for 1-2-3 Release 3.x and 1-2-3 for Windows have an extension of FM3, while worksheet files have an extension of WK3.

To translate Lotus 1-2-3 Release 3.x and Lotus 1-2-3 for Windows files, follow these steps:

1. On the PC, use the Save **A**s command on the **F**ile menu to save the file, making sure that you place the file on a 3 1/2-inch DOS-formatted floppy disk. For more information on saving in 1-2-3 for DOS, see Chapter 8 of *The Mac User's PC.* For more information on saving in 1-2-3 for Windows, see Chapter 9 of *The Mac User's PC.*

2. On the Mac, make sure that the disk translation utility is active, and insert the DOS disk into the floppy disk drive. If you're using Apple File Exchange, make sure that you "translate" the file you want to open in 1-2-3 for the Mac, and place the file in a folder of your choice on the Mac hard disk. Then, quit Apple File Exchange.

3. Start 1-2-3 for the Mac by using one of the techniques described in Chapter 2 of *The PC User's Mac.*

4. Choose the **Open** command from the **File** menu. For more information on opening in 1-2-3 for the Mac, see Chapter 6 of *The PC User's Mac.*

   1-2-3 for the Mac displays the Open dialog box.

5. In the Show pop-up menu, choose 123DOS (WK3,FM3).

   Because you just told 1-2-3 for the Mac to display only files with an extension of FM3, you may not see any files in the list on the left.

6. Choose the Desktop button on the right side of the dialog box.

7. Navigate to the DOS file. If you are using Apple File Exchange, you already copied the DOS file to someplace on the hard disk. If you are using PC Exchange, the DOS file may still be on the floppy disk.

   The Open dialog box you see should now appear similar to the one in Figure 13.18.

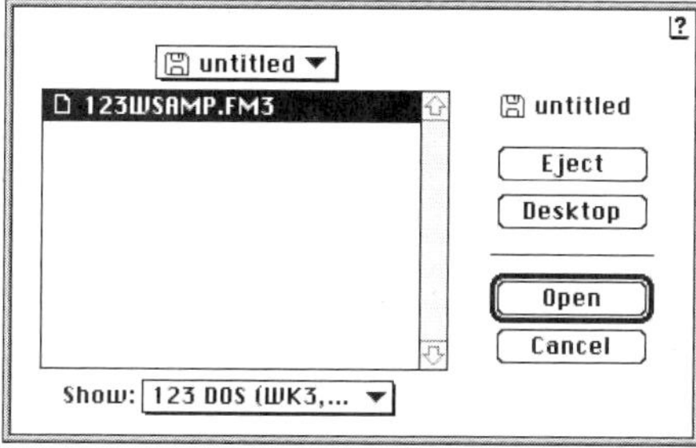

Figure 13.18. The Open dialog box displaying a 1-2-3 for Windows file.

8. Click the name of the file you want to open. Then, choose the Open button.

   1-2-3 for the Mac opens the 1-2-3 Release 3.x or 1-2-3 for Windows file with the majority of publishing and presentation formatting in place.

PC CAUTION

Any PIC files (graphs) and CGM files (clip art pictures) used in your spreadsheets *will not* translate from the PC. Instead, you will see gray squares representing these files. If you save the files and move them back to the PC, you still will see gray squares wherever you had included graphs or clip art.

Translating a 1-2-3 for the Mac File

To translate a Lotus 1-2-3 for the Mac file to a PC version of Lotus 1-2-3, you use Lotus 1-2-3 for the Mac. Translating a 1-2-3 for the Mac file to a PC version of 1-2-3 is not difficult. At this time, however, 1-2-3 for the Mac cannot translate all information you may store in a 1-2-3 for the Mac file to all PC versions of 1-2-3. You can translate all information to 1-2-3 Release 3.x and 1-2-3 for Windows, but you are limited to translating only single worksheet files to 1-2-3 Release 2.x. If you have added any formatting (such as bold or italics), the formatting will be lost because 1-2-3 for the Mac cannot translate formatting information for 1-2-3 Release 2.x.

To translate a Lotus 1-2-3 for the Mac file so that it can be read by Lotus 1-2-3 Release 2.x, follow these steps:

1. In 1-2-3 for the Mac, open the file you want to move to 1-2-3 Release 2.x. For more information on opening in 1-2-3 for the Mac, see Chapter 6 of *The PC User's Mac.*

2. Open the **File** menu and choose the **Save As** command. For more information on saving in 1-2-3 for the Mac, see Chapter 6 of *The PC User's Mac.*

   1-2-3 for the Mac displays the Save As dialog box.

3. From the File Type pop-up menu, choose 123 DOS (.WK1).

   1-2-3 for the Mac adds an extension of WK1 to the file name that appears in the Save As text box (see Figure 13.19).

4. If you want to change the name of the file on the floppy disk, click in the Save As text box and type a new name. Be sure to follow the DOS naming conventions—eight characters for the first name, a period, then WK1 as the three-character extension. (For more information on DOS file-naming conventions, see Chapter 12 of *The Mac User's PC.*)

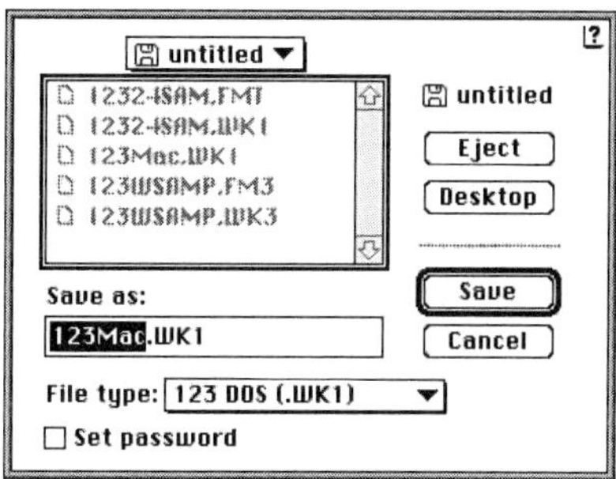

Figure 13.19.

The Save As dialog box after choosing the file type to show.

5. Click the Save button.

1-2-3 for the Mac saves the file in a format that can be read by 1-2-3 Release 2.x. You lose the majority of publishing and presentation formatting, such as bold and italics. Typically, you see a dialog box warning you that incompatible worksheet information was lost during saving.

6. Make sure that the disk translation utility is active, and insert (and, if necessary, format) a DOS disk into the floppy disk drive. See the first part of this chapter for more information on disk translation utilities and formatting DOS disks.

7. If PC Exchange is active, copy (by dragging) the file from the hard disk to the floppy disk. If Apple File Exchange is active, navigate to the file you want to move to the PC and "translate" it to the DOS-formatted floppy disk.

8. Eject the floppy disk from the floppy disk drive on the Mac and place the disk into the floppy disk drive on the PC.

9. Using one of the techniques described in Chapter 2 of *The Mac User's PC*, start 1-2-3 Release 2.x.

10. Use the **R**etrieve command from the **F**ile menu to open the worksheet in 1-2-3 Release 2.x. For more information on retrieving in 1-2-3 for DOS, see Chapter 8 of *The Mac User's PC*.

To translate a Lotus 1-2-3 for the Mac file so that it can be read by Lotus 1-2-3 Release 3.x or Lotus 1-2-3 for Windows, follow these steps:

1. In 1-2-3 for the Mac, open the file you want to move to 1-2-3 Release 3.x for DOS or 1-2-3 for Windows. For more information on opening in 1-2-3 for the Mac, see Chapter 6 of *The PC User's Mac.*

2. Open the **File** menu and choose the **Save As** command. For more information on saving in 1-2-3 for the Mac, see Chapter 6 of *The PC User's Mac.*

   1-2-3 for the Mac displays the Save As dialog box.

3. From the File Type pop-up menu, choose 123DOS (WK3,FM3).

   1-2-3 for the Mac adds an extension of FM3 to the file name that appears in the Save As text box (see Figure 13.20).

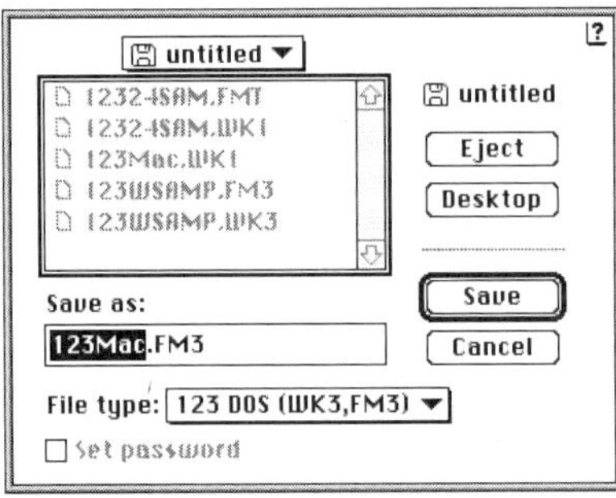

Figure 13.20. The Save As dialog box after choosing the file type to show.

4. If you want to change the name of the file on the floppy disk, click in the Save As text box and type a new name. Be sure to follow the DOS naming conventions—eight characters for the first name, a period, then FM3 as the three-character extension. (For more information on DOS file-naming conventions, see Chapter 12 of *The Mac User's PC.*)

5. Click the Save button.

   1-2-3 for the Mac saves the file in a format that can be read by 1-2-3 Release 3.x or 1-2-3 for Windows with the majority of publishing and presentation formatting in place.

6. Make sure that the disk translation utility is active, and insert (and, if necessary, format) a DOS disk into the floppy disk drive. See the first part of this chapter for more information on disk translation utilities and formatting DOS disks.

7. If PC Exchange is active, copy (by dragging) the file from the hard disk to the floppy disk. If Apple File Exchange is active, navigate to the file you want to move to the PC and "translate" it to the DOS-formatted floppy disk.

8. Eject the floppy disk from the floppy disk drive on the Mac and place the disk into the floppy disk drive of the PC.

9. Using a technique described in Chapter 2 of *The Mac User's PC,* start 1-2-3 Release 3.x or 1-2-3 for Windows.

10. Use the **O**pen command on the **F**ile menu to open the document in 1-2-3 Release 3.x or 1-2-3 for Windows. For more information on opening in 1-2-3 for DOS, see Chapter 8 of *The Mac User's PC.* For more information on opening in 1-2-3 for Windows, see Chapter 9 of *The Mac User's PC.*

Chapter Summary

In this chapter, you learned how to use floppy disks to transfer files between a Mac and a PC. But getting the file to the other computer doesn't necessarily mean that you can use the file. Therefore, you also learned about file translation utilities that convert Mac-formatted files to DOS format and DOS-formatted files to Mac format.

You then learned that you often can use an application itself to perform the translation, and you learned how to use the applications discussed in this book to translate files to the corresponding application on the other computer.

By the way, you now have reached the end of *The Mac User's PC,* except for the PC Glossary. I have the urge to say something such as "I hope you have found useful information in this book," but that sounds a lot like the written version of "Have a nice day." Anyone with a better idea for an ending, jump right in here. My personal favorite is "And they all lived happily ever after."

Glossary

BOOTING

C DRIVE

DOS PROMPT

PATH

ROOT DIRECTORY

A drive See *drive name.*

active cell The worksheet cell that contains the cell pointer.

active document The document that contains the insertion point.

active pane The portion of the window that contains the insertion point.

active window The window that contains the active document.

active worksheet The worksheet that contains the active cell.

alphanumeric keys The "typewriter keys" on a keyboard. The alphanumeric keys include the alphabetic keys, the numbers (and symbols) that appear above the alphabetic keys, and all the keys immediately next to the alphabetic keys that help form the block into a symmetrical rectangular group on the keyboard.

Alt key A special-purpose key that has no function by itself. When pressed in combination with another key, the Alt key may generate a special action in the current software package. "Alt" is an abbreviation for "Alternate." See also *Ctrl* key.

B drive See *drive name.*

blocking The process of selecting text. The term "blocking" is used in WordPerfect for DOS. See also *selecting.*

booting (or **boot process**) The sequence of steps the computer follows when you start it. You can start the computer by using either a cold boot or a warm boot. You use the on/off switch to perform a cold boot. You hold down the Ctrl and Alt keys as you press the Del key to perform a warm boot.

C drive See *drive name.*

C prompt See *DOS prompt.*

cell The intersection of a column and a row in a worksheet.

cell pointer The name of the mouse pointer or cursor shape when in a cell in a worksheet.

Central Processing Unit (CPU) A microchip that serves as the hardware brain of the computer.

check box A box or a pair of square brackets ([ ]) next to an option in a dialog box. You can choose more than one check box from a group of related options. An X appears in the check boxes of the activated options. See also *dialog box.*

choosing The process of selecting a menu, a command on a menu, or an option in a dialog box. The way in which you choose varies, depending on whether you are working in a DOS-based program or a Windows-based program. See also *highlighting* and *selecting.*

clicking The process of pressing and releasing a mouse button, usually the left mouse button. See also *double-clicking, dragging,* and *pointing.*

command An item that appears on a menu. You choose a command to accomplish a task in a program. See also *menu.*

command button An oblong button that performs an action, such as accepting or canceling choices, in a dialog box. See also *tunnel-through command button.*

Control menu button A button in Windows programs that opens either the window or the program Control menu, which contains commands you can use to control the size of windows.

copying The process of placing an additional version of a file or text at a second location, leaving the original file or text in its original location. See also *moving* and *renaming.*

CPU The acronym for Central Processing Unit. See *Central Processing Unit (CPU).*

Ctrl key A special-purpose key that has no function by itself. When pressed in combination with another key, the Ctrl key may generate a special action in the current software package. "Ctrl" is an abbreviation for "Control." See also *Alt* key.

cursor A video bar or a blinking underline that designates the location where your next action will occur. The cursor is the

equivalent of the insertion point in a Mac program. See also *insertion point.*

cursor-movement keys The keys you use to move the cursor (or the insertion point, in Windows programs). A PC usually contains two sets of cursor-movement keys: one set on the numeric keypad (which functions only when the Num Lock light is off), and the other (gray) set between the numeric keypad and the alphanumeric keys. The cursor-movement keys include the arrow keys and Home, End, PgUp, and PgDn. On the gray set that appears between the numeric keypad and the alphanumeric keys, PgUp may be labeled Page Up, and PgDn may be labeled Page Down. These keys perform the same functions, and, in this book, when you see "PgUp" or "PgDn", you can use either key.

database A collection of related information. On computers, database programs are used to build databases. See also *field* and *record.*

dialog box A small window you use to supply additional information required by a program. See also *check box, command button, list box, option button, text box,* and *tunnel-through command button.*

directional keys The cursor- or insertion point-movement keys. When the Num Lock light is off, the directional keys on the numeric keypad include the arrow keys and the Home, End, PgUp, and PgDn keys. The gray arrow keys and the gray Home, End, PageUp, and PageDown keys between the numeric keypad and the alphanumeric keypad are also directional keys. See also *cursor-movement keys.*

directory A computer-based "file folder" (comparable to a folder on a Mac) in which users place related files. People use directories to organize the files on their PCs. The structure of the directories created on a PC is hierarchical. See also *parent directory, root directory,* and *subdirectory.*

document Typically, in word processing applications, a file.

DOS The acronym for Disk Operating System. DOS acts as the software brain of the computer.

DOS prompt A place holder that designates where you type commands when you query DOS directly. The DOS prompt representation includes the letter name of the current drive. The prompt for the C drive might look like `C>` or `C:\>`.

double-clicking The process of quickly pressing and releasing the left mouse button twice. See also *clicking, dragging,* and *pointing.*

dragging The process of moving an item from one location to another by using the mouse. To drag, point to the item you want to drag. Then, hold down the left mouse button as you slide the mouse to move the mouse pointer to the new location. See also *clicking, double-clicking,* and *pointing.*

drive A See *drive name.*

drive B See *drive name.*

drive C See *drive name.*

drive name A letter designating a disk drive. Usually, floppy disk drives are named A: or B:, while hard disks are named C:, and network drives are named F:. Additional hard disk drive names increment alphabetically. The network drive name (F:) is a convention, and is not always used.

drop-down list box A box that contains a list of options in a dialog box. To open a drop-down list box, click on the down arrow at the right end of the box; or, hold down the Alt key and type the underlined letter in the list box name. See also *dialog box* and *list box.*

editing keys The editing keys include the Backspace key, the Del (or Delete) key, and the Ins (or Insert) key.

extended keyboard A keyboard that contains two sets of directional keys. One set appears on the numeric keypad on the right side of the keyboard, and the other set appears between the numeric keypad and the alphanumeric keys.

extension The second portion of a DOS file name. The extension is the portion of the DOS file name that appears after the period (.).

FAT The acronym for File Allocation Table, the device DOS uses to keep track of the location of files in a directory. See also *DOS.*

field Each separate piece of information in a database record. In a telephone book (the database) the last name is an example of a field. See also *database* and *record.*

file A unit in which information is stored on a computer. The same as a file on a Mac.

formatting The process of preparing a disk for use on a PC. The same general process as initializing a disk on a Mac.

function keys The function keys typically include F1 through F12. The purpose of a function key is defined by the software program you are using.

hardware The parts of a computer you physically can see and feel. These parts include, at the most basic level, the monitor, the keyboard, and the box containing the CPU and other components.

highlighting The process of identifying the menu or command you want to choose or the text you want to select. When a menu, command, or text is highlighted, a reverse video bar appears on it. See also *choosing* and *selecting.*

hot key A key used as a shortcut. The appearance of the key (so that you can identify it to use it) changes from one software package to another. In Windows, the hot key letters are always the underlined letters in commands or key combinations that appear on menus. In DOS programs, the hot key letter may appear underlined or in boldface or uppercase type.

icon An image that represents program or data files in Windows. You choose an icon (by using the mouse or the keyboard) to start a program. Also, if you minimize a program after starting it, its image is represented as an icon. You choose a minimized program's icon to return the program to a working size onscreen.

insert mode A typing mode in which the program places characters at the current location of the cursor or insertion point and moves all existing characters to the right. (The only typing mode on a Mac is insert mode.) See also *overtype mode* and *typeover mode.*

insertion point The flashing black vertical bar that identifies where text will appear when you type. See also *cursor.*

list box A box that contains a list of options in a dialog box. A drop-down list box shows only the active option when the dialog box appears. (To open a drop-down list box, click the down arrow at the right end of the box; or, hold down the Alt key and type the underlined letter in the list box name.) The other type of list box is already open when the dialog box appears. See also *dialog box* and *drop-down list box.*

Maximize button A button you choose in Windows programs or Word for DOS to increase the size of a window to fill the entire screen. See also *Minimize button* and *Restore button.*

menu An item that appears in the menu bar of a Windows-based program or somewhere onscreen (program-dependent) for a DOS-based program. Usually, in a Windows-based program, a menu contains a list of commands. In a DOS-based program, a menu may contain programs or commands. See also *command* and *menu bar.*

menu bar A bar that contains menu names. In Windows programs, the menu bar appears at the top of the screen just below the title bar. In DOS programs, the menu bar may appear anywhere onscreen. See also *menu.*

menu command See *command.*

Microsoft Windows A product which provides PC users with a graphical user interface (making the PC look more like your Mac) and the capability for multitasking. See also *multitasking.*

Minimize button A button you choose in Windows programs to reduce a window to an icon. See also *Maximize button* and *Restore button.*

moving The process of removing a file or text from its original location and placing it at a new location. See also *copying* and *renaming.*

multitasking The process of performing two or more tasks simultaneously. In a multitasking environment such as Windows, for example, the user can send data over a modem and work in a word processor while the data transmission takes place.

numeric keypad The numeric keypad appears at the right end of the keyboard. If the Num Lock feature (and Num Lock light) is on, pressing a numeric keypad key produces a number. You turn on and off the Num Lock feature by pressing the Num Lock key.

option button A small round button you use to choose one option from a group of related options in a dialog box. A black dot appears in the button of the currently selected option. See also *dialog box.*

overtype mode A typing mode in which a program places characters at the current location of the cursor or insertion point and replaces all characters that exist at that location. See also *insert mode* and *typeover mode.*

parent directory A directory that contains a subdirectory. The term "parent" is used to denote the hierarchical relationship between the two directories. See also *directory, root directory,* and *subdirectory.*

path The shortened name of "search path." See also *search path.*

pointing The process of identifying an item you want to choose. To point by using a mouse, slide the mouse until the mouse pointer onscreen appears on top of the item you want to choose. To point by using the keyboard, press the arrow keys until you highlight the item. See also *clicking, double-clicking,* and *dragging.*

program group A window (which can collapse to an icon) that contains icons you use to start programs in Windows. Program groups in Windows are comparable to directories in DOS and folders on the Mac.

Program Manager The program that manages the computer's resources in Windows.

record An entry in a database. In a telephone book (the database) all the information about one person is an example of a record. See also *database* and *field.*

renaming The process of changing the name of an existing file. When you rename, you do *not* create an additional copy of the file. See also *copying* and *moving.*

Restore button A button in Windows programs that changes the size of a window to a size somewhere between minimum and maximum. See also *Maximize button* and *Minimize button.*

retrieve The term used in many DOS programs to describe the action you take when you open a file.

reverse video bar A bar that appears on top of a command in a menu (often called a "highlight"). You use a reverse video bar to identify a command you want to choose. When a reverse video bar appears on a command and you press Enter, you choose the command and the program executes the command. See also *highlighting.*

root directory Based on the hierarchical structure of directories, the highest level directory on a disk. See also *directory, parent directory,* and *subdirectory.*

search path The drive and directory used when looking for files.

selecting The process of identifying the text on which you want to work. When you select text, it appears highlighted. See also *choosing* and *highlighting.*

subdirectory A directory within a directory. The equivalent to a folder inside a folder on a Mac. See also *directory* and *parent directory.*

text box A rectangular box in which you enter text in a dialog box. When a dialog box that contains a text box opens, the current text is usually selected. To replace the selected text, simply type the new information. See also *dialog box.*

title bar A bar that appears at the top of a window or a dialog box, and contains the name of the window or dialog box. See also *dialog box* and *window.*

TSR The acronym for Terminate/Stay Resident. TSRs are programs that load when you start a PC—the equivalent of INITs on a Mac. TSRs stay loaded until you turn off the computer.

tunnel-through command button A command button in a dialog box that opens another dialog box. See also *command button* and *dialog box.*

turbo mode A faster speed at which a computer can operate. For most programs, you want the computer to operate in turbo mode.

typeover mode A typing mode in which a program places characters at the current location of the cursor and replaces all characters that exist at that location. See also *insert mode* and *overtype mode.*

window A rectangular area onscreen that contains a title bar, scroll bar(s), and boxes you can use to close the window or adjust its size.

workbook A collection of Excel for Windows worksheets that are conceptually related to one another.

worksheet A document or file in a spreadsheet program.

NDEX

BOOTING

CHECK BOXES

DOS

FILES

MENUS

KEYBOARDS

PRINTING

WINDOWS

Symbols

A

B

C

D

E

G-H

I-J

K

L

M

N

O

P

Q-R

S

T

U-V

W

X-Z

Elaine J. Marmel

Elaine Marmel is president of Marmel Enterprises, Inc., an organization which provides PC and Macintosh software training and support and specializes in assisting small- to medium-sized businesses to computerize their accounting systems.

Elaine is the author of *Word for Windows 2 QuickStart, Quicken 1.0 for Windows Quick Reference, Quicken 6 for DOS Quick Reference,* and *Using Quicken 2.0 for Windows,* and a contributing author to *Look Your Best with 1-2-3* and *Using Ami Pro 3 for Windows,* Special Edition.

Elaine left her native Chicago for the warmer climes of Florida (by way of Cincinnati, Ohio; Jerusalem, Israel; Ithaca, New York; and Washington, D.C.) where she basks in the sun with her PC, her Mac, and her cats, Tonto and Cato. Elaine also enjoys cross-stitching, and she sings in an internationally recognized barbershop chorus, the Toast of Tampa.

CREDITS

Publisher

Mike Britton

Developmental Editor

Laura Wirthlin

Editors

Dave Ciskowski

Pamela Wampler

Laura Wirthlin

Technical Editors

Dave Ciskowski

Gloria Schuler

Cover Designer

Scott Cook

Interior Designer

Scott Cook

Interior Illustrator

Roger Morgan

Production Team

Jeanne Clark, Tim Cox, Mark Enochs, Joelynn Gifford, Tim Groeling, Phil Kitchel, Tom Loveman, Michael J. Nolan, Joe Ramon, Carrie Roth, Mary Beth Wakefield, Barb Webster, Kelli Widdifield

Book Acknowledgments

Dedicated to Terry Higdon, for courage and bravery and, most of all, friendship.

I would like to thank the following people:

Brian Low and Mike Pearse of Lotus Corporation for background technical help on the various versions of Lotus 1-2-3.

Earl Martin and the staff at TechForce for providing evaluation copies of software.

Glenda Kilpatrick for information on Clipper.

Gloria Schuler for the excellent technical editing job she did (although she enjoyed it far too much, and I think she ought to give the money back) and for providing an ear when I needed one.

Dave Ciskowski for keeping me on the right track with outstanding technical comments.

Pamela Wampler for her gentle guidance to help me make this a better book.

Laura Wirthlin for the opportunity to write this book.

All the people on the Hayden production team for a terrific job making the book look great.

TRADEMARK ACKNOWLEDGMENTS

This book mentions too many companies and products to list every trademark on this page. Because we are environmentalists, and because paper is a valuable (and costly) commodity, we limit our trademark acknowledgments to the following statements:

All terms mentioned in this book that are known to be trademarks or service marks have been appropriately capitalized. Hayden cannot attest to the accuracy of this information. Use of a term in this book should not be regarded as affecting the validity of any trademark or service mark.

IBM is a registered trademark of International Business Machines. Lotus and 1-2-3 are registered trademarks of Lotus Development Corporation. Microsoft, Microsoft Excel, Microsoft Windows, Microsoft Word, and MS-DOS are registered trademarks of Microsoft Corporation. WordPerfect is a registered trademark of WordPerfect Corporation. Apple, Mac, Macintosh, and Performa are registered trademarks of Apple Computer, Inc.

The PC User's Mac Contents

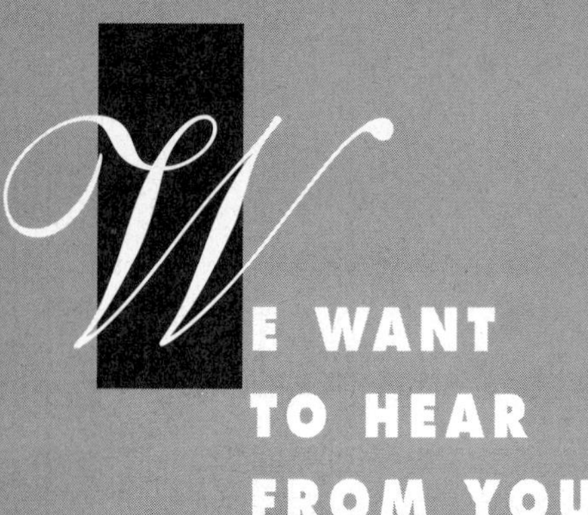

We Want to Hear from You

What our readers think of Hayden is crucial to our sense of well-being. If you have any comments, no matter how great or small, we'd appreciate your taking the time to send us a note, fax us a fax, rhyme us a rhyme, and so on.

We can be reached at the following address:

Hayden Books
11711 North College Avenue
Carmel, Indiana 46032
(317) 573-6880 voice
(317) 573-2583 fax

If this book has changed your life, please write and describe the euphoria you've experienced. Do you have a book idea? Please contact us at the above address.

Introduction

The war between the Macintosh and the PC continues, each side claiming its own computer as the best. Which computer *is* the best? This book does not answer that question. It doesn't even try. (If this text sounds familiar, then you have read the introduction to *The Mac User's PC*. This introduction is the same, so you can skip ahead to Chapter 1 if you want.)

Who Should Use This Book?

Are you a PC user confronted with the task of using a Macintosh? Are you trying to use a Macintosh, for example, to copy a file to a floppy disk that you can take to your PC and use? Oh, sure, your friend the Mac user keeps telling you how easy the Macintosh is. But where's your DOS prompt? Or where's the menu you always use to start programs? And what do all the pictures mean? Is this Windows on the Macintosh? How do you find what you're looking for? How do you use the mouse?

Or, are you a Mac user who has been forced to use a PC, if only for a small task such as copying a file from a hard disk to a floppy disk? If you're lucky, perhaps Windows started automatically. But, if not, what does `C>` (or `C:\>`) mean? What's the blinking square or underline next to it? Maybe you see a menu, but where's the mouse pointer? How do you find the file you want, let alone copy it to a floppy disk?

In either case, you may have found yourself in an environment that's entirely unfamiliar. This book is created for PC users who are experienced on PCs but have an occasional need to work on a Mac, and for Mac users who are experienced on Macs but have a similar occasional need to work on a PC. This book will not make you an expert at either the Macintosh or the PC—it does not provide an exhaustive look at either computer. This book covers software that exists for both platforms; for example, you will find chapters on WordPerfect for DOS, WordPerfect for Windows, and WordPerfect for the Mac (and, yes, I did have trouble keeping them all straight after a while!). This book will help you get by when you have to use the computer with which you are not familiar, and, I hope, this book will prepare you to read other books (or even the manuals) with greater understanding.

What Does This Book Contain?

The book consists of two parts, and you use each part independently. In fact, this book can be viewed as two books in one: *The PC User's Mac* and *The Mac User's PC.* In each part of the book, you find information that helps you identify the parts and understand the basic differences between the PC and the Macintosh. You learn to start popular programs; get help in those programs; open, edit, print, and save files in the programs; copy the files to a floppy disk; and exit the programs. You also learn to transfer and translate files between PCs and Macs.

The PC User's Mac

This part of the book, *The PC User's Mac*, contains nine chapters that describe a typical Macintosh and how to use popular Macintosh programs, plus a glossary of common Macintosh terms.

You may not want to read *The PC User's Mac* from front to back (or front to middle). But because Chapters 1 and 2 contain basic background information about Mac hardware, be sure to read these chapters first. Then, read the chapters that pertain to the Mac software you need to use.

Chapter 1, "Examining the Parts of a Mac," focuses on the Macintosh hardware. You learn to identify what you typically see when you look at the Macintosh from the front and from the back.

Chapter 2, "Turning On the Mac and Starting a Program," first explains, in a general way, the differences in philosophy behind the original construction of the PC and the Macintosh. In this chapter, you learn to experiment with the Macintosh without fear of "breaking" things. This chapter also describes what you typically see when you turn on a Macintosh, and you learn the basics of using a mouse. You also learn how to start a program on a Mac.

Chapters 3 through 6 contain the same basic information for different popular software programs: how to get help in the program; how to open, edit, print, and save a file; how to copy a file to a floppy disk; and how to exit from the program. In Chapter 3, you learn about WordPerfect for the Macintosh. Chapter 4 covers Microsoft Word for the Macintosh. Chapter 5 discusses Microsoft Excel for the Macintosh. Chapter 6 describes Lotus 1-2-3 for the Macintosh.

In Chapter 7, "Avoiding Database Programs," you learn what a database program is and what it can do for you. You also learn why you shouldn't use somebody else's database unless you really know what you're doing. You learn the names of some popular database programs so that you can avoid them while working on someone else's Macintosh.

In Chapter 8, "Working with Disks, Folders, and Files," you learn how to use the Finder on the Desktop to manage disks, folders, and files. You first review how to identify, select, and open disks, folders, and files. Then, you learn how to create disks, folders, and files; rename, move, and copy folders and files; use the Trash; and get help.

In Chapter 9, "Transferring and Translating Files between a PC and a Mac," you learn some of the ways you can move a file from a PC to a Macintosh and from a Macintosh to a PC.

The Mac Glossary provides definitions of popular Macintosh terms, and this part of the book concludes with a comprehensive index of *The PC User's Mac.*

The Mac User's PC

The other part of the book, *The Mac User's PC,* contains 13 chapters that describe a typical IBM-compatible PC and how to use popular PC programs, plus a glossary of common PC terms.

You may not want to read *The Mac User's PC* from front to back (or front to middle) either. But because Chapters 1 and 2 contain basic background information about PC hardware, be sure to read these chapters first. Then, read the chapters that pertain to the PC software you need to use. Some of the information may be repetitive; for example, each chapter about a Windows-based program contains basic information about using Windows. This repetition is intentional. Because Chapters 3 through 9 are independent and self-contained, you can rely on one chapter alone to use a particular software package. This way, you don't have to hunt for information throughout the book.

Chapter 1, "Examining the Parts of a PC," focuses on the PC hardware. You learn to identify what you typically see when you look at the PC from the front and from the back.

Chapter 2, "Turning On the PC and Starting a Program," first explains, in a general way, the differences in philosophy behind the original construction of the Macintosh and the PC. To help you identify the PC environment in which you are working, this chapter describes the various screens you might see when you start a PC. You then learn how to start a program in each of these environments. Chapter 2 also contains tips on starting programs not specifically covered in this book.

Chapters 3 through 9 contain the same basic information for different popular software programs: how to get help in the program; how to open, edit, print, and save a file; how to copy a file to a floppy disk; and how to exit from the program. In Chapter 3, you learn about WordPerfect for DOS; in Chapter 4, about WordPerfect for Windows. Chapter 5 covers Microsoft Word for DOS. Chapter 6 covers Microsoft Word for Windows. Chapter 7 discusses Microsoft Excel for Windows. Chapter 8 describes Lotus 1-2-3 for DOS, and Chapter 9 describes Lotus 1-2-3 for Windows.

In Chapter 10, "Avoiding Database Programs," you learn what a database program is and what it can do for you. You also learn why you shouldn't use somebody else's database unless you really know what you're doing. You learn the names of some of the more popular database programs so that you can avoid them while working on someone else's PC.

In Chapter 11, "Working with the MS-DOS Shell," you learn how to use the MS-DOS Shell, which is one of the PC environments described in Chapter 2. (In Chapter 2, you learned how to identify the MS-DOS Shell screen.) In this chapter, you learn to understand the MS-DOS Shell screen and to use the MS-DOS Shell to view, copy, and print files, and to start programs. The MS-DOS Shell is available to any user working under MS-DOS Version 4.0 or later. (In Chapter 2, you also learned how to identify the version of DOS you are using.) Even if the MS-DOS Shell doesn't appear when you start the computer, you may want to try using it if it is available.

Chapter 12, "Working with Basic DOS Commands (When All Else Fails)," teaches you the basics of the dreaded DOS. You review how to identify the version of DOS with which you are working, and learn how to copy and erase files. You also learn about directories and how to list their contents, switch to another directory, make a new directory, and delete a directory. PC users also may want to review this chapter. (But then again, maybe not.)

In Chapter 13, "Transferring and Translating Files between a Mac and a PC," you learn some of the ways you can move a file from a Macintosh to a PC or from a PC to a Macintosh.

The PC Glossary provides definitions of popular PC terms, and the other part of the book concludes with a comprehensive index of *The Mac User's PC.*

Conventions Used in This Book

The conventions used in this book were established to help you use the book more easily.

Information that appears onscreen and information that you type appears in a `special typeface`.

In numbered steps, menus, commands, and shortcut keys appear in **boldface type**.

When you see two or more keys separated by a plus sign (+), you hold down the first key(s) as you press the last key. When you see two or more keys separated by a comma (,), you press the keys in sequence.

Terms that appear in the glossary appear in **boldface type**.

Examining the Parts of a Mac

You have received the dreaded assignment: on Mary's Mac, find a file and print it. All you know about a Mac is that there's one sitting on Mary's desk. And until now, that's all you ever wanted to know. But now you must use Mary's Mac. Oh, sure, Mary says the Mac is much easier to use than your PC. Easy for her to say—she uses it every day.

The first step is to identify what you see when you look at the Mac. In this chapter, you learn about the hardware you can view from the outside of the computer.

Looking at the Computer from the Front

When you get to Mary's desk, you probably see a machine that closely resembles your IBM-compatible PC (at least physically) from the front. There are several different Macintosh models, but they generally have the same basic layout. Unless Mary is working on a Mac Classic or a Mac Performa 200, you should see four pieces of equipment: a monitor, a keyboard, a mouse, and a box containing other hardware components (on the Classic and the Performa 200, the monitor and the box are combined into one piece of equipment). For lack of a better term, the box containing these other hardware components is called "the box" throughout this book (just think of this as another technical term). In Figure 1.1,

you see a typical Mac Classic or Mac Performa 200. In Figure 1.2, you see a typical Mac LC II or Mac Performa 400. In Figure 1.3, you see a typical Mac IIsi, Mac IIci, or Mac Performa 600. Not all Macs look the same, but you will see the same types of buttons, lights, and so forth on most Macs.

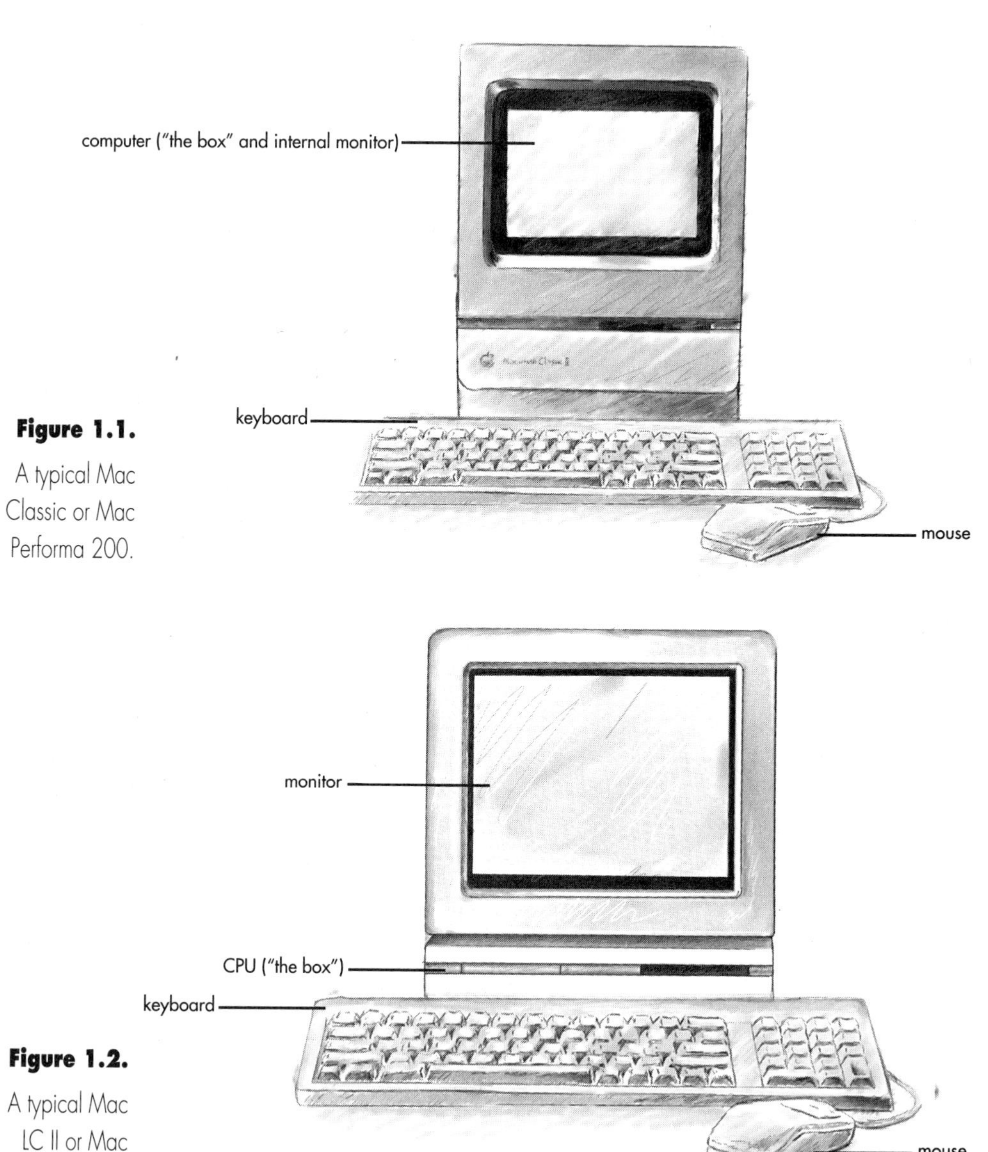

Figure 1.1. A typical Mac Classic or Mac Performa 200.

Figure 1.2. A typical Mac LC II or Mac Performa 400.

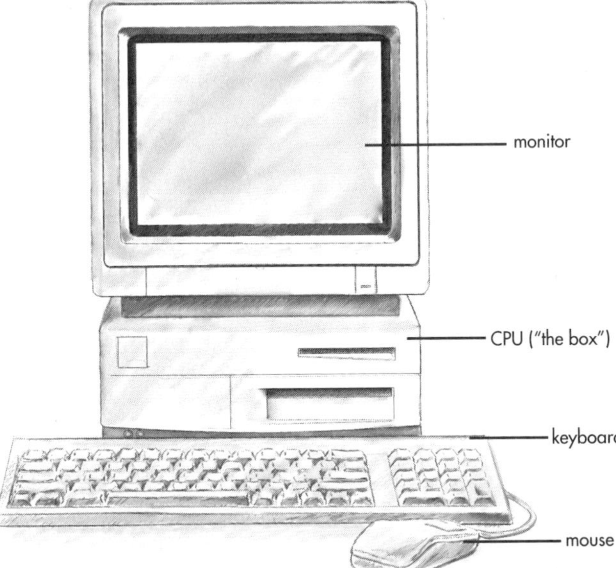

Figure 1.3.

A typical Mac IIsi, IIci, IIvx, or Mac Performa 600.

Another possibility is that Mary has a Macintosh Quadra, which resembles a typical IBM-compatible computer. The Quadras are the most powerful (and most expensive) Macs, so they're fairly uncommon. I won't show one here, but rest assured: they're not very different from the other Macs.

As you can see from Figure 1.1, the computer and monitor are combined into one piece on the Mac Classic and the Performa 200. Unlike the Mac Classic and the Performa 200, the box and the monitor are separate on the rest of the Macs, making them look more like a typical IBM-compatible PC. Aside from these dissimilarities, the basic components of a Mac don't change much from one Mac to the next, except that you might see more on the front and back of the Mac as you work on Macs with more options. To simplify identifying the parts of a Mac, you will be reading about a Performa 600, which includes options that you find on most smaller Macs as well as some additional options. Because of this, the Macintosh you are using might not have all of the elements discussed in this chapter.

The Front of the Monitor

Except for the Mac Classic and the Mac Performa 200, which include the monitor and the box in a single unit, you probably will see the monitor on top of the box. The (separate) monitor has a switch (located either on the front or the back) you can use to turn on or off the monitor. The monitor also has a light somewhere on the front that tells you whether the monitor is on (see Figure 1.4). The light is usually green when the monitor is on.

Also, the monitor usually has controls you can use to adjust the brightness of the image and the contrast (see Figure 1.4). These controls work like the brightness and contrast control knobs on your television set. On the Classic and the Performa 200, the monitor controls appear on the left side of the rear of the unit toward the bottom.

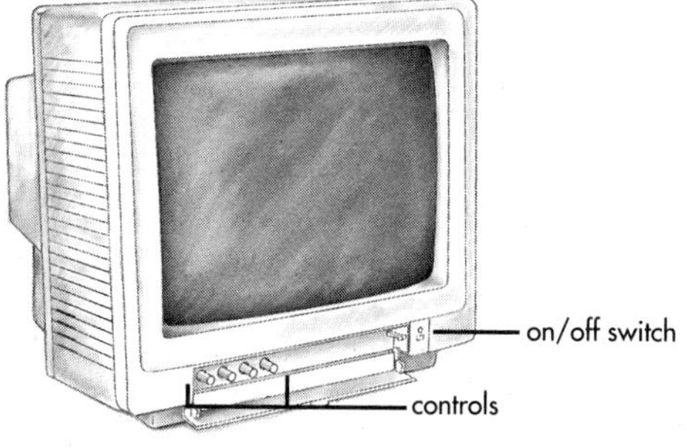

Figure 1.4.

A typical monitor and its parts.

The Front of the Box

Inside the box, you will find, among other hardware items, the **Central Processing Unit** (the **CPU**), memory chips, disk drives, and connection ports. Because you probably will not need to open the box, this section focuses on what you might see from the outside of the box. As you see from Figure 1.5, you probably can find a light, a few buttons, and a floppy disk drive somewhere on the outside of the box.

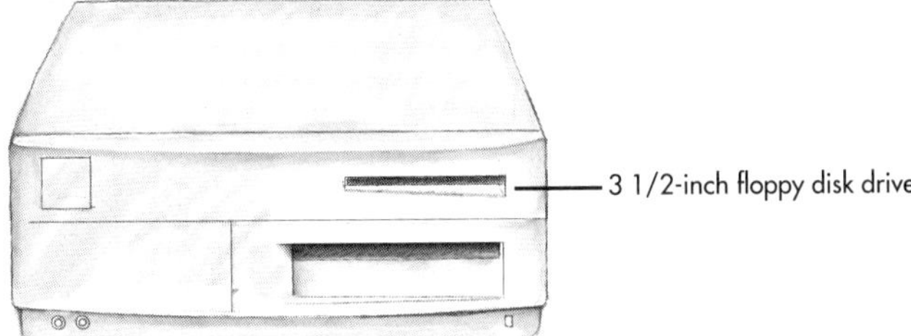

Figure 1.5. A typical Mac box.

Usually, you see a green light when the computer is turned on; this light indicates that the computer has power. Unlike a PC, which has a light that indicates activity on the hard drive and possibly a light that identifies whether the computer is running in turbo mode, the Mac has only one light—the power light.

Some Macs have two buttons as well: the Reset button and the Interrupt button. These two buttons are collectively referred to as the programmer's switch. These buttons can wreak havoc with the computer unless you're used to working with them, so it's best to leave them alone.

Unlike a PC, the floppy disk drive on a Mac doesn't have a name like A: or B:. It's just called "the floppy disk drive." Since 1989, Apple has been shipping all Macs with a 3 1/2-inch high-density floppy disk drive known as the Apple SuperDrive. A Mac with an Apple SuperDrive can read both high-density and double-density (or low-density) floppy disks, but some older Macs can read and write only double-density disks. If you think your disk should work with the Mac but it doesn't, you might be trying to use a high-density disk in an older Mac; if so, you will have to use a newer Mac to read the disk or copy the files you need onto a double-density disk.

The disks you buy to use with your PC also work on a Mac. You can tell the difference between a high-density 3 1/2-inch disk and a double-density 3 1/2-inch disk by the number of square holes you see at the sides of the disk. If you see a square hole on only one side

of the disk (as shown in Figure 1.6), you are looking at a double-density disk. If you see a square hole on each side of the disk (as shown in Figure 1.7), you are looking at a high-density disk.

Figure 1.6. A 3 1/2-inch double-density disk.

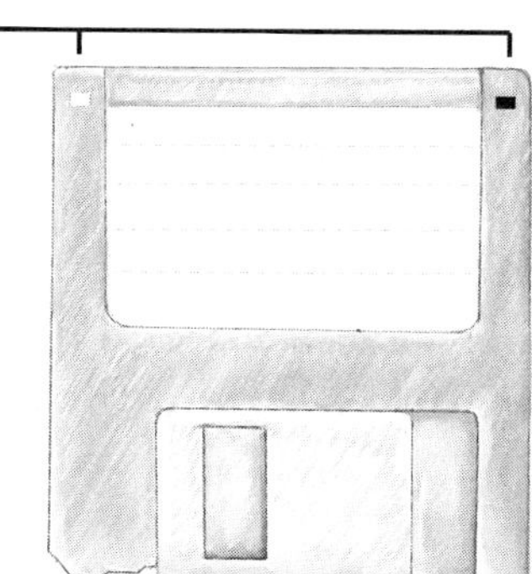
A high-density disk has two holes

Figure 1.7. A 3 1/2-inch high-density disk.

High-density 3 1/2-inch disks can hold 1.4 M of information. Double-density 3 1/2-inch disks can hold 800 K of information.

You might see another drive directly below the floppy drive. Some Macs have the capacity to support a 5 1/4-inch device such as a floppy disk drive or a CD-ROM drive. As an occasional user of a Mac, you probably won't have much need to use this drive. If you have a CD-ROM drive and some music CDs, however, you can use the Mac to play music in the background while you work. As you will learn later, you can even plug a set of headphones into the Mac and listen to the music "privately." If you are working on a Performa 600 CD (a Performa 600 with a CD-ROM drive just below the floppy disk drive), see Chapter 2 for basic instructions on using

the CD-ROM drive. If the Mac has an externally attached CD-ROM drive, you will have to do some hunting around to learn how to use it.

The Keyboard

You may see either of two basic keyboards on the Mac: the Apple Keyboard II or the Apple Extended Keyboard II. The Apple Keyboard II is similar to the keyboard shown in Figure 1.8, and the Apple Extended Keyboard II is similar to the keyboard shown in Figure 1.9.

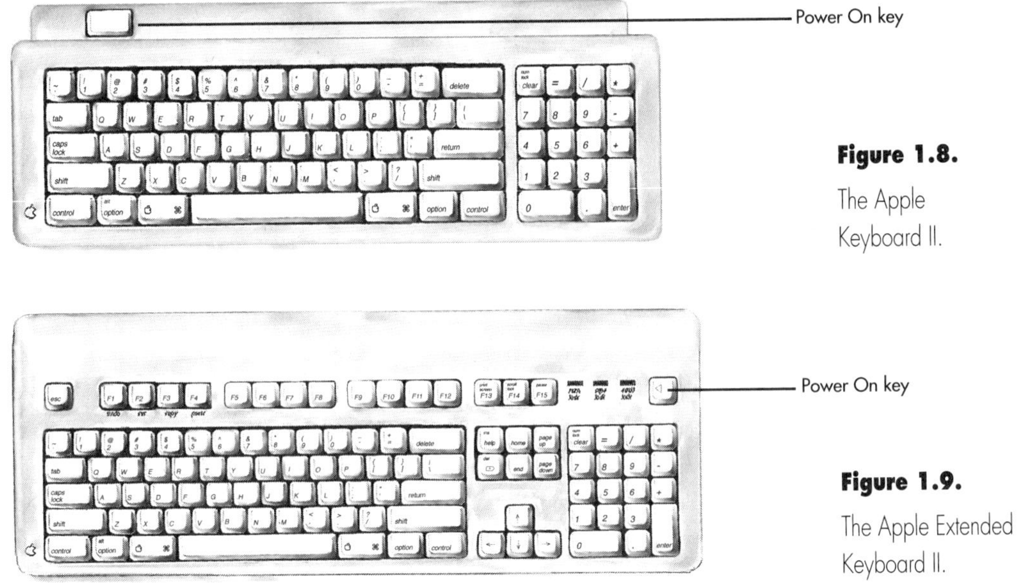

Figure 1.8. The Apple Keyboard II.

Figure 1.9. The Apple Extended Keyboard II.

Note that both keyboards are quite similar to PC keyboards—except for the Power On switch. Unlike the PC, the Power On switch for most Macs is actually a key on the keyboard. (Some of the entry-level Macintosh models have only a standard on/off switch on the back of the box which you must use instead.) On the Apple Keyboard II, the Power On key appears in the upper left

corner of the keyboard. On the Apple Extended Keyboard II, the Power On key appears in the upper right hand corner of the keyboard. Also, unlike the power switch on a PC, the Power On key only turns *on* the computer; you use a software command (which you will learn about in Chapter 2) to turn off the computer. (If the computer crashes to the point that you can't turn it off in the normal way, you must use a more traditional power button on the back of the box. This situation is discussed later in this chapter.)

On the sides of the keyboard, you will find two ports. These ports allow you to connect your keyboard to the box; you can use them interchangeably. You generally use one of the ports to connect the keyboard to the box and the other to connect a mouse to the keyboard.

For the sake of discussion, you can think of the keys on the keyboard in five different groups:

- The alphanumeric keys
- The editing keys
- The special-purpose keys
- The insertion point movement keys
- The numeric keypad
- The function keys

The Apple Keyboard II doesn't have function keys, but the Apple Extended Keyboard II does. (In the following sections, where you learn about the purposes of these groups of keys, you will see illustrations of the Apple Extended Keyboard II.)

In the following sections, you learn about the functions of each of these groups of keys as if you were using them to perform actions you might take in application software. Be aware, however, that the

actions of most keys can be redefined by application software (just like on the PC). Some keys, such as the alphanumeric keys, typically retain their actions as you move from one software package to another. Other keys, such as the function keys, usually change their actions as you move from one piece of software to another.

The Alphanumeric Keys

The **alphanumeric keys** on a Mac keyboard are arranged in the way they appear on a typewriter or on your PC keyboard (see Figure 1.10).

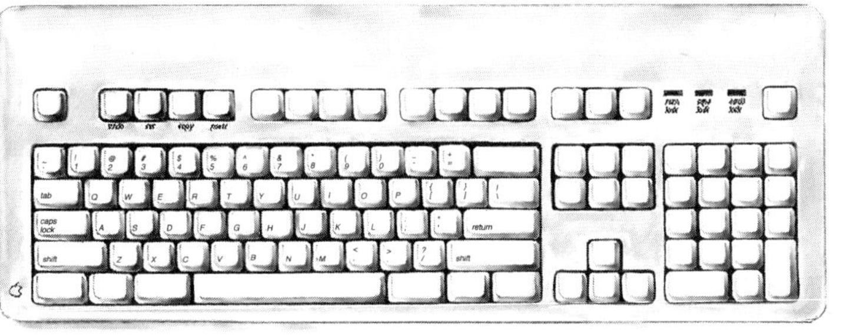

Figure 1.10.
The alphanumeric keys.

The alphanumeric keys produce letters and symbols. These keys operate, for the most part, like the keys on a typewriter. When enabled, the Caps Lock key lets you produce uppercase letters for the 26 alphabetic characters without pressing the Shift key. If you want to produce one of the symbols that appears in the top row of the alphanumeric keys (above the numbers), however, you still must press the Shift key.

The Editing Keys

The **editing keys**—Delete (Backspace on some keyboards), and Del (on an extended keyboard only)—enable you to modify text you already have typed (see Figure 1.11).

Figure 1.11.
The editing keys.

The Delete key (the Backspace key on some keyboards) enables you to remove the character immediately to the left of the insertion point. (The **insertion point** in a Mac program is the equivalent of the cursor in a DOS program and the insertion point in a Windows program: it designates the location where your next action will take place. The insertion point appears as a flashing vertical bar.) In some software packages, the Del key (on an extended keyboard only) enables you to remove the character to the right of the insertion point.

Special-Purpose Keys

You see the Esc key ("Esc" is an abbreviation for "escape") somewhere near the upper left corner of the keyboard. The Esc key is often (but not always) defined by software vendors to cancel the current action.

The keyboard contains a several other special-purpose keys (see Figure 1.12).

Figure 1.12.
The special-purpose keys.

The following keys have no function by themselves, but are used quite often in combination with other keys:

- The Option key (also labeled "alt," which is an abbreviation for "alternate").
- The Control key (labeled "Ctrl" on the Apple Keyboard II).
- The Command key, which appears next to the Option key and has both the Apple logo (an Apple with a bite out of it) and a funky symbol that has no name (see Figure 1.13).

Figure 1.13. The symbol that appears on the Command key.

Like the Alt key and the Ctrl key on a PC keyboard, when pressed in combination with another key, the Option key, the Control (or Ctrl) key, and the Command (⌘) key produce different results. The Option key is most often used to produce characters not available on the standard alphanumeric keyboard (such as accents), while the Command key is used to enter keyboard shortcuts for common commands. The Control key is used by only a few software packages, typically in a manner similar to the use of the Option key or Command key.

The Insertion Point Movement Keys

The **insertion point movement keys** (or simply "movement keys") appear between the numeric keypad and the alphanumeric keys (see Figure 1.14).

Pressing an arrow key moves the insertion point in the direction that the arrow points.

Figure 1.14.
The insertion point movement keys.

Certain keys on the numeric keypad also are programmed by many applications to function as movement keys. Normally, however, the numeric keypad functions only as a means for entering numbers. On a PC keyboard, you would press the Num Lock key to toggle these keys between movement keys and number keys. You also press the Num Lock key on a Mac to toggle between movement keys and number keys; however, the Num Lock light on the keyboard does not light, and you can make this switch only in programs that specifically use the numeric keypad to control insertion point movement.

The set of keys above the cursor movement keys are programmed to do different things by different applications. Most often, pressing the Home key moves the insertion point to the upper left corner of the screen or to the left end of the current line. Pressing the End key typically moves the insertion point to the end of the current line. Pressing PgUp (or Page Up) usually moves the view up one screen, and pressing PgDn (or Page Down) moves the view down one screen. Not all programs use these keys, however, and some use them in different ways.

The Tab key works like the Tab key on a typewriter and typically moves the insertion point to the next preset tab stop.

The Return key serves the same purpose as the Enter key on a PC keyboard. You press Return to send information to the computer—that is, you press Return to indicate that you're done typing and want the computer to act on the information you typed. In a word

processing program, pressing Return usually causes the insertion point to move to the beginning of the next paragraph. In a spreadsheet program, pressing Return transfers typed information into a cell. The Enter key on the numeric keypad typically performs the same functions as the Return key.

The Numeric Keypad

The **numeric keypad** (see Figure 1.15) does just what you'd expect it to do—it enters numbers. Some software packages, however, program the numeric keypad keys so that they serve two purposes. When you press the Num Lock key and then press a key on the numeric keypad, a number appears onscreen. When you press the Num Lock key again and then press a key on the numeric keypad, the insertion point changes positions.

Figure 1.15.

The numeric keypad.

The numeric keypad also contains keys that represent mathematical operations:

+	add
-	subtract
*	multiply
/	divide
=	equals

The Enter key on the numeric keypad generally works the same as the Return key in the alphanumeric keys.

The Function Keys

On the Apple Extended Keyboard II, you also see **function keys** across the top of the keyboard (see Figure 1.16).

Figure 1.16.
The function keys.

Function keys on the Mac work similarly to the way function keys work on a PC. The purpose of the function keys changes as you move from one software package to another; most programs use these keys to simplify work by assigning often-used tasks to the function keys. While the F1 key on a PC displays help information in most software packages, however, the F1 key on a Mac operates as the Undo key in most software packages, and undoes your last action. On an extended keyboard, where the F1 key is the Undo key, the Help key appears with the insertion point movement keys next to the Home key.

Looking at the Computer from the Back

You may never need (or want) to look at a Mac from the back. (In fact, you may decide to let somebody else do it for you if you think it's necessary.) On the other hand, you may want to try to fix a

problem that requires you to look at the back of a Mac. So, I have included information to identify the parts you may find on the back of a Mac. Not all Macs look alike from the back, but most have the standard basic parts described in this section. Also, the parts may not appear in the same place you see in the figures.

More powerful Macs have more features on the back, but the basic set of ports, connectors, and slots found on the Mac Classic or Performa 200 are also found on the most complex Macs. The Mac you are using might not have some of the connections described here, or might have some connections not described here, but the items discussed here are common to almost every Macintosh.

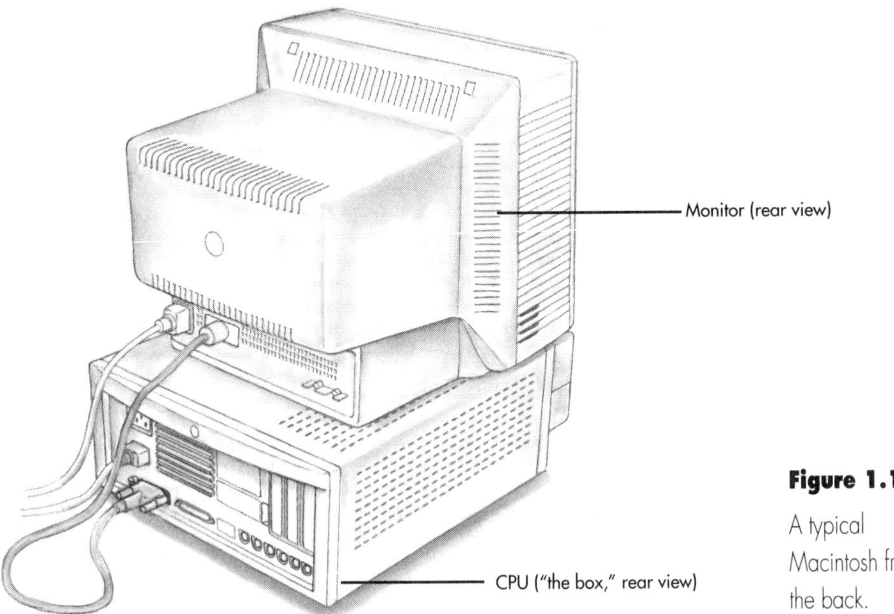

Figure 1.17.

A typical Macintosh from the back.

When you look at the back of the Mac, you see cables running out of connectors, ports, and slots. In the figures that appear in this section, however, you don't see all the cables; you see the actual connectors, ports, and slots that appear on the back of the equipment.

The Back of the Monitor

On the back of the monitor (see Figure 1.18), you see a cable that enables you to connect the monitor to the video port on the CPU box. Except on the Mac Classic and the Mac Performa 200, you also see the connector for the cable that connects the monitor to a source of electricity. On a Mac Classic or Mac Performa 200, you won't see a power cable connector, because the computer is an "all-in-one" unit, powered by one power source. You can, however, attach an external monitor to a Mac Classic or a Performa 200, so you will see a video port (discussed later in this chapter) on the Mac Classic and Mac Performa 200.

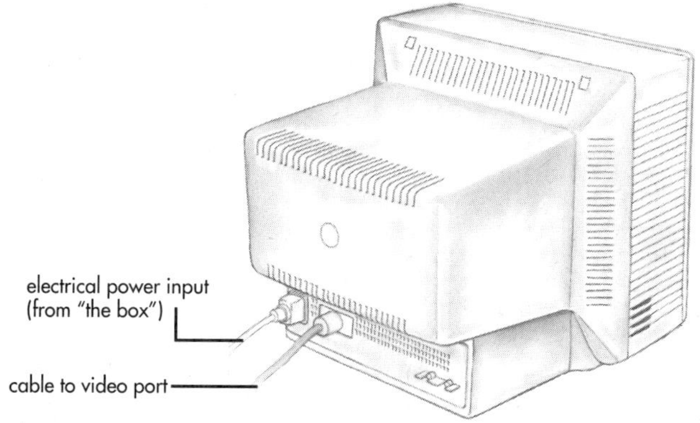

Figure 1.18. The back of a typical monitor.

The Back of the Box

On the back of the box, you see a variety of connectors, ports, and slots (see Figure 1.19). The position of these various connectors, ports and slots may change from Mac to Mac, but, in general, the appearance of each is similar.

On the back of a Mac, the connectors, ports, and slots are labeled with **icons**. Often, you find the same icon on the end of the cable that plugs into a particular connector, port, or slot. You can use the icons to align the cable with the connector, port, or slot by "matching" the icons.

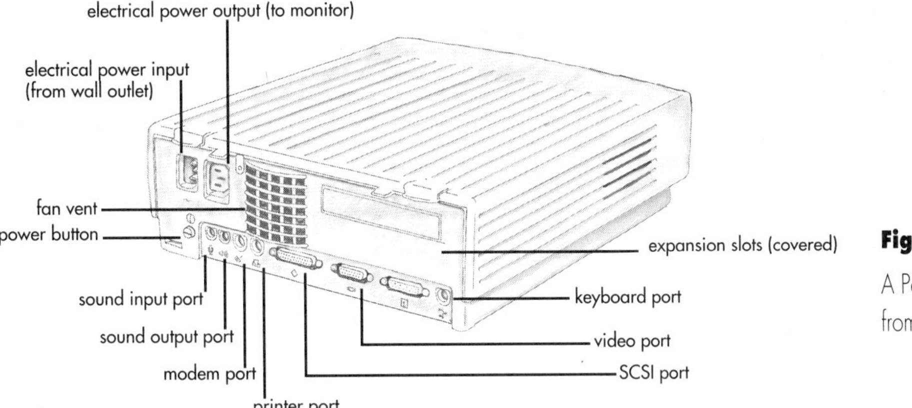

Figure 1.19.

A Performa 600 from the back.

You may see two power connectors—one input and one output. You use the input power connector to connect the Mac to a source of electricity. You can use the output power connector to connect a monitor to the power supply of the computer. You can then leave the monitor switched "on" all the time, and let the on/off switch on the box determine whether or not electricity travels to the monitor. In this way, when you turn on the Mac, you also turn on the monitor; similarly, when you turn off the Mac, you also turn off the monitor.

The fan vent keeps the power supply (which generates significant heat) cool.

On most Macs, you see an on/off switch somewhere on the back of the box which you can use to turn off the Mac if, for some reason, the mouse freezes onscreen and you can't turn off the computer. Unlike on a PC, the Power On switch on the keyboard is *not* a Power Off switch as well. Typically, you shut down (turn off) a Mac by using a software command you will learn about in Chapter 2. If, however, the computer locks up so that you can't use the software command, you can use the on/off switch on the back of the computer. On the back of many Macs, you won't find an on/off switch as such. Instead, you will find a power button, which serves the same purpose as an on/off switch: you can use it as an "emergency off" switch to shut down the Mac.

The video port allows you to connect the monitor to the box. You will see a video port on the back of a Mac Classic and a Mac Performa 200, even though they have a built-in monitor; you can use this video port to connect a second monitor.

You usually use the 25-pin SCSI port to connect external devices (such as additional hard drives) to the Mac.

You use the printer port, represented by an icon that looks like a printer, to connect the Mac to a printer or to an AppleTalk network.

You use the modem port to connect an external modem to the Mac to communicate over telephone lines with other computers.

You use the keyboard port (you may see more than one on the back of the Mac) to connect input devices, such as the keyboard and mouse, to the box.

You can use the sound output port to connect a set of headphones or speakers to the Mac. The sound produced by newer Macs is in stereo, so you will hear stereo sound if you connect stereo headphones or speakers to a new Mac.

You also might see a sound input port, which you can use to connect a microphone to the Mac. You can use the microphone and Mac to record sound. Certain applications specifically support sound; for example, in Microsoft Word for the Mac, you can create a voice annotation for your text.

Last, you see a series of metal strips. The strips are called slot covers because they cover the expansion slots (called **NuBus slots**) inside the Mac and keep them free from dust and debris. You use NuBus slots to add additional pieces of equipment (such as video cards or accelerator cards); various Macs come with varying numbers of NuBus slots. Note that many of the items you place in a NuBus slot require “access to the outside”; if you add a video card, it must be connected from the box to the monitor.

When you use a NuBus slot, therefore, you no longer use its slot cover, so you won't see slot covers in the expansion slots that contain additional hardware items.

Chapter Summary

In this chapter, you learned to identify the parts of a Mac, both from the front and the back. You learned that although all Macs do not look the same, they each contain some basic elements in common.

Putting aside Mac Classics and Mac Performa 200's for a moment, most Macs closely resemble PC's. You see a monitor, a box, and a keyboard. The monitor looks and works almost exactly like a monitor on any PC, except that the monitor controls on a Mac may not appear in the same place as the monitor controls on a PC. The Apple keyboards look very much like PC keyboards, with the exception that the Power On switch for most Macs is on the keyboard and the keyboard contains a Command key (which operates like the Ctrl and Alt keys on a PC keyboard). The box appears similar to most PC boxes; in some cases, the box may appear smaller on a Mac, but the box still contains the same basic components that you find inside a PC box—the CPU, the hard drive, a floppy drive, and expansion slots (called NuBus slots).

The Mac Classic and the Mac Performa 200 don't look like PC's until you realize that the monitor is built into the box—an "all-in-one" unit. Once you make the distinction, you realize that these Macs have all the basic parts of any other Mac or PC.

Turning On the Mac and Starting a Program

When you turn on a PC, the computer performs an automatic startup process. What you see at the end of the startup process may be a menu, the MS-DOS Shell, Microsoft Windows, or a DOS prompt. From any of these screens, you then can start a program.

When you turn on a Mac, the computer also performs an automatic startup process. After the startup process, you see the Desktop. Different things may appear on the Desktop, but the Desktop always remains onscreen. To explain why you always see the Desktop, the first section in this chapter briefly examines the difference in design philosophies that makes PCs different from Macs. After that, you learn to turn on a PC, and then how to start a program from any of the screens that may appear at the end of the computer's automatic startup process.

Understanding Design Philosophies: PC vs. Macintosh

As you already know, the PC and the Macintosh work very differently. Of course, technology is responsible for the major differences in the way these computers process information, but their design philosophies account for the differences in technology.

When IBM builds a computer, it attempts to build the most flexible computer available. An IBM-compatible personal computer will do almost anything you want it to do—you simply must learn how to tell it what you want it to do. And that means *everyone*, end users and programmers alike, must learn how to tell the computer what they want it to do. Typically, people tend to view flexibility as a "good" thing; however, flexibility has its price.

First, no specific standards exist that require software developers to make their programs look alike or operate in the same basic way. For this reason, developers have few restrictions and can work freely to design programs as they want. As users move from one program to another, they must learn how to operate each program from the ground up. Further, although PCs offer a great deal of flexibility to the users, this flexibility comes at the price of added complexity—the users must be well versed in making the computers do what they want them to do. This requirement usually means that users must learn, at a minimum, some basics about operating systems. And any PC user will tell you that working with the operating system on a PC is not a user-friendly experience.

On the other hand, the driving design philosophy behind the Macintosh was to make the computer user-friendly. And, as any Mac user will tell you, the Mac is easy to use. In the user-friendly environment, many of the details of how the software works have been predetermined. The users find that, regardless of the programs they are using, they can accomplish certain basic tasks by using the same basic commands. But, as with the PC's design philosophy, user-friendliness has its price—lack of flexibility. Mac programmers must operate under certain constraints.

Rather than focusing on which approach is "better" (which is a debate that's been going on for years), this chapter focuses on how a PC user can adjust to a flexible but controlled environment.

Although the screens you see on a Mac don't typically look like the screens you see in DOS programs and the commands that perform similar functions often have different names, most of the tasks you want to perform on the Mac are similar to the ones you perform on the PC. Therefore, when working in the Mac environment, look for similar commands to the ones you use on your PC (for example "open" and "retrieve") and try them. Remember that you probably won't hurt anything as long as you don't delete files. Don't be afraid to experiment.

If you have used Windows, you probably will find that working on the Mac reminds you of working in Windows. You will see menus and dialog boxes, and many of the commands you use in Windows programs are the same as the commands you use in Mac programs.

Turning On the Mac

On a PC, you find a switch somewhere on the box that you use to turn on the computer. To turn on most Macs, you usually use a key on the keyboard. On the Apple Keyboard II, the key appears in the upper left corner of the keyboard. On the Apple Extended Keyboard II, the key appears in the upper right corner of the keyboard. (See Chapter 1 for more information about the Power On key.)

The entry-level Macintosh models (such as the Classic, the Performa 200, the LC, and the Performa 400) do not use the Power On key, even though it is present on the keyboard. Instead, you must use the power switch located on the back of the box. Turning on this kind of Mac by using the power switch has the same effect as pressing the Power On key on the other Macs.

When you press the Power On key or power switch to turn on the box, you may also have to press the monitor's power switch to turn on the monitor (unless, of course, you are using a Mac Classic or Mac Performa 200, where the monitor and the box are "all in one").

When you turn on a Mac, instructions stored in the hardware chips tell the computer to "take an inventory" of parts and test them to make sure they are working properly. The computer tests the memory chips and the keyboard (you may notice the Num Lock, Caps Lock, and Scroll Lock lights flash on). After testing the hardware components of the computer, the next instruction tells the computer to search the hard disk for the operating system files (called "the **System**" in Mac lingo) and execute the instructions found there, loading the System and the INITs and CDEVs.

When you begin to see images onscreen, a small arrow (the **mouse pointer**) appears in the upper left corner of the screen. Shortly after that, you see in the center of the screen an image of a Mac with a smiling face. This image is known as the "happy Mac" and indicates that the Macintosh has found the System and is loading it. If you see an image of a floppy disk with a question mark, the Macintosh can't find the System files. This may indicate a problem with the hard disk. If you see an image of a frowning face (the "sad Mac"), you probably have a problem with the Macintosh hardware or with the System.

After you see the "happy Mac," you see the "Welcome to Macintosh" logo in a box in the center of the screen. You then see a series of **icons** appear along the bottom of the screen. These icons represent INITs and CDEVs—the Mac equivalent of the PC's TSR (Terminate/Stay Resident) programs, also known as "pop-up" programs, such as SideKick. INITs and CDEVs are small programs that are loaded while the Mac boots, adding features to the Macintosh operating system.

Understanding the Desktop

When the start-up process is complete, you see a Desktop similar to the one in Figure 2.1. If you are working on any of the Macintosh Performas, you might see a Desktop containing additional items, similar to the one in Figure 2.2.

The Desktop on a Performa may look different from the Desktop on other varieties of Macs because the Performa includes a software program called the Launcher, which you can use to start programs. Further, with the Performa software, Apple has defined a Documents folder, which acts as the default storage location for files you create. You learn more about the Launcher and the

Documents folder later in this chapter. And, because I'm working on a Performa, you will see the Performa Desktop in the full-screen figures in this book unless otherwise noted.

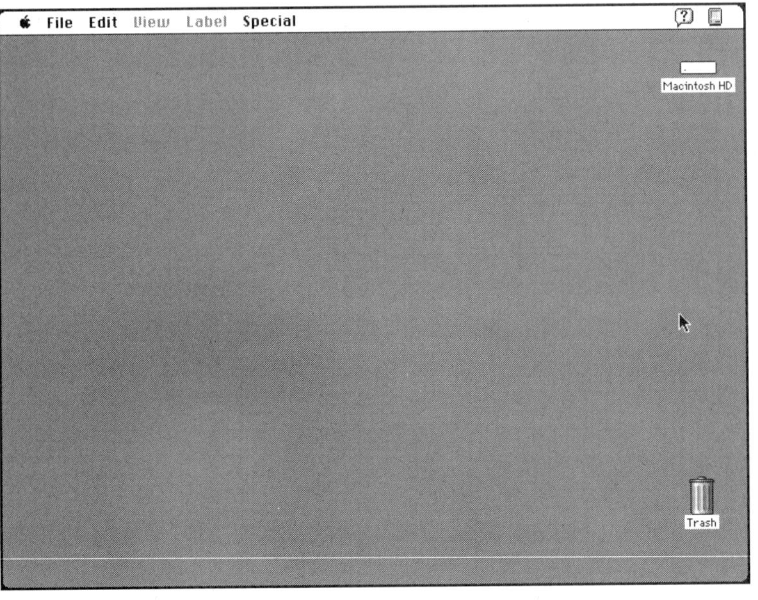

Figure 2.1.

A typical Mac Desktop.

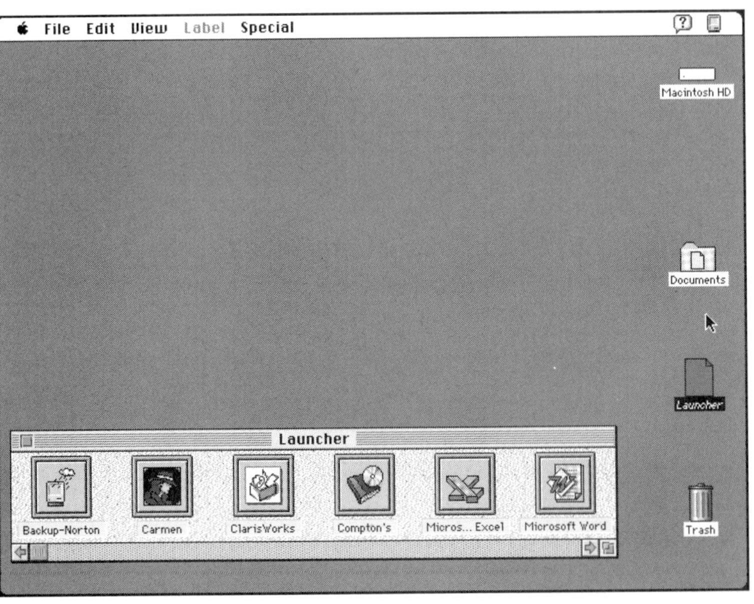

Figure 2.2.

A typical Mac Performa Desktop.

When you first start the Mac, the active program is the program that controls the activities on the Desktop—the **Finder**. (For versions of the System earlier than System 7, the active program may be the Finder or the **MultiFinder**—you learn how to determine which version of the System you are running later in this chapter.) If you are familiar with Windows, you can think of the Finder on the Mac as like the Program Manager in Windows.

MAC NOTE

As in Windows, you can use multitasking on a Mac. **Multitasking** enables the user to perform two or more functions simultaneously. For example, in a multitasking environment, the user can send data over a modem and work in a word processor while the data transmission takes place.

Operating the Mouse on a Mac

Although you can accomplish many tasks on a Mac by using just the keyboard, you primarily use a mouse to start programs, choose commands from menus, and choose options in dialog boxes. Typically, a Mac mouse has only one button, but the mouse you're using may have one, two, or three buttons. If this is the case, use the left mouse button. (The right and middle buttons—if your mouse has them—operate differently depending on the software that controls the mouse; if you stick to the left button, however, you will be fine.)

The mouse on a Mac operates differently from the way a mouse operates in DOS or Windows. Some terms require defining. **Pointing** is the process of sliding the mouse on the desk until the mouse pointer onscreen rests on the item to which you want to point. **Clicking** is the process of pressing and releasing the mouse

button one time. **Clicking and holding** is the process of pressing and holding down the mouse button. **Dragging** is the process of pressing and holding down the mouse button while sliding the mouse to move the mouse pointer (and whatever item you clicked on) to the new location. And **double-clicking** is the process of quickly pressing and releasing the mouse button two times.

Working with Icons and Windows on a Mac

The most basic task on any computer is to find documents and programs; on the Macintosh, you do this by using the Finder. This section explains what the icons mean and how to manipulate the Mac's windows.

Understanding Icons

On the Desktop, you see icons that represent various things on the Mac. For example, you see an icon representing the hard drive and you see the Trash can (which you use to erase information). You *may* also see some icons that represent programs and other icons that represent data files (see Figure 2.3).

If you work on a Performa, you see a folder icon labeled Documents and an icon that represents the Launcher—a software program bundled with Performas that is designed to make it easy for users to start programs.

With the exception of the Trash can, which has a special function, the other icons you might see on the Desktop represent three basic things: disks, folders, and files.

Somewhere on the Mac Desktop, you see a hard disk icon (like the one shown in Figure 2.4) and, when you insert a floppy disk into the floppy disk drive, you see an icon that resembles the one in Figure 2.5.

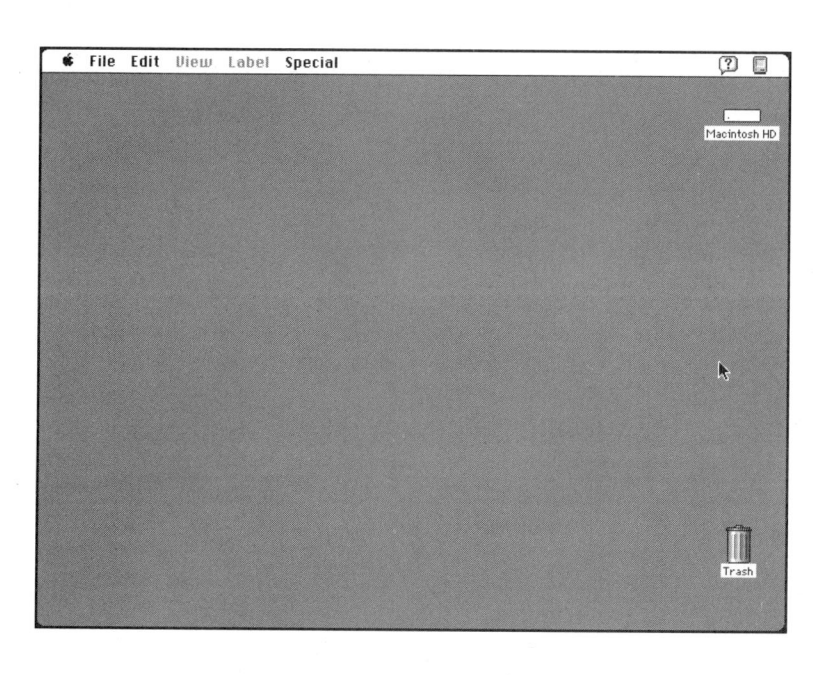

Figure 2.3.

A typical Desktop.

Figure 2.4.

A hard disk icon.

Figure 2.5.

A floppy disk icon.

If PC Exchange (a file translation utility) is installed, and the disk you insert is a floppy disk that was formatted on a PC, the floppy disk icon contains the letters PC (see Figure 2.6). You learn more about PC Exchange and transferring files between a PC and a Mac in Chapter 9.

On a PC, you would use the DIR command to display the contents of a floppy disk, the hard disk, or a directory. On a Mac, you open a floppy disk, the hard disk, or a folder to display its contents. You open a disk or folder by selecting it (clicking on the icon to **highlight** it) and then choosing the Open command from the File menu (which you'll learn about later in this chapter), or by double-clicking on the icon.

Figure 2.6.

A PC floppy disk icon when PC Exchange is active.

When you open the hard disk, the System displays a window in which you see folders and in which you may see files. **Folders** are the equivalent of directories, and they contain files. **Files** on a Mac correspond to files on a PC, and include such things as applications, documents, and worksheets. Folders are easy to identify: the folder icon looks like a file folder. The file icon looks like a piece of paper with the upper right corner folded over; some are plain and some include a symbol assigned to them by the application software that created them. In Figure 2.7, you see the System Folder, the Applications folder, the Mouse Basics folder, the Mouse Practice folder, and the Pictures folder. You also see a file named Picture 1.

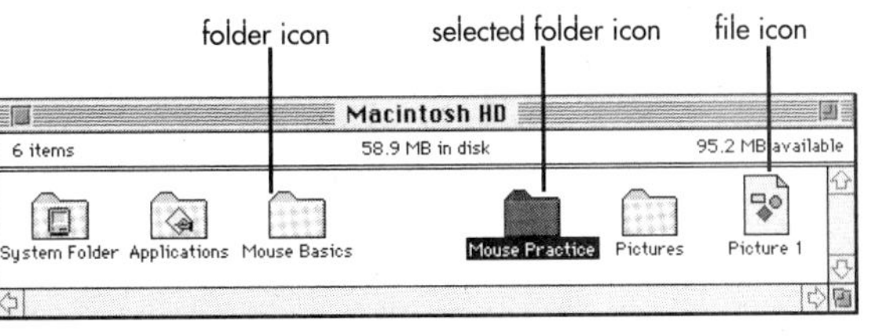

Figure 2.7.

Folders and files.

Working with Windows

As you just learned, when you open a disk or folder, the Finder opens a **window** on the Desktop to display the contents of the disk or folder. When you open the hard disk and view its window, you are doing the equivalent of viewing the root directory on a PC (which you would do by using the DIR command).

As you can see from Figure 2.8, windows contain several important features.

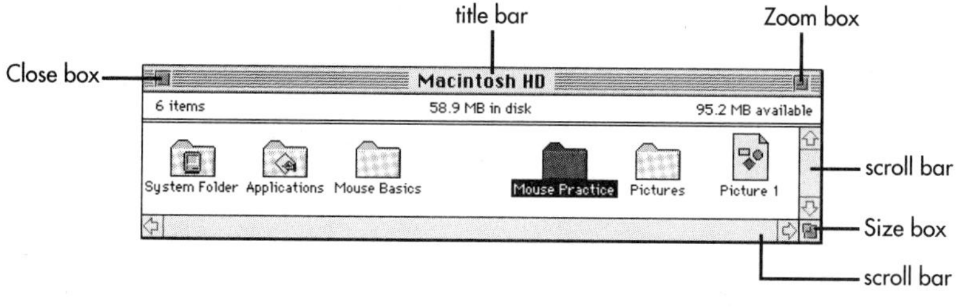

Figure 2.8. The parts of a window.

You can use the **title bar** of the window to move the window to a different location on the Desktop. Point to the title bar of the dialog box and drag it. You can see the outline of the window as you drag. When you release the mouse button, the Finder positions the window in the new location.

To see information that appears beyond the edges of the window, click on the arrows that appear at the ends of the **scroll bars** on the right side and bottom of the window.

To make the window big enough to show everything it contains (or as big as the Finder can make it onscreen), click on the **Zoom box** at the right end of the title bar.

To increase or decrease the size of the window, drag the **Size box** in the lower right corner of the window. You can drag in any direction: up, down, left, right, or diagonally.

To close the window, click on the **Close box**, located at the left end of the title bar.

As you continue to open disk or folder icons, the Finder continues to open windows. You can switch from one window to another simply by clicking anywhere in the window you want to activate. If you mistakenly select a disk, folder, or file, simply click anywhere on the Desktop to deselect it, or select something else instead.

On a Mac, you can change the way in which the icons appear in windows by using the commands on the View menu. In Figure 2.8, the icons in the window appear by Icon. In Figure 2.9, the icons in the hard drive window appear by Small Icon. In Figure 2.10, the

icons appear alphabetically organized by Name. Using other commands on the View menu, you can change the arrangement of icons in a window so that the icons appear organized by Size, by Kind, by Label, or by Date. For each of these arrangements, the icons look like the ones in Figure 2.10; they simply appear in a different order. Don't worry if you don't understand *what* each of these arrangements means; it's more important for you to be aware that icons in windows can appear differently.

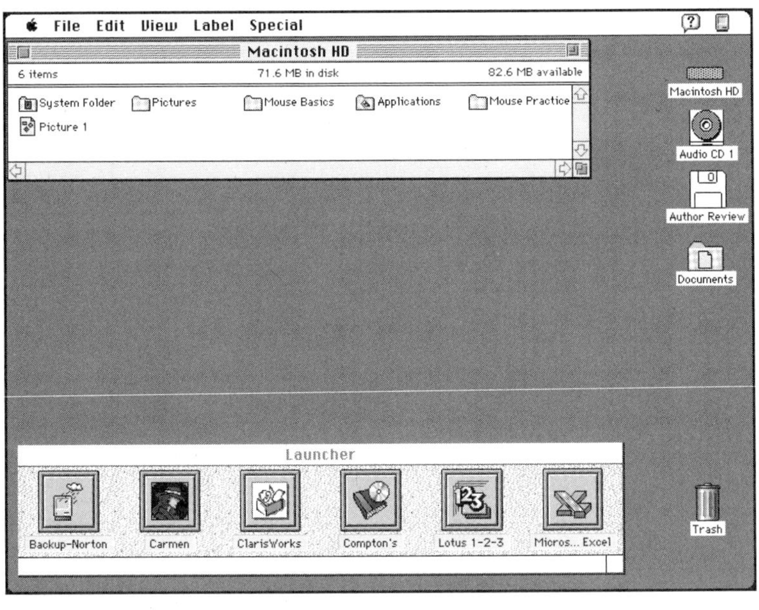

Figure 2.9.
The hard drive window viewed by Small Icon.

Working with Menus, Commands, and Dialog Boxes

At the top of the Desktop (see Figures 2.1, 2.2, and 2.3), you see the **menu bar**, which contains **menus**. The Finder has eight menus: from the left end of the menu bar, the Apple menu (represented by the icon), the File menu, the Edit menu, the View menu, the Label menu, the Special menu, and then—at the right end of the menu bar—the Help menu (represented by a balloon icon) and the

Application menu (also represented by an icon). Each menu contains **commands** you use on a Mac.

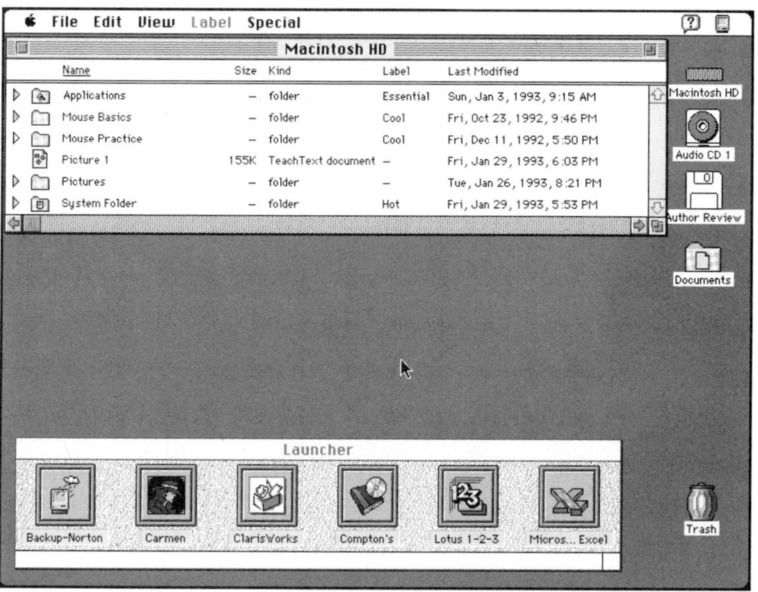

Figure 2.10. The hard drive window viewed by Name.

Ellipses (...) appear after some commands on the menus. The program (in this case, the Finder) requires additional information about these commands before it can execute them. When you choose a command that includes an ellipsis, a **dialog box** (in which you supply the additional required information) appears.

Opening a Menu and Choosing a Command

Most of the time, on a Mac, you use the mouse to open menus and choose commands. When you're working in the Finder, the commands you choose typically work on the selected icon. If you're used to working with a mouse and menus on a PC, you will find that opening a menu and choosing a command on the Mac is slightly different. To open a menu and choose a command, follow these steps:

1. Point to the menu that contains the command you want to choose.

2. Click and hold the left mouse button.

   The menu opens.

> **MAC TIP**
>
> If you move the mouse pointer along the menu bar while holding down the mouse button, each menu opens as the pointer passes across it.

3. Drag the mouse pointer down the menu until a highlight (a reverse video bar) appears over the command you want to choose.

4. Release the mouse button.

   The Finder executes the command you chose (or, if an ellipsis appears after the command, the Finder opens a dialog box).

Note the important difference between choosing commands in a Windows or DOS program and choosing commands on a Mac: When you open a menu to choose a command in a Windows or DOS program, you generally don't need to hold down the mouse button because the menu remains open after you release the mouse button. On a Mac, you must click and *hold* the mouse button to open a menu and choose a command; if you release the mouse button, the menu closes immediately.

You also can use **keyboard shortcuts** to choose a command. When you open a menu, you might notice characters that appear to the right of some commands. For example, to the right of the Find command on the File menu, you see ⌘ **F** (see Figure 2.11). To choose the Find command by using its keyboard shortcut, simply

press and hold the Command (⌘) key as you press the F key, regardless of where the mouse pointer appears on the Desktop. To use keyboard shortcuts, you must remember them. You can refresh your memory by using the mouse to open the menu, but once you have the menu open, you can simply choose the command. Because you are, in theory, an occasional user of the Mac, you probably will find it easier to use the menus to choose commands; however, in case you prefer to use the keyboard, the keyboard shortcuts also appear in this book.

Figure 2.11.
The commands on the File menu.

MAC NOTE

In this book, when you see two or more keys separated by a plus sign (+), you hold down the first key(s) as you press the last key. When you see two or more keys separated by a comma (,), you press the keys in sequence.

When you open a menu, some of the commands on the menu appear in black, and other commands appear in gray. The commands that appear in black are available and you can choose them. The commands that appear in gray are currently unavailable, so you can't choose them. Figure 2.11 shows the commands on the File menu; the Find command is black and available, while the Print command is gray and unavailable.

Now let's practice opening a menu and choosing a command. On the Apple menu, the first command is About this Macintosh. When you are running another program (for example, Microsoft Word), the first command on the Apple menu changes (for example, to become About Microsoft Word); the first command on the Apple menu always provides you with information about the program you are currently running. The About this Macintosh command helps you determine what version of the System software you are running and what programs, if any, are active.

To open this window, follow these steps:

1. Point to the **Apple** menu.
2. Click and hold the left mouse button.

   The Apple menu opens.
3. Drag the mouse down the menu until the first command, **About this Macintosh**, is highlighted.
4. Release the left mouse button.

   The About this Macintosh dialog box appears (see Figure 2.12).

Working with Dialog Boxes

Dialog boxes on the Mac serve the same purpose and work the same way as dialog boxes in Microsoft Windows. Next to some commands on menus (such as the About this Macintosh command on the Apple menu), you see ellipses (...). An ellipsis generally indicates that the program requires additional information before it can execute the command. Typically, when you choose a command that includes an ellipsis, a dialog box appears. You use a dialog box to supply additional information to the program that displayed the dialog box.

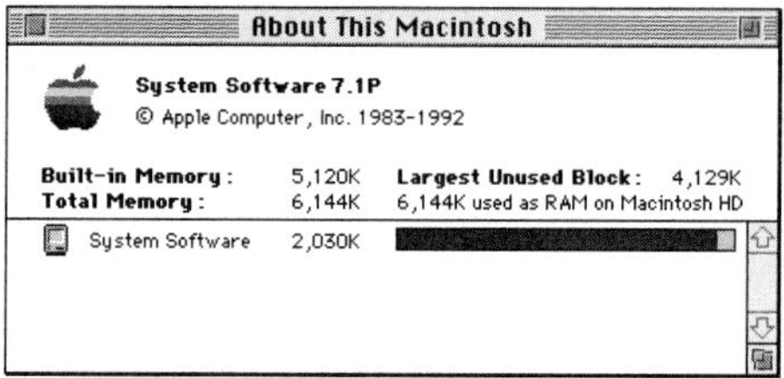

Figure 2.12. The About This Macintosh dialog box.

Figure 2.13 shows the Open dialog box that you see in Microsoft Word for the Mac. Figure 2.14 shows the Print dialog box. These two dialog boxes contain samples of the various kinds of options you may see in a dialog box.

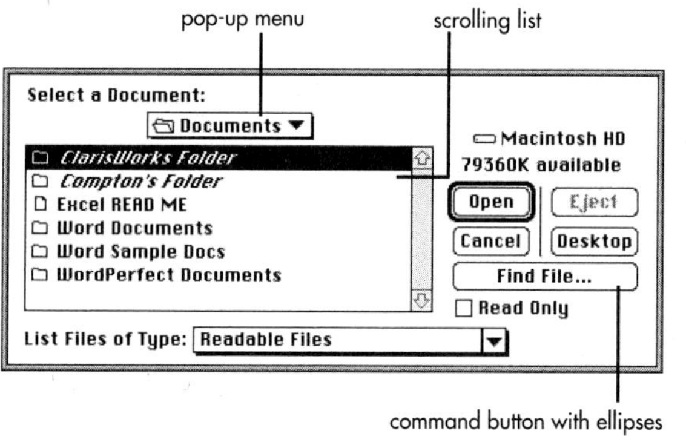

Figure 2.13. The Open dialog box in Word for the Mac.

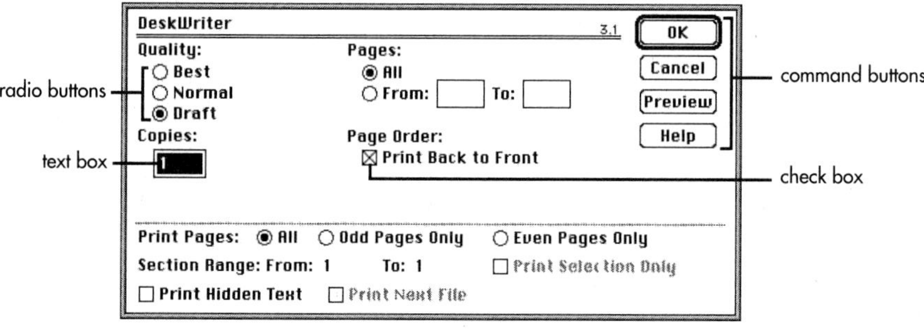

Figure 2.14. The Print dialog box for an HP Deskwriter.

Not all dialog boxes contain all kinds of options. But, you may find any of the following items in a dialog box:

- A **command button** is the same as a command button in a Windows program and is an oblong button that you use to perform an action. For example, in Figure 2.14, the OK command button accepts the settings in the dialog box. The Cancel button cancels your changes to the settings in the dialog box. To perform the action indicated by a command button, click on the button.

  Some command buttons include ellipses. As with menu commands that include ellipses, these command buttons open another dialog box. They work just like regular command buttons—click on the button for the action you want to perform.

- A **scrolling list** is the same as a list box in a Windows program and contains a list of options; the Open dialog box in Figure 2.13 lists files that you can open. You use a scrolling list to select an item on which you want to perform a command. To choose an item, highlight the item by clicking on it, then click the appropriate command button. If the scrolling list is not long enough to display all the available items in the list, click on an arrow at the end of the scroll bar to move beyond the items that appear in the box.

- A **pop-up menu** is similar to a drop-down list box in a Windows program and also contains a list of options. The List Files of Type item in Figure 2.13 is an example of a pop-up menu. The active option is displayed when the pop-up menu is closed; in Figure 2.13, Readable Files is the active option. Pop-up menus work just like regular menus: click on the pop-up menu and hold down the mouse button to display the list of options, drag the mouse to highlight the option you want to select, and then release the mouse button. The option then is displayed when the pop-up menu is closed.

- A **radio button** is the same as an option button in a Windows program and is a small round button you use to choose one option from a group of related options. Radio buttons are used when only one of the options can be used at a time—they take their name from the station preset buttons on a radio. (You can listen to only one station at a time!) To choose a radio button, click on it. A black dot appears in the button of the active option. In Figure 2.14, the Best, Normal, and Draft choices are radio buttons, and the active option is Draft.

- A **text box** is the same as a text box in a Windows program—a rectangular box where you type information. In Figure 2.14, the Copies box is a text box, and the From item in the Pages area has two text boxes in which you can type information. To enter information into a text box, click on the box and type the information.

- A **check box** is a small square box you use to choose an option. You can choose more than one check box from a group of related options (unlike a group of radio buttons, from which you can choose only one option). An **X** appears in the check boxes of the active options. To choose a check box, click on the check box. To deactivate the option and remove the **X** from the box, click on the check box again. In Figure 2.14, the Print Back to Front check box is active while the Print Hidden Text check box is not.

In dialog boxes, unavailable options appear in gray (like unavailable menu commands). In Figure 2.13, the Eject button is unavailable; in Figure 2.14, the Print Selection Only and Print Next File check boxes are unavailable.

Starting a Program on the Mac

You can start a program on a Mac in several ways:

- You may be able to use the Apple menu.
- You may be able to use the Launcher.
- You can double-click on the program's icon.
- You can double-click on the icon of a file created by that program.

Using the Apple Menu To Start a Program

If the program you want to start appears on the Apple menu, the easiest way to start the program is to open the Apple menu and choose the program. In this section, you practice using the Apple menu to start a program by starting the Calculator. And, just in case the Mac you are using has a CD-ROM drive, you learn how to use the CD-ROM drive to play music while you work. (Remember, I promised you in Chapter 1 that I'd tell you how to do this!)

Starting the Calculator

The Calculator is exactly what it's name implies: an onscreen version of a calculator you can use to perform arithmetic operations. You can use the Cut, Copy, and Paste commands to place the answers into other applications.

To start the Calculator, open the Apple menu and choose the Calculator command. The Calculator appears onscreen (see Figure 2.15).

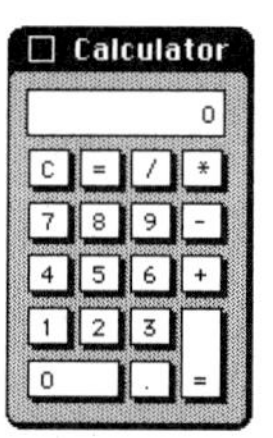

Figure 2.15.
The Calculator.

The calculator works just like any hand-held calculator. You can click on the keys to "press" them, or you can use the numeric keypad (or the number keys) on the keyboard to type the numbers. Use the + key to add entries and the - key to subtract entries. Use the * key to multiply entries, and the / key to divide the first entry by the second entry. Use the = key to find the result of the calculation. Use the C (Clear) key if you make a mistake while keying and want to retype the entry. During the entry of a list of numbers, you can press the C key and continue the calculation. If you press the C key after pressing the = key, the C key clears all entries from the memory of the calculator.

Using the CD ROM Drive To Play Music

If you use a Mac that has a built-in CD-ROM drive (such as the Performa 600 CD), you can play music on the Mac. First, you must have a music CD and the software to control the CD-ROM drive must be installed. To check, open the Apple menu and look for the CD Remote command. If you find this command and you have a music CD, follow these steps:

1. To open the CD caddy, hold it in one hand with the metal strip away from you. Pinch the corners of the caddy with one hand as you lift the plastic lid with the other hand.

2. Place the CD in the caddy, label side up, sliding the disk under the lip on the hinged side of the caddy.

3. Close the plastic lid.

4. Place the caddy in the CD-ROM drive, label side up and metal end first.

   After a few seconds, the CD-ROM icon appears on the Desktop.

5. Open the Apple menu and choose the CD Remote command.

   The CD Remote control appears (see Figure 2.16).

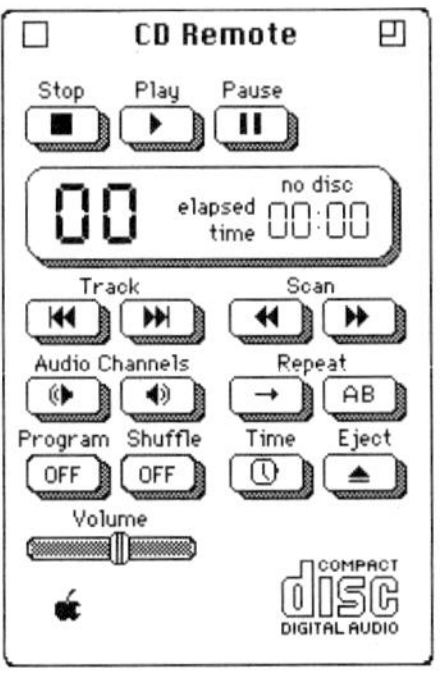

Figure 2.16.
The CD Remote control.

6. Click on the Play button.

   The CD begins to play.

Now, enjoy the music while you continue your Macintosh session! If you need to stop the CD, select the CD Remote command from the Apple menu again and click on the Stop button. To eject the caddy from the drive, click on the Eject button. To close the CD Remote control, click on its Close box (in the upper left corner) or open the File menu and choose the Quit command.

Starting Other Programs from the Apple Menu

You can start any program that appears in the Apple menu simply by choosing its name from the menu, just like you started the Calculator and the CD Remote. The Apple menu includes several small programs (called Desk Accessories) designed to be started from the Apple menu; examples include the Calculator, CD Remote, Note Pad, and Scrapbook; however, any program can be placed on the Apple menu, and you probably will find several other programs listed there. You can start all the programs on the Apple menu in the same way.

Using the Launcher To Start a Program

If you are working on a Performa, you may be able to use the Launcher to start the program you want to use; however, the Launcher window must contain the program you want to open. In the Launcher window (see Figure 2.17), you see icons representing programs. You can use the scroll bar in the window to see additional programs that have been set up in the Launcher.

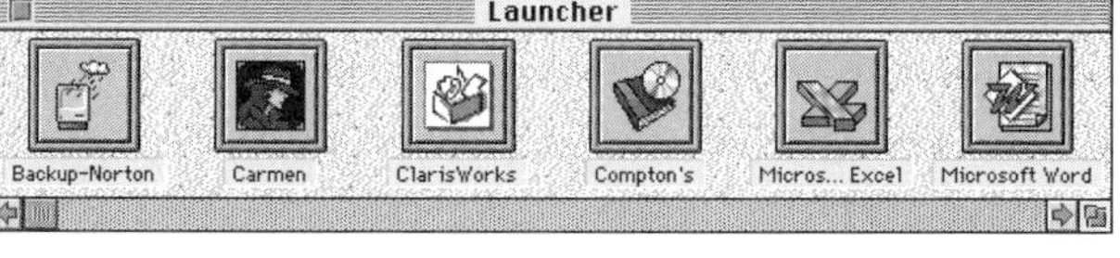

Figure 2.17. The Launcher window.

The Launcher may appear horizontally onscreen, as you see it in Figure 2.17, or it may appear vertically. If it appears horizontally, the scroll bar appears at the bottom of the window, and the scroll arrows appear in the lower left and right corners. If the Launcher window appears vertically onscreen, the scroll bar appears along the right side of the window, and the scroll arrows appear in the upper and lower right corners of the window. Click the scroll arrows to see additional programs set up in the Launcher.

To use the Launcher to start a program, just click on the icon that represents the program.

Using a Program Icon To Start a Program

As a PC user, you are most familiar with the concept of starting the program you want to run first and then opening (or retrieving) the file on which you want to work. You also can follow this sequence on a Mac.

To use a program icon to start a program, you double-click on the icon. To double-click on the program icon, though, you first must find it. The icon will appear in a Finder window, or on the Desktop. If the program icon appears on the Desktop, your job is easy: just double-click on it.

If the icon that represents the program you want to start doesn't appear on the Desktop, you must open the Finder window that contains it so that you can see the icon.

To find the correct window, you can guess by opening likely folders (a common habit among PC users), or you can use the Find command. To use the Find command, follow these steps:

1. Open the **File** menu and choose the **Find** command. (You can also use the keyboard shortcut shown on the menu: ⌘+**F**.)

   The Finder displays the Find dialog box (see Figure 2.18).

2. In the Find text box, type the name of the program for which you are searching. You don't need to type the whole name, because the Finder searches for all file and folder names that contain the letters you supply in the Find text box.

3. Click on the **Find** button.

   If the Finder finds the program you specified on the Desktop, the Finder opens a dialog box telling you that it found the program file on the Desktop. Click on the OK button and skip to step 5.

   If the Finder finds something on the Desktop that *isn't* what you wanted, click on the OK button to close the dialog box and continue with step 4.

   If the program isn't on the Desktop, the Finder opens the window containing the file or folder it found and highlights the file or folder.

4. If the Finder did not find the icon for the program you want to start, continue the search by opening the **File** menu and choosing the **Find Again** command (or use the keyboard shortcut ⌘+**G**).

   The Finder finds the next occurrence of the letters you typed in the Find dialog box. Each time you select **Find Again**, the Finder opens a window that contains a file or folder whose name contains the letters you supplied in the Find dialog box. When the Finder can't find any more files or folders that contain those letters, you hear a beep sound.

5. When you see the icon that represents the program you want to start, double-click on it.

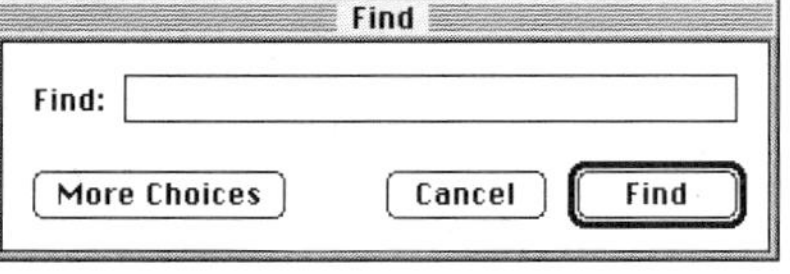

Figure 2.18. The Find dialog box.

MAC NOTE

These instructions are for System 7. If the Mac you are using has an earlier version of the System, you probably can use the Find File command on the Apple menu. It operates essentially the same way.

Using a File Icon To Start a Program

As a PC user, you're familiar with starting the program first and then the file on which you want to work. On a Mac, however, you can use the file on which you want to work to start the program and then open the specified file.

If the icon for the file on which you want to work appears on the Desktop, double-click on it. The Finder loads the program, and the program opens the file.

If the file doesn't appear on the Desktop, use the Find command to find the file (see the steps in the preceding section). When you find the file, double-click on its icon. The Finder loads the program, and the program opens the file.

Using the Application Menu To Switch between Programs

On a Mac, you can open and run more than one program at a time. To switch between programs, you use the Application menu, represented by the icon at the right end of the menu bar. (The icon changes to match the program icon of whatever program is active.)

To work in multiple programs, start each program, using one of the methods previously described. Then, to switch between them, open the Application menu and choose the program you want to use.

Turning Off the Mac

I know that to a PC user this seems like a silly section, but you are used to turning off a PC the same way you turn it on, and—that's right, you guessed it—you don't turn off a Mac the same way you turn it on.

Shutting Down the Mac

As a matter of good practice, before you shut down the computer, you should save any files on which you are working and quit any programs that are running. If you leave any programs running, the Finder will switch to them and quit them for you before you shut down the Mac; however, although most programs will ask whether you want to save open files before the programs close, you risk losing data if the programs in which you are working don't ask before they close.

To turn off the Mac, switch to the Finder. Then, open the Special menu and choose the Shut Down command. If you have left any programs running, you can see them flash onscreen as the Finder closes them. What happens next depends on what type of Mac you are using. If you're using a Mac that you can turn on with the Power On key on the keyboard, the Mac will shut itself off. If you have a Mac that you must turn on with a switch on the box, a dialog box tells you when it is safe to turn off the computer. You then flip the switch on the box to turn off the power.

Don't forget to turn off the monitor if necessary.

Restarting the Mac

On a PC, you occasionally need to perform a "warm boot" on the computer if, for example, the keyboard seems to freeze. You may occasionally need to perform a "warm boot" on the Mac as well. You can restart a Mac by choosing the Restart command on the Finder's Special menu. Be aware that, just as on a PC, you may lose data if you restart the Mac without saving any open files.

If the Mac should freeze so that you can't move the mouse pointer to choose the Restart command, the only recourse may be to turn off the computer by using the switch or button on the back of the box. This should be your last resort, however, because it can cause problems for the System software when you restart, and because it can cause you to lose data in any files that you haven't saved.

Chapter Summary

In this chapter, you learned how to turn on (and turn off) the Mac. You learned how to use the mouse with the Mac. You learned how to recognize and select icons for disks, folders, and files, and you learned how to work with windows. You learned how to choose commands from menus and options from dialog boxes. You also learned different ways to start programs on the Mac.

You turn on some Macs the same way that you turn on a PC—by using a switch or a button on the back of the Mac. On other Macs, you can use the Power On key on the keyboard to start the Mac. On Macs, you work with both floppy and hard disks, and you store information in files, as you do on a PC. You can organize your files on the Mac by grouping them in folders, which are the equivalent to directories on a PC. The Desktop on a Mac most closely resembles what you see onscreen on a PC when you start Microsoft Windows. A mouse on a Mac works differently than a mouse on a PC—on the Mac, you must hold down the mouse button while opening a menu to choose a command.

Now you're ready to learn about some of the more popular software packages and how to perform basic tasks in them. In the next chapter, you learn how to work with WordPerfect for the Mac files. As you know, Chapters 3 through 6 in *The PC User's Mac* focus on specific software packages. You should read the chapters that pertain to the software you want to use. Chapter 7 tells you about database programs you may want to avoid. Chapter 8 provides information for working at the System level on a Mac. If you need to transfer and translate files between a Mac and a PC, read Chapter 9.

Working with WordPerfect for the Mac Files

In the first two chapters of *The PC User's Mac*, you learned about the physical appearance of a Mac, how to turn on a Mac, how to recognize what you may see onscreen, and how to start programs. In Chapter 2, specifically, you learned how to open menus, choose commands, work with dialog boxes, and start programs. You will need these skills to proceed through this chapter

In this chapter, you will learn very basic information about using WordPerfect for the Mac. This chapter is not intended to make you an expert at using WordPerfect for the Mac; this chapter simply teaches you how to perform some basic tasks. You will learn how to open, edit, save, and print a WordPerfect for the Mac document; how to copy a WordPerfect for the Mac file to a floppy disk; and how to exit the program properly. And you will learn one other important thing—how to get help in WordPerfect for the Mac so that you can teach yourself to do the things that aren't covered in this book!

Identifying WordPerfect for the Mac Screen Parts

Using one of the techniques described in Chapter 2, start WordPerfect for the Mac. The opening screen appears as shown in Figure 3.1.

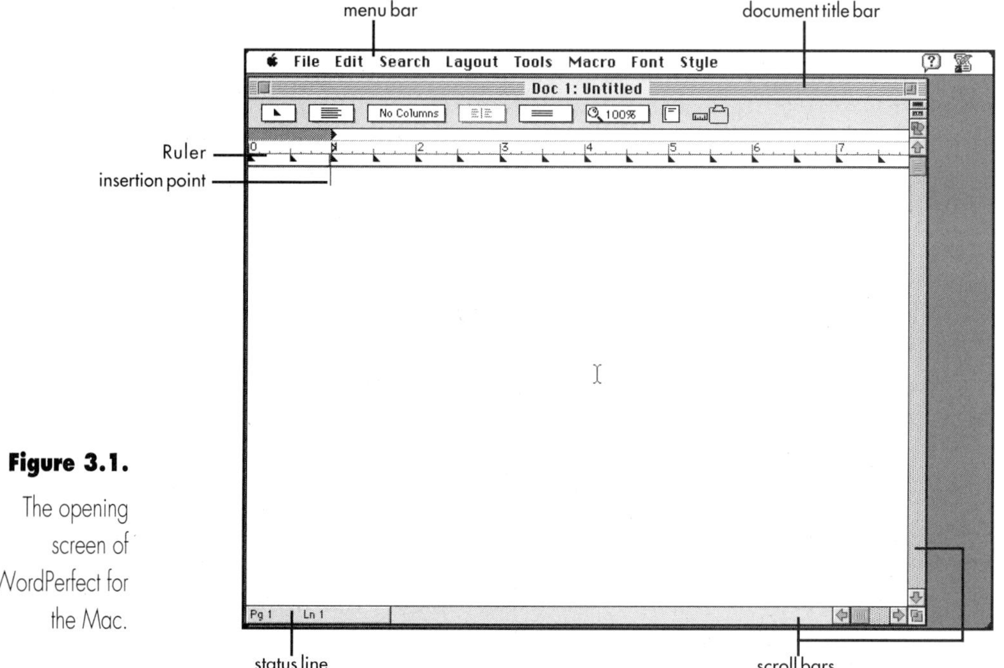

Figure 3.1.

The opening screen of WordPerfect for the Mac.

At the top of the screen, you see the WordPerfect **menu bar**, which also contains the Apple menu, the Help menu, and the Applications menu. Below the menu bar, you see the name of the current document, **Doc 1: Untitled**, in the **title bar** of the document window. Below the title bar, you see (unless someone has turned it off) the Ruler.

The Ruler actually consists of two parts. You use the bottom of the Ruler to move and remove tab stops, set margins, and control first line indention and column placement. You use the top part of the Ruler to perform a variety of functions. Working from the left edge of the Ruler, you use the first button to set tab types. You use the next button to control text alignment. The third button controls column layout, while the fourth button controls line spacing and formatting. Use the fifth button to change the size of text onscreen. Use the sixth button to center-align the page, and use the seventh button to copy Ruler settings to the Clipboard (more about the Clipboard later).

Just next to the status line, and also along the right side of the document window, you see the horizontal and vertical scroll bars. Each scroll bar has a scroll box on the bar and scroll arrows at both ends of the bar. The horizontal scroll bar enables you to scan the width of the page in your document, if the window isn't wide enough to display the entire document width. The vertical scroll bar enables you to move from top to bottom through each page, and from page to page through the length of the document.

The insertion point appears as a flashing vertical bar in the upper left corner of the empty document area. The **insertion point** indicates where text will appear when you type. When you start WordPerfect for the Mac, you always see an empty document window, in which you can start creating a new document. (Unless, of course, you started WordPerfect for the Mac by opening a document created by the program. In this case, you see the document you opened rather than an empty document.)

The status line, at the bottom of the screen, always indicates where the insertion point is located. In an empty document, the insertion point is located on Page 1, Line 1, as you can see in Figure 3.1. In the right half of the status line, you see the name of any style that has been assigned to the paragraph.

You can customize options that appear on the screen; if another WordPerfect for the Mac user has changed these options, something slightly different may appear. Figure 3.2 shows another WordPerfect for the Mac screen that you may see.

In this version of the opening screen, notice that some additional information appears in the status line at the bottom of the window. Next to the insertion point information, you see the Style buttons, which enable a user to apply formatting (for example, italics or underlining) to text easily. Next to the Style buttons, you see the exact vertical and horizontal position of the insertion point.

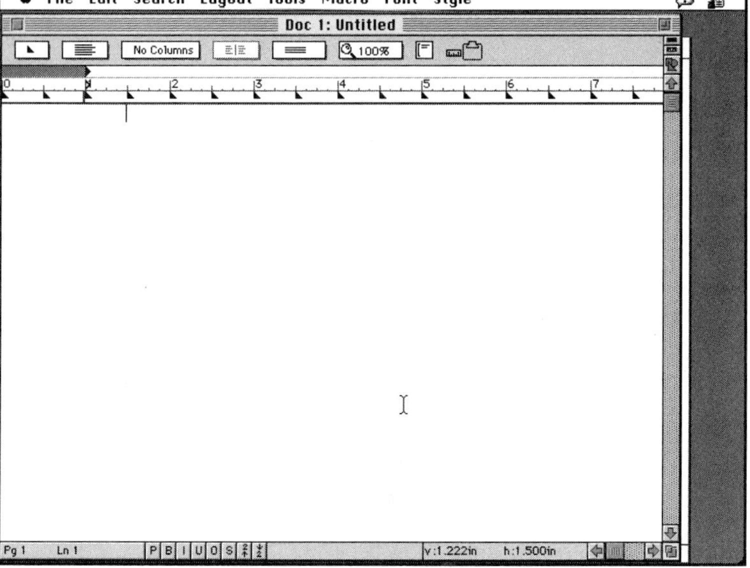

Figure 3.2. A customized opening WordPerfect for the Mac screen.

These additional features appear onscreen because the user opened the Environmental Preferences dialog box and made selections from the options and menus that appear in that dialog box. You can modify these preferences, but be aware that any changes you make remain in effect until you open the Environmental Preferences dialog box again and change your selections. If you want to modify the settings WordPerfect for the Mac uses, refer to the WordPerfect for the Mac reference manual for instructions, and note the changes you make so that you can change them back again.

Finding the WordPerfect 5.x Keyboard

When installing WordPerfect for the Mac, the user can choose to install the standard keyboard used by WordPerfect for the Mac *and*

the WordPerfect 5.0/5.1 keyboard. Because the two keyboards are very different, using the WordPerfect 5.0/5.1 keyboard can help PC users who use WordPerfect (either for Windows or for DOS) easily work in WordPerfect for the Mac. This keyboard enables users to use the function keys they "already know" to execute commands.

To find out which keyboard is active, press F5. If you see the Open dialog box, the WordPerfect 5.0/5.1 keyboard is active. If, instead, the insertion point moves to the first tab stop, the WordPerfect for the Mac keyboard is active.

Even if the WordPerfect for the Mac keyboard is active, you may be able to switch to the WordPerfect 5.0/5.1 keyboard while you are working in WordPerfect for the Mac. To do so, follow these steps:

1. Open the **File** menu and highlight the **Preferences** command, but don't release the mouse button.

   The **Preferences** submenu appears to the side of the **File** menu, displaying more choices.

2. Move the mouse pointer onto the **Preferences** submenu and select the **Keyboards** command (and release the mouse button).

   The Keyboard Management dialog box appears (see Figure 3.3).

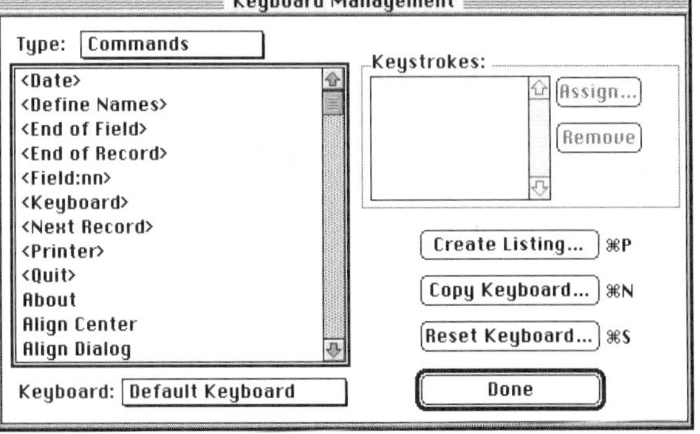

Figure 3.3. The Keyboard Management dialog box.

3. Open the Keyboard pop-up menu. If the WordPerfect 5.x choice appears in the list, choose it.

4. Click on the Done button.

5. Test the success of the procedure by pressing **F5**.

   If you successfully activated the WordPerfect 5.x keyboard, you should see the Open dialog box.

If the WordPerfect 5.x keyboard doesn't appear in the Keyboard list in step 3, all is not yet lost. You may be able to add it to the list. To try to add the WordPerfect 5.x keyboard to the list, follow these steps:

1. Open the **File** menu and choose the **Librarian** command.

   The Librarian dialog box appears.

2. Open the Resource pop-up menu and choose Keyboards.

   If you're lucky, three keyboards (one of which is the WordPerfect 5.x keyboard) will appear in the scrolling list on the left side of the dialog box (see Figure 3.4).

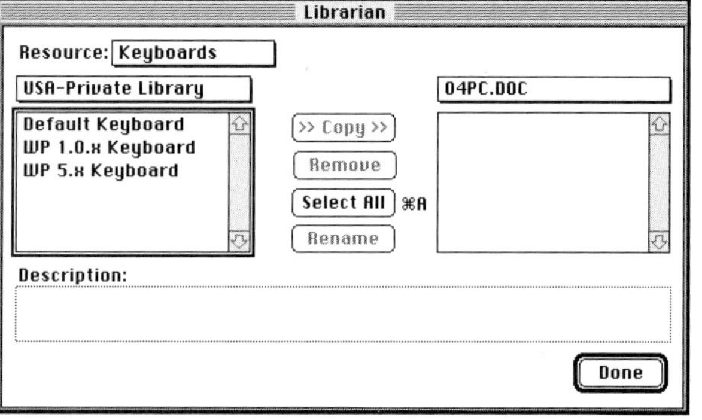

Figure 3.4. The Librarian dialog box.

3. Select the WordPerfect 5.x keyboard.

4. Click on the Copy button.

The WordPerfect 5.x keyboard appears in the scrolling list on the right side of the dialog box.

5. Click on the Done button.

Now, retry the steps for activating the WordPerfect 5.x keyboard.

Getting Help in WordPerfect for the Mac

You can use Balloon Help to get help about elements you point to onscreen. To turn on Balloon Help, open the Balloon Help menu and choose the Show Balloons command. Then, use the mouse pointer to point to the onscreen element you want to identify. Although Balloon Help briefly describes the effects of a menu command if you open the menu and highlight the command, Balloon Help doesn't provide detailed help, nor does it help you find a specific command you're looking for.

WordPerfect for the Mac also includes an excellent online Help facility which you can use to provide more help for commands. While WordPerfect for the Mac does include a template (like WordPerfect for DOS and WordPerfect for Windows), you probably have already noticed that the commands on the template don't bear much resemblance to the commands you use in WordPerfect for DOS or WordPerfect for Windows. If you haven't managed to activate the WordPerfect 5.x keyboard, you will want to use the Help window to quickly and easily familiarize yourself with the WordPerfect for the Mac basics.

You can open the Help window in three ways:

- You can open the Apple menu and choose the Help command.

- You can open the Balloon Help menu and choose the WordPerfect Help command.

- If you are working on an Apple Extended Keyboard II, you can press the Help key (next to the Home key).

After you open the Help window (see Figure 3.5), you see an alphabetical listing of WordPerfect commands on the left side. The left side of the window always displays a list of available Help topics.

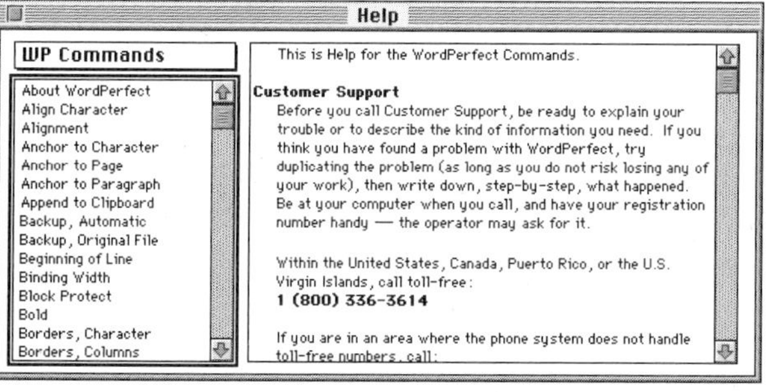

Figure 3.5.
The WordPerfect for the Mac Help window.

On the right side of the window, you see an explanation of the currently selected command. Just above the list of Help topics, you see a pop-up menu that contains a list of the other WordPerfect elements for which you can see Help topics: Draw Commands, Draw Macro Commands, Macro Commands, Variables, WP Commands, and WP Macro Commands. If you switch from WP Commands to one of the other options, the list of Help topics on the left side of the window changes, and the help displayed in the right side of the window changes accordingly.

While the Help window is open, you can view information about a topic in three ways:

- You can scroll through the list by using the scroll bar.

- You can open a menu and choose a command; WordPerfect for the Mac moves to the command in the Help topics list and displays help for the command in the right side of the window.

- You can type a few letters of the command for which you are searching; WordPerfect for the Mac moves to the word in the Help topics list that most closely matches the letters you typed.

If you use the last method, be aware that the speed with which you type the letters determines the topic about which you will see help. If you type letters fairly quickly in sequence, WordPerfect for the Mac treats the letters as part of the same word. If you type more slowly, WordPerfect for the Mac doesn't treat the letters as part of the same word, but as separate requests for separate Help topics. For example, if you want information about copying, and you type **co** fairly quickly, WordPerfect for the Mac moves to the Color, Background Help topic, which is the first topic that begins with the letters **co**. If, however, you type the letters **co** slowly, WordPerfect for the Mac moves first to the Cancel Help topic, which is the first Help topic that begins with the letter **c**. Then, WordPerfect for the Mac moves to the Open topic, which is the first Help topic that begins with the letter **o**.

You can get help about any key on the keyboard by pressing that key while the Help window is open. If you press the up- or down-arrow key, however, WordPerfect for the Mac does not provide help about that key; instead, the pointer moves to the topic above or below the current topic, and the help in the right side of the window changes to correspond to the new topic. If you press the left- or right-arrow key, though, WordPerfect for the Mac displays help about the arrow keys in general. If you press the Tab key, you see help about the Tab key. If you press Shift+Tab, you see help about the Margin Release key.

Opening a WordPerfect for the Mac File

Suppose that someone brings you a letter, asks you to make some minor changes to it, and then wants you to print the revised letter. In this section, you learn how to open an existing WordPerfect for the Mac file, also called a **document**. In the next three sections, you learn how to edit, save, and print a WordPerfect for the Mac document.

You can open as many documents at one time as the memory available to WordPerfect for the Mac permits. The document that contains the insertion point is called the **active document**, and is displayed in the **active window**.

When you start WordPerfect for the Mac, an empty document, Doc 1: Untitled, appears. If you need to type a new document, use the first window that appears when you start WordPerfect for the Mac, or start in a clean window by choosing the New command from the File menu (or by pressing ⌘+N). To switch between windows, open the Edit menu and choose the window you want to make active from the choices listed below the Cycle Windows command.

Opening a Document into a New Document Window

To open an existing document into its own document window, follow these steps:

1. Open the **File** menu and choose the **Open** command (or press ⌘+**O**).

   WordPerfect for the Mac displays the Open dialog box (see Figure 3.6).

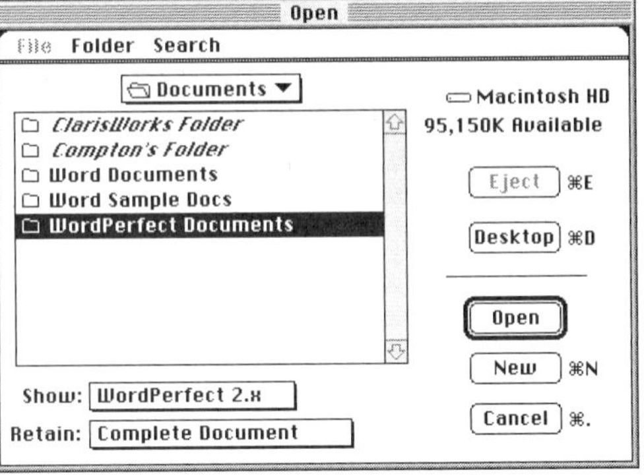

Figure 3.6.

The Open dialog box.

2. Navigate to the folder that contains the file you want to open. To open a folder, click on the folder name (to select it) in the scrolling list and then click on the Open button (or double-click on the folder name).

   If you need to back out of a folder, you can click on the Desktop button to list everything on the Desktop, then click on the icon of the hard disk to list the contents of the hard disk window. Or, if you opened a nested folder (a folder inside a folder), you can open the pop-up menu above the scrolling list and choose the parent folder.

3. When the file you want to open appears in the scrolling list, click on its name to select the file and then click on the Open button (or double-click on the file name).

   The document appears onscreen and you can edit it.

Combining Two Documents in One Document Window

You also can combine two documents by opening the first document and then inserting the second document instead of opening it. (This command is comparable to the **R**etrieve command in

WordPerfect for Windows.) When you insert one document into another, WordPerfect for the Mac doesn't open a new window before opening the document you choose. Therefore, when you insert, you effectively "merge" two documents together.

If you launch WordPerfect directly (rather than double-clicking on a WordPerfect document), the first document window you see after starting the program is empty. If you open an existing document, the empty window remains open and empty because the document you opened appears in a second document window. If, however, you insert a document while viewing the first empty document window, WordPerfect for the Mac places the document into the empty window *instead* of opening a second window.

To combine two documents in one document window, follow these steps:

1. Position the insertion point at the place where you want the second document to appear. If you are inserting a document into the empty window that appears when you start WordPerfect for the Mac, you do not need to move the insertion point.

2. Open the **File** menu and choose the **Insert** command.

   WordPerfect for the Mac displays the Insert dialog box, which looks and operates exactly like the Open dialog box shown in Figure 3.6.

3. Navigate to the folder that contains the file you want to open. To open a folder, click on the folder name (to select it) in the scrolling list and then click on the Open button (or double-click on the folder name).

   If you need to back out of a folder, you can click on the Desktop button to list everything on the Desktop and then click on the icon of the hard disk to list the contents of the hard disk window. Or, if you opened a nested folder (a folder

inside a folder), you can open the pop-up menu above the scrolling list and choose the parent folder.

4. When the file you want to insert appears in the scrolling list, click on its name to select the file and then click on the Insert button (or double-click on the file name).

   The document appears onscreen and you can edit it.

Performing Basic Editing in WordPerfect for the Mac

By default, when you type in WordPerfect for the Mac, you are working in insert mode. In **insert mode**, WordPerfect for the Mac places characters at the current location of the insertion point and moves all existing characters to the right. Unlike WordPerfect for DOS or WordPerfect for Windows, you cannot work in typeover mode in WordPerfect for the Mac. (In typeover mode, characters are placed at the current location of the insertion point and, if you type at that location, characters that exist at that location are replaced with those you type.)

You can use the Delete key to delete the character immediately to the left of the insertion point. You can use the Del key to delete the character immediately to the right of the insertion point.

Moving around a Document

You move around a WordPerfect for the Mac document by using the mouse and the scroll bars, or pressing the directional keys (the arrow keys, Home, End, Page Up, and Page Down). The results you

get when you press these keys, however, depends on whether the default WordPerfect for the Mac keyboard or the WordPerfect 5.x keyboard is active.

Table 3.1 summarizes the most common ways in which you can use the WordPerfect for the Mac keyboard to move the insertion point in an existing WordPerfect for the Mac document.

Table 3.1. WordPerfect for the Mac insertion point-movement keys (in an existing document).

Key(s)	Effect
← or →	Moves right or left one character.
↓ or ↑	Moves down or up one line.
Option+→	Moves right one word.
Option+←	Moves left one word.
Page Down (or Option+↓)	Moves down one page.
Page Up (or Option+↑)	Moves up one page.
⌘+←	Moves to the beginning of the current line.
⌘+→	Moves to the end of the current line.
Home	Moves to the beginning of the document.
End	Moves to the end of the document.
⌘+↓	Moves to the top of the next window.
⌘+↑	Moves to the top of the preceding window.

Table 3.2 summarizes the most common ways in which you can use the WordPerfect 5.x keyboard to move the insertion point in an existing WordPerfect for the Mac document.

Table 3.2. WordPerfect 5.x insertion point-movement keys (in an existing document).

Key(s)	Effect
→ or ←	Moves right or left one character.
↓ or ↑	Moves down or up one line.
Option+→	Moves right one word.
Option+←	Moves left one word.
End	Moves to the end of the document.
Home+→	Moves to the end of the current line.
Home+←	Moves to the beginning of the current line.
Home+↓	Moves to the bottom of the current or next window.
Home+↑	Moves to the top of the current window.
Home, Home+↓	Moves to the end of the document.
Home, Home+↑	Moves to the beginning of the document.
Page Down	Moves the insertion point to the top of the next page.
Page Up	Moves the insertion point to the top of the preceding page.

Selecting Text

You may want to make changes to the appearance of text. For example, you may want certain text to appear underlined, in

italics, or in boldface type. You may want to change the alignment of certain text. You may want to delete certain text.

In WordPerfect for the Mac, you select text whenever you want to "operate" on it—that is, when you want to format, align, edit, or even print text. **Selecting** is the process of highlighting the text so that WordPerfect for the Mac can identify the text you want to change. If you are a WordPerfect for DOS user, you call this operation **blocking**.

To use the mouse to select text, you drag the mouse pointer. Follow these steps:

1. Place the mouse pointer in front of the text you want to select. Click and hold down the mouse button.

2. Slide the mouse to the right.

   As you slide the mouse, a colored bar appears over the text you are selecting.

3. Continue sliding the mouse until you reach the end of the text you want to select.

4. Release the mouse button.

   The text you want to select is **highlighted**—a colored bar appears over it.

You can select a word by double-clicking on it. You can select a sentence by placing the insertion point in the sentence and pressing F6. You can select a paragraph by triple-clicking anywhere in the paragraph. You can select a page by placing the insertion point on that page and pressing Option+F6. You can cancel a selection by clicking the mouse anywhere else onscreen.

Another selection technique is to place the insertion point at the beginning of the text you want to select. Move to the end of the text

you want to select (even if it's pages away), hold down the Shift key, and click again (as if you were moving the insertion point to the new location). All the text between the original insertion point and the place you "Shift-clicked" is selected.

You also can add the Shift key to any of the keyboard shortcuts listed in Tables 3.1 and 3.2 to select the corresponding text. For example, pressing Shift+→ selects one character to the right of the insertion point.

When text is selected, the actions you perform affect that text. For example, if you press the Delete key while text is selected, all the selected text is deleted. If you type any characters while text is selected, those characters replace all the selected text. This is handy if you want to delete or replace large sections of text.

Using the Function Keys To Execute Commands

You may see a template similar to the one shown in Figure 3.7 on the keyboard next to the function keys. If your template came with the software or was purchased, you see words printed in red, green, blue, or black ink next to each function key.

WordPerfect® for the Macintosh®

	F1	F2	F3	F4	F5	F6	F7	F8	F9	F10	F11	F12	F13	F14	F15
Opt	Show ¶	Show Codes	Document Info	Char Map	Center Line	Select Page	Page Border	Page Format	Center Page	Edit Style	Generate	Tab Align	Go to	Uppercase	Lowercase
Shift	Move Together	Move Apart	Smart Quotes	Paste Special	Flush Right	Select Column	Column Border	Line Format	Edit Macro	Update Style	Index	Start Merge	View at 200%	Small Caps	Double Underline
⌘	New Graphic	New Text Box	Copy Ruler	Paste Text	♦Indent♦	Select ¶	¶ Border	¶ Format	Record Macro	New Style	ToC Level 2	End Of Record	View Full Page	Superscript	Subscript
	Undo	Cut	Copy	Paste	♦Indent	Select Sentence	Char Border	Char Format	Run Macro	Apply Style	ToC Level 1	End of Field	View at 100%	Redline	Strikeout

Figure 3.7. A sample template for WordPerfect for the Mac.

The words represent commands listed on the menus in WordPerfect for the Mac. Somewhere on the template, you see instructions that tell you to use the Command, Shift, and Option keys in combination with the function keys. Table 3.3 summarizes the way you use the function keys in WordPerfect for the Mac.

Table 3.3. Function keys and WordPerfect commands.

Color	Keystrokes
Red	Hold down the ⌘ key and press the appropriate function key.
Blue	Hold down the Option key and press the appropriate function key.
Green	Hold down the Shift key and press the appropriate function key.
Black	Press the appropriate function key.

Okay, so what happens if your template isn't color-coded, or you don't have a template? Unlike WordPerfect on the PC, which has incorporated an onscreen representation of the template for either keyboard within its online Help facility, you are dependent on this book or on the WordPerfect for the Mac reference manual, which contains a graphic representation of the keyboard (in the Keyboard Layout section).

Saving a WordPerfect for the Mac File

After you have made the changes you need to make, you will want to save the document. Like WordPerfect for Windows, WordPerfect for the Mac provides three ways to save a document, and each of these ways is described in detail in this chapter. One of these methods, the Save As command, lets you save a document using a different name. Because you may not want to overwrite the work that existed before you edited, you may want to read the detail sections on these three methods before you use any of them.

- You can use the Close command to save the document under its current name and into its current folder, and then "put away" the document (remove it from the screen).

- You can use the Save command to save the document under its current name and into its current folder, and then continue working on the document.

- You can use the Save As command to save the document under a different name or to a different folder or disk. You may want to save the document under a different name or to a different folder to avoid changing the original.

When you exit from WordPerfect for the Mac, the program also prompts you to save any documents that contain changes before you exit—but more about that later in this chapter.

Using the Close Command

You can use the Close command when you finish working with a document and you want WordPerfect for the Mac to save the document under its current name and into its current folder and put it away.

To close a document, open the File menu and choose the Close command (or press ⌘+W). If you have not made any changes to the document since the last time you saved it, WordPerfect for the Mac simply removes the document from the screen. If, however, you have made changes, WordPerfect for the Mac displays the dialog box shown in Figure 3.8.

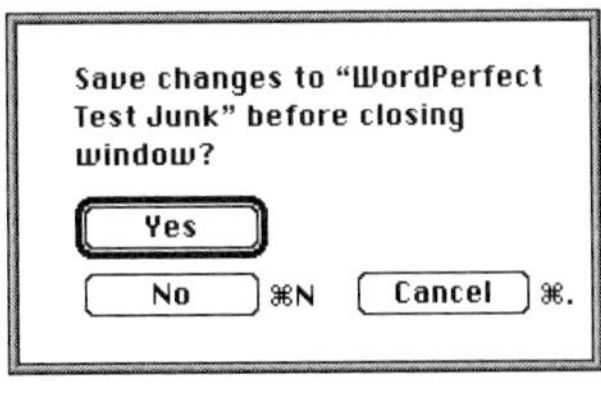

Figure 3.8.

The **Save changes to?** dialog box.

If you click on the Yes button, WordPerfect for the Mac saves the changes you have made and removes the document from the screen. If you click on the No button, WordPerfect for the Mac *does*

not save the changes you made since the last time you saved, but WordPerfect for the Mac *does* remove the document from the screen. (This discards all the changes you have made!) If you click on the Cancel button, WordPerfect for the Mac *does not* save the changes you made since the last time you saved and *does not* remove the document from the screen.

Using the Save Command

You can use the Save command to save the active document under its current name and into its current folder, and then continue working on the document. When you use the Save command, WordPerfect for the Mac saves the changes you have made to a disk (either hard or floppy) and leaves the document onscreen.

To save a document by using the Save command, open the File menu and choose the Save command (or press ⌘+S). WordPerfect for the Mac saves the document. (If you pay close attention to the status line at the bottom of the screen, you can see a message that indicates WordPerfect for the Mac is saving the document.)

If you choose the Save command the first time you save a new document, WordPerfect for the Mac executes the Save As command because it needs more information.

Using the Save As Command

You may want to leave the original document available in cases where your changes may not be final. If you are unsure of the changes you have made, for example, and somebody else is going to come back and check your work, you might want to keep the original document. You then can show that person your version, and let him or her decide which version to continue using.

To save your version of an existing document and leave the original version intact, follow these steps:

1. Open the **File** menu and choose the **Save As** command.

   WordPerfect for the Mac displays the Save As dialog box in Figure 3.9.

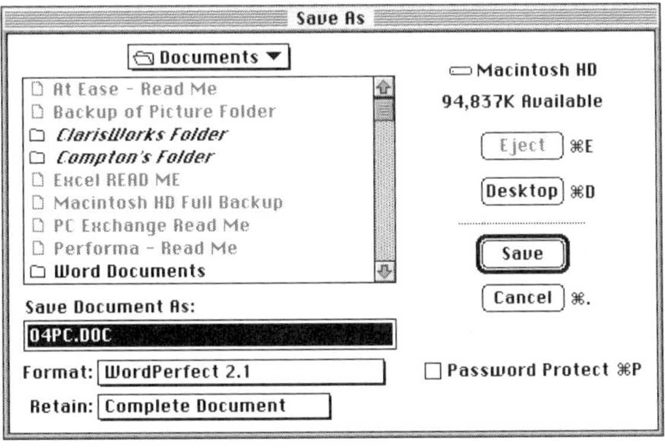

Figure 3.9. The Save As dialog box.

2. Open the folder into which you want to save the document. (You can save the document with a new name into the same folder as the original document.)

3. Type the new name for the document in the Save Document As text box. You can use up to 32 characters for the name you want to assign to the document.

   If you choose a name that appears in the Files scrolling list, WordPerfect for the Mac asks whether you want to replace that document. (If you do, you will effectively erase the other file with that name!) Because you probably don't want to replace the original version, click on the No button and then type another name—preferably one that doesn't appear in the Files scrolling list.

4. If you want, you can use the Format pop-up menu to choose a format other than WordPerfect in which to save the document. For example, you could choose to save the document as a WordPerfect 5.1 document, for export to WordPerfect for DOS or WordPerfect for Windows.

5. Click on the Save button.

   WordPerfect for the Mac saves the document under the name you specify, leaving the original version (under the original name) intact. The new document remains in a window onscreen; any additional changes you make and save are changes to the new document. The old document is "put away"; it no longer appears onscreen.

Printing a WordPerfect for the Mac File

After you edit and save a document, you may need to print it. Before you print the document, you might want to preview the document onscreen to ensure that it will print the way you expect. To preview a document in WordPerfect for the Mac and then print it, open the File menu and choose Print Preview. WordPerfect for the Mac displays onscreen the layout of your document as it will appear when you print it (see Figure 3.10). The image you see is 52% of its normal size.

Although you cannot edit on this screen, you can see the layout of the document as it will print. If text and graphics are not aligned properly on this screen, they won't be aligned properly when you print. You can use the Print Preview Button Bar along the side of the window, or the menus at the top of the window, to look at facing pages (as in a book), to look at the next or previous page, to

adjust the size of the view, or to print the document. If you click on the document, the image zooms to 100%. You can close the Preview window by using the Close box (on the window title bar). If you close the Preview window, WordPerfect for the Mac returns you to the editing window. If you choose to print the document from the Preview window (by clicking on the button that looks like a printer), WordPerfect for the Mac displays the Print dialog box (see Figure 3.11).

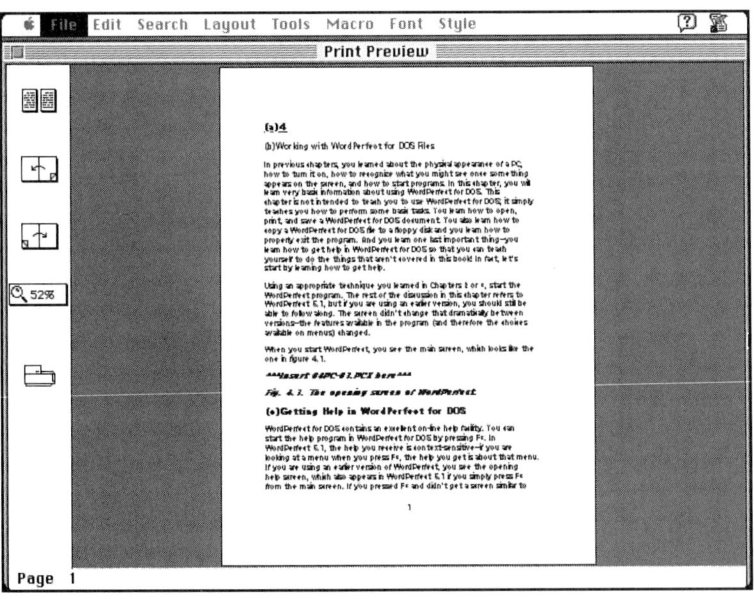

Figure 3.10.

A sample Print Preview screen.

MAC NOTE

If you want to print the document without previewing it, you can display the Print dialog box directly. Open the File menu and choose the Print command (or press ⌘+P).

The actual dialog box that appears depends on the printer connected to the Mac. But, regardless of the printer, you should be able to type the number of copies you want to print in the Copies text box. And you should be able to choose whether to print all the

pages in the document or only selected pages. If you choose to print only selected pages, specify the page numbers in the From and To text boxes. If you are working on a dot-matrix or inkjet printer, you can specify the Quality of the print; the meaning of the choices Best, Normal, and Draft changes from printer to printer, so you may have to experiment. For "final" copies, try Normal first.

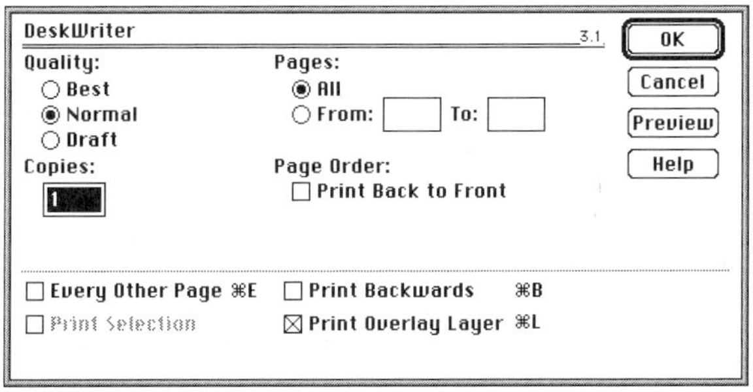

Figure 3.11. The Print dialog box.

You may need to check the Page Setup to set the paper type and orientation before you actually print. To check the Page Setup, open the File menu and choose the Page Setup command. A Page Setup dialog box, similar to the one in Figure 3.12, appears. This dialog box enables you to choose a paper type, a page orientation, and printing size (among other options).

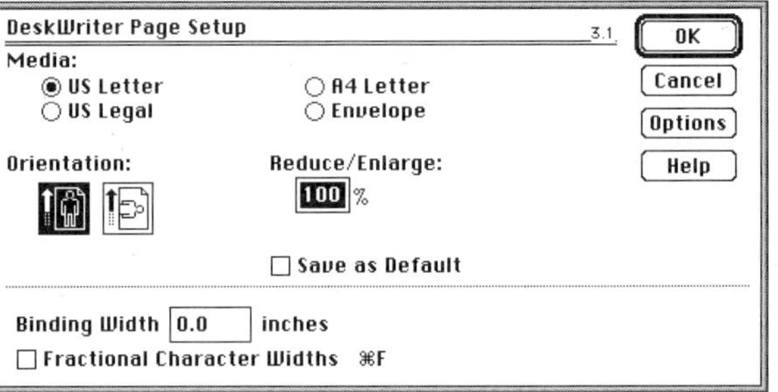

Figure 3.12. The Page Setup dialog box.

If you see any check boxes already selected when you open the Print dialog box or the Page Setup dialog box, and you don't really know what they represent, you probably should leave them selected. WordPerfect for the Mac may determine that certain options are required when it identifies the printer connected to the Mac.

Copying a WordPerfect for the Mac File to a Floppy Disk

You may find that you need to copy a WordPerfect for the Mac file to a floppy disk (perhaps to take the file to another Mac to print it). You can do this by using commands inside WordPerfect, or, if you prefer, you can work from the Desktop using Finder commands (see Chapter 8 for more information on using the Finder). If you are working in WordPerfect for the Mac Version 2.0 or earlier, you use the File Manager dialog box. In WordPerfect for the Mac Version 2.1, the options that appeared in the File Manager dialog box were combined into the Open dialog box, so you use the Open dialog box.

The File Manager commands enable you to perform a variety of functions. You may want to explore some of these functions on your own. To use the File Manager commands to copy a file to a floppy disk, follow these steps:

1. Insert an initialized disk into the floppy disk drive. If you plan to move this file to a PC, see Chapter 9 for more information on transferring files between computers before you proceed.

2. Open the **File** menu and choose the **File Manager** command (or the **Open** command, if you're using WordPerfect for the Mac Version 2.1).

   WordPerfect for the Mac displays the File Manager dialog box or the Open dialog box, both of which are similar to the dialog box in Figure 3.13. The only difference between the two dialog boxes is the name that appears in the title bar.

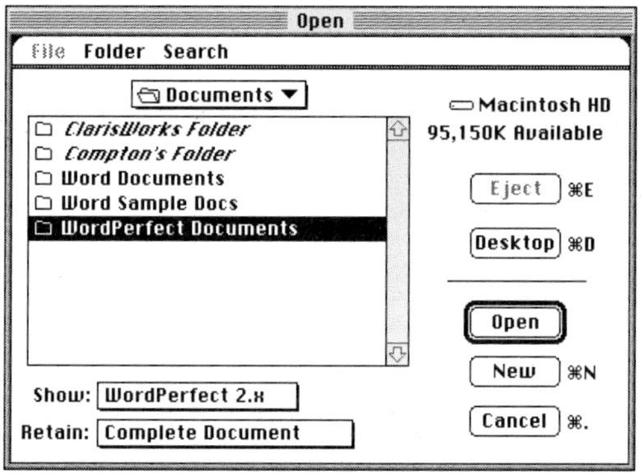

Figure 3.13.

The Open dialog box.

3. Navigate to the folder that contains the file you want to copy to a floppy disk.

   If you need to back out of a folder, you can click on the Desktop button to list everything on the Desktop and then click on the icon of the hard disk to list the contents of the hard disk window. Or, if you opened a nested folder (a folder inside a folder), you can open the pop-up menu above the scrolling list and choose the parent folder.

4. Click on the name of the file you want to copy to a floppy disk.

5. At the top of the dialog box (*not* at the top of the screen), you see a menu bar. Open the **File** menu and choose the **Copy** command.

   WordPerfect for the Mac displays the Copy dialog box shown in Figure 3.14.

6. Click on the Desktop button.

   WordPerfect for the Mac displays the items available on the Desktop in the scrolling list.

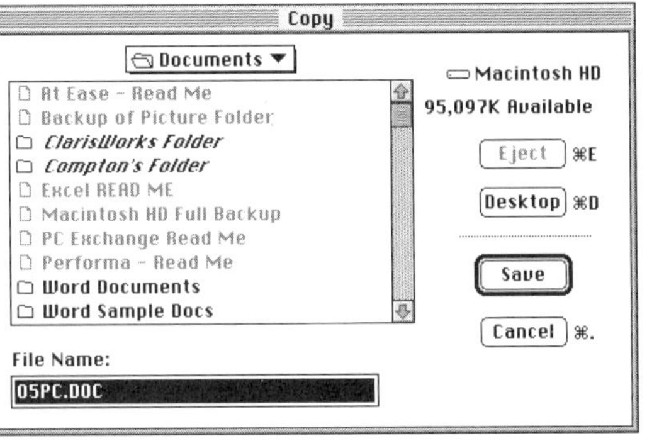

Figure 3.14. The Copy dialog box.

7. Click on the floppy disk icon to select it. In Figure 3.15, the floppy disk is named “untitled.”

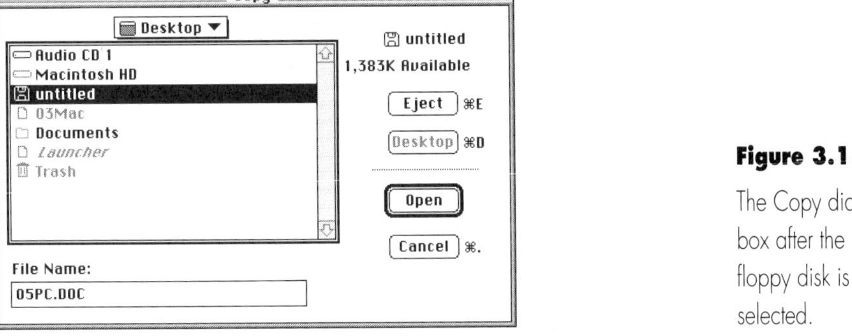

Figure 3.15. The Copy dialog box after the floppy disk is selected.

8. Click on the Open button.

9. If you want, type a new name for the document in the File Name text box. The new name will be assigned to the document on the floppy disk. The original file on the hard disk will retain its original name.

10. Click on the Save button.

WordPerfect for the Mac copies the file to the floppy disk.

If a file with the name you typed is already on the floppy disk, WordPerfect for the Mac prompts you to replace the file on the floppy disk or cancel the operation. If you replace the version on the floppy disk, you write over it and it is gone forever, so if you have *any* doubts, cancel the operation.

11. To close the Copy dialog box, click on the Cancel button.

Exiting WordPerfect for the Mac

When you are finished using WordPerfect for the Mac, you can exit by choosing the Quit command from the File menu (or by pressing ⌘+Q). If any of your open documents contain changes you didn't save, WordPerfect for the Mac displays a dialog box asking whether you want to save the changes before you exit. Choose Yes to save the changes and exit. Choose No to ignore the changes and exit. Choose Cancel to return to editing in WordPerfect for the Mac.

When you exit from WordPerfect for the Mac, you return to the Desktop. You can safely shut down the Mac from the Desktop by choosing the Shut Down command from the Special menu. If necessary, remember to turn off the monitor.

Chapter Summary

In this chapter, you learned how to use the online Help facility in WordPerfect for the Mac. You also learned how to open, edit, save, and print a WordPerfect for the Mac document. You learned how to copy a document to a floppy disk, and you learned how to exit from WordPerfect for the Mac.

As you noticed throughout this chapter, there is, unfortunately, very little resemblance between WordPerfect for the Mac and WordPerfect for DOS, unless you managed to find the WordPerfect 5.x keyboard in WordPerfect for the Mac. Some terms changed, but others are the same:

- In WordPerfect for DOS you *retrieve* a document; in WordPerfect for the Mac, you *open* or *insert* a document.
- In WordPerfect for DOS you *block* text on which you want to operate; in WordPerfect for the Mac, you *select* the text.
- In both packages, you *save, print,* and *copy* documents.
- You *exit* from WordPerfect for DOS, while you *quit* from WordPerfect for the Mac.

The standard keyboard in WordPerfect for Windows does not resemble the standard keyboard in WordPerfect for the Mac, but the terminology is the same. In both packages, you open, save, print, and copy documents and you select text. In both packages, you can use function keys or menus to execute commands.

In the next chapter, you learn how to work with Microsoft Word for the Mac files. As you know, Chapters 3 through 6 in *The PC User's Mac* focus on specific software packages. You should read the chapters about the software you want to use. Chapter 7 tells you about database programs you may want to avoid. Chapter 8 provides information for working at the System level on a Mac. If you need to transfer and translate files between a Mac and a PC, read Chapter 9.

Working with Word for the Mac Files

In the first two chapters of *The PC User's Mac*, you learned about the physical appearance of a Mac, how to turn it on a Mac, how to recognize what you may see onscreen, and how to start programs. In Chapter 2, for example, you learned how to open menus, choose commands, work with dialog boxes, and start programs. You will need these skills to proceed through this chapter.

In this chapter, you will learn very basic information about using Microsoft Word for the Mac. This chapter is not intended to make you a Word for the Mac expert; this chapter simply teaches you how to perform some basic tasks. You will learn how to open, edit, save, and print a Word for the Mac document; how to copy a Word for the Mac file to a floppy disk; and how to exit the program properly. And you will learn one other important thing—how to get help in Word for the Mac so that you can teach yourself to do the things that aren't covered in this book!

MAC NOTE

This book covers Word for the Mac Version 5.1. Version 5.0 is very similar to Version 5.1, except that Word 5.0 does not have the extensive Toolbars that version 5.1 has. The operation of the two versions is very similar unless otherwise noted.

Identifying Word for the Mac Screen Parts

Using one of the techniques described in Chapter 2, start Word for the Mac. The default screen appears as shown in Figure 4.1. This

screen is very similar to the screen you see when you start Word for Windows.

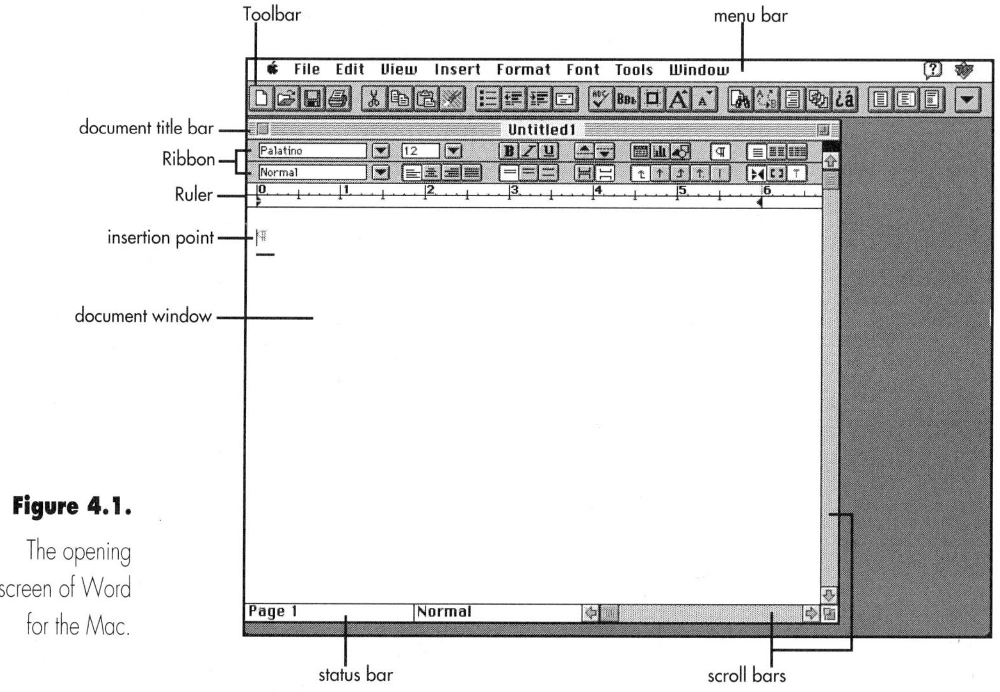

Figure 4.1.

The opening screen of Word for the Mac.

At the top of the screen, you see the **menu bar** for Word for the Mac that also contains the Apple menu, the Help menu, and the Applications menu.

Just below the menu bar (in Version 5.1 only), you may see the default Toolbar. (The opening screen of Word for the Mac can be customized by using commands on the View menu; as a result, the Toolbar may not be visible.) Like Word for Windows, Word for the Mac uses the Toolbar to assign common commands to buttons. You use the mouse to click buttons on the Toolbar. Figure 4.2 displays the Toolbar; its functions are described in the list that follows the figure. Because the Toolbar can be customized, you may not see the same icons on your screen as the ones shown in Figure 4.2.

Figure 4.2.

The Toolbar.

There are six groups of buttons on the Toolbar. The following list describes the commands executed by the buttons, starting from the left end of the Toolbar. Many of these commands are described in greater detail later in the chapter.

- The first group of buttons represents commands that manipulate files. Respectively, these buttons execute the New, Open, Save, and Print commands.
- The second group of buttons controls editing functions. Respectively, these buttons execute the Cut, Copy, Paste, and Undo commands.
- The third group of buttons controls certain formatting options. Respectively, these buttons enable you to format bulleted text, shift a paragraph to the left, shift a paragraph to the right, and set up an envelope.
- The fourth group of buttons controls several functions. The first button brings up the spelling checker. The other buttons control more formatting options, including text case, paragraph borders, increased font size, and decreased font size.
- The fifth group of buttons represent, respectively, the Find File command, the Replace command, the Insert Page Break command, the Repaginate command, and the Insert Symbol command.
- The sixth group of buttons switch between different views of the document. The first button represents the Normal view; the second button represents the Page Layout view, and the third button represents the Print Preview view.
- The lone button at the right end of the Toolbar enables the user to customize the Toolbar.

Below the Toolbar, you see the **title bar** for the current document window. When you start Word for the Mac, you always see an empty document window in which you can create a new document. The name of the first empty document (which appears in the title bar) is always Untitled1, and each new document you open is named incrementally—Untitled2, Untitled3, Untitled4, and so on. You can open as many documents as permitted by the memory available to Word for the Mac.

Just below the document window title bar, you might see the Ribbon and the Ruler, with which you must use a mouse, as you do in Word for Windows. (Like the Toolbar, the Ruler and Ribbon can be hidden by using commands on the View menu, so they may not be visible.) The commands available on the Ribbon and the Ruler also can be accessed by using menu commands.

The Ribbon appears as two rows in Word for the Mac, and you can use the Ribbon to perform a variety of functions. Figure 4.3 displays the Ribbon; the buttons on the Ribbon are described below.

Figure 4.3.
The Ribbon.

The first row of the Ribbon generally controls the formatting of text:

- The first two boxes are drop-down menus that change the font and font size, respectively.
- The second group of buttons applies Bold, Italic, and Underlined text formatting.
- The third group, which has two buttons, enables the user to set superscript and subscript formatting.
- The fourth group enables the user to create, respectively, tables, graphs, and drawings to insert into the document.

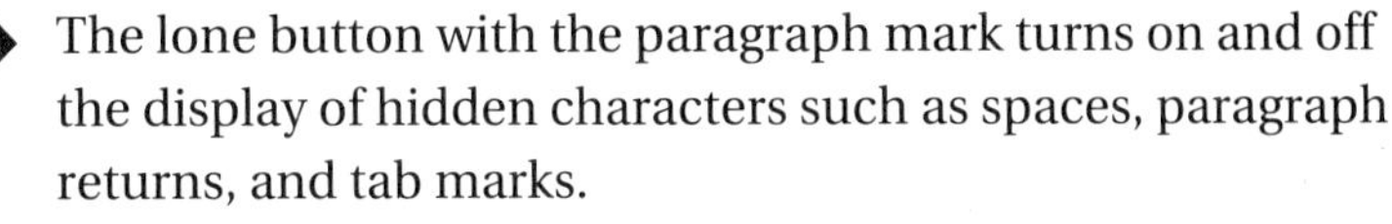

- The lone button with the paragraph mark turns on and off the display of hidden characters such as spaces, paragraph returns, and tab marks.
- The final group of buttons sets the text into one, two, or three columns, respectively.

The second row in the Ribbon contains buttons that generally control where the text appears on the page:

- The first box is a drop-down menu that enables you to change the style applied to the currently selected paragraphs.
- The second group of buttons controls the alignment of the currently selected paragraphs: left-aligned, centered, right-aligned, and justified.
- The third group of buttons controls the space between the lines of text: single-spaced, 1 1/2-spaced, and double-spaced.
- The fourth group of buttons controls the space between paragraphs: normal line spacing or an extra line space.
- The fifth group of buttons sets different types of tab stops in the Ruler: left-aligned tab, centered tab, right-aligned tab, and decimal tab; the final button in the group inserts a vertical line in the paragraph.
- The last group of buttons controls the current Ruler view: the Tab ruler, the Margin ruler, and the Table ruler.

You use the Ruler (see Figure 4.4) to set, move, and remove tab stops; to move the left and right margins; and to set column widths.

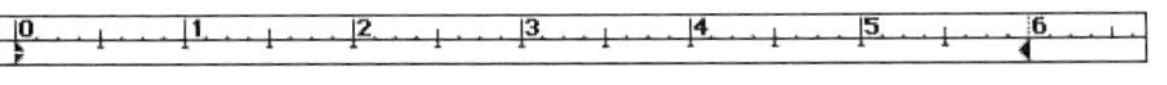

Figure 4.4.

The Ruler.

At the bottom of the screen, you see the status bar. The status bar is divided into two parts and tells you the current location of the insertion point, a flashing black vertical bar. The **insertion point** is where text will appear when you type. In the status bar, you also see the current page number, and the style of the current paragraph.

Just next to the status bar, and also along the right edge of the document window, you see the horizontal and vertical scroll bars. Each scroll bar has a scroll box on the bar and scroll arrows at both ends of the bar. The horizontal scroll bar enables you to scan the width of the page in your document, if the window isn't wide enough to display the entire document width. The vertical scroll bar enables you to move from top to bottom through each page, and from page to page through the length of the document.

Getting Help in Word for the Mac

In Word for the Mac, you can get context-sensitive help about areas of the screen by pressing the Help key, or by activating Balloon Help. When you press the Help key, the mouse pointer changes shape into a question mark. Move the mouse pointer to the area of the screen for which you want help, and click. Word for the Mac displays help for the area on which you clicked.

You also can use Balloon Help to get help about onscreen elements. To turn on Balloon Help, open the Balloon Help menu and choose the Show Balloons command. Then, point to the onscreen element for which you want help. A brief description of the element appears.

Word for the Mac also provides an excellent online Help facility. You can open the Help window in Word for the Mac by choosing the Help command from the Window menu, or by choosing the Microsoft Word Help command from the Balloon Help menu (see Figure 4.5).

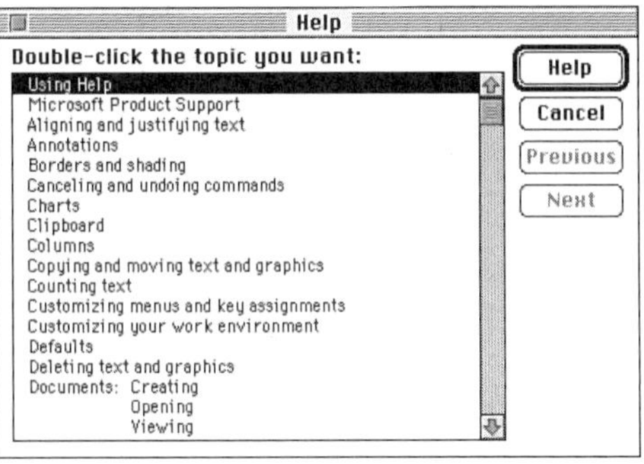

Figure 4.5.

The Help Index.

When you open the Help window, you see an alphabetical list of Word Help topics. You can move through the list by using the scroll bar or the arrow keys. Or, you can type the first letter of the topic for which you are searching; Word for the Mac moves to the first word in the Help topics list that begins with the letter you typed.

You can view information about a topic by double-clicking on the topic or by highlighting the topic and clicking the Help button. Word then displays an explanation of the currently selected topic.

When you select a topic to view, Word for the Mac displays the help information in the Help window, and the command buttons change (see Figure 4.6).

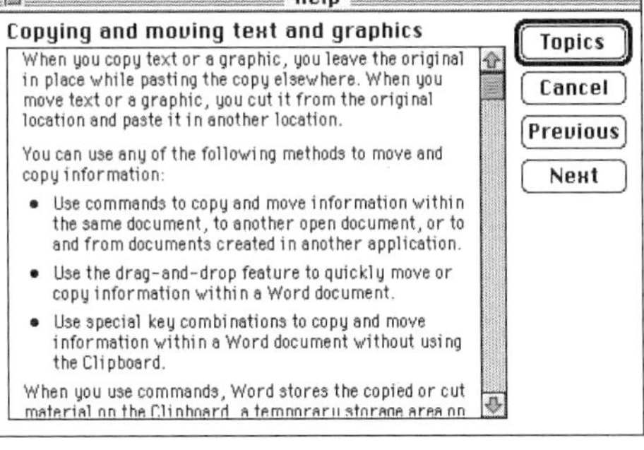

Figure 4.6.

The Help window when a topic appears.

You can return to the Help Index by clicking on the Topics button. You can close Help by clicking on the Cancel button, or by clicking on the Close box in the Help window title bar. You can view the next topic in the list by clicking on the Next button, and you can view the previous topic in the list by clicking on the Previous button.

Opening a Word for the Mac File

Suppose that someone brings you a letter, asks you to make some minor changes to it, and then wants you to print the revised letter. In this section, you learn how to open an existing Word for the Mac file, also called a **document**. In the next three sections, you learn how to edit, save, and print a Word for the Mac document.

You can open as many documents at one time as the memory available to Word for the Mac permits. The document that contains the insertion point is called the **active document**, and is displayed in the **active window**.

When you start Word for the Mac, an empty document called Untitled1 appears. You can start typing a new document in Untitled1. If you open an existing document without typing in Untitled1, the existing document replaces Untitled1. If you need to type a new document, use Untitled1, or start in an empty document by choosing the New command from the File menu (or by pressing ⌘+N). You also can click on the New button on the Toolbar (the first button on the left).

To open an existing document, follow these steps:

1. Open the **File** menu and choose the **Open** command. You also can press ⌘+**O**, or you can click on the **Open** button on the Toolbar (the second button from the left).

   Word for the Mac displays the Open dialog box (see Figure 4.7).

2. Navigate to the folder that contains the file you want to open. To open a folder, click on the folder name (to select it) in the scrolling list and then click on the Open button (or double-click on the folder name).

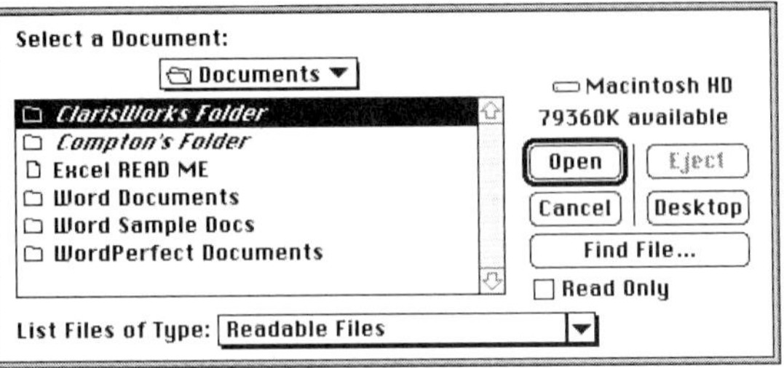

Figure 4.7.

The Open dialog box.

If you need to back out of a folder, you can click on the Desktop button to list everything on the Desktop and then click on the icon of the hard disk to list the contents of the hard disk window. Or, if you opened a nested folder (a folder inside a folder), you can open the pop-up menu above the scrolling list and choose the parent folder.

3. When the name of the file you want to open appears in the scrolling list, click on its name to select the file and then click on the Open button (or double-click on the file name).

   The document appears onscreen and you can edit it.

Performing Basic Editing in Word for the Mac

By default, when you type in Word for the Mac, you are working in insert mode. In **insert mode**, Word for the Mac places characters at the current location of the insertion point and moves all existing characters to the right, just like insert mode in Word for Windows and Word for DOS. Unlike in Word for Windows and Word for DOS, however, you cannot switch to overtype mode.

You can use the Delete key to delete the character immediately to the left of the insertion point. You can use the Del key to delete the

character immediately to the right of the insertion point. You can press ⌘+Option+Delete to delete the word immediately to the left of the insertion point. You can press ⌘+Option+G to delete the word immediately to the right of the insertion point.

Moving around a Document

You move around a Word for the Mac document by using the mouse and the scroll bars or by pressing the directional keys (the arrow keys, Home, End, Page Up, and Page Down).Table 4.1 summarizes the most common ways in which you can use the keyboard to move around a Word for the Mac document. You will notice that most of the keystrokes are quite similar to the ones you use in Word for Windows.

Table 4.1. Word for the Mac insertion point-movement keys (in an existing document).

Key(s)	Effect
→ and ←	Moves right or left one character.
↓ and ↑	Moves down or up one line.
⌘+→	Moves right one word.
⌘+←	Moves left one word.
⌘+↓	Moves down one paragraph.
⌘+↑	Moves up one paragraph.
7 (numeric keypad)	Moves to the beginning of the current line.
1 (numeric keypad)	Moves to the end of the current line.
Home	Moves to the top of the window.
End	Moves to the bottom of the window.
Page Down	Moves to the top of the next window.
Page Up	Moves to the top of the preceding window.
⌘+Home	Moves to the beginning of the document.
⌘+End	Moves to the end of the document.

Selecting Text

You may want to make changes to the appearance of text. For example, you may want certain text to appear underlined, in italics, or in boldface type. You may want to change the alignment of certain text. You may want to delete certain text.

Just as in Word for Windows and Word for DOS, in Word for the Mac, you select text whenever you want to "operate" on it—that is, when you want to format, align, edit, or even print text. **Selecting** is the process of highlighting the text so that Word for the Mac can identify the text you want to change.

You can select text by using the mouse or the keyboard. Both methods work just like they do in Word for Windows and Word for DOS. To use the mouse to select text, you drag the mouse pointer. Follow these steps:

1. Place the mouse pointer in front of the text you want to select. Click and hold down the mouse button.

2. Slide the mouse to the right.

   As you slide the mouse, a colored bar appears over the text you are selecting.

3. Continue sliding the mouse until you reach the end of the text you want to select.

4. Release the mouse button.

   The text you want to select is **highlighted**—a colored bar appears over it.

You also can use shortcuts with the mouse to select a word, a sentence, or a paragraph:

- You can select a word by double-clicking on it.

- You can select a sentence by holding down the ⌘ key as you click anywhere in the sentence.

- You can select a paragraph by triple-clicking anywhere in the paragraph.

- You can select consecutive paragraphs by using a combination of clicking and dragging. Click three times anywhere in the first paragraph, holding down the mouse button on the last click, and then drag to select consecutive paragraphs.

You can cancel a selection by clicking anywhere else onscreen.

Another selection technique is to place the insertion point at the beginning of the text you want to select. Move to the end of the text you want to select (even if it's pages away), hold down the Shift key, and click again (as if you were moving the insertion point to the new location). All text between the original insertion point and the place you "Shift-clicked" is selected.

You also can add the Shift key to any of the keyboard shortcuts listed in Table 4.1 to select the corresponding text. For example, pressing Shift+→ selects one character to the right of the insertion point.

You can cancel a selection by pressing any arrow key (or by clicking the mouse anywhere in the document).

When text is selected, the actions you perform affect that text. For example, if you press the Delete key while text is selected, all the selected text is deleted. If you type any characters while text is selected, those characters replace all the selected text. This is handy if you want to delete or replace large sections of text.

Executing Commands

As in Word for Windows and Word for DOS, to execute a command, you open a menu and choose the command. You also can

use the Toolbar if the command you want to execute appears there. You use the mouse techniques described in Chapter 2 to open menus and choose commands.

Also like Word for Windows and Word for DOS, Word for the Mac uses **keyboard shortcuts** (also known as "hot keys") to execute commands without opening any menus. You may notice key combinations appearing next to certain commands on the menus. These key combinations are the keyboard shortcuts or "hot keys." For example, if you want to open a new, empty window, you can press ⌘+N.

In addition, you can open Word for the Mac menus and choose commands by using the keyboard. The technique you use is similar but not identical to the one you use in Word for Windows and Word for DOS. Follow these steps:

1. Press the period (.) on the numeric keypad to activate the menu bar.

   The menu bar appears highlighted (see Figure 4.8).

Figure 4.8. The menu bar after being activated from the keyboard.

2. Press the left- or the right-arrow key.

   If you press the right-arrow key, the **File** menu opens and remains open (see Figure 4.9). If you press the left-arrow key, the **Window** menu opens and remains open.

3. Press the down-arrow key until the command you want to choose is highlighted.

4. Press **Return** to choose the command.

   Word closes the menu and executes the command.

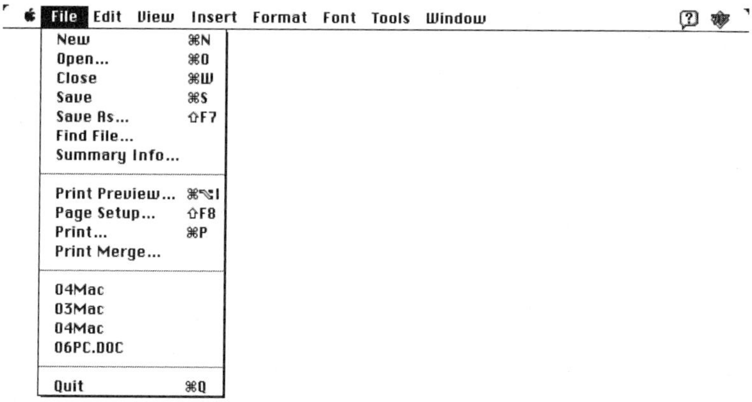

File Edit View Insert Format Font Tools Window

New ⌘N
Open... ⌘O
Close ⌘W
Save ⌘S
Save As... ⇧F7
Find File...
Summary Info...

Print Preview... ⌘⌥I
Page Setup... ⇧F8
Print... ⌘P
Print Merge...

04Mac
03Mac
04Mac
06PC.DOC

Quit ⌘Q

Figure 4.9.

The File menu opens if you press the right-arrow key.

Saving a Word for the Mac File

After you have made the changes you need to make, you will want to save the document. Like Word for Windows and Word for DOS, Word for the Mac provides three ways to save a document, and each of these ways is described in detail in this chapter. One of these methods, the Save As command, lets you save a document using a different name. Because you may not want to overwrite the work that existed before you edited, you may want to read the sections on these three methods before you use any of them.

- You can use the Close command to save the document under its current name and into its current folder, and then "put away" the document (remove it from the screen).

- You can use the Save command to save the document under its current name and into its current folder, and then continue working on the document.

- You can use the Save As command to save the document under a different name or to a different folder or disk. You may want to save the document under a different name or to a different folder to avoid changing the original.

MAC NOTE

It's a good idea to save a previously created document under another name before you edit it to ensure that your changes can be removed if necessary. See the "Using the Save As Command" section to learn how to do this.

When you exit from Word for the Mac, the program also prompts you to save any documents that contain changes before you exit—but more about that later in this chapter.

Using the Close Command

You can use the Close command when you finish working with a document and you want Word for the Mac to put it away. When you choose the Close command, Word for the Mac gives you the option of saving any changes you have made before the program puts away the document.

To close a document, open the File menu and choose the Close command (or press ⌘+W). If you have not made any changes to the document since the last time you saved it, Word for the Mac simply removes the document from the screen. If, however, you have made changes, Word for the Mac displays the dialog box shown in Figure 4.10.

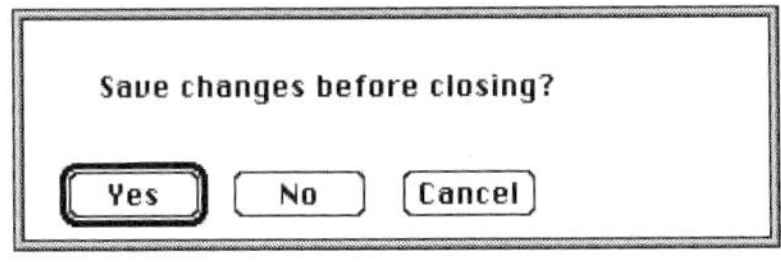

Figure 4.10. The **Save changes before closing?** dialog box.

If you click on the Yes button, Word for the Mac saves the changes you made and removes the document from the window. If you click on the No button, Word for the Mac *does not* save the changes you made since the last time you saved, but *does* remove the

document from the screen. This has the effect of throwing your changes away! If you choose Cancel, Word for the Mac *does not* save the changes you made since the last time you saved and *does not* remove the document from the screen.

Using the Save Command

You can use the Save command to save the active document under its current name and into its current folder, and then continue working on the document. When you use the Save command, Word for the Mac saves the changes you have made to a disk (either hard or floppy) and leaves the document onscreen.

To save a document by using the Save command, open the File menu and choose the Save command. Alternatively, you can press ⌘+S, or you can click on the Save button on the Toolbar (the third button from the left). Word for the Mac saves the document. (If you pay close attention to the status bar at the bottom of the screen, you can see a message that indicates Word for the Mac is saving the document.)

If you choose the Save command the first time you save a new document, Word for the Mac executes the Save As command because it needs more information.

Using the Save As Command

You may want to leave the original document available in cases where your changes may not be final. If you are unsure of the changes you have made, for example, and somebody else is going to come back and check your work, you might want to keep the original document. You then can show that person your version, and let him or her decide which version to continue using.

To save your version of an existing document and leave the original version intact, follow these steps:

1. Open the **File** menu and choose the **Save As** command (or press **Shift+F7**).

   Word for the Mac displays the Save As dialog box shown in Figure 4.11.

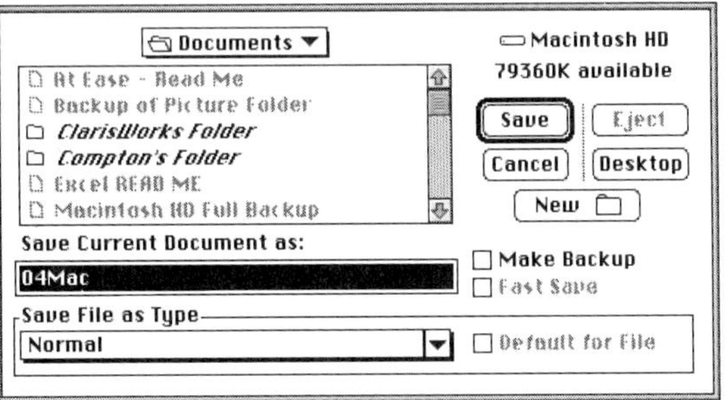

Figure 4.11.

The Save As dialog box.

2. Open the folder into which you want to save the document. (You can save the document with a new name into the same folder as the original document.)

3. Type the new name for the document in the Save Current Document As text box. You can use up to 32 characters for the name you want to assign to the document.

   If you choose a name that appears in the Files scrolling list, Word for the Mac asks whether you want to replace that document. (If you do, you will erase the other file with that name!) Because you probably don't want to replace the original version, click on the No button and then type another name—preferably one that doesn't appear in the Files scrolling list.

4. If you want, you can use the Save File as Type pop-up menu to choose a file format other than Word in which to save the document. For example, you could choose to save the document as a Word for Windows document, a Word for DOS document, or a WordPerfect 5.x document.

5. Click on the Save button.

Word for the Mac saves your document under the name you specify, leaving the original version (under the original name) intact. The new document remains in a window onscreen; any additional changes you make and save are changes to the new document. The old document is "put away"; it no longer appears onscreen.

Printing a Word for the Mac File

After you edit and save a document, you may need to print it. Before you print the document, you might want to preview the document onscreen to ensure that it will print the way you expect. To preview a document in Word for the Mac and then print it, open the File menu and choose Print Preview (or press ⌘+Option+I), or click on the Print Preview button on the Toolbar (the second button from the right). Word for the Mac displays onscreen the layout of the document as it will appear when you print it (see Figure 4.12).

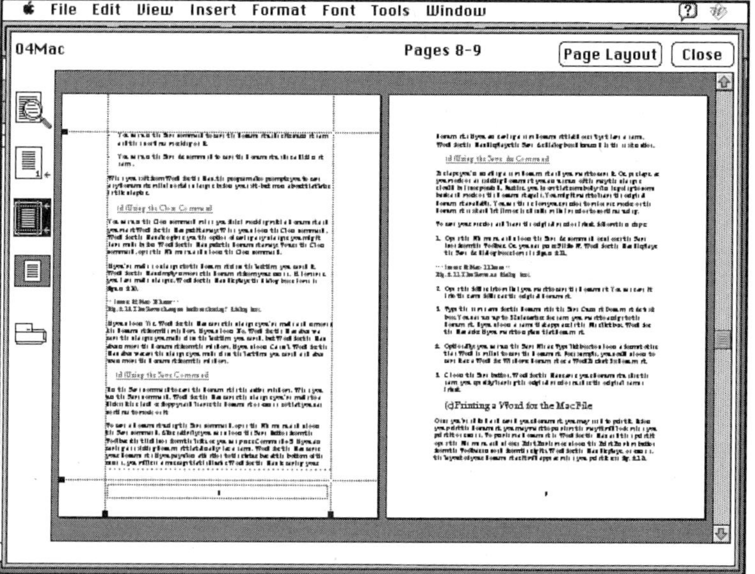

Figure 4.12.

A sample Print Preview Screen.

Although you cannot edit in this screen, you can move the margins and the page breaks and see the layout of the document as it will print. If text and graphics are not aligned properly on this screen, they won't be aligned properly when you print. You can use the Page Layout button at the top of the window to save any changes you make in Print Preview mode and return to editing in Page Layout View. You can click on the Close button to save any changes you make in Print Preview mode and return to editing in the same view you were using when you switched to Print Preview mode. You can use the buttons along the side of the Print Preview window to perform the following functions:

- If you click on the first button, Word for the Mac enlarges the view so that you can read what you see on the Print Preview screen. You cannot edit in the enlarged screen. Click on the button again to return to the default Print Preview screen.
- You can insert page numbers. Click on the second button, and then move the insertion point to the location onscreen where you want page numbers to appear and click again. To remove a page number, drag it off the page.
- You can hide or display the margins of your document by clicking on the third button. When you display margins, you can change them by dragging the black boxes.
- You can click on the fourth button to see one full page, or to see two pages (as shown in Figure 4.12) of a long document.
- You can click on the fifth button to print the document. Word for the Mac displays the Print dialog box shown in Figure 4.13.

MAC NOTE

If you want to print the document without previewing it, you can display the Print dialog box directly. Open the File menu and choose the Print command, or press ⌘+P, or click on the Print button on the Toolbar (the fourth button from the left).

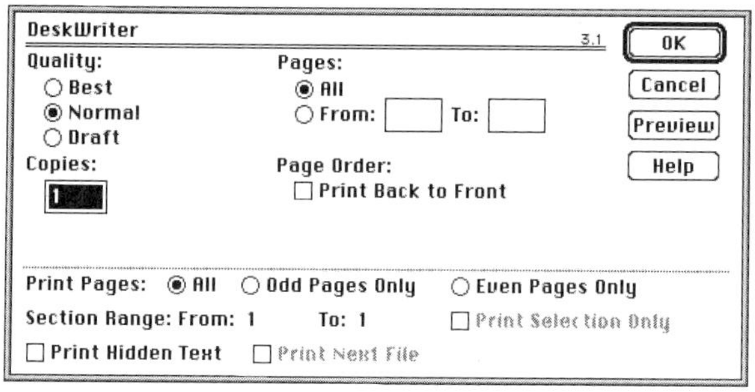

Figure 4.13.

The Print dialog box.

The actual dialog box that appears depends on the printer connected to the Mac. But, regardless of the printer, you should be able to type the number of copies you want to print in the Copies text box. And you should be able to choose whether to print all the pages in your document or only certain pages. If you choose to print only certain pages, specify the page numbers in the From and To text boxes. If you are printing on a dot-matrix or inkjet printer, you can specify the Quality of the print; the meaning of the choices Best, Normal, and Draft changes from printer to printer, so you may have to experiment. For "final" copies, try Normal first.

You may need to check the Page Setup to set the paper type and orientation before you actually print. To check the Page Setup, open the File menu and choose the Page Setup command (or press Shift+F8). A Page Setup dialog box, similar to the one in Figure 4.14, appears. This dialog box enables you to choose a paper type, a page orientation, and a printing size (among other options).

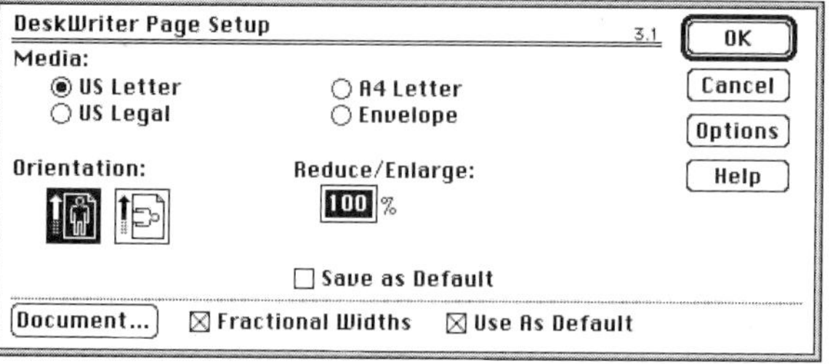

Figure 4.14.

The Page Setup dialog box.

If you see any check boxes already selected when you open the Print dialog box or the Page Setup dialog box, and you don't really

know what they represent, you should probably leave them selected. Word for the Mac may determine that certain options are required when it identifies the printer that is connected to the Mac.

Copying a Word for the Mac File to a Floppy Disk

You may find that you need to copy a Word for the Mac file to a floppy disk, perhaps to take the file to another Mac to print it. You can do this by using the Save As command inside Word, or, if you prefer, you can work from the Desktop by using Finder commands (see Chapter 8 for more information on using the Finder).

Earlier in this chapter, you learned to use the Save As dialog box to save new documents or to save an existing document under a different name. When you use the Save As command to copy a file, in effect you save the file to a different disk. Remember that the following set of steps saves the current document to a *different* disk. If you also want to save the current document to the hard disk, first use either the Save or Save As command (as you learned earlier) to save to the hard disk. Then, use the following set of steps to save the current document to a different disk.

To use the Save As dialog box to save a file to a floppy disk, follow these steps:

1. Insert an initialized disk into the floppy disk drive. If you plan to move this file to a PC, see Chapter 9 for more information on transferring files between computers before you proceed.

2. Open the **File** menu and choose the **Save As** command (or press **Shift**+**F7**).

Word for the Mac displays the Save As dialog box (see Figure 4.15), listing the files in the current folder. The name of the current folder appears at the top of the list.

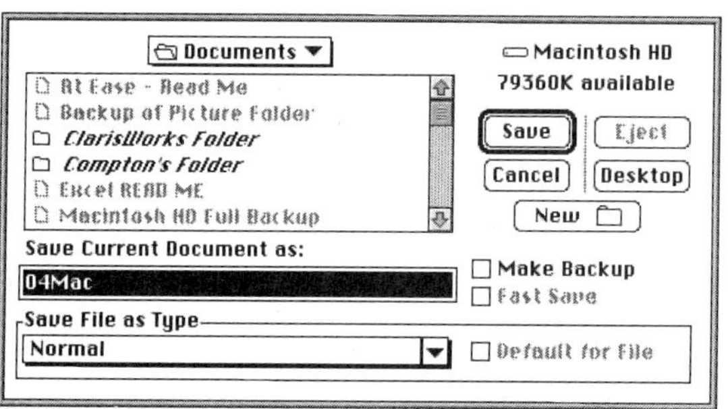

Figure 4.15. The Save As dialog box.

3. Click on the Desktop button. In the scrolling list, you now see the list of items on the Desktop, which includes the floppy disk you inserted into the floppy disk drive.

4. Click on the floppy disk icon. In Figure 4.16, the floppy disk is named "untitled."

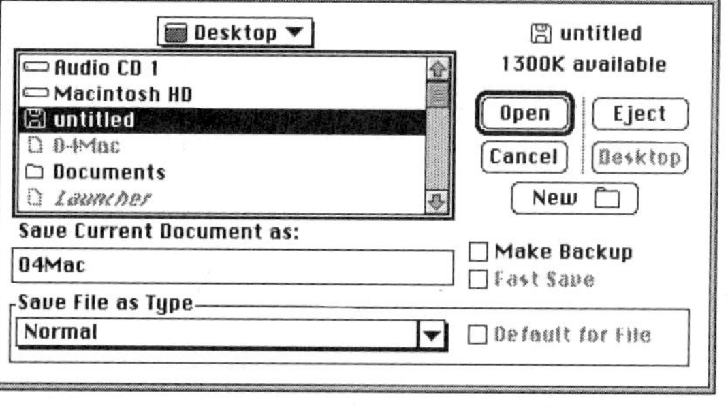

Figure 4.16. The Save As dialog box after the floppy disk is selected.

5. Click on the Open button.

6. If you want, type a new name for the document in the Save Current Document As text box.

   The new name is assigned to the document on the floppy disk. The original file on the hard disk retains its original name.

7. Click on the Save button.

Word for the Mac copies the file to the floppy disk.

If a file with the name you typed is already on the floppy disk, Word asks whether you want to replace the file on the disk. If you replace the version on the floppy disk, you write over that file and it is gone forever, so, if you have *any* doubts, cancel the operation.

You might see the Summary Information dialog box. Fill in the information requested in this dialog box, or click on OK to bypass it.

Exiting Word for the Mac

When you are finished using Word for the Mac, you can exit by choosing the Quit command from the File menu (or by pressing ⌘+Q). If any of your open documents contain changes you haven't saved yet, Word for the Mac displays a dialog box asking whether you want to save the changes to the document before you exit. Choose Yes to save the changes and exit. Choose No to ignore the changes and exit. Choose Cancel to return to editing in Word for the Mac.

When you exit from Word for the Mac, you return to the Desktop. You can safely shut down the Mac from the Desktop by choosing the Shut Down command from the Special menu. If necessary, remember to turn off the monitor.

Chapter Summary

In this chapter, you learned how to use the online Help facility in Word for the Mac. You also learned how to open, edit, save, and

print a document. You learned how to use Word for the Mac to copy a document to a floppy disk, and you learned how to exit from Word for the Mac.

As you have seen, apart from the appearance of the screens, Word for the Mac is quite similar to both Word for DOS and Word for Windows. You find predominantly familiar commands on the menus, and you use all the same basic commands to perform the functions of opening, saving, and printing a document. You can use the keyboard to move around a Word for the Mac document in many of the same ways you move around a Word for DOS or Word for Windows document; the basic dissimilarity appears on the keyboard itself—a PC keyboard doesn't have a Command key.

In the next chapter, you learn how to work with Microsoft Excel for the Mac files. As you know, Chapters 3 through 6 in *The PC User's Mac* focus on specific software packages. You should read the chapters that pertain to the software you want to use. Chapter 7 tells you about database programs you may want to avoid. Chapter 8 provides information for working at the System level on a Mac. If you need to transfer and translate files between a PC and a Mac, read Chapter 9.

ONE
TWO
THREE
FOUR
FIVE
SIX
SEVEN
EIGHT
NINE
GLOSSARY

Working with Excel for the Mac Files

In the first two chapters of *The PC User's Mac*, you learned about the physical appearance of a Mac, how to turn on a Mac, how to recognize what you may see onscreen, and how to start programs. In this chapter, you will learn very basic information about using Excel for the Mac. This chapter is not intended to make you an expert at using Excel for the Mac; this chapter simply teaches you how to perform some basic tasks. You will learn how to open, edit, save, and print an Excel for the Mac file, also called a **worksheet**; how to copy an Excel for the Mac file to a floppy disk; and how to exit the program properly. And you will learn one other important thing—how to get help in Excel for the Mac so that you can teach yourself to do the things that aren't covered in this book!

And, there's some wonderful news for PC users—Excel for the Mac is almost identical to Excel for Windows. The biggest difference you will notice is that the Mac keyboard has a Command key that you can use in keyboard shortcuts. Even the Help facility is almost identical.

Identifying Excel for the Mac Screen Parts

Using one of the techniques described in Chapter 2, start Excel for the Mac. The default screen, which looks like the screen in Figure 5.1, is very similar to the screen you see when you start Excel for Windows.

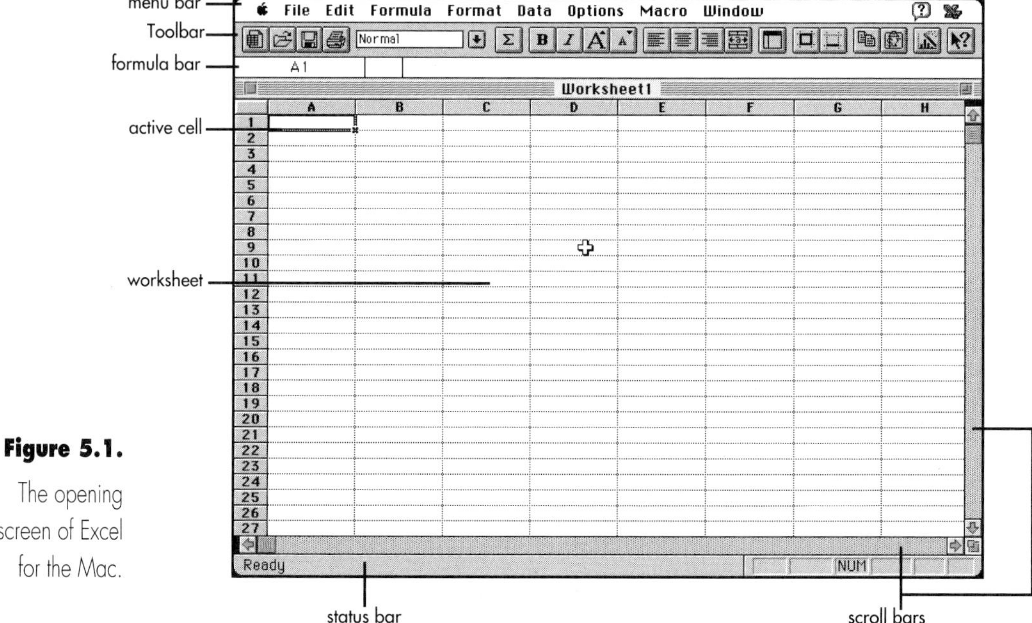

Figure 5.1.

The opening screen of Excel for the Mac.

When you start Excel for the Mac, you always see an empty worksheet in which you can create a new worksheet. The worksheet in Figure 5.1 fills the entire screen. When you start Excel for the Mac, the worksheet may not fill the entire screen. To increase the size of the worksheet so that it fills the entire screen, click on the **Zoom box** in the upper right corner of the worksheet window.

The worksheet area consists of lettered columns and numbered rows. The intersection of a column and a row is called a **cell**; you enter information into cells. The cell pointer, the darker rectangular outline, identifies the **active cell**—the location where text or numbers will appear when you type. You refer to a cell by its cell address, which is the name of its column and row. In Figure 5.1, the active cell is cell A1.

At the top of the screen, you see the **menu bar**. At the right end of the menu bar, you see the Help menu and the Applications menu. You can use Balloon Help in Excel for the Mac—but more about

that later when you learn about Help in Excel for the Mac. You can use the Applications menu to switch to other applications that might be running.

Just below the menu bar, you see the default Toolbar. Like Excel for Windows, Excel for the Mac assigns commonly performed tasks to tools on the Toolbar. You must use a mouse to select a tool on the Toolbar. Remember, however, that you also can use the menus or the keyboard to perform all the tasks assigned to tools on the Toolbar. Because the Toolbar can be customized, the tools shown in Figure 5.1 may not appear on your screen.

You can use the default Toolbar to perform a variety of functions. And there's good news here: the tools in Excel for the Mac are the same as the tools in Excel for Windows. Working from the left edge of the Toolbar, you can perform the following tasks:

- Create a new worksheet.
- Open an existing worksheet.
- Save the active worksheet.
- Print the active worksheet.
- Apply Styles to the selected cells.
- Sum a column or row of cells (all of which must contain numbers).
- Apply bold or italic formatting to selected cells.
- Increase or decrease the size of the font in the selected cells.
- Set left, center, or right text alignment for the selected cells.
- Center text across several cells.

- Automatically format cells based on the last automatic formatting you applied.
- Add (or remove) a border around the selected cells.
- Add (or remove) a border at the bottom of the selected cells.
- Copy the selected cells to the Clipboard.
- Paste formats you copied to the Clipboard into the currently selected cells.
- Start the ChartWizard to create or edit charts.
- Access context-sensitive Help about the area on which you click.

Below the Toolbar, you see the formula bar, which works just like the formula bar in Excel for Windows. From the formula bar, you can identify the current location of the cell pointer, and, if the active cell contains any information, you see that information in the formula bar. When you type in a cell, what you are typing appears in the formula bar. You use the formula bar to edit the contents of a cell.

At the bottom of the screen, you see the status bar. The status bar is divided into two parts. The left side of the status bar informs you about the current operation or command you are executing. The right side of the status bar shows you whether the Caps Lock and Num Lock features are on.

Just above the status bar and along the right edge of the screen, you see the horizontal and vertical scroll bars. The scroll bars contain scroll arrows at both ends, as well as a scroll box. Using a mouse, you can click on the arrows or drag the scroll box on the horizontal scroll bar to move the view of a worksheet right or left. Or, you can click on the arrows or drag the scroll box on the vertical scroll bar to move the view of a worksheet down or up.

Getting Help in Excel for the Mac

Excel for the Mac contains an excellent online Help facility. In this section, you learn the basics of using Help in Excel for the Mac.

You can use the online tutorials that come with Excel for the Mac, but you must have HyperCard 1.2 or later and you must start the tutorials from the Finder, rather than from within Excel for the Mac. You may not know whether you have HyperCard (any version), so follow these steps to try to start a tutorial:

1. From the Finder, navigate to the Excel folder and open it.
2. In the Excel folder, double-click on the icon for Introducing Microsoft Excel, a brief tutorial, or Learning Microsoft Excel, a more extensive tutorial.
3. If anything interesting appears onscreen, follow the onscreen instructions. If you see an error message, you can't run the Excel for the Mac tutorials.

Even if you can't run the tutorials, Excel for the Mac contains an excellent online Help facility that will remind you a lot of the Help facility in Excel for Windows. You can display the Help Contents window in Excel for the Mac by pressing the Help key, or by opening the Balloon Help menu and choosing the Microsoft Excel Help command (see Figure 5.2). In Excel for the Mac, the help you receive is context-sensitive—if you are looking at a command on a menu and you press the Help key, the help you get is about that menu command.

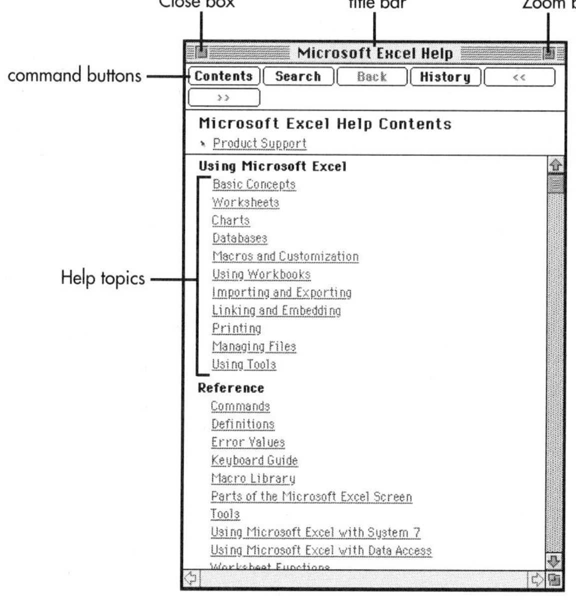

Figure 5.2. The Help Contents window.

When you view the Help Contents window, you see the Help topics. On a color monitor, these topics appear in green and are underlined. If the list of topics is too long to fit in one Help window, you can use the scroll bar on the right side of the window to view the rest of the topics. Using the mouse, you can click on the scroll arrows to move the topics in the window until you see the topic about which you want help. To choose the topic, click on it. Using the keyboard, you can press the down-arrow key to move the topics in the window. To choose the topic, use the Tab key to highlight the topic and then press Return.

As in Excel for Windows, you can get step-by-step instructions by using an "organizational" approach (the topics listed under **Using Microsoft Excel**) or by using a "reference" approach (the topics listed under **Reference**).

You also can use the Reference section of the Help Contents window to find definitions of terms and meanings of error messages you may encounter while working in Excel for the Mac.

When viewing a particular Help topic, you also may see a word underlined with a dotted line. If you choose that word, Excel for Windows displays its definition. Press Return or click on the word again to remove the definition.

The Reference section also can help you find information about the mouse and the keyboard. You can use the **Menu Commands** topic in the Reference section to get help about a specific command that appears on one of the Excel for the Mac menus.

Although you also can find information about parts of the Excel for the Mac screen in this way, the easiest way to get information about screen parts is to use Balloon Help. To turn on Balloon Help, open the Balloon Help menu and choose the Show Balloons command. Then, point to the onscreen element you want to identify. Excel displays a brief description of the element. Turn off Balloon Help by opening the Balloon Help menu and choosing the Hide Balloons command.

You can use the Search button in the Help window to open the Help Search dialog box (shown in Figure 5.3) and search for topics you specify.

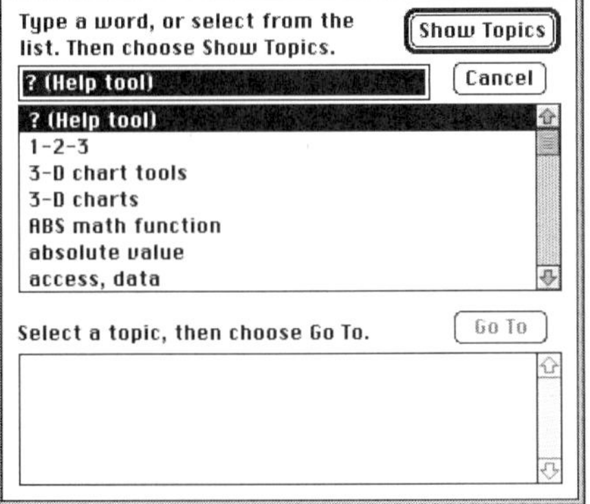

Figure 5.3.

The Help Search dialog box.

Use the Help Search dialog box just like you use the Help Search dialog box in Excel for Windows. Follow these steps:

1. Type a word that represents the topic for which you want to search.

   As you type, Excel for the Mac Help highlights the topic that most closely matches the characters you type.

2. Click on the Show Topics button.

   In the bottom portion of the dialog box, Excel for the Mac Help displays the topics that most closely match the characters you typed.

3. Choose a topic from the list, and then click on the Go To button.

   Excel for the Mac Help displays the topic you chose.

You can print the information that appears in Help windows by choosing the Print Topic command from the Help window's File menu—if your printer supports printing Help topics (my HP DeskWriter doesn't).

If you find a topic in Help to which you might want to return later (without having to remember how you got there in the first place), create a bookmark for the topic. Follow these steps:

1. While viewing the topic you want to mark, open the **Bookmark** menu (on the Help window's menu bar) and choose the **Define** command.

   Excel for the Mac Help displays the Bookmark Define dialog box shown in Figure 5.4. The name of the topic you are viewing appears in the Bookmark Name text box.

Figure 5.4. The Bookmark Define dialog box.

2. If you want to change the bookmark name, type a new name; otherwise, Excel for the Mac Help will use the topic name as the bookmark name.

3. Click on OK.

   Excel for the Mac stores the topic name on the Bookmark menu.

When you open the Bookmark menu again, you see below the Define command the topics for which you stored a bookmark. If you choose a topic from the Bookmark menu, Excel for the Mac Help displays the topic.

After viewing several topics, you can use the Contents button to redisplay the Help Contents window. Or, you can use the Back button to redisplay in reverse order the topics you viewed. You also can return directly to any topic you displayed by clicking on the History button. When you choose the History button, Excel for the Mac Help displays the Help History window, in which you can see every topic you viewed since you started Help. If you looked at a topic more than once, it appears more than once in the Help History window. To go to a topic listed in the Help History window, double-click on the topic; or, use the arrow keys to point to the topic, and then press Return.

MAC NOTE

If you close Help, Excel for the Mac also closes the history of your Help session and no longer maintains the history of the Help screens you viewed. When you open Help again, Excel for the Mac starts the history over again.

Opening an Excel for the Mac File

Suppose that someone brings you a worksheet, asks you to make some minor changes to it, and then wants you to print the revised worksheet. In this section, you learn how to open an existing Excel for the Mac worksheet. In the next three sections, you learn how to edit, save, and print an Excel for the Mac worksheet.

You can open more than one worksheet at a time. The worksheet that contains the insertion point is called the **active worksheet** and you are looking at it in the **active window**. When you start Excel for the Mac, Worksheet1, a blank worksheet, always appears. You can start typing a new worksheet in Worksheet1. If you open an existing worksheet without typing in Worksheet1, the existing worksheet becomes the active worksheet, but you can switch to Worksheet1 by using commands on the Window menu.

To open an existing Excel for the Mac worksheet, follow these steps:

1. Open the **File** menu and choose the **Open** command (or press ⌘+**O**). You also can click on the Open button on the Toolbar (the second button from the left).

   Excel for the Mac displays the Open dialog box (see Figure 5.5).

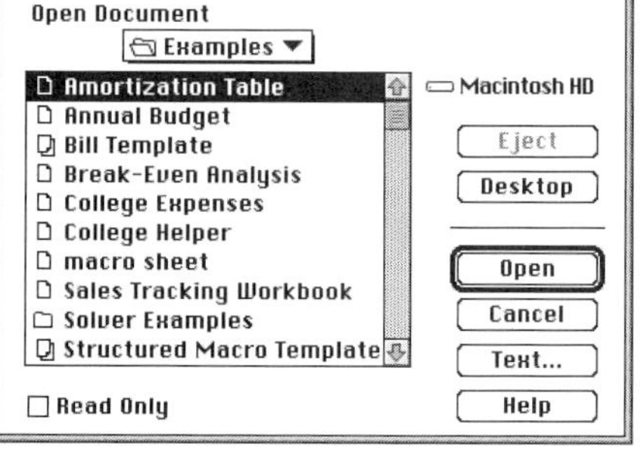

Figure 5.5. The Open dialog box.

2. Navigate to the folder that contains the file you want to open. To open a folder, click on the folder name (to select it) in the scrolling list box on the left and click on the Open button on the right.

   If you need to back out of a folder, you can click on the Desktop button to list everything on the Desktop and then click on the icon of the hard disk to list the contents of the hard disk window. Or, if you opened a nested folder (a folder inside a folder), you can open the pop-up menu above the scrolling list and choose the parent folder. Use these techniques to find the file you want to open.

3. When the name of the file you want to open appears in the list box, click on the file name.

4. Click on the Open button.

   The document appears onscreen and you can edit it.

MAC TIP

Be aware that the user can create a **workbook**, which is a collection of worksheets that are conceptually related to one another. When you retrieve a workbook, you retrieve all the worksheets in the workbook.

Performing Basic Editing in Excel for the Mac

In this section, you learn about basic editing in Excel for the Mac. You learn how to move around a worksheet, how to

enter information into a cell, how to change the contents of a cell, how to select a group of cells, and how to execute commands.

Moving around a Worksheet

You move around an Excel for the Mac worksheet by clicking the mouse or by pressing the directional keys (the arrow keys, Home, End, Page Up, and Page Down). Table 5.1 summarizes the most common ways in which you can use the keyboard to move around an Excel for the Mac document.

MAC NOTE

Excel for the Mac enables you to use many different keys on the keyboard to perform functions. The keystrokes you see in Table 5.1 are basic editing keystrokes. For more information on other keystrokes available, see Excel for the Mac Help, discussed earlier in this chapter.

Table 5.1. Directional keys in an Excel for the Mac worksheet.

Key(s)	Effect
→ or ←	Moves the cell pointer one cell in the direction of the arrow key—right or left one column.
↑ or ↓	Moves the cell pointer one cell in the direction of the arrow key—up or down one row.
⌘+← or ⌘+→	Moves the cell pointer in the direction of the arrow key to the last non-empty cell in a contiguous group of cells in the current row.
⌘+↑ or ⌘+↓	Moves the cell pointer in the direction of the arrow key to the last non-empty cell in a contiguous group of cells in the current column.

Key(s)	Effect
Page Down	Moves the cell pointer down one window length.
Page Up	Moves the cell pointer up one window length.
⌘+Page Down	Moves the cell pointer right one window width.
⌘+Page Up	Moves the cell pointer left one window width.
Home	Moves the cell pointer to the first cell in the current row.
⌘+Home	Moves the cell pointer to cell A1.
End	Turns End Mode on or off.
⌘+End	Moves the cell pointer to the last completed cell in the worksheet.
End+arrow key	Moves the cell pointer to the last non-empty cell in a contiguous group of cells in the direction of the arrow key.

Entering Information into a Worksheet

Entering text or numbers into an Excel for the Mac worksheet is a three-step process, just like entering text or numbers into an Excel for Windows worksheet. To enter text or numbers into a worksheet, follow these steps:

1. Select the cell into which you want to place text or numbers to make it the active cell. To select the cell, position the cell pointer on the cell into which you want to place text or numbers, and click there.

2. Type the text or numbers.

When you type, Excel for the Mac activates the formula bar, and the text or numbers you type appear in the formula bar. When Excel for the Mac activates the formula bar, you also see the Accept and Cancel buttons (as in Figure 5.6).

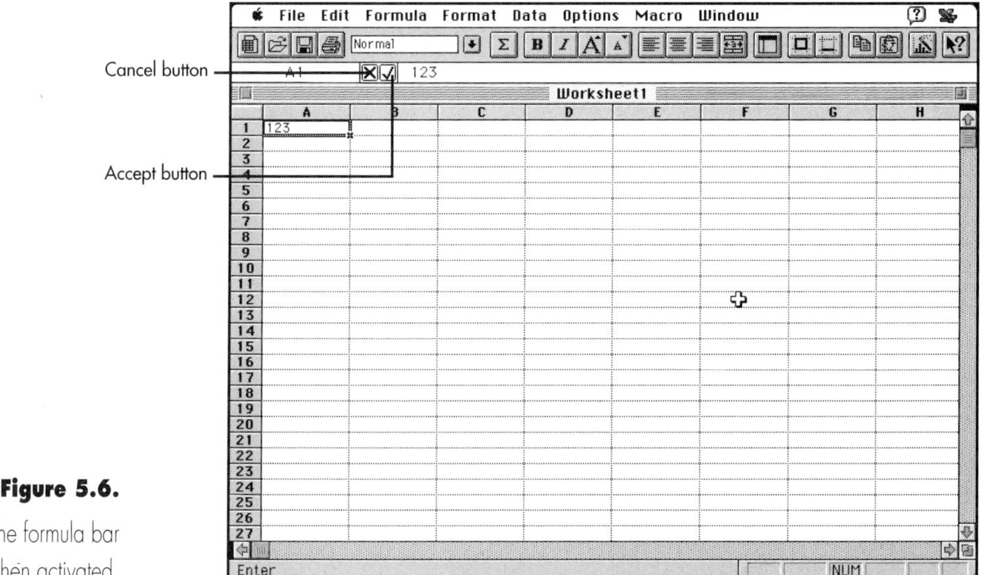

Figure 5.6.

The formula bar when activated.

By default, when you enter text into a cell, Excel for the Mac aligns the characters with the left edge of the current cell. Also by default, when you enter numbers into a cell, Excel for the Mac aligns the numbers with the right edge of the current cell.

3. To accept what you typed, press an arrow key (to accept the entry and move to another cell) or press the **Return** key, or click on the Accept button in the formula bar.

To cancel what you typed, press the Esc key or click on the Cancel button in the formula bar.

Changing the Contents of a Cell

You can use the Delete key to delete the character immediately to the left of the insertion point. You can use the Del key to delete the character immediately to the right of the insertion point. (The **insertion point**, the flashing black vertical bar, tells you where text will appear when you type.)

You can replace the contents of a cell simply by typing over what currently appears in the cell, or you can edit the contents of the cell. To edit the contents of the cell, position the cell pointer on the cell you want to edit. Then, press ⌘+U, or click on the cell's contents in the formula bar. If you press ⌘+U, the insertion point appears at the end of the cell's contents. If you click on the cell's contents in the formula bar, the insertion point appears at the location you clicked. If you accidentally click at the wrong location, you *cannot* use the arrow keys to move to the correct location unless you first press ⌘+U.

While you are editing a cell, you are working in insert mode. In **insert mode**, Excel for the Mac places characters at the current location of the insertion point and moves all existing characters to the right. Unlike Excel for Windows, Excel for the Mac has no overtype mode.

Selecting Cells

You may want to add up the contents of a group of cells, or make changes to the appearance of the worksheet. For example, you may want the contents of certain cells to appear in italics or in boldface type. You may want to change the alignment of the contents of certain cells or delete the contents of certain cells.

In Excel for the Mac, you select a cell or group of cells whenever you want to "operate" on the cell(s)—for example, when you want to add the column or row or center the information in the cell(s).

Selecting is the process of highlighting the cell(s) so that Excel for the Mac can identify the cell(s) on which you want to work. You can select more than one cell as long as the selection is contiguous.

To use the mouse to select cells, you drag the mouse pointer. Follow these steps:

1. Position the mouse pointer on the first cell you want to select. Click and hold down the mouse button.

2. Slide the mouse in the direction of the other cells you want to select.

   As you slide the mouse, a **reverse video bar** (a highlight) appears over all the cells you are selecting except the first cell. You can slide the mouse diagonally to select a rectangle that contains more than one row and more than one column of cells.

3. Continue sliding the mouse until you reach the end of the cells you want to select.

4. Release the mouse button.

   The cells you want to select appear highlighted—a reverse video bar appears over them.

In Figure 5.7, cells B7 through B9 are selected. When referring to a block of cells (such as B7 through B9), Excel for the Mac uses the notation B7:B9.

Now suppose that the selection should have included cells B7:E9. If you didn't select all the cells you meant to select, you can use a shortcut to extend a selection. Press and hold down the Shift key. Then, click on the cell to which you want to extend the selection. Alternatively, press F8. In the status bar, **EXT** appears (see Figure 5.8).

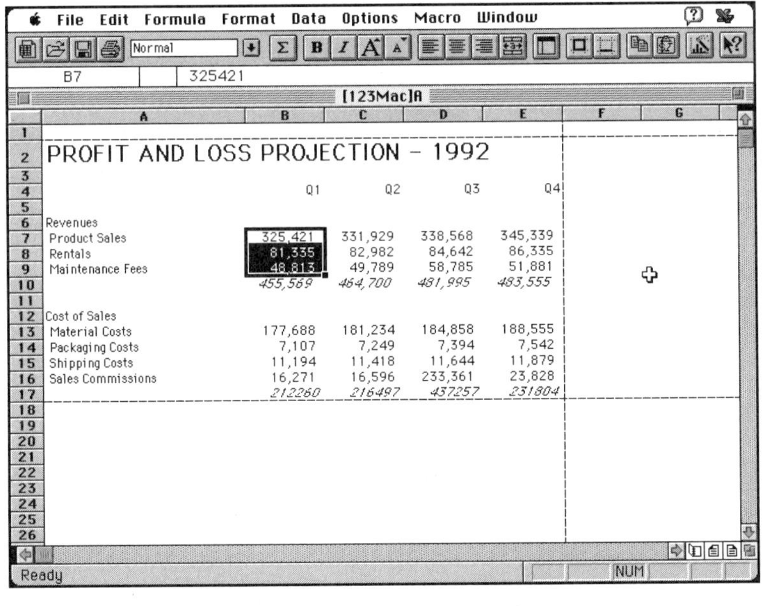

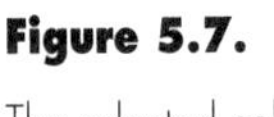

Figure 5.7.

The selected cells.

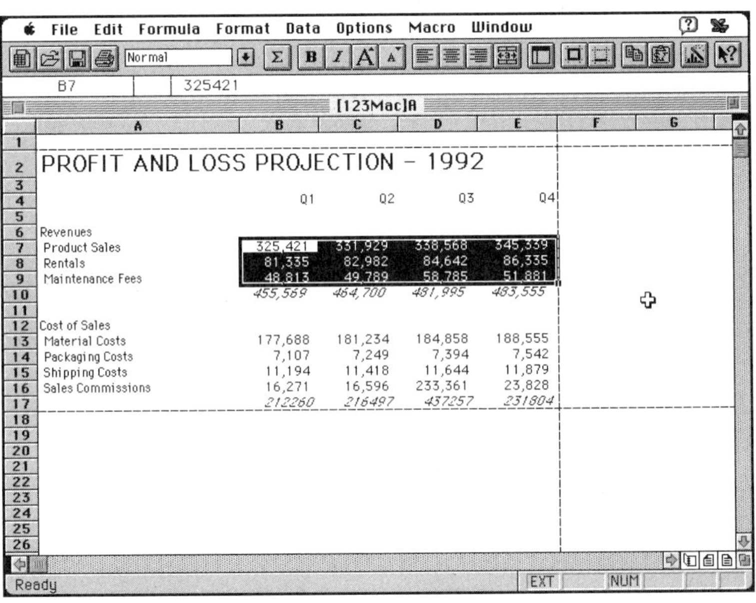

Figure 5.8.

The status bar after pressing F8 to activate the selection extender.

Click on the cell to which you want to extend the selection. Excel for the Mac adds to the selection all the cells between the original selection and the cell on which you clicked. After you have made the selection, press F8 again to deactivate the selection extended. (Otherwise, everywhere you click will extend the selection.)

You can cancel a selection by clicking the mouse anywhere else onscreen. (This action also selects the cell on which you clicked.)

To select cells by using the keyboard, place the cell pointer at the beginning of the cells you want to select. Then, use the keystrokes in Table 5.2 to select cells.

Table 5.2. Selecting Excel for the Mac cells by using the keyboard.

Key(s)	Results
Any arrow key	Selects the current cell.
Shift+arrow key	Extends the selection by one cell in the direction of the arrow.
⌘+Shift+arrow key	Extends the selection to the last non-empty cell in the direction of the arrow.
Shift+Home	Extends the selection to the beginning of the row.
⌘+Shift+Home	Extends the selection to the beginning of the worksheet.
⌘+Shift+End	Extends the selection to the last non-empty cell in the worksheet.
⌘+Shift+Page Up	Extends the selection left one window length.
⌘+Shift+Page Down	Extends the selection right one window length.
Shift+Page Up	Extends the selection up one window width.
Shift+Page Down	Extends the selection down one window width.

Key(s)	Results
⌘+spacebar	Selects the entire current column.
Shift+spacebar	Selects the entire current row.
⌘+Shift+spacebar	Selects the entire worksheet.
Shift+Delete	Collapses the selection to the active cell.

You can cancel a selection by pressing any arrow key.

Executing Commands

As in Excel for Windows, to execute a command, you open a menu and choose the command. You use the mouse techniques described in Chapter 2 to open menus and choose commands. (If the command you want to execute appears on the Toolbar, you also can use the Toolbar to choose the command.)

Like Excel for Windows, Excel for the Mac also provides "shortcut keys" or "hot keys"—you can use them to execute a command without opening its menu. For example, if you want to move the cell pointer to a specific place in the worksheet (a cell you named previously, for example), you can open the Formula menu and choose the Go To command, or you can press ⌘+G.

You also can open Excel for the Mac menus and choose commands by using the keyboard. The technique you use is similar but not identical to the one you use in Excel for Windows. Follow these steps:

1. Press **F10** to activate the menu bar.

   Excel for the Mac highlights the File menu, and displays all other menu names with one letter underlined.

2. To open a menu, either press the underlined letter in the name of the menu you want to open, or press the left- or right-arrow key until the menu you want to open is highlighted, and then press Return.

   Excel for the Mac opens the menu and *leaves it open.*

3. To choose a command from the menu, use either of the two methods described in the previous step (substituting the down- or up-arrow key for the left- or right-arrow key).

   When you select the letter of the command or press Return to choose the command, Excel for the Mac closes the menu and executes the command.

If you activate the menu bar accidentally, you can deactivate it by pressing F10 again or by pressing the Esc key until no menu name is highlighted.

Saving an Excel for the Mac File

After you have made the changes you need to make, you will want to save the worksheet. Like Excel for Windows, Excel for the Mac provides three ways to save a worksheet, and each of these ways is described in detail in this chapter. One of these methods lets you save a worksheet under a different name. Because you may not want to overwrite the work that existed before you edited, you may want to read the sections on the following three methods before you use them:

- You can use the Close command to save the worksheet under its current name and then "put it away" (remove it from the screen).

MAC NOTE

When you work with a workbook, the Close command becomes the Close Workbook command. The Close Workbook command works just like the Close command.

- You can use the Save command to save the worksheet under its current name, and then continue working on it.
- You can use the Save As command to save the worksheet under a different name.

When you exit from Excel for the Mac, the program prompts you to save any worksheets that contain changes before you exit—but more about that later in this chapter.

Using the Close Command

You can use the Close command when you finish working with a worksheet and you want Excel for the Mac to put it away, but you don't want to exit from the program. When you choose the Close command, Excel for the Mac also gives you the option of saving any changes you might have made before Excel for the Mac puts away the worksheet. To close a worksheet, open the File menu and choose the Close command (or press ⌘+W).

If you haven't made any changes to the worksheet since the last time you saved it, Excel for the Mac simply removes the worksheet from the screen. If, however, you have made changes, Excel for the Mac displays the dialog box shown in Figure 5.9.

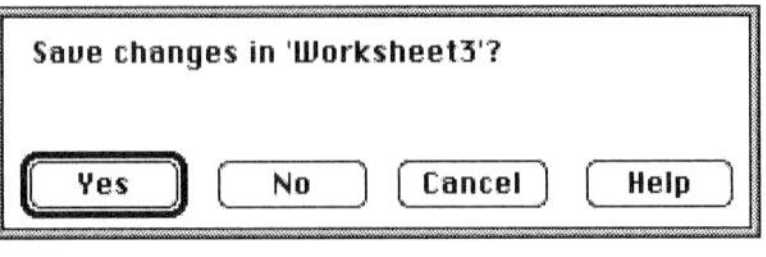

Figure 5.9. The **Save changes in?** dialog box.

If you choose Yes, Excel for the Mac saves the changes you have made and removes the worksheet from the screen. If you choose No, Excel for the Mac *does not* save the changes you have made since the last time you saved, but *does* remove the worksheet from the screen. (This has the effect of discarding all your changes!) If you choose Cancel, Excel for the Mac *does not* save the changes you have made since the last time you save and *does not* remove the worksheet from the screen.

Using the Save Command

Use the Save command to save the worksheet in the active window. When you use the Save command, Excel for the Mac saves the changes you have made to a disk (either hard or floppy) and leaves the worksheet onscreen so that you can continue to work on it.

To save a worksheet by using the Save command, open the File menu and choose the Save command (or press ⌘+S). Alternatively, you can click on the Save button on the Toolbar (the third icon from the left). If you are saving an existing worksheet that already has a name, Excel for the Mac saves the worksheet. (If you pay close attention to the status bar at the bottom of the screen, you will see a message that indicates Excel for the Mac is saving the worksheet.) If you are saving a new worksheet that doesn't yet have a name, Excel for the Mac displays the Save As dialog box discussed in the next section.

Using the Save As Command

You might want to leave the original worksheet available in cases where your changes may not be final. If you are unsure of the changes you have made, for example, and somebody else is going to come back and check your work, you might want to keep the original worksheet. You then can show the person your version, and let him or her decide which version to continue using.

You can save a worksheet under another name in Excel for the Mac similarly to the way you save a worksheet under a different name in Excel for Windows. To save your version and leave the original version intact, follow these steps:

1. Open the **File** menu and choose the **Save As** command.

   Excel for the Mac displays the Save As dialog box shown in Figure 5.10.

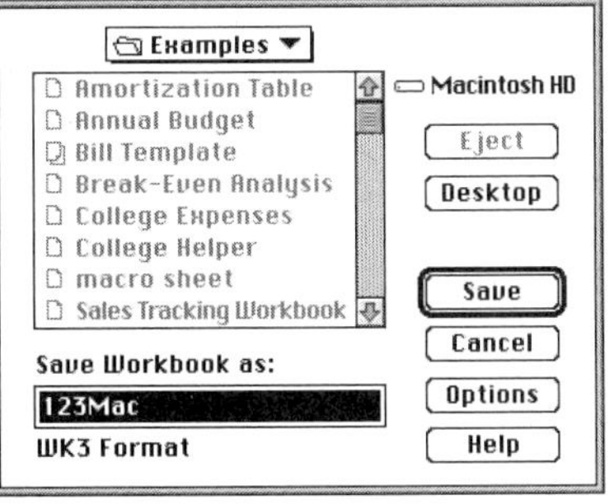

Figure 5.10.
The Save As dialog box.

2. Open the folder into which you want to save the worksheet. You can save the worksheet into the same folder as the original worksheet.

   If you need to back out of a folder, you can click on the Desktop button to list everything on the Desktop and then click on the icon of the hard disk to list the contents of the hard disk window. Or, if you opened a nested folder (a folder inside a folder), you can open the pop-up menu above the scrolling list and choose the parent folder.

3. Type the new name for the worksheet in the Save Worksheet As text box. You can use up to 32 characters for the name you want to assign to the worksheet.

   If you choose a name that appears in the Files scrolling list box, Excel for the Mac asks whether you want to replace that worksheet. (If you do, you will effectively erase the other file with that name!)

4. If you want, you can save the worksheet in a format other than Excel. For example, you can save it in Lotus 1-2-3 format. To do so, click on the Options button.

   Excel displays the Save Options dialog box. Choose the file format you want from the File Format pop-up menu, and then click on the OK button. Excel returns you to the Save As dialog box; the new format is listed below the Save Worksheet As text box.

5. Click on the Save button.

   Excel for the Mac saves the worksheet under the name you specified in the Save Worksheet As text box, leaving the original version (under the original name) intact.

Printing an Excel for the Mac File

After you have edited and saved the worksheet, you may need to print it. But before you print the worksheet, you may want to see onscreen the way it will look when you print it. To preview a worksheet in Excel for the Mac and then print it, open the File menu and choose Print Preview. Excel for the Mac displays onscreen the layout of the worksheet as it will appear when you print it (see Figure 5.11).

You cannot edit on this screen, but you can change the margins and see the layout of this worksheet as it will print. If, for example, you see gridlines appearing around the cells, gridlines will print. You can use the buttons along the top of the Print Preview window to adjust the view, adjust the margins, adjust the settings (such as whether or not gridlines print), return to the editing window, or print the worksheet:

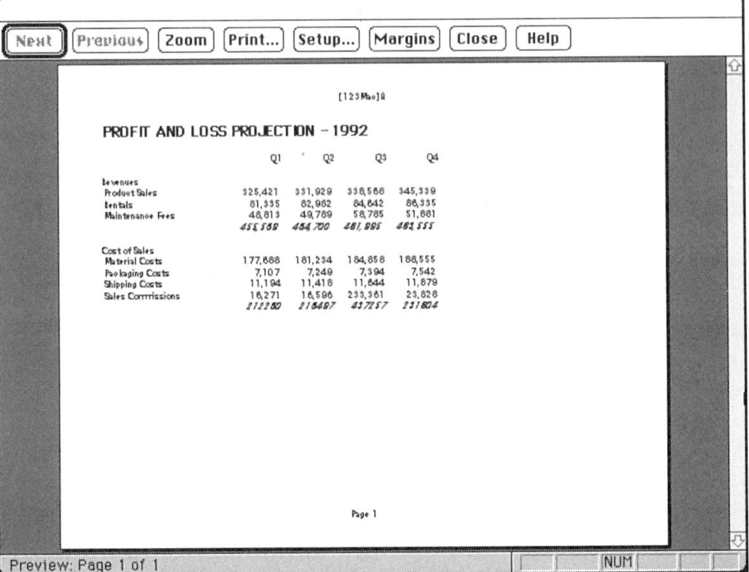

Figure 5.11.

A sample Print Preview screen.

- You can open Excel for the Mac Help by clicking on the Help button.
- If they are available, you can use the Next and Previous command buttons to page through your worksheet. (If they are not available, the worksheet will print on one sheet of paper.)
- You can use the Zoom button to switch to the full-page view (as shown in Figure 5.11) or to see the detailed information that appears in the cells.
- You can use the Setup button to open the Page Setup dialog box (see Figure 5.12). This is used to adjust page setup information, such as whether gridlines print.
- You can use the Margins button to hide or display the margins of the worksheet. When you display margins, you can change them by dragging with the mouse.
- You can use the Close button to return to the editing window without printing.

- You can use the Print button to print the worksheet. Excel for the Mac closes the Print Preview screen and displays the Print dialog box shown in Figure 5.13.

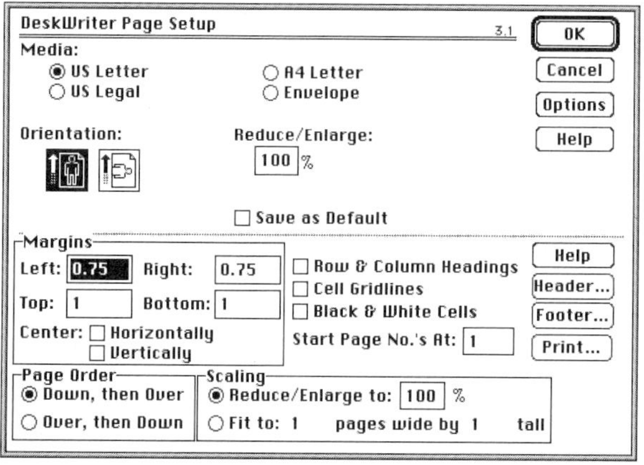

Figure 5.12. The Page Setup dialog box.

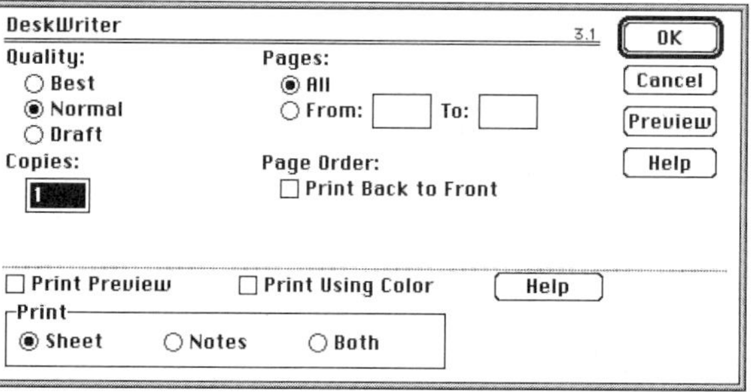

Figure 5.13. The Print dialog box.

Note that you can open the Page Setup dialog box from the Print dialog box by clicking on the Page Setup button. Also, you can preview the worksheet before you print by checking the Preview check box in the Print dialog box.

Although there are several other choices in this dialog box, the ones you are most likely to use are the choices among the Print Range radio buttons and the Copies text box.

From the choices among the Print Range radio buttons, you can choose the pages you want to print:

- To print the entire worksheet, choose All.
- To print selected pages, choose Pages, and then specify the page numbers in the From and To text boxes.

To print more than one copy of your document, change the number of copies in the Copies text box.

To open the Print dialog box (see Figure 5.13) without previewing the worksheet, choose the Print command from the File menu (or press ⌘+P).

MAC NOTE

When you preview first and then click on the Print button in the Preview window, Excel for the Mac displays the Print dialog box. When you open the Print dialog box and click on the Preview button, Excel for the Mac displays the Preview window; however, when you choose the Print button from the Preview window, Excel for the Mac *does not* redisplay the Print dialog box before printing the worksheet.

If you know that you want to use the default settings that appear in the Print dialog box (if you want to print one copy of the entire worksheet in the active window), you can print the worksheet without opening the Print dialog box by clicking on the Print button on the Toolbar (the fourth button from the left end).

Copying an Excel for the Mac File to a Floppy Disk

You may find that you need to copy an Excel for the Mac file to a floppy disk. You may need to print a file on another Mac, for example. (If you need to take the file to a PC, see Chapter 9 for

information on transferring and translating files between a Mac and a PC.) Using the Save As command is an easy way to copy an Excel for Windows worksheet to a floppy disk. Alternatively, you can copy the file from the Finder; this technique is discussed in Chapter 8.

Earlier in this chapter, when you were learning to save a worksheet, you used the Save As dialog box to save a new worksheet you created or to save an existing worksheet under a different name. When you use the Save As command to copy a file, in effect, you save the file to a different disk. Remember that the following set of steps saves the current document to a *different* disk. If you also want to save the current document to the hard disk, use either the Save command or the Save As command to save to the hard disk first.

To use the Save As dialog box to copy a file to a floppy disk, follow these steps:

1. Insert an initialized disk into the floppy disk drive.

2. Open the worksheet you want to copy to the floppy disk so that it appears in the active window.

3. Open the **File** menu and choose the **Save As** command.

   Excel for the Mac displays the Save As dialog box (see Figure 5.14), showing the files listed in the current folder. The name of the current folder appears at the top of the list.

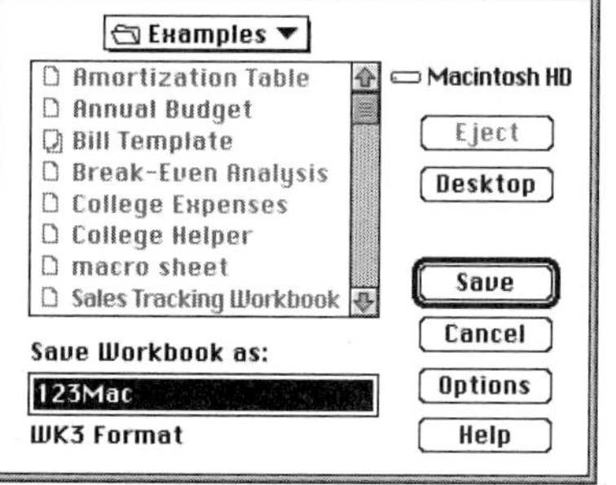

Figure 5.14.

The Save As dialog box.

4. Click on the Desktop button.

   In the scrolling list, you now see the list of available items on the Desktop, which includes the floppy disk you placed in the floppy disk drive.

5. Click on the floppy disk name to select it. In Figure 5.15, the floppy disk is named "untitled."

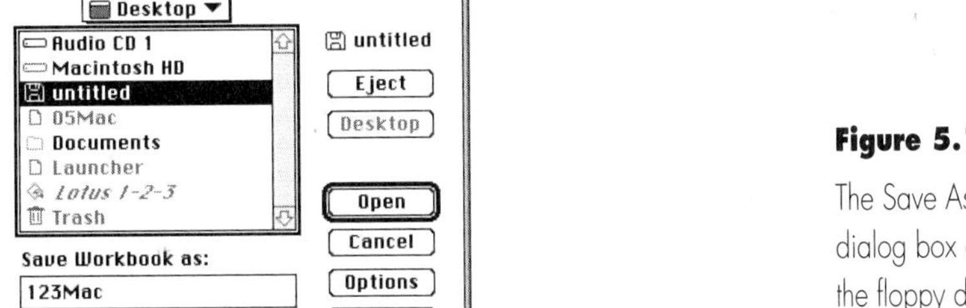

Figure 5.15. The Save As dialog box after the floppy disk is selected.

6. Click on the Open button.

7. If you want, type a new name for the document in the Save Current Document As text box. The new name will be assigned to the document on the floppy disk. The original file on the hard disk will retain its original name.

8. Click on the Save button.

   Excel for the Mac saves the file to the floppy disk. If a file with the same name already exists on the floppy disk, Excel for the Mac asks whether you want to replace the file on the floppy disk. If you replace the version on the floppy, you write over it and it is gone forever, so, if you have *any* doubts, cancel the operation.

When you complete these steps, Excel for the Mac places a copy of the current document on the floppy disk. Remember, if you want a copy of the current document on the hard disk, you must save it using the Save As command, as described earlier in this chapter.

Exiting Excel for the Mac

When you are finished using Excel for the Mac, you can exit by choosing the Quit command from the File menu (or by pressing ⌘+Q). If any of the open worksheets contain changes you didn't save, Excel for the Mac displays a dialog box asking whether you want to save the changes to the worksheet in question before you exit. Choose Yes to save the changes and exit. Choose No to ignore the changes and exit. Choose Cancel to return to editing in Excel for the Mac.

When you exit from Excel for the Mac, you return to the Desktop. You can safely shut down the Mac by using the Shutdown command after exiting from Excel.

Chapter Summary

In this chapter, you learned how to use the excellent online Help facility in Excel for the Mac. You learned how to open an Excel for the Mac worksheet, move around in it, and perform basic editing functions. You learned how to save and print a worksheet. You learned how to copy a worksheet to a floppy disk, and you learned how to exit from Excel for the Mac.

Excel for the Mac is almost completely identical to Excel for Windows (that, in your author's humble opinion, is the *definition* of cross-platform software—no learning curve!). I found the

biggest difference between the two packages to be the shortcut keys that appear on the menus so that you can bypass menus. In Excel for Windows, many of the shortcut keys include a function key, but in Excel for the Mac, the shortcut keys tend to include the ⌘ key and an alphabetic character. But the basic tasks (using Help, opening a worksheet, moving around in it, editing, saving, printing, and exiting) are all almost identical in the two packages.

In the next chapter, you learn how to work with Lotus 1-2-3 for the Mac files. As you know, Chapters 3 through 6 in *The PC User's Mac* focus on specific software packages. You should read the chapters that pertain to the software you want to use. Chapter 7 tells you about database programs you may want to avoid. See Chapter 8 for information on using the Finder on the Desktop to copy files. See Chapter 9 for information on transferring and translating files between the PC and the Mac.

Working with 1-2-3 for the Mac Files

In the first two chapters of *The PC User's Mac*, you learned about the physical appearance of a Mac, how to turn on a Mac, how to recognize what you might see once something appears on the screen, and how to start programs. In this chapter, you will learn very basic information about using Lotus 1-2-3 for the Mac. This chapter is not intended to make you an expert at using 1-2-3 for the Mac; this chapter simply teaches you how to perform some basic tasks. You will learn how to open, edit, save, and print a 1-2-3 for the Mac file, also called a **worksheet**. You will learn how to perform these tasks using both 1-2-3 for the Mac menus and commands and using the commands you may know from 1-2-3 for DOS (because 1-2-3 for the Mac contains the menus from 1-2-3 for DOS). You also will learn how to copy a 1-2-3 for the Mac file to a floppy disk and how to exit the program properly. And you will learn one last important thing—how to get help in 1-2-3 for the Mac, so that you can teach yourself to do the things that aren't covered in this book.

Using one of the techniques described in Chapter 2, start the 1-2-3 for the Mac program. The rest of the discussion in this chapter refers to 1-2-3 for the Mac Version 1.1, but if you are using a different version, you should still be able to follow along.

Identifying 1-2-3 for the Mac Screen Parts

When you start 1-2-3 for the Mac, you see the main screen, which looks like the one in Figure 6.1. Although you see some new things that you may not have seen in other versions of Lotus, the basic components of the screen are similar to other versions of Lotus.

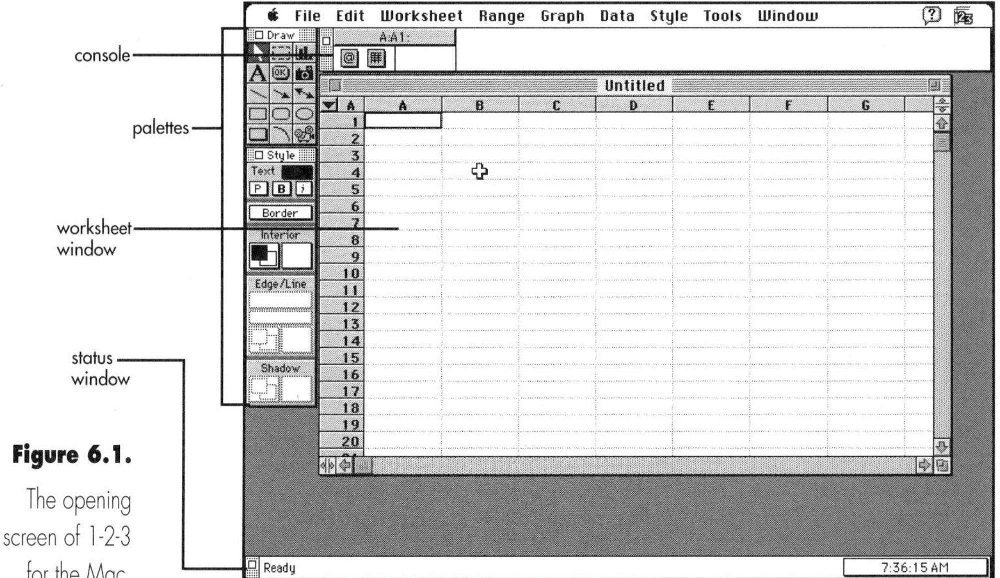

Figure 6.1.

The opening screen of 1-2-3 for the Mac.

You can use either the mouse or the keyboard to move around 1-2-3 for the Mac, select commands from menus, and choose options from dialog boxes. The mouse pointer changes shapes, depending on where you have placed it onscreen. In Figure 6.1, the mouse pointer is in the worksheet window.

For purposes of discussion, you can think of the screen in four different sections:

- The worksheet window
- The status window
- The console
- The palettes

The Worksheet Window

The center area of the screen is the worksheet window. The worksheet window consists of lettered columns and numbered

rows. The intersection of a column and a row is called a **cell**; you enter information into cells. The cell pointer, a rectangular outline in Figure 6.1, identifies the current cell location where text or numbers will appear if you type. The cell that is outlined by the cell pointer is called the **active cell**. You refer to a cell by its cell address, the name of its column and row. In Figure 6.1, the cell pointer is in cell A1.

Within the worksheet window, you see panes, which are the portions of the window that you can see onscreen at one time. In the current pane (also called the **active pane**) in Figure 6.1, you can see cells A1 through G20. Other cells, such as those in column H or in row 21, appear in a different pane.

The Status Window

Below the worksheet area, you see the status window, which displays information about what 1-2-3 for the Mac is doing. In the left portion of the status window, you see the mode indicator, which identifies the current mode in which 1-2-3 for the Mac is operating. In Figure 6.1, 1-2-3 for the Mac is in Ready mode. The mode that appears in the status window depends on the actions you are taking in 1-2-3 for the Mac. On the right portion of the status window, you see the time of your computer system's internal clock.

The Console

Above the worksheet area, you see the console, which contains some of the information you see in the control panel in 1-2-3 for DOS. The console consists of two parts. On the left side of the console, you see the location of the cell pointer. In Figure 6.1, the cell pointer is located in cell A:A1, which is cell A1 of Sheet A. In 1-2-3 for the Mac, you can create worksheet files that consist of more than one sheet, but more about that in a moment. Just below

the location for the cell pointer, you see two buttons that open pop-up menus. The left button opens the pop-up Function menu, which displays all the 1-2-3 functions (for example, @SUM). The right button opens the pop-up Range menu, which lets you create, list, and select named ranges. On the right side of the first line of the console, you see the contents of the current cell. In Figure 6.1, you see nothing but **A1**, indicating that the cell pointer is resting in cell A1, which doesn't contain anything. But, in Figure 6.2, you see **456** on the right side of console, because the active cell will contain the number 456 after you press Enter.

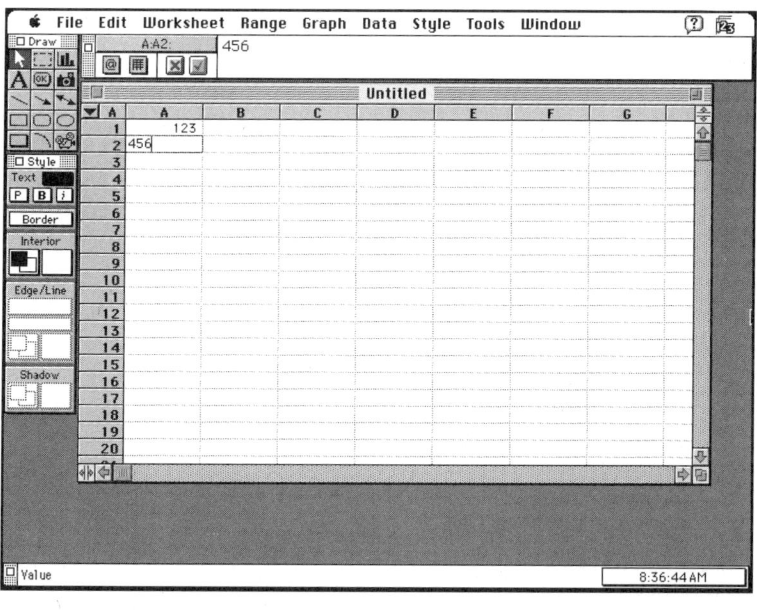

Figure 6.2.

As you start to type, the text appears in the console.

Also in Figure 6.2, you see two additional buttons on the left side of the console. If you have used Lotus 1-2-3 for Windows, you recognize these buttons as the Accept and Cancel buttons. These buttons appear when you type new information into a cell or when you edit the contents of the active cell. If you make a mistake while typing or editing, click on the left button (the one that looks like an **X**) or press the Esc key. 1-2-3 for the Mac ignores your typing or editing, and returns the cell's contents to what it originally

contained. If you click on the right button (the one that looks like a check mark) or press Return, 1-2-3 for the Mac accepts your typing or editing and places the change in the active cell.

MAC NOTE

If you start to type a number, the mode indicator in the status window changes to **VALUE**.

The Palettes

On the left side of the screen, you see the Draw palette and the Style palette. You also can display the Graph palette by choosing the Show All Palettes command from the Hide | Show submenu of the Window menu. In Figure 6.3, you see all the palettes.

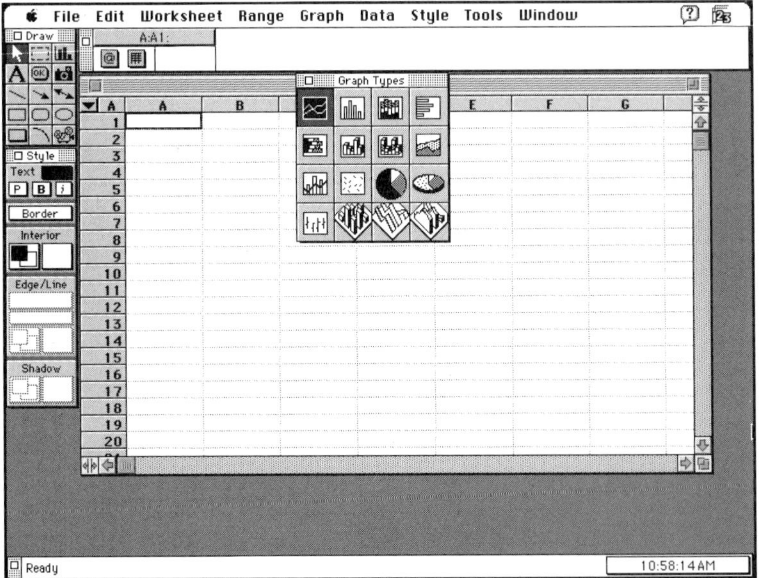

Figure 6.3. 1-2-3 for the Mac with all the palettes displayed.

You use the Draw palette to work with drawing tools and the Graph palette to select graph types. You use the Style palette as a shortcut to set some of the options in the Font dialog box (which you open by choosing the Font command from the Style menu). Be aware that the Font dialog box contains options you can't set from the Style palette, and the Style palette contains options you can't set from the Font dialog box.

Working with the Menus

Good news, here. 1-2-3 for the Mac contains both its own menus and the menus used in 1-2-3 for DOS. In 1-2-3 for the Mac, the menus and commands you know from 1-2-3 for DOS are called the "1-2-3 Classic menus." Whenever you can use either 1-2-3 for the Mac menus or 1-2-3 Classic menus, each of the following sections contains notes in the margin that effectively divide the section into two parts. One part describes how to perform the operation using 1-2-3 Classic menus and commands, and the other part describes how to perform the operation using 1-2-3 for the Mac menus and commands.

If you're familiar with 1-2-3 for DOS and you want to use the menus you already know, you can press the forward slash (/) key. As an alternative technique, you can operate the 1-2-3 for the Mac menu bar, which closely resembles the 1-2-3 for Windows menu bar, with the keyboard by pressing Option+/. Press Return when you have selected the command you want to use. If, on the other hand, you have been using 1-2-3 for Windows or you simply want to use the 1-2-3 for the Mac menu bar, you can open a 1-2-3 for the Mac menu and choose a command using either the keyboard or the mouse.

If you find that you can't activate the 1-2-3 Classic menus or the 1-2-3 for the Mac menu bar using the forward slash key (and Option+/), someone may have changed the default setting from the forward slash key (and Option+/) to the less than sign (<) (and Option+<). If neither / nor < (and their corresponding keystrokes Option+/ and Option+<) activate the 1-2-3 Classic menus and the 1-2-3 for the Mac menu bar, someone may have eliminated keyboard access to the menus. You can reinstate keyboard access to the menus for the current session only (which we recommend) or permanently (which we don't recommend because this isn't your computer).

To enable keyboard access to either the 1-2-3 for the Mac menu bar or the 1-2-3 Classic menus, follow these steps using the mouse:

1. Open the **Tools** menu.

2. Open the **User Setup** submenu.

3. Choose the **Preferences** command. 1-2-3 for the Mac displays the Preferences dialog box (as shown in Figure 6.4).

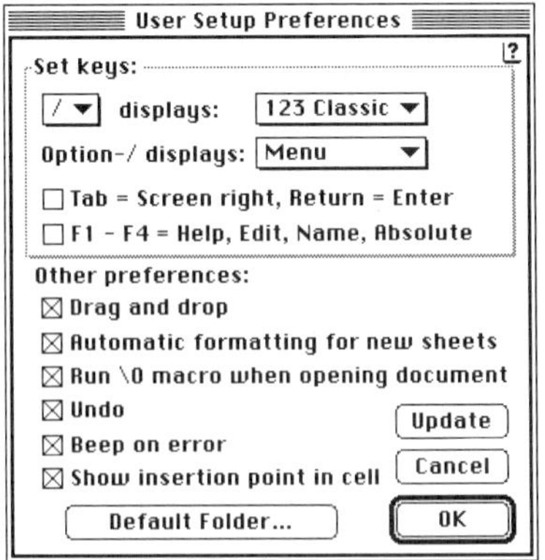

Figure 6.4.

The User Setup Preferences dialog box.

4. In the first pop-up menu, choose the key you want to use to display the 1-2-3 Classic menus.

5. In the next pop-up menu, choose **1-2-3 Classic**.

6. In the third pop-up menu, choose **Menu** to assign Option+/ as the keystroke combination to activate the 1-2-3 for the Mac menu bar.

7. Click on OK to save the settings for just this session of 1-2-3 for the Mac. Click on Update to save the settings permanently.

MAC TIP

To use the < key to activate 1-2-3 Classic menus (and the corresponding Option+< to activate 1-2-3 for the Mac menu bar), you must press the Shift key. So, all lazy people (including me) use the forward slash. For the sake of simplicity and laziness, you will read in this book that the / key activates the 1-2-3 Classic menus and that Option+/ activates the 1-2-3 for the Mac menu bar.

1-2-3 Classic Menus

The 1-2-3 Classic menus enable you to use your 1-2-3 for DOS knowledge. When you press /, 1-2-3 for the Mac opens the 1-2-3 Classic window shown in Figure 6.5.

The 1-2-3 Classic menus appear in a window in the console, and work exactly as you would expect the menus to operate in 1-2-3 for DOS, including "disappearing" if you press Esc enough times or press Control+Pause. You can choose commands from the 1-2-3 Classic menus only by using the keyboard. Note that the mode indicator in both the 1-2-3 Classic window and the status window at the bottom of the screen changes to **MENU** when you activate the 1-2-3 Classic menus.

Figure 6.5.

The 1-2-3 Classic window in 1-2-3 for the Mac.

The 1-2-3 Classic window contains three lines, referred to as the "control panel" in 1-2-3 for DOS. The first line of the console contains the same information as part of the control panel: information about the location of the cell pointer and the contents of the active cell.

The second line of the console contains the actual menu choices. What you see on the third line of the console depends on what menu choice you highlighted on the second line of the console. In some cases, on the third line of the console, you see submenus that will appear if you choose the currently highlighted menu choice. For example, if you choose the Worksheet command, 1-2-3 for the Mac will display another menu, containing the Global, Insert, Delete, Column, Erase, Titles, Window, Status, Page, and Learn commands.

Alternatively, you might see, on the third line of the console, some descriptive text, as in Figure 6.6.

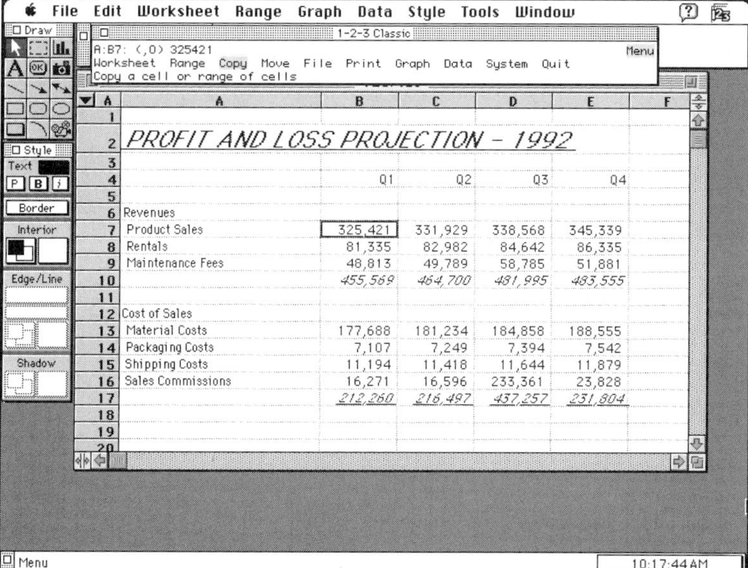

Figure 6.6. The third line of the console of the 1-2-3 Classic window when you highlight the Copy command.

When descriptive text appears in the third line of the console, 1-2-3 for the Mac will not display a submenu if you choose the highlighted command; instead, 1-2-3 for the Mac will perform the highlighted command. If you chose the Copy command, 1-2-3 for the Mac would start the process of copying information from one cell to another, and the mode indicator, both in the 1-2-3 Classic window and in the status window, would change to **POINT**.

To choose a command from the 1-2-3 Classic menus, follow these steps:

1. Select the cell or cells on which you want to operate.
2. Press **/** to activate the 1-2-3 Classic menu bar.
3. Use the right- and left-arrow keys to highlight the command (or submenu).
4. Press **Return** to choose the command (or submenu).

5. If the command you want is in a submenu, repeat steps 3 and 4 until you have found the command you want.

As in 1-2-3 for DOS, you can press the first letter of the name of the command on the 1-2-3 Classic menu. The first letter of the command acts as a **hot key**, and automatically chooses the command. You won't be able to read the Help information that appears when you highlight the command, and you won't need to press Return to choose the command. For example, if you wanted to choose the Copy command from the 1-2-3 Classic menu, you could press C. The hot keys appear in bold letters in this book.

1-2-3 for the Mac Menus

To choose commands from the 1-2-3 for the Mac menu bar by using the keyboard, follow these steps:

1. Select the cell or cells on which you want to operate.

2. Press **Option**+/ to activate the 1-2-3 for the Mac menu bar. The 1-2-3 for the Mac menu bar appears in reverse video (see Figure 6.7).

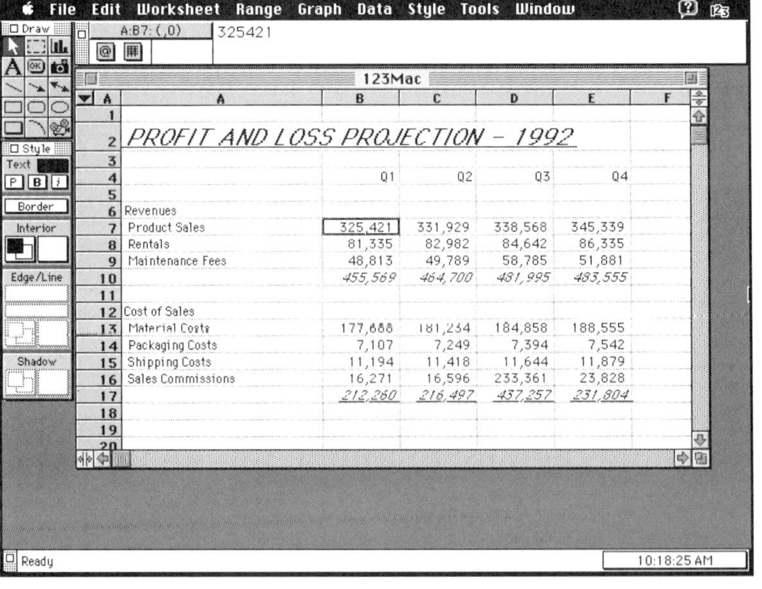

Figure 6.7. The 1-2-3 for the Mac menu bar after you activate it using the keyboard.

3. Use the left- or right-arrow key to open menus, starting from the left or right side (depending on which arrow key you press) of the menu bar. Continue pressing the left- or right-arrow key until the menu from which you want to choose a command opens.

4. Press the up- or down-arrow key to highlight the command you want to choose. Press **Return** to choose the command.

Alternatively, you can press the first letter of the name of the menu you want to open. The first letter of the command acts as a hot key, and automatically opens the menu. You also can press the first letter of the command you want to choose. If more than one command on the menu begins with the same letter (on the File menu, you see four commands that begin with P), press the letter repeatedly until the command you want is highlighted. Press Return to choose the command.

To choose a command from a 1-2-3 for the Mac menu using the mouse, point to the menu, click and hold the mouse button, slide the mouse pointer until the command you want is highlighted, and then release the mouse button.

MAC NOTE

You cannot move the cell pointer around the worksheet area while a menu is activated onscreen. To remove the menu from the screen, press Csontrol+Pause, or press Esc until the menus disappear.

As with all Macintosh menus, you can bypass opening menus and simply choose commands directly by using keyboard shortcuts. On each menu, you see certain key combinations appearing next to command names. For example, next to the Print command on the File menu, you see ⌘+P. To open the Print dialog box without opening the File menu and choosing the Print command, press ⌘+P.

Getting Help in 1-2-3 for the Mac

You can use Balloon Help to get help about onscreen elements to which you point. To turn on Balloon Help, open the Balloon Help menu and choose the Show Balloons command. Then, move the mouse pointer to the onscreen element you want to identify.

You also can get context-sensitive help in 1-2-3 for the Mac. You can get help about a dialog box by clicking on the Help icon in the dialog box (the question mark in the upper left corner). You can get context-sensitive help about commands on menus by first activating Help, and then choosing a command from a menu. 1-2-3 for the Mac displays help about the command.

1-2-3 for the Mac contains an excellent online Help facility. Start Help by pressing the Help key, or by opening the Balloon Help menu and choosing the 1-2-3 Help command. When you start Help, you see the opening Help screen (see Figure 6.8).

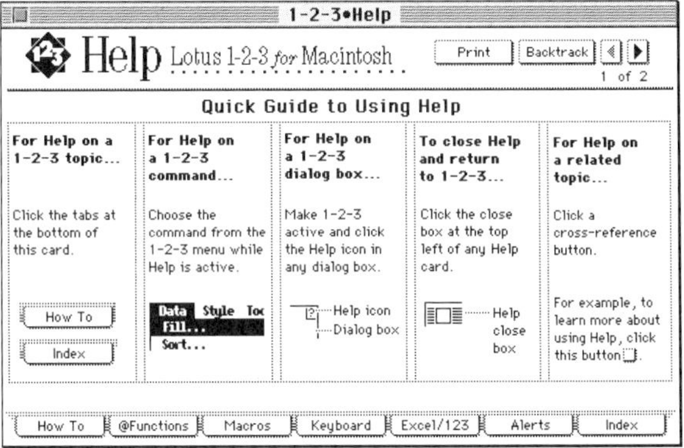

Figure 6.8.

The opening Help screen.

The opening Help screen in 1-2-3 for the Mac shows you how to use Help. Notice the buttons that appear in the upper right corner of the Help dialog box. You can print part or all of the current Help topic by clicking on the Print button. As you view topics in Help,

1-2-3 for the Mac keeps track of the topics and the order in which you view them. You can use the Backtrack button to return to previously viewed Help topics. (You will see the topics in the opposite order from which you originally view them.) Last, you can use the buttons next to the Backtrack button to view any additional screens for the current Help topic. The number of screens available for each Help topic appears just below these buttons. For example, you can see that, in addition to the opening screen at which you are looking, one additional opening screen exists.

In addition to the context-sensitive help described previously, you can click on a card located at the bottom of the Help screen. If you choose the How To card, you see (as shown in Figure 6.9) a list of topics organized by subject. To view one of the topics, click on the box located to the left of the topic.

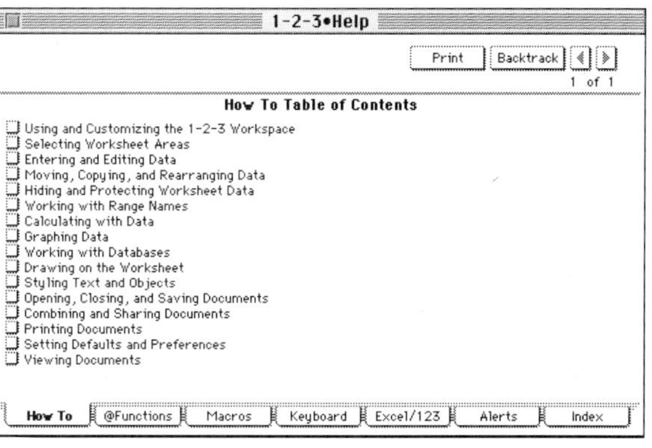

Figure 6.9. The How To Help topic card.

If you choose the @Functions, Macros, Keyboard, or Excel/1-2-3 cards, you will see cards that look like the How To card. Each card lists topics specific to the subject.

If you choose the Alerts card, you see an alphabetical listing of error messages that can occur while you are using 1-2-3 for the Mac. If you click on one of the messages, 1-2-3 for the Mac displays an explanation of the message.

If you choose the Index card, you see the index of topics for which help is available (see Figure 6.10).

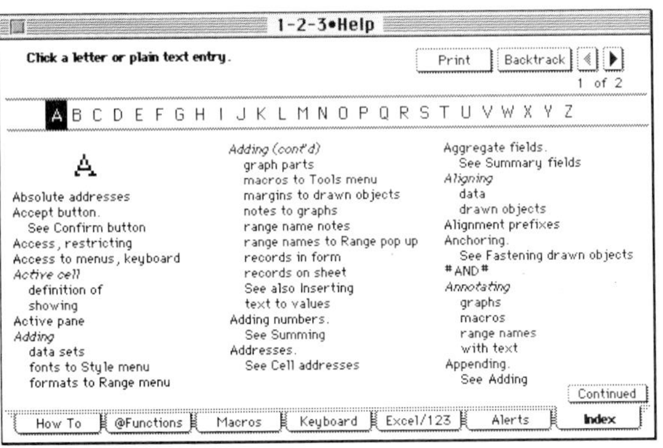

Figure 6.10.

The Help Index.

You can view topics by clicking on any topic that does *not* appear in italicized type. If you want to see more of the topics listed under the letter A, click on the forward arrow in the upper right corner, or click on the Continue button at the bottom right corner of the window. If you want to view the index topics that begin with a specific letter, click on that letter in the alphabet list.

Opening a 1-2-3 for the Mac File

Suppose that someone brings you a worksheet, asks you to make some minor changes to it, and then wants you to print the revised worksheet. In this section, you learn how to open an existing 1-2-3 for the Mac worksheet. In the next three sections, you learn how to edit, save, and print a 1-2-3 for the Mac worksheet. For each set of operations, you will find steps to follow if you are using 1-2-3 Classic menus and alternate steps to follow if you are using 1-2-3 for the Mac menus.

1-2-3 Classic Menus

When you use the 1-2-3 Classic menus, opening a 1-2-3 worksheet on the Mac isn't very different from opening a 1-2-3 worksheet on the PC. To open a worksheet using the 1-2-3 Classic menus, follow these steps:

1. Press **/** (or **<**) to activate the 1-2-3 Classic Main Menu; choose the **F**ile command.

2. Choose the **R**etrieve command from the **F**ile menu. 1-2-3 for the Mac displays the names of the first five available worksheets on the third line of the console (see Figure 6.11).

Figure 6.11.

The names of the worksheets you can retrieve.

```
1-2-3 Classic
A:A1:                                                                  Files
Enter name of file to retrieve: Macintosh HD:Desktop Folder:Documents:Lotus 1-2-
12324SAM.FMT     12324SAM.WK1     123Mac          123WSAMP.FM3
```

MAC NOTE

You might see only 1-2-3 for DOS files. You might not see any 1-2-3 for the Mac files because, by default, the 1-2-3 Classic menus display only 1-2-3 for DOS files. To see 1-2-3 for the Mac files, press Esc until you reach the 1-2-3 Classic Main Menu. From the 1-2-3 Classic Main Menu, choose **W**orksheet, **G**lobal, **D**efault, **E**xt, **L**ist. Change WK* to *. Then, retry the preceding steps.

3. To see additional available worksheets, press the right-arrow key, and 1-2-3 for the Mac scrolls through the names along the third line of the console. Or, you can press F3 to see the names of worksheet files in a columnar list format (see Figure 6.12). You can retrieve a file from either the list on the third line of the console, or from the columnar list that appears when you press F3.

```
1-2-3 Classic
A:A1:                                                              Files
Enter name of file to retrieve: Macintosh HD:Desktop Folder:Documents:Lotus 1-2-
          12324SAM.FMT    17-Dec-92
12324SAM.FMT        12324SAM.WK1        123Mac              123WSAMP.FM3
123WSAMP.WK3        junk                Evaluation Sample   Learning Guide Doc
Sample Database:    Worksheet Template
```

Figure 6.12. The columnar list format from which you can retrieve a file.

4. Using the arrow keys, choose the name of the worksheet you want to open from the list.

The worksheet appears onscreen and you can edit it.

1-2-3 for the Mac Menus

To open a worksheet using the standard 1-2-3 for the Mac commands, follow these steps:

1. Open the **File** menu and choose the **Open** command (or press ⌘-O).

1-2-3 for the Mac displays the Open dialog box (see Figure 6.13). The list on the left of the dialog box shows the contents of the current folder.

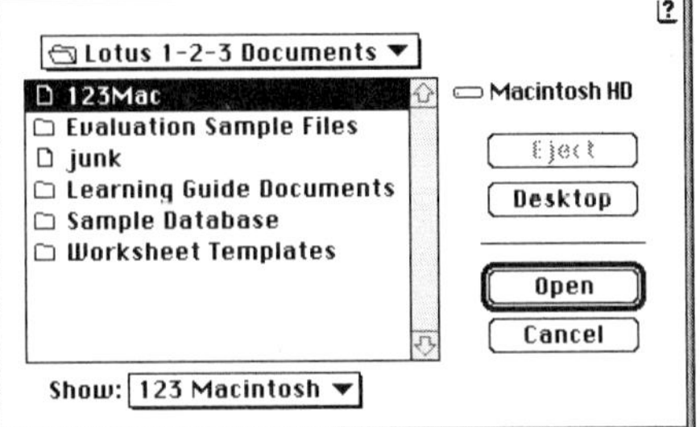

Figure 6.13. The Open dialog box.

2. Select the file you want to open by clicking on its name.

   It may be necessary to navigate through folders to find the file you want to open. If the file you want to open doesn't appear in the current folder, you need to back out of the folder. You can click on the Desktop button to list everything on the Desktop, and then click on the icon of the hard disk to list the contents of the hard disk window. Or, if the current folder is a nested folder (a folder inside a folder), you can open the pop-up menu above the scrolling list and choose the parent folder.

3. When you have selected the file you want to open, click on the **Open** button.

   1-2-3 for the Mac opens the file you selected and displays it onscreen.

Performing Basic Editing in 1-2-3 for the Mac

In this section, you learn about basic editing in 1-2-3 for the Mac. You learn how to move around a worksheet, how to enter information into a cell, how to change the contents of a cell, how to select a group of cells, and how to execute commands.

Moving around a Worksheet

You can use the mouse to move around a 1-2-3 for the Mac worksheet. To move to a particular cell, click on that cell. When you click on a cell, you select that cell. **Selecting** is the process of identifying the cell or cells upon which you want to operate. You will learn more about selecting cells later in this chapter.

You move around a 1-2-3 for the Mac worksheet by pressing the directional keys on the keyboard (the arrow keys, Home, End, Page Up, and Page Down) or by using the mouse.

For the most part, you use the same keys to move around a worksheet in 1-2-3 for the Mac as you do in 1-2-3 for DOS. However, in 1-2-3 for the Mac, the numeric keypad only enters numbers, even if the Num Lock key is toggled.

Table 6.1 summarizes the most common ways you can use the keyboard to move around a 1-2-3 for the Mac worksheet. All references to keys refer to the directional keys, not any corresponding keys you might use on the numeric keypad on the PC.

Table 6.1. Directional keys in a 1-2-3 for the Mac worksheet.

Key(s)	Effect on Insertion Point
→ or ←	Moves one cell in the direction of the chosen arrow key; one column to the right or left.
↑ or ↓	Moves one cell in the direction of the chosen arrow key; one row up or down.
Page Down	Moves down one window length.
Page Up	Moves up one window length.
Control+→	Moves one window width to the right.
Control+←	Moves one window width to the left.
Home	Moves to cell A1.
End	Turns End mode On and Off.
End, Home	Moves to the last non-empty cell in the worksheet.
End, arrow key	Moves to the last non-empty cell in the direction of the arrow key.

Entering Information into a Worksheet

Entering text or numbers into a 1-2-3 for the Mac worksheet is a three-step process, just like entering text or numbers in 1-2-3 for DOS or 1-2-3 for Windows. To enter text or numbers into a worksheet, follow these three basic steps:

1. Position the cell pointer on the cell into which you want to place text or numbers.

2. Type the text or numbers.

3. Press **Return**.

Changing the Contents of a Cell

While typing characters or numbers into a cell, you can use the Delete key to delete the character or number immediately to the left of the insertion point. You can use the Del key to delete the character or number immediately to the right of the insertion point. The **insertion point**, a flashing vertical bar that appears in the cell, marks the place where text will be inserted when you type.

You can replace the contents of a cell simply by typing over what currently appears in the cell, or you can edit the contents of the cell. To type over the current contents of the cell, select the cell that contains the contents you want to replace, type, and press Return. 1-2-3 for the Mac replaces the original contents of the cell with the new information you type.

To edit the contents of the cell, position the cell pointer on the cell you want to edit. Then, click in the console; the insertion point appears at the end of the cell's contents. While you are editing a cell, you are working in insert mode (and you cannot switch to

typeover mode). In **insert mode**, 1-2-3 for the Mac places characters to the left of the insertion point and moves all existing characters to the right. Press the Delete key to delete the character immediately to the left of the insertion point; press the Del key to delete the character immediately to the right of the insertion point. When you finish making changes to the contents on the console, press Return. 1-2-3 for the Mac places the new information in the active cell.

If you are working with 1-2-3 for the Mac Version 1.1, you can use "in-cell editing," which enables you to edit a cell in the worksheet window. Double-click on the cell you want to edit. 1-2-3 for the Mac displays the contents of the cell on which you double-clicked in the worksheet (not in the console), with the insertion point in the cell. As with the other method of editing, you are working in insert mode. Press the Delete key to delete the character immediately to the left of the insertion point; press the Del key to delete the character immediately to the right of the insertion point. When you finish making changes to the contents in the worksheet window, press Return. 1-2-3 for the Mac places the new information in the active cell.

Selecting Cells

You might want to add up the contents of a group of cells or make changes to the appearance of the worksheet. For example, you may want the contents of certain cells to appear in italics or in boldface type. You may want to change the alignment of the contents of certain cells or delete the contents of certain cells. To accomplish any of these tasks, you select cells and then choose commands from the 1-2-3 for the Mac menus. When you select cells, you highlight the cell(s) so that 1-2-3 for the Mac can identify the cell(s) you want to change. You can select more than one cell as long as the selection is contiguous.

MAC NOTE

In some cases, such as copying or moving, you must select cells more than once to complete the command. For example, to copy cells, you first must select the range of cells you want to copy; then, you must select the target location of cells where the copy should appear.

To select a single cell using the mouse, click on the cell you want to select. To select a contiguous group of cells using the mouse, you **drag** the mouse pointer. Follow these steps:

1. Position the mouse pointer on the first cell you want to select. Click and hold down the left mouse button.

2. Slide the mouse in the direction of the other cells you want to select. As you slide the mouse, a **reverse video bar** (a highlight) appears over all the cells you are selecting. You can slide the mouse diagonally to select a rectangle that contains more than one row and more than one column of cells.

3. Continue sliding the mouse until you reach the end of the cells you want to select.

4. Release the mouse button. The cells you want to select appear highlighted—a reverse video bar appears over them.

In Figure 6.14, cells A:B7 through A:B9 are selected. When referring to a block of cells (such as A:B7 through A:B9), 1-2-3 for the Mac, like 1-2-3 for Windows uses the notation **A:B7..A:B9**.

You can cancel a selection by clicking the mouse anywhere onscreen.

To select a single cell using the keyboard, make it the active cell by using the directional keys or the Go To command to place the cell pointer in the cell. In Table 6.2, you see the keystrokes you use to select contiguous groups of cells in the active sheet. You can find additional keystroke combinations for selecting cells in multi-sheet

worksheets using Help in 1-2-3 for the Mac. Notice that the keystrokes in Table 6.2 bear a strong resemblance to the keystrokes you use to select cells in 1-2-3 for DOS and 1-2-3 for Windows.

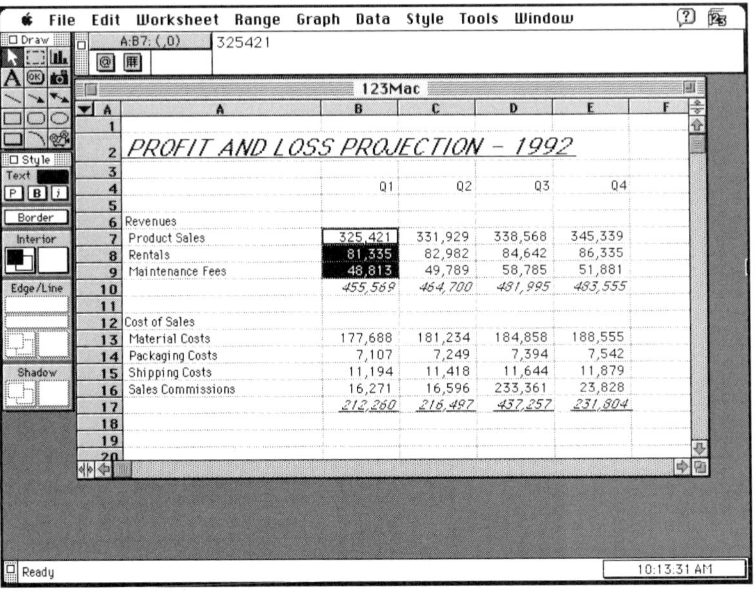

Figure 6.14. Cells A:B7..A:B9 are selected.

Table 6.2. Key combinations to select cells.

Keys	Effect
Shift+→	Extends the selection one cell to the right.
Shift+←	Extends the selection one cell to the left.
Shift+↑	Extends the selection one cell up.
Shift+↓	Extends the selection one row down.
Shift+Home	Selects all cells between the current cell and cell A1.
Shift+Page Up	Selects all cells in the column above the cell pointer.
Shift+Page Down	Selects all cells in the column below the cell pointer.

continues

Table 6.2. Continued

Keys	Effect
Shift+Control+→	Selects all cells in the row to the right of the cell pointer.
Shift+Control+←	Selects all cells in the row to the left of the cell pointer.

You can cancel a selection by pressing any arrow key.

Saving a 1-2-3 for the Mac File

Once you have made the changes you need to make, you will want to save the worksheet. You can use either 1-2-3 for the Mac menus and commands or 1-2-3 Classic menus and commands to save a worksheet. If, however, you are editing someone else's worksheet, you may want to save your work to a different file so that you don't change the original file. You can save your changes to a different file using 1-2-3 Classic menus and commands or by using 1-2-3 for the Mac menus and commands. You may therefore want to read through this section before you try any of the steps to identify which method of saving best suits your purposes.

1-2-3 Classic Menus

1-2-3 Classic menus default to saving files with a WK3 extension, in the format suitable for 1-2-3 for DOS or 1-2-3 for Windows. If you plan to use 1-2-3 Classic menus to save worksheet files in Macintosh format, you should first change the default extension. From the 1-2-3 Classic Main Menu, choose **W**orksheet, **G**lobal, **D**efault, **E**xt, **S**ave. If you see **WK3**, change **WK3** to a blank character (remove **WK3** and then press Return). If you don't see **WK3**, simply press Return. Choose the **Q**uit command to return to Ready mode.

To save an existing worksheet under its original name, follow these steps:

1. Activate the 1-2-3 Classic Main Menu by pressing **/**.

2. Choose the **F**ile command.

   1-2-3 for the Mac displays the File menu.

3. Choose the **S**ave command.

   1-2-3 for the Mac displays the current name of the file on the second line of the console.

4. To use the same name, press **Return**.

   1-2-3 for the Mac displays a menu from which you choose **C**ancel, **R**eplace, or **B**ackup. To abort saving, choose **C**ancel. To replace the original worksheet with the one you have modified, choose **R**eplace. To save both the original worksheet and the one you have modified, choose **B**ackup. The original file will not automatically appear in the list that appears when you retrieve files, but an experienced 1-2-3 for the Mac user should know how to retrieve it.

If you want to save the changes you have made, but you don't want to write over the original because you (an inexperienced 1-2-3 for the Mac user) want to work further with the original worksheet, save the modified version under a different name. In step 3 above, type a new name and press Return. 1-2-3 for the Mac *does not* display the menu asking you to Cancel, Replace, or Backup, unless the new name you typed is the name of an existing worksheet. Instead, 1-2-3 for the Mac saves the modified worksheet as a new worksheet with the name you supplied. The names of both the original worksheet and the modified version will appear in the list that appears when you retrieve files.

1-2-3 for the Mac Menus

To save an existing worksheet under its original name using the 1-2-3 for the Mac menus, open the File menu and choose the Save command (or press ⌘+S). 1-2-3 for the Mac saves the file, writing over the existing version with the same name.

If you want to save the changes you have made, but you don't want to write over the original because it was created by someone else who may not like the changes you have made, you can save the modified version under a different name. Follow these steps:

1. Open the **File** menu and choose the **Save As** command. 1-2-3 for the Mac displays the Save As dialog box (see Figure 6.15).

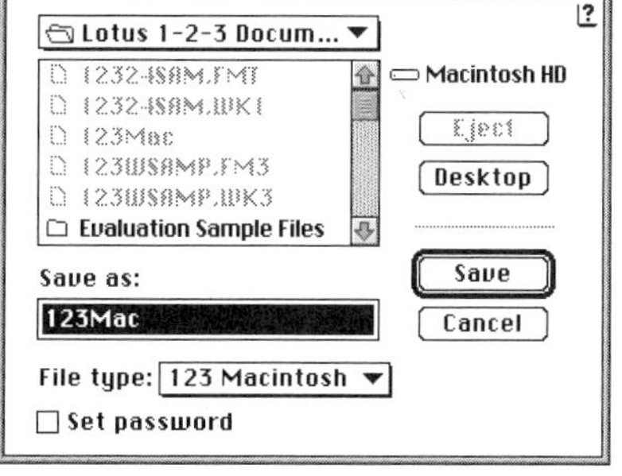

Figure 6.15. The Save As dialog box.

2. The Save As dialog box works like the Open dialog box. If necessary, use the buttons in the dialog box to navigate to and open the folder in which you want to save the worksheet.

3. Type a new name for the worksheet in the Save As text box. Click on the Save button. 1-2-3 for the Mac saves the worksheet in the current folder under the new name, leaving the existing worksheet untouched under the original name.

MAC NOTE

If you don't type a new name in the Save As text box, or you type the name of a worksheet that already exists in that folder, 1-2-3 for the Mac displays a dialog box asking if you want to replace the existing worksheet. If you click on the Yes button, you write over the existing worksheet. If you click on the No button, 1-2-3 for the Mac redisplays the Save As dialog box so that you can type a worksheet name in the Save As text box that doesn't exist in the current folder (or you can switch to a different folder). If you click on the Backup then Replace button, 1-2-3 for the Mac backs up the closed file and then replaces it with the open file.

Removing a Worksheet from the Screen

You may want to stop working on one worksheet and put it away before you open a different worksheet. You can put a worksheet away using either 1-2-3 Classic menus and commands or 1-2-3 for the Mac menus and commands.

1-2-3 Classic Menus

To clear the screen, activate the 1-2-3 Classic Main Menu by pressing / and choosing the **W**orksheet command. From the Worksheet menu, choose the **E**rase command. 1-2-3 for the Mac reconfirms that you chose the **E**rase command by displaying a submenu asking if you want to erase all worksheets in memory. After you choose the **Y**es command (to say that you really want to erase all worksheets in memory), 1-2-3 for the Mac checks to see if any of your worksheets in memory contain changes that you didn't

save. If any worksheets do contain changes you didn't save, 1-2-3 for the Mac displays another submenu asking if you want to erase worksheets from memory without saving the changes. Choose **Y**es to erase all worksheets from memory without saving changes, or choose **N**o to return to the worksheet. If you choose **N**o, you then can save the worksheet using the information described previously in "Saving a 1-2-3 for the Mac File."

1-2-3 for the Mac Menus

You can use the Close command when you finish working with a worksheet and you want 1-2-3 for the Mac to "put away" the worksheet. When you choose the Close command, 1-2-3 for the Mac also gives you the option of saving any changes you might have made before 1-2-3 for the Mac puts away the worksheet. To use the Close command, click on the Close box in the title bar of the worksheet, or open the File menu and choose the Close command (or press ⌘+W).

If you have not made any changes to the worksheet since the last time you saved it, 1-2-3 for the Mac simply removes the worksheet from the screen. If, however, you have made changes, 1-2-3 for the Mac displays the dialog box shown in Figure 6.16.

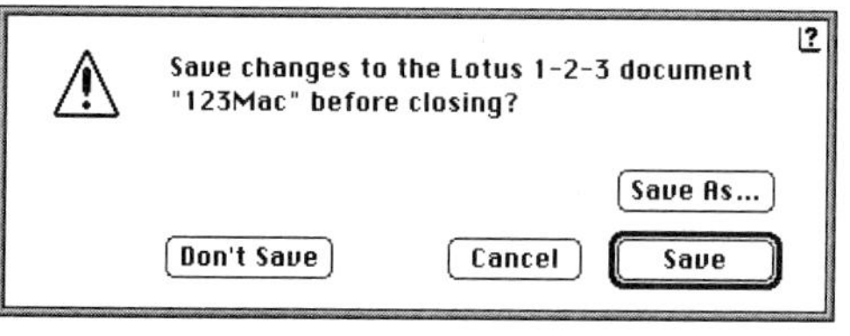

Figure 6.16. The **Save changes to the Lotus 1-2-3 document "x" before closing?** dialog box.

Based on the command button you choose, 1-2-3 for the Mac performs the actions listed in Table 6.3:

Table 6.3.

Command button effects.

Command Button	Action
Save	1-2-3 for the Mac saves the changes you have made and removes the worksheet from the window.
Save As	1-2-3 for the Mac opens the Save As dialog box and gives you the opportunity to supply a different name under which to save the worksheet before closing. After you supply the new name, 1-2-3 for the Mac removes the worksheet from the screen.
Don't Save	1-2-3 for the Mac *does not* save the changes you have made since the last time you saved, but 1-2-3 for the Mac *does* remove the worksheet from the window. This will discard all your changes!
Cancel	1-2-3 for the Mac *does not* save the changes you have made since the last time you saved and *does not* remove the worksheet from the window.

MAC NOTE

If you want to clear only one (of several) worksheets from the screen, you must use 1-2-3 for the Mac commands.

Printing a 1-2-3 for the Mac File

Once you have edited the worksheet, you may need to print it. You can preview the print job, but only if you use 1-2-3 for the Mac commands.

1-2-3 Classic Menus

To print your worksheet using the 1-2-3 Classic menus, follow these steps. (If you want to preview your worksheet before printing, you must use 1-2-3 for the Mac menus and commands.)

1. Activate the 1-2-3 Classic menu by pressing **/**.

2. Choose the **P**rint command.

3. From the Print menu, choose the **P**rinter command.

4. From the Printer menu, choose the **R**ange command.

   1-2-3 for the Mac displays the currently selected range in the console and highlights the range onscreen (see Figure 6.17). Change the range as needed. When you finish, 1-2-3 for the Mac redisplays the Printer menu.

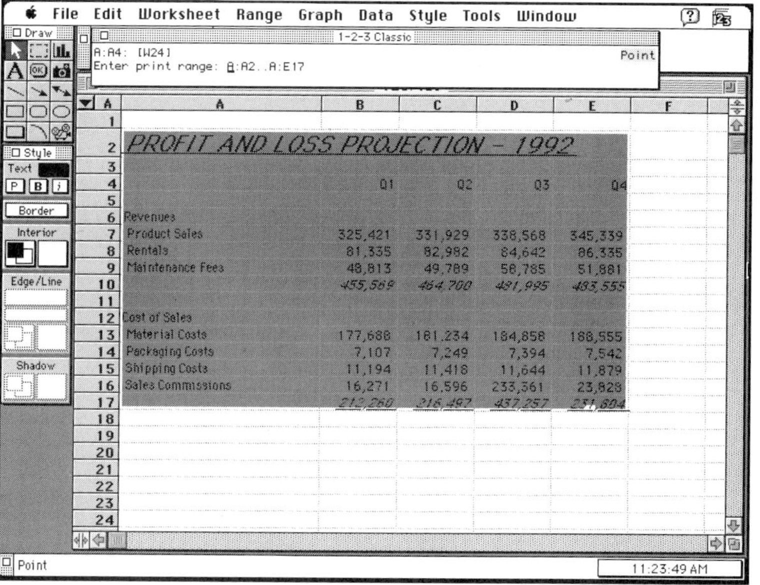

Figure 6.17.
The worksheet while setting a print range.

5. As needed, choose other commands on the Printer menu—**O**ptions, **C**lear, **I**mage, **G**o, or **Q**uit.

Use the **O**ptions command to specify such items as headers, footers, borders, and margins. Use the **C**lear command to clear some or all previous settings. Use the **I**mage command to choose a graph to print.

6. When you are ready to print, use the **G**o command. Use the **Q**uit command to return to Ready mode without printing. The other commands on the menu (besides **O**ptions, **C**lear, **I**mage, **G**o, and **Q**uit) are not available.

1-2-3 for the Mac Menus

Before you print the worksheet, you may want to preview onscreen the way it will look when you print it. To preview worksheets, you use 1-2-3 for the Mac commands. Follow these steps to preview a worksheet and then print it.

1. Open the **File** menu and choose the **Print Preview** command. 1-2-3 for the Mac displays a Print Preview window similar to the one you see in Figure 6.18.

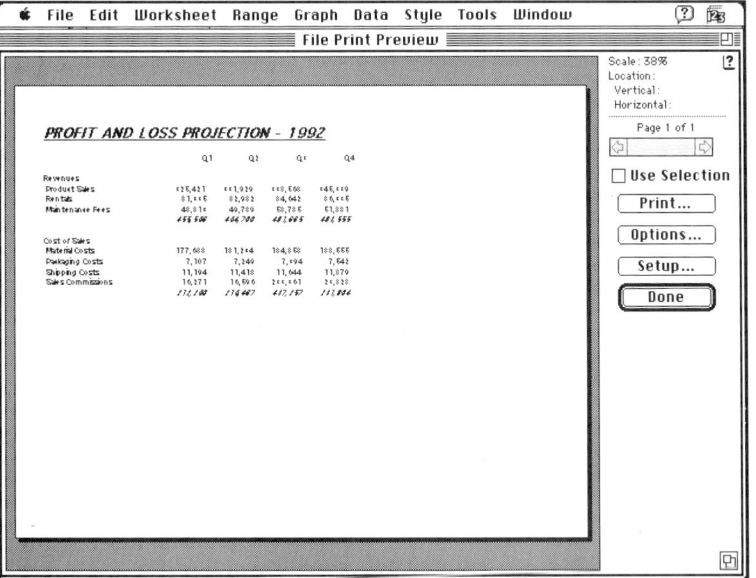

Figure 6.18.

The Print Preview window.

2. 1-2-3 for the Mac assumes you want to print the entire document. Click on the Options button to set a specific print range. From the Option dialog box you also can change other print options such as layout, which includes margins, headers, and footers. 1-2-3 for the Mac "remembers" print settings when you save a worksheet. For this reason, if you are editing an existing worksheet, you may not need to change many settings—someone may have already "set it up" for you.

3. Click on the Setup button to change printer setup information, such as the orientation of the print (landscape or portrait).

4. Click on the Done command button to return to the worksheet without printing.

5. Click on the Print button to print the worksheet.

You can independently change printer settings and printing options by choosing the Page Setup or the Print Options commands from the File menu. You also can print without previewing by opening the File menu and choosing the Print command (or by pressing ⌘+P). If you choose the Print command from the File menu, 1-2-3 for the Mac displays the same Print dialog box that you see when you click on the Setup button from the Print Preview window (see Figure 6.19).

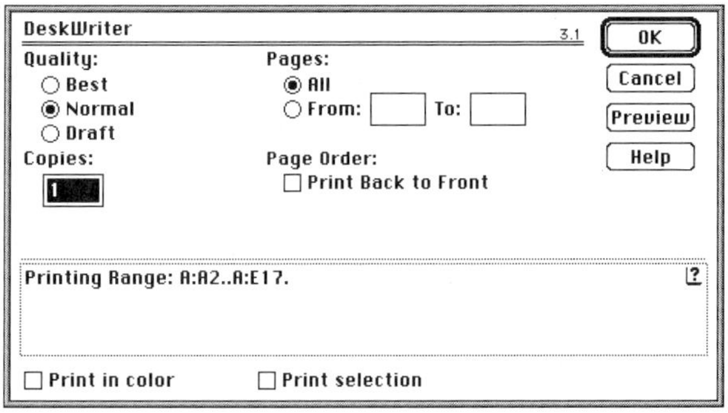

Figure 6.19. The Print dialog box.

Copying a 1-2-3 for the Mac File to a Floppy Disk

You may find that you need to copy a 1-2-3 for the Mac file to a floppy disk. You may need to print a file on another Mac, for example. If you need to take the file to a PC, review Chapter 9 for information on translating and transferring files between a Mac and a PC. If you are copying files for use with another Mac, however, you can use the Save As command to save the worksheet to a floppy. Alternatively, you can use the Finder and copy the file from the Desktop; this technique is discussed in Chapter 8.

Earlier in this chapter, when you were learning to save a worksheet using 1-2-3 for the Mac menus and commands, you used the Save As command on the File menu to save a file under a different name to the hard disk drive. To use the Save As command to copy a file to a floppy disk, follow these steps:

1. Insert a formatted diskette into the floppy disk drive.

2. Open (Retrieve) the worksheet you want to copy to the floppy disk.

3. Open the **File** menu and choose the **Save As** command.

   1-2-3 for the Mac displays the Save As dialog box, which works like the Open dialog box.

4. Click on the Desktop button. The list on the left changes to display the available items on the Desktop, including the floppy disk in the floppy disk drive.

5. Click on the floppy disk icon to select it. In Figure 6.20, the floppy disk is named "untitled."

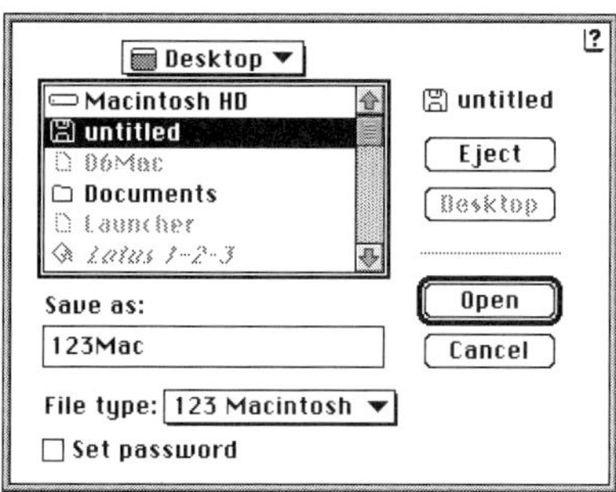

Figure 6.20. The Save As dialog box after the floppy disk is selected.

6. Click on the Open button.

7. If you want, type a new name for the worksheet in the Save As text box. The new name will be assigned to the worksheet on the floppy disk. The original file on the hard disk will retain its original name.

8. Click on the Save button.

   1-2-3 for the Mac saves the file to the floppy disk.

   If you typed a new name in step 7 and the name you chose belongs to a file already on the floppy disk, 1-2-3 for the Mac displays a dialog box asking if you want to replace the existing worksheet. If you click on the Yes button, you write over the existing worksheet.

   If you click on the No button, 1-2-3 for the Mac redisplays the Save As dialog box so that you can type a worksheet name in the Save As text box that doesn't exist in the current folder (or you can switch to a different folder).

   If you click on the Backup then Replace button, 1-2-3 for the Mac backs up the closed file and then replaces it with the open file.

Note that if you save your worksheet to a floppy disk using the Save As command, 1-2-3 will consider the worksheet on the floppy disk

to be the active worksheet. Use the Save As command to save the worksheet to the hard disk again; the worksheet will be saved in both places, and you then will be editing the worksheet saved on the hard disk.

Exiting from 1-2-3 for the Mac

Just as on your PC, when you are finished using 1-2-3 for the Mac, you should exit from the program properly. You don't have to save all the open worksheets before you exit from the program; like 1-2-3 for DOS and 1-2-3 for Windows, 1-2-3 for the Mac will prompt you to save any worksheets to which changes were made since the last time you saved. And, as you might expect, you can use 1-2-3 Classic menus and commands or 1-2-3 for the Mac menus and commands to exit from the program.

1-2-3 Classic Menus

When you are finished using 1-2-3 for the Mac, you can exit by choosing the **Q**uit command from the 1-2-3 Classic Main Menu. 1-2-3 for the Mac displays a submenu asking if you want to quit or return to editing. After you choose the **Y**es command (to say that you really want to quit), 1-2-3 for the Mac checks to see if the worksheet contains changes that you didn't save. If the worksheet does contain changes you didn't save, 1-2-3 for the Mac displays another submenu asking if you want to quit without saving the changes. Choose **Y**es to quit without saving changes, or choose **N**o to return to the worksheet. If you choose **N**o, you then can save the worksheet using the techniques described earlier in "Saving a 1-2-3 for the Mac File."

When you exit from 1-2-3 for the Mac, you return to the Finder. At this point, you can shut down the Mac safely.

1-2-3 for the Mac Menus

When you are finished using 1-2-3 for the Mac, you can exit by choosing the Quit command from the File menu. If you saved changes before choosing Quit from the File menu, 1-2-3 for the Mac immediately returns you to the Finder. If, however, you made changes to the worksheet and didn't save them, 1-2-3 for the Mac displays a dialog box asking if you want to save changes. Click on the Save button to save the changes and quit 1-2-3 for the Mac. Click on the Don't Save button to quit 1-2-3 for the Mac *without* saving the changes to the worksheet. Click on the Cancel button to return to the worksheet.

When you exit from 1-2-3 for the Mac, you return to the Desktop. At this point, you can shut down the Mac safely.

Chapter Summary

In this chapter, you learned how to use the online Help facility in 1-2-3 for the Mac. You also learned how to open a 1-2-3 for the Mac worksheet, move around in it, and perform basic editing functions. You learned how to save and print a worksheet using either 1-2-3 Classic menus and commands or 1-2-3 for the Mac menus and commands. You learned how to copy a worksheet to a floppy disk, and you learned how to exit from 1-2-3 for the Mac.

At a glance, 1-2-3 for the Mac closely resembles 1-2-3 for Windows. The existence, however, of 1-2-3 Classic menus in both 1-2-3 for the Mac and 1-2-3 for Windows, makes all versions of 1-2-3 similar to use. In 1-2-3 for the Mac and 1-2-3 for Windows, you open worksheets; in 1-2-3 for DOS (or using 1-2-3 Classic menus in 1-2-3 for the Mac and 1-2-3 for Windows), you retrieve worksheets instead of opening them. In all three packages, you print and save worksheets.

In the next chapter, you learn about database programs you may want to avoid. As you know, Chapters 3 through 6 in *The PC User's Mac* focus on specific software packages. You should read the chapters that pertain to the software you want to use. See Chapter 8 for information on using the Finder on the Desktop to copy files. See Chapter 9 for information on transferring and translating files between the PC and the Mac.

Avoiding Database Programs

A strange title for a chapter, I know, but appropriate. In this brief chapter, you will learn to identify some of the more popular Mac-based database design and development programs—for the express purpose of avoiding them.

Databases are repositories of related information. Typically, each entry in a database is called a **record**, and each piece of information in the record is stored in a **field**. A telephone book is a database of names, addresses, and phone numbers within a specified geographic area. A dictionary is a database of words and their meanings. A thesaurus is a database of words of related meanings.

People initially use databases (automated or otherwise) to store related information. Later, users retrieve information from the databases and, usually, sort the retrieved information in some desired order to suit a specified purpose. For example, name and address information could be sorted alphabetically to prepare an address book. Alternatively, name and address information could be sorted in ZIP code order to prepare mailing labels for a bulk mailing.

You use a database design and development program, which is generic in nature, to build a database geared toward some aspect of your job and specific to your needs. For example, you might build a database to store information about customers—their names, addresses, phone numbers, and the last time they purchased anything from you. Or, you might build a database to store information about employees—when they were hired, where they live, how much they earn, how many payroll deductions they claim, when their last performance review was, and so on.

Databases are highly personalized, both in their content and their function. When you build a database, you are "programming." In

some cases, you don't perform a lot of programming, but, nevertheless, you are programming. To *use* a database, you really don't need to know the database design and development program in which the database was created. Instead, you need to know the database itself because each database is designed to fit the unique needs of its users.

Because database design and development programs are generic in nature, the database designer can customize the screens and functions of the database to suit his or her own needs. And, because the database designer can customize the database, it is impossible to predict the appearance of database screens. Two different people might use the same database design and development program to build a database of the same information, but the appearance and functioning of those databases are likely to be very different.

You can draw two conclusions from this discussion:

- It is impossible for me to show you the database screens you might see if you accidentally (or on purpose) start a database program.
- You are not likely to have much need to use someone else's database. In fact, unless you know how to use that database, you just might mess it up.

So, in this brief chapter, I'm going to try to familiarize you with the names of some popular database programs, so that if you happen to start one of these programs accidentally, you can start looking for the Quit command immediately.

Among the more popular database programs you might find on the Mac are:

- FileMaker Pro
- Double Helix

- 4th DIMENSION
- FoxBASE
- dBASE for the Mac

In addition, many integrated programs (such as ClarisWorks and GreatWorks), while not exclusively databases, include database capabilities.

Of the database design and development programs listed above, all are relational database programs except FileMaker Pro, which is a flat-file database program. Relational database programs are more complex to use, but also more powerful. You often find them in use for large, complex, company-wide databases. Flat-file database programs are easy to use, but less powerful. You are likely to find them when one or two users have a relatively simple need.

Be aware that, on a Mac, you can start a program by double-clicking on the icon of a file created by that program. For example, if you double-click on a FileMaker Pro file, FileMaker Pro starts and automatically loads the document whose icon you double-clicked. Further, be aware that the programmer who builds a database can assign *any* name to the database file he or she creates. If you are wandering around on the Mac and you run into a file name or an icon that you don't recognize, you don't have to double-click the icon and start the program to find out what kind of file you have encountered. You can use the Finder to identify what program created the file.

To check what program created a file, you work in the Finder. Follow these steps:

1. Open the folder containing the file in which you are interested.
2. Click (one time only) on the file's icon.
3. Open the **File** menu and choose the **Get Info** command.

The Finder displays a window similar to the one in Figure 7.1.

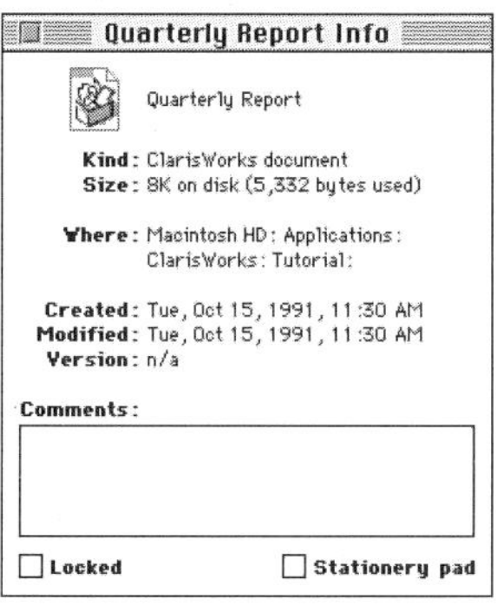

Figure 7.1. The Get Info window.

Note that the Get Info window tells you what program created the file as well as the file size, the place where the file is stored, and the dates the file was created and modified.

4. Click the Close box on the Get Info window to close the window.

If you inadvertently double-click on the file's icon or otherwise start a database program, you can always click the Close box in the title bar (or choose the Close command on the File menu) to close the file you opened. Then, choose the Quit command on the File menu to exit the program.

Chapter Summary

To maintain friendships, avoid database design and development programs as well as other people's databases unless you have been trained to use them. If you choose to use a database or a database design and development program, consult the user's manual that comes with that database or program—or someone who knows how that database works.

In the next chapter, you learn how to work with disks, folders and files at the System level on a Mac. In Chapter 9, you learn to transfer and translate files between a PC and a Mac.

Working with Disks, Folders, and Files

In the beginning of Chapter 2, you learned to identify, select, and open disks, folders, and files. At the beginning of this chapter, you review these Finder basics. Then, you learn how to create disks, folders, and files, and how to rename, move, and copy folders and files. At the end of the chapter, you learn how to use the Trash and how to get help in the Finder.

Reviewing Disk, Folder, and File Basics

On the Desktop, you see **icons** that represent various things on the Mac. For example, you see an icon representing the hard disk and you see the Trash, which you use to erase information (see Figure 8.1). You also may see some icons that represent programs and other icons that represent data files.

If you work on a Performa, you see a folder icon labeled Documents and an icon representing the Launcher—a software program bundled with Performas that is designed to make it easy for users to start programs (see Figure 8.2).

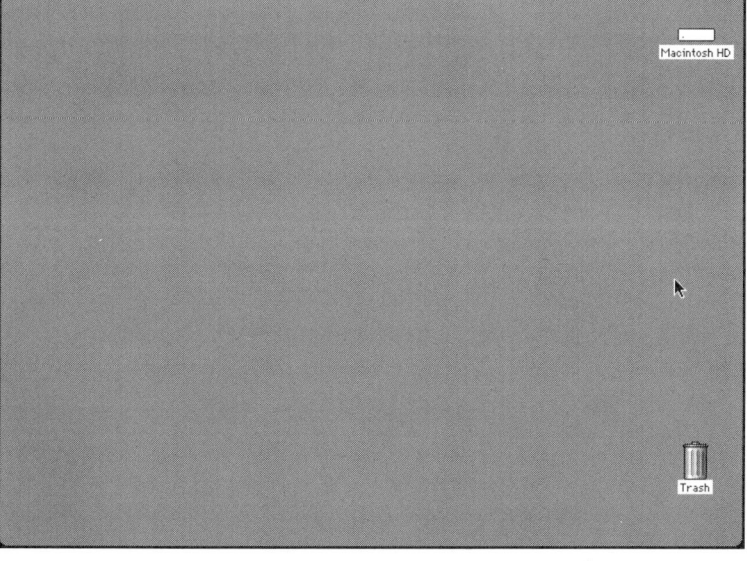

Figure 8.1. A typical Desktop.

Figure 8.2. A typical Performa Desktop.

With the exception of the Trash can, which has a special function, the other icons you might see on the Desktop represent three basic things:

- Disks
- Folders
- Files

As you may recall from Chapter 2, the hard disk icon on a Mac Desktop resembles the ones shown in Figures 8.1 and 8.2. When you insert a Mac-formatted floppy disk into the floppy disk drive, you see an icon that resembles the one in Figure 8.3.

Figure 8.3. A floppy disk icon.

If PC Exchange, a file translation utility, is installed and you insert a floppy disk that was formatted on a PC, the floppy disk icon contains the letters PC (see Figure 8.4). You learn more about PC Exchange and transferring files between a PC and a Mac in Chapter 9.

Figure 8.4. A PC floppy disk icon when PC Exchange is active.

On a PC, you would use the DIR command to display the contents of a floppy disk, the hard disk, or a directory. On a Mac, you open a floppy disk, the hard disk, or a folder to display its contents. You open a disk or folder by **selecting** it (clicking on the icon to **highlight** it) and then choosing the Open command from the File menu

(which you learn about later in this chapter), or by double-clicking on the icon.

When you open the hard disk, a **window** appears. In the window you see **folders** (the equivalent of directories); folders contain files. You also may see **files**, which correspond to files on a PC and include such things as applications, documents, and worksheets (see Figure 8.5).

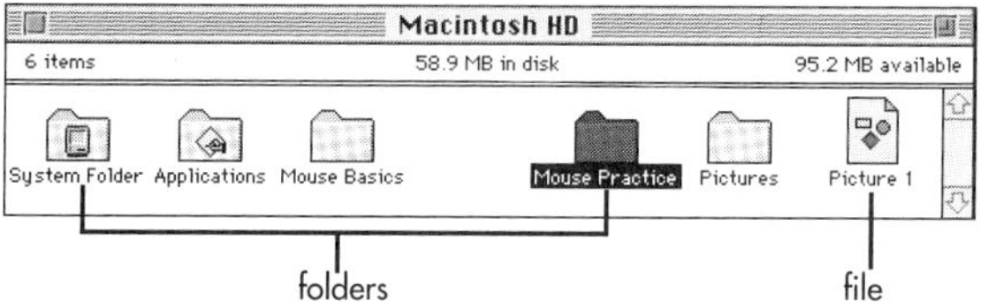

Figure 8.5. Folders and files in the hard disk window.

Creating Disks, Folders, and Files

In the next few sections, you will learn how to rename, move, and copy folders and files by using the hard disk and a floppy disk. To work through these sections, you need to create a disk (by initializing a floppy disk), a folder, and a file with which you can experiment.

Initializing a Floppy Disk

To work through the upcoming sections of this chapter, you need a floppy disk that doesn't contain any necessary files. You will be safest using a brand new disk or a 3 1/2-inch disk you have used previously on your PC (one that you know doesn't contain any critical information). Just as you must format a disk on a PC before you can use it, on a Mac, you must **initialize** the disk.

You really don't need to initialize a floppy disk unless you see a message from the Finder that asks whether you want to initialize the disk. You will see such a message (shown in Figure 8.6) if you insert any new disk into the floppy disk drive.

Figure 8.6. One of the messages you may see when you insert an uninitialized disk into the floppy disk drive.

Unless PC Exchange is active, you see a similar message if you insert a disk that was formatted on a PC into the Mac's floppy disk drive. Unless you want to destroy the data on the disk, cancel the action by clicking the Eject button.

To initialize the floppy disk, click the Initialize button. If you have a file translation utility installed, you may see a different dialog box with more options available. In Figure 8.7, for example, you see the dialog box that appears when PC Exchange is installed. In this dialog box, you can name the disk by typing a name over the current name of **untitled** in the Name text box. You also can create a DOS , Pro-DOS, or Macintosh disk by choosing the appropriate option from the Format pop-up menu.

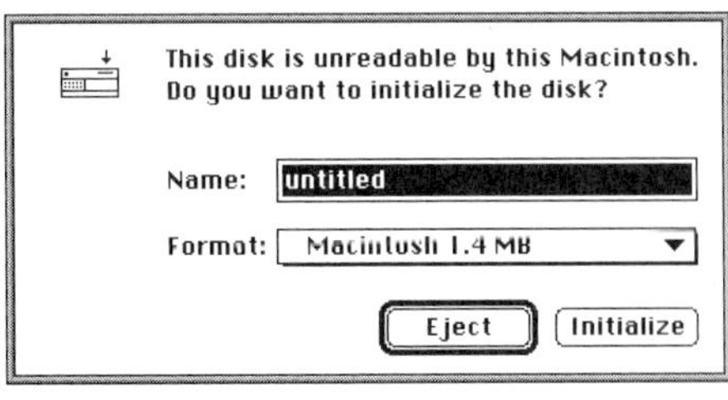

Figure 8.7. The PC Exchange version of the Initialize dialog box.

You can force the Finder to initialize any disk you place in the disk drive by erasing the disk.

MAC CAUTION

Erasing a disk on a Mac is the same as formatting a disk on a PC—erasing removes all the data that was stored on the disk. You cannot recover this information without special utilities. Make sure that you don't want to keep the data on a disk before you erase it!

To erase a disk, follow these steps:

1. Insert the disk you want to erase into the floppy disk drive.

   The icon for the floppy disk appears on the Desktop.

   MAC CAUTION

   Be sure the highlighted icon is the one for the floppy disk so that you don't erase the hard disk!

2. Open the **Special** menu and choose the **Erase Disk** command.

   The Finder displays a dialog box similar to the one shown in Figure 8.8.

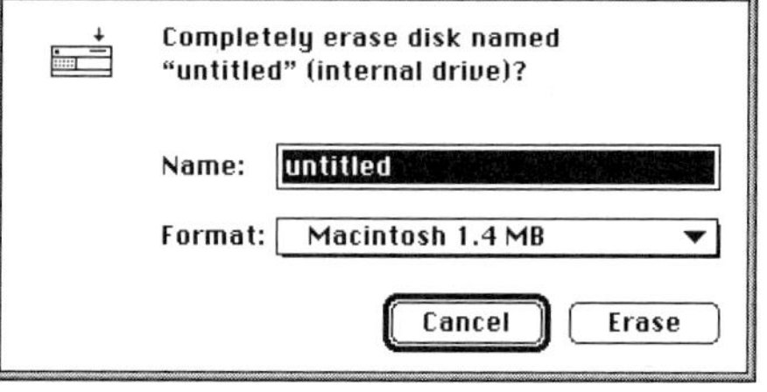

Figure 8.8. The dialog box when PC Exchange is active.

3. Click the Erase button to erase the contents of the disk and initialize it.

Ejecting the Floppy Disk

It was easy to get the floppy disk into the drive, but how do you get it out? On a PC, you can use the eject button on the 3 1/2-inch floppy disk drive, but on a Mac, there is no eject button.

You can remove a floppy disk from the floppy disk drive by using either of two commands. Regardless of which command you use, select the floppy disk icon first. Then, to remove the disk from the drive, open the File menu and choose the Put Away command (or use the keyboard shortcut by pressing ⌘+Y). Alternatively, open the Special menu and choose the Eject Disk command (or press ⌘+E).

What's the difference between the two commands? When you choose the Put Away command, the Finder ejects the disk and removes the disk's icon from the Desktop. You might see, if you watch closely, an image of the disk being tossed into the Trash, and you can accomplish the same result by manually dragging the disk icon to the Trash. (Don't worry—this doesn't erase your disk!)

When you choose the Eject Disk command, the Finder ejects the disk, but the image remains on your Desktop. Sound messy? Well, not really, because you can use that image to copy the entire contents of one floppy disk to another floppy disk. (This procedure is covered a little later in this chapter.)

Creating a Folder

You can create a new folder on the Mac so that you can separate the files you create from files already stored on the Mac. You use folders on the Mac the same way you use directories on a PC—a

folder on the Mac provides a new category into which you can place files and other folders.

Open the hard disk window, if it isn't already open. Now, to create a new folder in the hard disk window, open the File menu and choose New Folder (or press ⌘+N). A new folder appears in the hard disk window, with the name **Untitled Folder**. The text is selected when the folder is created, so that you can name the folder immediately. Name the folder **Practice Items**. To deselect the text or deselect the folder, click on any blank space within the window.

MAC NOTE

You don't have to name a new folder immediately; later in this chapter, you learn how to rename disks, folders, and files.

Creating a File

To work through the upcoming sections of this chapter, you need a file with which to practice. You can create a file that contains a screen image of your Desktop by using a command that doesn't appear on the menus. Press ⌘+Shift+3. You hear a faint crunching sound (similar to the sound a camera's shutter makes when you take a photograph), and the mouse pointer freezes for a few moments. When the mouse pointer becomes available again, look in the hard disk window. You will see a file named **Picture 1**. Its icon looks like a piece of paper with the upper right corner folded forward, and it contains some symbols in the center of the icon.

As you reviewed earlier in this chapter, you can open this file by double-clicking on it. When you double-click on Picture 1, a program called TeachText starts and opens the Picture 1 file. Onscreen, you see what looks like another image of your screen, but the title bar at the top contains only two menus: the File menu and the Edit menu. To close the file (and clear your double-

vision!), open the File menu and choose the Quit command (or press ⌘+Q). TeachText closes both the Picture 1 file and itself.

In the next sections, you use the floppy disk, the Practice Items folder, and Picture 1 file to learn how to rename, move, and copy disks, folders, and files.

Renaming Folders and Files

The title of this section is misleading: you can rename your hard disk, too, but because you are an "occasional" user of the Mac and the hard disk may not be *your* hard disk, this section concentrates on folders and files.

As an example, let's **rename** the file (currently named Picture 1) that we created in the preceding section:

1. Select the Picture 1 file.

2. Click on the name of file.

   After a moment, the Finder selects the text that appears underneath the icon that represents the file.

3. Type a new name, or click anywhere in the existing name to begin typing at that location. For this exercise, type **Desktop Image**.

4. Press **Return** when you're done typing.

   This tells the Macintosh that you're done typing, and saves the new name of the file.

You can use this procedure to rename anything—files, folders, even disks. There are a few exceptions; for example, you can't

rename the Trash. You can use these steps to rename the floppy disk you initialized earlier or to rename the folder you created earlier. Simply substitute “floppy disk” or “folder” in the appropriate places.

Macintosh names aren’t as limited as PC names. File and folder names can include up to 32 characters, with uppercase and lowercase letters; disk names can include up to 27 characters. The only character you can’t use is the colon. This feature can help you better remember what is in the files and folders—the longer names can be more descriptive.

Moving Folders and Files

You can **move** a file or a folder to any other location on the same disk by dragging it. That is, you can move a file from one folder to another folder on a floppy disk by dragging it. Or, you can move a file from one folder to another on the hard disk by dragging it.

In this section, you move the Desktop Image file (which you renamed in the preceding section) to the Practice Items folder (which you created earlier in this chapter). To move the Desktop Image file into the Practice Items folder, follow these steps:

1. Make sure the hard disk window is open.
2. Drag the Desktop Image file onto the Practice Items folder until the icon and name of the Practice Items folder are highlighted. (You don’t have to open the Practice Items folder first.)
3. Release the mouse button.

   The Desktop Image file disappears from the hard disk window.

4. Open the Practice Items folder by double-clicking it.

   You now can see the Desktop Image file inside the Practice Items folder.

You can move the Desktop Image file back to the hard disk window by dragging it back, or you can place it directly on the Desktop (not inside any window) by dragging it anywhere onto the Desktop. To follow the rest of the examples in this chapter, move the Desktop Image file back into the hard disk window.

When you drag a file (or folder) from one *disk* to another, the Mac actually creates a copy of the file (or folder) in the new location; that is, it doesn't erase the original file from the original disk. (This is discussed in greater detail in the next section.) You can *move* a folder or file from a floppy disk to a hard disk (or from a hard disk to a floppy disk) by making a copy of the folder or file (see the next section) and then erasing the original folder or file. For more information on erasing folders and files, see the section "Using the Trash" later in this chapter.

Remember, although the examples in this section focus on moving a file, you can move folders the same way you move files.

Copying Folders and Files

When you move a folder or file, you drag it from one location to another (perhaps into a different folder), and it no longer appears in its original location. After you move a folder or file, you still have only one copy of that folder or file.

Sometimes, however, you want to create a duplicate of the original folder or file. Copying on a Mac has the same end result as copying on a PC—ultimately you have two identical versions of the same file. When you **copy** a folder or file, you make a duplicate of the

folder or file, which you can then place in a different location. After you copy a folder or file, you have two of the same folder or file; after you move a folder or file, you still have only one folder or file. In this section, you learn to copy folders and files from one disk to another disk. You also learn to copy folders or files from one location to another on the same disk.

The examples in this section focus on copying a file, but remember: you can copy entire folders the same way you copy files. If you copy a folder, you also copy all the folders and files it contains.

Copying to a Different Disk

As was mentioned earlier, you can copy a folder or file from a hard disk to a floppy disk (or from a floppy disk to a hard disk) by dragging it. To copy the Desktop Image file on the hard disk to a floppy disk, for example, follow these steps:

1. Insert an initialized floppy disk in the floppy disk drive.

2. Open the hard disk window (by double-clicking on the hard disk icon) and select the Desktop Image file.

3. Drag the Desktop Image file from the hard disk window to the floppy disk icon, until the icon and name of the floppy disk are highlighted.

4. Release the mouse button.

   The Finder places a copy of the Desktop Image file onto the floppy disk. You briefly see a dialog box that tells you the Finder is copying the file.

You can open the floppy disk (by double-clicking it) to see that the Desktop Image file appears on that disk.

The procedure is exactly the same for copying a file from a floppy disk to a hard disk, but in reverse. Insert and open the floppy disk, drag the file you want to copy from the floppy disk to the hard disk icon, and release the mouse button. The Finder copies the file onto the hard disk.

In this section, you learned how to copy a folder or file to a different disk. Occasionally, however, you need to copy folders or files to a different location on the same disk. You can make another copy of a file or a folder by using the Duplicate command.

Using the Duplicate Command to Copy

You can use the Duplicate command to copy a file or folder to any location on the hard disk or to the Desktop. For example, to copy the Desktop Image file to the Practice Items folder by using the Duplicate command, follow these steps:

1. Make sure that the hard disk window is open.
2. Select the Desktop Image file (by clicking on it).
3. Open the **File** menu and choose the **Duplicate** command (or press ⌘+**D**, the keyboard shortcut).

   The Finder copies the file and places another version of it, named Desktop Image copy, partly on top of the original (see Figure 8.9).

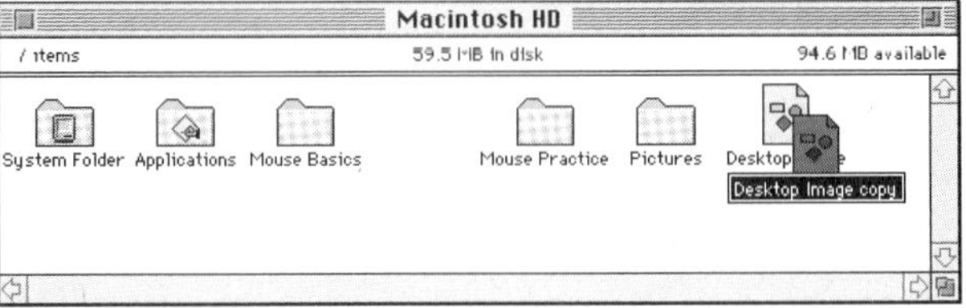

Figure 8.9. The results of the Duplicate command.

4. Drag the copy onto the folder named Practice Items (which you created earlier in this chapter), until the Practice Items name and icon are highlighted.

5. Release the mouse button.

   When you release the mouse button, the original Desktop Image file still appears in the hard disk window. When you open the Practice Items folder, you see the Desktop Image copy file.

MAC NOTE

You also can use the Option key to copy folders or files to a different location on the same disk. Usually, if you drag a file onto a folder, you are moving the file to that folder—the file is no longer where it was when you began. If you want to place only a copy of the file in the folder, hold down the Option key as you drag the file. This procedure places a duplicate of the file in the folder, rather than moving the original file.

Copying Entire Disks

Although I don't think that you, as an occasional user of a Mac, are going to have much need to copy the contents of one floppy disk to another floppy disk, my editors thought it would be interesting for you to know how, just in case. So, here goes—the Mac equivalent of the DISKCOPY command in DOS.

Just like on a PC, you have a source disk and a target disk for this operation. The source disk contains the information you want to copy; the target disk is the disk onto which you want to copy the information.

To copy information from a source floppy disk to a target floppy disk, follow these steps:

1. Place the source disk in the floppy disk drive.

   The Finder reads the directory of the floppy disk and places an icon that represents the source disk on the Desktop.

2. After the icon appears, open the **Special** menu and choose the **Eject Disk** command (or press ⌘+**E**).

   The Finder ejects the source disk from the disk drive, but the source disk's icon remains on the Desktop as a broken outline (see Figure 8.10)

Figure 8.10. The image that remains on the Desktop when you choose Eject Disk from the Special menu.

3. Place the target disk in the floppy disk drive.

   The Finder reads the directory of the target floppy disk and places an icon that represents the target disk on the Desktop.

4. Drag the source disk icon on top of the target disk icon until the icon and title of the target disk are highlighted, and then release the mouse button.

   The Finder displays a dialog box that asks whether you really want to copy the information on the source disk onto the target disk.

5. Click the OK button.

After you click the OK button, the Finder starts copying. You will be prompted several times to swap the source and target disks before the copying process is complete (just like on a PC).

Using the Trash

In previous sections, you learned how to move and copy files, and, in the process, you may have a few files on the hard disk that you really don't want. On a Mac, you use the Trash to erase files and folders (see Figure 8.11).

Figure 8.11.
The Trash icon.

To erase a file or folder, you drag it to the Trash. The Trash acts as a temporary holding tank for files and folders you intend to erase. But you can recover those items (by dragging them back out of the Trash) right up until the time you empty the Trash.

If you worked through all the examples in this chapter, you have a copy of the Desktop Image file in the hard disk window and in the Practice Items folder (inside the hard disk window).

To erase the Desktop Image file in the hard disk window, drag it on top of the Trash until the Trash icon is highlighted. Then, release the mouse button. As you can see from Figure 8.12, the Trash icon appears to bulge (as if it has so much garbage in it that it might explode—but don't worry, it won't).

Figure 8.12.
The Trash when it contains items.

To erase any other Desktop Image files (including the one named Desktop Image copy in the Practice Items folder), open each window where the file appears and drag the file to the Trash.

To see the contents of the Trash, open the Trash by double-clicking it. To remove an item from the Trash, drag it back out of the Trash to any location you desire. To empty the Trash (which permanently erases the items in the Trash), open the Special menu and choose the Empty Trash command. The Finder reports the number of items you are about to erase and the amount of space they occupy and asks whether you really want to remove them. Click the Continue button to erase the items.

Getting Help

You can use Balloon Help to remind you of things as you work. When you turn Balloon Help on and move the mouse pointer, a balloon (like the kind you see in the comics) displays information about the item to which the mouse pointer is pointing. For example, when Balloon Help is active and you point to a floppy disk icon, a balloon like the one in Figure 8.13 appears.

To activate Balloon Help, open the Help menu and choose the Show Balloons command. The Help menu appears toward the right end of the menu bar and looks like a balloon with a question mark inside it. As you move the mouse pointer, you will see balloons containing help information.

Figure 8.13. Balloon Help for a floppy disk.

To deactivate Balloon Help, open the Help menu and choose the Hide Balloons command.

The Help menu for the Finder also contains the Finder Shortcuts command. You can use this command to review shortcuts and tricks that can streamline working with the Finder. These shortcuts don't let you do anything you can't do by using standard methods, but they can speed up your work a bit.

Chapter Summary

In this chapter, you learned to work with the Desktop of the Mac. You reviewed how to identify, select, and open disks, folders, and files. You learned how to initialize (format) a floppy disk and how to eject the floppy disk from the floppy disk drive. You learned how to create, rename, and move folders and files. You learned how to copy files to a different disk (either from a floppy disk to the hard disk or from the hard disk to a floppy disk). You also learned how to copy the entire contents of one floppy disk to another floppy disk (the equivalent of the DOS DISKCOPY command). You learned how to use the Trash to erase files, and you learned how to use Balloon Help.

You learned that similar concepts exist in both the PC world and the Mac world. For example, renaming is renaming, moving is moving, and copying is copying on both computers. You learned, however, that the ways you accomplish these tasks on the Mac are very different from the ways you perform the same tasks on a PC.

In the next chapter, you learn how to transfer and translate files between the PC and the Mac. As you know, Chapters 3 through 6 in *The PC User's Mac* focus on specific software packages. If you skipped ahead to read this chapter, you might want to go back and read the chapters about the Mac software programs you want to use. (Or perhaps, read Chapter 7, which tells you about database programs you may want to avoid.)

Transferring and Translating Files between a PC and a Mac

If you live or work in an environment where there are both PCs and Macs, someone invariably will need to move a file between the two platforms. The good news is that you can do this. And, as time has gone on, this task has become easier to accomplish. In this chapter, you will learn the basics of the simplest approach to transferring and translating files between a PC and a Mac—you will learn how to use a floppy disk and a disk (or file) translation utility to move a file between the computers and how to use application software to open the file on the "other" computer.

Remember, no matter what you do while working in this chapter, you can't "break" anything unless you start deleting files. Don't be afraid to experiment if you see something unfamiliar. (My technical editor said you would need a reminder here.)

The techniques described in this chapter work for the PC user who needs to move a file to a Mac or for the Mac user who needs to move a file to a PC. Therefore, you will find that this chapter is the same in both parts of this book. If you have read this chapter while reading *The Mac User's PC*, you don't need to read it again while reading *The PC User's Mac* (unless you really liked it).

Using Floppy Disks To Transfer Files

You may think that the most logical way to move a file from one computer to the other is to copy the file onto a floppy disk. But because both hard and floppy disks for a PC are prepared (or "formatted" or "initialized") differently than disks for a Mac, neither computer can directly read disks prepared by the other computer.

Because people sometimes need to use files on both PCs and Macs, software manufacturers have developed disk (or file) translation products that enable one computer to read disks prepared by the other computer. For both the PC and the Mac, a variety of such products exist. Apple ships PC Exchange with System 7 on Performas and Apple File Exchange with System 6.0.x and System 7 on non-Performa Macs. (PC Exchange is also available separately.) In the next two sections, you learn about using these products. Then, you will find some information on products available from other vendors.

It's important to understand that, whether you want to take a PC file to a Mac or a Mac file to a PC, you need to place the file on a DOS-formatted floppy disk. You can use a PC, PC Exchange, or Apple File Exchange to create a DOS-formatted disk.

Using PC Exchange

For users of System 7 who have PC Exchange available and enabled, transferring files is disgustingly easy. As long as PC Exchange is running, you can simply insert a DOS-formatted disk into the floppy disk drive on the Mac, and the Mac will recognize the disk as a DOS-formatted disk. You then can open the disk just like you would open any other disk and copy files to or from that disk. The Mac may not be able to read the files on the disk directly, though; you may need a file translation utility for that process. Reading the file is discussed at the end of this section. First, you learn to determine whether you have System 7 and PC Exchange. Then, you learn how to use PC Exchange to format (initialize) a DOS disk or a Mac disk. After you have a DOS-formatted disk (which the Mac will recognize), you can copy a Mac file onto the disk and then move the disk back to a PC. Or, you can copy a PC file onto the disk and then move the disk to the Mac.

Checking for System 7

To check whether you're using System 7, switch to the Finder, open the Apple menu, and choose About This Macintosh. The window you see identifies the version of the System software with which you are working. (You can close the About This Macintosh window after you identify the version of the System software.)

Checking for PC Exchange

To check for PC Exchange the easy way, insert any DOS-formatted disk into the floppy disk drive of the Mac. If you see a disk icon that resembles the icon shown in Figure 9.1 on the Macintosh desktop, PC Exchange is installed and active. Notice that the icon is different from the typical icon you see for a floppy disk on a Mac, because it contains the letters PC in the center of the icon. If you see the dialog box shown in Figure 9.2, PC Exchange is not installed and active. (This dialog box appears when you insert an unformatted disk or a disk that the Mac cannot recognize.)

Figure 9.1. The icon for a DOS-formatted floppy disk when PC Exchange is active.

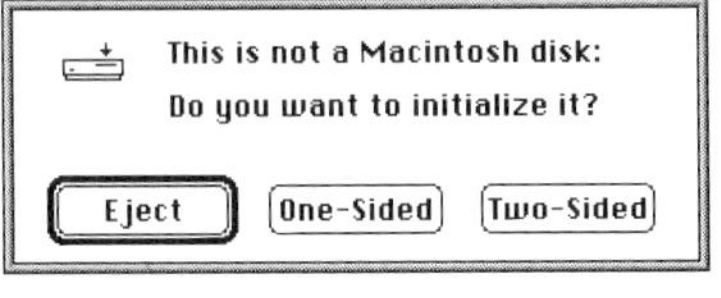

Figure 9.2. The dialog box you see when PC Exchange is not active.

If PC Exchange is not available, you can use Apple File Exchange or a third-party product to transfer files.

Formatting a Disk

If you determine that PC Exchange is installed and active, you can use PC Exchange to create a DOS-formatted disk or a Mac-formatted disk. Follow these steps:

1. Insert a disk you want to format (initialize) into the floppy disk drive on the Mac.

   If you insert a disk that has never been formatted, the Finder displays a dialog box similar to the dialog box in Figure 9.3.

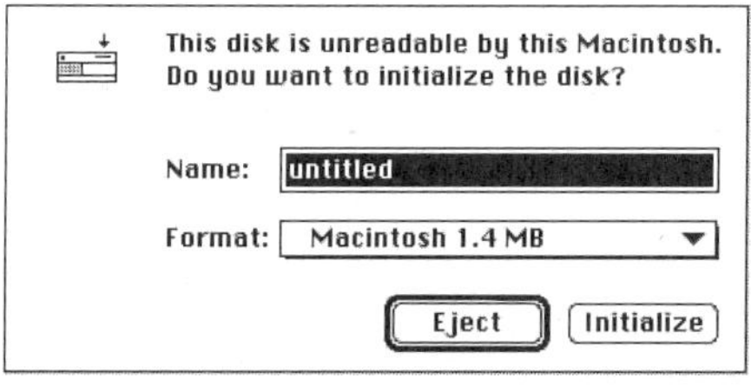

Figure 9.3. The dialog box you see when you insert a blank disk.

   If you inserted a previously formatted disk, open the **Special** menu and choose the **Erase Disk** command. The Finder displays a dialog box similar to the one in Figure 9.4.

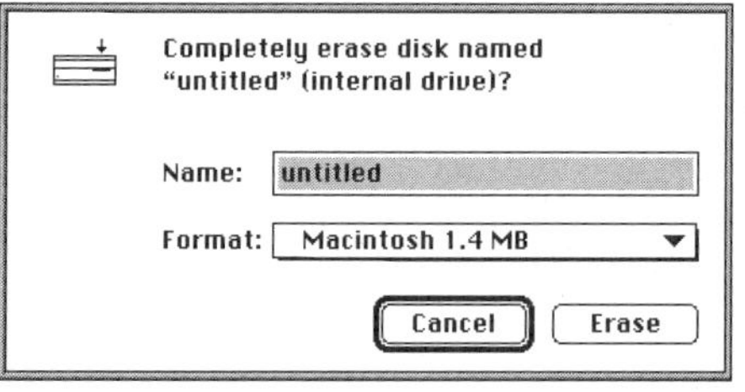

Figure 9.4. The dialog box you see when you choose the Erase Disk command from the Special menu.

2. In the Name text box, type a name you want to assign to the disk. If you plan to use this disk on a PC, use no more than 11 contiguous characters (no spaces).

3. Open the Format pop-up menu to select the format you want to assign to the disk. You can choose from Macintosh, ProDOS, or DOS. If you inserted a high-density disk, each of the choices also shows a related density of 1.4 MB. If you inserted a double-density disk, you see related density choices of 720K for DOS and of 800K for Macintosh and ProDOS.

4. To format the disk to work on a PC, choose the DOS format.

5. If you inserted a disk that has never been formatted, choose the Initialize button. If you inserted a previously formatted disk, choose the Erase button.

   The Finder formats (or initializes) the disk.

After you have used PC Exchange to format the disk so that it can be read by either the Mac or a PC, you can copy onto the floppy disk the file(s) you want to move.

But simply creating a disk that either computer can read still doesn't mean that you will be able to open a file and use it on either computer. You still need to translate the file. The solution to this problem appears in two forms:

- Software manufacturers have developed file translation utilities as well as disk translation utilities.
- Software manufacturers of products for both the Mac and the PC often build into their products the capability to read files created on the "other" computer.

For the most part today, if you have a disk translation utility (such as PC Exchange) and the same software on both the Mac and the PC, you can easily use a floppy disk to move a file between the computers. If you don't have the same software on both computers, you may be able to use a similar software program to translate the file you transferred. For example, Microsoft Word for Windows

can open not only Word for Windows documents, but also Word for DOS, Word for the Mac, WordPerfect for DOS, and WordPerfect for Windows documents (among others). So, even if you need to create a word processing document on one computer in a certain word processing program, you may be able to open the document in a different word processing program on the other computer.

In the last part of this chapter, you find sections that describe the translation process for each software program discussed in the earlier chapters of this book. If you have used PC Exchange to transfer the file to the other computer, you should refer to the section in this chapter that describes the translation process for the software in which you created the file.

Using Apple File Exchange

If you use System 6.0.x, or don't have PC Exchange, you can use Apple File Exchange to transfer files between a Mac and a PC. In addition, if you need to create a file on one computer and then transfer it to the other computer where no comparable software exists, Apple File Exchange can act as a file translator.

In this section, you learn how to start Apple File Exchange, how to use Apple File Exchange to format a DOS disk, and how to use Apple File Exchange to transfer and translate a file.

Starting Apple File Exchange

Unlike PC Exchange, Apple File Exchange is not typically running when you start the computer. In addition, unlike other programs on the Mac, you must start Apple File Exchange *before* you try to copy or translate a file; otherwise, the Mac assumes it is reading an unformatted disk and displays the dialog box that asks whether you want to initialize the disk.

Apple File Exchange is stored in the System Folder. To start Apple File Exchange, follow these steps:

1. On the Mac, make sure that the hard disk is open.

2. Open the System Folder.

3. Open the Apple File Exchange folder. If you don't see the Apple File Exchange folder, use the Find command to search for Apple File Exchange (System 6 users can use the Find File command).

4. Double-click on the Apple File Exchange application icon.

   The Apple File Exchange dialog box appears (see Figure 9.5).

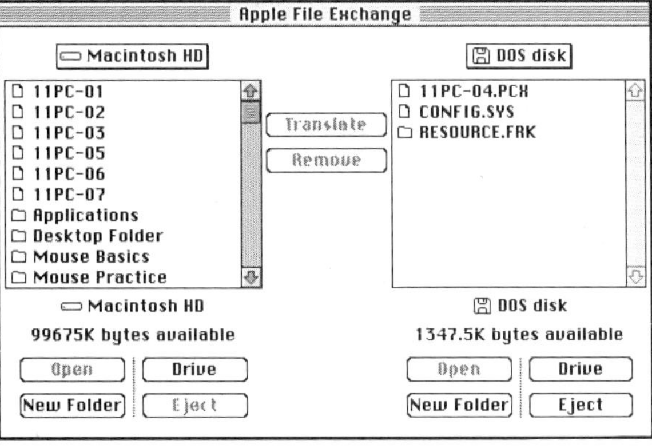

Figure 9.5. The Apple File Exchange dialog box.

Formatting a Disk

On occasion, you may need to format a DOS disk on a Mac so that you can transfer information created on the Mac to the PC. For example, if you are a Mac user and you need to supply a PC user with a file, you need to place your file on a DOS-formatted disk. Or, if you have a Mac at home and a PC at work, and you do some work at home that you want to bring to the office, you must place the file on a DOS-formatted disk. You can use Apple File Exchange to format a DOS disk (so that you can transfer a file from the Mac to a PC). Follow these steps:

1. Start Apple File Exchange as described in the preceding section.

2. Insert the disk you want to format into the floppy disk drive.

3. Choose the **Erase Disk** command from the **File** menu.

   A dialog box appears, asking whether you want to erase the information on the floppy disk (see Figure 9.6).

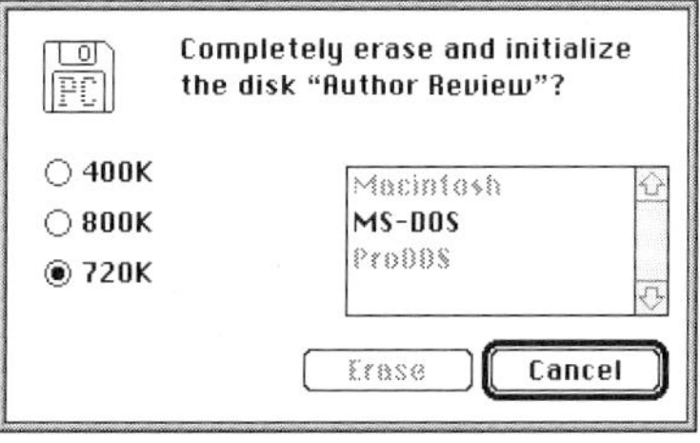

Figure 9.6. The Apple File Exchange Erase Disk dialog box.

4. Choose a radio button on the left side of the dialog box to identify the density of the floppy disk. Use the scrolling list on the right side of the dialog box to choose the format you want Apple File Exchange to use on the floppy disk. If you inserted a high-density disk, you see only 1440K on the left side of the dialog box, but you can choose Macintosh or MS-DOS from the scrolling list on the right. If you inserted a double-density disk, the choices are 400K, 800K, or 720K. If you choose either 400K or 800K, you can choose Macintosh or ProDOS from the scrolling list on the right. If you choose 720K, you can choose only DOS from the scrolling list.

5. Click the Erase button.

   Apple File Exchange formats (initializes) the disk in the format you specified. When the process is complete, Apple File Exchange asks you to supply a name for the disk. If you plan to use the disk on a PC, limit the disk name to 11 contiguous characters (no spaces). Then, click OK.

MAC NOTE

When you first place a DOS-formatted disk in the floppy disk drive, Apple File Exchange assumes you want to format the disk as an MS-DOS disk. If you, for some reason, want to format the disk as a Mac disk, choose the 800K option on the left side of the dialog box. On the right side of the dialog box, MS-DOS no longer is available, but Macintosh is.

Transferring and Translating a File

To use Apple File Exchange to transfer and translate a file between a Mac and a PC, follow these steps:

1. If you want to transfer a file from a PC to the Mac, save the PC file to a 3 1/2-inch DOS-formatted floppy disk. For more information on saving a file, see the section on saving in the chapter about the software program you are using.

2. On the Mac, start Apple File Exchange as described earlier in the chapter.

3. If you want to transfer a file from a PC to the Mac, insert the DOS-formatted floppy disk containing the file you want to transfer into the Mac's floppy disk drive. If you want to transfer a file from the Mac to a PC, format a DOS disk as described earlier in the chapter.

   On the right side of the dialog box, Apple File Exchange displays the names of the files (if any) on the floppy disk (see Figure 9.7).

4. On the left side of the window, if necessary, click on the Drive button until you display the drive on which you want to store the transferred file or from which you want to transfer a file.

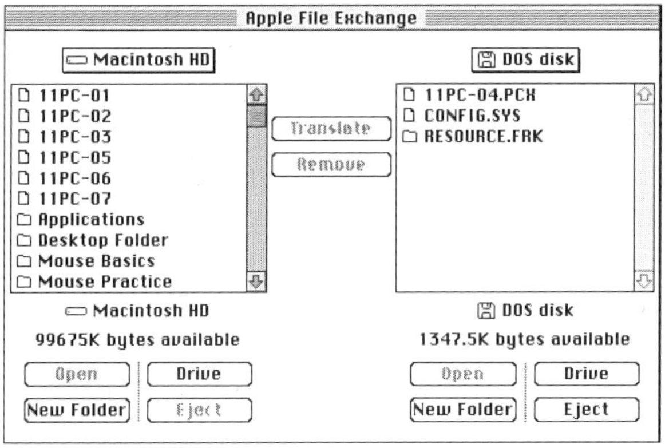

Apple File Exchange

Macintosh HD | DOS disk

11PC-01
11PC-02
11PC-03
11PC-05
11PC-06
11PC-07
Applications
Desktop Folder
Mouse Basics
Mouse Practice

Translate
Remove

11PC-04.PCH
CONFIG.SYS
RESOURCE.FRK

Macintosh HD
99675K bytes available
Open | Drive
New Folder | Eject

DOS disk
1347.5K bytes available
Open | Drive
New Folder | Eject

Figure 9.7. The Apple File Exchange dialog box.

MAC NOTE

If you happen to switch floppy disks during this process, you may see the sides of the window switch. You can still transfer files; just make sure that you are aware of the drive *from* which you are translating and the drive *to* which you are translating.

5. On the left side of the window, open the folder into which you want to place the translated file or from which you want to transfer a file.

6. On the appropriate side of the window, highlight the name(s) of the file(s) you want to translate. You can Shift-click or Command-click to select more than one file.

7. Use the menus to make choices about the type of translation (if any) you want to perform. If you want to transfer a file from a PC to the Mac, open the **MS-DOS to Mac** menu and make sure that you see a diamond in front of the **Default format** command. If you see a check mark in front of any other command, remove the check mark by choosing the command again.

8. When you finish setting up the translation, choose the Translate button.

Apple File Exchange shows the progress of the translation. When the translation is complete, the dialog box reappears.

9. On the right side of the window, choose the Eject button to remove the DOS-formatted floppy disk from the floppy disk drive.

10. Open the **File** menu and choose the **Quit** command to close Apple File Exchange.

Simply transferring a file doesn't mean that you will be able to open the file and use it on the other computer. You may still need to translate the file. The solution to this problem appears in two forms:

- Software manufacturers have developed file translation utilities as well as disk translation utilities.

- Software manufacturers of products for both the Mac and the PC often build into their products the capability to read files created on the "other" computer.

For the most part today, if you use Apple File Exchange to transfer a file between the Mac and the PC, you can use the same or similar software to translate the file you transferred. For example, Microsoft Word for Windows can open not only Word for Windows documents, but also Word for DOS, Word for the Mac, WordPerfect for DOS, and WordPerfect for Windows documents (among others). So, even if you need to create a word processing document on one computer in a certain word processing program, you may be able to open the document in a different word processing program on the other computer.

In the last part of this chapter, you find sections that describe the translation process for each software program discussed in the earlier chapters of this book. If you have used Apple File Exchange to transfer the file to the other computer, you should refer to the section in this chapter that describes the translation process for the software in which you created the file.

Exploring Third-Party Translation Utilities

In addition to the two products shipped by Apple, some third-party vendors have developed disk translation utilities. You may find Access PC 2.0 on the Mac. Access PC 2.0 supports both 5 1/4- and 3 1/2-inch disks, in case you don't have a 3 1/2-inch disk drive on both computers (not the likely case, because Apple has been shipping the 3 1/2-inch SuperDrive as an internal drive on most Macs since 1989). Or, you may find DOS Mounter 3.0 on the Mac.

On the PC, you may find that hardware has been installed to let the PC "talk" to the Mac. Matchmaker, which consists of software and an internal card, enables you to connect an external Mac floppy disk drive to a PC. The PC recognizes the Mac floppy disk drive as the M drive; you basically add an "M" to the beginning of the various DOS commands you want to perform on the disk in the external Mac floppy disk drive. Or, on the PC, you may find the Deluxe Option Board and its Macintosh Control Program, which temporarily enables a PC drive to read a Mac disk.

Or, on the PC, you may find Mac-in-DOS or Mac-to-DOS, which reads high-density 3 1/2-inch floppy disks. Because Mac-to-DOS also supports Mac SyQuest, Bernoulli, and erasable optical cartridges, Mac-to-DOS is most useful for transferring large files that won't fit on floppy disks.

To use most of these products, you must follow the manufacturer's instructions.

MacLinkPlus/PC is a third-party vendor product that translates files created in one format on one platform to a different format on the other platform. For example, you can use MacLinkPlus/PC to translate a PCX file created on a PC to a PICT file readable on a Mac. MacLinkPlus/PC also includes DOS Mounter, the disk translation utility mentioned previously.

Using Applications To Translate Files

In most cases, when you are transferring files between platforms, you are transferring the files between the same application on both platforms. For example, most of the time, if you need to transfer a WordPerfect for DOS file to the Mac, you want to use it in WordPerfect for the Mac.

There's good news. Most of the software vendors who manufacture products for both platforms have built into the products the capability to read files from the other platform. For this reason, you often don't need a file translation utility; you simply need a disk translation utility that lets the Mac work with a DOS-formatted disk. Because I have already discussed those utilities in the previous sections, in this section I will focus on what you do inside each software program to translate a file to the format of the corresponding program on the other platform.

There's more good news. It's usually very easy to move between platforms. Follow these two basic rules when transferring files:

- Regardless of the platform you are transferring from, start with a DOS-formatted disk. You can format the disk on the PC or on the Mac (by using a disk translation utility such as PC Exchange or Apple File Exchange to create a DOS-formatted disk).

- If you are using Apple File Exchange as your disk translation utility, you must translate the PC-based files and store them on your hard disk (in the folder of your choice) before you try to open the files in Mac programs.

Translating a WordPerfect for DOS File

Translating a WordPerfect for DOS file to WordPerfect for the Mac is very easy and works well. Follow these steps:

1. On the PC, save the open file by pressing **F7** or **F10**, making sure that you place the file on a DOS-formatted floppy disk. For more information on saving in WordPerfect for DOS, see Chapter 3 of *The Mac User's PC.*

2. On the Mac, make sure that the disk translation utility is active, and insert the DOS disk into the floppy disk drive. If you're using Apple File Exchange, make sure that you "translate" the file you want to open in WordPerfect for the Mac, and place the file in a folder of your choice on the Mac hard disk. Then, quit Apple File Exchange.

3. Start WordPerfect for the Mac by using one of the techniques described in Chapter 2 of *The PC User's Mac.*

4. Choose the **Open** command from the **File** menu. For more information on opening in WordPerfect for the Mac, see Chapter 3 of *The PC User's Mac.*

   WordPerfect for the Mac displays the Open dialog box in Figure 9.8.

Figure 9.8. The Open dialog box.

5. In the Show pop-up menu, choose All to see all files. (WordPerfect for the Mac defaults to showing only WordPerfect for the Mac files.)

6. Choose the Desktop button on the right side of the dialog box.

7. Navigate to the WordPerfect for DOS file. If you are using Apple File Exchange, you already copied the WordPerfect for DOS file to someplace on the hard disk. If you are using PC Exchange, the WordPerfect for DOS file may be on the floppy disk.

8. In the scrolling list, highlight the WordPerfect for DOS file you want to open. Then choose the Open button on the right side of the dialog box.

   WordPerfect for the Mac translates and opens the WordPerfect for DOS document.

MAC TIP

WordPerfect for the Mac translates the file using the default font in WordPerfect for the Mac, *not* the font you were using in WordPerfect for DOS. You may want to consider changing the font in WordPerfect for DOS to your WordPerfect for the Mac default font before you create the file, or you may want to change fonts in WordPerfect for the Mac after you translate the file.

Translating a WordPerfect for Windows File

Translating a WordPerfect for Windows file to WordPerfect for the Mac is very easy and works well. Follow these steps:

1. On the PC, save the file by using the Save **A**s command on the **F**ile menu, making sure that you place the file on a DOS-formatted floppy disk. For more information on saving in WordPerfect for Windows, see Chapter 4 of *The Mac User's PC.*

2. On the Mac, make sure that the disk translation utility is active, and insert the DOS disk into the floppy disk drive. If you're using Apple File Exchange, make sure that you "translate" the file you want to open in WordPerfect for the Mac, and place the file in a folder of your choice on the Mac hard disk. Then, quit Apple File Exchange.

3. Start WordPerfect for the Mac by using one of the techniques described in Chapter 2 of *The PC User's Mac.*

4. Choose the **Open** command from the **File** menu. For more information on saving in WordPerfect for the Mac, see Chapter 3 of *The PC User's Mac.*

   WordPerfect for the Mac displays the Open dialog box in Figure 9.9.

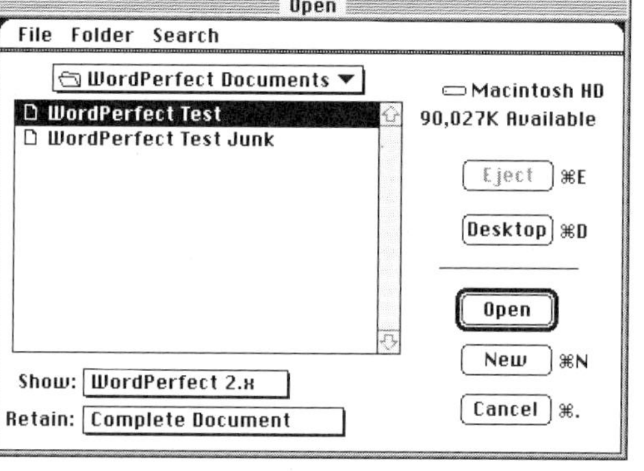

Figure 9.9. The Open dialog box.

5. In the Show pop-up menu, choose All to see all files. (WordPerfect for the Mac defaults to showing only WordPerfect for the Mac files.)

6. Choose the Desktop button on the right side of the dialog box.

7. Navigate to the DOS file. If you are using Apple File Exchange, the DOS file is somewhere on the hard disk. If you are using PC Exchange, the DOS file may be on the floppy disk.

8. In the scrolling list, highlight the WordPerfect for Windows file you want to open. Then, choose the Open button on the right side of the dialog box.

   WordPerfect for the Mac translates and opens the WordPerfect for Windows document.

MAC TIP

WordPerfect for the Mac translates the file using the default font in WordPerfect for the Mac, *not* the font you were using in WordPerfect for Windows. You may want to consider changing the font in WordPerfect for Windows to your WordPerfect for the Mac default font before you create the file, or you may want to change fonts in WordPerfect for the Mac after you translate the file.

Translating a WordPerfect for the Mac File

Translating a WordPerfect for the Mac file to WordPerfect for DOS or WordPerfect for Windows is only a little more complicated than saving a file in WordPerfect for the Mac. Follow these steps:

1. In WordPerfect for the Mac, use the **Open** command on the **File** menu to open the file you want to move to WordPerfect for DOS or WordPerfect for Windows. For more information on opening in WordPerfect for the Mac, see Chapter 3 of *The PC User's Mac.*

2. Open the **File** menu and choose the **Save As** command. For more information on saving in WordPerfect for the Mac, see Chapter 3 of *The PC User's Mac.*

   The Save As dialog box in Figure 9.10 appears.

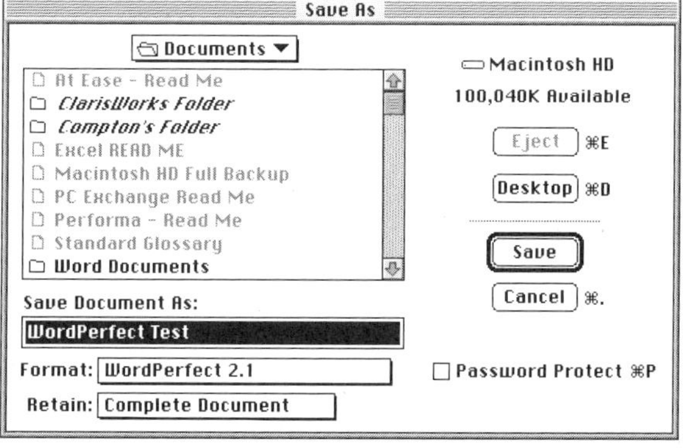

Figure 9.10.
The Save As dialog box.

3. From the Format pop-up menu, choose the appropriate version of WordPerfect for DOS (Version 4.2, Version 5.0, or Version 5.1) or WordPerfect for Windows (Version 5.1).

4. Click in the Save Document As text box and type a name for the file. Be sure to follow DOS naming conventions—eight characters for the first name, a period, then three characters for the extension. (For more information on DOS file-naming conventions, see Chapter 12 of *The Mac User's PC*).

5. Choose the Save button.

   WordPerfect for the Mac saves the file on the hard disk in the format you specified.

6. Make sure that the disk translation utility is active, and insert (and, if necessary, format) a DOS disk into the floppy disk drive. See the first part of this chapter for more information on disk translation utilities and formatting DOS disks.

7. If PC Exchange is active, copy (by dragging) the file from the hard disk to the floppy disk. If Apple File Exchange is active, navigate to the file you want to move to the PC and "translate" it to the DOS-formatted floppy disk.

8. Eject the floppy disk from the floppy disk drive on the Mac and place the disk into the floppy disk drive on the PC.

9. Using one of the methods described in Chapter 2 of *The Mac User's PC*, start WordPerfect for DOS or WordPerfect for Windows.

10. Retrieve or open the file as you usually would in WordPerfect for DOS (press **F10**) or WordPerfect for Windows (use the **Open** command on the **File** menu). For more information on retrieving or opening in WordPerfect for DOS or Word Perfect for Windows, see Chapter 3 or 4 of *The Mac User's PC*.

Translating a Word for DOS File

Translating a Word for DOS file to Word for the Mac is fairly easy. Follow these steps:

1. On the PC, save the file by using the Save **A**s command on the **F**ile menu, making sure that you place the file on a DOS-formatted 3 1/2-inch floppy disk. For more information on saving in Word for DOS, see Chapter 5 of *The Mac User's PC*.

2. On the Mac, make sure that the disk translation utility is active, and insert the DOS disk into the floppy disk drive. If you're using Apple File Exchange, make sure that you "translate" the file you want to open in Word for the Mac, and place the file in a folder of your choice on the Mac hard disk. Then, quit Apple File Exchange.

3. Start Word for the Mac by using one of the techniques described in Chapter 2 of *The PC User's Mac.*

4. Choose the **Open** command from the **File** menu. For more information on opening in Word for the Mac, see Chapter 4 of *The PC User's Mac.*

   Word displays the Open dialog box in Figure 9.11.

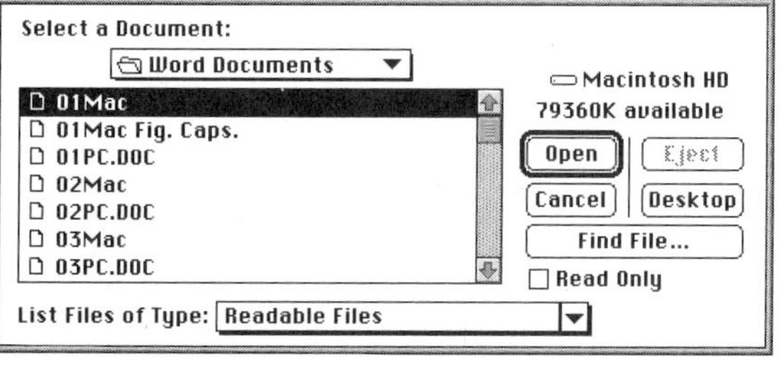

Figure 9.11. The Open dialog box.

5. Choose the Desktop button on the right side of the dialog box.

6. Navigate to the DOS file. If you are using Apple File Exchange, you already copied the DOS file to someplace on the hard disk. If you are using PC Exchange, the DOS file may still be on the floppy disk.

7. In the scrolling list, highlight the Word for DOS file you want to open. Then choose the Open button on the right side of the dialog box.

   Unless you copied NORMAL.STY along with the document onto the floppy disk (and, unless NORMAL.STY has been modified, you *won't* be able to find it on the PC to copy it to the floppy disk), a message appears at the bottom of the dialog box that asks you to find and attach the style sheet NORMAL.STY. If you didn't copy NORMAL.STY, choose the Ignore button.

   Word for the Mac translates and opens the Word for DOS document.

Translating a Word for Windows File

Translating a applicationsWord for Windows file to Word for the Mac is only a little more complicated than saving a file in Word for Windows. Follow these steps:

MAC NOTE

You may have some trouble (for example, Type 1 errors) transferring a Word for Windows file to Word for the Mac without first converting the file to Word for the Mac format. In these steps, therefore, you save the Word for Windows file as a Word for the Mac file before you try to open the file in Word for the Mac.

1. On the PC, in Word for Windows, open the file you want to move to Word for the Mac. For more information on opening in Word for Windows, see Chapter 6 of *The Mac User's PC.*

2. Open the **F**ile menu and choose the Save **A**s command. For more information on saving in Word for Windows, see Chapter 6 of *The Mac User's PC.*

   The Save As dialog box in Figure 9.12 appears.

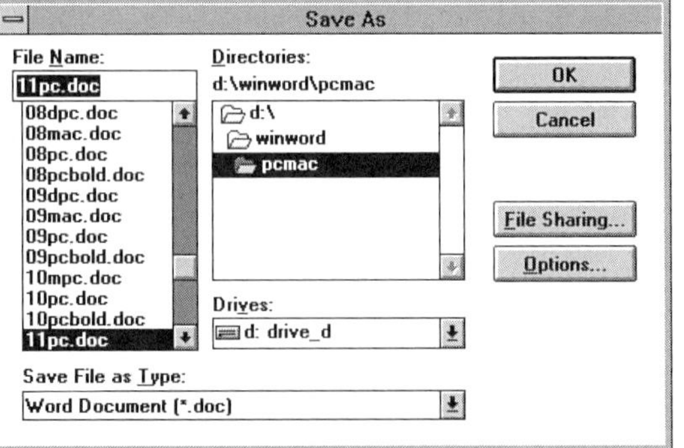

Figure 9.12.

The Save As dialog box.

3. Insert the 3 1/2-inch DOS-formatted disk on which you want to store the translated file into the floppy disk drive.

4. Open the Dri**v**es drop-down list box and choose the floppy disk drive.

5. Open the Save File as **T**ype drop-down list box and choose Word for the Macintosh (4.0 or 5.0, depending on the version you use on the Mac).

6. Choose OK.

   Word for Windows saves the file in Word for the Mac format.

7. On the Mac, make sure that the disk translation utility is active, and insert the DOS disk into the floppy disk drive. If you're using Apple File Exchange, make sure that you "translate" the file you want to open in Word for the Mac, and place the file in a folder of your choice on the Mac hard disk. Then, quit Apple File Exchange.

8. Start Word for the Mac by using one of the techniques described in Chapter 2 of *The PC User's Mac.*

9. Choose the **Open** command from the **File** menu. For more information on opening in Word for the Mac, see Chapter 4 of *The PC User's Mac.*

   Word displays the Open dialog box in Figure 9.13.

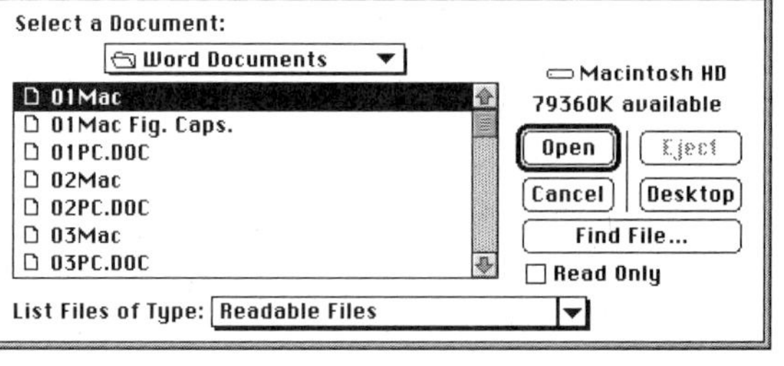

Figure 9.13.
The Open dialog box.

10. Choose the Desktop button on the right side of the dialog box.

11. Navigate to the DOS file. If you are using Apple File Exchange, you already copied the DOS file to someplace on the hard disk. If you are using PC Exchange, the DOS file may still be on the floppy disk.

12. In the scrolling list, highlight the DOS file you want to open on the left side of the dialog box. Then, choose the Open button on the right side of the dialog box.

    Word for the Mac translates and opens the Word for Windows document.

Translating a Word for the Mac File

Translating a Word for the Mac file to Word for DOS or Word for Windows is only a little more complicated than saving a file in Word for the Mac. Follow these steps:

1. In Word for the Mac, use the **Open** command on the **File** menu to open the file you want to move to Word for DOS or Word for Windows. For more information on opening in Word for the Mac, see Chapter 4 of *The PC User's Mac.*

2. Open the **File** menu and choose the **Save As** command. For more information on saving in Word for the Mac, see Chapter 4 of *The PC User's Mac.*

    The Save As dialog box in Figure 9.14 appears.

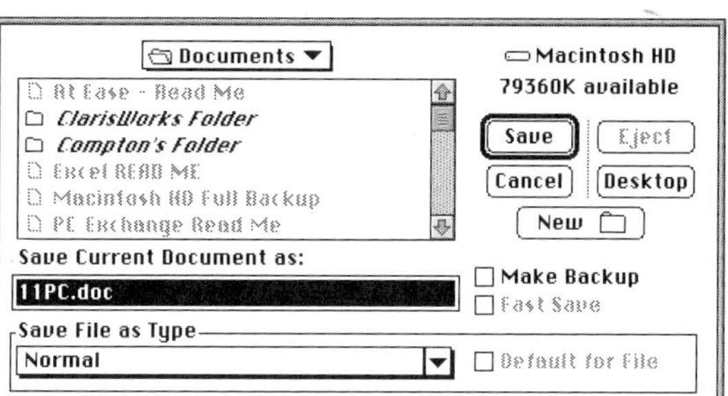

Figure 9.14.

The Save As dialog box.

3. Open the Save File as Type pop-up menu and choose the appropriate version of Word for Windows (Version 1.0 or Version 2.0) or Word for DOS.

4. Click in the Save Current Document As text box and type a name for your file. Be sure to follow the DOS naming conventions—eight characters for the first name, a period, then three characters for the extension. (For more information on DOS file-naming conventions, see Chapter 12 of *The Mac User's PC*.)

MAC NOTE

When you translate a file to Word for DOS format, you see a dialog box asking you to attach a style sheet to the document. Because you probably don't have a separate style sheet on the Mac, you can't attach one, so choose No. When you open the document in Word for DOS, you may need to do some reformatting.

5. Choose the Save button.

Word for the Mac saves the file to the hard disk in the format you specified.

6. Make sure that the disk translation utility is active, and insert (and, if necessary, format) a DOS disk into the floppy disk drive. See the first part of this chapter for more information on disk translation utilities and formatting DOS disks.

7. If PC Exchange is active, copy (by dragging) the file from the hard disk to the floppy disk. If Apple File Exchange is active, navigate to the file you want to move to the PC and "translate" it to the DOS-formatted floppy disk.

8. Eject the floppy disk from the floppy disk drive on the Mac and place the disk into the floppy disk drive on the PC.

9. Using one of the techniques described in Chapter 2 of *The Mac User's PC,* start Word for DOS or Word for Windows.

10. Use the **O**pen command on the **F**ile menu to open the document in Word for DOS or Word for Windows. For more information on opening in Word for DOS or Word Perfect for Windows, see Chapter 5 or 6 of *The Mac User's PC.*

MAC TIP

In step 5, if you are translating to Word for Windows, you can save the document as a Normal type of document, in which case Word for the Mac saves the document in Word for the Mac format. When you open the document in Word for Windows, Word for Windows recognizes the Mac format and suggests that you convert the file from Word for the Mac. Simply choose OK. The conversion to Word for Windows format works equally well whether you convert in Word for the Mac or in Word for Windows.

Translating an Excel for Windows File

Translating an Excel for Windows file to Excel for the Mac is very easy and works well because both versions of Excel use the same file format. Follow these steps:

1. On the PC, use the Save **A**s command on the **F**ile menu to save the file, making sure that you place the file on a floppy disk. For more information on saving in Excel for Windows, see Chapter 7 of *The Mac User's PC.*

2. On the Mac, make sure that the disk translation utility is active, and insert the DOS disk into the floppy disk drive. If you're using Apple File Exchange, make sure that you "translate" the file you want to open in Excel for the Mac, and place the file in a folder of your choice on the Mac hard disk. Then, quit Apple File Exchange.

3. Start Excel for the Mac by using one of the techniques described in Chapter 2 of *The PC User's Mac.*

4. Choose the **Open** command from the **File** menu. For more information on opening in Excel for the Mac, see Chapter 5 of *The PC User's Mac.*

   Excel displays the Open dialog box shown in Figure 9.15.

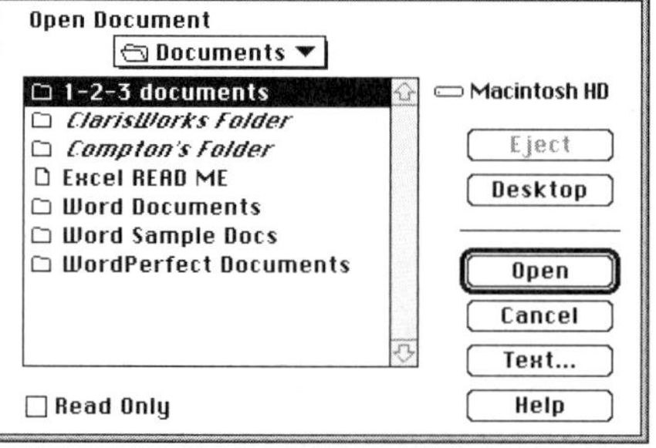

Figure 9.15. The Open dialog box.

5. Choose the Desktop button on the right side of the dialog box.

6. Navigate to the Excel for Windows file. If you are using Apple File Exchange, you already copied the Excel for Windows file to someplace on the hard disk. If you are using PC Exchange, the Excel for Windows file may still be on the floppy disk.

7. In the scrolling list, highlight the Excel for Windows file you want to open. Then, choose the Open button from the right side of the dialog box.

   Excel for the Mac opens the worksheet.

Translating an Excel for the Mac File

Translating an Excel for the Mac file to Excel for Windows is only a little more complicated than saving a file in Excel for the Mac. Follow these steps:

1. In Excel for the Mac, use the **Open** command on the **File** menu to open the file you want to move to Excel for Windows. For more information on opening in Excel for the Mac, see Chapter 5 of *The PC User's Mac.*

2. Open the **File** menu and choose the **Save As** command. For more information on saving in Excel for the Mac, see Chapter 5 of *The PC User's Mac.*

   The Save As dialog box in Figure 9.16 appears.

3. Click in the Save Worksheet As text box and type a name for your file. Be sure to follow the DOS naming conventions—eight characters for the first name, a period, then XLS as the three-character extension. (For more information on DOS file-naming conventions, see Chapter 12 of *The Mac User's PC.*)

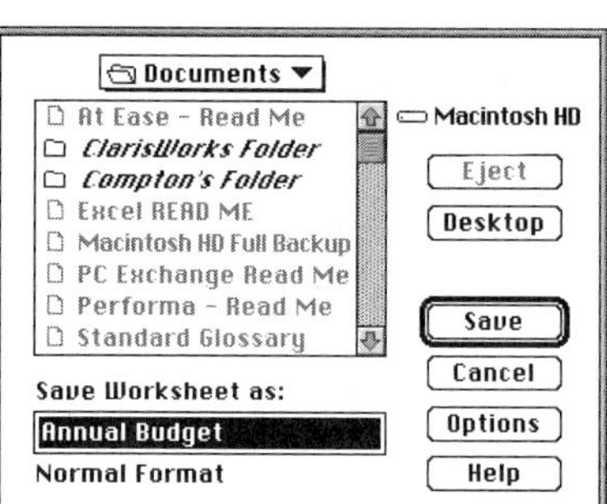

Figure 9.16.
The Save As dialog box.

4. Choose the Save button.

Excel for the Mac saves the file to the hard disk.

5. Make sure that the disk translation utility is active, and insert (and, if necessary, format) a DOS disk into the floppy disk drive. See the first part of this chapter for more information on disk translation utilities and formatting DOS disks.

6. If PC Exchange is active, copy (by dragging) the file from the hard disk to the floppy disk. If Apple File Exchange is active, navigate to the file you want to move to the PC and "translate" it to the DOS-formatted floppy disk.

7. Eject the floppy disk from the floppy disk drive on the Mac and place the disk into the floppy disk drive of the PC.

8. Using one of the methods described in Chapter 2 of *The Mac User's PC*, start Excel for Windows.

9. Use the **O**pen command on the **F**ile menu to open the file in Excel for Windows. For more information on opening in Excel for Windows, see Chapter 7 of *The Mac User's PC*.

Excel for Windows opens the worksheet.

Translating a 1-2-3 for DOS File

To translate PC versions of Lotus 1-2-3 files, you use Lotus 1-2-3 for the Mac. Translating 1-2-3 files created on a PC is not difficult. At this time, however, 1-2-3 for the Mac cannot translate all files created with all PC versions of 1-2-3. You can translate all files created by 1-2-3 Release 3.x and 1-2-3 for Windows (see the next section), but you are limited to translating only worksheet files created by Release 2.x. You cannot translate formatting files for 1-2-3 Release 2.x, which have an extension of FMT or ALL. Worksheet files have an extension of WK1.

When you use Release 2.x of 1-2-3 to create publishing and presentation information, you create that information using one of three add-in products: Allways, Impress, or Wysiwyg. The publishing and presentation information is not stored in the worksheet file with your data; it is stored in a file with an extension of ALL or FMT. The data in your worksheet is stored in a file with an extension of WK1. You can translate Release 2.x worksheet files, but you cannot translate Release 2.x publishing and presentation files.

To translate Lotus 1-2-3 Release 2.x files, follow these steps:

1. On the PC, use the **S**ave command on the **F**ile menu to save the file, making sure that you place the file on a floppy disk. For more information on saving in 1-2-3 for DOS, see Chapter 8 of *The Mac User's PC.*

2. On the Mac, make sure that the disk translation utility is active, and insert the DOS disk into the floppy disk drive. If you're using Apple File Exchange, make sure that you "translate" the file you want to open in 1-2-3 for the Mac, and place the file in a folder of your choice on the Mac hard disk. Then, quit Apple File Exchange.

3. Start 1-2-3 for the Mac by using one of the techniques described in Chapter 2 of *The PC User's Mac.*

4. Choose the **Open** command from the **File** menu. For more information on opening in 1-2-3 for the Mac, see Chapter 6 of *The PC User's Mac.*

   1-2-3 for the Mac displays the Open dialog box.

5. From the Show pop-up menu, choose All Types.

   1-2-3 displays all files in the scrolling list.

6. Choose the Desktop button on the right side of the dialog box.

7. Navigate to the 1-2-3 for DOS file. If you are using Apple File Exchange, you already copied the 1-2-3 for DOS file to someplace on the hard disk. If you are using PC Exchange, the 1-2-3 for DOS file may still be on the floppy disk.

   The Open dialog box you see should now appear similar to the one in Figure 9.17.

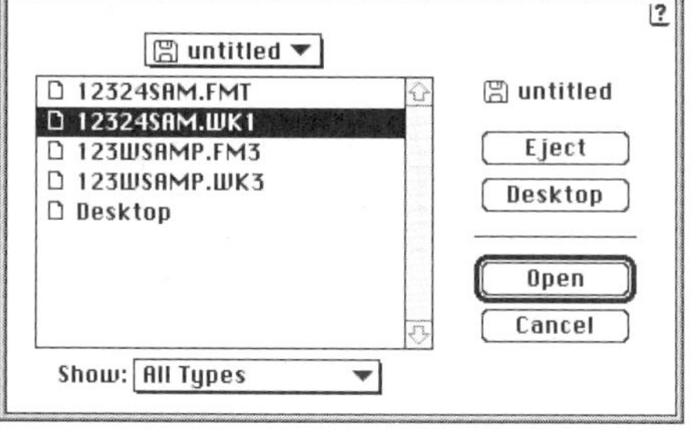

Figure 9.17. The Open dialog box after choosing the file type to show and navigating to the 1-2-3 for DOS file.

8. In the scrolling list, highlight the name of the WK1 file you want to open. Then choose the Open button on the right side of the dialog box.

1-2-3 for the Mac opens the 1-2-3 Release 2.x file. None of the formatting you applied using 1-2-3 Release 2.x appears.

MAC CAUTION

Any PIC files (graphs) and CGM files (clip art pictures) used in the worksheet *will not* translate from the PC. Instead, you will see gray squares representing these files. If you save the files and then move them back to the PC, you still will see gray squares wherever you had included graphs or clip art.

Translating a 1-2-3 for Windows File

You can translate all files created by Lotus 1-2-3 Release 3.x and Lotus 1-2-3 for Windows; the process for translating either kind of file is the same. When you add publishing and presentation information to any worksheet you create in any release of Lotus 1-2-3, the publishing and presentation information is stored in a separate formatting file, while the data is stored in a worksheet file. Typically, formatting files for 1-2-3 Release 3.x and 1-2-3 for Windows have an extension of FM3, while worksheet files have an extension of WK3.

To translate Lotus 1-2-3 Release 3.x and Lotus 1-2-3 for Windows files, follow these steps:

1. On the PC, use the Save **A**s command on the **F**ile menu to save the file, making sure that you place the file on a 3 1/2-inch DOS-formatted floppy disk. For more information on saving in 1-2-3 for DOS, see Chapter 8 of *The Mac User's PC.* For more information on saving in 1-2-3 for Windows, see Chapter 9 of *The Mac User's PC.*

2. On the Mac, make sure that the disk translation utility is active, and insert the DOS disk into the floppy disk drive. If you're using Apple File Exchange, make sure that you "translate" the file you want to open in 1-2-3 for the Mac, and place the file in a folder of your choice on the Mac hard disk. Then, quit Apple File Exchange.

3. Start 1-2-3 for the Mac by using one of the techniques described in Chapter 2 of *The PC User's Mac.*

4. Choose the **Open** command from the **File** menu. For more information on opening in 1-2-3 for the Mac, see Chapter 6 of *The PC User's Mac.*

   1-2-3 for the Mac displays the Open dialog box.

5. In the Show pop-up menu, choose 123DOS (WK3,FM3).

   Because you just told 1-2-3 for the Mac to display only files with an extension of FM3, you may not see any files in the list on the left.

6. Choose the Desktop button on the right side of the dialog box.

7. Navigate to the DOS file. If you are using Apple File Exchange, you already copied the DOS file to someplace on the hard disk. If you are using PC Exchange, the DOS file may still be on the floppy disk.

   The Open dialog box you see should now appear similar to the one in Figure 9.18.

8. Click the name of the file you want to open. Then, choose the Open button.

   1-2-3 for the Mac opens the 1-2-3 Release 3.x or 1-2-3 for Windows file with the majority of publishing and presentation formatting in place.

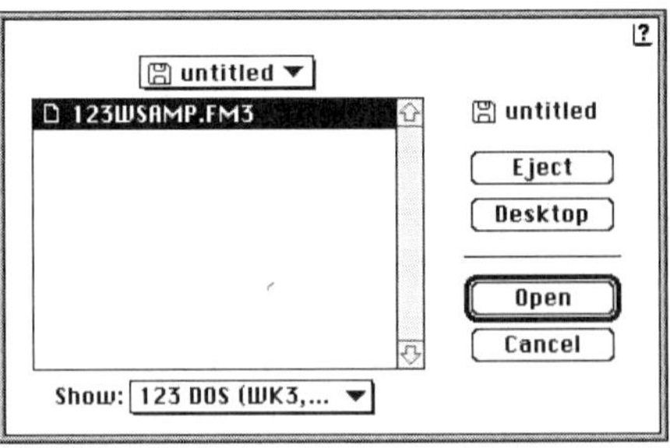

Figure 9.18.
The Open dialog box displaying a 1-2-3 for Windows file.

MAC CAUTION

Any PIC files (graphs) and CGM files (clip art pictures) used in the worksheet *will not* translate from the PC. Instead, you will see gray squares representing these files. If you save the files and move them back to the PC, you still will see gray squares wherever you had included graphs or clip art.

Translating a 1-2-3 for the Mac File

To translate a Lotus 1-2-3 for the Mac file to a PC version of Lotus 1-2-3, you use Lotus 1-2-3 for the Mac. Translating a 1-2-3 for the Mac file to a PC version of 1-2-3 is not difficult. At this time, however, 1-2-3 for the Mac cannot translate all information you may store in a 1-2-3 for the Mac file to all PC versions of 1-2-3. You can translate all information to 1-2-3 Release 3.x and 1-2-3 for Windows, but you are limited to translating only single worksheet files to 1-2-3 Release 2.x. If you have added any formatting (such as bold or italics), the formatting will be lost because 1-2-3 for the Mac cannot translate formatting information for 1-2-3 Release 2.x.

To translate a Lotus 1-2-3 for the Mac file so that it can be read by Lotus 1-2-3 Release 2.x, follow these steps:

1. In 1-2-3 for the Mac, open the file you want to move to 1-2-3 Release 2.x. For more information on opening in 1-2-3 for the Mac, see Chapter 6 of *The PC User's Mac.*

2. Open the **File** menu and choose the **Save As** command. For more information on saving in 1-2-3 for the Mac, see Chapter 6 of *The PC User's Mac.*

   1-2-3 for the Mac displays the Save As dialog box.

3. From the File Type pop-up menu, choose 123 DOS (.WK1).

   1-2-3 for the Mac adds an extension of WK1 to the file name that appears in the Save As text box (see Figure 9.19).

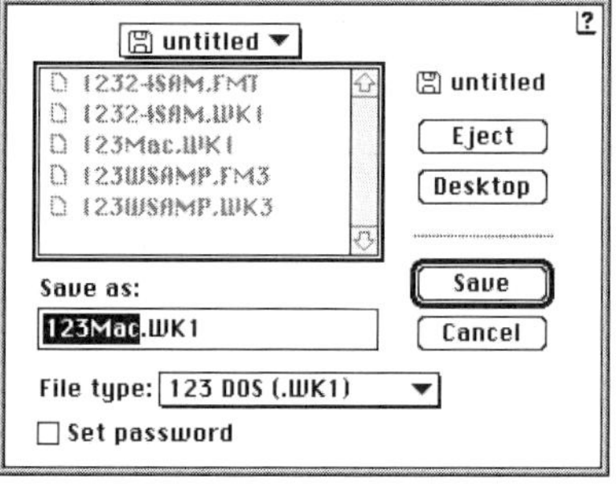

Figure 9.19. The Save As dialog box after choosing the file type to show.

4. If you want to change the name of the file on the floppy disk, click in the Save As text box and type a new name. Be sure to follow the DOS naming conventions—eight characters for the first name, a period, then WK1 as the three-character extension. (For more information on DOS file-naming conventions, see Chapter 12 of *The Mac User's PC.*)

5. Click the Save button.

   1-2-3 for the Mac saves the file in a format that can be read by 1-2-3 Release 2.x. You lose the majority of publishing and presentation formatting, such as bold and italics. Typically, you see a dialog box warning you that incompatible worksheet information was lost during saving.

6. Make sure that the disk translation utility is active, and insert (and, if necessary, format) a DOS disk into the floppy disk drive. See the first part of this chapter for more information on disk translation utilities and formatting DOS disks.

7. If PC Exchange is active, copy (by dragging) the file from the hard disk to the floppy disk. If Apple File Exchange is active, navigate to the file you want to move to the PC and "translate" it to the DOS-formatted floppy disk.

8. Eject the floppy disk from the floppy disk drive on the Mac and place the disk into the floppy disk drive on the PC.

9. Using one of the techniques described in Chapter 2 of *The Mac User's PC*, start 1-2-3 Release 2.x.

10. Use the **R**etrieve command from the **F**ile menu to open the worksheet in 1-2-3 Release 2.x. For more information on retrieving in 1-2-3 for DOS, see Chapter 8 of *The Mac User's PC.*

To translate a Lotus 1-2-3 for the Mac file so that it can be read by Lotus 1-2-3 Release 3.x or Lotus 1-2-3 for Windows, follow these steps:

1. In 1-2-3 for the Mac, open the file you want to move to 1-2-3 Release 3.x for DOS or 1-2-3 for Windows. For more information on opening in 1-2-3 for the Mac, see Chapter 6 of *The PC User's Mac.*

2. Open the **File** menu and choose the **Save As** command. For more information on saving in 1-2-3 for the Mac, see Chapter 6 of *The PC User's Mac.*

   1-2-3 for the Mac displays the Save As dialog box.

3. From the File Type pop-up menu, choose 123DOS (WK3,FM3).

1-2-3 for the Mac adds an extension of FM3 to the file name that appears in the Save As text box (see Figure 9.20).

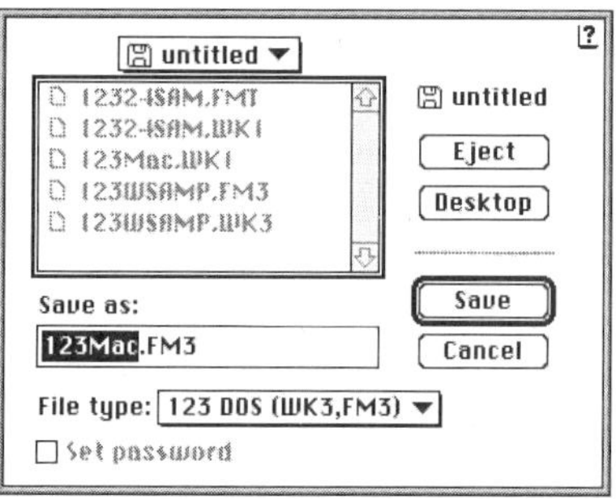

Figure 9.20. The Save As dialog box after choosing the file type to show.

4. If you want to change the name of the file on the floppy disk, click in the Save As text box and type a new name. Be sure to follow the DOS naming conventions—eight characters for the first name, a period, then FM3 as the three-character extension. (For more information on DOS file-naming conventions, see Chapter 12 of *The Mac User's PC.*)

5. Click the Save button.

   1-2-3 for the Mac saves the file in a format that can be read by 1-2-3 Release 3.x or 1-2-3 for Windows with the majority of publishing and presentation formatting in place.

6. Make sure that the disk translation utility is active, and insert (and, if necessary, format) a DOS disk into the floppy disk drive. See the first part of this chapter for more information on disk translation utilities and formatting DOS disks.

7. If PC Exchange is active, copy (by dragging) the file from the hard disk to the floppy disk. If Apple File Exchange is active, navigate to the file you want to move to the PC and "translate" it to the DOS-formatted floppy disk.

8. Eject the floppy disk from the floppy disk drive on the Mac and place the disk into the floppy disk drive of the PC.

9. Using a technique described in Chapter 2 of *The Mac User's PC*, start 1-2-3 Release 3.x or 1-2-3 for Windows.

10. Use the **O**pen command on the **F**ile menu to open the document in 1-2-3 Release 3.x or 1-2-3 for Windows. For more information on opening in 1-2-3 for DOS, see Chapter 8 of *The Mac User's PC*. For more information on opening in 1-2-3 for Windows, see Chapter 9 of *The Mac User's PC*.

Chapter Summary

In this chapter, you learned how to use floppy disks to transfer files between a PC and a Mac. But getting the file to the other computer doesn't necessarily mean that you can use the file. Therefore, you also learned about file translation utilities that convert Mac-formatted files to DOS format and DOS-formatted files to Mac format.

You then learned that you often can use an application itself to perform the translation, and you learned how to use the applications discussed in this book to translate files to the corresponding application on the other computer.

By the way, you now have reached the end of *The PC User's Mac*, except for the Mac Glossary. I have the urge to say something such as "I hope you have found useful information in this book," but that sounds a lot like the written version of "Have a nice day." Anyone with a better idea for an ending, jump right in here. My personal favorite is "And they all lived happily ever after."

LOSSARY

CLICKING

DESKTOP

FINDER

MOUSE POINTER

SYSTEM

active cell The worksheet cell that contains the cell pointer.

active document The document that contains the insertion point.

active pane The portion of the window that contains the insertion point.

active window The window that contains the active document.

active worksheet The worksheet that contains the active cell.

alphanumeric keys The "typewriter keys" on a keyboard. The alphanumeric keys include the alphabetic keys, the numbers (and symbols) that appear above the alphabetic keys, and all the keys immediately next to the alphabetic keys that help form the block into a symmetrical rectangular group on the keyboard.

blocking The process of selecting text. The term "blocking" is used in WordPerfect. See also *selecting*.

booting (or **boot process**) The sequence of steps the computer follows when you start it. You can start the computer by using either a cold boot or a warm boot. You use the on/off switch to perform a cold boot. You choose the Restart command from the Special menu to perform a warm boot.

cell The intersection of a column and a row in a worksheet.

cell pointer The name of the mouse pointer when in a cell in a worksheet.

Central Processing Unit (CPU) A microchip that serves as the hardware brain of the computer.

check box A box next to an option in a dialog box. You can choose more than one check box from a group of related options. An X appears in the check boxes of the activated options. See also *dialog box.*

choosing The process of selecting a menu, a command on a menu, or an option in a dialog box. See also *highlighting* and *selecting.*

clicking The process of pressing and releasing a mouse button (usually the left mouse button, if the mouse has more than one button). See also *dragging, double-clicking,* and *pointing.*

clicking and holding The process of opening a menu. Pressing and holding down the mouse button.

Close box The small square box located at the left end of a title bar. You can click the Close box to close a window or dialog box.

command An item that appears on a menu. You choose a command to accomplish a task in a program. See also *menu.*

command button An oblong button that performs an action, such as accepting or canceling choices, in a dialog box. To choose a command button, click on the button. See also *dialog box.*

Command key The key that appears next to the Option key. On the Command key, you see both the Apple logo () and a funky symbol (⌘) that has no name. A special-purpose key that has no function by itself. When pressed in combination with another key, the Command key may generate a special action in the current software package. See also *Control key* and *Option key.*

Control key A special-purpose key that has no function by itself. When pressed in combination with another key, the Control key (also labeled "Ctrl" on an Apple Keyboard II) may generate a special action in the current software package. See also *Command key* and *Option key.*

copying The process of placing an additional version of a file or text at a second location, leaving the original file or text in its original location. See also *moving* and *renaming.*

CPU The acronym for Central Processing Unit. See *Central Processing Unit (CPU).*

database A collection of related information. On computers, database programs are used to build databases. See also *field* and *record.*

Desktop The screen you see when a Mac finishes booting. Working on the Desktop of a Mac is similar to working at a DOS prompt on a PC, from which you can navigate to any location on any disk, or working in the Program Manager in Windows, from which you can access any program group.

dialog box A small window you use to supply additional information required by a program. See also *check box, command button, radio button, scrolling list,* and *text box.*

directional keys See *insertion point-movement keys.*

document Typically, in word processing applications, a file.

double-clicking The process of quickly pressing and releasing the mouse button twice (usually the left mouse button, if the mouse has more than one button). See also *clicking, dragging,* and *pointing.*

dragging The process of moving an item from one location to another by using the mouse. To drag, point to the item you want to drag. Then, hold down the mouse button (usually the left mouse button, if the mouse has more than one button) as you slide the mouse to move the mouse pointer to the new location. See also *clicking, double-clicking,* and *pointing.*

editing keys The editing keys include the Delete key and the Del key.

field Each separate piece of information in a database record. In a telephone book (the database) the last name is an example of a field. See also *database* and *record.*

file A unit in which information is stored on a computer. The same as a file on a PC.

Finder The active program that controls the activities that take place on the Desktop. Equivalent to the Program Manager in Windows. See also *MultiFinder*.

folder The Mac equivalent of a directory. You use folders to store and organize related files.

function keys The function keys typically include F1 through F12. The purpose of a function key is defined by the software program you are using.

hardware The parts of a computer you physically can see and feel. These parts include, at the most basic level, the monitor, the keyboard, the mouse, and the box containing the CPU and other components.

highlighting The process of identifying the menu or command you want to choose or the text you want to select. When a menu, command, or text is highlighted, a reverse video bar appears on it. See also *choosing* and *selecting*.

icon An image that represents program or data files on the Macintosh.

INIT The Mac equivalent of Terminate/Stay Resident (TSR) programs such as Sidekick. INITs are loaded as the Mac boots and stay loaded until you turn off the computer.

initialize The process of preparing a disk for use on a Mac. The same general process as formatting a disk on a PC.

insert mode The typing mode in which the program places characters at the current location of the insertion point and moves all existing characters to the right. The standard typing mode on a Mac is insert mode.

insertion point The flashing black vertical bar that identifies where text will appear when you type. The equivalent of the cursor in a DOS-based program.

insertion point-movement keys The keys you use to move the insertion point. The insertion point-movement keys include the arrow keys and Home, End, PgUp, and PgDn. PgUp may be labeled Page Up, and PgDn may be labeled Page Down. These keys perform the same functions, and, in this book, when you see PageUp or PageDown, you can use either key.

keyboard shortcut A key combination you can use as a shortcut to bypass opening menus. The keyboard shortcut for a command typically appears next to the command on the menu. See also *Command key, Control key,* and *Option key.*

Launcher A software program that comes with Performas only. The Launcher serves as a menu from which you can start programs.

menu An item that appears in the menu bar of a Mac program. Usually, a menu contains a list of commands. See also *command* and *menu bar.*

menu bar The bar that contains menu names. On a Mac, the menu bar always appears at the top of the screen. See also *menu.*

menu command See *command.*

mouse pointer The small arrow (or other shape) onscreen that represents the mouse's position on your desk. When you slide the mouse on your desk, the mouse pointer moves in a corresponding direction onscreen.

moving The process of removing a file or text from its original location and placing it at a new location. See also *copying* and *renaming.*

MultiFinder In versions of the System software earlier than System 7, an alternative program to control the activities that take place on the Desktop. The MultiFinder enables users of earlier System versions to run more that one application at the same time. Equivalent to the Program Manager in Windows. See also *Finder.*

multitasking The process of performing two or more tasks simultaneously. In a multitasking environment, for example, the user can send data over a modem and work in a word processor while the data transmission takes place.

NuBus slot An expansion slot used to add additional pieces of equipment, such as a fax board or a network board, to a Mac.

numeric keypad The numeric keypad appears at the right end of the keyboard. If the Num Lock feature is on, pressing a numeric keypad key produces a number. You turn on and off the Num Lock feature by pressing the Num Lock key.

Option key A special-purpose key that has no function by itself. When pressed in combination with another key, the Option key (also labeled "Alt") may generate a special action in the current software package. See also *Command key* and *Control key.*

pointing The process of identifying an item you want to choose. To point by using a mouse, slide the mouse until the mouse pointer onscreen appears on top of the item you want to choose. See also *clicking, double-clicking,* and *dragging.*

pop-up menu A box that contains a list of options in a dialog box. To open a pop-up menu, click on the down arrow at the right end of the box. See also *dialog box.*

radio button A small round button you use to choose one option from a group of related options in a dialog box. A black dot appears in the button of the currently selected option. See also *dialog box.*

record An entry in a database. In a telephone book (the database) all the information about one person is an example of a record. See also *database* and *field.*

renaming The process of changing the name of an existing file. When you rename, you do *not* create an additional copy of the file. See also *copying* and *moving.*

reverse video bar A bar that appears on top of a command in a menu or an option in a list (often called a "highlight"). You use a reverse video bar to identify a command or option you want to choose. See also *highlighting.*

scroll bar The vertical bar at the right side of a window or the horizontal bar at the bottom of a window that enables you to shift the view of the window's contents up, down, left, or right. A scroll bar also may appear at the side of a scrolling list. See also *scrolling list* and *window.*

scrolling list A box that contains a list of options in a dialog box. See also *dialog box.*

Size box The small square box that appears in the lower right corner of a window (where the ends of the vertical and horizontal scroll bars converge). You can drag the Size box to increase or decrease the size of the window.

selecting The process of identifying the text on which you want to work. When you select text, it appears highlighted. See also *choosing* and *highlighting.*

System The operating system of a Mac. The equivalent of DOS or Windows on a PC.

text box A rectangular box in which you enter text in a dialog box. When a dialog box that contains a text box opens, the current text is usually selected. To replace the selected text, simply type the new information. See also *dialog box.*

title bar A bar that appears at the top of a window or a dialog box, and contains the name of the window or dialog box. See also *dialog box* and *window.*

window A rectangular area onscreen that contains a title bar, scroll bar(s), and boxes you can use to close the window or adjust its size.

workbook A collection of Excel for the Mac worksheets that are conceptually related to one another.

worksheet A document or file in a spreadsheet program.

Zoom box The small square box at the right end of a title bar. You can click the Zoom box to reduce the window to its preceding size or to enlarge the window to the maximum size that fits onscreen.

Index

BOOTING

CHECK BOXES

MACINTOSH

FILES

MENUS

DOCUMENTS

PRINTING

WINDOWS

Symbols

A

B

C

D

E

F

G-H

I-J

K

L

M

N

O

P

Q-R

S

T

V-W

X-Z